The Revell

TARBELL'S

Teacher's Guide

to the International
Sunday School Lessons
includes the RSV and KJV

78th Annual Volume
September 1982—August 1983

Edited by FRANK S. MEAD

FLEMING H. REVELL COMPANY
OLD TAPPAN, NEW JERSEY

This volume is based on The International Sunday School Lessons; the International Bible Lessons for Christian Teaching, copyright © 1970 by the Committee on the Uniform Series.

The text of the Revised Standard Version of the Bible and quotations therefrom are copyright 1946 and 1952 by the Division of Christian Education, National Council of Churches, and used by permission.

Unless otherwise identified all biblical quotations in the material used by the author to illustrate the lesson are from the King James Version.

Scripture quotations identified TLB are from The Living Bible, copyright © 1971 by Tyndale House Publishers, Wheaton, Illinois. Used by permission.

Printed in the United States of America

ISBN: 0-8007-1284-6
ISSN: 0730-2622

CONTENTS

LIST OF LESSONS
SEPTEMBER–NOVEMBER 1982
ORIGINS OF GOD'S CHOSEN PEOPLE

DECEMBER 1982–FEBRUARY 1983
THE GOSPEL OF LUKE

MARCH–MAY 1983
THE BOOK OF ACTS

JUNE–AUGUST 1983
OLD TESTAMENT PERSONALITIES

A WORD TO THE TEACHER

In a recent survey on youth and religion, Dr. George Gallup, Jr. suggested that we "Encourage parents to cooperate with teachers in teaching their children *and their grandparents.*" Grandparents? Yes, come to think of it, grandparents need teaching in the Scriptures as well as youth needs it. At *every* age, there is work for the teacher to do.

No scientist is ever satisfied with what he knows; he must know more, more, more! No learned naturalist knows all there is to know about nature, no astronomer knows all about space and the universe, no historian knows all there is to know about history. They keep seeking, seeking, seeking. The author of the 119th Psalm realized this when he wrote, "Teach me, O Lord . . . Give me understanding." He was wise, wise enough to know that none of us can learn all there is to know about God and His Word in ten easy lessons. It takes a lifetime.

This was brought home to me recently when I read a letter from a kindly teacher who complained that "In TARBELL'S for this year, you have twenty-one lessons on Matthew. Isn't that too much?" I know what she meant, but then I looked at a bookshelf in my study and found no less than fifteen *books* on Matthew. I used every one of them in preparing the twenty-one lessons on Matthew—and I still feel that I have a lot to learn about this Matthew and his Gospel.

Rome wasn't built in a day. Neither is a sufficient Christian faith. Yes, we have answers to most of the questions of life in our Bible, but the trouble is that so few know where to look for them. The teacher must tell them.

When I was very young, I knew a delightful old lady who lived in a little house built long before the Civil War; in her dooryard was an old, old well that seemed to be bottomless. You couldn't *see* the coolest, clearest, most refreshing water I have ever known; you had to drop a bucket into its depths and draw it out.

The Bible is God's well of *living* water, but we will never taste of it until we learn that we have to let down our buckets of study and understanding and draw it out. If at first you do not go deep enough, try again, and again, and again. It is there; when you find it, you shall never thirst again.

As a teacher of His Word, you have an awesome responsibility; God has put His bucket in your hands, and He trusts you to use it well.

God bless you all.
Frank S. Mead

SEPTEMBER, OCTOBER, NOVEMBER 1982

ORIGINS OF GOD'S CHOSEN PEOPLE

LESSON I—SEPTEMBER 5

GOD CREATES PERSONS

Background Scripture: Genesis 2:4–25
Devotional Reading: Genesis 1:26–2:4

KING JAMES VERSION

GENESIS 2 4 These *are* the generations of the heavens and of the earth when they were created, in the day that the LORD God made the earth and the heavens,

5 And every plant of the field before it was in the earth, and every herb of the field before it grew: for the LORD God had not caused it to rain upon the earth, and *there was* not a man to till the ground.

6 But there went up a mist from the earth, and watered the whole face of the ground.

7 And the LORD God formed man *of* the dust of the ground, and breathed into his nostrils the breath of life; and man became a living soul.

8 And the LORD God planted a garden eastward in Eden; and there he put the man whom he had formed.

9 And out of the ground made the LORD God to grow every tree that is pleasant to the sight, and good for food; the tree of life also in the midst of the garden, and the tree of knowledge of good and evil.

18 And the LORD God said, *It is* not good that the man should be alone; I will make him an help meet for him.

19 And out of the ground the LORD God formed every beast of the field, and every fowl of the air; and brought *them* unto Adam to see what he would call them: and whatsoever Adam called every living creature, that *was* the name thereof.

20 And Adam gave names to all cattle, and to the fowl of the air, and to every beast of the field; but for Adam there was not found an help meet for him.

21 And the LORD God caused a deep sleep to fall upon Adam, and he slept: and he took one of his ribs, and closed up the flesh instead thereof:

REVISED STANDARD VERSION

GENESIS 2 4 These are the generations of the heavens and the earth when they were created.

In the day that the LORD God made the earth and the heavens, 5 when no plant of the field was yet in the earth and no herb of the field had yet sprung up—for the LORD God had not caused it to rain upon the earth, and there was no man to till the ground; 6 but a mist went up from the earth and watered the whole face of the ground— 7 then the LORD God formed man of dust from the ground, and breathed into his nostrils the breath of life; and man became a living being. 8 And the LORD God planted a garden in Eden, in the east; and there he put the man whom he had formed. 9 And out of the ground the LORD God made to grow every tree that is pleasant to the sight and good for food, the tree of life also in the midst of the garden, and the tree of the knowledge of good and evil.

18 Then the LORD God said, "It is not good that the man should be alone; I will make him a helper fit for him." 19 So out of the ground the LORD God formed every beast of the field and every bird of the air, and brought them to the man to see what he would call them; and whatever the man called every living creature, that was its name. 20 The man gave names to all cattle, and to the birds of the air, and to every beast of the field; but for the man there was not found a helper fit for him. 21 So the LORD God caused a deep sleep to fall upon the man, and while he slept took one of his ribs and closed up its place with flesh; 22 and the rib which the LORD God had taken from the man he made into a

22 And the rib, which the LORD God had taken from man, made he a woman, and brought her unto the man.

23 And Adam said, This *is* now bone of my bones, and flesh of my flesh: she shall be called Woman, because she was taken out of Man.

24 Therefore shall a man leave his father and his mother, and shall cleave unto his wife: and they shall be one flesh.

25 And they were both naked, the man and his wife, and were not ashamed.

woman and brought her to the man. 23 Then the man said,

"This at last is bone of my bones and
flesh of my flesh;
she shall be called Woman,
because she was taken out of Man."

24 Therefore a man leaves his father and his mother and cleaves to his wife, and they become one flesh. 25 And the man and his wife were both naked, and were not ashamed.

KEY VERSE: . . . the Lord God formed man of dust from the ground, and breathed into his nostrils the breath of life; and man became a living being. Genesis 2:7 (RSV).

HOME DAILY BIBLE READINGS

Aug. 30. *M.* *In the Beginning God.* Genesis 1:1–8.
Aug. 31. *T.* *God Created Natural Wonders.* Genesis 1:9–19.
Sept. 1. *W.* *God Declared His Creation Good.* Genesis 1:20–25.
Sept. 2. *T.* *God Created People.* Genesis 1:26–2:4a.
Sept. 3. *F.* *God Provided for People's Needs.* Genesis 2:4b–9.
Sept. 4. *S.* *God Set Standards.* Genesis 2:10–17.
Sept. 5. *S.* *Man and Woman—Complementary.* Genesis 2:18–25.

BACKGROUND

For the next three months, we shall be studying the origins of God's chosen people, Israel, so we deal in this first lesson with the first of the Israelites, indeed with the first living creatures. Our scriptural references are found in the Book of Genesis. The word *Genesis* means origin or creation; this is why we call the Book of Genesis "The Book of Beginnings." Martin Luther said that "Nothing is more beautiful than Genesis, nothing more useful." He spoke the truth. Genesis is beautiful as a Hymn of Creation; it is useful and highly valuable in its highlighting of the major Hebrew literature and theology. It is the background of Jewish thinking and religious faith.

We are dealing here not with historical record, but with the manner in which the primitives of Israel thought of their God and Creator revealing Himself before any man walked the earth—indeed, before the earth was even formed.

NOTES ON THE PRINTED TEXT

In the beginning—God! Before the earth was formed, when all was chaos and darkness, there was God. Most primitive men believed this and told stories about how God—or pagan gods—brought order out of that chaos and darkness. The Egyptians and the Babylonians, for instance, had accounts of creation which in some places resemble the account of Genesis, but they were poor and often ridiculous accounts of a whole galaxy of squabbling, quarreling gods who sound more like fighting clowns than intelligent men. They are of little help in our effort to understand the place and work of a sovereign, all-intelligent God.

Then came Genesis, which, compared with the old pagan stories, is as different as a rose is different from a poisonous weed. Just when Genesis was written, we do not know. According to one tradition, Moses wrote it; according to another, it is the work of many writers who over a period of years gathered together the old Hebrew concepts of how the world began and how man came into being in the world. It is possible that Moses did this "gathering" of material, but what is valuable for us, here, is not the matter of authorship but the adequacy of the record as we find it in Genesis.

Actually we have not one but two accounts of Creation in Genesis—one in Genesis 1:1,2–4a, and the other in Genesis 2:4b–25. They differ in language, style, and theology. "The first account begins with the creation of the animals first and ends with the creation of man; the second begins with the creation of man. They are two different stories, both borrowed from the past, but they both come out with the same lesson—the lesson that the one true and living God is the sovereign Lord of creation."—Charles T. Fritsch.

Stories! What we have here is a collection of stories told by the fathers of Israel. These fathers told and retold them around the campfires of their wandering days, told by mothers and fathers to their children in their homes. In time, these ancient tales took on a definite form, in which, in story form, the great basic beliefs of the Hebrew people about the beginnings of the universe and the nature and the unique importance of man in his relation to God are clarified. They were not told as accurate history, nor accurate science. That was not their purpose—and we have no reason to interpret Genesis as a record of creative *science.* The scientists ask, "*How* was man and the universe created?" The author or authors of Genesis ask, "*Why?*"

Now read the Scripture, and you will see why, and what God's purpose was in His Creation. Generation after generation, the children or descendants were taught by their parents of the making of heaven and earth (2:4). At a day (time) when no shrub or plant grew on the barren earth, God causes rain to fall. Before that rain, earth was a Death Valley; God, with His rain, turned it into fertile land. Let man try to perform the miracle of making rain! Only an all-powerful God could work that miracle. Man knows that deserts can be changed into gardens with a little water; man, with God's help, can be changed from sinner to saint. The rain gave man plants and trees for food and for beauty all around him.

After giving life to the plants, God formed man of the dust of the ground. Dust we are, and to dust we return! There is rich symbolism here: (Read Jeremiah 18:1–11.) The Hebrew word *formed* describes the work of a potter—and God, like a potter, uses the ground moistened by His rain to create man. It is true: we are all like so much clay in the hand of the Creator; He creates us, nourishes us, teaches us, uses us for His purpose.

But God did something more. He did not want man to be a mere plant or a mere animal: He breathed into man's nostrils the breath of life—spiritual as well as physical life—and that made man "a little lower than God." This creating and breathing made man the crowning glory of the whole creative act. The earth and all within it *was made for man's enjoyment and health.* To help man to increase in the love and knowledge of his Maker, God provided two trees in a garden called Eden ("paradise"); one was a tree of life that would give man fruit and immortality; the other was a tree of the knowledge of good and evil (spiritual insight and wisdom).

To this man (Adam), God gave dominion over the beasts of the land and the fowls of the air. That was good, for the animals are the least of His Creation. Animals have no souls; animals cannot know God. Man is spiritually superior to the beast; therefore God "chose" (made) this Adam the first of His Chosen People. He put great faith in him and looked to his descendants to bring all men into a new relationship with Him, to spread His love and will across the world that was to come.

One more thing was necessary in the mind of the Creator: this man should not live *alone.* Can you imagine the loneliness of a man living without a family, without neighbors? Can we imagine a world in which there are only *men?* To give this Adam a "helper," a companion—a *woman,* guaranteed the births of future generations. "The supreme message (of Genesis)," says Charles R. Erdman, "is contained in relating the creating of woman. Made not simply from 'the dust of the ground,' but taken from the side of man, molded and fashioned to be his equal and counterpart, she is presented to Adam as 'his other self,' and the inspired writer adds the divine injunction quoted by our Lord: 'Therefore shall a man leave his father and his mother, and shall cleave unto his wife; and they shall be one flesh.' Thus the ordinance of marriage was established and sanctified. Thus the blessedness of man was made complete."

So there is the whole story of "the beginnings," written in typical oriental imagery. The whole thing has one great basic emphasis, best described in the words of the eighth Psalm: "what is man that thou art mindful of him, and the son of man that thou dost care for him? Yet thou has made him little less than God, and dost crown him with glory and honor "(Psalms 8:4,5 RSV).

On the curtain of Ford's Opera House in Baltimore, we read these words:

> God conceived the world, that was Poetry;
> He formed it, that was Sculpture;
> He colored it, that was Painting;
> He peopled it with living beings, that was
> The grand, divine, eternal Drama.
>
> —Credited to Charlotte Cushman.

SUGGESTIONS TO TEACHERS

Nearly every child has said to a parent, "Mummy, where did I come from?" Upon being told that he or she comes from Mummy and Daddy, little Dougie or Debbie asks, "But where did *you* come from, Mummy?" The answer, "From Grandpa and Grandma," merely inspires further probing about origins. "Where did Grandpa and Grandma come from?" Every youngster needs to know something about his or her origins.

The same thing is true regarding our community of faith. What are our origins as God's people? Where did we come from? How did we come to be the way we are? These are some of the questions being asked in this quarter.

As teacher, your assignment is to help each person in your class to appreciate his or her "roots." September's lessons especially focus on the origins of God's people as found in Genesis. Today, you will work with the Genesis 2:4–25 account of the Creation story in which the Lord creates human life.

1. *COMPASSIONATE CREATOR.* Call attention to the fact that the Genesis story is unique in that it presupposes a benevolent yet powerful Lord at work. Our existence as humans is not the result of mere chance. Human life did not come into being because of an accident in nature but by the design of the Creator. Let your people ponder the ramifications of realizing their lives come from God's action. Ask them to discuss why God brought human life into being. Also point out that the Genesis account makes clear that the Creator continues to be interested and involved in His Creation, brings "new creation" through the Resurrection of Jesus Christ.

2. *CULTIVATOR OF CREATION.* Take time in your lesson to talk about the nature and the destiny of human existence, as suggested in Genesis 2. Point out, for example, that the Hebrew word for *human* means something like "earthling," and is derived from the Hebrew for *earth.* The earthling part of human existence must be acknowledged. Yet earthlings also have received the gift of the breath of the Creator, making them alive. You should remind your class that the word for *breath* is also the Hebrew word for *spirit.* Furthermore, indicate that earthlings with the Creator's breath have been put in a beautiful garden or world. The Creator intends His special Creation—humans—to care for the garden, not exploit it or destroy it. Here are the biblical ideas for this concept.

3. *CONFINES FOR CREATIVITY.* The Creator, you should make clear, puts limits on His creatures. The Lord tells humans that they must live within certain bounds. You may want to jump ahead briefly to Genesis 3, and refer to the way the earthlings refused to accept the bounds put on them by the Lord, and by eating from the forbidden tree brought misery to themselves and their descendants.

4. *COMPANION IN COMMUNITY.* Allow sufficient time to discuss the significance of the creation of male and female. Each respects and cares for the other. Neither tries to lord it over the other. Furthermore, the Creator intends a wholesome joy in the relationship between the man and the woman. According to the Genesis story, there is no shame or guilt in the enjoyment of sex between partners permanently committed to one another. Marriage, according to the Bible, is intended as companionship and community-building. Contrast this with the destructive notions of relationships between the sexes today.

TOPIC FOR ADULTS
GOD CREATES PERSONS

Offering. "We are the agents of the Creative Spirit in this world. Real advance in the spiritual life, then, means accepting this vocation with all it involves. Not merely turning over the pages of an engineering magazine and enjoying the pictures, but putting on overalls and getting on with the job. The real spiritual life must be horizontal as well as vertical; spread more and more as well as aspire more and more. It must be larger, fuller, richer, more generous in its interests than the natural life alone can ever be; must invade and transform all homely activities and practical things. For it means an offering of life to the Father of life, to Whom it belongs; a willingness—an eager willingness—to take our small place in the vast operations of His Spirit, instead of trying to run a poky little business on our own."—Evelyn Underhill, *The Spiritual Life.* Harper & Row, Publishers, Inc., 1955, 1977. Reprinted by permission.

Perfection of a Tree. There are wonderful things all around us, if only we could see. What may be commonplace to one man may be a living miracle to another. In his 1939 book *Wind, Sand, and Stars,* Antoine de Saint-Exupéry told how he had talked to some Bedouin chieftains on their return to the North African desert from a tour of France. Saint-Exupéry expected them to be full of admiration for the achievements of civilization they had witnessed. But, he said, they evinced a "freezing indifference" to the Eiffel Tower, the steamships, the locomotives. "What they thought admirable was not a locomotive, but a tree. When you think of it, a tree does possess a perfection that a locomotive does not know."

Meant to Be Together. Thomas and Zena Mohr of Orefield, Pennsylvania, had been married for seventy-three years when they decided they should move to a retirement home in Elizabethtown. Mr. Mohr, ninety-four and Mrs. Mohr, ninety-three, found that they were having difficulties managing their own house. Their applications at the Elizabethtown Home were accepted, and the Mohrs prepared to move. Then they learned that they would have to be separated. Thomas and Zena declined to move. Fervent Christians and long-time members of their Lutheran congregation, they understand that their marriage vows are "for as long as they both shall live." They intend to remain together as husband and wife. "Always work together. Be kind. Be happy," Thomas Mohr says is the philosophy of his long, successful marriage. They reflect the understanding of marriage in Genesis 2, when God created man and woman to bring care and fulfillment to each other as lifetime partners.

Questions for Pupils on the Next Lesson. 1. How do you find a purpose in life that is open to change and direction? 2. Where do you go for help in making decisions? 3. What are the most powerful competitors for supreme allegiance in your life? 4. What covenants have you made in life? 5. Why is it so hard to trust God?

TOPIC FOR YOUTH
BEGINNING WITH ONE AND ONE

Care and Power. "The average woman owns 750 movable muscles, 500 of which work in pairs. Her skin covers an area of 20 square feet. 'In any piece of her skin the size of a postage stamp there are four yards of nerves, a hundred sweat glands, fifteen oil glands, a yard of blood vessels and three million assorted cells!'

"Now this is what we might call God working in a square inch; this tells us of the detailed marvel of creation; this is seeing God in the infinitesimally small thing.

"But then we go on to the other end of the scale, and we look at the universe. The astronomers measure the distance that stars are away in light years. A light year is the distance that light travels in a year. Light travels 186,000 miles per second. Therefore in one year light travels 186,000 multiplied by 60 for minutes, multiplied by 60 for hours, multiplied by 24 for days, multiplied by 365 for years.

"Put this another way. The light we see shining from the Pole Star left that star just about when Shakespeare was writing his plays, when the Authorised Version of the Bible was being written, and has been travelling ever since at 186,000 miles per second to get here.

"The point about all this is that we see God in two things. First, we see in God the *most detailed care.* Nothing is too small for God. God's love of detail can be seen in the delicate tracery of every snowflake. The very structure of the universe shows us a God for whose care nothing is too small. We need never fear that, as far as God is concerned, we are lost in the mass. The very form of the universe makes it easy to believe in a God whose love is over every creature whom his hands have made.

"Secondly, we see a God of *infinite power.* Nothing is too great to be beyond the control of God. The immensities of the universe obey the laws of the universe just as much as the atom or the molecule do. Just as the issues of the individual life are in the hands of God, so are the issues of the universe."—William Barclay, *In the Hand of God.*

Unfinished Products. "We do not speak of the creation of a pot of jam; though we might speak of the creation of a salad, for there freedom and choice play a major part. No two salads are ever quite alike. Creation is the activity of an artist possessed by the vision of perfection; who, by means of the raw material with which he works, tries to give more and more perfect expression to his idea, his inspiration or his love. From this point of view, each human spirit is an unfinished product, on which the Creative Spirit is always at work."—Evelyn Underhill, *The Spiritual Life.* Harper & Row, Publishers, Inc., 1955, 1977. Reprinted by permission.

Sauntering Through Our Resources? "America is now sauntering through her resources and through the mazes of her politics with easy nonchalance; but presently there will come a time when she will be surprised to find herself grown old—a country crowded, strained, perplexed—when she will be obliged to fall back upon her conservatism, obliged to pull herself together, adopt a new regimen of life, husband her resources, concentrate her strength, steady her methods, sober her views, restrict her vagaries, trust her best, not average, members."

Words by a "far out" ecologist in this morning's paper?

Believe it or not, the above words were prophesied by Woodrow Wilson way back in 1889!

As God's people, taking Genesis seriously (as Wilson did), will we heed the biblical message which Wilson echoed?

Sentence Sermon to Remember: The world embarrasses me, and I cannot dream that this watch exists and has no watchmaker.—Voltaire.

Questions for Pupils on the Next Lesson. 1. What are the most important promises you have made? Why are these promises so important? 2. What are God's promises to His people? 3. How does God relate to persons? 4. How is the Jewish sense of being distinctive rooted in history? 5. What others do you trust, and why?

LESSON II—SEPTEMBER 12

GOD MAKES A COVENANT

Background Scripture: Genesis 15
Devotional Reading: Hebrews 6:13–20

KING JAMES VERSION

GENESIS 15 1 After these things the word of the LORD came unto Abram in a vision, saying, Fear not, Abram: I *am* thy shield, *and* thy exceeding great reward. 2 And Abram said, Lord GOD, what wilt thou give me, seeing I go childless, and the steward of my house *is* this Eliezer of Damascus?

3 And Abram said, Behold, to me thou hast given no seed: and, lo, one born in my house is mine heir.

4 And, behold, the word of the LORD *came* unto him, saying, This shall not be thine heir; but he that shall come forth out of thine own bowels shall be thine heir.

5 And he brought him forth abroad, and said, Look now toward heaven, and tell the stars, if thou be able to number them: and he said unto him, So shall thy seed be.

6 And he believed in the LORD; and he counted it to him for righteousness.

12 And when the sun was going down, a deep sleep fell upon Abram; and, lo, a horror of great darkness fell upon him.

13 And he said unto Abram, Know of a surety that thy seed shall be a stranger in a land *that is* not theirs, and shall serve them; and they shall afflict them four hundred years;

14 And also that nation, whom they shall serve, will I judge: and afterward shall they come out with great substance.

15 And thou shalt go to thy fathers in peace; thou shalt be buried in a good old age.

16 But in the fourth generation they shall come hither again: for the iniquity of the Amorites *is* not yet full.

17 And it came to pass, that, when the sun went down, and it was dark, behold a smoking furnace, and a burning lamp that passed between those pieces.

18 In that same day the LORD made a covenant with Abram, saying, Unto thy seed have I given this land, from the river of Egypt unto the great river, the river Euphrates:

REVISED STANDARD VERSION

GENESIS 15 1 After these things the word of the LORD came to Abram in a vision, "Fear not, Abram, I am your shield; your reward shall be very great." 2 But Abram said, "O Lord GOD, what wilt thou give me, for I continue childless, and the heir of my house is Eliezer of Damascus?" 3 And Abram said, "Behold, thou hast given me no offspring; and a slave born in my house will be my heir." 4 And behold, the word of the LORD came to him, "This man shall not be your heir; your own son shall be your heir." 5 And he brought him outside and said, "Look toward heaven, and number the stars, if you are able to number them." Then he said to him, "So shall your descendants be." 6 And he believed the LORD; and he reckoned it to him as righteousness.

12 As the sun was going down, a deep sleep fell on Abram; and lo, a dread and great darkness fell upon him. 13 Then the LORD said to Abram, "Know of a surety that your descendants will be sojourners in a land that is not theirs, and will be slaves there, and they will be oppressed for four hundred years; 14 but I will bring judgment on the nation which they serve, and afterward they shall come out with great possessions. 15 As for yourself, you shall go to your fathers in peace; you shall be buried in a good old age. 16 And they shall come back here in the fourth generation; for the iniquity of the Amorites is not yet complete."

17 When the sun had gone down and it was dark, behold, a smoking fire pot and a flaming torch passed between these pieces. 18 On that day the LORD made a covenant with Abram, saying, "To your descendants I give this land, from the river of Egypt to the great river, the river Euphrates."

KEY VERSE: On that day the Lord made a covenant with Abram saying, "To your descendants I give this land." Genesis 15:18 (RSV).

HOME DAILY BIBLE READINGS

Sept. *6.* *M.* *God's Call to Abram.* Genesis 12:1–5.
Sept. *7.* *T.* *God's Promise to Abram.* Genesis 15:1–6.
Sept. *8.* *W.* *The Covenant Made.* Genesis 15:7–21.
Sept. *9.* *T.* *The Covenant Restated.* Genesis 17:1–8.
Sept. *10.* *F.* *The Birth of Isaac.* Genesis 21:1–7.
Sept. *11.* *S.* *Abram Obeyed God.* Genesis 22:15–19.
Sept. *12.* *S.* *God Kept His Promise.* Hebrews 6:13–20.

BACKGROUND

Last week we talked about Adam, who by any standard was a weak individual of doubtful strength and faith. Then, as the record in Genesis is written, came Cain and Abel, the one good and the other bad—then Noah more notable for his ark than for godly character. Now we have Abraham, the most colossal man to appear in the pages of history before the birth of Jesus Christ. Abraham ruled no nation or country, enacted no laws, but was a giant in the field of religion. Christians and Mohammedans hold him in reverence; the Jews called him Father Abraham, the founder of their faith. Abraham, of Ur of the Chaldees, son of Terah . . . *Father* Abraham, who at God's command led his people out of Ur to march to Canaan, a land of which Abraham knew nothing. But "he went out, not knowing whither he went" (Hebrews 11:8).

That was an act of superb courage and faith, but his faith and courage were to be tried by fire before he saw Canaan.

NOTES ON THE PRINTED TEXT

On the road to Canaan, Abraham had troubles that would kill an ordinary man, but this was no ordinary man. He was far from perfect at times; at one point he was ready to give up. He had trouble with his ambitious nephew Lot; famine drove him into Egypt, where he had trouble with the Pharaoh of the day. He insulted the King of Elam and rebuffed the King of Sodom. A stranger in a strange country, surrounded by hostile, potential enemies, he had just about "had it." But not quite. God came to him in a vision at this darkest hour. (How many of us find God when the darkness is terrifying?)

Loud and clear came the voice of God: "Fear not, Abram, I am your shield; your reward shall be very great" (Genesis 15:1 RSV). *Reward?* Reward in a future that seemed a lost hope to the harassed Abram? How could that be? (Poor Abram: he had forgotten the promise God had made to him when he left Ur: "I will make of thee a great nation, and I will bless thee, and make thy name great; and thou shalt be a blessing" (Genesis 12:2). How, Lord?

Now two Hebrew customs and beliefs are involved here. A Hebrew father must have *sons* to perpetuate his name—and Abram was childless! The only male in his family besides himself was a servant, or slave, named Eliezer, and the Jewish Law said that if a man had no natural son, his estate would pass into the hands of the senior slave in his household.

So Eliezer would be his heir. How could that make Abram great, and a blessing?

God had the answer for *that* problem: "You will have a son to inherit everything you own. Don't predict your own future, Abram; that is in my hands. Go out and look up at the stars in the heavens above you; your descendants will be as numerous as that! Stop worrying and trust Me. I have promised you this, and I will keep My promise." It turned out just so.

The teaching for us, here, is that it is not what a man is but what a man trusts God to do that saves him. Abram, now certain that God would shield him from trouble, doubt, and harassment, "believed God; then God considered him righteous on account of his faith" (Genesis 15:6 TLB). Not out of any good works that we may do, not out of observance of any rite or ceremony does righteousness come, but out of our trust in God and submission to His will. Paul says the same thing when he says that justification is by faith alone.

The second thing that bothered Abram had to do with his possession of the Land of Promise—Canaan. In another vision—or was it a dream?—God repeats His promise concerning the Land, saying that the descendants of Abram would surely take and keep Canaan, but only after a flood of troubles. The conquest would not be easy; there would be four hundred years of bondage and affliction in Egypt, and there would be enemy tribes (like the Amorites). All in God's time, as *He* planned it, the people of Abram would possess and rule the Land He had promised them, but the road to Canaan would be a road of suffering and travail.

The ratification of this promise and this covenant between Abram (Israel) and God was publicly announced by the use of another custom or rite familiar to all covenant-making Hebrews. The bodies of slain animals were laid out in two parallel rows, and the two parties to the covenant involved walked between them. Behind them, as they walked, was a blazing light, the visible symbol of the Deity. That sealed the covenant concerning the Land for all time. In yet another covenant, the Lord made yet another promise, outlining the territory over which the descendants would spread. It was quite a territory: it reached from "the river in Egypt unto the great river, the river Euphrates (15:18). (The Egyptian river was probably the southern border of Judah.)

Great were these promises made to Abram, as he struggled to keep his faith, and God made them to him because in him God had a man He could trust! Again and again, Abram had doubts, and conquered them, and in conquering became *righteous*. Most of us are like that, but all of us do not march with our eyes on God through our troubles, or in strange, forbidding crises.

In the pre-Civil War days in our country, slaves often attempted to escape to Canada or to the "free" northern states. They traveled by night; through dismal, deadly swamps and through strange territory. They learned one very important thing: so long as they kept their eyes on one star in the sky and moved toward it, they would be moving north, toward freedom. Most of the stars shifted, moved around during the night. But the North Star was constant, in one place, like a fixed beacon or shining light. So long as they kept their eyes on that one star, they had a chance.

That is true about God, too. He is as fixed and steady as the North Star. If we could only learn, as Abram learned, that so long as we keep our heart's eyes on Him, we will enter the Promised Land which we call salvation! He walks with us, leads us through every darkness, past every doubt, to an ultimate goal of victory.

What God requires of us is not so much words of praise, or rituals, or creeds, but that righteousness which is the fruit of unconquerable faith and trust in Him.

SUGGESTIONS TO TEACHERS

How many times have you heard the expression, "A man is as good as his word!"? One woman illustrated this by describing her grandfather. The old man, a devout Mennonite, was a cabinet-maker who was widely respected for his fine work. According to his granddaughter, he never needed to sign a contract or swear an oath in a courtroom. He was so deeply respected as a man whose handshake meant an agreement was sealed and would be honored that everyone said, "He keeps his word!"

God keeps His word. God is as good as His word. This is the thrust of your lesson today. The saga of Abram is more than "ancient religious soap opera," as one critic once irreverently put it. Abram's story is the account of God giving His word—and keeping His word. Be sure to make clear to your class that God continues to keep His covenant.

1. *A PROMISE IN THE PRESENT.* Abram and Sarai were childless. They lamented that God had not seen fit to send them offspring. However, the Lord gave Abram His word that Abram would have more descendants than there are stars in the sky. How did Abram know that God would not back out on His promise? Because God had covenanted with Abram. God had given His word. The details of the covenant-making ceremony may seem gory to our ears, but halving the carcasses and the passing of the fire was understood as God Himself giving His word that He would keep His promise. God and Abram had an unbreakable pact. Take time in your lesson to comment on God's unbreakable pact through Abram and renewed through Jesus Christ with us.

2. *A PURPOSE TO THE PAST.* Because of God's covenant, Abram is able to understand that history has meaning. The events in his life make sense. Urge your people to trace the pattern of God's activity in their personal histories. God's word-giving needs to be noted in each believer's past, and you may even wish to have your class break into groups of two or three in order to permit each person the opportunity to "read" God's purposes into his or her own story.

3. *A PEEK AT THE FUTURE.* The dream episode in Genesis 15:12 offers Abram a glimpse at the end of the story. He understands that in spite of hardships and heartaches in life God keeps His word. God may be trusted to bring a successful conclusion to what He promises. Ask your people if they honestly believe that human existence has any purpose or that life is going anywhere. The covenanting Lord assures the Abrahams and Sarahs of each generation that, with Him, the human story ultimately has a happy ending. After all, it is a love story!

TOPIC FOR ADULTS
GOD MAKES A COVENANT

On Believing Without Seeing. The famous swimmer, Florence Chadwick, tells of the first time she tried to swim from Catalina Island to the California coast, on July 4, 1952. After nearly sixteen hours, numb with cold and discouraged by the poor visibility because of fog, she was forced to give up, just a mile from her goal. To a reporter she confessed afterward, "I'm not trying to excuse myself, but if I could have seen land I might have made it." It was the sighting of land that had given her the spur to go on when she first swam the English Channel in 1950.

Miss Chadwick, as a deeply religious woman who always prays before she undertakes one of her remarkable swims—and she later did successfully cross the Catalina Channel—has herself pointed to the lesson in faith she was taught by her failure.

God has made a covenant—a promise—with us that He may be trusted to keep His word. Although we may have to struggle onward at times, weary from the struggle and unable to see our goal, we may be certain that our faith is not in vain. We, like Abram, will live as sojourners and strangers, but we may be certain that God holds to His commitments.

Sterling Hallmark. Fine silver bears the hallmark *Sterling* stamped on it. "Sterling" stands for honesty and quality. If a piece of silverware carries that stamp, everyone knows that the piece is genuine silver. Few, however, know the background for the term.

In the thirteenth century, a man by the name of Easterling was a famous silversmith in England. He had a reputation for integrity. When Easterling gave his word that a piece he had crafted was truly silver, people knew they could trust him. Easterling founded the Easterling Guild, a group of Saxon craftsmen and merchants in silverware who moved to London. The Easterling Guild was so renowned for standards of excellence of quality and workmanship that Easterling's word became synonomous for trustworthiness. Today, the Easterling name, shortened to "Sterling," is used everywhere as the standard for silver.

God's word to Abram, called the Covenant, became the hallmark of the biblical story. God kept His word, Abram learned. Throughout the centuries, God's people have learned that God continues to keep His covenant.

Covenant Calls for Promise-Making to Children. Baptism stands for covenant-making. The sacrament reiterates God's covenant through Abram and, finally, Jesus Christ. In response to God's covenant, all present covenant with Him and each other to keep promises with the children.

"Once there was a little boy. When he was six weeks old, his parents turned him over to a baby sitter while they worked and danced. When he was two, they dressed him up as a cowboy and gave him a gun. When he was three, everybody said, 'How cute,' as he went about lisping a beer commercial jingle. When he was five, his parents taught him the latest rock and roll rhythms and popular tunes; he soon learned to dance.

"When he was six, his father occasionally dropped him off for Sunday school on his way to the golf course, but more often took him to the lake for the day and taught him neglect of the church in favor of swimming, water-skiing, and fishing. When he was eight, he learned to play cards by watching and being taught by his parents. When he was ten, he spent his after-school hours at the drugstore newsstand reading comic books and getting his first taste of poor and scummy literature. His mother wasn't home and his father was busy.

"When he was thirteen, he told his parents that other boys his age didn't have to go to Sunday school or church, and they said he could do as he wished. (It was easy that way.) When he was fourteen, he seldom went to church, but frequented dance halls and the movies, got his first taste of beer, and ran with the crowd. When he was sixteen, the police called at his home one night and said, 'We have your boy, he's been in trouble.' 'In trouble?' said the father, 'It can't be my boy.' BUT IT WAS!"—*Pulpit Helps.*

Questions for Pupils on the Next Lesson. 1. What are some of the times your have found yourself in trouble because of your moral failures? 2. Why do we sometimes try to use our possessions to restore right relationships with those we have injured? 3. Why does a sense of guilt produce a moral struggle? 4. Have you known persons who have had a nominal relationship with God, then, in a crisis, have had a new, life-changing experience with Him?

TOPIC FOR YOUTH
MAKING PROMISES

No Risks, No Woes. Buddhism states, "Those who love a hundred have a hundred woes. Those who love ten have ten woes. Those who love one have one woe. Those who love none have no woe."

The Bible shows that God loves not one or two, or even a few hundred, but has given His word that He cares about each and all. His covenant with Abram is that love for Abram and all future generations.

God's covenant is also the risk of woes. And what woes God endured and continues to endure because of His covenant with us!

Promise to Those Inside and Outside. In 1893, the Lafayette Presbyterian Church of Brooklyn erected an expensive building. They commissioned a famous studio to create a large stained-glass window showing the Apostle Paul preaching to a crowd. The most generous contributors in the congregation were rewarded by having their faces portrayed in the glass as members of Paul's audience. The congregation wished to emphasize God's covenant with the Church, particularly with those who responded with financial contributions.

Eighty-one years later, the church commissioned artist Hank Prussing to paint a series of murals on the walls to complement its Tiffany treasures. Prussing photographed hundreds of persons on the neighborhood streets to get faces and figures for his work. Prussing's panels on the walls depict the people that exist outside the doors of the church, just as the earlier stained-glass windows show those inside. Collectively called *Clouds of Witness,* the decorations symbolize God's covenant with both "insiders" and "outsiders." The windows and murals also can be understood to portray the promise-making by a local congregation with its own members and those in the community.

How would you depict the covenant between God and your church? How would you show in graphic form the commitment your church has to others?

Snail's Pace. Because God makes promises to us, especially through Abram and later through Jesus Christ, we make promises to one another. In fact, Christians use the word *covenant* to describe the promise-making in marriage.

When Christopher and Deborah Hudson of Hove, England, were married only four months ago, Mr. Hudson promised faithfully that he would give up his hobby of breeding snails. But it was a hard-to-keep promise, since Mr. Hudson gained some fame a few years ago when he bred the giant snail Geronimo, which grew to a length of almost a foot before it died last year. This week Mr. Hudson admitted that he had been unable to divest himself of his devotion to snails, and he had, in fact, signed a contract calling for him to appear on television to talk about them. "That was the last straw for Deborah," he said. "We have now decided to go our separate ways."

How sad that Christopher and Deborah Hudson failed to realize God's covenant with them so that they could keep promises to each other!

Have you considered the marriage relationship in terms of a covenant to devote attention to each other?

Sentence Sermon to Remember: An honest belief, while hard to come by, is humanity's main asset and hope.—Peabody Journal of Education.

Questions for Pupils on the Next Lesson. 1. What is the basis for your relationship with members of your family, with members of your peer group, and with significant adults? 2. Why do you feel comfortable or uncomfortable with these? 3. How do you resolve conflicts in your relationships with these others? 4. What is the most significant encounter you have had with spiritual reality? 5. What are you doing to understand God's will for your life?

LESSON III—SEPTEMBER 19

GOD GIVES JACOB A NEW NAME

Background Scripture: Genesis 27–28;31,32
Devotional Reading: Genesis 35:1–15

KING JAMES VERSION

GENESIS 32 9 And Jacob said, O God of my father Abraham, and God of my father Isaac, the LORD which saidst unto me, Return unto thy country, and to thy kindred, and I will deal well with thee:

10 I am not worthy of the least of all the mercies, and of all the truth, which thou has shewed unto thy servant; for with my staff I passed over this Jordan; and now I am become two bands.

11 Deliver me, I pray thee, from the hand of my brother, from the hand of Esau: for I fear him, lest he will come and smite me, *and* the mother with the children.

12 And thou saidst, I will surely do thee good, and make thy seed as the sand of the sea, which cannot be numbered for multitude.

22 And he rose up that night, and took his two wives, and his two women-servants, and his eleven sons, and passed over the ford Jabbok.

23 And he took them, and sent them over the brook, and sent over that he had.

24 And Jacob was left alone; and there wrestled a man with him until the breaking of the day.

25 And when he saw that he prevailed not against him, he touched the hollow of his thigh; and the hollow of Jacob's thigh was out of joint, as he wrestled with him.

26 And he said, Let me go, for the day breaketh. And he said, I will not let thee go, except thou bless me.

27 And he said unto him, What *is* thy name? And he said, Jacob.

28 And he said, Thy name shall be called no more Jacob, but Israel: for as a prince hast thou power with God and with men, and hast prevailed.

29 And Jacob asked *him,* and said, Tell *me,* I pray thee, thy name. And he said, Wherefore *is* it *that* thou dost ask after my name? And he blessed him there.

30 And Jacob called the name of the place Peniel: for I have seen God face to face, and my life is preserved.

REVISED STANDARD VERSION

GENESIS 32 9 And Jacob said, "O God of my father Abraham and God of my father Isaac, O LORD who didst say to me, 'Return to your country and to your kindred, and I will do you good,' 10 I am not worthy of the least of all the steadfast love and all the faithfulness which thou hast shown to thy servant, for with only my staff I crossed this Jordan; and now I have become two companies. 11 Deliver me, I pray thee, from the hand of my brother, from the hand of Esau, for I fear him, lest he come and slay us all, the mothers with the children. 12 But thou didst say, 'I will do you good, and make your descendants as the sand of the sea, which cannot be numbered for multitude.' "

22 The same night he arose and took his two wives, his two maids, and his eleven children, and crossed the ford of the Jabbok. 23 He took them and sent them across the stream, and likewise everything that he had. 24 And Jacob was left alone; and a man wrestled with him until the breaking of the day. 25 When the man saw that he did not prevail against Jacob, he touched the hollow of his thigh; and Jacob's thigh was put out of joint as he wrestled with him. 26 Then he said, "Let me go, for the day is breaking." But Jacob said, "I will not let you go, unless you bless me." 27 And he said to him, "What is your name?" And he said, "Jacob." 28 Then he said, "Your name shall no more be called Jacob, but Israel, for you have striven with God and with men, and have prevailed." 29 Then Jacob asked him, "Tell me, I pray, your name." But he said, "Why is it that you ask my name?" And there he blessed him. 30 So Jacob called the name of the place Peniel, saying, "For I have seen God face to face, and yet my life is preserved."

KEY VERSE: "Your name shall no more be called Jacob, but Israel, for you have striven with God and with men, and have prevailed." Genesis 32:28 (RSV).

HOME DAILY BIBLE READINGS

Sept. 13. *M.* *Jacob Deceived Isaac.* Genesis 27:19–29.
Sept. 14. *T.* *Esau Denied Birthright and Blessing.* Genesis 27:30–36.
Sept. 15. *W.* *Jacob Sent to Laban.* Genesis 28:1–5.
Sept. 16. *T.* *Jacob's Dream at Bethel.* Genesis 18:10–22.
Sept. 17. *F.* *God Sent Jacob Home.* Genesis 31:1–16.
Sept. 18. *S.* *Jacob Prepared to Meet Esau.* Genesis 12:1–12.
Sept. 19. *S.* *Jacob Becomes Israel.* Genesis 32:22–30.

BACKGROUND

Three great names resound through early Jewish history: Abraham, Isaac, and Jacob. When we look at the background life of Jacob, we may wonder why he should be called great. He was a tricky, unattractive man for a long, long time, and a cheat. He cheated Esau his brother, Laban his uncle, and even his poor old meek, peace-loving, dying father! He left his father's house and for years wandered as a prodigal son. But God could see something fine and good in this Jacob, which men could not see, and God changed him into a new man, a Prince of God, one worthy of having his name changed by God to *Israel!*

His life is worth careful studying, for there is a bit of the prodigal in all of us.

NOTES ON THE PRINTED TEXT

The prodigal Jacob is "on the run" when we meet him in the Scripture for this lesson, but somewhat a better man than he was on the day when he left the house of Isaac. He is running, and he is desperately afraid: news comes to him that Esau, whom he had cheated of his birthright (the right of inheritance of the bulk of the father's estate, given under law to the eldest son—Esau) was on his way to meet Jacob—with an army of 400 men! It was an army led by a man determined on vengeance.

Have you ever felt sorry for Esau? Don't be sorry. This man was a playboy, a neer-do-well. He thought little or nothing of that birthright. He thought more of his stomach than he did of his soul—or of communion with God. For what a cheap price did he sell that birthright!

Jacob was a better man than that. Prodigal he may have been, but he was a troubled prodigal who could not quiet a conscience that told him he had done a great wrong and deserved God's punishment for it. He prayed at this moment, half in fear, half in repentance: "I am not worthy of the least of all the mercies" (Genesis 32:10). That sense of sin had been increased at the time of the dream (in Genesis 28) in which he saw that ladder between earth and heaven with the Lord at the top of it. No, he was not all bad!

But fear dominated him now. Fearful of destruction at the hand of his infuriated brother, he divided his company (people) into two bands; if Esau destroyed one company, the other might escape the disaster and become what God had promised Abraham: the descendant seed, and a people outnumbering the stars.

In an effort to soften the anger of Esau, Jacob sent Esau herds of goats, rams, camels, cows, bulls, and donkeys. Surely, that would satisfy him, and put an end to the old conflicts between the brothers.

It settled nothing. Left alone that night, Jacob is still in a panic of fear over what might happen the next day. What he has done to Esau still haunts him; his conscience is a knife stabbing deep. That night, for the first time, he understands that his real battle is not with Esau but with God. Things will never be right for him until he is right with God. Alone in the darkness, smitten with remorse, he is approached by "a man" who seizes him and wrestles with him until the dawn of another day.

Just who or what this "man" may have been, the Scripture does not say. There are many guesses, many "explanations." All that is certain in the story is that Jacob sees him as a supernatural being (Genesis 32:30). Hosea (12:3,4) says that it was a sympathetic angel. Martin Luther sees in this man an appearance of the preincarnate Christ. Whoever he was, Jacob knew that he was dealing with none other than the God of Israel. "It is God who is wrestling with Jacob, not Jacob with God."—Charles T. Fritsch. God, who would not give up the struggle to overcome the old Jacob and bring him at last to the stature of a greater, more Godlike servant. At the end of the struggle, God lays His finger on Jacob's thigh and Jacob, in defeat, hangs helpless on the neck of his divine adversary.

"Now let me go," says the adversary.

"No," says Jacob. "Not until you bless me."

"What is your name," asks the Man.

"It is Jacob."

"No more is it Jacob. Now it is Israel, for you have striven with God and with men, and have prevailed. Because you have been striving with God, you shall prevail with men" (verse 28 TLB).

Then Jacob saw it clearly: he called the place where the struggle had been won Peneil, *"for I have seen God face to face, and my life is preserved."* He had a *new* life and a new name. He was sinful, crafty Jacob no more. The rest of his life he walked closer to God.

"Jacob was in many respects as despicable a character as you could hope to find; he was crafty and shrewd and cunning and deceptive, and there were many other things you could say about him. But Jacob was also a man who was true to the faith that had been given him by his father, and God was true to the promise that He had given to Abraham. God will bless you and He will bless me, not for what we are but for what He is, because He is God and because He has promised to be our God and the God and Father of our children. We should be deeply grateful to Him, as Jacob came to be, for all His blessings, and we should serve Him faithfully and well."—William Sanford LaSor, in *Great Personalities of the Bible.*

SUGGESTIONS TO TEACHERS

A hang-glider enthusiast with the name of Eagle Marmont attempted to fly his hang-glider across the Atlantic in the summer of 1980, but was stopped by Canadian officials for violating aviation rules. Reporters interviewing the angry, frustrated would-be hero asked him how he had acquired the unusual name of Eagle Marmont. Marmont acknowledged that he had been born Joseph Carter Whitmore, but had taken the name *Eagle* for himself because it is the boldest, highest flying bird, and *Marmont* because it was the name of a mountain in his favorite science-fiction story. His new name, legally assumed, gave him his sense of identity and destiny, he claimed.

Although few of us will change our names, we should understand the importance of a name. People in the Bible certainly did. A name was a badge. A name bestowed personhood and was something to remind one constantly of who he was.

Your lesson today on God giving Jacob a new name is meant to be more than antique lore. Basically, it is intended to help each person in your class to understand his or her new name of "Christian."

1. *SNEAKY SINNER.* Take a few minutes to present the biblical portrait of Jacob. It is not very pretty. Jacob is a man with a past. Remind your class that the Bible never tries to "pretty up" the account of the heroes of the faith, but shows Jacob as the liar, the cheat, and the opportunist which he was. In fact, Jacob even lies about the Lord. However, God uses such unpromising raw material to carry out His purposes. Emphasize to your class that if God can take a hated, hunted sneak like Jacob, He can also call them, regardless of their pasts.

2. *SURPRISING STAIRWAY.* "Jacob's ladder" is more than a kid's campfire song. It is the unexpected encounter of Jacob with the Lord. The same Lord who introduced Himself to Jacob has introduced Himself to us through the life, death, and Resurrection of Jesus Christ. Let your class members share ways in which they might have been surprised by the Lord presenting Himself to them when they least expected Him. Have your people also notice that the Lord's words to Jacob apply to them: ". . . I will not leave you until I have done that of which I have spoken to you" (Genesis 28:15).

3. *SAVING STRUGGLE.* Devote enough time in the lesson to Jacob's all-night wrestling match with the Lord. Sometimes, a person must struggle alone, contending with God until God wins out. Is this not what prayer must often be? Don't be afraid to share some of your personal spiritual struggles and permit your class to share some of theirs.

4. *SETTLED SELFHOOD.* Jacob receives a new name, *Israel.* The one-time cheat and liar also understands who he is and for what he is meant to live. He no longer lives as a fugitive. With the Lord, Jacob-Israel has a sense of security and purpose. Talk with your class about the "identity crises" which beset so many in various stages of life today. How does the Christian faith bestow a notion of selfhood?

TOPIC FOR ADULTS
GOD GIVES JACOB A NEW NAME

Pilgrimage. "I think as I write this of Dürer's wonderful drawing of the Knight, Death, and the Devil: the Knight of the Spirit on his strong and well-kept horse—human nature, treated as it ought to be, and used as it ought to be—riding up a dark rocky defile. Beside him travels Death, a horrible, doddering figure of decay, saying, 'All things perish—time is passing—we are all getting older—is this effort really worthwhile?' On his flank is a yet more hideous fellow pilgrim—the ugly, perverse, violent element of our mixed human nature, all our animal part, our evil impulses, nagging at him, too. In one way or another, we all hear those two voices from time to time; with their discouragements and sneers, their unworthy invitations, their cynical comments and vile suggestions. 'Don't forget me, I am your future,' says Death. 'Don't forget me,' says animal man, 'I am your undying past.' But the Knight of the Spirit does not look at them. He has had his hand-to-hand struggle farther back; and on his lance is impaled the horrid creature, his own special devil, which he has slain. Now he is absorbed in the contemplation of something beyond the picture, something far more real than the nightmarish landscape through which he must travel; and because of that, he rides steadily forth from that lower world and its phantasies to the Eternal World and its realities. He looks at that which he loves, not at that which he hates, and so he goes safely out of the defile into the open; where he will join the great army of God. There we see the spiritual life as humanity is called to live it; based on the deep conviction that the Good, the Holy, is the Real, and the only thing that matters, fed and supported by the steadfast contemplation of the Holy and the Real—which is also the Beautiful and the Sane—and expressed in deliberate willed movements towards it, a sturdy faithful refusal to look at that which distracts us from it. Always looking the same way, always moving the same way; in spite of obstacles, discouragements, mockery and fatigue. 'Thou hast made us for thyself, and our hearts find no rest save in thee.' But we must be willing to undertake the journey, whatever it may cost."—Evelyn Underhill, *The Spiritual Life.*

Naming the Child. Missionaries to New Guinea in the Pacific were shocked to discover the horrid names which the Moni people gave to their children. Vile names such as "dog-dung" and "pig-dung" were frequently used. When the missionaries asked why such repulsive names were given, they were told that these were used so that the evil spirits would not be as inclined to harm the babies. The missionaries, of course, pointed out that the coming of Jesus means the presence and power of One greater than the evil spirit, and that He offers new life and the new name of "Christian."

Secret Name. The Aranda tribe of Aborigines in Australia's "outback" customarily give two names to each person. One name is known to everyone. The other name is the secret and sacred name and may be used only on solemn occasions. This special name, in fact, is so secret that the women never learn what their own sacred names are. The old men guard these names to themselves.

Many persons in our culture go through life without realizing that God has bestowed a special name on every person: "forgiven sinner." It is no secret that through Jesus Christ God has come conferring a new status and a new identity. He intends us who respond to His coming to carry the family name "Christian."

Questions for Pupils on the Next Lesson. 1. Why do people find that it is so hard to believe that they are forgiven? 2. How does faith in God's preserving power over events and persons free us to be forgiving? 3. Why can broken relationships be best restored when the offended persons take the initiative? 4. How can people avoid being corrupted by power? 5. How can we strengthen our trust in God when it seems that evil prevails?

TOPIC FOR YOUTH
BEGINNING A NEW LIFE

Delivered From a No-World. Helen Keller was left totally blind and deaf from disease when she was a baby. The girl lived in a world of total darkness and silence until she was seven years old. At that point, the family hired a young Boston teacher Anne Sullivan to work with the "hopeless" girl. Anne Sullivan patiently began to gain entry into Helen Keller's world and, most importantly, into the girl's heart. Finally, one day, holding Helen's hand under a spout of cool water and hand-spelling *water* into Helen's palm through the running water, Anne enabled the blind, deaf-and-dumb girl to understand that there was such a thing as language. More important, Anne Sullivan the teacher introduced Helen to a new life.

Helen Keller learned to read, write, and speak. With her brilliant teacher at her side over the next fifty years, she graduated from Radcliffe College and became a world celebrity and author. Describing her new life after Anne Sullivan came to her, Helen Keller wrote, "Before my teacher came to me, I did not know what I am. I lived in a world that was a no-world."

This was Jacob's experience after his encounter with the Lord. These same words can be used by every person who knows the meaning of Jesus Christ. He offers a new beginning. He brings us out of a no-world into a new life.

Names, Not Numbers. Several years ago, during a census, a census-taker called at an apartment in a teemingly crowded part of Detroit. A woman came to the door, holding a baby and with five other small children clinging to her. The census-taker started his questions, and soon came to the one inquiring, "And how many children do you have?" The woman deliberately answered, "Well, there is Debbie Sue, there is Jimmy, there is Tracy Lynne, there's Beth Anne, there is. . . ." The census-taker impatiently cut her off. "Forget the names, lady. Just give me the number." The woman's eyes blazed. "In the home, the children are *not* numbers. They are names!" she replied indignantly.

Through Jesus Christ, we understand that we are not mere numbers but are names known and loved by God.

Santa With Amnesia. Parents of a little five-year-old boy in North Carolina took him to visit the Santa Claus at a local department store. The boy perched himself in Santa's lap and when Santa asked him his name eagerly replied, "Johnny Reno." The following Christmas season, Johnny's parents took him to a different store to see Santa. The opening question was the same as the previous year: "What's your name, Sonny?" Johnny looked up with a disgusted expression. "Why, you know my name. I was here last year!"

Santa may forget; God remembers your name. Jacob learned his real identity from the Lord. He also found that God enabled him to begin a new life. Have you?

Sentence Sermon to Remember: God loves to help him who strives to help himself.—Aeschylus: *Fragments.*

Questions for Pupils on the Next Lesson. 1. Why is the desire for revenge so destructive? 2. What evidence do you find that God is at work in the world today? 3. How do you respond to those who try to tell you that there is no future? 4. How do you know that God overrules evil for good?

LESSON IV—SEPTEMBER 26

GOD PRESERVES HIS PEOPLE

Background Scripture: Genesis 37;42–45;50
Devotional Reading: Genesis 37:12–28

KING JAMES VERSION

GENESIS 50 15 And when Joseph's brethren saw that their father was dead, they said, Joseph will peradventure hate us, and will certainly requite us all the evil which we did unto him.

16 And they sent a messenger unto Joseph, saying, Thy father did command before he died, saying,

17 So shall ye say unto Joseph, Forgive, I pray thee now, the trespass of thy brethren, and their sin; for they did unto thee evil: and now, we pray thee, forgive the trespass of the servants of the God of thy father. And Joseph wept when they spake unto him.

18 And his brethren also went and fell down before his face; and they said, Behold, we *be* thy servants.

19 And Joseph said unto them, Fear not: for *am* I in the place of God?

20 But as for you, ye thought evil against me; *but* God meant it unto good, to bring to pass, as *it is* this day, to save much people alive.

21 Now therefore fear ye not: I will nourish you, and your little ones. And he comforted them, and spake kindly unto them.

22 And Joseph dwelt in Egypt, he, and his father's house: and Joseph lived a hundred and ten years.

23 And Joseph saw Ephraim's children of the third *generation:* the children also of Machir the son of Manasseh were brought up upon Joseph's knees.

24 And Joseph said unto his brethren, I die; and God will surely visit you, and bring you out of this land unto the land which he sware to Abraham, to Isaac, and to Jacob.

25 And Joseph took an oath of the children of Israel, saying, God will surely visit you, and ye shall carry up my bones from hence.

26 So Joseph died, *being* a hundred and ten years old: and they embalmed him, and he was put in a coffin in Egypt.

REVISED STANDARD VERSION

GENESIS 50 15 When Joseph's brothers saw that their father was dead, they said, "It may be that Joseph will hate us and pay us back for all the evil which we did to him." 16 So they sent a message to Joseph, saying, "Your father gave this command before he died, 17 'Say to Joseph, Forgive, I pray you, the transgression of your brothers and their sin, because they did evil to you.' And now, we pray you, forgive the transgression of the servants of the God of your father." Joseph wept when they spoke to him. 18 His brothers also came and fell down before him, and said, "Behold, we are your servants." 19 But Joseph said to them, "Fear not, for am I in the place of God? 20 As for you, you meant evil against me; but God meant it for good, to bring it about that many people should be kept alive, as they are today. 21 So do not fear; I will provide for you and your little ones." Thus he reassured them and comforted them.

22 So Joseph dwelt in Egypt, he and his father's house; and Joseph lived a hundred and ten years. 23 And Joseph saw Ephraim's children of the third generation; the children also of Machir the son of Manasseh were born upon Joseph's knees. 24 And Joseph said to his brothers, "I am about to die; but God will visit you, and bring you up out of this land to the land which he swore to Abraham, to Isaac, and to Jacob." 25 Then Joseph took an oath of the sons of Israel, saying, "God will visit you, and you shall carry up my bones from here." 26 So Joseph died, being a hundred and ten years old; and they embalmed him, and he was put in a coffin in Egypt.

KEY VERSE: As for you, you meant evil against me; but God meant it for good, to bring it about that many people should be kept alive, as they are today. Genesis 50:20 (RSV).

HOME DAILY BIBLE READINGS

Sept. 20. M. *Joseph's Dreams About His Family.* Genesis 37:1–11.
Sept. 21. T. *Joseph Sold to Traders.* Genesis 37:12–28.
Sept. 22. W. *Joseph's Family Seeks Grain.* Genesis 42:1–8.
Sept. 23. T. *Back to Egypt for Grain Again.* Genesis 43:1–15.
Sept. 24. F. *Concern for a Father.* Genesis 44:18–34.
Sept. 25. S. *Joseph Reveals His Identity.* Genesis 45:1–15.
Sept. 26. S. *Joseph Reassured His Brothers.* Genesis 50:15–26.

BACKGROUND

The story of Joseph (called by some the most Christlike figure in the Old Testament) is too familiar to be described in full detail here. We all know him as the eleventh of Jacob's twelve sons, as a child spoiled because his father loved him too much—more than any of the other eleven. Spoiled, conceited, boastful, so obnoxious that the older brothers first envied and then wickedly sold him into slavery in Egypt. That would finish him! That would get him out of their way. But, alas, as Robert Burns put it, "The best laid schemes o' mice and men gang aft a-gley." What the murderous brothers did not know was that God had plans for Joseph, and went with him into Egypt.

NOTES ON THE PRINTED TEXT

The little "spoiled kid" named Joseph died in Egypt, and a great man was born. This evil thing that his brothers had done to him was the best thing that could have happened to Joseph, and, growing, Joseph knew it. He gained great favor with the Pharaoh of the day, who came to love and trust him not as talented enough to hold high office but as a man of spotless, incorruptible character. Never for a moment did Joseph sin in the face of Egypt's king or in the face of God. Over and over again in the story, we read that "Jehovah was with Joseph," or "Joseph was a goodly person, and well-favored" (*see* chapter 39)—so well-favored that the old Pharaoh put him second in command over his whole kingdom. Joseph was thirty years old when that happened. He may never have forgotten his brothers back in Canaan, but they had forgotten him. They thought he was surely dead.

Then a famine struck Canaan, and most of the rest of the Mediterranean world. Poor old Jacob and his sons were threatened with death. They had nowhere to go to find food except to Egypt, for Egypt was the granary of that world. So Jacob sent ten of Joseph's brothers (all except Benjamin), to "buy corn in Egypt" (42:3)—and right into the hands of Joseph!

If this Joseph had been like the most of us, he would have thrown those brothers into prison. After all those years, here was his chance to "get even," to punish them. But no—the brother they had sold into slavery was too great a man for that. For a while, he played a game of cat-and-mouse with them, humiliating them, making them cringe as they were reminded of what they had done to him. When that was over, he asked them, "Doth my father yet live?" (45:3). Yes, Jacob still lived. Joseph wept, when he heard that. He made himself known to them, forgave them, and ordered them to go and bring Jacob to live with them in peace in Egypt. Jacob came; he lived with his reunited family in the region called Goshen, in Egypt, for seventeen more years, and then he died.

Forgiveness! Joseph is the personification of forgiveness among the people called Israel. It runs through the Old Testament from beginning to end; it is also a belief of high priority among those Christians who hear their Master say, "Father, forgive them; for they know not what they do!"

It is hard to believe, but it is fact: when poor old Jacob died, his sons flew into panic. Now that he was gone, they feared Joseph just might take vengeance on them! Even now, they did not see the majesty of their powerful brother. Quaking, they sent a messenger (lacking the courage to go themselves?), who told Joseph that before he died, Jacob had told them to ask his forgiveness for the evil they had done. Were they sincere, or was this just another trick? They begged forgiveness—only because they were frightened? Who knows? It made no difference to Joseph whether they were sincere or not. He asked them, "Do you think I am *God?* Go in peace, my brothers; it is up to God to judge and punish in the end." God, said Joseph, had turned into good the evil they had done him; *He* had brought Joseph to Egypt, and brought it about that His people should not die, but live on in Canaan. And Israel lived!

God does not *create* evil, but He uses it to serve good ends for those who trust Him. (Is He using the evil of a Godless Russia to bring us to our senses, and to stand for Him, today?)

So they lived on in Egypt for many a year to come. And when God was ready, He took Joseph. Joseph was ready for that; there was no fear in his voice when he told the brothers that now he should die; there was only serenity and faith. With his last words, he asked them to take his body back to Canaan and bury it there. He wanted no such elaborate and costly burial as was given to King Tut! Bury him in the Land, the Land of his fathers! They did that; they kept the body in a sealed coffin until Moses came to lead them back home again, to lay His great Joseph to rest in the land of Abraham, Isaac, and Jacob.

What a nobleman of God he was! His love and forgiveness was much like Christ's, passing understanding. He left with his people and with us two mighty convictions: *all of life is in the hands of God, and no living, good man can ever put himself beyond God's love and care.*

SUGGESTIONS TO TEACHERS

"Miracles?" snorted the scoffer. "The biggest miracle I know of is the survival of the Church," he added incredulously. "It should have sputtered out centuries ago, according to all the rules of institutional survival."

This skeptic and critic of the Church could not comprehend how the people of God continue to exist. The answer, of course, is that God preserves His people.

Your lesson this week takes up this idea. Explore with your class the reasons why and the manner in which God continues to preserve the community of the faith by studying the Joseph stories.

1. *LEADERS WITH DREAMS.* Joseph had great dreams. God seems to raise up men and women who will have a sense of vision. The Bible recounts many such stories. Help your class members to do some dreaming as members of the community of God's people today. What dreams do they have for your class? For your congregation? For the Church in your community? For each other as members of God's family? What dreams do you have for your class members? Take plenty of time to share these dreams.

2. *LIFE IN THE PITS.* Joseph, despised by jealous brothers, suffered. Being a leader and dreamer in God's community does not mean exemption from hardship. In fact, it more often means being resented. Don't forget that Jesus was so resented that He was killed and put in the pit of a tomb. God, however, stands with His people, even in the pits.

3. *LEAP OF FAITH.* Joseph, the immigrant slave boy in Egypt, remembered who he was, in spite of adversity and loneliness. He persevered in the faith. He persisted in remembering that he belonged to the Lord. Although Joseph ultimately became the Number Two man in the country, he never assumed that his faith "paid off." Joseph remained faithful without expecting rewards. Devote some of your lesson time on the subject of being steadfast in faith without calculating the prizes you deserve. Some of your class may listen to the electronic church on TV, and be led to think that faith always brings success, and that lack of success may be attributed to lack of faith. Let the biblical message set the record straight: be faithful not because of what you're going to get out of it, but simply because God is faithful to His people!

TOPIC FOR ADULTS
GOD PRESERVES HIS PEOPLE

No Private Haven. "The transcendent God is not the prisoner, much less the mascot, of the Christian community. His presence and work in Jesus means that He is about His humanizing work not just in the church or in Christians but in the world—wherever human beings live together, whether they know or acknowledge Him or not. Nevertheless, if we ask how we can recognize Him and be open to experience and participate in what He is doing, we have to talk about the community gathered, judged, and condemned, but also constantly reclaimed and put to work by the disturbing centrality of the man Jesus in its midst. Openness to the presence of the transcendent God means openness to find Him not only hidden but revealed in the worldly, human, fallible, guilty community of 'Jesus people.' If we are not open to recognize Him in this worldly form, we will not be able to recognize Him in any other worldly form.

"From a Christian perspective, the quest for transcendence and mystery cannot mean the search for a private haven or communal ghetto of 'our kind of people,' where we can find peace and quiet, security and comfort, and the solution to all our problems. It can only mean the willingness to discover the transcendent God who is hidden in the world, in unpleasant as well as pleasant human encounters, among the weak and suffering, where humanizing change is taking place. And most offensive of all, it can only mean the willingness to put up with the Christian community where (however reluctantly) people are confronted with a first-century Jew who is the clue to what this hidden God is doing in the modern world."—Shirley C. Guthrie, Jr., *Transcendence and Mystery*, Earl D. C. Brewer, editor.

Three Word Telegram. Years ago, a distinguished minister in Boston numbered among the members of his congregation an individual who kept up a running vendetta against him. This parishioner was responsible for poison-pen letters, mysterious calls, cliques of opposition, open movements to dismiss the man from his post. Eventually, this member moved to the West Coast. There, under calmer circumstances and, perhaps, under the pressure of advancing years, her heart was penitent. She wrote to ask pardon of the man whose trail she had dogged so many years. Dr. Conrad's response was in the form of a three-word telegram: "Forgiven! Forgotten! Forever!"

This is also God's message for us! He preserves His people through the news that we are forgiven for the purpose of forgiving others.

Questions for Pupils on the Next Lesson. 1. How do you cope with the feelings of rebellion and hopelessness which you sometimes feel? 2. What does Scripture suggest when we experience broken relationships, failures, and disappointments with which we cannot cope? 3. How can Christians make the claim that God continues to rule this world with authority and power? 4. On what basis do God's people state that there is ultimately justice in the world? 5. Why did both the Pharaoh and the Israelites not want to listen to Moses?

TOPIC FOR YOUTH
GOD CARES FOR YOU

Delayed Worship Service. "Because we know through Scripture that God continues to preserve his people, we can be certain of God's care. Sometimes, astonishingly, this means that we must learn to forgive God!

"The story is told that on one *Kol Nidre* Rabbi Levi Yitzhak of Berditchev stood before his congregation, but he prevented the *chazan* (cantor) from chanting *Kol Nidre* (public declaration canceling all forced or harmful personal vows). The congregation waited in silence while the rabbi began to pray. 'Master of the universe, there is a man among us with whom you have dealt very badly. You have taken away his livelihood through his illness, and his wife through hers. And as if that weren't enough, you caused him to lose a precious prayerbook in a fire, a prayerbook that he treasured. I will not permit this service to continue until he has forgiven you.' "—Richard F. Steinbrink, *The Presbyterian Outlook*, 512 E. Main St., Richmond, Va. 23219. Published weekly. $14. per year. Issue of March 26, 1979.

Sharing Family. "I collect 'giving' stories. They're an instant antidote for the ordinary garden variety 'blahs' and they aren't fattening. Recently, a friend of mine, the Rev. Vic Seidel of Wheeling, West Virginia, added a new treasure to my collection.

"It seems that his travels once took him to Mexico, where he decided to buy gifts to take back to his elderly mother. After he'd selected a handsome handwoven tablecloth, his eyes fell on a beautiful carved cane.

So he bought them both for her. And then, who can leave the West without a cowboy hat? So Vic also bought a fancy lid.

"When he got home, he gave his dear mother the cane and the linen. She was delighted, exclaiming over and over how much she liked them. Then, she thought a minute and said, 'You know I got the cloth, but you know who'd just love that cane?'

" 'Who?' asked my friend.

" 'Why, your Uncle Bill. He'd really like that cane. Why don't you just give him the cane?'

"So Vic took the cane, added the cowboy hat and gave them both to his Uncle Bill. Needless to say, his uncle was very, very pleased. He tried on the hat; he strode about with the cane. Then he paused, scratched his chin and said, 'You know, these are both great presents, but you know who'd really like that cowboy hat?'

" 'Who?' asked Vic.

" 'Why your Uncle Joe, I got the cane. Why don't you just take that cowboy hat over to Joe?' So he did.

"Later, when he told the story to me, he reflected, 'That's just the kind of people they are, my mother and my uncles, each always thinking of the others. If I'd had a hundred souvenirs I'd still be giving them away.' "—"Comment" column by Linda Robbins, SERVICE NEWS, Vol. 33, No. 3, June 1980.

As the Church, we are God's "family," and we are preserved for a purpose. That purpose is to share God's care. Vic Seidel's family is a model of what every congregation is intended to be.

Drop-Out. Parents put little Dougie to bed one night and settled down to watch their favorite program. Suddenly, there was a loud THUMP! upstairs. The father and mother bounded up to Dougie's room and found him sitting dazedly on the floor beside his bed. Before they had an opportunity to say anything, Dougie, rubbing his eyes, announced in a sleepy voice, "I guess I fell asleep too close to where I got in."

Isn't this also the experience of many church members after joining the Church? They attend a meeting of the board and are welcomed into membership. Then, they drop out. They "fall asleep too close to where they got in."

As God's community, we must remember that God's preserving power involves each of us. No one of us may be a "drop-out" from passing on his care.

Sentence Sermon to Remember: Joseph proves to us that a good man, wherever he go, cannot put himself beyond God's care.—Frank S. Mead in *Who's Who in the Bible.*

Questions for Pupils on the Next Lesson. 1. Are you sometimes confused about what is going on in the world and what God has to do with it? 2. What, exactly, do you believe God is doing in your daily life? 3. Why are you sometimes unwilling to listen to significant adults who could give you some guidance? 4. Have you ever seen yourself as a leader in the Church? Why or why not? 5. Who are the leaders you respect the most? Why?

LESSON V—OCTOBER 3

GOD REAFFIRMS HIS PROMISE

Background Scripture: Exodus 3:1–6:13
Devotional Reading: Exodus 1:1–14

KING JAMES VERSION

EXODUS 5 22 And Moses returned unto the LORD, and said, Lord, wherefore hast thou *so* evil entreated this people? why *is* it *that* thou hast sent me?

23 For since I came to Pharaoh to speak in thy name, he hath done evil to this people; neither hast thou delivered thy people at all.

6 1 Then the LORD said unto Moses, Now shalt thou see what I will do to Pharaoh: for with a strong hand shall he let them go, and with a strong hand shall he drive them out of his land.

2 And God spake unto Moses, and said unto him, I *am* the LORD:

3 And I appeared unto Abraham, unto Isaac, and unto Jacob, by *the name of* God Almighty; but by my name JEHOVAH was I not known to them.

4 And I have also established my covenant with them, to give them the land of Canaan, the land of their pilgrimage, wherein they were strangers.

5 And I have also heard the groaning of the children of Israel, whom the Egyptians keep in bondage; and I have remembered my covenant.

6 Wherefore say unto the children of Israel, I *am* the LORD, and I will bring you out from under the burdens of the Egyptians, and I will rid you out of their bondage, and I will redeem you with a stretched out arm, and with great judgments:

7 And I will take you to me for a people, and I will be to you a God: and ye shall know that I *am* the LORD your God, which bringeth you out from under the burdens of the Egyptians.

8 And I will bring you in unto the land, concerning the which I did swear to give it to Abraham, to Isaac, and to Jacob; and I will give it you for a heritage: I *am* the LORD.

9 And Moses spake so unto the children of Israel: but they hearkened not unto Moses for anguish of spirit, and for cruel bondage.

REVISED STANDARD VERSION

EXODUS 5 22 Then Moses turned again to the LORD and said, "O LORD, why hast thou done evil to this people? Why didst thou ever send me? 23 For since I came to Pharaoh to speak in thy name, he has done evil to this people, and thou hast not delivered thy people at all." 1 But the LORD said to Moses, "Now you shall see what I will do to Pharaoh; for with a strong hand he will send them out, yea, with a strong hand he will drive them out of his land."

2 And God said to Moses, "I am the LORD. 3 I appeared to Abraham, to Isaac, and to Jacob, as God Almighty, but by my name the LORD I did not make myself known to them. 4 I also established my covenant with them, to give them the land of Canaan, the land in which they dwelt as sojourners. 5 Moreover I have heard the groaning of the people of Israel whom the Egyptians hold in bondage and I have remembered my covenant. 6 Say therefore to the people of Israel, 'I am the LORD, and I will bring you out from under the burdens of the Egyptians, and I will deliver you from their bondage, and I will redeem you with an outstretched arm and with great acts of judgment, 7 and I will take you for my people, and I will be your God; and you shall know that I am the LORD your God, who has brought you out from under the burdens of the Egyptians. 8 And I will bring you into the land which I swore to give to Abraham, to Isaac, and to Jacob; I will give it to you for a possession. I am the LORD.' " 9 Moses spoke thus to the people of Israel; but they did not listen to Moses, because of their broken spirit and their cruel bondage.

13 And the LORD spake unto Moses and unto Aaron, and gave them a charge unto the children of Israel, and unto Pharaoh king of Egypt, to bring the children of Israel out of the land of Egypt.

13 But the LORD spoke to Moses and Aaron, and gave them a charge to the people of Israel and to Pharaoh king of Egypt to bring the people of Israel out of the land of Egypt.

KEY VERSE: . . . I am the Lord and I will bring you out from under the burdens of the Egyptians . . . and I will take you to me for a people, and I will be to you a God. Exodus 6:6,7.

HOME DAILY BIBLE READINGS

Sept. 27. *M.* *Cruel Treatment.* Exodus 1:1–14.
Sept. 28. *T.* *God Intervenes.* Exodus 3:1–10.
Sept. 29. *W.* *The God of Abraham, Isaac, and Jacob.* Exodus 3:11–17.
Sept. 30. *T.* *Clear Evidence.* Exodus 4:1–9.
Oct. 1. *F.* *Needed Help.* Exodus 4:14–16,27–31.
Oct. 2. *S.* *Confrontation.* Exodus 5:1–5.
Oct. 3. *S.* *Complaining.* Exodus 5:15–23.

BACKGROUND

The "Sojourn" of the Israelites in Egypt lasted, according to Exodus 12:40, four hundred and thirty years, and while accurate dates are hard to determine at this time, that is probably approximately correct. Over that long period, between Joseph and Moses, the children of Israel multiplied in Goshen—and became almost the slaves of Rameses II, the greatest boaster and the greatest builder in Egyptian history. In a strictly literal sense, they were not slaves; they were in Egypt of their own accord, but they were pressed into laboring *like* slaves. Driven mercilessly, they built the great hypostyle at Karnak, the magnificent colonnade at Luxor—in front of which they set up six tremendous statues of Rameses!

They were a good labor force, but to Rameses they were also something of a threat to the throne of Egypt; there were just too many rebel-minded Jews in his kingdom, and that meant the danger of rebellion. He was driving them to slow death, and the time came when they could stand it no longer. Along about 1250 B.C., with the approval of Rameses, they made their "Exodus" from Egypt and started back to their own land. They left because God sent them a giant of a leader named Moses.

NOTES ON THE PRINTED TEXT

Moses! He was the brightest star in the galaxy of Israel's great leaders, their deliverer, their lawgiver, a great rock of a man who turned the tide of history, who forced Rameses to "let his people go." Like Joseph, he grew up in Egypt and became a high official in the Egyptian government—a "lord of all Egypt" (Genesis 45:9). He might have lived out his days in the luxuries of the Egyptian court, but he was a Jew and not an Egyptian, and the labor enslavement of his fellow Jews fell on his heart like a stinging whip. One day this sting erupted in a fit of anger: Moses killed an Egyptian slave driver who was abusing a Jewish laborer, buried his body in the sand and fled into Midian, beyond the grasp of Rameses. That was a great mistake. Moses made three great mistakes—when he killed that Egyptian, when he was stubbornly resistant against God's command and will, and when he sinned against God at the rock of Meribah (for which he was denied entrance into the Promised Land).

Actually, Moses did not want to go back to Egypt and bring out his people to freedom. God had to *draft* him! To the great credit of Moses, *he went back.* He went back to lead a people whose suffering had almost destroyed their faith in the God of Abraham, Isaac, and Jacob; at other times, they had lost faith in Moses. They had come to think that both God and Moses had deserted them, and in a moment of despondency Moses himself complained to God that "thou hast not delivered my people at all!" (Exodus 5:23). How could God expect me, Moses, to do what He has not done? The old covenant promise of God to Abraham, to establish this people in the Promised Land, seemed to have been broken. You, God, want *me* to bring them out? They will not even *listen* to me! (What sins do we commit when frustration and abject humility overcomes us!)

God has the perfect answer for all this: "I am Jehovah (a new name for God!), the almighty God who appeared to Abraham, Isaac, and Jacob . . . and I entered into a solemn covenant with them. . . . And now I have heard the groaning of the people of Israel, and I remember my promise" (Exodus 6:2-5, TLB). The almighty Jehovah, not Moses, had promised this; Moses was only the instrument of freedom not its author. This was a divine recital of faith on the nature of the God of Israel. If God were their leader and their hope, what could a puny king like Rameses do to stop it? Go, Moses, and tell your people that. Go and stand before Pharaoh and command him, in the name of God, "Let my people go!" And he went, and Pharaoh let His people go.

Yes, the great Moses made mistakes. Who doesn't? "We can eliminate his mistakes . . . and look only at his splendid achievements—a nation rescued from bondage, trained to righteousness and power, and the laws and religion of the whole world placed on their immutable foundations. All this, under God, we owe to Moses. Mistakes are sad things, but they may become occasions of joy! They are the black soil out of which may grow lovely flowers and sturdy trees. When a great man makes mistakes, it is indeed calamitous. But when from all his mistakes he comes off more than conqueror, we can all thank God, take courage, gird up our loins, and do the same."—Amos R. Wells, in *Bible Miniatures.*

Kings like Rameses are but puppets after all. Men like Moses are the great benefactors of this world. In them lies our only hope in our day when godless Pharaohs terrorize our world. But the terrifiers will pass when God grows tired of them, and God will still be here.

SUGGESTIONS TO TEACHERS

A brilliant young engineering consultant sat next to a Christian clergyman on the fifteen-hour flight from Los Angeles to Sydney, Australia. After several hours of conversation, the engineer felt comfortable enough with his seatmate to tell him that he felt a little like he was talking with a member of the flat-earth society. The pastor laughed, in spite of being regarded as a something of a curiosity and source of amusement. The engineering consultant insisted that anyone clinging to a view of the universe in which the idea of a God is taken seriously is as much of a back number as someone thinking that the world is flat, and also as obstinate in refusing to acknowledge the "evidence."

What "evidence" can God's people muster to "prove" that the consultant is mistaken? None, actually, except God's own reaffirmation of His promises. God is greater than cynical young consultants, and wisely maintains that He keeps His promises as He did with Moses, the Prophets, and through Jesus.

The account of Moses coming to terms with God's promise is the gist of your lesson today.

1. *GOD INTRODUCES.* You have so much rich material from the Exodus report of God calling Moses that you will have to select certain parts for emphasis and slide over others. Point out, however, that God calls Moses and each of us by name. God knows us personally, not as statistics. Moreover, when God introduces Himself, He reminds Moses and each of us that He is the God of our spiritual ancestors. He tells us that we are part of an ongoing saga of His people. God makes it clear that He reaffirms the promise made earlier to our fathers and mothers in the faith.

2. *GOD INHABITS.* Make sure that your class members understand how God identifies with the oppressed and suffering in the world. Point out the passages in the Scripture in today's lesson which deal with the Lord telling Moses, "I have seen . . . I have heard . . . I know. . . ." God is very much in this world! Make your class aware that God is aware of world conditions. However, there is more than being aware that God is aware. Moses learned that such an awareness of God at work also meant that God had put His finger on him. Are your class members conscious of the way the Lord also has fingered each of them for service in His world?

3. *GOD INSISTS.* You should have some fun by noting Moses' excuses. In fact, you may wish to have your class make a list of these. The class will quickly see similarities between Moses' evasions and those of believers today. ("I am nobody. How can I go?" . . . "Suppose they don't believe me?" . . . "I am not a good speaker" . . . "Send someone else.") More important, point out how God bats down every excuse. The Lord insists that Moses return to Egypt and deliver His people. Where is God sending you and your people today? What is the "Egypt" to which He insists you go?

4. *GOD INSTRUCTS.* Moses finds the Pharaoh opposes the Lord's plans. Even the Hebrews resist. Moses complains to God, "Why do you mistreat your people? Why did you send me here?" (Exodus 5:22). The Lord reaffirms His promises, telling Moses, "Now you will see what I will do . . . I am the Lord. I appeared to Abraham, to Isaac, to Jacob . . . established my covenant with them" (Exodus 6:1–4). Help those in your class with wobbly faith to grow in confidence that they will see what God will do.

TOPIC FOR ADULTS
GOD REAFFIRMS HIS PROMISE

The Promise in a Penicillin Vial. A Filipino college student once described the first Communion service of a Hill Tribe from one of the Philippine Islands. A missionary had preached the Gospel to them and taught them until they had accepted Christ as their Lord and Savior. They came to him and asked if they might partake of the Sacrament of the Lord's Supper. He agreed and set the day for the service. On that day, before the elements were distributed, he preached a sermon in which he told them they could not commune with the living Christ if there was hatred or an unforgiving spirit in their hearts.

As he walked the pulpit to the Table, an old man got up and went to the other side of the room. There he put his head on another man's shoulder and said, "Forgive me, my brother, I have hated you for years because once you stole a chicken from me." After they had demonstrated understanding and peace between them, the old man returned to his seat. Hardly had he seated himself, when a second man got up and going to another man reenacted the same confession and forgiveness with him. Soon people were getting up all over the room and cleansing their hearts as they asked forgiveness of each other.

When they had all returned to their places, the Sacrament was given in the peace and stillness of Christ's presence and Christ's love. The Communion was served in empty penicillin vials which had deep meaning for them. From these same little bottles had come healing for their bodies, even as they were now receiving healing for their souls, as the living Christ had helped them cast out hatred and an unforgiving spirit.

Holy Ground for Future Moseses. In the country church of a small village, an altar boy serving the priest at Sunday Mass accidentally dropped the cruet of wine. The village priest struck the altar boy sharply on the cheek and in a gruff voice shouted: "Leave the altar and don't come back!" The boy became Tito. "In the cathedral of a large city, an altar boy serving the bishop at Sunday Mass accidentally dropped the cruet of wine. With a warm twinkle in his eyes, the bishop gently whispered: 'Someday you will be a priest.' " The result: Fulton Sheen, Archbishop, was on his way up from altar boyhood.

Daydreams. Novelist Kurt Vonnegut, speaking to the congregation at St. Clement's Episcopal Church, New York City, a couple of years ago, told why he thought people attended worship services. "People come to church not for preachments," observed Vonnegut, "but to daydream about God."

God invariably intrudes Himself on our daydreams. Moses reflecting in the midst of his sheep-tending daydreamed about God. Those daydreams led to a startling encounter. Ultimately, Moses' daydreams propelled him back to Egypt. He discovered that God frees and instructs His chosen people.

Are you providing time for daydreams about God? Are you pondering how God reaffirms His promise to you and to His people today?

Questions for Pupils on the Next Lesson. 1. What is the Christian equivalent to the Jewish Passover? 2. How can Christians use memorial services as means of personal spiritual growth? 3. Who are the oppressed and exploited people in your community? 4. How are you teaching the young people in your congregation the meaning of God's deliverance?

TOPIC FOR YOUTH
WHEN THE GOING GETS TOUGH

End of the Stymie. You have heard the expression, *stymied,* but you probably don't know the origin of the word. In golf, if your ball is on the green and your opponent's ball is between you and the hole, you are "stymied." This is because a basic rule of golf states that the player farthest from the hole must putt first. Obviously, you could not putt past your opponent's ball, and had to use extra strokes to go around it. Almost a century ago, however, the stymie rule was changed when the game became popular in America. The new rule declared that it was polite and proper for your opponent to "mark" the spot where his ball is so that you can putt over him instead of going around him.

God has delivered us from being stymied by hopelessness. The Bible message is that He has instituted a new beginning in the game of life.

Funny Excuses. Moses tried many excuses to avoid going to Egypt. We are all masters at making excuses.

Recently, an insurance company publicized some of the excuses for claims which have been filed in its New York office. Here are a few:

"An invisible car came out of nowhere, struck my car, and vanished."

"The other car collided with mine without warning me of its intention."

"I had been driving my car for forty years when I fell asleep at the wheel and had the accident."

"As I reached an intersection, a hedge sprang up obscuring my vision."

"I pulled away from the side of the road, glanced at my mother-in-law, and headed over the embankment."

"The pedestrian had no idea which direction to go, so I ran over him."

"The telephone pole was approaching fast. I attempted to swerve out of its path when it struck my front end."

"The guy was all over the road. I had to swerve a number of times before I hit him."

"The indirect cause of this accident was a little guy in a small car with a big mouth."

Amusing? Yes, but not as absurd as the excuses we try to make to the Lord.

End of a Community. St. Kilda is a remote island west of Scotland. Today, it is a bird sanctuary. Once, however, this outermost island of the Hebrides had a stable population of 200 people who lived by fishing and farming. Forty-two islanders emigrated to Australia in 1851 and 1856, and during the following years the young men began to leave as soon as they were old enough. By 1930, there were only thirty-five St. Kildans. Discouraged, the thirty-five gave up. They petitioned the government to be evacuated to the mainland.

Even before their petition was delivered and any decision was made, however, the St. Kildans had given up. They had planted no crops for the coming year.

When there is no hope for the future, we plant no crops for the coming year. Without an awareness of God's promise, we despair. A famous football coach used to tell his teams, "When the going gets tough, the tough get going," and we of the Church know we can get going because of God's freeing and instructing His people.

Sentence Sermon to Remember: God never made a promise to any man that He didn't keep.—J. C. Cook.

Questions for Pupils on the Next Lesson. 1. What are the main forces that have shaped the history of the Christian Church? 2. What are the principal forces which have shaped your personal faith? 3. What are the most significant celebrations for you in the Church? 4. How involved are you in the lives of people struggling to achieve liberation and identity? 5. Does your family provide a setting for growing in the Christian faith?

LESSON VI—OCTOBER 10

GOD ESTABLISHES THE PASSOVER

Background Scripture: Exodus 11, 12
Devotional Reading: Exodus 12:37–42

KING JAMES VERSION

EXODUS 12 11 And thus shall ye eat it; *with* your loins girded, your shoes on your feet, and your staff in your hand; and ye shall eat it in haste: it *is* the LORD's passover.

12 For I will pass through the land of Egypt this night, and will smite all the firstborn in the land of Egypt, both man and beast; and against all the gods of Egypt I will execute judgment: I *am* the LORD.

13 And the blood shall be to you for a token upon the houses where ye *are:* and when I see the blood, I will pass over you, and the plague shall not be upon you to destroy *you,* when I smite the land of Egypt.

14 And this day shall be unto you for a memorial; and ye shall keep it a feast to the LORD throughout your generations: ye shall keep it a feast by an ordinance for ever.

15 Seven days shall ye eat unleavened bread; even the first day ye shall put away leaven out of your houses: for whosoever eateth leavened bread from the first day until the seventh day, that soul shall be cut off from Israel.

16 And in the first day *there shall be* a holy convocation, and in the seventh day there shall be a holy convocation to you; no manner of work shall be done in them, save *that* which every man must eat, that only may be done of you.

17 And ye shall observe *the feast of* unleavened bread; for in this selfsame day have I brought your armies out of the land of Egypt: therefore shall ye observe this day in your generations by an ordinance for ever.

24 And ye shall observe this thing for an ordinance to thee and to thy sons for ever.

25 And it shall come to pass, when ye be come to the land which the LORD will give you, according as he hath promised, that ye shall keep this service.

26 And it shall come to pass, when your children shall say unto you, What mean ye by this service?

REVISED STANDARD VERSION

EXODUS 12 11 "In this manner you shall eat it: your loins girded, your sandals on your feet, and your staff in your hand; and you shall eat it in haste. It is the LORD's passover. 12 For I will pass through the land of Egypt that night, and I will smite all the first-born in the land of Egypt, both man and beast; and on all the gods of Egypt I will execute judgments: I am the LORD. 13 The blood shall be a sign for you, upon the houses where you are; and when I see the blood, I will pass over you, and no plague shall fall upon you to destroy you, when I smite the land of Egypt.

14 "This day shall be for you a memorial day, and you shall keep it as a feast to the LORD; throughout your generations you shall observe it as an ordinance for ever. 15 Seven days you shall eat unleavened bread; on the first day you shall put away leaven out of your houses, for if any one eats what is leavened, from the first day until the seventh day, that person shall be cut off from Israel. 16 On the first you shall hold a holy assembly, and on the seventh day a holy assembly; no work shall be done on those days; but what every one must eat, that only may be prepared by you. 17 And you shall observe the feast of unleavened bread, for on this very day I brought your hosts out of the land of Egypt: therefore you shall observe this day, throughout your generations, as an ordinance for ever.

24 "You shall observe this rite as an ordinance for you and for your sons for ever. 25 And when you come to the land which the LORD will give you, as he has promised, you shall keep this service. 26 And when your children say to you, 'What do you mean by this service?' 27 you shall say, 'It is the sacrifice of the LORD's passover, for he passed over the houses of the people

27 That ye shall say, It *is* the sacrifice of the LORD's passover, who passed over the houses of the children of Israel in Egypt, when he smote the Egyptians, and delivered our houses. And the people bowed the head and worshipped.

of Israel in Egypt, when he slew the Egyptians but spared our houses.' " And the people bowed their heads and worshiped.

***KEY VERSE:* "This day shall be for you a memorial day, and you shall keep it as a feast to the Lord, throughout your generations you shall observe it as an ordinance forever."** Exodus 12:14 (RSV).

HOME DAILY BIBLE READINGS

Oct. 4. M. One More Punishment. Exodus 11:1–8.
Oct. 5. T. A Lasting Memorial. Exodus 12:1–14.
Oct. 6. W. Once Slaves. Deuteronomy 16:1–12.
Oct. 7. T. Seeing the Blood. Exodus 12:21–28.
Oct. 8. F. The Final Straw. Exodus 12:29–36.
Oct. 9. S. Setting Out. Exodus 12:37–42.
Oct. 10. S. Participation. Exodus 12:43–50.

BACKGROUND

Tourists in modern Egypt stare in awe at the ruins of great stone buildings erected by Rameses II, and at his ridiculously tall statues cut out of stone. But the Jews who knew this Pharaoh while he lived knew that he had a heart of stone. They never forgot the command of this king who ordered the death of countless Hebrew children, who made them make bricks without straw, nor the anguish of Jewish laborers, the hiss of the master's whip, the broken promises, the hard heart of this fiendish Pharaoh.

This agony was at its peak when Moses stood face to face with Rameses and demanded that he set his labor prisoners free to leave his land. But neither the voice of an enraged Moses or even the voice of God did anything to soften that murderous heart. So God used another method of persuasion. In what the Hebrews saw as God's divine retribution, a series of plagues fell upon Egypt; water in the rivers turned to blood, frogs and insects came in clouds, locusts ate crops from the ground, the cattle died, men and beasts suffered the affliction of boils or carbuncles, hailstorms further destroyed the crops ("only in Goshen was there no hail"), and an impenetrable darkness fell on the whole land. Pharaoh trembled, but still refused to let the Jews of Goshen go.

Then came the worst of all. Moses tells Pharaoh that the Almighty God would take the lives of every first-born Egyptian son! Only the first-born of the Jews would be spared. And after that, the Jewish people would go out of Egypt.

Pharaoh couldn't believe it. But the Jews did.

NOTES ON THE PRINTED TEXT

Moses and Aaron moved among the people and told them what to do before the slaughter began. They were to prepare themselves for the long march to Canaan. To protect them against the killing of their first-born, they were to take and kill a lamb, a lamb without blemish, "a male of the first year," and sprinkle its blood on their doorposts and lintels. Then they were to eat the lamb and burn whatever might be left over. They were to partake of this feast with shoes on their feet and their staffs close at hand, ready to move. God would see to it that they should escape; the devastating angels of death would see that blood sign on every Jewish door, and He would spare the lives of all within the house. This was to happen on the tenth day of the month Abib, later known as Nisan on the fourteenth day, in the early evening. Henceforth this was to be the first month of the sacred Jewish year. And the feast of lamb, this night, would be known forever as The Feast of Passover—or the feast of the night when God "passed over" every Jewish home and saved its occupants.

Blood! The blood of a lamb! We read the same words in the story of One offering up His blood as the Lamb of God on Calvary, to save not only His own people, but the people of all the world! Said Paul, "For even Christ our Passover is sacrificed for us: Therefore let us keep the feast, not with the old leaven, neither with the leaven of malice and wickedness, but with the unleavened bread of sincerity and truth" (*see* 1 Corinthians 5:7,8).

Thus was born the deathless Passover of the Jewish people, who never forgot the passing over of their God. Their commemoration of this Passover has kept the event as much alive in New York as in Jerusalem.

Closely linked with this observance of the Feast of the Passover is the Feast of Unleavened Bread. Unleavened bread (the Jewish *mazzoth*) is bread without yeast. Yeast had a *fermenting* value; it was the symbol of corruption; it is also a symbolism of the abolition of corruptness in the people of a God who would have fellowship only with a *holy* people, a totally *incorrupt* people. For seven days after Passover, then, let the people of God celebrate that fellowship in eating unleavened bread.

Passover meant *redemption* to the Jews. It meant deliverance from bondage and from death at the hands of the Egyptians. God said to them, "You shall observe this rite (this annual celebration of Passover) as an ordinance for you and for your sons for ever" (verse 24 RSV). They should celebrate it in *remembrance* of their deliverance from the land of the Pharaohs.

The Christian too, has his rite of remembrance of another day or night of deliverance; he repeats, in his rite of the Last Supper the words of another Deliverer: "Do ye this in remembrance of me!" He, too, has been saved, redeemed, by way of the shed blood of another Lamb on a cross, the blood of another Lamb without blemish and without spot (*see* 1 Peter 1:18). He, too, has a security which depends upon his trust in the promises of God. The relation of the Feast of the Passover and the Last Supper is vital and familiar. The Christian too, has his Pascal Lamb, and he feeds upon Him by faith.

SUGGESTIONS TO TEACHERS

An artist lecturing on Michelangelo's sculpture *Pieta* described the artist as one who "liberated" the beautiful figures by chipping away the pieces of marble enslaving them in the block.

God's activity at the time of Moses and the Pharaoh was also a case of seeing something beautiful hidden and trapped in the rough block of hopeless circumstances but chipping away until the work of art was complete. What we call Passover was an act of liberation.

Your Jewish neighbors or the local rabbi can help you on the details of the Passover celebration today if necessary. Don't fuss too much over the ceremonial aspects, however. The important matter is what God was doing then, and how He is liberating now.

1. *THE ACTOR.* Call attention to the way that the Lord is the chief actor, not the Pharaoh and not Moses. The Lord establishes the miraculous deliverance in spite of the power and willfulness of the mightiest ruler on earth at the time. Do those in your class see God at work in the world today? What acts do they see Him doing in these days? Help them to profit from understanding the Passover account in coping with the cruel "pharaohs" in their world. You should encourage the members of your class to describe the "pharaohs" oppressing them. Emphasize that the Lord, not these two-bit rulers, is the chief Activator in the universe.

2. *THE INITIATOR.* You may have some in your class who are uncomfortable with the way so many apparently perished during the Passover and who accuse God of cruelty or capriciousness. Remind your class that disobedience to God always has social consequences. Refusal to heed the Lord is more than merely a personal affair. It affects others. The Pharaoh's cavalier disregard of God's rule ("Who is the Lord?" he repeatedly sneers) and callous unconcern for the suffering Hebrews meant that God had to take counter steps. Wherever there is oppression or injustice, God initiates deliverance. Ask your class to identify areas where God may be initiating deliverances today.

3. *THE CONQUEROR.* The death of the Pharaoh's son, who was thought to be the personification of the highest Egyptian deity, signified the triumph of the Lord over all rival gods. God is never stymied. He reigns supreme. The Lord is Conqueror, and enables us also to conquer when lesser gods try to claim us. What are some of the rival gods trying to displace the Lord and capture our allegiance?

4. *THE LIBERATOR.* Discuss with your class the parallels between the Jewish Passover and the Christian celebration of Easter, sometimes referred to as the Christian "Passover." How is the Resurrection a liberation experience for us Christians? Why do believers often refer to Jesus Christ as the Liberator?

TOPIC FOR ADULTS
REMEMBERING THE PASSOVER

King Bestows Citizenship. Benny Gyaw, a Karen tribesman forced to flee from Burma to Thailand, is a Christian serving as a house parent in the Maessering Christian Hostel for orphans and as a translator of the Bible into the Karen dialect. When rats destroyed the rice seedlings of a group of tribesmen in northern Thailand, Benny Gyaw organized a feeding program among the Christians in the area. Although desperately poor themselves, because of Benny Gyaw's leadership and inspiration they kept the hill tribes from starving to death. Benny Gyaw also instituted a fish pond for the hill people to help them feed themselves. Prince Pitsadet, the Thai King's right-hand man, heard of Benny Gyaw's efforts and had the King of Thailand pay a personal visit to him. The King arrived in the village in a helicopter and inspected the fish pond. Knowing that the village had no chair for the King, Benny Gyaw carried a folding chair the many miles along the steep mountain trails so that the King could be received properly. Duly seated on the folding chair, the King received Benny Gyaw. The King, impressed with Gyaw's service, granted Benny Gyaw, the Karen refugee, Thai citizenship on the spot. Today, that folding chair hangs on the wall of Benny Gyaw's house in northern Thailand. No one is allowed to sit on it. The grateful Benny Gyaw memorializes the visit of the King.

As Benny Gyaw was surprised by the visit of the King, and commemorated the announcement of citizenship through that folding chair, so believers are reminded that there has been a Passover in their everyday lives. The Good News of God's promise breaks in on Moses and each of us, often when we least expect it. God has remembered us! He has visited His people and made us citizens of His realm.

Remembering the Past and Future. "Our world indeed is full of problems and the signs of the times are clear: the dignity and rights of all men, women, and children must be asserted and achieved, the hungry must be fed, peace between nations must be worked for, the environment protected, human life respected.

"You know well that you cannot now see the fullness of the light, which will be the reward of all who are faithful, but you can catch a glimpse of that mystery as a warm, gentle glow . . . the present generation wants to hear about God, and what they hear must have the ring of authenticity born of experience."—Basil Hume, Archbishop of Westminster, at the celebration of 1,500 years of Benedictine Order at Westminster Abbey, London, July 1980.

Lessons for God's People. "In Germany, the Nazis first came for the Communists and I didn't speak up because I was not a Communist.

"Then they came for the Jews, and I did not speak up because I was not a Jew.

"Then they came for the Trade Unionists and I didn't speak up because I wasn't a Trade Unionist.

"Then they came for the Catholics and I was a Protestant so I didn't speak up.

"Then they came for ME . . . by that time there was no one to speak up for anyone."—Pastor Martin Niemoller at the Council of the Evangelical Church in Germany, October 18, 1945.

Questions for Pupils on the Next Lesson. 1. How would you list your responsibilities to God, to others, and to yourself? 2. What are "golden calves" in contemporary culture? 3. What is the greatest failure of the Church in our times in your opinion? 4. Does God persist in bringing up the sins and failures of the past? 5. How does irresponsibility disrupt relationships?

TOPIC FOR YOUTH
TRACING YOUR RELIGIOUS ROOTS

Sense of Identity and Destiny. "Christopher Columbus was one of the most remarkable Christian laymen of all time.

"Columbus believed that his own name, given to him at his baptism, was a special sign that God had predestinated him to be the evangelist (*Christophoros*—Christ-bearer) who would open up the unreached tribes of the 'distant isles' to the saving knowledge of the Gospel of the Lord Jesus Christ. He believed that the Holy Spirit had given him special assistance in understanding both the Scriptures and the sciences of navigation and geography required for his life's mission.

"As Columbus urged his near-mutinous sailors to sail on through uncharted seas in the fall of 1492, his zeal and assurance were not derived from love of adventure or greed for gold and glory, but were founded wholly upon the revealed word of God in Scripture. He regarded the successful outcome of his voyages as confirmation of the truth of Scripture and the faithfulness of the sovereign God who had graciously decreed the opening of new lands and tribes to the Gospel of the Saviour Jesus Christ.

"Columbus named his first landfall *San Salvador* (Holy Saviour), and in February 1502, while making preparations for his fourth voyage, he wrote to Pope Alexander VI asking for priests and friars to assist him, 'in the name of the Lord Jesus to spread his name and Gospel everywhere.' Columbus specified that he wanted to select these evangelists himself.

"All of Columbus's sailing journals and most of his private letters give evidence of his biblical knowledge and his devout love for Jesus Christ.

" 'Our Lord Jesus desired to perform a very obvious miracle in the voyage to the Indies, to comfort me and the whole people of God.

" 'No one should fear to undertake any task in the name of our Saviour, if it is just and if the intention is purely for His holy service.' "—August J. Kling. Reprinted from *The Presbyterian Layman.*

The Good and The Best. George E. Washington Carver, the great black American scientist, had to make his choice between the good and the best. Just as he was beginning his work at Tuskegee, a painting of his received honorable mention at the World's Columbian Exposition. He was invited to exhibit his paintings in Paris. The possibility of a great career in art opened before him. Should he give his life to art—a worthy ambition—or should he remain at Tuskegee to serve the members of his race? For months the conflict burned within him. Would it never end? Then came the day which all of us face. Dr. Carver remembered his roots. He recalled that he was a Christian. The Passover story had always had special meaning for him, a black man, because he could identify with the way that God delivered the Israelites from slavery. Remembering the Passover, Dr. Carver made his decision. He would remain at Tuskegee and lift the social, economic, and spiritual level of the Negro. He chose the best. Painting—the good—remained with him as a hobby.

Fake Roots. Hans Hermann Weyer noticed that titles still count in West Germany. Even the general manager of the Hamburg soccer team uses "Dr." before his name, and the woman who reads the weather reports on German television refers to herself as "Doktor." Weyer figured that people would be willing to pay for status and lineage. A few years ago, he began to manufacture titles. By his own count, Weyer sold 350 doctoral degrees, 76 certificates of nobility, 80 consular titles and 23 other orders of distinction—all bogus. Weyer is now in jail, convicted of fraud and falsification, but defends his deception on the grounds that he was giving his clients a sense of roots.

Christ's people need no such flimflamery. We trace our religious roots to the Passover. Our sense of who we are comes from being part of the community of faith that stretches back 5,000 years to Abraham and down through Isaac, Jacob, Moses, the Prophets, and Jesus Christ. This is identity enough!

Sentence Sermon to Remember:

Christ is our Passover!
And we will keep the feast
With the new leaven
The bread of heaven:
All welcome, even the least!
—A, R. Thompson, from
The Roman Breviary.

Questions for Pupils on the Next Lesson. 1. Why does being irresponsible always eventually disrupt relationships? 2. How do you define sin? 3. How do you reconcile the statements that God both judges and forgives? 4. What is the story of the Golden Calf? 5. What idols do people make for themselves in these times?

LESSON VII—OCTOBER 17

GOD FORGIVES HIS PEOPLE

Background Scripture: Exodus 32:1–34:10
Devotional Reading: Exodus 20:1–17

KING JAMES VERSION

EXODUS 32 9 And the LORD said unto Moses, I have seen this people, and, behold, it *is* a stiffnecked people:

10 Now therefore let me alone, that my wrath may wax hot against them, and that I may consume them: and I will make of thee a great nation.

11 And Moses besought the LORD his God, and said, LORD, why doth thy wrath wax hot against thy people, which thou hast brought forth out of the land of Egypt with great power, and with a mighty hand?

12 Wherefore should the Egyptians speak, and say, For mischief did he bring them out, to slay them in the mountains, and to consume them from the face of the earth? Turn from thy fierce wrath, and repent of this evil against thy people.

13 Remember Abraham, Isaac, and Israel, thy servants, to whom thou swarest by thine own self, and saidst unto them, I will multiply your seed as the stars of heaven, and all this land that I have spoken of will I give unto your seed, and they shall inherit *it* for ever.

14 And the LORD repented of the evil which he thought to do unto his people.

34 5 And the LORD descended in the cloud, and stood with him there, and proclaimed the name of the LORD.

6 And the LORD passed by before him, and proclaimed, The LORD, The LORD God, merciful and gracious, long suffering, and abundant in goodness and truth,

7 Keeping mercy for thousands, forgiving iniquity and transgression and sin, and that will by no means clear *the guilty;* visiting the iniquity of the fathers upon the children, and upon the children's children, unto the third and to the fourth *generation.*

8 And Moses made haste, and bowed his head toward the earth, and worshipped.

9 And he said, If now I have found grace in thy sight, O Lord, let my Lord, I pray thee, go among us; for it *is* a stiffnecked people; and pardon our iniquity and our sin, and take us for thine inheritance.

REVISED STANDARD VERSION

EXODUS 32 9 And the LORD said to Moses, "I have seen this people, and behold, it is a stiff-necked people; 10 now therefore let me alone, that my wrath may burn hot against them and I may consume them; but of you I will make a great nation."

11 But Moses besought the LORD his God, and said, "O LORD, why does thy wrath burn hot against thy people, whom thou hast brought forth out of the land of Egypt with great power and with a mighty hand? 12 Why should the Egyptians say, 'With evil intent did he bring them forth, to slay them in the mountains, and to consume them from the face of the earth'? Turn from thy fierce wrath, and repent of this evil against thy people. 13 Remember Abraham, Isaac, and Israel, thy servants, to whom thou didst swear by thine own self, and didst say to them, 'I will multiply your descendants as the stars of heaven, and all this land that I have promised I will give to your descendants, and they shall inherit it for ever.'" 14 And the LORD repented of the evil which he thought to do to his people.

34 5 And the LORD descended in the cloud and stood with him there, and proclaimed the name of the LORD. 6 The LORD passed before him, and proclaimed, "The LORD, the LORD, a God merciful and gracious, slow to anger, and abounding in steadfast love and faithfulness, 7 keeping steadfast love for thousands, forgiving iniquity and transgression and sin, but who will by no means clear the guilty, visiting the iniquity of the fathers upon the children and the children's children, to the third and the fourth generation." 8 And Moses made haste to bow his head toward the earth, and worshiped. 9 And he said, "If now I have found favor in thy sight, O LORD, let the LORD, I pray thee, go in the midst of us, although it is a stiff-necked people; and pardon our iniquity and our sin, and take us for thy inheritance."

KEY VERSE: The Lord is merciful and gracious, slow to anger and abounding in steadfast love. Psalms 103:8 (RSV).

HOME DAILY BIBLE READINGS

Oct. 11. *M.* *God's Commands.* Exodus 20:1–17.
Oct. 12. *T.* *Disobedience.* Exodus 32:1–6.
Oct. 13. *W.* *Justifiable Anger.* Exodus 32:15–24.
Oct. 14. *T.* *Punishment.* Exodus 32:30–35.
Oct. 15. *F.* *Not Angry Forever.* Psalms 103:1–12.
Oct. 16. *S.* *Father, Forgive Them.* Luke 23:26–34.
Oct. 17. *S.* *Forgiving Presence.* Exodus 33:12–23.

BACKGROUND

Three months after the Israelites had left Egypt, they set up a camp at the foot of the holy mountain of Sinai. They were a weary, cheerless, almost a hopeless company, and no wonder: they had fought their way over one hundred and fifty miles of wilderness, and it seemed that they would *never* reach Canaan. And they were rebellious. Moses, they felt, had led them into a trap to die, and even God had deserted them. If they had only stayed in Egypt, where life was better than this, even in slavery! Where was Moses, at this moment? He was not in the camp.

Moses was where God wanted him to be: up at the crest of Sinai, alone with God. He was up there for a long time; Exodus 24:18 tells us that he was up there forty days and nights, but we must not take that literally. Forty was a symbolic number used generally for a period of time—here, a long, long time. "We wot not what is become of him," wailed the people in the camp. Something must have happened to him. Maybe he is dead.

He was far from dead. He was receiving the Ten Commandments from God, and his instructions for the future.

Sinfully impatient and afraid, the Israelites decided to go their own way, without God or Moses. They set up a golden calf, or young bullock, and worshiped *that!*

NOTES ON THE PRINTED TEXT

What these frightened, discouraged people wanted was a visible manifestation of God—an image, an *idol* they could *see* and worship. They had been warned against such idolatry in Egypt, but they had forgotten that. (It is a familiar sin; only last week, on TV, we heard a frightened woman with a son captured in Iran, exclaim, "If there is a God up there, what is He *doing*?") Aaron, the brother of Moses, gave them a calf made of gold, and they worshiped it in a wild night of drinking and sexuality.

God saw this, though Moses did not; God sent Moses down the Mount to stop it. He came with the tablets of the Law in his hands, and in anger against "this stiff-necked" (obstinate, selfish, spiritually blind) people. He smashed their idol, smashed the tablets of the Law. It was a bitter anger; he was punishing a people who had broken their covenant with God.

God, according to the record, was mad, too. Why not? Why shouldn't He have been mad? God is just, but He can be a God of wrath, too. God would "consume" them for this sin, He would destroy them, and "I will make of thee (Moses) a great nation" (verse 10).

Destroy them? Wipe them out? Moses cannot bear even the thought of that. Please, Lord, *no,* he prays in the most notable act of his career. Please, not *now.* You have saved, redeemed them, Lord, and made them a Chosen People. To destroy them now would be regarded as a triumph by the Egyptians. It would nullify the promises God had made to Abraham, Isaac, and Jacob. Yes, Lord, they have sinned but give them another chance! And God repented (changed His mind), and gave them another chance, and another, and another, and another, as the years wore on.

Let's face it: every one of us *deserves* punishment for our sins. God is not to be mocked by our denial of Him, our desertion of Him. But there is always the possibility of a second chance, provided we repent and go His way. God takes no joy in punishment. In one sense, men punish *themselves;* in choosing the way of sin instead of the way of obedience to God, they throw their lives "down the drain." Now Moses goes up the Mount again, and answers the call of God, who bids him bring two new tablets of stone on which the Commandments will be written all over again. So is the Law renewed; so is the covenant renewed. Once more, God reveals Himself as "merciful and gracious, longsuffering, slow to anger" (34:6). And He forgives, but He does not leave unpunished those who deny Him; He "visits" (inflicts) the sins of the fathers upon the third and fourth generations to come. That sounds rather drastic, doesn't it? Maybe so—but it is true. We who live in the twentieth century have only to look back across the years to see that what one generation does has its effect, good or bad, upon the following generations. The brutality of the old emperors of Rome brought suffering to Romans who lived long after those Caesars were dead; *Rome collapsed.* Germans who live today are paying a hideous price for the wickedness of Hitler. One generation established the Communistic Fidel Castro as chief executive of their land; today another generation of Cuban refugees is flocking by the thousands to the United States, crying out for freedom from Castro. Yes, the children do pay for the sins of their fathers.

Moses was well aware of the iniquity of the fathers of Israel—and of the iniquity of their children who were with him at Sinai. He offers up a prayer to the God against whom both fathers and children have sinned: "Oh, Lord, let the Lord, I pray thee, go in the midst of us, although it is a stiff-necked people; and pardon our iniquity and our sin, and take us for thy inheritance (accept us as your own)" (Exodus 34:9 RSV). Turn back from your idol-worship, Israel for God and God alone is able to guide you through this wilderness into the Promised Land. It was true then and it is true today: only obedience to God will bring *us* through the fear that runs like a devastating plague all across our modern world.

SUGGESTIONS TO TEACHERS

God's people seem to have muted their talk about Him. In the 1920's, U.S. President Calvin Coolidge, asked what the Sunday sermon was about, replied laconically, "Sin." (When pressed to tell what the preacher had said about sin, Coolidge drawled, "He was agin' it.") Recently, Dr. Earl Menninger, a perceptive Christian psychotherapist, wrote a book with the provocative title, *Whatever Became of Sin?* Dr. Menninger notes that the present-day Church seems to gloss over the disobedience and faithlessness of its people. Coolidge would not hear many sermons today in which sin was mentioned. Neither Dr. Menninger nor any other responsible Christian leader wants to see a morbid preoccupation with sin. However, the situation of human sinfulness must be acknowledged before God's mercy can be appreciated.

Your lesson today will be an excellent opportunity for you and your class to explore new dimensions of the experience of forgiveness. The biblical story of the golden calf offers meaning into human nature and God's nature in every generation.

1. *INCLINATION TO IDOLATRY.* Remind your people that they also have a propensity to make idols. Although they may not deliberately construct a bull shrine like the Israelites, they may be just as guilty of idol worship through putting something else ahead of the Lord. Make clear that placing any other cause or interest as Number One in life is turning that cause or interest into an idol. People "worship" what they consider most important. Perhaps it would help to pass out sheets of paper and have each person make a personal list in private of his or her priorities. It may also be helpful to ask the class to consider the idols of the Church, such as membership statistics, buildings, or other "sacred cows."

2. *ABILITY FOR EXCUSES.* Aaron tried to exonerate himself from responsibility in the calf-making, saying he was just carrying out the people's wishes and "out came this calf" (Exodus 32:24). Like Aaron, we are all masters at deceiving ourselves. We also have the silly notion that our shabby excuses impress God. The Lord, of course, sees through them and also sees us as the phonies we so often are.

3. *INSIGHT INTO EXODUS.* The point of this lesson is that God forgives His people, so budget plenty of lesson time to discuss this emphasis. Have your people reflect on the way the Lord reintroduces Himself to Moses, and announces, "I will be gracious . . . I will show mercy . . ." (Exodus 33:19). The Lord even gives a new start to His community by having Moses cut new stone tablets with the Commandments inscribed on them. The Good News of God's forgiveness is that He brings new beginnings! Tie in the new beginning God brings His community now through Jesus Christ.

4. *INTERCESSION FOR THE INSINCERE.* Christians sometimes tend to become judgmental toward those who don't seem as pious or pure as they. Moses' prayer in which he interceded for his people needs to be studied carefully (Exodus 32:11–13). God calls us to pray for others in mercy, not to denounce them in disgust. Talk together in your class about ways in which your church intercedes in the spirit of Christ's forgiveness for others.

TOPIC FOR ADULTS
HOPE FOR SINNERS

Conscience at Fault. Charles de Foucauld was a Frenchman who wasted the early part of his life as a drifter and soldier. Thrown out of the army, he spent most of his time in the slum bars of French-speaking North Africa and entered into an illicit affair with a woman. Meanwhile, he felt a restlessness. De Foucauld returned to France. Always a nonbeliever, he wandered into a Paris church one day. He told the priest, Abbe Huvelin, "I have not come to confessional; I have no faith."

The Abbe replied, "It is not your faith that is at fault, my friend, but your conscience."

Charles de Foucauld later confessed his sins and learned the experience of Christian forgiveness. He began a spiritual pilgrimage that led him to join the Trappist Order of monks. He subsequently was sent to Algeria with the Little Brothers. His service in the Sahara became legendary. Charles de Foucauld was killed during World War II sharing the forgiving love of God which he had learned personally brings hope for all sinners. His work continues in Algeria today, respected by Moslems and Christians alike.

Law and Gospel One. "The truth is good news, even when it speaks of God's demand, of the law enclosed in the Gospel. The law and the Gospel are one. Nowhere in Scriptures is there pure condemnation with no good news, even through the unheard of good news be simply that it is God who speaks. For even though God speaks to condemn me, it is the God of love who speaks. The only bad news would be that God ceases to speak to me."—Jacques Ellul

Twentieth Century Sin. Economist Peter Drucker writes about some "good people" who went along with Nazism, employing the fiction that they could reform it from within and keep their careers intact. No, evil works through such folk "precisely because evil is monstrous and men are petty. The Lord's Prayer knows how small man is and how weak, when it asks the Lord not to lead us into temptation but to deliver us from evil. And because evil is never banal and men so often are, men must not treat with evil on any terms—for the terms are always the terms of evil and never those of man. Man becomes the instrument of evil when . . . he thinks to harness evil to his ambition, and he becomes the instrument of evil when . . . he joins with evil to prevent worse.

"But maybe the greatest sin . . . may be the new, the twentieth-century sin of indifference, the sin of the distinguished biochemist-physiologist who neither kills nor lies but refuses to bear witness when, in the words of the old gospel hymn, 'they crucify my Lord.' "—Peter Drucker, *Adventures of a Bystander.*

Questions for Pupils on the Next Lesson. 1. Why are people so concerned about their own income and possessions? 2. How can possessions confer a measure of freedom from helpless dependency? 3. What does it mean to say that we are "trustees for God" of all that we have? 4. What is the basis for the biblical claim that we have a responsibility for other persons? 5. How do you decide between the welfare of others and your own rights of possession?

TOPIC FOR YOUTH
GOD WILL FORGIVE YOU

The Gracious Yes. Theologian Karl Barth once wrote a devastating book called *NEIN* ("No") against his fellow Swiss theologian Emil Brunner. The two great thinkers conducted a running battle in print for years, bringing deep personal estrangement between them. Finally, near the end of his life, Barth said, "If Brunner is still alive and it is possible, tell him again, 'Commended to *our* God,' even by me. And tell, '*Yes*' that the time I thought I had to say *Nein* to him is now long past, since we all live only by virtue of the fact that the great and merciful God says His gracious Yes to all of us." We are told that these were the last words that Brunner heard before he lapsed into unconsciousness before he died.

Silly Explanations. Why are fire trucks red? Well, fire trucks have four wheels and eight men, and everybody knows that four and eight make twelve. There are twelve inches in a foot, and a foot is a ruler. Queen Elizabeth II, a ruler, is also the name of the largest ship on the seven seas. Seas have fish and fish have fins. Finns fought the Russians; Russians are "Reds." Fire trucks are always rushin'. Therefore, fire trucks are red.

If you think that is wild, you ought to hear how some people try to explain why they do not believe God will forgive them, or that they do not think they have to obey God's commandments. Haven't you tried such "logic" to excuse yourself? Does it not remind you of Aaron and the Israelites explaining their idolatry?

Forgiven and Forgiving. In the latter part of the third century A.D., Christians were still frequently persecuted by Roman authorities. Had these believers been carnal, they would have fought back, exhibiting anger, criticism, and condemnation. The record of history reveals, however, that they instead showed love and forgiveness. For example, during a plague in the Egyptian city of Alexandria, "the Christians distinguished themselves by selfless behaviour, tending the sick and burying the dead while the pagan inhabitants fled like panic-stricken animals. There were plenty of cases where sick pagans were abandoned by their own families in the streets, only to be picked up and nursed by Christians. . . . Some of those sick and dying pagans who were cared for had probably been members of the Alexandrian mob which ten years before had been on the rampage lynching any Christians that they could find."—Taken from *From Christ to Constantine* by Michael K. Smith. © InterVarsity Press–London, and used by permission of InterVarsity Press.

Sentence Sermon to Remember: Among the attributes of God, although they are all equal, mercy shines with even more brilliance than justice.—Miguel de Cervantes.

Questions for Pupils on the Next Lesson. 1. What exactly does freedom mean to you as a Christian? 2. Why are so many people in our culture so "hung up" on money, property, and possessions? 3. How does a Christian decide between his/her own interests and the needs of others? 4. Why must Christians sometimes talk about economic concerns of others?

LESSON VIII—OCTOBER 24

GOD PROCLAIMS THE YEAR OF JUBILEE

Background Scripture: Leviticus 25
Devotional Reading: Leviticus 26:3–5,40–46

KING JAMES VERSION

LEVITICUS 25 1 And the LORD spake unto Moses in mount Sinai, saying,

2 Speak unto the children of Israel, and say unto them, When ye come into the land which I give you, then shall the land keep a sabbath unto the LORD.

8 And thou shalt number seven sabbaths of years unto thee, seven times seven years; and the space of the seven sabbaths of years shall be unto thee forty and nine years.

9 Then shalt thou cause the trumpet of the jubilee to sound on the tenth *day* of the seventh month, in the day of atonement shall ye make the trumpet sound throughout all your land.

10 And ye shall hallow the fiftieth year, and proclaim liberty throughout *all* the land unto all the inhabitants thereof: it shall be a jubilee unto you; and ye shall return every man unto his possession, and ye shall return every man unto his family.

11 A jubilee shall that fiftieth year be unto you: ye shall not sow, neither reap that which groweth of itself in it, nor gather *the grapes* in it of thy vine undressed.

12 For it *is* the jubilee; it shall be holy unto you: ye shall eat the increase thereof out of the field.

23 The land shall not be sold for ever: for the land *is* mine; for ye *are* strangers and sojourners with me.

24 And in all the land of your possession ye shall grant a redemption for the land.

39 And if thy brother *that dwelleth* by thee be waxen poor, and be sold unto thee; thou shalt not compel him to serve as a bondservant:

40 *But* as a hired servant, *and* as a sojourner, he shall be with thee, *and* shall serve thee unto the year of jubilee:

41 And *then* shall he depart from thee, *both* he and his children with him, and shall return unto his own family, and unto the possession of his fathers shall he return.

42 For they *are* my servants, which I brought forth out of the land of Egypt: they shall not be sold as bondmen.

REVISED STANDARD VERSION

LEVITICUS 25 1 The LORD said to Moses on Mount Sinai, 2 "Say to the people of Israel, When you come into the land which I give you, the land shall keep a sabbath to the LORD.

8 "And you shall count seven weeks of years, seven times seven years, so that the time of the seven weeks of years shall be to you forty-nine years. 9 Then you shall send abroad the loud trumpet on the tenth day of the seventh month; on the day of atonement you shall send abroad the trumpet throughout all your land. 10 And you shall hallow the fiftieth year, and proclaim liberty throughout the land to all its inhabitants; it shall be a jubilee for you, when each of you shall return to his property and each of you shall return to his family. 11 A jubilee shall that fiftieth year be to you; in it you shall neither sow, nor reap what grows of itself, nor gather the grapes from the undressed vines. 12 For it is a jubilee; it shall be holy to you; you shall eat what it yields out of the field.

23 "The land shall not be sold in perpetuity, for the land is mine; for you are strangers and sojourners with me. 24 And in all the country you possess, you shall grant a redemption of the land.

39 "And if your brother becomes poor beside you, and sells himself to you, you shall not make him serve as a slave: 40 he shall be with you as a hired servant and as a sojourner. He shall serve with you until the year of the jubilee; 41 then he shall go out from you, he and his children with him, and go back to his own family, and return to the possession of his fathers. 42 For they are my servants, whom I brought forth out of the land of Egypt; they shall not be sold as slaves. 43 You shall not rule over him with harshness, but shall fear your God."

43 Thou shalt not rule over him with rigour; but shalt fear thy God.

KEY VERSE: "And you shall hallow the fiftieth year, and proclaim liberty throughout the land to all its inhabitants, it shall be a jubilee for you, when each of you shall return to his property and each of you shall return to his family. Leviticus 25:10 (RSV).

HOME DAILY BIBLE READINGS

Oct. 18. *M.* *The Year of Jubilee.* Leviticus 25:1–6,10,18,19.
Oct. 19. *T.* *The Blessings of Obedience.* Leviticus 26:3–13.
Oct. 20. *W.* *The Consequences of Disobedience.* Leviticus 26:14–20.
Oct. 21. *T.* *The Results of Repentance.* Leviticus 26:40–46.
Oct. 22. *F.* *The Year of the Lord's Favor.* Isaiah 61:1–7.
Oct. 23. *S.* *The Acceptable Year of the Lord.* Luke 4:16–21.
Oct. 24. *S.* *God's Ultimate Plan for Liberty.* John 8:31–36.

BACKGROUND

There are many references in the Old Testament that would lead us to think that the Israelites who left Egypt were an unruly, unlearned, almost vulgarian mob. But that is not quite true. Some of them may have been like that, but with them on their long march were many fine, consecrated, highly intelligent men. There were, for instance, the priests and the Levites. The priests were all descendants of Aaron, who had served as their high priest. The Levites were members of the tribe of Levi, and they were designated as priests and aides to the priests. The Book of Leviticus lays down laws for the priests and the Levites. So we might call it a directory of divine worship or, better, a Code of Laws dealing both with religious worship and with the practical conduct of life.

Most of it was written during the Persian period (583–333 B.C.), but it reaches back far beyond this period, dealing with laws laid down in the lifetime of Moses.

NOTES ON THE PRINTED TEXT

The Jewish people were long on feasts and fasts, holy days and holy convocations. Their sacred seasons included the sacred Sabbath or seventh day of the week, a seventh week, a seventh month, a Sabbatical Year and a Year of Jubilee. The "Sabbath Year" came every seventh year, and the Year of Jubilee came on the fiftieth year, after "seven weeks of years."

The Sabbath Year was one during which they were to celebrate God as *the giver and owner of the land.* God told Moses on the Mount, that when they entered the Promised Land, "then shall the land keep a sabbath unto the Lord" (25:2). For six years they were to sow seed on this, the Lord's land, prune their vines and gather their harvests, but every seventh year they were to "let the land rest"—lie fallow. They were to sow no crops, prune no vines, reap no crops, for this was the year of *rest* for the land. Any crops that *did* grow, without their help, were to be eaten by their servants, by any foreigners living in the land, and by themselves.

There was great significance in that, great religious teaching. As the weekly Sabbath honored God as Creator of the world, this Year honored

Him as Owner of the land. Those who lived on the land lived there only as temporary tenants—just as modern apartment dwellers are temporary tenants who must pay their rent and move on when other tenants move in. Without this land offered and supplied by their God, they could not and would not exist. Thank God for that! Thank Him at least at the time of the Sabbatical Year.

We do not know how well or enthusiastically the Hebrews observed this Sabbatical Year, but it is likely that some observed it faithfully, while others did not. That is not too important; what is important is that a great principle was laid down which they never forgot. The fertile, life-giving land was *a gift of God to man, and to God account must be made for its use.* It might be well for *us* to have such a Sabbatical Year in which to remember Him, and thank Him for what we think is "our" land. We sing lustily of "America the beautiful," but it was God who made it beautiful, not us! We seem to be despoiling our land feverously.

The Year of Jubilee was something different. While it carried on the idea that God was the ultimate owner of the land, it added to this certain principles that just might solve certain social problems and economic problems of their day—*and our day.* This word *Jubilee* is a Greek form of the Hebrew word for *trumpet.* On the day of Atonement in the fiftieth year, let the trumpets of Israel sound loud and clear throughout the land. Let every man return to his family and property (sounds like Christmas, doesn't it, the day when *we* go home?). Let every man listen to the blowing of the trumpets which proclaimed "liberty throughout all the land unto all the inhabitants thereof" (verse 10). These words are carved on the rim of our Liberty Bell, and they mean much for us.

But—liberty for *whom?* It meant, first of all, a liberty applied to the ownership of the land. Specifically, in Leviticus 25:23, land in the new country was not to be sold forever—in perpetuity, "for the land is mine (God's)," and not yours. So, in the Year of Jubilee, all property in land was to be returned to its original proprietors. This meant that inasmuch as God was the supreme Owner of the land, He could impose the conditions on which it could be held by His tenants; it was a law made to protect those who might fall into slavery through loss of their property and through debts accumulated in days of poverty.

Beyond this, provisions were made for the *redemption* of land lost under these circumstances. "This might be done by the former tenant in case he became unable so to do, or by someone next of kin, who might secure the land for himself and thus retain it as a possession of the family. In fact, it was regarded as the duty of the nearest relative to 'redeem' the property which the poverty of the kinsman had compelled him to sell. It became a custom, almost obligatory, for such a 'kinsman-redeemer' to marry the childless widow of a former owner."—Charles R. Erdman.

Last but not least, Moses struck a blow at the institution of slavery in the Jubilee laws. He did not *abolish* slavery, but he made life more tolerable for the slaves by warning against severity and heartlessness. He told his Israelites not to forget that *they* had once been slaves in Egypt and that they had been delivered from it at the hand of a merciful God. So let them be merciful to *their* slaves, bondsmen, and servants. And he added to that the law that at Jubilee time all slaves should "go out free." These laws applied only to those who were in bondage to fellow Israelites and not to slaves captured from some other nation.

No, he did not put an end to slavery. But it is startling to see that such a people, so early in Hebrew history, laid down a principle of liberty and equality which in time brought an end to the slavery of *any* of God's children. It hasn't been *completely* abolished, but we have come to the place were slave-owning nations are considered anathema in our world, and that is a long step forward.

SUGGESTIONS TO TEACHERS

"The Church should keep out of social issues. If it would stick to the Gospel, we wouldn't keep losing members and getting embroiled in controversy," exploded an active lay person at a church board meeting.

Little did he realize that if the sections of the Bible dealing with "social issues" were cut out, there would be little left. From Genesis to Revelation, the record shows God's deep involvement in all aspects of human society.

Your lesson today on the Year of Jubilee is more than research into part of the Hebrew legal and economic system. Basically, this lesson deals with God's concern for justice for the poor and oppressed everywhere. With this in mind, direct your class throughout your lesson time to think specifically of the poor and oppressed in your community and in the world at this time.

1. *A LORD LEANING TOWARD THE LEFT-OUT*. Start the lesson with the biblical and theological rationale for the Year of Jubilee. Make sure that the class clearly understands that God definitely identifies with and involves Himself with the poor and the oppressed. Review the story of the Lord's concern for the Israelites in the slave camps of Egypt before the Exodus. Throughout the Scriptures, God seems to show a partiality toward the underdog and the exploited. God, who saw the misery and heard the groans of the Hebrews, brought them out of bondage. He continues to work toward delivering from bondage those who are trampled. Where in particular do you and members of your class think that God may be wanting to be working today?

2. *A PEOPLE PARTIAL TOWARD THE POOR*. The community of God's people have been appointed to be God's agents for redressing injustice. God's family, if they are to carry His name, must be spokesmen and champions for the oppressed. This will frequently mean being out of step with the ruling powers. It will almost certainly mean criticism. Have your class talk candidly about forms of involvement which the Church may have to take. Discuss how this involvement may often be corporate as well as individual and applies to changing systems as well as changing persons.

3. *A SYSTEM SENSITIVE TO THE SUFFERING*. Although the Levitical law of the Year of Jubilee was designed to deliver from bondage those who had been forced into poverty or hopeless debt, the idea behind it remains true today. The Jubilee Year regulations are not a legal system to be applied literally today. God, however, continues to call for each society to be organized to heed and help the poor. Whenever any society—our own included—ignores the cries and groans of the downtrod-

den and exploited, God pronounces harsh judgment on its leaders. In the face of the substratum of poor in the nation and world today, what does your class think God intends?

TOPIC FOR ADULTS
PROCLAIM LIBERTY

Like Mighty Waters. "At the height of U.S. involvement in Southeast Asia, William Sloane Coffin, pastor of New York City's Riverside Church, was one of a group of ministers who urged Henry Kissinger to withdraw U.S. troops. Mr. Kissinger, pushing them on the complexities of such a proposal, asked, 'How would you get the boys out of Vietnam?' To which Bill Coffin, turning to the Prophet Amos, responded, 'Mr. Kissinger, our job is to proclaim that "justice must roll down like waters, and righteousness like a mighty stream." Your job is to work out the details of the irrigation system.'

"There is an important truth in the response. Christians do not have any inside track on political action. Prayer and piety alone do not produce good politics. Indeed, some of those who pray most in public seem to have the worst politics. Christians have to do their homework, listen to the experts, and learn from them—just like everybody else. But when they have done that, they have the right to challenge unjust actions and press for policies more reflective of what life in the global village—our earth—ought to be."—Robert McAfee Brown, *A.D.*, March 1980.

Stewards for Neighbors' Needs. "Let this, then," Calvin wrote in his *Institutes,* "be our rule for benignity and beneficence—that whatever God had conferred on us, which enables us to assist our neighbors, we are stewards of it, and must one day render an account of our stewardship. All," he says, "is to be used not for ourselves but for the advantage of others."

Definition of Scriptures. John Fry, a Christian with a gift for satire, penned this tongue-in-cheek definition of the Bible for his fellow Presbyterians at their national gathering a few years ago.

"HOLY BIBLE (variously referred to also as the Bible, the Scriptures, the Word, the Word of God, and is also found holding up the broken leg of the Church). The Holy Bible supersedes even the Standing Rules of the General Assembly. It has been declared 'the only rule of faith and practice.' As a 'rule,' the Holy Bible guides the General Assembly in large matters, such as, the value of faith, trust in God, and stewardship, but is seldom appealed to as a rule when ministry to the poor, hungry, or imprisoned is being discussed. On these occasions, the Bible as a rule becomes mere advice which the GA can take or leave as it chooses. Wags sometimes suggest that looseleaf copies would be useful so that the hard parts could be slipped out without destroying the whole book." Copies of John Fry's magazine *frying pan* were passed around UPCUSA General Assembly in Philadelphia in 1976. The issue contained a "Glistening Glossary of Common General Assembly Terms and Expressions," of which the above was one of the entries.

Questions for Pupils on the Next Lesson. 1. Why do some people respond to a national or personal crisis by suddenly turning to religion? 2. How can the Church help people in your community restrain themselves from wholesale condemnation of other racial, national, or religious outsiders? 3. What is the destiny of your congregation as "people of God"? 4. What is the message of the story of Balaam to you? 5. Why do some people worry about the future of the Church?

TOPIC FOR YOUTH
CELEBRATE LIBERTY

Soldier's Cloak. St. Martin, the beloved bishop of Tours in France, was a military man when he was converted. After he committed his life to Jesus Christ, he asked to be baptized as a Christian. He was going to Tours to be baptized when he encountered a shivering, unbelieving beggar. It was almost night. Martin cut his soldier's cloak in two, gave a half to the beggar, and crawled into the culvert with the beggar to help keep him warm during the cold night. Some of his fellow soldiers saw what he had done and laughed scornfully. That night, Martin had a dream in which the Crucified One came to him—wearing half a cloak. When Martin awoke, he realized it was not so much he, Martin, taking Jesus to the beggar as it was finding Jesus in the beggar!

The despised outsider and the oppressed beggar is where Jesus stands. If we shunt aside the poor and the hungry, we shunt aside the Living Lord who comes to encounter us. Ignoring the helpless and hurting will cost us meeting Jesus.

Need to "Liberate" Young People. In 1930, President Herbert Hoover opened a White House conference on child health and protection with these words: ". . . If we could have but one generation of properly born, trained, educated, and happy children, a thousand other problems of government would vanish."

While their condition has improved significantly in the past fifty years, here are some shocking facts about our young.

(1) A total of 17.6 million U.S. children are barely surviving in families with incomes below poverty level.

(2) Ten million children under sixteen receive no regular medical attention.

(3) A third of all children under seventeen have never seen a dentist.

(4) More than 7 million Americans under nineteen have some physical handicap, but only 55 percent receive the necessary care.

(5) One-fourth of those now entering fifth grade will become high school dropouts.

(6) Almost 77,000 of America's inmates in prisons for adult offenders are under eighteen, costing taxpayers more than $18,000 annually per youth.

Need for Jubilee Year for Minorities. "The past decade saw a widening of the yawning gap between black and whites. Black family income fell from over 60 percent of white family income at the beginning of the decade to barely 57 percent at the end of the 1970s. Over a half million more black people were poorer in 1979 than in 1970.

"Black gains in the 1980s will be largely dependent on new job opportunities for female heads of families. Over a third of black families are headed by women, and most are poor because of the failure to provide full-time employment, a situation likely to continue and even worsen in the decade ahead.

"If the 1970s were a decade of benign neglect, the 1980s threaten to render black people, their needs, and their aspirations, invisible.

So we enter the 1980s with the nation's attention focused on military weapons, energy, and inflation to the neglect of racial equality, full employment, and urban revitalization. The inevitable result will be further deterioration of the living conditions of poor people and black people.

"But the state of America is interwoven with the state of black America, a strong economically healthy and just America is as essential to national security as any missile arsenal—even more so."—Vernon Jordan, Jr., *Column,* March 6, 1980. Reprinted from Call-Chronicle Newspapers, Inc. Allentown, Pennsylvania.

Sentence Sermon to Remember:

> The poor too often turn away, unheard,
> From hearts that shut against them with a snap
> That will be heard in heaven.
>
> Henry Wadsworth Longfellow.

Questions for Pupils on the Next Lesson. 1. What are the chief threats to your well-being? 2. Why do you feel you are incapable of speaking out for God? 3. How may youth such as yourself be used to bless others more? 4. What concerns you most about the future?

LESSON IX—OCTOBER 31

GOD SPEAKS THROUGH A GENTILE

Background Scripture: Numbers 22–24
Devotional Reading: Proverbs 16:1–11

KING JAMES VERSION

NUMBERS 22 4 And Moab said unto the elders of Midian, Now shall this company lick up all *that are* round about us, as the ox licketh up the grass of the field. And Balak the son of Zippor *was* king of the Moabites at that time.

5 He sent messengers therefore unto Balaam the son of Beor to Pethor, which *is* by the river of the land of the children of his people, to call him, saying, Behold, there is a people come out from Egypt: behold, they cover the face of the earth, and they abide over against me:

6 Come now therefore, I pray thee, curse me this people; for they *are* too mighty for me: peradventure I shall prevail, *that* we may smite them, and *that* I may drive them out of the land: for I wot that he whom thou blessest *is* blessed, and he whom thou cursest is cursed.

23 7 And he took up his parable, and said, Balak the king of Moab hath brought me from Aram, out of the mountains of the east, *saying,* Come, curse me Jacob, and come, defy Israel.

8 How shall I curse, *whom* God hath not cursed? of how shall I defy, *whom* the LORD hath not defied?

9 For from the top of the rocks I see him, and from the hills I behold him: lo, the people shall dwell alone, and shall not be reckoned among the nations.

10 Who can count the dust of Jacob, and the number of the fourth *part* of Israel? Let me die the death of the righteous, and let my last end be like his!

11 And Balak said unto Balaam, What has thou done unto me? I took thee to curse mine enemies, and, behold, thou has blessed *them* altogether.

12 And he answered and said, Must I not take heed to speak that which the LORD hath put in my mouth?

24 17 . . . there shall come a Star out of Jacob, and a Sceptre shall rise out of Israel,

REVISED STANDARD VERSION

NUMBERS 22 4 And Moab said to the elders of Midian, "This horde will now lick up all that is round about us, as the ox licks up the grass of the field." So Balak the son of Zippor, who was king of Moab at that time, 5 sent messengers to Balaam the son of Beor at Pethor, which is near the River, in the land of Amaw to call him, saying, "Behold, a people has come out of Egypt; they cover the face of the earth, and they are dwelling opposite me. 6 Come now, curse this people for me, since they are too mighty for me; perhaps I shall be able to defeat them and drive them from the land; for I know that he whom you bless is blessed, and he whom you curse is cursed."

23 7 And Balaam took up his discourse, and said,

"From Aram Balak has brought me,
the king of Moab from the eastern mountains:
'Come, curse Jacob for me,
and come, denounce Israel!'

8 How can I curse whom God has not cursed?
How can I denounce whom the LORD has not denounced?
9 For from the top of the mountains I see him,
from the hills I behold him;
lo, a people dwelling alone,
and not reckoning itself among the nations!
10 Who can count the dust of Jacob,
or number the fourth part of Israel?
Let me die the death of the righteous,
and let my end be like his!"

11 And Balak said to Balaam, "What have you done to me? I took you to curse my enemies, and behold, you have done nothing but bless them." 12 And he answered, "Must I not take heed to speak what the LORD puts in my mouth?"

24 17 ". . . a star shall come forth out of Jacob,

and shall smite the corners of Moab, and destroy all the children of Sheth.

and a scepter shall rise out of Israel;
it shall crush the forehead of Moab,
and break down all the sons of Sheth."

KEY VERSE: "Must I not take heed to speak what the Lord puts in my mouth?" Numbers 23:12 (RSV).

HOME DAILY BIBLE READINGS

Oct. 25. *M.* *A Spokesman for God.* Numbers 22:31–38.
Oct. 26. *T.* *Careful to Obey.* Numbers 23:4–12.
Oct. 27. *W.* *The Power of God's Word.* Numbers 23:16–23.
Oct. 28. *T.* *Power Without Limit.* Isaiah 45:1–7.
Oct. 29. *F.* *God Enables Those He Calls.* Jeremiah 1:4–10.
Oct. 30. *S.* *The Source of Sound Speech.* Proverbs 16:1–11.
Oct. 31. *S.* *No Need to Worry.* Matthew 10:7–20.

BACKGROUND

The arm of Israel stands at the gate of Canaan, encamped in the plains of Moab; Balak, King of Moab, is in a panic. This Israeli host has whipped the Amorites into submission and marched on to confront the Moabites. Such victories bring fear and desperation to all the tribes of Canaan: who can stop the Israelites? Balak hastens to make an alliance with the Midianites, a tribe of nomads who roam the desert to the east and south of Moab, in an effort to weaken the Israelites with a devilish scheme. But in his heart Balak knows that it will take something more than a military alliance to stop this horde that seems unconquerable. He looks around to find someone among the sorcerers and magicians of the pagan gods of Canaan who with his magic could put a curse on the people of Israel.

For this purpose he employs a man named Balaam. It was a bad move, for while this Balaam loved gold and probably would take a bribe to inflict his curse, he happened to be a man who feared the God of Israel!

NOTES ON THE PRINTED TEXT

Balaam! Most of us laugh at the mention of his name, for we know him only as a fool who had a long talk with his donkey (*see* Numbers 22:21–35). But there is a lot more involved in the story of Balaam than this. In Balaam when we read his *whole* story, we find a man who was not an Israelite but a Gentile, a man deeply sincere at times and crafty and money-wise at others, a man who had trouble making up his mind in choosing the God of Israel above the gods of Canaan, a man chosen to speak as the mouthpiece of God. He had the gift but lacked the grace of a great prophet.

Balaam was good at blessing or cursing with his magic. Knowing his reputation, Balak sent a little embassy of the top leaders of Moab and Midian, who came with bribe money in their hands—"rich rewards of devination." Balaam looked long at the money, but he couldn't quite bring himself to put on Israel the curse that Balak wanted. He stalled for time, for time in which he might consult in prayer with the God of Israel! God gave him His answer: "Don't do it, Balaam. Don't curse those I have blessed." In the morning, he told the princes of Balak to go home and forget it (he would have *liked* to curse Israel, but he didn't dare)!

Balak was disappointed, but he tried again; he sent another embassy of more honorable princes with more gold. Balaam pretends to be insulted at the offer of more gold: "If Balak would give me his house full of silver and gold, *I cannot go beyond the word of the Lord my God. . . .*" *His* God? Yes, it was his God; in his heart, he fought to decide whether to follow this universal God or remain a money-hungry devotee of Baal. So he stalls again. Stay here, he says to the princes, while I go and talk with God and find out whether He will add anything to what He has already told me! Maybe God will change His mind and let me go with you.

It was hypocrisy. God would not change His mind, and Balaam knew it. God tells him, *yes,* he may go with these men, but he will go *only to deliver a message from God*—only say and do what God had ordered him to say and do. So he goes. It is on this journey that he had the serio-comic conversation with his donkey. The main figure in the donkey story, however, is not the donkey but an angel of God who repeats the Lord's commandment: "Go, but say only what I tell you to say."

Later he stood with Balak on a mountain height, among the idols of Baal—and once again, for the third time, he tried to fight off the temptation to put a curse upon the host of Israel which he could see clearly in the valley below. Once more, God puts words in his mouth; he says to Balak, "How shall I curse whom God has not cursed? . . . Let me die the death of the righteous . . ." (23:8, 10).

Three times! Balaam, here, seems to be a deeply sincere man struggling against any denial of God—a brave man surrounded by an alien people who might well kill him if he refuses to help them. He *was* brave, up to this point, for even here he tries one last compromise in preparing seven altars to the God Baal, on which are sacrificed a bull and a ram, in the forlorn hope that the divine powers (of Baal) might curse and confound the Israelites. It is a sacrifice credited to Balak—but Balaam stood by and watched it and made no effort to stop it. Yes, Balaam was one who couldn't make up his mind.

The rest is epilogue. Courageous as he was, at times, poor Baalam ended miserably. Falling at last completely, he sought to bring the curse upon Israel after all by inducing the Israelites to commit sensuous (sexual) sins and to eat food sacrified to idols. That finished him. In a battle with the Midianites, five kings and Balaam the son of Beor were slain with the sword. The star of Balaam fell; the star of Balak and the Moabites fell, and the star of Jacob (Israel) rose high. Balaam, prophet to the Gentiles though he was, passed into obscurity while Israel moved on to glory.

And what does the whole sad story tell us? It tells us that there were really two Balaams—the Balaam of indecision and treachery, and the Balaam who couldn't quite come to walk in truth with God. It tells us that Israel regarded their God as a *universal* God rather than a national deity. It tells us that sin is never condoned, that it is *not* all right for any of us to compromise and sin under certain crucial circumstances as long as it all comes out right—as in Balaam's weak turning to the pagan gods of Moab. It tells us that *no* man can worship both God and Mammon.

Three times Balak tempted him; three times Balaam fought it down. It was not easy for him to bless Israel while he was in Balak's camp with wealth and high position calling. He did let God speak through him, and that was hard. If his sense of holiness had been as keen as his sense of magic, we would link his name with the great Isaiah's.

SUGGESTIONS TO TEACHERS

The committee to select a new pastor was talking with a prospective candidate. "Now, Reverend," spoke the chairman of the committee, "We want a preacher who will fit in here as one of us and not upset us. We like the way we are here in Washington County, and we don't like outsiders comin' in here tryin' to change things."

Heard those sentiments before? Perhaps you and people in your class have even thought them yourselves.

Your lesson today is aimed at helping God's people to listen to the way He sometimes speaks through outsiders. Balaam's place in the story of God's people is merely one of many times when God spoke through strangers. The main idea to remember today is that God may still be trying to get through to us through people with different accents or colors or backgrounds.

Sometimes, too, we as God's people feel like outsiders. As such, we may feel constrained to keep silent. God, however, may require us to speak on His behalf.

Your lesson on how God speaks through an outsider may unfold in several directions as you work with Numbers 22–24.

1. *COMMANDED.* Balaam will not be bought or browbeaten by Balak but insists that he must obey the Lord. Have your class reflect with you how God's people are sometimes put under pressure to "go along." Balak still speaks, trying to push God's men and women where he wants. Ask your class members to identify some of the "Balak's" or pressurers trying to own or control them. Point out that an obstinate sense of obedience to God is needed by believers nowadays as well as in Balaam's time.

2. *CONTRADICTION.* The amusing story of Balaam's ass (Numbers 22:21–35) was undoubtedly told and retold to successive generations. Teller and listener chuckled over the ass's greater spiritual perceptivity. Behind all folktales, however, there are usually profound truths, and this one is no exception. Even Balaam misses the Lord who stands immediately before him on the road. "I did not know that thou didst stand in the road against me," Balaam gasps when he discovers why the animal had been balking (22:34). Have your class recount occasions when its members were not aware that the Lord had been with them all the time. Like Balaam, our faith proves to have contradictions.

3. *CLARIFICATION.* Balaam the outsider is able to interpret the contemporary scene because of his knowledge of what God had done for the Israelites in Egypt. Because of his knowledge of God's acts in Israel's past, Balaam could unscramble the present. Furthermore, Balaam realizes that God is greater than magic charms or witchcraft. Outsiders sometimes have remarkable powers of discernment. What are others trying to say to the Christians in our nation today? Why must we take them seriously?

TOPIC FOR ADULTS
GOD SPEAKS THROUGH AN OUTSIDER

Challenges From Third World Christians. "The Bible was originally a revolutionary book ('good news to the poor . . .'), we tamed it. Now our sisters and brothers in the Third World are freeing it up once again to communicate its liberating message.

"Two different Bibles emerge, depending on the perspective from which the one Bible is read. One perspective very skillfully justifies our Western capitalist culture. That is the comforting Bible we have read. The other challenges all the assumptions of that culture and offers the ingredients for creating an alternative world, with something about the Kingdom of God being like a little child ('and the only privileged ones will be the children')."—Robert McAfee Brown, "Starting Over: New Beginning Points for Theology," Copyright 1980 Christian Century Foundation. Reprinted by permission from the May 14, 1980, issue of *The Christian Century.*

Prophetic Word. "What was significant about this conference was that, for the first time at any major gathering of this kind, the scientists and technologists overwhelmed the theologians numerically. The theologians were prepared to listen attentively to what the scientists were saying about today's world and to accept that God has a word, given in thoroughly secular terms, from those whose discipline it is to wrestle with the secrets of the physical universe, to struggle, to interpret and direct the world's economies or to analyse trends in contemporary society. This conference was, in fact, a paradigm for the kind of process which is required, if the Church is to take seriously the contribution of the whole people of God in pursuing the purposes of God within the political, economic, research and industrial structures of their working lives. Every opportunity needs to be given in every gathering place of God's people for those working within secular structures to share their insights into God's ways with the world, as was attempted at this conference.

"There was a large number of participants from the Southern world, and they have a knack of bringing discussion down to earth and of uttering a prophetic word. One young participant from the Tonga stated, 'As countries with small populations spread across a vast ocean, we are very vulnerable to exploitation. It is a very safe place in which to make nuclear tests—for the West, that is, but not for us. The Pacific is on the way to becoming a radioactive paradise.' Over such technology the people of the Pacific have very little control and share little in decision-making about it. The plea of the vast number of nations of the world, who are not involved in the nuclear arms race, yet threatened by it, was declared to be, 'No annihilation without representation!' From every side the question was raised of the purposes technology serves. It had already been revealed at the conference that 50 percent of the world's scientists and technologists are engaged in arms research and development."—Graeme Brown, Reporting on World Council of Churches Conference on "Faith, Science and the Future" held at Cambridge, Massachusetts, 1979.

Voice of God Through Voices of Other Denominations. We need to heed those outside our own denomination. God sometimes speaks through these "Gentiles." All responsible Christian leaders realize this, including Billy Graham.

Some twenty-five years ago Billy caused a sensation by refusing to hold an evangelistic campaign.

A big Texas city had invited him. The money was pledged and the workers were signed up. A huge hall was rented. The publicity was all planned. And it was his own denomination, the Southern Baptists, who was to sponsor the "crusade." But that was precisely the trouble. The moment Billy Graham learned that it was a one-denomination project, he pulled out. He knew quite well that to get a missionary job done in the best way it takes all denominations working together.

Many people who differ strongly with Billy Graham about the mission of the church will agree with him about the importance of churches working together for that mission. "In union there is strength" is not only a national motto; it seems to be God's plan for His people, too.

Questions for Pupils on the Next Lesson. 1. Where do you find assurance of God's presence during times of crisis and change? 2. What symbols of God's faithfulness do you cherish the most? Why? 3. What are some of the occasions in which reflecting on the past helped you to cope in the present? 4. What parallels do you see between the wandering in the wilderness of the Israelites and your own spiritual pilgrimage? 5. How do you memorialize significant events involving God in your life and the life of your family?

TOPIC FOR YOUTH
AN UNLIKELY SPEAKER FOR GOD

Strange People at the Wedding. "What does Johnny Carson have in common with Paul . . . ?

"Johnny: 'What do you get when you cross an aardvark with a rhino?' Answer: 'A lot of strange people at the wedding!'

"Paul warns us to expect a lot of strange guests at the wedding of Christ and His Bride, the Church. (*See* 1 Corinthians 12:12–30.) The metaphors get mixed but our denominationalistic culture fosters three mistaken images of the Church, the Body of Christ. False Statement #1: 'I'm leaving the church because. . . .' This, said by a person or a whole congregation, is just as ludicrous as: 'If the foot should say because I am not a hand I don't belong to the body. . . .' There are no voluntary withdrawals from the Church any more than self-amputation. F.S. #2: 'You must be/do/believe the following or you're not in the "true church." Uniformity of Christian expression—a great deformity of the Body, the Church. 'If the whole body were an eye, where would we smell the roses?' A body with only an eye would look silly rolling down the street. So does the denomination/individual whose bumper sticker says, '(Be) Like Us—or Leave Us!' F.S. #3: 'Just me and God—I don't need you to be a Christian.' Said another way: 'The eye cannot say to the hand, "I have no need of you." ' No interorgan wars, or jealousy, or pride are permitted. 'If one member suffers/is honored, all members suffer/rejoice together. . . . We are all the Body of Christ . . . Nazarenes, Episcopals, Assemblies of God, Roman Catholics, Northern/Southern Presbys. . . .'

" 'Hey, Maude,' Elder Elmer blurted out, 'You'll never guess who joined the church today. . . .' "—Ron Guinn, *Highland Herald,* Highland Presbyterian Church, Tyler, Texas.

A New Church. Dr. Robert Lee, professor at San Francisco Theological Seminary in San Anselmo, California, and Frank Mar, pastor of the Chinese Church in Oakland, California, recently visited ten major Chinese cities. They reported on the revival of several Christian churches.

"Slowly, the People's Republic of China is permitting its citizens to practice their religious beliefs. Worship services are packed to overflowing, and Bible study and Sunday schools are well attended. In one mountain district, for instance, where the church had been forced to close during the cultural revolution, about twenty-five pastors organized a factory for the manufacturing of classroom supplies. In this way, the pastors kept themselves and others employed, and also kept a Christian community alive. When the church reopened, the community was intact, and from memory—all church records had been destroyed—the organizers reconstructed the membership rolls. When the first service was held, 800 people gathered. Everyone was surprised, including the pastors, who didn't expect such a turnout."

The State of the Church. "If reading the Gospel does not both drive us to our knees and to the streets, we will not be faithful in either of these aspects of our discipleship.

"In a world of growing uncertainties there will be a growing demand for cultural and theological absolutes. The church's role as teacher in such a world is crucial.

"The church can no longer think of itself as solving great human problems. Its calling is more profound: witness to the inbreaking Kingdom of God.

"Before the 1980s are over the majority of the world's Christian population will be in the Southern hemisphere. If that fact does not change our Christian practice, we have not been practicing Christianity.

"What then is the State of the Church? Why do we want to know? Does it really matter? If it matters, in what way does it matter? If we are strong and faithful, will it make us hopeless? Or will we find in strength and weakness the occasion to repent and to give thanks? Will we find the occasion for reflection, search, and expectation, as the Lord of all fulfills His purpose both through our weakness and through our strength? Will we find our belongings in the worldwide Church? Will we seek the health and strength of Christ's body AROUND the globe? Will we pray from our deep need and hope, 'Thy Kingdom come . . . On earth'?

"Our concern is not so much the State of the Church as it is the promise of God and how the State of the Church everywhere is the occasion to understand and live in His promises."—From "An Essay on the State of the Church" presented to the UPCUSA General Assembly, 1980, by its Mission Council.

Sentence Sermon to Remember: Who dares to say that he alone has found the truth?—H. W. Longfellow.

Questions for Pupils on the Next Lesson. 1. What are the main obstacles you are encountering in your pilgrimage of faith? How can you recognize leaders who have an obligation to God to serve the best interests of all people? 3. Why do you sometimes feel cynical about political leaders? 4. What does the Bible mean by "Judges" in the Old Testament?

LESSON X—NOVEMBER 7

GOD LEADS HIS PEOPLE INTO THE PROMISED LAND

Background Scripture: Joshua 3–4
Devotional Reading: Joshua 4:19–14

KING JAMES VERSION

JOSHUA 3 14 And it came to pass, when the people removed from their tents, to pass over Jordan, and the priests bearing the ark of the covenant before the people;

15 And as they that bare the ark were come unto Jordan, and the feet of the priests that bare the ark were dipped in the brim of the water, (for Jordan overfloweth all his banks all the time of harvest,)

16 That the waters which came down from above stood *and* rose up upon a heap very far from the city Adam, that *is* beside Zaretan; and those that came down toward the sea of the plain, *even* the salt sea, failed, *and* were cut off; and the people passed over right against Jericho.

17 And the priests that bare the ark of the covenant of the LORD stood firm on dry ground in the midst of Jordan, and all the Israelites passed over on dry ground, until all the people were passed clean over Jordan.

4 1 And it came to pass, when all the people were clean passed over Jordan, that the LORD spake unto Joshua, saying,

2 Take you twelve men out of the people, out of every tribe a man,

3 And command ye them, saying, Take you hence out of the midst of Jordan, out of the place where the priests' feet stood firm, twelve stones, and ye shall carry them over with you, and leave them in the lodging place, where ye shall lodge this night.

4 Then Joshua called the twelve men, whom he had prepared of the children of Israel, out of every tribe a man:

5 And Joshua said unto them, Pass over before the ark of the LORD your God into the midst of Jordan, and take you up every man of you a stone upon his shoulder, according unto the number of the tribes of the children of Israel:

6 That this may be a sign among you, *that* when your children ask *their fathers* in time to come, saying, What *mean* ye by these stones?

7 Then ye shall answer them, That the

REVISED STANDARD VERSION

JOSHUA 3 14 So, when the people set out from their tents, to pass over the Jordan with the priests bearing the ark of the covenant before the people, 15 and when those who bore the ark had come to the Jordan, and the feet of the priests bearing the ark were dipped in the brink of the water (the Jordan overflows all its banks throughout the time of harvest), 16 the waters coming down from above stood and rose up in a heap far off, at Adam, the city that is beside Zarethan, and those flowing down toward the sea of the Arabah, the Salt Sea, were wholly cut off; and the people passed over opposite Jericho. 17 And while all Israel were passing over on dry ground, the priests who bore the ark of the covenant of the LORD stood on dry ground in the midst of the Jordan, until all the nation finished passing over the Jordan.

4 1 When all the nation had finished passing over the Jordan, the LORD said to Joshua, 2 "Take twelve men from the people, from each tribe a man, 3 and command them, 'Take twelve stones from here out of the midst of the Jordan, from the very place where the priests' feet stood, and carry them over with you, and lay them down in the place where you lodge tonight.' " 4 Then Joshua called the twelve men from the people of Israel, whom he had appointed, a man from each tribe; 5 and Joshua said to them, "Pass on before the ark of the LORD your God into the midst of the Jordan, and take up each of you a stone upon his shoulder, according to the number of the tribes of the people of Israel, 6 that this may be a sign among you, when your children ask in time to come, 'What do those stones mean to you?' 7 Then you shall tell them that the waters of the Jordan were cut off before the ark of the covenant of the LORD; when it passed over the Jordan, the waters of the Jordan were cut off. So these stones shall be to the people of Israel a memorial for ever."

waters of Jordan were cut off before the ark of the covenant of the LORD; when it passed over Jordan, the waters of Jordan were cut off: and these stones shall be for a memorial unto the children of Israel for ever.

KEY VERSE: "Behold, the ark of the covenant of the Lord of all the earth is to pass over before you into the Jordan." Joshua 3:11 (RSV).

HOME DAILY BIBLE READINGS

Nov. 1. *M.* *God Promises His Presence.* Joshua 1:1–9.
Nov. 2. *T.* *God Calls to Action.* Joshua 3:5–13.
Nov. 3. *W.* *God Honors His Word.* Joshua 4:11–18.
Nov. 4. *T.* *Remembering God's Faithfulness.* Joshua 4:19–24.
Nov. 5. *F.* *Assurance of God's Direction.* Psalms 23:1–6.
Nov. 6. *S.* *Assurance of God's Provision.* Matthew 6:25–34.
Nov. 7. *S.* *God's Ultimate Presence and Provision.* Ephesians 1:3–14.

BACKGROUND

At long last, the tormenting trek through the wilderness is over, behind them, gone but never to be forgotten. The Israelites have a new leader, following the death of Moses: he is a young, aggressive man of God charged with the taking of the Promised Land. They stand at the river Jordan, the last barrier between them and the hostile tribes in Canaan. Joshua is the ideal man for this hour; he is an officer and a gentleman, one of the precious few whose memory bears no stain. Moses, dying, named him as his successor. A good choice! Joshua knew what was ahead of him; he had been one of the twelve spies who went into Canaan, one of two who told the truth of what he saw there. A Babe born in a manger was given his name: *Jesus* is Greek for Joshua.

Joshua stands now at Jordan, and he has a problem: Jordan has overflowed its banks. Jordan was not so much a river as it was a flood; the snows on Lebanon had melted, causing the flood, as it often did—and does. Only a fool would dare to attempt a crossing. Joshua was no fool; he knew it was dangerous, but he led them into the flood. They murmured, but they went into the raging waters.

And they made it—with the help of God.

NOTES ON THE PRINTED TEXT

Before they took the fateful plunge into the swollen waters, Joshua sent his officers among the people to say to them, "When ye see the ark of the covenant of the Lord your God, and the priests the Levites bearing it, then ye shall remove from your place, and go after it . . . for to morrow the Lord will do wonders among you" (Joshua 3:3,5).

The ark! The very word is more precious to old and modern Israel than mountains of gold. The word *ark* means "chest" or "box" in Hebrew, and there were several arks. The first is mentioned in Genesis 6:14–16, and here it was "Noah's ark"—the houseboat in which his family and the animals sought refuge from the Babylonian Flood. Exodus 2:3 mentions an ark in which the infant Moses was placed; it was made of bulrushes (papyrus) and hidden in the flags on the banks of the Nile. The ark mentioned in our Scripture for our lesson today was called the Ark (notice the capital A) of God, or the Ark of the Testimony. This was an elaborate ark made of shittim (acacia) wood overlaid with gold and having four rings by which it was carried. The golden lid was known as the mercy seat, over which stood two golden cherubim looking down toward the place *where the very Presence of God was believed to dwell as He communicated with His people.* Inside the Ark were believed to be the two stone Tablets of the Law delivered to Moses on Sinai. This was the Ark that went through the Wilderness with Israel—a constant reminder that God marched with them and would see them through—even through flooded Jordan.

At the command of Joshua, the priests took up the Ark and moved down to a place where their feet touched the water. There must have been fright in their hearts at that moment, but there was also, in their minds, the promise that God would work a miracle for them—and God did just that. Far up the river, at the city of Adam, the waters were stopped, cut off, and piled up as though behind a dam. (Remember the miracle when God did the same thing when they crossed the Red Sea?) The riverbed was *dry.* The priests bore the Ark out to the middle of Jordan and waited there until the people passed across to the other shore.

An Arab historian tells us that there was a similar occurrence in 1226, and another in 1909, and yet another in 1927, when an earthquake collapsed the banks of the river near the city of Adam, and that the waters were held back for twenty-one hours. Maybe so. But, says Edward P. Blair, "The miracle is not minimized by a suggestion of the means by which it happened." To Israel, it was pure miracle.

When they were all safely across, Joshua picked out twelve men (one from every tribe) to mark the locale of the miracle. They were ordered to pick up twelve stones, set them in the ground and leave them there as monuments of remembrance. Actually, there were two piles of stones—one in the bed of Jordan where the priests had stood and one at Gilgal, the place of encampment after they had crossed the river. Why? Their children, who would come after they were gone, must never forget what God did for them that day at Jordan's banks. They must always *remember.* Yesterday has a meaning for today; any nation and people have strength only as they keep alive the faith and the courage of their past. Our modern Aleksandr Solzhenitsyn puts it well when he says that "A people that no longer remembers has lost its history and its soul." Right!

The appeal to remembrance was one of the great, dominant emphases of Israel's faith, and it should be dominant in *our* faith. We who think of the Church as "*our* church" are talking nonsense; we should remember that we would have no church at all were it not for the labors and the faith of whole generations of men and women who gave them "their" church. We who boast of "our" America should remember Valley Forge. The crossing of Jordan was not accomplished by the brilliant genius of any leader; without a faith in God, without His plan, that crossing would not have succeeded.

Why do we forget? Why do we worship God and then ignore Him? Why do we read our Bible and then refuse to let it guide us? Why do we almost worship our famed Declaration of Independence, preserve it in

Washington, and then forget to put its principles to work in our time and day? Israel never forgot but we do!

There is another lesson to be learned in all this: God lays His plans, *but we must carry them out!* He has no hands but our hands. Israel had not accomplished all that God had chosen for her to accomplish when they crossed Jordan. There was work for her to do beyond and after that. They had come to their Land, yes—but that Land was filled with enemies who would do their best to drive them out, to kill every one of them. They had conquered their wilderness; now there was more conquering ahead of them, and every one of them must do his part, must not only remember Abraham, Isaac, and Jacob, but must put his life on the line in the struggle.

The Hebrews, while they often stumbled, never forgot *that.* The infamous Nazis murdered millions of them in Hitler's Germany, but they never denied their God. In their temples today, an ark is placed in the walls of their synagogues facing Jerusalem (in the United States, facing east). The congregation rises whenever from this holy portion of the wall are removed the scrolls of the Law which are kept there. They still remember!

SUGGESTIONS TO TEACHERS

How would you write the history of your Church? One way would be merely to list names and dates. Chronology, however, would not truly tell the story. The history of your Church is more than a record of organizational meetings and cornerstone-layings. It is the astonishing account of the Lord choosing, leading, and delivering a group of people for a special task.

As you investigate the scriptural account of God's people settling in the Promised Land, use it as a model for tracing God's choosing, leading, and delivering you and your congregation and denomination, and also the larger Church.

1. *RISK OF ADVANCING.* Joshua 3–4 describes the Israelites venturing into an uncharted land. Joshua knew the feelings of apprehension in entering an area where he and his people had not been before. The pilgrimage of faith, however, is always filled with uncertainty. Trusting in the Lord means taking risks. You may well have your class talk together for a few minutes about the risks which the founders of your congregation and your denomination had to take. Also have your class enumerate some of the risks which they feel the Church will have to take in the immediate future.

2. *RESOURCE FOR THE JOURNEY.* Joshua pointed out to the people of Israel, ". . . you shall know that the living God is among you . . ." (Joshua 3:10). The Lord was resource enough. A miraculous deliverance—a repeat of the Red Sea Crossing, except a Jordan River Crossing this time—showed that the Lord truly was capable of leading His people through any challenge. The Risen Christ likewise leads us, God's people today across whatever Jordans we may encounter.

3. *REMINDER OF THE HAPPENING.* The twelve stones became a permanent sign of how God had brought Israel across the Jordan into the Promised Land. Think of the "signs" of God's activity and deliverance

which we may cherish, such as the sacraments of Baptism and the Lord's Supper. Every community, including Christ's, needs to take time to recall the miraculous happenings which God made possible. What are some of the other "twelve-stone events" in the life of your congregation?

4. *REFERENCE FOR HOPING.* Allow some of your lesson period to do some "futuristic thinking." Note the phrase, "When your children ask their fathers in time to come, 'What do these stones mean?' " (Joshua 4:23). The biblical account always looks ahead to the coming generations. What should your church do to share the faith more effectively with your children? How are the members of your class personally telling young persons what the "stones" of the Christian experience mean?

TOPIC FOR ADULTS
INTO THE PROMISED LAND

Wahlstrom's Wonder. "Wahlstrom is a tinkering man, and, a few years ago, looking for recreation, he bought an old bombsight and took it apart to see what made it work. When he started to put it back together, he discovered that he had some parts from other projects that could be added to the mechanism. This became his hobby. Neighbors brought parts and pieces, and Wahlstrom's genius was turned to putting them to use. He was able to use almost every cog, wheel, belt, and screw he could find. The result is a machine that the neighbors call Wahlstrom's Wonder. It has ten thousand parts. When he throws the switch, three thousand of them begin to move. Lights flash, bells ring, big wheels run belts that turn little wheels, and the whole thing revolves on a turntable. It's a wonderful machine—only it doesn't do any work. It just runs.

"No one familiar with the organization of a modern church—especially a large church—needs to have this parable interpreted! It is entirely possible for us to be buried by our boards, commissions, and committees."—C. Willard Fetter, *Pulpit Digest,* October 1964.

Into New Promised Lands! "The times—they are achanging. We still send missionaries to Korea, of course. But we now read of 16 Korean-speaking congregations in the United States in the Presbyterian Church U.S., and we are told that the Presbyterians in Korea have themselves sent out a dozen foreign missionaries!

"Changing times. Arab oil dominates. So the largest Christian church in the Middle East is a Korean Presbyterian congregation in Saudi Arabia!

"We read of the challenge of the new population explosion. If all the people in the world were suddenly moved to the United States they still would not pack this country as tightly as Bangladesh is crowded. So now we read of our new mission work there, concentrating on health services so desperately needed. Or we read of a letter from Zaire missionary Annette Kriner working with baby clinics, nutrition, education, and family planning services, knowing that the latter might bring her all kinds of trouble.

"We read of new abject poverty in Latin America. But we also read of beggars being taught carpentry in missionary vocational schools in Haiti. As some progress, at least, is made in Brazil, we read that vast government programs of housing and slum clearance offer splendid opportunity for evangelism and the establishment of new Protestant churches.

The mission-sponsored 'Land for the Landless' program has helped at least a few. And Taiwanese Presbyterians not only are sending 19 missionaries abroad; they are themselves making sacrificial contributions to emergency relief funds for the poor and hungry around the world.

"Thus even today one reads of growing churches. Though often beset by immature leadership which sometimes places corrupt people in power, the church in Africa takes in almost more new members than it can handle. A missionary in Brazil wonders how to assign the twenty-five graduates of a Bible training school when there are fifty places wanting them. World changes are making incredible hardships for the church in many places around the world. But, believing in Easter now, missionaries that our gifts support are seeing changes as challenges. Here and there they are reporting resurrection and new life."—William Ramsey, *Presbyterian Outlook,* March 31, 1980.

Questions for Pupils on the Next Lesson. 1. How do leaders influence others for good and ill in our culture? 2. Does God continue to judge nations as He judged Israel in Old Testament times? 3. Does the Lord raise up leaders in our time? 4. What are some of the lessons of history which you wish that the coming generation would remember? 5. Do you see yourself as a leader? Why or why not?

TOPIC FOR YOUTH
GOD KEEPS HIS WORD

Carried. "A short time ago I heard a very well-known Glasgow minister tell of an incident which he had never forgotten.

"More than thirty years ago now he had been at a service conducted by a very famous preacher who for many years had occupied a great pulpit with the greatest distinction. After the service my friend went round to speak to the famous man. 'Sir,' he said, 'when I think of the strain of preaching from this famous pulpit, I do not know how you have carried on all these years.' The great preacher answered: 'In this job you do not carry on; you are carried on.'

"My friend went on to say that at the time it had seemed to him almost a 'slick' answer, but the years had taught him that it was nothing but the truth.

"The Bible is full of this truth of the support of God. 'Cast your burden on the Lord,' said the Psalmist, 'and he will sustain you' (Psalms 55:22). 'When you pass through the waters, I will be with you,' Isaiah heard God say, 'and through the rivers, they shall not overwhelm you' (Isaiah 43:2). 'The eternal God is your dwelling-place,' said Moses, 'and underneath are the everlasting arms' (Deuteronomy 33:27). Again and again the promise recurs."—William Barclay, *In the Hands of God.*

Move on to The Promised Land. A man who worked in a paper factory came to Samuel Johnson. He had taken from the factory two or three sheets of paper and some pieces of string to tie up parcels of his own; and by doing so had convinced himself that he had committed a deadly sin. He would not stop talking and lamenting about this trivial business. At last Dr. Johnson burst out: "Stop bothering about paper and packthread when we are all living together in a world that is bursting with sin and sorrow."

Sometimes, we are so preoccupied with trivia and so oblivious to

God's promise that we think only of our paper-and-packthread sins. God calls us to take the risk of taking Him at His word and moving into the uncharted future. He holds out a Promised Land for us, His people, in these times.

Sentence Sermon to Remember: God could have kept Daniel out of the lion's den. . . . He could have kept Paul and Silas out of jail. . . . He could have kept the three Hebrew children out of the fiery furnace. . . . But God has never promised to keep us out of hard places. . . . What He has promised is to go with us through every hard place, and to bring us through victoriously.—Merv Rosell.

Questions for Pupils on the Next Lesson. 1. Why do you sometimes feel cynical about political leaders? 2. Do you think that God raises up leaders in our times? 3. What qualities in a leader do you think are most important? 4. What leadership qualities do you think you have been given by God?

LESSON XI—NOVEMBER 14

GOD PROVIDES JUDGES FOR HIS PEOPLE

Background Scripture: Judges 1–2
Devotional Reading: Joshua 24:19–29

KING JAMES VERSION

JUDGES 2 6 And when Joshua had let the people go, the children of Israel went every man unto his inheritance to possess the land.

7 And the people served the LORD all the days of Joshua, and all the days of the elders that outlived Joshua, who had seen all the great works of the LORD, that he did for Israel.

11 And the children of Israel did evil in the sight of the LORD, and served Baalim:

12 And they forsook the LORD God of their fathers, which brought them out of the land of Egypt, and followed other gods, of the gods of the people that *were* round about them, and bowed themselves unto them, and provoked the LORD to anger.

13 And they forsook the LORD, and served Baal and Ashtaroth.

14 And the anger of the LORD was hot against Israel, and he delivered them into the hands of spoilers that spoiled them, and he sold them into the hands of their enemies round about, so that they could not any longer stand before their enemies.

15 Whithersoever they went out, the hand of the LORD was against them for evil, as the LORD had said, and as the LORD had sworn unto them: and they were greatly distressed.

16 Nevertheless the LORD raised up judges, which delivered them out of the hand of those that spoiled them.

17 And yet they would not hearken unto their judges, but they went a whoring after other gods, and bowed themselves unto them: they turned quickly out of the way which their fathers walked in, obeying the commandments of the LORD; *but* they did not so.

18 And when the LORD raised them up judges, then the LORD was with the judge, and delivered them out of the hand of their enemies all the days of the judge: for it repented the LORD because of their groanings by reason of them that oppressed them and vexed them.

19 And it came to pass, when the judge

REVISED STANDARD VERSION

JUDGES 2 6 When Joshua dismissed the people, the people of Israel went each to his inheritance to take possession of the land. 7 And the people served the LORD all the days of Joshua, and all the days of the elders who outlived Joshua, who had seen all the great work which the LORD had done for Israel.

11 And the people of Israel did what was evil in the sight of the LORD and served the Baals; 12 and they forsook the LORD, the God of their fathers, who had brought them out of the land of Egypt; they went after other gods, from among the gods of the peoples who were round about them, and bowed down to them; and they provoked the LORD to anger. 13 They forsook the LORD, and served the Baals and the Ashtaroth. 14 So the anger of the LORD was kindled against Israel, and he gave them over to plunderers, who plundered them; and he sold them into the power of their enemies round about, so that they could no longer withstand their enemies.

15 Whenever they marched out, the hand of the LORD was against them for evil, as the LORD had warned, and as the LORD had sworn to them; and they were in sore straits.

16 Then the LORD raised up judges, who saved them out of the power of those who plundered them. 17 And yet they did not listen to their judges; for they played the harlot after other gods and bowed down to them; they soon turned aside from the way in which their fathers had walked, who had obeyed the commandments of the LORD, and they did not do so. 18 Whenever the LORD raised up judges for them, the LORD was with the judge, and he saved them from the hand of their enemies all the days of the judge; for the LORD was moved to pity by their groaning because of those who afflicted and oppressed them. 19 But whenever the judge died, they turned back and behaved worse than their fathers, going after other gods, serving them and

was dead, *that* they returned, and corrupted *themselves* more than their fathers, in following other gods to serve them, and to bow down unto them; they ceased not from their own doings, not from their stubborn way.

bowing down to them; they did not drop any of their practices or their stubborn ways.

KEY VERSE: Whenever the Lord raised up judges for them, the Lord was with the judge. . . . Judges 2:18 (RSV).

HOME DAILY BIBLE READINGS

Nov. *8. M.* *Remember Your Past.* Joshua 24:1–13.
Nov. *9. T.* *Serve the Lord.* Joshua 24:14–25.
Nov. *10. W.* *New Direction.* Judges 1:1–8.
Nov. *11. T.* *United to Fight.* Judges 1:9–17.
Nov. *12. F.* *Failure to Obey.* Judges 1:27–36.
Nov. *13. S.* *A Time for Weeping.* Judges 2:1–6.
Nov. *14. S.* *The Lord Raised Up Judges.* Judges 2:16–19.

BACKGROUND

Having led in the Jewish conquest of Canaan, Joshua supervised the allotment of the land among the twelve tribes. For himself, he asked only for a small town. Timnath-serah, in the hill country of Ephriam: "So Joshua let the people depart, every man unto his inheritance" (Joshua 24:28). His age has been called "Israel's Golden Age." The old soldier preached a brilliant sermon at Shechem, urging them never to forsake their God. Then he died at the ripe old age of one hundred and ten.

Now what? Now they had no great, capable leader; now they were widely scattered across the Land, each tribe being a law unto itself and not even bound loosely together, as they had been in the wilderness. And now God instituted an institution of "Judges". . . . They were tribal heroes, and, hopefully, strong men who would hold the tribe together. The period of the Judges ran from the time of Joshua's death to the days in which Saul was made king—some 230 years. There were thirteen of them; they are named in Judges 3–16.

They had problems. Great problems.

NOTES ON THE PRINTED TEXT

Their problems can be summed up in two categories: one was social and national, and the other was religious.

Here they were, a band of nomads settling down in a strange country. Here they were surrounded by hostile, Baal-worshipping Canaanites. Their problem here was: how could they, should they, get along with them? Should they adopt whatever Canaanite customs would help them to live in peace together, or should they remain strictly Jewish? "When you are in Rome," said someone, "you do as the Romans do." For the sake of peace and survival, should they yield just a little, and adopt some Canaanite ways? It is quite possible that some among them said that the only way to survival was to kill every Canaanite in the land!

Now keep in mind the fact that this was a whole new generation in Canaan. The fathers who lived in Joshua's time gradually passed away, and a whole new Israel which had never seen Joshua took over. Neither did this new generation know God at first hand; that made it easier for them to fall into apostasy.

Remember, too, that they were now an *agricultural* people and no longer nomads. They had to live on the new land. They had to plant crops, and they needed all the help they could get to raise their crops. *That* was the stumbling block that nearly ruined them.

In the land of Canaan, Baal was god. Baal was their *male* god, and Astarte (Ashtaroth) was his female consort—and a goddess of fertility. Their religion was tied up with sustaining the fertility of the soil; they prayed to Astarte to give them good crops. They had other deities, male and female, who could give fertility to the soil,—but little if any *morality.* Their worship of these deities was often nothing more than a sexual orgy.

What to do? Should they cultivate the help of Astarte or not? We can condemn them for bowing down to Baal, but wasn't it natural for them to get whatever help they could, if they were to survive? Natural or sinful, that is just what the Hebrews did: they fell away from their desert ways of strict morality, into the repulsive worship of Baalism simply because falling away seemed to promise them success in their new, agricultural life.

It was a matter of self-preservation—and it brought down on them the fearful anger of God: ". . . and he (God) gave them over to plunderers, who plundered them; and he sold them into the power of their enemies . . ." (Judges 2:14 RSV).

It was at this precise moment that "the Lord raised up judges, who saved them out of the power of those who plundered them" (verse 16 RSV).

All through the long story of this era, there runs a cycle of apostasy, judgment, repentance, and deliverance. Certainly, God had reason to be angry with their turning away from Him to Baal; certainly He had the right of judgment against them. But always, God stood ready to be merciful as well as angry and just, provided that they showed signs of repentance. The tears of repentance—*tears*—moved Him and brought mercy, and forgiveness.

All through human history, men have been playing a game of "follow the leader." At times, they follow leaders who are basically evil (Hitler, Mussolini, Castro, Amin, Khomeini); following them meant only trouble. This was not the case, however, at this point in Hebrew history. The judges appointed of God were, on the whole, good and consecrated judges or leaders. They were truly "deliverers" who saved their people time and again from disaster, when the people forsook their God. (There was even great goodness in Samson, who was also something of a clown.) Most of them, in action, echoed the stirring challenge of Joshua to their erring people: "Choose ye this day whom ye will serve." (Joshua 24:15). They taught their people that they could not serve two masters—God and Baal. But the people had a bad habit: "And it came to pass, when the judge was dead, that they returned, and corrupted themselves more than their fathers . . ." (Judges 2:19). For that, they paid a bitter price; they were plundered by the Canaanite enemy. And they were forgiven by a God whose patience is beyond understanding, whose mercy is wider and deeper than the sea!

What do we learn from all this? We learn that doing evil brings its own punishment upon us, that we cannot break God's laws, but we can and do break ourselves against them; that every new generation must honor the faith of its fathers and must find its own way to God; that to "adjust" our Christian morality to that of the non-Christian world spells spiritual death; that God gives us a second, third, fourth chance to repent our neglect of Him and return to do His will, and that God often strengthens us by way of competition with evil forces.

"And God *saved* them." This is the whole lesson of Judges. He *can* save us. He never gives up on men. His hand is always out to them. Even in a day when a godless Communism threatens us, when millions of Jews are murdered in an unspeakable holocaust, when a "new" morality seems about to undermine our moral strength, when truth seems to be on the gallows and evil on the throne and the Church is plagued with great losses in membership—even *then,* He can save us—but only if we reach out and touch His outstretched hand.

There never was and never will be a darkness through which God can't come with the light and hope and faith which we saw in His Son.

SUGGESTIONS TO TEACHERS

"Plus ça change, plus la même chose," is a famous cynical phrase in French, which translates roughly, "The more things change, the more they are the same." Or, in today's vernacular: "Nothing new; it's the same old messy world."

At first reading, Judges 1,2 seems to be such a dreary message. The human record is, after all, a dismal story. And if there was nothing more to history except a procession of suffering and deaths, the final word would be merely *"Plus la même."*

God, however, injects His plans and His presence into the story. The Bible is the record of His doings. The Book of Judges describes one segment in Israel's history of God's activity. Your task as teacher is to extrapolate God's activity in today's world from the record of His work in the Judges's world.

1. *COST OF DISOBEDIENCE.* The Israelites did not obey the Lord and drive out the Canaanites from their land. That act of disobedience cost God's people dearly. They began to pick up the attitudes and customs of the Canaanites. They forgot their identity as God's people. Without getting into pointless wrangling over the command of God in regard to the Canaanites, have your class come to understand that God calls His people to obey, not to argue. To disobey brings dire consequences.

2. *CULTURE OF DISASTER.* As teacher, devote a little time to researching the Canaanites's religion and culture. You will find that their Baal worship was more than a preoccupation with little clay fertility figurines, but involved an entire culture involving violence, power, possessions, and eroticism. Let your class pick out the similarities between the Canaanite culture of 1200 B.C. and the contemporary culture of A.D.

1982. Without great watchfulness, the Canaanite mentality can easily take over. The Israelites "forsook the Lord . . . they went after other gods" (Judges 2:11), and so can we!

3. *CONFEDERATES ON DISCERNMENT.* The Judges, you should make clear to your class, were not judicial officials presiding over a courtroom, but leaders raised up by God to bring the Israelites back to their heritage and destiny. Not all of them lived blameless lives. But these men and women (and be sure to remember that Deborah was one of the Judges!) understood what God had done and what God had in mind for His people still. Encourage your class to think who the "Judges" are for the Church in today's world. Who are the most discerning people in present-day society? How should people in your class be interpreting conditions now?

4. *CALL TO DISCIPLINE.* Each of the Judges summoned God's people in his own day to remember the covenant God had with them and to return to the Lord. God's people were to stop their flirtation or "affair" ("They played the harlot after other gods" as Judges 2:17 says) with Canaanite gods. God's people today are also called to be resolute and serve only Him as Lord!

TOPIC FOR ADULTS
NEW LEADERS FOR NEW TIMES

Alert Leader Captures the Impregnable. When Cyrus was besieging Sardis, he was told the city was unconquerable. High above him loomed the Acropolis of Sardis—an impregnable spur of solid rock, heavily fortified, well-manned. Cyrus offered a special reward to anyone who could find a way in.

One day, a soldier named Hyeroeades was watching the Sardian Acropolis, and saw a soldier from the Sardis fortress at the top accidentally drop his metal helmet. The helmet clattered down over the battlements. Hyeroeades carefully observed as the Sardian soldier climbed down the cliffs to retrieve the helmet. That night, Hyeroeades led a handpicked band of commandos up that same path and found the top unguarded. They rushed in and captured the citadel which was believed by the Sardians to be completely safe and unconquerable.

The Judges, like Hyeroeades, were alert to opportunities. Although the situation seemed impossible, with the help of the Lord and a relatively small force, these leaders were able to save the nation.

Bound Together as a Community of Leaders. "In the face of the overwhelming needs all around us which the world represents, we cannot afford our quarrels and bickering. We are bound together by more than a system of rules, important though the rules may be. Our polity may force us to learn to tolerate one another, but it cannot make us learn from each other. Only the presence of the Holy Spirit and our receptivity to the working of the Spirit can enable us to discover that we actually need each other with all our diversity.

"*The peace* of the church is more than keeping the lid on, or trying a new structure or program which will prevent open warfare among us, peace is not simply the absence of conflict. . . .

"Schism takes two parties and it is always the end result of a period of unwillingness to take others seriously. The high price of schism is that it never accomplishes what it seeks to do."—Howard Rice, Sermon preached at Detroit, May 27, 1980.

Casino Reflections Set Boardwalk on Fire. The golden glitter of one of Atlantic City's new casinos is causing an unexpected problem on the Boardwalk. Officials say the sun's rays are bouncing off Caesar's new casino hotel and causing fires on the wooden way.

Officials say some panels of the angular, plexiglass facade around Caesar's new Boardwalk Regency are warping inward, causing the concentration of the sun's rays onto a small area of the Boardwalk.

A solar energy professor told fire officials that temperatures in the treated pine planks can reach up to 400 degrees in areas up to eighteen inches in diameter.

Fire fighters have been called out several times to put out small fires and smoldering wood on the Boardwalk.

The situation of the gambling casino's reflections igniting blazes is a type of parable. Greed ultimately burns. Selfishness and irresponsibility eventually cause destruction. Evil, whether in ancient Israel or a modern-day nation, seems to have its own built-in ruin effects. God runs a moral universe.

Questions for Pupils on the Next Lesson. 1. Have you ever faced the question of pondering whether or not to accept a position of power? 2. What do you do when you feel inadequate in the face of life's problems? 3. How do you test your perceptions of God's call? 4. Do some in your church feel you are too few to make an impact in society today? 5. What relevance do you find in the story of Gideon for your life?

TOPIC FOR YOUTH
NEW LEADERS FOR NEW TIMES

Qualities of Leadership. What are the qualities which you think a leader should have? Try making your list. Others have.

Most lists emphasize awareness of one's limitations and humility. We need to remember our own ignorance. Quintilian, the Roman teacher of oratory, said of certain of his students: "They would doubtless have been excellent students, if they had not been convinced of their own knowledge." As the old proverb reminds us: "He who knows not, and knows not that he knows not is a fool—avoid him; he who knows not and knows that he knows not is a wise man—seek his company."

Does your list also include an experience of Jesus Christ? It is told that when the Church at Ecclefechan was looking for a minister, Thomas Carlyle's father, who was an elder there, said simply: "What this kirk wants is a minister who knows Jesus Christ other than at secondhand."

God calls leaders in each generation, including ours. He intends you to accept responsibilities. Do you have the above qualities of leadership?

Sheltered. Newspapers reported in April 1980 that a Missoula, Montana, religious leader was certain that the destruction of the world was coming, and that there was no hope. Leland Jensen and his small band of religious followers headed for their fallout shelters to await the destruction of the world by a nuclear war that they said would come April 29, 1980.

Mr. Leland, a former Missoula chiropractor, and his members of a splinter group of the Baha'i faith planned for the doomsday for months.

Other members of the religious group, called Baha'i Under the Provisions of the Covenant, planned to go underground in such places as Sheridan, Wyoming; Durango, Colorado, and Fort Smith, Arkansas.

Contrast Jensen and this group with the leaders in ancient Israel in today's lesson. Instead of retreating with a "shelter-mentality," because of difficult days, they became deliverers who roused the people to advance with God's help.

God continues to raise up new leaders for new times, and impells them and us to stand boldly for him.

Look Up. Israel often failed to be thankful to God. It assumed that it had no obligations. It failed to live up to its destiny.

In a sense, every time any community fails to look up to the Lord as the Giver of all life and to accept responsibilities to God, it declines into something less than human.

Turn a hog loose in an orchard and it will eat the apples as they fall without looking up to see from where they came. This is a whole new parable of a large part of the human race. They receive many gifts from the hand of the great Giver, but never look up to the Source of every good and perfect gift.

Sentence Sermon to Remember: Without judges who are truly just, life is nothing more than anarchy.—J. L. Healey.

Questions for Pupils on the Next Lesson. 1. What are the most overwhelming negative forces trying to work in your life? 2. Do you see many evidences of God's leadership in crises in your life or your community? 3. Why do you sometimes feel a lack of self-confidence in dealing with problems? 4. Have you ever considered a career in service to others? 5. What particular task of responsibility to others is God fitting you to do?

LESSON XII—NOVEMBER 21

GOD EMPOWERS GIDEON

Background Scripture: Judges 6:1–8:21
Devotional Reading: Psalms 105:7–15

KING JAMES VERSION

JUDGES 6 3 And *so* it was, when Israel had sown, that the Midianites came up, and the Amalekites, and the children of the east, even they came up against them;

4 And they encamped against them, and destroyed the increase of the earth, till thou come unto Gaza, and left no sustenance for Israel, neither sheep, nor ox, nor ass.

5 For they came up with their cattle and their tents, and they came as grasshoppers for multitude; *for* both they and their camels were without number: and they entered into the land to destroy it.

6 And Israel was greatly impoverished because of the Midianites; and the children of Israel cried unto the LORD.

11 And there came an angel of the LORD, and sat under an oak which *was* in Oparah, that *pertained* unto Joash the Abiezrite: and his son Gideon threshed wheat by the winepress, to hide *it* from the Midianites.

12 And the angel of the LORD appeared unto him, and said unto him, The LORD *is* with thee, thou mighty man of valour.

13 And Gideon said unto him, O my Lord, if the LORD be with us, why then is all this befallen us? and where *be* all his miracles which our fathers told us of, saying, Did not the LORD bring us up from Egypt? but now the LORD hath forsaken us, and delivered us into the hands of the Midianites.

14 And the LORD looked upon him, and said, Go in this thy might, and thou shalt save Israel from the hand of the Midianites: have not I sent thee?

15 And he said unto him, O my Lord, wherewith shall I save Israel? behold, my family *is* poor in Manasseh, and I *am* the least in my father's house.

16 And the LORD said unto him, Surely I will be with thee, and thou shalt smite the Midianites as one man.

7 20 And the three companies blew the trumpets, and brake the pitchers, and held the lamps in their left hands, and the trumpets in their right hands to blow

REVISED STANDARD VERSION

JUDGES 6 3 For whenever the Israelites put in seed the Midianites and the Amalekites and the people of the East would come up and attack them; 4 they would encamp against them and destroy the produce of the land, as far as the neighborhood of Gaza, and leave no sustenance in Israel, and no sheep or ox or ass. 5 For they would come up with their cattle and their tents, coming like locusts for number; both they and their camels could not be counted; so that they wasted the land as they came in. 6 And Israel was brought very low because of Midian; and the people of Israel cried for help to the LORD.

11 Now the angel of the LORD came and sat under the oak at Ophrah, which belonged to Joash the Abiezrite, as his son Gideon was beating out wheat in the wine press, to hide it from the Midianites. 12 And the angel of the LORD appeared to him and said to him, "The LORD is with you, you mighty man of valor." 13 And Gideon said to him, "Pray, sir, if the LORD is with us, why then has all this befallen us? And where are all his wonderful deeds which our fathers recounted to us, saying, 'Did not the LORD bring us up from Egypt?' But now the LORD has cast us off, and given us into the hand of Midian." 14 And the LORD turned to him and said, "Go in this might of yours and deliver Israel from the hand of Midian; do not I send you?" 15 And he said to him, "Pray, Lord, how can I deliver Israel? Behold, my clan is the weakest in Manasseh, and I am the least in my family." 16 And the LORD said to him, "But I will be with you, and you shall smite the Midianites as one man."

7 20 And the three companies blew the trumpets and broke the jars, holding in their left hands the torches, and in their right hands the trumpets to blow; and they

withal: and they cried, The sword of the LORD, and of Gideon.
21 And they stood every man in his place round about the camp: and all the host ran, and cried, and fled.

cried, "A sword for the LORD and for Gideon!" 21 They stood every man in his place round about the camp, and all the army ran; they cried out and fled.

KEY VERSE: . . . the angel of the Lord appeared to him and said to him, "The Lord is with you, you mighty man of valor." Judges 6:12 (RSV).

HOME DAILY BIBLE READINGS

Nov. 15. M. One Among Many. Judges 3:1–6.
Nov. 16. T. Othniel the Judge. Judges 3:7–11.
Nov. 17. W. Ehud Delivers. Judges 3:12–30.
Nov. 18. T. Deborah and Barak Prepare. Judges 4:1–9.
Nov. 19. F. A Victory Song. Judges 5:1–5,31.
Nov. 20. S. Away With False Gods. Judges 6:25–32.
Nov. 21. S. The Victory Gained. Judges 7:9–22.

BACKGROUND

Joshua and his army entered Canaan by way of Jericho; he entered the land right in the middle and so cut off the north from the south, and then, one by one, proceeded to crush the Canaanite tribes within the land. (British General Allenby used exactly the same strategy in Palestine in World War I.) We might think that this would bring peace and security to Israel and the end of war. Not so!

Beyond the borders of the occupied land, other enemies arose to harass them. These were Midianites in the country south and east of Moab and Edom; they were actually kin of the Hebrews, according to Genesis 25:1–6. With them came the Amalekites, and Bedouins who lived in the east, beyond Jordan. These were maraudering people who preyed on any other tribes or people who had something they wanted; they raided Israel all across her territory, as far as Gaza (a land occupied by the Philistines). If they were not checked and driven out, Israel faced sudden death. Stopping them would be difficult for an Israel scattered and disjointed as they were.

But it was not in God's plan that they should win. In the tribe of Manasseh, in the village of Ophrah, He had a shy, self-effacing young man working on his father's farm.

Gideon!

NOTES ON THE PRINTED TEXT

Gideon, like all the rest of Israel, lived in constant fear of the raiding Midianites and Amalekites who specialized in raiding Jewish farms at the time of harvest, who came with their cattle and tents, and "as grasshoppers for multitude" (Judges 6:5). They also came on camels—something new in warfare! They came and killed, "and they left no sustenance for Israel, neither sheep, nor ox, or ass (verse 4). They took the fruit of the crops, leaving Israel nothing to eat.

Food! Let a raiding enemy cut off a nation's food supply and their war is won; even spiritual values and virtues cannot survive without food.

The author or authors of Judges makes it plain that this threatened starvation was a punishment for Israel for her desertion of God to other gods.

Gideon was faithful to God—but he couldn't quite understand why God had let this happen. Like the rest of his people, he and his father had fled to hideouts and strongholds in the mountains. For seven long years, they did that—and the Midianites still came, plundering the farms and vineyards in the valleys.

One day, the story goes, Gideon was busy threshing his wheat in his wine press; the Midianites wouldn't find him there, and neither would they find his hidden wheat. An enemy might not find him there, but God did: he looks up from his work to see an angel of the Lord sitting under a nearby oak tree, and they talked together. It is difficult for us to determine whether this was a vision, or the appearance of an actual man, but to Gideon this man or angel was God Himself in visible form. Verse 14 says that "The Lord looked upon him (Gideon), and said, Go in this thy might, and thou shalt save Israel from the hand of the Midianites: *have not I sent thee?*"

And Gideon wondered what many a man has wondered when God called him to a hard task—why *me?* He was an obscure man in a small, almost obscure tribe (Manasseh). How could a man like this lead the army of Israel against the powerful Midianites? Odd, isn't it, that God so often chooses such modest men to lead other men through great crises? It happened when God called Moses to lead the revolt against Egypt. "Who am I," said Moses, "that I should go unto Pharaoh?" When God called Isaiah, the prophet pleaded that he was a man of unclean lips, a most unworthy man. Gideon not only pleads his humility; he can't help wondering why God had let His people into this conflict with Midian! Why didn't God crush the Midianites earlier than this? God might have taken offense at this, but no—He said, gently, "Surely I will be with thee, and thou shalt smite the Midianites as one man" (verse 16).

There comes a moment in the experiences of man, when the divine overwhelms the human, a moment in which man understands that with the assurance of God's help he can accomplish the impossible. Weak men become heroes, with that assurance. It worked out that way with hesitant Gideon. He made ready to face the Midianites.

We do not know how many thousands of men there were in the army of the Midianites and the Amalekites, but we do know that Gideon had some 32,000 men under arms. Out of these, he picked out only 300 of the best of them, and equipped each man with a trumpet and a jar in which a lighted torch was hidden—and, quite likely, with sword and spear. They moved out at night, and when they reached the Midianite camp they blew a blast on the trumpets which must have sounded like the noise of doom, and with their flaming torches fell upon the enemy camp, screaming, "The sword of the Lord, and of Gideon!" Taken by surprise, the Midianites ran about wildly in the darkness, killing each other! By the time dawn came, they had been driven back across Jordan.

So, with only 300 men—*and God*—Gideon saved Israel. Dr. Harry Emerson Fosdick once told his students that "The hope of the world lies in its minorities." History proves that to be true. God is *not,* as Napoleon once sneered, "On the side of the largest battalions." God is on the side of those who are *right.*

Gideon was far from being perfect; he was often wrong. Wrong, when he questioned the presence of God in Israel. Wrong, when he was over-cautious. Wrong, when he made an ephod of the golden spoils of Midian. But he was right more often than wrong. He knew the voice of God when he heard it, and he did as God commanded. He was more of a local hero in Israel, than a national hero, but the mark of Gideon is upon his people yet, and upon us. Today we have a group of people who call themselves "The Gideons"; they go about the country placing Bibles in hotel rooms, so that the guests of the hotels, often weary, lonely, or dispirited, may read and learn that God is with them there and everywhere. How many have been lifted up and strengthened in reading their Gideon Bibles, we will never know.

Gideon had one more mark of credit: he refused to be a king over Israel. He died as he lived, humbly.

SUGGESTIONS TO TEACHERS

"What can I do? I'm just one insignificant person," you may sigh.

"What can we accomplish?" a leader in a small church complains. "We're so few and don't have the resources."

The Gideon story, the basis of today's lesson, answers those who complain of being so inadequate. As was the case with so many biblical heroes, God chose an unknown character from Nowheresville to save the situation. The point of your lesson will be that the Lord continues to summon ordinary persons such as those in your class to be champions of the faith.

1. *UNPROMISING TIMES.* "When things are different, I'll try to do something for God," someone says. Christians stall in serving until "the situation shows signs of improving" or "the conditions are right." The human scene is nearly always a crisis. The days of Gideon or the days of the guys and girls in your class will always appear to be unpromising, even hopeless. The Midianites seem to prevail. But *today,* in spite of the problems and perils, the Lord calls each in your class to champion His cause.

2. *UNLIKELY HERO.* Take time to present a good character sketch of Gideon. Let your students see that Gideon was hardly the stuff from which heroes are made. Point out how Gideon tried to back out, and how Gideon argued with the Lord. You may find Paddy Chayefsky's play about this fascinating personality offering you suggestions and insights into the Gideon story. Your class is filled with Gideons, waiting to be challenged. They may seem like unlikely heroes, but so was Gideon himself! Your lesson today may help rouse these latent Gideons.

3. *UNENCUMBERED ARMY.* From the horde of undisciplined armed rabble, the Lord screens out a small, highly mobile strike force of 300. Each of the 300 is superbly self-reliant and well-trained. This elite battalion can be depended upon to overcome the mighty Midianites. The Church is often compared to such a military unit. Each member is meant to be part of a spiritual commando force. Discuss what it means to be mo-

bilized for service for God. What qualities are needed to be an alert, equipped, and dependable Christian Church member today?

4. *UNEXPECTED VICTORY.* God brings His own victory in His own way and in His own time. Although the "Midianites" may seem overwhelmingly powerful, when we are enlisted and trained for duty, God promises us that He will prevail. The Resurrection of Jesus Christ is God's complete assurance of final victory even over the last great enemy—death!

TOPIC FOR ADULTS
CALLED TO BE A CHAMPION

Anybody—Where Are You? This is a story about four men named Everybody, Somebody, Anybody, and Nobody.

There was an important job to be done and Everybody was asked to do it. Everybody was sure that Somebody would do it. Anybody could have done it, but Nobody did it. Somebody got angry about that because it was Everybody's job. Everybody thought that Anybody could do it, and Nobody realized that Everybody wouldn't do it. It ended up with Everybody blaming Somebody when actually Nobody blamed Anybody.

Called from Grief to Champion the Poor. "To the Christian soul many a time a personal sorrow, or disappointment, or loss has been a turning point in life, an occasion for deeper consecration and wider service. In Morley's *Life of Cobden,* there is a quotation from one of John Bright's speeches, which explains how he was led to devote his life first of all to the anti-Corn Law agitation and so to many noble causes. 'At that time I was at Leamington, and I was, on the day when Mr. Cobden called on me, in the depths of grief, I might almost say of despair; for the light and sunshine of my house had been extinguished. All that was left on earth of my young wife, except the memory of a sainted life and of a too brief happiness, was lying still and cold in the chamber above us. Mr. Cobden called upon me as his friend, and addressed me, as you might suppose, with words of condolence. After a time he looked up and said, "There are thousands of houses in England at this moment where wives, mothers, and children are dying of hunger. Now," he said, "when the first paroxysm of your grief is past, I would advise you to come with me, and we will never rest till the Corn Law is repealed." ' That was chastening, yielding its noble fruit, sympathy born of sorrow. John Bright's rich, useful life might have been lost to England, if he had only brooded over his grief and hardened his heart, and refused to listen to the evident call which came to him."—Hugh Black, *Comfort.*

A Person's Duty. As a boy in Toronto, Canada, young Joseph Tyrrell liked wild life. He even had his own zoo of creatures captured on the banks of the Humber River near his home. When he reached manhood, he studied to become a lawyer. He was afflicted with lung diseases, and his doctor warned him that he would have to get out of the city and into the wilds if he expected to live. Tyrrell quit law and joined the Geological Survey of Canada. The next three-quarters of a century were used by Tyrrell in an incredible series of careers as an explorer, a historical scholar, and a mining tycoon. In June, 1884, Tyrrell discovered the first dinosaur skeletons in Alberta's Red Deer Valley, a seam of bituminous coal on the present site of Drumheller, the largest coal deposit in Canada. Tyrrell, who died at age of ninety-nine, was accorded nearly every honor imaginable. A few years earlier, this man of faith declared, "It's a man's duty to live as long as he can." For Tyrrell, the emphasis was on the living of life, not on the length.

God calls Gideons in every age to live as much as they can in the years given them.

Questions for Pupils on the Next Lesson. 1. Is having power moral or immoral, or does it depend on how one uses it? 2. What are some of the examples of power which you have? 3. What does the Bible say to those in the "success-at-any-cost" syndrome? 4. What is the point of Jotham's parable in Judges 9:9–15? 5. What are some of the false gods worshiped in our culture?

TOPIC FOR YOUTH
CALLED TO BE A CHAMPION

Champion for God, not Critic. One day a man came up to Dwight L. Moody and criticized him for the way he went about winning souls. Moody listened courteously and then asked, "How would you do it?" The man, taken aback, mumbled that he didn't do it. "Well," said Moody, "I prefer the way I do it to the way you don't do it."

The Power of One Vote. Remember that it was one vote that gave Oliver Cromwell control of England in 1656.

It was one vote that gave America the English instead of the German language in 1776.

It was one vote that changed France from a Monarchy into a Republic in 1875.

It was one vote that gave the Presidency of the United States to Rutherford B. Hayes in 1876.

And it was one vote that gave Adolf Hitler the leadership of the Nazi Party in Germany in 1923.

Never underestimate the power of one vote or of one witness.

Thanksgiving Note Missing. According to an old Jewish legend, Lucifer, son of the morning, after he had fallen from heaven, was asked what he most missed. His reply was, "I miss most of all the trumpets that are sounded in heaven each morning."

Is not this the one great lack in many lives today? There is needed more and more the clear trumpet note of joy and thanksgiving. Many persons are more ready to sing a dreary *Miserere* than a joyous song of praise to God. We need less of the spirit of sadness and melancholy and more of the abandonment of joy that thrilled in the heart of the Psalmist when he summoned God's people to "praise him with the sound of the trumpet," to "praise him upon the loud cymbals," to "praise him upon the high sounding cymbals."

We miss from many lives the sound of the morning trumpet. God must miss hearing from many who ought to be glad to hear the sound of the joy trumpet of thanksgiving. At this Thanksgiving season let us blow the trumpet of thanksgiving—and then let us keep on blowing it as an every morning expression of our gratitude.

Sentence Sermon to Remember: Don't let us think that we need to be "stars" in order to shine. It was by the ministry of a candle that the woman recovered her lost piece of silver.—John Henry Jowett.

Questions for Pupils on the Next Lesson. 1. What examples have you noticed of God's justice being the final word after all? 2. Can you recall instances of the results of ruthless amibition? 3. If your top allegiance is to God, how should you choose leaders in your peer group? 4. What do you think is the point of Jotham's fable in Judges 9:9–15?

LESSON XIII—NOVEMBER 28

GOD IS ISRAEL'S TRUE KING

Background Scripture: Judges 8:22–9:57
Devotional Reading: Isaiah 12:1–6

KING JAMES VERSION

JUDGES 8 22 Then the men of Israel said unto Gideon, Rule thou over us, both thou, and thy son, and they son's son also: for thou hast delivered us from the hand of Midian.

23 And Gideon said unto them, I will not rule over you, neither shall my son rule over you: the LORD shall rule over you.

9 6 And all the men of Shechem gathered together, and all the house of Millo, and went and made Abimelech king, by the plain of the pillar that *was* in Shechem.

7 And when they told *it* to Jotham, he went and stood in the top of mount Gerizim, and lifted up his voice, and cried, and said unto them, Hearken unto me, ye men of Shechem, that God may hearken unto you.

8 The trees went forth *on a time* to anoint a king over them; and they said unto the olive tree, Reign thou over us.

9 But the olive tree said unto them, Should I leave my fatness, wherewith by me they honour God and man, and go to be promoted over the trees?

10 And the trees said to the fig tree, Come thou, *and* reign over us.

11 But the fig tree said unto them, Should I forsake my sweetness, and my good fruit, and go to be promoted over the trees?

12 Then said the trees unto the vine, Come thou, *and* reign over us.

13 And the vine said unto them, Should I leave my wine, which cheereth God and man, and go to be promoted over the trees?

14 Then said all the trees unto the bramble, Come thou, *and* reign over us.

15 And the bramble said unto the trees, If in truth ye anoint me king over you, *then* come *and* put your trust in my shadow; and if not, let fire come out of the bramble, and devour the cedars of Lebanon.

55 And when the men of Israel saw that Abimelech was dead, they departed every man unto his place.

56 Thus God rendered the wickedness

REVISED STANDARD VERSION

JUDGES 8 22 Then the men of Israel said to Gideon, "Rule over us, you and your son and your grandson also; for you have delivered us out of the hand of Midian." 23 Gideon said to them, "I will not rule over you, and my son will not rule over you; the LORD will rule over you."

9 6 And all the citizens of Shechem came together, and all Beth-millo, and they went and made Abimelech king, by the oak of the pillar at Shechem.

7 When it was told to Jotham, he went and stood on the top of Mount Gerizim, and cried aloud and said to them, "Listen to me, you men of Shechem, that God may listen to you. 8 The trees once went forth to anoint a king over them; and they said to the olive tree, 'Reign over us.' 9 But the olive tree said to them, 'Shall I leave my fatness, by which gods and men are honored, and go to sway over the trees?' 10 And the trees said to the fig tree, 'Come you, and reign over us.' 11 But the fig tree said to them, 'Shall I leave my sweetness and my good fruit, and go to sway over the trees?' 12 And the trees said to the vine, 'Come you, and reign over us.' 13 But the vine said to them, 'Shall I leave my wine which cheers gods and men, and go to sway over the trees?' 14 Then all the trees said to the bramble, 'Come you, and reign over us.' 15 And the bramble said to the trees, 'If in good faith you are anointing me king over you, then come and take refuge in my shade; but if not, let fire come out of the bramble and devour the cedars of Lebanon.' "

55 And when the men of Israel saw that Abimelech was dead, they departed every man to his home. 56 Thus God requited the crime of Abimelech, which he com-

of Abimelech, which he did unto his father, in slaying his seventy brethren:

57 And all the evil of the men of Shechem did God render upon their heads: and upon them came the curse of Jotham the son of Jerubbaal.

mited against his father in killing his seventy brothers; 57 and God also made all the wickedness of the men of Shechem fall back upon their heads, and upon them came the curse of Jotham the son of Jerubbaal.

KEY VERSE: Gideon said to them, "I will not rule over you, and my son will not rule over you; the Lord will rule over you." Judges 8:23 (RSV).

HOME DAILY BIBLE READINGS

Nov. 22. *M.* *King Over All.* Psalms 47.
Nov. 23. *T.* *A Song to the King.* Psalms 74:1–12.
Nov. 24. *W.* *The Lord Is Our King.* Psalms 89:8–18.
Nov. 25. *T.* *King of Glory.* Psalms 24.
Nov. 26. *F.* *The King Remembers.* Isaiah 43:14–21.
Nov. 27. *S.* *Treachery by the King's Son.* Judges 9:1–15.
Nov. 28. *S.* *The Meaning of Jotham's Fable.* Judges 9:16–21.

BACKGROUND

Judges 8:28 tells us that "The country was in quietness forty years in the days of Gideon." This was mainly due to the fact that the powerful Midianites had been crushed. Gideon then put aside his weapons of war and went back to his plowshares and pruning hooks. "And Gideon had threescore and ten sons of his body begotten: for he had many wives" (Judges 8:30). We cannot help but wonder how much "quietness" there could be in such a multitudinous family!

Once Gideon was dead, trouble reared its ugly head. He had refused to be made king over Israel; as the great popular hero in the land, he certainly deserved that honor, but he rejected it. Kingship was not for him. He knew well that kingship could and often did bring corruption, that "power tends to corrupt and absolute power corrupts absolutely." And he had another reason for spurning the crown: he believed that kingship over Israel belonged to God, and that no man had the right to put himself in the high place of God.

The seventy sons thought otherwise. One of them, they knew, would be the heir apparent to the leadership of their father. Which one would get it?

The least of the seventy got it by way of wholesale murder. Abimelech, an unprincipled adventurer, ruthlessly ambitious, snarling, sinister, one of the worst rogues in the Bible, made himself king by simply killing every last one of his brothers, save one. Jotham got away.

NOTES ON THE PRINTED TEXT

Poor Gideon, unknowingly, may have made a great mistake when he intermarried with a Shechemite woman, not strictly as a wife but as a concubine, and by this concubine he had Abimelech as an illigitimate son. That was accepted, by the Jews, but it was also tragic, for it signaled an alliance with the heathen Shechemites. Abimelech, the youngest of his sons and least entitled to take over the leadership of his father, made the most of it; he used the Shechemites to lift himself to the place of supreme power. Furthermore, he helped himself to funds that had been donated by the people to the worship of Baal-berith! Then he killed off his brothers and announced that he and he alone was king over Israel.

But he had trouble convincing Israel that he had the right to say or do that. The one who got away from the slaughter led the opposition. Jotham was determined that Abimelech should be toppled from his throne.

Jotham might have recruited an army to march against Abimelech, but he chose to go out alone to the top of Mount Gerizem, above Shechem, to deliver a speech that was ablaze with condemnation. He spoke by way of a parable—a parable of trees. The trees, he said, decided that it was time they had a king tree to rule over them. They offered the kingship, first, to an olive tree, which declined the honor; olive trees were supposed to supply oil for the anointing of religious leaders and religious feasts. Then they offered the honor to a fig tree—which also declined, on the ground that the function of fig trees was to produce food—figs—and not kings. Then they asked a vine to be their king; the vine rejected it on the ground that vines were created to produce wine. One last attempt was made; they turned to the lowly bramble, a miserable bit of briar covered with thorns, good enough only to be burned. The bramble accepted! The meanest, most useless weed in treedom was made king.

The meaning of this parable isn't hard to find. The Israelites had the chance to pick a far more worthy man as their king, but they chose the meanest, the lowest of them, in Abimelech. They chose a man who lacked integrity, who had neither the brains nor the capacity to rule anything or anybody. That, shouted Jotham, would destroy Shechem. "Let fire come out from Abimelech, and devour the men of Shechem . . . and let fire come out from the men of Shechem, and from the house of Millo, and devour Abimelech" (Judges 9:20). It was a bitter curse; having delivered it, Jotham ran for his life and hid in a place called Beer on the border of Moab.

It happened. Three years later, there were shouts of "Down with Abimelech!" Shechem turned against him—and he killed its people and levelled their city to the ground. But alas for Abimelech, he, too, died; a *woman* dropped a stone on his head. What a way to die at the hands of a woman!

Now we can say, "Good! Abimelech deserved what he got, and so did Shechem." But let's look at ourselves before we condemn him. Why do we allow greedy, overambitious, inadequate men to take public office? Why do so many of our really talented men stay out of politics and let lesser men seize office while they stay in business or become great in other occupations? Corruption in high office runs riot in our day from Washington to the humblest hamlet. Why? Why, because *we* elect them! We seem to enjoy putting in office garrulous, ill-equipped political hacks whose only recommendation for office is that they have served well one or another of our political machine. Why do we allow "the boys (bosses) in a smoke-filled room" to decide for us who shall have high places in government?

On the border between Chile and Argentina on a high mountain, there stands *The Christ of the Andes,* a statue of Jesus Christ; it bears the inscription, "Sooner shall these mountains crumble into dust than the Argentines and Chilians break the peace sworn at the feet of Christ the Redeemer." That is the ideal of good government, but—is it practiced?

Jotham may have wanted that kingship for himself, but that may be hard to prove. He made history in predicting that "The wages of sin is *death.*" It is the sin of charlatans who steer the ship of state while better men stay clear.

There are two lessons, then, in all of this for us: 1. Only God is or can be the true King of mankind to be worshiped and followed. 2. Rear a throne anywhere, and we will find a host of quarreling "heirs" at your palace door.

It is our duty to guard that door and guard it well.

SUGGESTIONS TO TEACHERS

Critics of a conceited old czar in the Labor Movement used to grumble that he had the ability to strut while sitting down. The same also could have been said of most of Israel's kings. Inevitably, the nation stumbled from crisis to crisis.

The biblical material for today's lesson makes dismal reading. You may wish for some pleasant "inspirational" verses. However, the conversation of God through Scripture includes the stern stuff about rulers who try to strut sitting down, who think they can place themselves above God as King. You will discover startling parallels between the biblical narrative and present-day life.

1. *SAD SEQUEL.* Although Gideon had driven out the Midianites, thereby saving the nation, and had turned down the offer of being king and establishing a royal line, he took a collection of gold and fashioned it into an idol. The predictable result: "all Israel played the harlot after it and it became a snare to Gideon and his family," to use the salty language of Judges 8:27. After Gideon's faith had saved the nation, Gideon's lack of faith led him to idolatry and almost destroyed the nation. How could such an outstanding leader later cause such dismal effects? What does the close of Gideon's story suggest to successful and religious people like us?

2. *SQUALID SAGA.* Abimelech's coup and the later bloodbath in today's scriptural material are more than the petty politics and intrigues of a minor-league power 3,000 years ago. The Book of Judges is a case history of a people who willfully had the wrong allegiances. God is meant to be honored as Israel's King, but Israel hankers after gods. Conduct the class discussion along lines which make each person think of the need of the Church and the nation to give allegiance to the Lord with more than mottos ("In God we trust") and lip service.

3. *SAGE'S STORY.* Call attention to Jotham's fable (Judges 9:9–15) about the trees selecting a king. Encourage discussion about accepting the responsibilities of leadership in the community. This account in Judges makes it clear that Christians have an obligation to take their civic obligations seriously. When people become too busy or too disinterested to be actively involved in their government, they will be ruled by "brambles."

4. *STEADY SAVIOR.* Throughout Scripture, the claim stands that God is Israel's true King. He claims ultimate allegiance. Behind the blood-and-gore in the scriptural material in today's class period is the inescapable lesson that failure to put God first as a Church, as a nation, and as an individual brings ruin to all. However, retell the Good News running throughout the story of God's people that God saves! His steadfast love continues to our generation!

TOPIC FOR ADULTS
GIVING ALLEGIANCE TO GOD

Reminder Who Is King. Andrew Melville understood that if Christ was Lord, everyone, kings included, must be in subjection to Him. He spoke directly to James VI of Scotland in 1596. "There are two kings and two kingdoms in Scotland; there is King James the head of the Commonwealth, and there is Christ Jesus the King of the Church, whose subject King James VI is, and of whose Kingdom he is not a king nor a lord nor a head, but a member."

Growth Through Failure. "Learning to accept losing as an integral part of living, makes us keenly aware that we are all vulnerable. There is no guarantee against failure in life. . . .

"Experience in failing also reminds us of our limitations. While it is important to have ambition, striving without a sense of possible limitations can only frustrate and depress us. On the other hand, if we are too cautious to take on any risks, we will never realize our limitations or potential. . . . Losing itself can be a time for reflection and reassessment of life's goals. Were our previous dreams and visions too self-serving, too unrealistic? . . .

"Losing underlines the fact that life offers us no promises, only a journey. The journey which the biblical witness throughout invites us to take is a trusting relationship with the living God. Losing confronts us once again with this living God, who is Lord over all aspects of life. . . .

"Finally, a failing experience brings us to Christ's cross . . . It is only through our experience of and confession of losing that we can understand the depth and pain involved in Christ's cross. The temptations are always there to rationalize around the failing events that confront us. Such rationalizations make phonies of us. On the other hand, ironically, as we admit our failures in the presence of Christ's cross we are not only forgiven, but discover strangely a fulfillment and identity that enables us to be true to ourselves. It is time for us realistically and biblically to uphold losing as an important part of God's saving effort to reconcile us to Himself."—Carnegie Samuel Calian, *For All Your Seasons: Biblical Direction through Life's Passages.* John Knox Press, 1979.

Keep on Giving Allegiance. The Scottish scholar, preacher, and teacher, A. J. Gossip, lived a full life when he was a professor at Trinity College and Glasgow University. When he was about to retire from teaching, one of his colleagues, thinking of the changes that would come, asked him, "What will you do when you retire?" Gossip promptly answered, "What will I do when I retire? Why, man, keep on living till I'm dead!"

And when Gossip said *living*, he meant living with trust and obedience to his king, Jesus Christ.

Questions for Pupils on the Next Lesson. 1. Why do you think Luke wrote a Gospel account? 2. Can you make a contribution in life without being a member of the "in group"? 3. What does the verse mean, "I have not come to call the righteous but sinners to repentance"? 4. What happens when a person tries to get ahead without accepting the high cost of responsibility? 5. What are some of the needs of people to which Luke shows that Jesus ministered?

TOPIC FOR YOUTH
NO KING BUT GOD

Reminder of Responsibility. "In Ystad, Sweden, a church of fairly conventional design save that on the pillar opposite the pulpit stands a crucifix, life-size and lifelike, 'with human hair matted under the crown of actual thorns.' Why this strange arrangement?

"The story, as it turned out, goes back to a visit to Ystad, and to Mariakyrchen, the great warrior hero king, Charles XII, in 1716. The visit was unexpected, and the pastor was so overwhelmed by this sudden burst of glory that he put aside his prescribed text and substituted an ardent eulogy of the king and the royal family. Some few months later, the Church received a gift from King Charles. It was this second crucifix, and with it these instructions: 'This is to hang on the pillar opposite the pulpit, so that all who shall stand there will be reminded of their proper subject.' "—R. M. Brown, *The Spirit of Protestantism.*

Ill-Equipped Guide. "There was a king of Spain once, Philip III, who is said to have died of a fever he contracted from sitting too long near a hot brazier, helplessly overheating himself because the functionary whose duty it was to remove the brazier when summoned could not be found. In the late 20th century it begins to appear as if mankind may be approaching a similar state of suicidal incompetence. . . . No woodenheadedness is so impenetrable to that of a religious zealot. Because he is connected with a private wire to the Almighty, no idea coming in on a lesser channel can reach him, which leaves him ill-equipped to guide his country in its own best interests."—Barbara Tuchman. Reprinted from *CONTEXT* by permission of Claretian Publications, 221 W. Madison St., Chicago, Ill. 60606.

Secret of Courage. When they laid John Knox to rest in his grave, the Earl of Morton looked down. "Here lies one," he said, "who feared God so much that he never feared the face of any man."

If we truly respect God as King, we will never fear anyone or anything. To fear God in the biblical sense means to find the secret of courage. Have you recognized the Lord God as Ruler in your life? Are you aware that there is no King but Jesus Christ?

Sentence Sermon to Remember:

Behind the dim unknown
Standeth God within the shadow, keeping
watch above His own.
—James Russell Lowell.

Questions for Pupils on the Next Lesson. 1. Why may we rely on Luke's Gospel account as a reliable source about Jesus? 2. Why did Luke write his version of the Good News of Jesus? 3. Why were the scribes and Pharisees so critical of Jesus? 4. How can a person find any meaning in the suffering and death in life?

DECEMBER, 1982–FEBRUARY, 1983

THE GOSPEL OF LUKE

LESSON I—DECEMBER 5

THE NATURE OF LUKE'S GOSPEL

Background Scripture: Luke 1:1–4; 5:29–32; 8:19–21; 9:18–22
Devotional Reading: 2 Timothy 4:1–8

KING JAMES VERSION

LUKE 1 1 Forasmuch as many have taken in hand to set forth in order a declaration of those things which are most surely believed among us,

2 Even as they delivered them unto us, which from the beginning were eyewitnesses, and ministers of the word;

3 It seemed good to me also, having had perfect understanding of all things from the very first, to write unto thee in order, most excellent Theophilus,

4 That thou mightest know the certainty of those things, wherein thou hast been instructed.

5 29 And Levi made him a great feast in his own house: and there was a great company of publicans and of others that sat down with them.

30 But their scribes and Pharisees murmured against his disciples, saying, Why do ye eat and drink with publicans and sinners?

31 And Jesus answering said unto them, They that are whole need not a physician; but they that are sick.

32 I came not to call the righteous, but sinners to repentance.

8 19 Then came to him *his* mother and his brethren, and could not come at him for the press.

20 And it was told him *by certain* which said, Thy mother and thy brethren stand without, desiring to see thee.

21 And he answered and said unto them, My mother and my brethren are these which hear the word of God, and do it.

9 18 And it came to pass, as he was alone praying, his disciples were with him; and he asked them, saying, Whom say the people that I am?

19 They answering said, John the Baptist; but some *say*, Elias; and others *say*,

REVISED STANDARD VERSION

LUKE 1 1 Inasmuch as many have undertaken to compile a narrative of the things which have been accomplished among us, 2 just as they were delivered to us by those who from the beginning were eyewitnesses and ministers of the word, 3 it seemed good to me also, having followed all things closely for some time past, to write an orderly account for you, most excellent Theophilus, 4 that you may know the truth concerning the things of which you have been informed.

5 29 And Levi made him a great feast in his house; and there was a large company of tax collectors and others sitting at table with them. 30 And the Pharisees and their scribes murmured against his disciples, saying, "Why do you eat and drink with tax collectors and sinners?" 31 And Jesus answered them, "Those who are well have no need of a physician, but those who are sick; 32 I have not come to call the righteous, but sinners to repentance."

8 19 Then his mother and his brothers came to him, but they could not reach him for the crowd. 20 And he was told, "Your mother and your brothers are standing outside, desiring to see you." 21 But he said to them, "My mother and my brothers are those who hear the word of God and do it."

9 18 Now it happened that as he was praying alone the disciples were with him; and he asked them, "Who do the people say that I am?" 19 And they answered, "John the Baptist; but others say, Elijah; and others, that one of the old prophets has

that one of the old prophets is risen again.

20 He said unto them, But whom say ye that I am? Peter answering said, The Christ of God.

21 And he straitly charged them, and commanded *them* to tell no man that thing;

22 Saying, The Son of man must suffer many things, and be rejected of the elders and chief priests and scribes, and be slain, and be raised the third day.

risen." 20 And he said to them, "But who do you say that I am?" And Peter answered, "The Christ of God." 21 But he charged and commanded them to tell this to no one, 22 saying, "The Son of man must suffer many things, and be rejected by the elders and chief priests and scribes, and be killed, and on the third day be raised."

KEY VERSE: I came not to call the righteous, but sinners to repentance. Luke 5:32.

HOME DAILY BIBLE READINGS

Nov. *29.* *M.* *A Writer Led by God.* Luke 1:1–4; Acts 1:1–3.
Nov. *30.* *T.* *Luke, Faithful Friend.* 2 Timothy 4:6–11.
Dec. *1.* *W.* *The Guide for Believers' Growth.* 2 Timothy 3:12–17.
Dec. *2.* *T.* *A Doctor for the Sick.* Luke 5:27–32.
Dec. *3.* *F.* *A Family of Believers.* Matthew 12:46–50.
Dec. *4.* *S.* *A Leader Who Must Die.* Luke 9:18–22.
Dec. *5.* *S.* *The Lord Is Merciful.* Psalms 103:1–12.

BACKGROUND

Now, in the lessons for this quarter, we shall be studying one of the most beautiful ever written by any man—the sublime picture of Jesus Christ as Luke saw Him.

Luke was not the first to attempt the writing of the biography of Jesus. Mark did that, first, in A.D. 65–70, Luke's Gospel was written in A.D. 80–85, Matthew in A.D. 90–100, and John toward the end of the first century. They were all inspiring—and all different accounts. What was "different" about Luke?

One outstanding difference was the Luke wrote for the Gentiles, and not for the Jews. Luke was a physician: he was called "the *Beloved* Physician" by his friend Paul. He never *saw* Jesus as Matthew and Mark saw Him; he was a convert living in the Apostolic Age—so enthusiastic a convert that he wrote not one but two books: his Gospel, and another called The Acts of the Apostles.

Why did he write these two imperishable books?

NOTES ON THE PRINTED TEXT

Luke wrote his Gospel in the form of a letter to a friend: "the most excellent Theophilus." This Theophilus was evidently a Roman official—another Gentile—and a sponsor of Luke. He wrote, as he says, because he was anxious to "compile a narrative of the things which have been accomplished among us" (Luke 1:1 RSV). That is a much better translation than the King James, "to set forth in order a declaration of those things which are most surely believed among us." Up to his time, what had been accomplished by Jesus and His followers was described in a host of confusing oral traditions. Luke, a born writer, wanted to write an *orderly* account of the eyewitnesses and ministers of the day. He went at this task with a rare writer's intelligence.

He had as his sources the words passed down from man to man about Jesus. He was of course aware of the fact that most of these words and writings dealt with the influence of Jesus upon the Jews. But, Gentile that he was, he wanted also to tell what Jesus had done for the Gentiles. He believed, with John (John 12:47), that Jesus had come to save not only the Jews, but the *world*, and all through his writing he stresses his conviction that the mercy and compassion of Jesus reached out to Gentiles as well as Jews.

Now there were many, in Luke's day, who did not want to accept that. Most Jews hated most Gentiles—and that idea, though the Jews did not see it, would have slammed the door in the face of the world's Gentiles, who were *anathema!* It would have made of Christianity nothing more than a little Jewish sect, and it would have died quickly. Jesus threw open to *all* men the promise of salvation. Read it and weep today when we have many churches which bar from their sanctuaries all who they do not accept as Christians, who figuratively put up a sign over their church doors which reads, "Only our *kind* of Christians may enter here." Too many of us practice the "shunning" of those non-Christians who stand in the need of being saved. Theirs, alas, is not the compassionate Jesus of whom Luke wrote.

Luke pushed the idea further and deeper in his plea for a *universal* Christ and Church. Being a physician, he was keenly aware of the sufferings of humanity, and of their need of the Great Physician. "It is because of this Gospel that we know the Jesus who looked with redeeming pity upon a sinful woman who knelt at His feet; the Jesus whose quick understanding marked the boastful Pharisees and the humbled publican in the temple; the Jesus who told His parables of the Good Samaritan, the Lost Sheep, and the Prodigal Son; who went home with the despised Zaccheus and stopped to answer the cry of blind Bartimaeus by the roadside, and who on the cross would say to the dying thief beside him, 'Today thou shalt be with me in Paradise.' These are the imperishable pictures of Jesus which are due to this third Gospel."—Walter Russel Bowie, *The Compassionate Christ,* by permission of Abingdon Press, publishers.

A despised tax-collector named Levi (Matthew), with a great reputation as a thief, fell under the spell of Jesus and followed Him. He even invited Jesus to a dinner made up of several of his tax-collector friends. (Stand up, any of you who love your tax collector enough to invite him to dinner!) The Pharisees and the scribes were furious at that; how could He sit and eat with such depraved characters? Ah, said Jesus, they should know that He had come into the world not to save the spiritually healthy, but the spiritually *sick.* Luke, as a physician, *would* write that. Doctors do not spend much time with the healthy; they concentrate on the sick.

Luke stressed, again and again, the concept of Jesus as One who came to save the *world.* That got Jesus into trouble on a day when His mother and His brothers came to talk with Him and beg Him to come home. Mark tells the same incident: "and his friends . . . went out to seize him, for they said, 'He is beside himself' " (Mark 3:21). There is no suggestion in Luke that His mother and brothers wanted to "seize" Him; they came simply because they were afraid of the hostility that was rising against

Him; they did not want to be involved in the risks He was running. These brothers could not understand that Jesus had a divine mission to perform, and that there was a divine relationship in Him that would supersede any relationship of birth and kinship; they did not follow Him because they could not understand Him. They had lived with him, day by day, but as one poet puts it, they never understood "the vision that glorified his clay."

It was not an easy moment for Jesus; here He had to choose between loyalty to His human family and loyalty to His Father, God. It must have torn His heart when He said to His family and to the crowd gathered around Him, "My mother and my brothers are those who hear the word of God and *do* it." All men were His brothers—and these blood brothers He would not allow to stand in His way. Many a family has been disrupted by the decision of a son so determined to serve the Christ that he is ready to leave family and home to serve Him. Often, alas, it is sadly true, as Matthew says, "A man's foes shall be they of his own household" (Matthew 10:36).

It has been suggested that Luke's Gospel might well be entitled, "This Is What Jesus Means to Me." As a Gentile, he had fought his way upward to a truly magnificent concept of his Lord; he knew well what the people among whom he lived thought of this Man from Galilee, but, while he listened to them, he became convinced that he had to find his own way to fellowship with his Lord. All of us must do that: what people say may be wrong; what they believe about Christ may, too, be believed in error.

The grand climax in his thinking is expressed in his account of Jesus talking with Peter and the disciples about just who and what Jesus was. After Jesus had heard the disciples say that to some people He was John the Baptist or Elijah come to life in their midst, He asked Peter, "But who do *you* say that I am?" and Peter cries out, "The Christ of God!" Whatever else Luke wanted men to understand about Jesus, this was paramount. What do *you* think He is and was? Never mind what uninformed people say; what do *you* think?

Now Jesus tells them that it will not be easy to follow One who will suffer the bitter pains of persecution and death; they, too, would have to suffer. He was saying that to be a Christian is *never* easy. Christianity is not an escape from the world; it is a battle, a constant battle, *with* the world. If you can't pay the price in suffering, if you cannot go from creed to sacrificial living—then don't profess belief in Christ. Verbal loyalty will never get us into heaven!

Luke wasn't merely passing out advice; he was speaking out of his experience. He suffered, too. He followed Paul through suffering to the end of the long, long trail from Jerusalem to Rome; at the end of the road Paul said, "Only Luke is with me!" A good doctor, Luke! He faced storms, heat, cold, even death itself to tend the sick. He was the first medical missionary.

SUGGESTIONS TO TEACHERS

Suppose you were engaged in medical research and discovered a cure for a type of cancer. Even if it would be possible for you, a researcher, to keep such a discovery to yourself, you would not. You would feel impelled to share it with others. You would also quickly encounter reporters eager to write how you came upon this great medical breakthrough and what you hope will result from it.

Today's lesson takes on some of the characteristics of such an interview. Luke, a medical man himself, discloses the greatest breakthrough of divine healing in history. Opening a series of thirteen lessons on Luke's Gospel account, this unit "interviews" Luke and presents the nature of his version of the Good News of Jesus Christ.

1. *FACTS.* Luke opens his Gospel by stating that it is reliably researched. To use his words, it is intended to be "an orderly account" (1:3) so "that you may know the truth" (1:4). Here is a carefully trained observer telling about Jesus. Who, after all, would be more factual and perceptive than a medical man? And, if traditions about Luke's origins are true, here is one writing from a "Western World" point of view. Doctor Luke, in other words, writes like "one of us"—a person anxious to get the facts straight. Here is a witness we must take seriously!

2. *FORGIVENESS.* As one devoted to healing, Luke is convinced of the relationship between forgiveness and health. His Gospel account stresses the mercy of God which Jesus brings to persons. The nature of Luke's Gospel, emphasizing Jesus' forgiveness to people willing to accept it, is summarized in the account of Levi (5:29–32). Have your class put themselves into the roles of the various people in this passage so that they can better appreciate who Jesus Christ is as "physician" (5:31).

3. *FAMILY.* Direct your class's attention to the important verses about Jesus' family (8:19–21). Luke, who was not Jewish, knew he had absolutely no blood kinship to Jesus. However, realizing that Jesus calls *family* anyone hearing and obeying God's Word through Him, Luke knows that he is now related to Jesus as brother! How much does each person in your class feel related to Jesus by this standard? What does it mean to them to "hear the word of God and do it"?

4. *FULFILLMENT.* The nature of Luke's Gospel also is that Jesus was the Messiah who suffered for others, and completely fulfills the hopes and expectations in the spiritual quest of every human. Do those in your class feel this way? Guide the discussion along lines of what they in particular might have been raised to think about God (Stern Judge? Distant Designer?). Help them to appreciate the way Jesus answers every religious longing.

TOPIC FOR ADULTS
THE NATURE OF LUKE'S GOSPEL

Let It Be Heard! Fritz Kreisler, the famous violinist, going down a back street, heard the liquid, penetrating tones of a violin. He stopped and listened. Eagerly, he followed the sound and found a shabby, little secondhand shop. He offered to buy the violin but was told that it had already been promised to a wealthy man who had a hobby of collecting violins.

"That this beautiful voice should be doomed to silence under the glass case of a collector," said Kreisler, "was a tragedy that rent my heart. From that moment I was determined to have it and to endow it with life. I laid siege to the place that held it and I gave the owner no peace. . . . At last he took it from its resting place to grant me a small concession, the right to play upon it. I opened the case tenderly, took it out and caressed it. And then I poured my whole soul into it. I played as a man might play for his ransom." When the great musician had finished there was silence except for the halting words of the owner who stood pale and deeply moved. He said, "I have no right to it. It belongs to you. Keep it. Go out into the world and let it be heard."

No person has the right to keep the news of Jesus to himself or herself. The Good News belongs to everyone. Luke knew this. He knew he had to go out into the world and let it be heard.

Do you have such a compulsion to share the priceless message of hope through Jesus Christ? Will you let the harmony which He brings be heard by others?

In Terms We Can Understand. Gilbert Highet in *Art of Teaching* describes how Robert Browning's father interested young Robert in the classics in ways which the boy could comprehend.

When he was five Robert Browning saw his father reading and ask him what he was reading about. Looking up from his Homer, his father said, "The siege of Troy." "What's a siege?" said the little boy, "and what is Troy?" Now, at this point most fathers would reply, "Troy is a city in Asia, now run off and play with your trains." Browning's father was different. He leapt up and began to build Troy there in the living room. He built a city of tables and chairs. On top he put an armchair for a throne and popped little Robert into it. "There now," he said, "that's Troy, and you're King Priam, and let me see, here's Helen of Troy, beautiful and sleek," and he pointed to the cat beneath the footstool. "Outside, you know the two big dogs in the yard, always trying to get in and catch Helen? They are the fighting kings, Agamemnon and Menelaus, and they are making a siege of Troy so as to catch Helen." And so he told the child as much of the story as could interest him, in just the terms he could understand.

Luke, like Browning's father, determined to present the story of Jesus in just the terms we can understand. He selected his materials and arranged them in ways which make us appreciate Jesus as Lord and Savior of all persons, especially us! Luke enables us, his readers, to feel as if we are part of the drama of Jesus' life, and wants us to see Jesus as the most important person of our lives.

"No One Spoke to Me." A man and his wife complained to Dwight L. Moody that no one had spoken to them when they attended a certain church that morning, and they were never going to attend any church again.

"Didn't speak to you, you say?" replied Moody: "Well, maybe they thought you were dead!"

Luke, writing his two-volume work, would have appreciated this retort because he knew that Jesus came bringing healing and life. No person touched by Jesus Christ could leave His presence grumpily waiting for someone else to speak first. In fact, the mark of a Christian is to want to speak up and tell others about the joy and vitality Jesus has brought to him or her.

Questions for Pupils on the Next Lesson. 1. How should Protestants regard Mary, the Mother of Jesus? 2. What kind of a world would we have if Jesus had not been born? 3. What is the role of the Holy Spirit in understanding the significance of Jesus Christ's birth? 4. What do you do when you need assurance that you are needed and wanted? 5. Why do you sometimes feel you cannot reach out to others in time of need?

TOPIC FOR YOUTH
A LOOK AT LUKE'S GOSPEL

Fit the Picture. An exasperated father, attempting to read the evening paper amid the distracting actions of his young daughter, finally cut a large map out of the paper and cut it into small pieces. He handed it to his daughter, telling her to reassemble the map, expecting to keep her busy for quite some time. A minute later she returned with the map perfectly assembled. Dumbfounded, the father asked how she had done it. "Oh," said the girl. "That was easy; all you have to do is put together the face of the man on the other side and everything else fits right in."

Luke knew that we can find a pattern and meaning to our shredded lives only as we fit them together on the picture of God which we see in Jesus Christ. Our world, torn into pieces, can only be reassembled as we study the face of the Lord.

Accept the Invitation. Bob Lilly, the great defensive tackle for the Dallas Cowboys, was inducted into the Football Hall of Fame in Canton, Ohio, in 1980. At the impressive ceremony, Lilly spoke humbly not so much about football, which he loved and played so superbly, but about his faith. "There are many highways to travel and many to advise you which to travel," stated Bob Lilly, "however, most lead to emptiness, to loneliness, to the proverbial nowhere. The most important decision I ever made was to adhere to, to listen to, and to accept the invitation of my Lord and Savior . . . an invitation to travel the road of salvation . . . the invitation to quench my thirst at my Savior's well of salvation . . . an invitation to live life eternal. Yes, I chose the highway of life, God's path to heaven."

Luke, the physician, often used similar expressions about Jesus Christ. The word *salvation* means wholeness or health, and Jesus the Great Physician invited everyone to walk the road of wholeness with Him for eternity.

Respect Him for His Own Sake. Luke wants his readers to have a new relationship with God through Jesus Christ. Luke pleads, in effect, for others to respect and honor Jesus Christ for His own sake, not for what they can "get" from Him.

In similar vein, a famous Medieval Christian named Meister Eckhart once said, "Some people want to see God with their eyes as they see a cow, and love Him as they love a cow—for the milk and cheese and profit it brings them."

How do you view Jesus Christ? As an object to be used, or as friend to relate to?

Sentence Sermon to Remember: I have read in Plato and Cicero sayings that are very wise and very beautiful; but I never read in either of them: "Come unto me all ye that labour and are heavy laden."—St. Augustine.

Questions for Pupils on the Next Lesson. 1. How should Protestants look upon Mary, Jesus' Mother? 2. How do you understand the references to "angels" in the New Testament? 3. How does Jesus Christ bring a person a sense of worth? 4. Why is it so hard to accept yourself? 5. When are you most aware of God's presence in your daily life?

LESSON II—DECEMBER 12

PROMISE OF JESUS' BIRTH

Background Scripture: Luke 1:26–56
Devotional Reading: Hebrews 3:1–6

KING JAMES VERSION

LUKE 1 39 And Mary arose in those days, and went into the hill country with haste, into a city of Juda;

40 And entered into the house of Zacharias, and saluted Elisabeth.

41 And it came to pass, that, when Elisabeth heard the salutation of Mary, the babe leaped in her womb; and Elisabeth was filled with the Holy Ghost:

42 And she spake out with a loud voice, and said, Blessed *art* thou among women, and blessed *is* the fruit of thy womb.

43 And whence *is* this to me, that the mother of my Lord should come to me?

44 For, lo, as soon as the voice of thy salutation sounded in mine ears, the babe leaped in my womb for joy.

45 And blessed *is* she that believed: for there shall be a performance of those things which were told her from the Lord.

46 And Mary said, My soul doth magnify the Lord,

47 And my spirit hath rejoiced in God my Saviour.

48 For he hath regarded the low estate of his handmaiden: for, behold, from henceforth all generations shall call me blessed.

49 For he that is mighty hath done to me great things; and holy *is* his name.

50 And his mercy *is* on them that fear him from generation to generation.

51 He hath shewed strength with his arm; he hath scattered the proud in the imagination of their hearts.

52 He hath put down the mighty from *their* seats, and exalted them of low degree.

53 He hath filled the hungry with good things; and the rich he hath sent empty away.

54 He hath holpen his servant Israel, in remembrance of *his* mercy;

55 As he spake to our fathers, to Abraham, and to his seed for ever.

56 And Mary abode with her about three months, and returned to her own house.

REVISED STANDARD VERSION

LUKE 1 39 In those days Mary arose and went with haste into the hill country, to a city of Judah, 40 and she entered the house of Zachariah and greeted Elizabeth. 41 And when Elizabeth heard the greeting of Mary, the babe leaped in her womb; and Elizabeth was filled with the Holy Spirit 42 and she exclaimed with a loud cry, "Blessed are you among women, and blessed is the fruit of your womb! 43 And why is this granted me, that the mother of my Lord should come to me? 44 For behold, when the voice of your greeting came to my ears, the babe in my womb leaped for joy. 45 And blessed is she who believed that there would be a fulfillment of what was spoken to her from the Lord."
46 And Mary said,

"My soul magnifies the Lord,
47 and my spirit rejoices in God my Savior,

48 for he has regarded the low estate of his handmaiden.
For behold, henceforth all generations will call me blessed;
49 for he who is mighty has done great things for me,
and holy is his name.
50 And his mercy is on those who fear him from generation to generation.
51 He has shown strength with his arm,
he has scattered the proud in the imagination of their hearts,
52 he has put down the mighty from their thrones,
and exalted those of low degree;
53 he has filled the hungry with good things,
and the rich he has sent empty away.
54 He has helped his servant Israel, in remembrance of his mercy,
55 as he spoke to our fathers,
to Abraham and to his posterity for ever."

56 and Mary remained with her about three months, and returned to her home.

KEY VERSE: Blessed art thou among women, and blessed is the fruit of thy womb. Luke 1:42.

HOME DAILY BIBLE READINGS

Dec. 6. M. Preparing the Lord's Way. Isaiah 40:3–5,10,11.
Dec. 7. T. New Growth From David's Line. Isaiah 11:1–5,10.
Dec. 8. W. A Child Will Be Born. Isaiah 9:2–4,6,7.
Dec. 9. T. Gabriel's Startling Word to Mary. Luke 1:26–33.
Dec. 10. F. Mary's Song of Wonder. Luke 1:46–55.
Dec. 11. S. The Angel's Message to Joseph. Matthew 1:18–25.
Dec. 12. S. Christ and God's House. Hebrews 3:1–6.

BACKGROUND

We know very little about the family background of Mary the Mother of Jesus. The second century Protevangelium of James identifies her parents as Joachim and Anna, and this may be a reliable tradition. When we first meet her in Luke's Gospel, she is a young Jewish girl about fourteen years of age, engaged or "espoused" to a man named Joseph, a man of the Davidic line; it is also claimed that Mary, too, was of that line.

According to the legends written down about Anna and Joachim, an angel appears to this childless couple, announcing that they will have a child; the child was Mary; Anna cares for her until she is three, and then takes her to the temple, where Mary is dedicated to lifelong service to God. This is pure legend, but it reveals an Old Testament background for Mary the Mother of Jesus.

An angel appears to Mary, too, announcing that she was to "bring forth a son, and thou shalt call his name Jesus" (Luke 1:31). Jesus—the long-expected Messiah!

Beyond herself, ecstatic, overwrought at the thought that she was to be the very Mother of One who was not the son of Joseph but the Son of God, Mary did the natural thing: she ran for help and advice from an elderly cousin, Elizabeth, in the hills of Hebron.

NOTES ON THE PRINTED TEXT

Elizabeth was the wife of a country priest, Zachariah. All through their long lives together, these two had prayed that they might have a son, and in their old age they had almost given up hope of having that son. But just before Gabriel had appeared to Mary, he came to Zachariah in the temple, to bring the good news that he and Elizabeth were to have a son, and they should call his name John. John! John the Baptist, the forerunner of Jesus Christ!

There they sat, old age and young. Young Mary could not yet grasp the truth, the magnificence of what was happening to both of them, but Elizabeth, "filled with the Holy Spirit," did understand it. Her babe "leaped in her womb." She must have been a woman of great persuasion, for after this first moment together, Mary *did* seem to understand, and she prepared herself for "the great divine event." She quietly surrendered herself to the spirit and the will of God.

That took rare courage in a girl of her age. She knew what she would have to face back in her home town. She faced frightening social consequences and the misunderstanding of Joseph. She faced, possibly, death by stoning at the hands of strictly orthodox Jews who still held to the old practice of stoning adulterers and adulteresses to death. That *could* happen, and Mary knew it all too well. (Jesus was to put an end to that when He rescued a woman taken in adultery.)

Mary did not cringe; she *rejoiced.* She *sang!* Sang what we call the *Magnificat* (which is the first word of her song in the Latin Bible). "Oh," she exulted, "how I praise the Lord" (Luke 1:46 TLB). She rejoiced not only because of her unexpected lofty position (verses 47–49) but because now she understood that through her God was fulfilling His promise to Israel (54,55). Some attribute this *Magnificat* to Elizabeth, but most accredit it to Mary. Jesus was not only *her* son, but Abraham's son, and "great David's greater Son." Her song seems to be modeled on the song of Hannah, in 1 Samuel 2, but it goes far beyond that Old Testament song.

One might think that such a song of glory would be recorded by all of the Gospel writers, but no, it is found only in Luke, and in it we see again Luke's Savior of mercy and power and of sympathy with the poor. "He (God) hath regarded (looked upon) the low estate of his handmaiden" Luke was peculiarly concerned with those of low estate in his book. "And his mercy is on them that fear him." Luke *despised* the well-to-do who saw no need of Him. (Jesus did not despise the rich; He pitied them.) Luke went out of his way to identify himself with the lowly folks who welcomed Jesus with all their hearts. "He (Jesus) put down the mighty, and exalted them of low degree." Luke's church was not made up of the affluent, but of those poor in spirit because they were poor in the things of the world. "He hath filled the hungry with good things." Luke filled them, too, as a missionary physician.

Luke knew a compassionate Christ, a Lord who satisfied the hungry heart!

Rose Trumbull has a heartrending little poem about this Jesus born of Mary:

Mary, when that little child
  Softly kissed your cheek benign,
Did you know O Mary mild,
  Judas's sign?

Mary, when that little child
  Gooed and prattled at your knee,
Did you see with heartbeat wild,
  Calvary?

She saw, saw it all, and she suffered with Him and for Him all the way to the cross.

Some worship her and some adore. All the world stands mute before her peaceful, patient face. Mary, Mother of Jesus. Mary, mother of love.

SUGGESTIONS TO TEACHERS

"Why does Christmas have to turn into such a hassle every year?" snapped a tired mother of three two weeks before the big day.

Most people in your class agree with her. There is too much stress in life in any case, but with the stepped-up pressures of shopping and entertaining, this season brings an emotional overload. It's time to stop everything, sit quietly, and reflect on Jesus' Coming. Today's lesson is the welcome pause in the busy preholiday push to contemplate the Promise of Jesus' birth.

Don't fuss too much over trying to "prepare a lesson." Let the words of Scripture conveying facets of the Promise speak for themselves.

1. *ANNOUNCEMENT.* Let the angel Gabriel's words be pondered by having those in your class paraphrase them in present-day speech. Next, ask each person to list at least two reasons or two ways in which that announcement applies to him/her.

2. *ANGEL.* Like all angels in the Bible, Gabriel was a messenger, or an agent, or an announcer for the Lord. Without veering off toward pointless arguments over the existence of supernatural beings (which led ancient theologians into silly debates over how many angels could dance on the head of a pin), comment on ways each one in your class is an "angel" in the sense of being God's messenger or announcer.

3. *AGENT.* Allow enough time to reflect on Mary, Mother of Jesus, and what she understood about the Promise of Jesus' birth. She was willing to be God's agent in spite of fear and uncertainty. Mary can be a model for each believer today. Let the soliloquy of Mary containing the Promise be read in the light of a commission to each in your class to be an agent "birthing" new evidence of Jesus Christ today.

4. *AID.* Move on to the words and ways of Elizabeth as one of the players in the Drama of the Birth. How she encouraged Mary! How important the Elizabeths are! Discuss ways whereby each person may be used to reassure others in the faith at times.

5. *ADORATION.* Set aside plenty of minutes for the great song, the *Magnificat* in Luke 1:46–55. Perhaps creative persons in your class can be asked to present these words through the media of dance or music. Maybe even a time of silence in which each person reflects on the Promise through these words may be helpful. Some teachers have found that darkening the room, playing quiet classical music, and having a person able to speak slowly and expressively read these verses aloud.

TOPIC FOR ADULTS
ANNOUNCEMENT OF JESUS' BIRTH

Promise of Hope. The Coming of Jesus is God's personal visit to us. He comes in concern. The ancient world was relieved to hear that the Lord of the universe was not a capricious deity, teasing and toying with humans.

Robert C. Holland expresses the contrast between the Announcement of Jesus' birth and some of the ancient Greek legends remembered vaguely such as a legend from Mt. Olympus. . . . "Aurora, goddess of the dawn, falls in love with Tythonus, son of the king of Troy, a mere mortal. Aurora goes to Zeus, chairman of the gods, and prays that Tythonus might be raised above the troubles and trials of the earth, be made immortal, and live forever. Her prayer is answered. But remember, Zeus is not nice! Just when you think he is doing you a favor, invariably he has some nasty trick up his sleeve. On this occasion, as on others, he is up to no good.

"Zeus answers Aurora's prayer. Tythonus becomes a sort of third-class god, and he and Aurora are delirious in their love. But Aurora has forgotten to pray that her handsome, virile, robust lover, now immortal, might also stay youthful forever. So, as the years go by, he grows older but cannot die. So the answer to Aurora's prayer becomes a curse. Eventually, when she loses interest in the elderly, undying Tythonus, Aurora changes him into a grasshopper upon Mt. Olympus.

"When Aurora prayed unwisely, selfishly, thoughtlessly, her prayer was answered almost viciously. She remained everlastingly young, while her lover grew eternally old.

"Zeus was capricious—a player of pranks. The God of Jesus Christ, in honor of whom we are gathered here this morning, does not ever stoop to the unkindness of a practical joke. But neither will the God of Jesus Christ answer any prayer in a way which does not fit into His pattern of good. Not only for you and me. Not only for everyone in this room or this State or this Nation, but for everyone on this earth. In this universe, God has a plan."—Robert C. Holland, *Layman*, August/September 1980.

Act of God. The Federal Register, October 25, 1979, page 61,548, gets into theology by defining an act of God. It appears in federal regulation 50 CFR Part 258, Subpart C, Paragraph 285.21 (a). An act of God "means any act, event or circumstance . . . whose effect could not reasonably have been prevented, avoided or ameliorated by human care, skill or foresight (either before or after the act, event or circumstance) or a type, degree and timeliness which would normally be expected from an ordinarily prudent person in the same situation and under the prevailing circumstances." Who devised it? The National Marine Fisheries Service.

Federal bureaucracies may try to define an act of God in such cumbersome prose. God Himself announced His great act of mercy by promising the birth of a baby named Jesus.

The Angel in Evangelism. "The root of the word *evangelism* is 'angel.' The Bible has two words for *angel.* Both words in Bible times meant 'messenger,' a unique kind of messenger, so the author of Hebrews tells us. An angel is a messenger carrying news of salvation.

"Is this not the meaning conveyed by our word *ev-ANGEL-ist?* The prefix *ev* means good, implying the Gospel, or Good News about Jesus Christ. An ev-ANGEL-ist, like the angel in the Christmas story, is one who brings good news.

"Ev-ANGEL-ism in this sense has been central to the church's mission. Historically, the church has majored in five kinds of ev-ANGEL-ism."—Robert W. Youngs.

Questions for Pupils on the Next Lesson. 1. How was Jesus' birth the fulfillment of prophecy? 2. How did Joseph and Mary play a role in Jesus' childhood? 3. In what ways was Jesus raised according to the Jewish faith and ritual? 4. How can adults in the church help young people to grow intellectually, spiritually, and socially? 5. What enables you to look with expectancy toward the future?

TOPIC FOR YOUTH
A STARTLING ANNOUNCEMENT

Jesus' Birth in Life of a Champion. Darrell Porter, catcher for the World Series' Kansas City Royals, acknowledges that he "lost" six years of his life as an alcoholic and drug addict. Darrell Porter also tells about the promise of Jesus Christ's coming to him. Jesus meant a new beginning for this outstanding athlete in 1980.

"In 1974 . . . I was still with the Brewers. I realized, following all kinds of ugly incidents, that I was no longer the friendly guy who made friends easily. My attitude had basically changed. My outlook became constantly pessimistic, and I had a fear of people.

". . . I was too far gone. I was an alcoholic. It was a way for me to escape that emotional pain. I was losing touch with reality. The slightest things bothered me. Little problems. I felt I had to escape. Looking back, I think I was an alcoholic before I ever touched a drop.

"Alcohol was everywhere . . . Parties, restaurants, home . . . I drank until it became difficult to reach the euphoric feeling. Then I discovered I could escape quicker by smoking joints and popping quaaludes.

"All the time . . . Everyday . . . I needed more and more. Every time I would come down lower. The highs got lower and the lows got lower. I started taking pills to work against other pills to get normal.

"Everything got heavier. I tried to stay high all the time. I started popping grennies (speed) before games. My mind was gone. As soon as I'd swallow a supply, I'd feel good. And the stuff hadn't even had a chance to work yet.

"I felt everybody was driving me insane. I couldn't see that it was me. The alcohol and drugs made me magnify little things a thousand times. I'd hide from people. My playing went downhill; I lost my marriage; I lost my relationship with my parents and relatives.

"I didn't feel that drugs and alcohol were the reason for my problems. I felt everybody else was the problem. I thought anybody who said I was having a drinking problem was crazy. Not me!

"Like I said, I feared people. The drugs and booze did that to me. I was never rational. Maybe on the field I was. Baseball and drugs were my gods. There was nothing else. I let all the nice things people say go to my head, too. For some reason, maybe to get close, people tend to be nice to celebrities, which, I guess I was. Everything you do, friends praise.

"I'm confronted with booze all the time. But it's now no problem at all. This person has no desire to do those things again. This person is twenty-eight years old and has a lot to do to make up for six lost years of life.

"I'm simply a Christian. I've been fortunate He didn't abandon me. He's always right there in front of my eyes and lets me know if I'm in danger of slipping.

"I'm totally relaxed now. My priorities are God first, everything else second. I feel no pressure playing ball. Pressure is getting all blown away at night, then trying to get straight the next day. That was pressure. I have self-respect now. I had none before.

"All I can say, and it says everything, is that kids on drugs and alcohol are miserable. They don't think they are. I didn't either. But they are. They're only fooling themselves, and hey, I was lucky. Many are killing themselves. All the talk about a little here, a little there and it won't hurt . . . It's all wrong. I've been there.

"No, nothing worthwhile is easy. But God really is with us. He's a kind God. Sometimes we get too wrapped up and forget about him. That's when life gets dangerous."—From an interview by Gordon Smith, Associate Sports Editor, October 12, 1980.

"God's Town." In 1977, The Full Gospel Temple, a Pentecostal group, purchased Bridgeville, California. Bridgeville, located on eighty-seven acres in northern California, was up for sale for $450,000. The Full Gospel Temple took out a mortgage and announced that it would turn the town into "God's Town," a community where no sin or vice could flourish and which would be completely religious. By November, 1978, however, the dream was all but dead. The church was in default of its mortgage, and foreclosure was imminent. The town was scheduled to be auctioned. A San Jose businessman assumed the debt for $375,000, and the Full Gospel Temple left Bridgeville.

God does not claim eighty-seven acres in California but the entire world! Through the startling announcement of the Birth of Jesus, God states His claim over every town and city everywhere. He is the Lord of Bridgeville, and of your community.

Has the meaning of the startling announcement of His Coming dawned on you?

Detached Bystander. The great musician-theologian-missionary-doctor, Albert Schweitzer, was once working on the roof of one of his hospital buildings in Lambarene, in the heart of the African jungle. Holding a hammer and covered with sweat, the famous physician needed someone to come up the ladder to the roof to help him for a minute. Dr. Schweitzer saw a strong young African walking below and called to him, asking him to lend a hand. The young man haughtily refused, explaining, "I can read and write."

Dr. Schweitzer smiled and chuckled to the man, "My friend, I, too, have had a try at being an intellectual, but I haven't been able to make a go at it."

God has refused to be a detached bystander. He has not chosen to offer intellectual answers. Through the startling announcement of Jesus' birth, we realize that He has come among us in our need. The Lord promises that Jesus Christ's coming is God usefully and meaningfully involving Himself in our world for us.

Sentence Sermon to Remember: Every man hath a good and a bad angel attending on him in particular, all his life long.—Robert Burton, in *Anatomy of Melancholy.*

Questions for Pupils on the Next Lesson. 1. When do you find the restrictions and limitations placed on you by parents most frustrating? 2. Do you think that God has a plan for you? 3. How would you describe Jesus' relationship with Mary and Joseph? 4. Why did Jesus feel He had to obey His parents? 5. What are the values which seem to be shaping your life most noticeably?

LESSON III—DECEMBER 19

JESUS' EARLY LIFE

Background Scripture: Luke 2
Devotional Reading: Proverbs 23:15–25

KING JAMES VERSION

LUKE 2 22 And when the days of her purification according to the law of Moses were accomplished, they brought him to Jerusalem, to present *him* to the Lord;

23 (As it is written in the law of the Lord, Every male that openeth the womb shall be called holy to the Lord;)

24 And to offer a sacrifice according to that which is said in the law of the Lord, A pair of turtledoves, or two young pigeons.

25 And, behold, there was a man in Jerusalem, whose name *was* Simeon; and the same man *was* just and devout, waiting for the consolation of Israel: and the Holy Ghost was upon him.

26 And it was revealed unto him by the Holy Ghost, that he should not see death, before he had seen the Lord's Christ.

27 And he came by the Spirit into the temple: and when the parents brought in the child Jesus, to do for him after the custom of the law,

28 Then took he him up in his arms, and blessed God, and said,

29 Lord, now lettest thou thy servant depart in peace, according to thy word:

30 For mine eyes have seen thy salvation,

31 Which thou hast prepared before the face of all people;

32 A light to lighten the Gentiles, and the glory of thy people Israel.

33 And Joseph and his mother marveled at those things which were spoken of him.

34 And Simeon blessed them, and said unto Mary his mother, Behold, this *child* is set for the fall and rising again of many in Israel; and for a sign which shall be spoken against;

35 (Yea, a sword shall pierce through thy own soul also;) that the thoughts of many hearts may be revealed.

51 And he went down with them, and came to Nazareth, and was subject unto them: but his mother kept all these sayings in her heart.

52 And Jesus increased in wisdom and stature, and in favour with God and man.

REVISED STANDARD VERSION

LUKE 2 22 And when the time came for their purification according to the law of Moses, they brought him up to Jerusalem to present him to the Lord 23 (as it is written in the law of the Lord, "Every male that opens the womb shall be called holy to the Lord") 24 and to offer a sacrifice according to what is said in the law of the Lord, "a pair of turtledoves, or two young pigeons." 25 Now there was a man in Jerusalem, whose name was Simeon, and this man was righteous and devout, looking for the consolation of Israel, and the Holy Spirit was upon Him. 26 And it had been revealed to him by the Holy Spirit that he should not see death before he had seen the Lord's Christ. 27 And inspired by the Spirit he came into the temple; and when the parents brought in the child Jesus, to do for him according to the custom of the law, 28 he took him up in his arms and blessed God and said,

29 "Lord, now lettest thou thy servant
depart in peace,
according to thy word;
30 for mine eyes have seen thy salvation
31 which thou hast prepared in the presence of all peoples,
32 a light for revelation to the Gentiles,
and for glory to thy people Israel."

33 And his father and his mother marveled at what was said about him; 34 and Simeon blessed them and said to Mary his mother,

"Behold, this child is set for the fall and rising of many in Israel,
and for a sign that is spoken against
35 (and a sword will pierce through your own soul also),
that thoughts out of many hearts may be revealed."

51 And he went down with them and came to Nazareth, and was obedient to them; and his mother kept all these things in her heart.

52 And Jesus increased in wisdom and in stature, and in favor with God and man.

KEY VERSE: And Jesus increased in wisdom and in stature, and in favour with God and man. Luke 2:52.

HOME DAILY BIBLE READINGS

Dec. 13. *M.* *Born in a Stable.* Luke 2:1–7.
Dec. 14. *T.* *Glory to God in the Highest.* Luke 2:8–14.
Dec. 15. *W.* *Let Us Go Over to Bethlehem.* Luke 2:15–20.
Dec. 16. *T.* *Dedication.* Luke 2:22–28.
Dec. 17. *F.* *A Song of Praise.* Luke 2:29–35.
Dec. 18. *S.* *A Widow's Testimony.* Luke 2:36–40.
Dec. 19. *S.* *Jesus in the Temple.* Luke 2:41–52.

BACKGROUND

Have you noticed the great *singing* that burst out at the Coming of Jesus? Mary had her great hymn, the *Magnificat.* The Shepherds in the fields heard the heavenly hosts singing, "Glory to God in the highest. . . ." And there was the little man named Simeon who gave us the *Nunc Dimittis,* which has become one of the great songs of the Church. Any mother sings in her heart when her first child is born; here, heaven and earth sing joy to all the world.

Luke reaches back deep into Hebrew history and customs as he tells of what happened after the birth in Bethlehem. All was done "according to the law of Moses" (Luke 2:22). According to that law, every Jewish boy was circumcised on the eighth day after his birth, and so Jesus was circumcised. On that day, He was legally given the name of Jesus.

NOTES ON THE PRINTED TEXT

And there were certain other ceremonies, following this. One was the rite of "The Redemption of the Firstborn" (*see* Numbers 18:16). Behind this rite lay the conviction that every firstborn boy was sacred to God. At this time the sum of five shekels was paid to the priests officiating at the ceremony; this was to be performed before thirty-one days after the birth. The parents could, if they wished, buy back their son from God.

Second, there was the rite of "Purification After Childbirth." The mother was believed to be unclean for forty days if it were a boy, or for eighty days if it were a girl. During that time, she could not enter the temple. At the end of this time, she was required to bring to the temple a lamb and a young pigeon for sacrifice.

This rite of sacrifice was called "The Offering of the Poor." Mary and Joseph were very poor; they could not afford to give a lamb, so they were permitted to bring only a pair of young pigeons. Only Luke gives us the story of these rites, as performed by Mary and Joseph, and that is important. This Luke was an apostle to the *poor,* and all through his book he stands as champion of the poor. His sympathy for those who knew no luxuries and who were tortured in the endless fight to "make both ends meet" runs all through his writings. He seems more than anxious to make it clear that the poor loved and worshiped God—*and that God cared for them.* In this instance he is telling us that every child is the gift of God, and that every parent bears the responsibility of dedicating his children to the will and purpose of the God who gave them life.

But the real "hero" of this story, strangely, is not Mary nor Joseph. It is an obscure, humble man who "just happened" to be in the temple the day when His parents brought the baby Jesus to dedicate Him to God. Just happened? No, that is not quite right. Luke says that Simeon, a man "just and devout," came to the temple "by the Spirit," *led* there by the Holy Spirit. Simeon was not a priest, not a man of high estate, but he was a man who all his life had longed for the "consolation" of Israel—for the fulfillment of the messianic hopes of Israel. "And it was revealed unto him by the Holy Ghost, that he should not see death, before he had seen the Lord's Christ" (verse 26). The moment he looked at the young Child in the arms of Mary, he knew that he was looking at the young Christ. Now, he cried, he could die in peace, according to the promise of the Spirit.

With all his heart, Luke believed in the fulfillment of that promise of a Messiah to come. He pictures Simeon as a man of quiet faith. He was one of those Hebrews who were called "The Quiet in the Land." He expected no warrior Christ, no military genius sent to destroy the enemies of Israel, but one who prayed humbly for an humble Christ, and one who would be a light for revelation to the *Gentiles.* Here again it is a Gentile Luke who is speaking.

Simeon glimpsed another thing about this gentle Christ child: He would be "set for the fall and rising of many in Israel" (verse 34 RSV). This verse, and those following it, sum up the work and the fate of Jesus. He came into this world as a *light*—a Light which could guide us out of the darkness of sin into the revealing light of the Kingdom of God. Walk in the Light and we find salvation; walk in darkness and we fall away from God. Those who ignore or evade the Light which is in Christ fall back into the old ways which men walked before He came; those who accept Him will *rise;* they will be made new creatures. Jesus does *not* condemn those who reject Him; He leaves the choice of walking one way or the other to men. As one commentator puts it, "There is a great refusal and there is a great acceptance. . . . We either surrender to Him or we are at war with him." No man can remain neutral to Jesus Christ.

Up to this point, it has all been joy with Simeon, all singing and praise. But now, for the first time, he speaks words of infinite sadness about the Child of Mary. The shadow of the cross falls upon her and her Child; Simeon predicts "a sword shall pierce through thy own soul . . ." (verse 35). It was a sword forged by men of evil thoughts, it was a suffering that would harass Mother Mary all through her life. It is startling to hear such a statement made at a time when the Infant was only a few weeks old, and even more startling that the prediction was a true one; that was exactly what happened to Mary.

Holman Hunt painted a great picture which he entitled *The Lord of Time and All the Worlds.* He pictures Jesus as a young man in the carpenter shop at Nazareth; He stands, stretching out His arms perhaps in a moment of relaxation from His work. Kneeling at His right is Mary, sweeping up shavings from the floor; she looks up at a shadow cast on the wall—and the shadow is in the form of a man on a cross! "In this picture . . . we have an epitome of the life of Jesus. The gifts of the Magi recall His infancy; the carpenter's shop, His youth and manhood; the shadow, His awful sacrifice. The clouds of Golgotha throw their darkness and their sunset-crimson on the golden mists of Bethlehem and the holy innocence of Nazareth."—Frederic W. Farrar in *The Life of Christ*, by permission of The Macmillan Company, publishers.

All of these rites were performed in the temple at Jersualem. Mary and Joseph made many pilgrimages to that temple; Luke says that "His parents went to Jerusalem every year at the feast of the passover" (verse 41). There was one year when the boy Jesus was lost in the crowds—and found in the temple asking questions of the scholarly doctors (theologians)! But it was not in the temple that He was to be educated for the work He had come to do; that education was in His home. As he grew to boyhood and early youth, He was trained in the Jewish faith. This was the only school He ever knew. His most influential teacher was not a schoolmaster but His mother. Under her, He increased in body, mind, and spirit. He must have sensed a feeling of uneasiness, in this mother; she kept in her heart, silently, all that she heard people say about her Son; that must have "leaked through to Jesus" but Mary went on teaching, and hoping.

SUGGESTIONS TO TEACHERS

Rudolph the Red-Nosed Reindeer. Santa Claus. Elves in Santa's workshop at the North Pole. The Little Christmas Angel. Is Jesus merely one of the fictitious figures of Yuletide fantasy land?

Alas, for many people, the answer seems to be *Yes*. They hint that He exists only in a make-believe world. Some even doubt that He lived at all, or, if He did, He is hopelessly buried beneath that debris of piety and legend.

Today's lesson will be the time when you lift Jesus out of the obscurity of myth and make-believe to the reality of the human Jesus. Move your people beyond plastic manger scenes to examining the accounts of Jesus' early life.

1. *NOBODIES FROM NAZARETH*. The scriptural account of Jesus' birth is a healthy antidote to the silly, the phony, and the funny of the shopping-mart portrayal of this season. Draw your class's attention to the Where, the How and the When of God's choice of visiting our world. Note that the Birth occurred to real-life people enduring real-life pressures and problems. In fact, urge your class to list parallels they may note between Mary's and Joseph's situation and today's, such as uncertainty, worries, taxes, travel, etc. God came into the real world where your people live!

2. *NEWS AT NIGHT*. The Good News of the birth took place in darkness, in a cave, in a strange town. The birth was announced to shepherds at night. How is night the loneliest time for many? What are some other forms of "darkness"? Impress on your people that God seems to choose the loneliness of night for His appearance.

3. *NAME WITH MEANING*. Have your class members take note of the meaning of Jesus' name. Selecting a name for a Jewish baby was a serious matter, and Mary and Joseph recognized their baby had a unique role for the world. Your class may wish to reflect briefly on the naming of children as Christians through baptism. Reading Luke 2:21, remind your class of the many personal details about Jesus in the Gospel accounts, reinforcing their credibility.

4. *NOTHING YET KNOWING*. The visit to the Temple with the in-

fant Jesus tells a lot about the home into which the Saviour of the world was born. So poor that they could afford only the peasants' offering of two pigeons, Mary and Joseph had nothing of the world's riches or power. Yet they had all they needed: they served the Lord. They received confirmation of their assignment as God's agents when old Simeon blessed their baby and ancient Anna prophesied about Jesus. What do these details suggest about the home life of Christians nowadays? What about the priorities of those who would have Jesus as part of their homes?

5. *NORMAL BUT NEAR.* Alert your class to the fact that Luke refuses to portray the boy Jesus as Superkid. Instead, he shows Jesus experiencing the normal boyhood of a Jewish village lad, yet near to God the Father. Jesus was truly human in every way but also conscious from the beginning of His unique relationship ("My Father's House" in 2:49) with the Creator. What new insights into Jesus' character and career do these details suggest?

TOPIC FOR ADULTS
JESUS' EARLY LIFE

Christ in Our Neighbor. Martin Luther preached a sermon at Christmastime on the Nativity story. Having portrayed a wretched Bethlehem which forced Mary to give birth in a cow stall, he addressed his people: "There are some of us in this congregation who think to ourselves: 'If only I had been there! How quick I would have been to help the Baby. I would have washed His linen. How happy I would have been to go with the shepherds to see the Lord lying in the manger!' Yes, we would. We say that because we know how great Christ is, but if we had been there at that time, we would have done no better than the people of Bethlehem. . . . Why don't we do it now? We have Christ in our neighbor."

We have Christ in our neighbor. And there, too, is the offense of the ordinary: we are glad to worship an historical memory, but unwilling to see the living Lord who still comes in very human form among common people. Like the people of Nazareth, we also turn away in disappointment from a God who seems to be so ordinary. But still the voice follows us: "Blessed is he who takes no offense at me."

Throwaway Children. Two years ago, a New Jersey couple were charged with child abuse for trying to trade their fourteen-month-old son for a three-year-old black and silver Corvette valued at $8,800. The dealer, who contacted the police and played along with their request, reported, "They had the keys and the papers for the car and we were putting the license plates on. They left the baby on the showroom floor."

Shortly afterward, a Washington D.C. area suburban welfare agency reported that troublesome children expelled by parents from their homes comprise a substantial part of its case load. The director of a shelter for runaway youngsters states, "The 1960s idea of 'Do your own thing' has moved into the '80s with disposable relationships. If they don't work, if it's not perfect, I want something else." Another social worker at that agency reports that at least once a week a parent drives up and drops off a child with a suitcase and quick good-bye.

Every parent owes his/her child unconditional acceptance. A father or mother cannot calculate the relationship on the basis of convenience. The story of Joseph and Mary is more than pretty fantasy. As they discovered opportunities to serve the Lord through their parenting, so modern parents encounter Christ through accepting of responsibilities of parenthood.

Plant for Others. An ancient tale from the Middle East relates how a caliph traveled along an old road and noticed an elderly man planting olive trees. Knowing that olive trees require years and years to mature before they produce fruit, the surprised Caliph asked the old man why he bothered to plant olive trees. "You will not live to see the fruits of your labors," said the caliph.

"Yes, that is true," answered the wise, old man. "I will not live to eat any of the olives from these trees. But others planted so that we should eat. Therefore, we must plant so that they shall eat."

The caliph, moved by the old man's humility and devotion, reached into his purse and gave him a large gold coin.

Jesus' parents, Anna, Simeon, and others played an important role in Jesus' early life—far more than we usually think. And previous generations as well as others have been instrumental in the way our faith has been shaped in a positive way.

We, in turn, are called to plant and cultivate so that others may eat, so that children and future generations will be nurtured physically, spiritually, and socially.

Questions for Pupils on the Next Lesson. 1. Is there ever a time when you are free from temptation and testing? 2. How do you handle conflicting pressures and values? 3. Do you sometimes feel that the world is against you? 4. How is your faith in Christ meant to confer a sense of purpose and power for your life? Does it? 5. What were some of the times when you were able to withstand temptation, and what were some of the times when you were not?

TOPIC FOR YOUTH
FOLLOWING GOD'S PLAN

God's Plans for Two Boys? About a century ago, a boy was dangerously mired in a swampy bog near Darvel, Scotland. The boy's cries were heard by a man walking in the area. The man, at great personal risk, rescued the boy.

The boy, it turned out, was the son of a nobleman. The boy's father wanted to reward the rescuer, but the man refused to accept anything for himself. The boy's father finally persuaded the Scotsman to receive help to educate his own son.

The son of the rescuer was enabled to receive a good education and decided to enter medicine. Funded by the nobleman, he eventually graduated from St. Mary's Hospital Medical School. The boy went on to a distinguished career in medical research and became renowned as the discoverer of penicillin. The Scotsman's son's name was Alexander Fleming.

Interestingly, there was a sequel. During World War II, during a bleak hour, the son of the nobleman, the same boy who had been trapped in the bog, became ill with pneumonia. He would have died if he had not received injections of the then-new "miracle drug"—penicillin. The course of the war and Great Britain would have been substantially affected if he had died. His name was Winston Churchill.

Each boy was helped by others, and the entire world was enriched!

God's plan is that we reflect our Christian values by helping each other.

Dizzying Numbers. You seem surrounded by numbers—big numbers. Your Zip Codes now stretch half way across the bottom of an envelope. Your identity is reduced to 9 digits of a Social Security number. Big rows of numbers confront you daily, as reporters and politicians speak casually of 4.2 billion people in the world and $2.39 trillion in the nation's G.N.P. *The Guinness Book of Records* states that the world weighs 6,585,600,000,000,000,000,000 tons. Sir Arthur Eddington opened his *The Philosophy of Physical Science* with the sentence, "I believe that there are 15,747,724,136,275,002,577,605,653,961,181,555,468,044,717,-914,527,116,709,366,231,425,076,185,631,031,295 protons in the universe and the same number of electrons."

It makes you feel insignificant. It makes you question whether you have any value or importance.

The birth and the life of Jesus make clear that God has a plan for the universe. You are part of that plan, not a miserable fraction, not a trivial number. Although Jesus grew up in a minor peasant village named Nazareth in the home of two unknown persons named Joseph and Mary, God through Him tells you that you are never a statistic, forgotten or forgettable. You are known and valued.

God, Not Football or Ice-skating, Rules Lives. "She's here, and she's going to stay with me," said Terry Bradshaw in September 1980. With that firm statement, the Pittsburgh Steelers's quarterback announced that he and his wife, the ice-skating star Jo Jo Starbuck, had reunited. Ms. Starbuck had filed for a divorce after having spoken publicly about the strain two big-time sports careers can put on heart and home. But the couple have now put their problems "in the hands of the Lord," Bradshaw said. "We're going to live together," Bradshaw said, "God is going to come first in our lives, then our marriage and being together, and then our careers. Football and ice skating are not going to rule our lives."

Sentence Sermon to Remember: Christmas is a time for "giving up" sin, bad habits, and selfish pleasures. Christmas is a time for "giving in," surrender to Christ, acceptance of Him as King. Christmas is a time for "giving out," real giving, not swapping.—Anonymous.

Questions for Pupils on the Next Lesson. 1. What are the toughest temptations to deal with in your daily living? 2. Do you ever feel that you are being tested in life? 3. Where are the areas in your life where you feel the greatest conflicts of values? 4. Do you think that Jesus really experienced temptations? 5. How is the Christian faith supposed to help a person stand up to testing and temptation?

LESSON IV—DECEMBER 26

JESUS BEGINS HIS MINISTRY

Background Scripture: Luke 3:21–4:15
Devotional Reading: Luke 3:15–20

KING JAMES VERSION

LUKE 4 1 And Jesus being full of the Holy Ghost returned from Jordan, and was led by the Spirit into the wilderness,

2 Being forty days tempted of the devil. And in those days he did eat nothing: and when they were ended, he afterward hungered.

3 And the devil said unto him, If thou be the Son of God, command this stone that it be made bread.

4 And Jesus answered him, saying, It is written, That man shall not live by bread alone, but by every word of God.

5 And the devil, taking him up into a high mountain, shewed unto him all the kingdoms of the world in a moment of time.

6 And the devil said unto him, All this power will I give thee, and the glory of them: for that is delivered unto me; and to whomsoever I will, I give it.

7 If thou therefore wilt worship me, all shall be thine.

8 And Jesus answered and said unto him, Get thee behind me, Satan: for it is written, Thou shalt worship the Lord thy God, and him only shalt thou serve.

9 And he brought him to Jerusalem, and set him on a pinnacle of the temple, and said unto him, If thou be the Son of God, cast thyself down from hence:

10 For it is written, He shall give his angels charge over thee, to keep thee:

11 And in *their* hands they shall bear thee up, lest at any time thou dash thy foot against a stone.

12 And Jesus answering said unto him, It is said, Thou shalt not tempt the Lord thy God.

13 And when the devil had ended all the temptation, he departed from him for a season.

14 And Jesus returned in the power of the Spirit into Galilee: and there went out a fame of him through all the region round about.

15 And he taught in their synagogues, being glorified of all.

REVISED STANDARD VERSION

LUKE 4 1 And Jesus, full of the Holy Spirit, returned from the Jordan, and was led by the Spirit 2 for forty days in the wilderness, tempted by the devil. And he ate nothing in those days; and when they were ended, he was hungry. 3 The devil said to him, "If you are the Son of God, command this stone to become bread." 4 And Jesus answered him, "It is written, 'Man shall not live by bread alone.' " 5 And the devil took him up, and showed him all the kingdoms of the world in a moment of time, 6 and said to him, "To you I will give all this authority and their glory; for it has been delivered to me, and I give it to whom I will. 7 If you, then, will worship me, it shall all be yours." 8 And Jesus answered him, "It is written,

'You shall worship the Lord your God,
and him only shall you serve,' "

9 And he took him to Jerusalem, and set him on the pinnacle of the temple, and said to him, "If you are the Son of God, throw yourself down from here; 10 for it is written,

'He will give his angels charge of you,
too guard you,'

11 and

'on their hands they will bear you up,
lest you strike your foot against a
stone.' "

12 And Jesus answered him, "It is said, 'You shall not tempt the Lord your God.' "

13 And when the devil had ended every temptation, he departed from him until an opportune time.

14 And Jesus returned in the power of the Spirit into Galilee, and a report concerning him went out through all the surrounding country. 15 And he taught in their synagogues, being glorified by all.

KEY VERSE: And Jesus returned in the power of the Spirit into Galilee, and a report concerning him went out through all the surrounding country. Luke 4:14 (RSV).

HOME DAILY BIBLE READINGS

Dec. 20. M. A Call to Repentance. Luke 3:1–6.
Dec. 21. T. Proof of Repentance. Luke 3:7–14.
Dec. 22. W. My Beloved Son. Luke 3:15–22.
Dec. 23. T. Victory in Temptation. Luke 4:1–15.
Dec. 24. F. Behold the Lamb of God. John 1:29–36.
Dec. 25. S. Two Interested Men. John 1:37–42.
Dec. 26. S. Follow Me. John 1:43–51.

BACKGROUND

There come moments in the lives of busy, troubled men when they just have to "get away from it all," away from the "rat race" of life and in solitude sit down to "think it through." This happened to Moses during the days of Israel in the wilderness, when he climbed a mountain and stayed there with only God to find out just what he was to be and do. He stayed up there forty days and nights (Deuteronomy 9:9), and in that desolate place he did not eat or drink.

Jesus knew all about that experience of Moses. Often, He went off alone to some secret place to get away from the crowds and even from His disciples, to rest and to take counsel with His Father. Immediately after His baptism, He went out into the wilderness near the Dead Sea. It was a barren wasteland called Jeshimmon, which meant "The Devastation": it was a land of dust, broken limestone, and rocks, and it was cursed with the withering heat of a blast furnace. Nobody would find Him there, nobody but God—and, as it turned out, the Devil.

He knew, after His baptism, just who He was and what He had to do. He knew that His lifework was to be a crusade *to win men to God.* But He had questions in His mind: *how* was He to do this, what *methods* should He use, and where was He to *begin?* So He went up to a mountain in this cursed land, to the very mountain that the three kings had crossed when they came to worship Him in Bethlehem.

NOTES ON THE PRINTED TEXT

At the end of the forty days (as it was with Moses), by way of three conversations with the Devil, He found the answers to these vital questions. Many modern cynical critics will tell you that there is no personal Devil; they look upon the Devil as a symbol of human sin, but Jesus did *not* believe that; He believed in the reality of the Devil, and He saw in that Devil His most dangerous adversary. Either Satan or Christ would win the men of earth, in His mind. What happened in this confrontation of Jesus and the Devil is something that must have come from Jesus' own lips; there are no other sources describing this milestone experience in His life.

There were three temptations facing Jesus on that wilderness mountain. Or three evil *voices* tempting Him to use the Devil's methods in the work He had come to do. They were voices that still speak to *us* when we try to figure out how we are to live as Christians.

First, there was the evil suggestion that He demonstrate His power by changing the stones at His feet into bread. Jesus was hungry; "in those days he did eat nothing" (verse 2). All around Him, as He fasted, there were loaf-shaped stones. Why, asked the Devil, didn't He just turn those stones into bread and *eat?* Don't be foolish, Jesus; just perform a miracle (which, with your power, you could easily perform!) The Devil went even further: if Jesus really wanted to win men to God, He could do it easily and quickly just by giving bread to His hungry, poor people. A man must eat; men even kill that they may eat. Jesus was aware of that; He had been raised among the poor, and He knew their hunger. Now, says the sly Devil, you have the power to *feed* them. Do that, and they will flock to you by the thousand. Surely this would establish Him as the Messiah.

No, said Jesus; that would be an evil thing for me to do. I came to earth not to give bread to men's bodies, but bread for their souls. "Man," He tells the Devil, "shall not live by bread alone." We can feed a drunken derelict for days and weeks and years, but until he accepts the bread of salvation in his heart and soul, he will never by anything but a drunken derelict. *That* was the bread He would offer men. He refused to take the short road to what would be a short, cheap popularity.

The second temptation was the toughest of all; it was a temptation that had a political background, and a temptation to compromise with the Devil. In imagination Jesus stood on the mountain top and looked down on "all of the kingdoms of the world in a moment of time" (verse 5). This world, the Devil sneered, was *his* world; he claimed that *he* ruled it. Clarence Darrow once passed the rather cynical remark that "Certainly a devil who runs three-quarters of the world is worthy of our attention if not of our respect." Just compromise a little, Jesus, said the Devil, just worship me a little, and I will give you (my) world!

It was not his world. The Devil lied and assumed an authority that he did not have. *It was God's world,* and the people who inhabited it should and must worship God and God alone. Those people down there, those Israelites and Gentiles all wanted a better world than they had; the Israelites had for a long time looked forward to the coming of a Messiah with a sword in His hand, to deliver them from the oppression of Rome; they wanted to be *free.* Now, says the Devil to Jesus, all you have to do is to accept my way of the sword and deliver them from Rome. Arouse your people; lead them to battle, and I will see to it that you win. It was nonsense, fatal nonsense, and Jesus knew it.

Jesus had the power to do that, but He never used it. He never once compromised with evil, never once gave in to the standards of the world; rather than do that, He *died.* Not many men are willing to do that today. Most of them prefer the way of the world to the way of God, and they lead us to disaster when they do it and repent for it only on their deathbeds.

No man can compromise with God.

The third and last temptation was an utterly stupid suggestion by the Devil that Jesus go up to the pinnacle of the temple in Jerusalem and jump off just to prove that He was truly the Son of a God who would save Him from death. That would have been a drop of about 450 feet. Only a fool would make such a jump. (We still have men who jump off the tops of skyscrapers and make it. So what? What do they prove, in doing that? Within a week's time we even forget their names.)

No, said Jesus; He would not stoop to sensationalism to win men, for sensationalists are nine-day wonders. They never *last*. Sensationalists in our times are a dime a dozen; they attract gawking crowds, but they do no lasting good in the Kingdom; they come and go *quickly* and are soon forgotten.

Jesus scorched the Devil into silence—and departure—with the words, "You shall not tempt the Lord thy God" (verse 12). God will not protect a fool who risks death to prove nothing; His promises were never meant to be abused by senseless trickery. God's methods are unlike the methods of men. His methods include the giving of a spiritual bread greater than any bread men may eat; His method is not one calculated to entertain men but to *save* men; His method is not to tempt men but to lead them slowly past temptation to lasting fellowship with Him and obedience to Him.

There was still that other question in Jesus' mind: where was He to begin His ministry? Where would He start? Luke says that "Jesus returned in the power of the Spirit into Galilee. . . ." Galilee! This was a province made up of some 204 villages and towns, with a total population estimated at 3,000,000. They were a people living in a territory entirely surrounded by non-Jewish countries (the word *Galilee* means "a circle," and they were encircled by nonbelievers). They were also a highly courageous people with a rebel mind, fond of innovations and seditions. That made it a good place for Jesus to begin, for in Galilee He was sure of an audience ready to listen.

And He began in the Synagogues of Galilee. He might have started out from the temple in Jerusalem, but no, the temple was a place for sacrifice, but the Synagogue was a place for teaching. In the Synagogue, any man was privileged to stand and speak to the congregation. The stage of the Synagogue was therefore open to the Christ who came with a new message, and He began by bringing them a message that troubled their minds and their hearts.

SUGGESTIONS TO TEACHERS

It's the day after Christmas, and many (perhaps including you!) are nearly exhausted from preparing and celebrating the holiday. Yet you also felt some stirring during Christmas. Many in your class sense that something mysterious and great occurred. Some have told themselves, "Some day, I must study what the Coming of Jesus Christ signifies." Today, the day after Christmas, is the opportunity for everyone, yourself included, to begin that long-promised investigation. As the class leader, however, make today more than an academic exercise. You and the class are not here to "study" Jesus. Today must be the start of a new part of a pilgrimage with Jesus Christ, especially as a new year begins.

1. *DEDICATED.* Review the baptism of Jesus. Nudge your class into thinking why Jesus would be baptized and what it meant to Him. Have the class check the Old Testament significance in Psalms 2:7 and Isaiah 42:1 of the words of the voice from heaven (Luke 3:22). Suggest that the

descent of the Spirit upon Jesus after His baptism was affirmation of His commitment to be the divinely-anointed One. Also be sure that the class understand Jesus' commitment to suffer for others, as Isaiah 42 (and the following chapters) make clear.

2. *DESCENDED.* At first, the long geneology in Luke 3 may seem pointless. Jesus, however, had a lineage. He was part of a special community. He could trace His roots clear back to Adam. (Matthew's Gospel takes Jesus' ancestry only back to Abraham, but Luke insists on showing Jesus' connection to the entire human family.) Jesus belongs to everyone. Take some time to allow each person to say something about why Jesus has special meaning to him/her.

3. *DETERMINED.* Jesus endured the testing in the wilderness and hammered out the shape of His service as the Chosen One. Your class should investigate the significance of each of the three temptations or short-cuts presenting themselves to Jesus. Why did He reject each of these? How do some religious leaders today seem to adopt some of these sensational approaches? How did Jesus withstand these temptations? Discuss how Christians are "tested" and tempted today. How does Christian faith enable members of your class to endure such times?

4. *DIRECTED.* Have your class members put their minds on the way Jesus returned from His wilderness experience "in the power of the Spirit." Encourage comments on the part of your class about what this phrase suggests. Jesus was obviously conscious of being directed as God's own. Remind your class, however, that Jesus shares the power of the Spirit with us, His followers. When we live with Him and for Him, we may hope to be empowered!

TOPIC FOR ADULTS
JESUS BEGINS HIS MINISTRY

Prophet or Profit? In the early part of this century, German Kaiser Wilhelm did not mind affecting an air of religion when it was to his advantage. His unswerving goal, however, was to promote the prestige of Imperial Germany. He devoted his energies to building a powerful war machine and bristled at real or imagined slights at the hands of the British, French, or Russians. At his instruction, his Foreign Office wove webs of intrigue and his Generals devised strategies of attack which eventually led to the conflagration of 1914–1918. Beforehand, however, his policies won enthusiastic support of German industrialists because they kept Ruhr steel mills busy and produced handsome profits for German investors. When someone asked him whether he was sure he was acting according to the precepts of Christian morality, the Kaiser snorted, "Morality is all right, but what about dividends?"

Christians from the industrialized, technologically advanced nations of the West find themselves tempted to say the same words. Religion, we may think, has its place, but the main question is the bottom line on the balance sheet. "Morality is all right, but what about dividends?"

As Jesus began His ministry, He experienced the temptation to consider profit ahead of prophecy. Each day, as we take up our forms of ministry, we also must resolve the temptation to seek power for ourselves through force of various forms instead of serving the Lord who calls us to carry out His will. Pray to receive strength to resolve to place Him first.

Your Size. George Washington Carver, the great, black research scientist who achieved wonders with the humble peanut, liked to tell this story: "When I was young I said to God, 'God, tell me the mystery of the Universe.' But God answered, 'That knowledge is reserved for Me alone.' So I said, 'God, tell me the mystery of the peanut.' Then God said, 'Well, that is more nearly your size.' And He told me."

Erroneous Assumption. The college drama department was presenting Shakespeare's *Hamlet* at a well-known drama festival. The night before the big production, the man playing Hamlet was rushed to the hospital for an emergency appendectomy, and his understudy, a brash young sophomore with an exaggerated idea of his acting abilities, was thrust into the lead role. Unfortunately, the sophomore stand-in proved to be disastrously inexperienced as an actor. Although he knew the lines perfectly, he lacked sensitivity of the part of the young Prince of Denmark. Instead of acting the part of Hamlet in Shakespeare's magnificent tragedy, the young man was proving himself to be an egotistical ham. The audience grew increasingly restless. As the silly performance of the sophomoric replacement continued, muttering could be heard throughout the theater. The point of no return, however, was reached when the youngster mangled the moving soliloquy of Hamlet, and hisses and boos and catcalls broke out from the audience. Still not comprehending that his acting was the cause of the dissatisfaction, the lad stopped in the middle of the great soliloquy, stepped to the front of the stage, and announced innocently to the house, "Hey, look, I didn't write this stuff!"

One of our main temptations is to place the blame on someone else and to excuse ourselves. Our egos become so inflated that we imagine that the universe revolves around our whims.

Jesus began His ministry by withdrawing for a forty-day "retreat" in order to resolve once-and-for-all that He would not be a self-seeking actor instead of the divinely-anointed One.

Questions for Pupils on the Next Lesson. 1. What are some of the occasions recently in your life when you have experienced guilt? What have you done about these? 2. How do you deal constructively with attitudes and feelings which alienate you from others? 3. Why is it so hard to forgive others? 4. What reactions did Jesus cause among His hearers when He announced that the woman who anointed His feet was forgiven? 5. Why are we church members so often like Simon the Pharisee?

TOPIC FOR YOUTH
TESTED AND TRUE

Secret of Success. Herb Adderley is remembered as one of the great cornerbacks of all time in professional football. Adderley starred with the Green Bay Packers and the Dallas Cowboys for many seasons. He was also respected by teammates and opponents for his personal qualities as well as his professional achievements on the gridiron. People realized that Herb Adderley was a Christian athlete who, in spite of temptations and testing, lived his faith.

Once, in a talk, Herb quietly described how his trust in God's endearing love was the key to his success. In a highly competitive profession, where many athletes find themselves tempted in many unbelievable ways to be less or to do less than the Lord wants them to, Herb Adderley remained true. "A person must go back to the beginning," states Adderley, "and in the beginning was God."

There and Back. "I fully expected to die."

Chell Roberts, a Salt Lake City graduate student, was speaking for all eighty passengers aboard the Boeing 727 in April, 1980, that suddenly spun into a terrifying 27,000-foot dive near Detroit. Disaster was averted only at the last instant.

Are there lasting effects for a person placed, however briefly, on a modern equivalent of the executioner's block?

"It's made a big change in our life," says Louise Roberts, Chell's wife. "We try to get anything out of each day we can. It's made us realize what we almost didn't have."

The day after the near crash, the Robertses began a journal that they've kept up ever since—so they won't forget. And every so often, they go down to the airport and watch the planes land.

Your personal time of trial or testing may not come in as dramatic a form as Chell Roberts's, but you are being tested in your faith daily in other ways. Are you asking for Christ's help to remain true to Him?

Got What He Asked For. A little boy in the Pacific Northwest asked and asked Santa Claus for a volcano. After the eruption of Mount St. Helena in 1980, he suddenly decided he had got it.

Sometimes, in our relationship with God, we demand things for ourselves which, if they were granted, would prove destructive either to ourselves or others. Christian living means times of being tested to see whether or not our prayers are the "Gimme a volcano" type. Sometimes, we feel that the Lord and the world are against us because we don't get what we want. However, as Jesus Christ's people, we are called to ministry—just as He was called to minister to others.

Sentence Sermon to Remember: Learn to say no; it will be of more use to you than to be able to read Latin.—Charles H. Spurgeon.

Questions for Pupils on the Next Lesson. 1. What do you find hurts you the most deeply? 2. How do you handle these hurts from others? 3. Why do you have to learn to receive acceptance yourself before you can grant it to others? 4. When was the last time you felt guilty? What did you do about it? 5. How does Jesus bring forgiveness?

LESSON V—JANUARY 2

TEACHING ABOUT FORGIVENESS

Background Scripture: Luke 7:36–50
Devotional Reading: Luke 5:17–26

KING JAMES VERSION

LUKE 7 36 And one of the Pharisees desired him that he would eat with him. And he went into the Pharisee's house, and sat down to meat.

37 And, behind, a woman in the city, which was a sinner, when she knew that *Jesus* sat at meat in the Pharisee's house, brought an alabaster box of ointment,

38 And stood at his feet behind *him* weeping, and began to wash his feet with tears, and did wipe *them* with the hairs of her head, and kissed his feet, and anointed *them* with the ointment.

39 Now when the Pharisee which had bidden him saw *it,* he spake within himself, saying, This man, if he were a prophet, would have known who and what manner of woman *this is* that toucheth him; for she is a sinner.

40 And Jesus answering said unto him, Simon, I have somewhat to say unto thee. And he saith, Master, say on.

41 There was a certain creditor which had two debtors: the one owed five hundred pence, and the other fifty.

42 And when they had nothing to pay, he frankly forgave them both. Tell me therefore, which of them will love him most?

43 Simon answered and said, I suppose that *he,* to whom he forgave most. And he said unto him, Thou hast rightly judged.

44 And he turned to the woman, and said unto Simon, Seest thou this woman? I entered into thine house, thou gavest me no water for my feet: but she hath washed my feet with tears, and wiped *them* with the hairs of her head.

45 Thou gavest me no kiss: but this woman, since the time I came in, hath not ceased to kiss my feet.

46 My head with oil thou didst not anoint: but this woman hath anointed my feet with ointment.

47 Wherefore I say unto thee, Her sins, which are many, are forgiven; for she loved much: but to whom little is forgiven, *the same* loveth little.

REVISED STANDARD VERSION

LUKE 7 36 One of the Pharisees asked him to eat with him, and he went into the Pharisee's house, and took his place at table. 37 And behold, a woman of the city, who was a sinner, when she learned that he was at table in the Pharisee's house, brought an alabaster flask of ointment, 38 and standing behind him at his feet, weeping, she began to wet his feet with her tears, and wiped them with the hair of her head, and kissed his feet, and anointed them with the ointment. 39 Now when the Pharisee who had invited him saw it, he said to himself, "If this man were a prophet, he would have known who and what sort of woman this is who is touching him, for she is a sinner." 40 And Jesus answering said to him, "Simon, I have something to say to you." And he answered, "What is it, Teacher?" 41 "A certain creditor had two debtors; one owed five hundred denarii, and the other fifty. 42 When they could not pay, he forgave them both. Now which of them will love him more?" 43 Simon answered, "The one, I suppose, to whom he forgave more." And he said to him, "You have judged rightly." 44 Then turning toward the woman he said to Simon, "Do you see this woman? I entered your house, you gave me no water for my feet, but she has wet my feet with her tears and wiped them with her hair. 45 You gave me no kiss, but from the time I came in she has not ceased to kiss my feet. 46 You did not anoint my head with oil, but she has anointed my feet with ointment. 47 Therefore I tell you, her sins, which are many, are forgiven, for she loved much; but he who is forgiven little, loves little." 48 And he said to her, "Your sins are forgiven." 49 Then those who were at table with him began to say among themselves, "Who is this, who even forgives sins?" 50 And he said to the woman, "Your faith has saved you; go in peace."

KING JAMES VERSION

48 And he said unto her, Thy sins are forgiven.

49 And they that sat at meat with him began to say within themselves, Who is this that forgiveth sins also?

50 And he said to the woman, Thy faith hath saved thee; go in peace.

KEY VERSE: "Therefore I tell you, her sins, which are many, are forgiven, for she loved much; but he who is forgiven little, loves little." Luke 7:47 (RSV).

HOME DAILY BIBLE READINGS

Dec. 27. *M. The Authority of Jesus.* Luke 4:16–30.
Dec. 28. *T. His Authority Demonstrated.* Luke 4:31–37.
Dec. 29. *W. Jesus' Love for All People.* Luke 4:38–44.
Dec. 30. *T. Leaving Everything to Follow Jesus.* Luke 5:1–11.
Dec. 31. *F. Which Is Easier?* Luke 5:17–26.
Jan. 1. *S. They Found the Slave Well.* Luke 7:1–10.
Jan. 2. *S. Teaching About Forgiveness.* Luke 7:36–50.

BACKGROUND

The account of the temptations of Jesus ends with the words, "And Jesus returned in the power of the Spirit into Galilee, and a report concerning him went out . . ." (Luke 4:14). The reports were both good and bad. They were good in that the common people heard Him gladly and were wildly enthusiastic when they learned of His healings. He had healed a demoniac, and Simon's wife's mother, and a leper, and a man sick of the palsy, and He had raised the son of a widow in Nain. He had worked a miracle in healing the servant of a centurian, and another in providing a draught of fishes. These were works that demonstrated His *power.* The people loved it; the Pharisees feared it: this Jesus had done something they could not do!

But when we come to the lesson for today, we have a story and a parable that are demonstrations of His love and compassion. There is no miraculous healing here, only an account of the *love* which lies behind every miracle. Perhaps the miracle of salvation had already taken place in the woman who is the leading character in the story. However that may have been, this woman was a sinner who knew it, and some other highly respected Pharisees who were also sinners didn't know it.

NOTES ON THE PRINTED TEXT

The scene is the courtyard of the house of one Simon, a Pharisee who invited Jesus to dinner. The tables were laid out in a hollow square; the guests (fellow Pharisees) reclined around this table. They had come at Simon's invitation, to see and perhaps listen to this unorthodox rabbi (teacher) from Nazareth. Why was *Jesus* invited?

It could have been that Simon was merely curious about Jesus. Or he may have had just a hint of admiration for the humble Nazarene, but that is doubtful, for he insulted Jesus before the meal began. Courtesy, on such occasions, demanded that the host bestow upon his guest a kiss of peace, provide a basin of cool water in which the feet of the guest be cleansed of the dust of the road, and that a drop of perfume be placed on the guest's head. Simon granted this Guest no such courtesies. Simon, the great Pharisee, was a man superior to this Guest, and he had not so much invited Jesus as he had *enticed* Him, hoping that his Pharisee guests might trick Him into saying something that might convict Him of heresy. Simon was, in fact, a hypocrite who only patronised Jesus.

Now this courtyard in which the dinner was held was open to the streets beyond the walls of the house. If anyone in the street wanted to come in, they were free to do so—they could not eat, but they could listen to the words of wisdom spoken by the Pharisees. On this occasion, one came in who was truly a woman of the street: she was, to put it bluntly and sadly, a prostitute—one of the most despised in all Israel. We do not know her name. She was merely one of the great uninvited who most needed Jesus. She may have listened to Him as He spoke at that banquet, or she may have heard Him speak before that; what she heard warmed her heart strangely and gave her a hope she had never had before.

From around her neck she tore a little vial (called an alabaster) containing a precious perfume; that was the most precious material thing she had ever known, and she poured it out over His feet and then wiped His feet with her hair. She gave all she had—while the Pharisees only watched in anger.

What kind of man was this Jesus, Simon asked, to do a thing like this with such a disreputable woman as this? Consorting with a *prostitute!* He threw this additional insult to Jesus, thinking that it would surely put Him to shame. But the answer of Jesus put Simon to shame. He told Simon a little parable.

Suppose, Simon, that a man had loaned money to two other men, one of whom owed him $5,000 and the other $500, and the man forgave them their debt, and took none of their money. Which debtor would love him most for such an act of forgiveness? Simon had only one answer to that: of course, the man who owed most must have loved him most. Right, said Jesus. Now, Simon, this poor woman has done something you did not do: she washed the dust from my feet and wiped them with her hair. She had lived a life of sin, but in this act her sins have been forgiven: "Her sins, which are many, are forgiven; for she loved much: but to whom little is forgiven, the same loveth little" (verse 47).

Poor Simon must have hated that, for he was conscious of no need for Christ or for the forgiveness of God in Christ. He was not a man of love, but a man of mind—and a poor mind, at that. Jesus had come not to debate with this self-sufficient Pharisee *but to save sinners.* Simon commited the worst of sins because he had no consciousness of sin.

All of us have a little of Simon in our hearts. Only those are great and good men who know that they need forgiveness, who know that the greater the forgiveness, the greater is the love. Simon was too much like the prodigal son's brother who thought that by his own efforts he had the approval of the Father. It is faith and not works that brings salvation.

Only yesterday, we listened to a man pleading the cause of what we call "Humanism"; he held forth in fine oratory, endeavoring to prove that men had within themselves all the strength they needed to live a good life; they really had no need of God! Love, even the love of God, he said, was not *necessary;* men can and should lift themselves by their own bootstraps. We felt like asking him if he thought that Francis of Assisi was a good man; no doubt he would say *yes,* he "probably" was. Then what did Francis mean when he said, "There is nowhere a more wretched and a more miserable man than I." Francis could have gotten that from a man named Paul, who startled a sinful world when he said that without love he was nothing more than sounding brass, or a tinkling cymbal. Simon is long gone and forgotten; Paul stands like a colossus at the crossroads of history.

Every last one of us stands in need of love and forgiveness; hardly a day goes by in which we do not sin in one way or another. We shame God when we say that we love Him, and live as though He were not; too many of us pour out our lives in dependence on our own human powers; too many would never dream of pouring out the incense of love, as the gloriously penitent poured out not only the perfume in her vial but her life in love of a Savior whom Simon refused to believe.

SUGGESTIONS TO TEACHERS

As a teacher, you will be interested in seeing Jesus in action as a teacher in the scriptural material in the unit which commences today. Take note of His aims, His methods throughout these next five lessons. Most of all, remember that His teaching was a form of ministry. The same applies also to you!

Your lesson for this week centers on Jesus' teaching about forgiveness. The background Scripture describing the meal at Simon the Pharisee's house bubbles with insights into Jesus and forgiveness. Luke, who also understood good teaching techniques, vividly contrasts smug Simon with the "woman of the city . . . a sinner" (7:37) who anoints Jesus out of gratitude for being forgiven. Story-telling still stands as a successful teacher's tool. Let the story of Jesus, Simon, and the woman do your teaching for you.

1. *INVITATION.* As the story unfolds, describe Simon. Let your class find the many similarities between Simon and church people like themselves. Have your class also remark about the way Simon invited Jesus to his house but did not show much hospitality. What are situations in our lives in which we fail to show the Lord much of a warm welcome, in spite of our invitations?

2. *INTERRUPTION.* Urge your class to exercise their imaginations in picturing how upsetting it must have been to have had the woman intrude on the dinner party. Have your people consider the reasons behind her lavish expression of gratitude. In addition, comment on how opportunities often present themselves as interruptions. In fact, some of your most effective teaching may be done in the course of an interruption. Jesus certainly used this intrusion as an occasion to teach about forgiveness. How do you and your class use your interruptions?

3. *INTERPRETATION.* Jesus clarifies, as usual. He points out to Simon and the other guests the lavishness of love. Teacher Jesus also tells a story to get the point across. In your class, budget the greatest amount of time today for discussing that story, the parable of the two debtors. Make sure

that your people grasp how hopelessly in debt the 500 denarii offender was and how hopelessly dependent upon God's mercy each of us is.

4. *IMPLICATIONS.* "He who is forgiven little, loves little" (7:47) and *vice-versa.* No one can measure love, of course, but one can be certain that love calls for a response. Remind your class that if a person has been personally aware of divine mercy, he or she will *have* to show some care to others! God's care implies our caring out of gratitude. Furthermore, this passage in Luke implies God's mercy is conveyed most completely and most clearly to us through Jesus Christ. Have your class talk over the grumbling, behind-the-hand remarks by the Pharisees to one another about Jesus, "Who is this, who even forgives sins?" (7:29). Put the same question to your people. "Who is this . . . ?"

TOPIC FOR ADULTS
TEACHING ABOUT FORGIVENESS

Onion Parable. One of the most revealing parables of Jesus' requirement of mercy toward others outside of the New Testament is Dostoyevsky's story of the onion as told by the motherly Grushenka in *The Brothers Karamazov:*

"Once upon a time there was a peasant woman and a very wicked woman she was. And she died and did not leave a single good deed behind. The devils caught her and plunged her into the lake of fire. So her guardian angel stood and wondered what good deed of hers he could remember to tell to God: 'She once pulled up an onion in her garden,' said he, 'and gave it to a beggar woman.' And God answered: 'You take that onion then, hold it out to her in the lake, and let her take hold and be pulled out. And if you can pull her out of the lake, let her come to Paradise, but if the onion breaks, then the woman must stay where she is.' The angel ran to the woman and held out the onion to her; 'Come,' said he, 'catch hold and I'll pull you out.' And he began cautiously pulling her out. He had just pulled her right out, when the others sinners in the lake, seeing how she was being drawn out, began catching hold of her so as to be pulled out with her. But she was a very wicked woman and she began kicking them. 'I'm to be pulled out, not you. It's my onion, not yours.' As soon as she said that, the onion broke. And the woman fell into the lake and . . . the angel wept and went away."

Unforgiving Person Predisposed to Illness. "Drs. O. Carl Simonton and Stephanie Matthews-Simonton argue that there is a cancer-prone personality, that a certain combination of traits makes some people especially vulnerable to cancer. Simonton listed these characteristics in a 1975 article: 'First, a great tendency to hold resentment and marked inability to forgive; second, a tendency toward self-pity; third, a poor ability to develop and maintain meaningful long-term relationships; and fourth, a very poor self-image.' These qualities, Simonton proposes, make it difficult for a person to deal with emotions at a conscious level, to acknowledge negative feelings and then deal with them.

" 'The biggest single factor that I can find as a predisposing factor to the actual development of the disease,' Simonton wrote, 'is the loss of a serious love object, occurring 6 months to 18 months prior to the diagnosis.' Another emotional reverse that can precipitate cancer, he says, is the loss of a significant life role, perhaps through the death of a spouse or as a result of getting fired. The potential patient responds to the loss, whatever it is, with profound feelings of helplessness and hopelessness. But these feelings are not acknowledged inwardly or expressed to others; the cancer-prone patient puts on a happy face and denies any sense of loss, anger, distress, disappointment, or despair.

"But the feelings, which the Simontons term 'negative emotions,' are there just the same and are eventually given somatic expression. Malignancy is thus despair that has been experienced biologically, despair at the level of the cell."—Maggie Scarf, *Psychology Today.*

Mirrors With Love. The Elephant Man has been a well-received play recently on Broadway. It is based on events in the life of a hideously deformed man and the sensitivity of his friend. The real-life "elephant man" was a person with a huge, malformed head with what seemed to be the crude beginnings of a trunk and tusks protruding from his face. A distinguished surgeon, Sir Frederick Treaves, discovered this horrible-looking creature in a carnival sideshow. Dr. Treaves took the man from the carnival and gave him the best of medical care and personal kindness for the remainder of the "elephant man's" brief life. One of the rules which Dr. Treaves insisted upon, however, was that no mirrors were permitted anywhere in the house. He would not let the malformed man look at himself, saying, "He must not endure the agony of seeing himself as he is."

Commendable as Dr. Treaves' motives were, he was forcing the unfortunate victim to live a pretense. Jesus Christ, on the other hand, allows us to see ourselves as we really are. He comes with a mirror, so to speak, permitting us to see all the ugliness in our lives for what it is, *yet accepting us*—in spite of the hideousness of our sin, in spite of the ways we have defaced God's image within us. Jesus Christ assures us that we are loved! We can "look in the mirror" to see ourselves for what we really are, and we can also rest in the certainty of divine mercy. This, in turn, means we can forgive others in spite of the ugliness in their characters.

Questions for Pupils on the Next Lesson. 1. Do you ever feel affirmed and encouraged by those in your church? 2. How does your class help others in your church who may be experiencing doubts, fears, hurts, sorrows, and injustice? 3. Why do you grow when you engage in helpful acts? 4. What is the relationship between neighbor-love and self-love? 5. Why did Jesus' parable of the Good Samaritan upset so many of His hearers?

TOPIC FOR YOUTH
THANKFUL FOR FORGIVENESS

Words Stuck in His Throat. When Charles Peguy, the great French writer, published his masterpiece on Joan of Arc, critics cruelly panned both the poem and Peguy. Charles Peguy was deeply hurt. He also found himself deeply angry toward his critics. Retreating within himself, the sensitive poet could not bring himself to forgive his reviewers for their harsh words about him or his *Joan.* Much later, Peguy described his rage in a letter to a friend. "Would you believe it," he wrote, "that for eighteen months I could not say 'Our Father . . . Thy Will be done'? It was quite impossible to say. I could not accept His will. It was even more impossible for me to pray, 'Forgive us . . .' " The words, Charles Peguy reported, "would have stuck in my throat."

Without forgiving others, any requests for God's forgiveness seem to stick in our throats instead of reaching the Lord. Jesus' teaching about forgiveness are unmistakeable: we may receive forgiveness only as we extend it!

Your Religion Is Showing. Some little Girl Scouts were on a cookout. As their leader, a devout Roman Catholic, leaned over the fire, a religious medal on a chain around her neck slipped from behind her blouse and dangled in front of her. Noticing the medal suddenly prominently suspended in front of the leader, one little girl exclaimed, "Oh, Mrs. Halberson, your religion is showing!"

Your religion shows most, however, when you forgive. You show that you are Christ's. You share His mercy.

Is your religion showing?

Missing the Mark. The word *sin* in Greek means literally "missing the mark," and we often miss the mark. Sometimes, we try to excuse ourselves instead of being thankful for forgiveness. We are like the golfer who was having a bad day on the famed Monte Carlo course. Not one of the shots were right. At the eighteenth hole, he made a last swipe at the ball, missed completely, and tore up about a yard of turf. He strolled disgustedly from the tee and looked down at the blue Mediterranean, hundreds of feet below. Several sailboats were gliding lazily about, "How can anyone be expected to shoot a decent game," demanded the golfer passionately, "with those infernal ships rushing back and forth."

The Good News of Jesus Christ is that we don't have to blame something or someone else for missing the mark. We can accept ourselves because He accepts us—excuses and all!

Sentence Sermon to Remember: A Christian will find it cheaper to pardon than to resent. Forgiveness saves the expense of anger, the cost of hatred, the waste of spirits.—Hannah Moore.

Questions for Pupils on the Next Lesson. 1. Who are the most caring people you know? 2. Who are those toward whom it is the hardest for you to show compassion? Why? 3. How can your church help you and others to show compassion toward those who are of different racial or cultural backgrounds? 4. Why is it sometimes hard for people to accept themselves? 5. How would you retell the story of the Good Samaritan in today's world?

LESSON VI—JANUARY 9

TEACHING ABOUT COMPASSION

Background Scripture: Luke 7:11–23; 10:25–37
Devotional Reading: Luke 6:6–11

KING JAMES VERSION

LUKE 10 25 And, behold, a certain lawyer stood up, and tempted him, saying, Master, what shall I do to inherit eternal life?

26 He said unto him, What is written in the law? how readest thou?

27 And he answering said, Thou shalt love the Lord thy God with all thy heart, and with all thy soul, and with all thy strength, and with all thy mind; and thy neighbour as thyself.

28 And he said unto him, Thou hast answered right: this do, and thou shalt live.

29 But he, willing to justify himself, said unto Jesus, And who is my neighbour?

30 And Jesus answering said, A certain *man* went down from Jerusalem to Jericho, and fell among thieves, which stripped him of his raiment, and wounded *him*, and departed, leaving *him* half dead.

31 And by chance there came down a certain priest that way; and when he saw him, he passed by on the other side.

32 And likewise a Levite, when he was at the place, came and looked *on him*, and passed by on the other side.

33 But a certain Samaritan, as he journeyed, came where he was; and when he saw him, he had compassion *on him*,

34 And went to *him*, and bound up his wounds, pouring in oil and wine, and set him on his own beast, and brought him to an inn, and took care of him.

35 And on the morrow when he departed, he took out two pence, and gave *them* to the host, and said unto him, Take care of him: and whatsoever thou spendest more, when I come again, I will repay thee.

36 Which now of these three, thinkest thou, was neighbour unto him that fell among the thieves?

37 And he said, He that shewed mercy on him. Then said Jesus unto him, Go, and do thou likewise.

REVISED STANDARD VERSION

LUKE 10 25 And behold, a lawyer stood up to put him to the test, saying, "Teacher, what shall I do to inherit eternal life?" 26 He said to him, "What is written in the law? How do you read?" 27 And he answered, "You shall love the Lord your God with all your heart, and with all your soul, and with all your strength, and with all your mind; and your neighbor as yourself." 28 And he said to him, "You have answered right; do this, and you will live."

29 But he, desiring to justify himself, said to Jesus, "And who is my neighbor?" 30 Jesus replied, "A man was going down from Jerusalem to Jericho, and he fell among robbers, who stripped him and beat him, and departed, leaving him half dead. 31 Now by chance a priest was going down that road; and when he saw him he passed by on the other side. 32 So likewise a Levite, when he came to the place and saw him, passed by on the other side. 33 But a Samaritan, as he journeyed, came to where he was; and when he saw him, he had compassion, 34 and went to him and bound up his wounds, pouring on oil and wine; then he set him on his own beast and brought him to an inn, and took care of him. 35 And the next day he took out two denarii and gave them to the innkeeper, saying, 'Take care of him; and whatever more you spend, I will repay you when I come back.' 36 Which of these three, do you think, proved neighbor to the man who fell among the robbers?" 37 He said, "The one who showed mercy on him." And Jesus said to him, "Go and do likewise."

KEY VERSE: . . . "You shall love the Lord your God with all your heart, and with all your soul, and with all your strength, and with all your mind; and your neighbor as yourself." Luke 10:27 (RSV).

HOME DAILY BIBLE READINGS

Jan. 3. *M.* *A Demonstration of Compassion.* Luke 7:11–17.
Jan. 4. *T.* *From Bondage to Freedom.* Luke 8:26–39.
Jan. 5. *W.* *A Plea for Help.* Luke 8:40–42a; 49–56.
Jan. 6. *T.* *Jesus' Response to Faith.* Luke 8:42b–48.
Jan. 7. *F.* *Because He Cared.* Luke 9:1–6.
Jan. 8. *S.* *Feeding the Hungry.* Luke 9:10–17.
Jan. 9. *S.* *Who Is My Neighbor?* Luke 10:25–37.

BACKGROUND

When a scribe spoke in the Jerusalem of New Testament days, the people listened for a scribe was a man of great accomplishment and respect. The scribes were actually ecclesiastical lawyers or scholars who defended the Law and the ancient traditions laid down under the Law. They interpreted the Law that had come down from Moses, and generally their interpretations were accepted. They were not priests, though they often worked in conjunction with the priests; they were laymen, trained from the time they were thirteen until they were thirty years of age. They spoke with authority, and they did not like to be challenged when they interpreted. As time passed, the "words of the scribes came to be honored above the Law."

Jesus spoke often of the scribes, usually in denouncement along with the Pharisees; the scribes opposed Him from the start, for the simple reason that He challenged their authority and threatened their prestige. It seems too bad that it was "the most respectable people" who were the most opposed to Jesus, and who brought about His Crucifixion, but that was the way it was.

In today's lesson, a sly and crafty little scribe challenged Jesus not to learn of the truth, but to get Him to say something for which He might be arrested.

NOTES ON THE PRINTED TEXT

Luke (who is the only one of the Gospel writers to tell the story) says that the man was a lawyer; he did not call him a scribe, for scribes were Jewish and a part of Jewish life and belief; he called the man a lawyer because the Gentiles he was seeking to win would understand that term, *lawyer.* So both Jews and Gentiles (Samaritans) would know what this questioner of Jesus was, that he was an expert in interpreting the Law—or in confusing people with involved explanations of what the Law was about.

What, he asked Jesus, should a man do to inherit eternal life? He might have asked, "What does a man *have* to do in order to be *respectable?*" What did he have to do to be a *good* man, to live a life that God would like him to live? That was a tough question; the old rabbis debated it and often came up with rather poor answers.

But Jesus was ready for it. He said, in effect, "Sir, you are a lawyer. You know what the Law says. You plead with the people to obey the precedents of the Law. Now *you* tell *me:* what must we do to win the acceptance and the love of God according to Moses?"

The clever little lawyer had only one answer for that, and he knew it. "Thou shalt love the Lord thy God with all thy heart, and with all thy soul, and with all thy strength, and with all thy mind . . . *and thy neighbor as thyself*" (Luke 10:27).

It must have stung the lawyer to admit that. Lawyers are sticklers for the thing called *precedence:* if they can point back in the old law books to a rule laid down in a case similar to the one they are trying, *that* old law was to be obeyed. If they can only find a precedent, then "that's it," that settles everything! Jesus congratulated the lawyer; he had answered well—but the answer wasn't enough to satisfy *this* lawyer. He didn't like it when Jesus told him to obey this Old Testament Law, to love his God *and his neighbor* in order to follow this holy precept, and he would find eternal life.

So the lawyer quibbled. Some lawyers love quibbling; if they can only confuse a witness with endless, *confusing* questions, they just might win their case! So . . . "But who *is* my neighbor?" asked the quibbling lawyer. It was like hearing some lawyer in a case involving obscenity asking, "But what *is* obscenity"—and they quarrel for days over a definition that satisfies nobody!

To avoid that nonsense, Jesus replies to the "neighbor" question with one of the most dramatic parables in the New Testament; he tells the story of the Good Samaritan. Read it in Luke 10:30–35; it is too well-known to be repeated here in full; we need only look at the four characters in the story.

First, there was the man fallen among thieves on the road between Jerusalem and Jericho. In a way, this man was a fool to travel that road *alone.* It was infested with thieves; St. Jerome says it was called "The Red and Bloody Way." No man with any sense would travel it alone. But this man did. Thieves pounced on him, robbed him, left him for dead.

Second, there was the priest who came along just after it happened. This priest took one look at the man bleeding in the ditch and hurried off down the road. Maybe he was thinking of the rule (laid down in Numbers 19:11) that anyone who touched a dead body was unclean for seven days. He had work to do; he couldn't lose seven days! Besides, he just may have not wanted to become "involved"—like people who rush past an automobile accident because it's just none of their business, and they don't want to go to court "about another man's problems." (Some in our day have even witnessed murders and run away to avoid involvement.)

Then came a Levite. He ran from the scene, too; this man in the ditch might be a decoy, "playing dead" to lure anyone wanting to help him into the hands of the thieves. Safety first! Besides, he had ceremonial duties to perform in the temple; he couldn't be late in arriving at the temple.

Then—thank God—came a lowly, despised Samaritan, a man loathed and hated by every Jew (priest, Levite, or common man), a heretic, a breaker of the Jewish Law. Heretic he might have been, but he loved his God *and his neighbor.* He may have had an outlawed creed, but he had shoulders strong enough to pick up the blood-smeared man from the ditch and carry him to an inn and take care of him, paying the innkeeper for any expenses involved. Unorthodox, yes; beloved of God for his merciful act, yes.

The lesson is as clear as crystal. When Jesus forced this precedent-haunted lawyer to admit that the Samaritan was the good neighbor in this story, He was telling us that Christian compassion and not men's creeds is the standard by which we will be judged as good neighbors or good Christians. Hate your neighbor and lose the Kingdom. Love a neighbor who is in need and you are loved of Christ—which means eternal life. Pass him by and you will never know the mercy of God.

Long, long before Christ came, the Jews were cautioned to love their neighbors as they loved themselves (*see* Leviticus 18:19). But to the Jew that meant that he should love his *Jewish* neighbor! Jesus made no distinctions between races or nations: He taught that any man or nation who is in need is our neighbor, and our love of all men and all nations must be as wide and deep as the love of God, or it is a sham and a farce.

Yes, that is "hard to take," but we must take it—must accept it or we are of no use to Him. He left us no choice. When he left the little haggling lawyer who admitted that love of one's neighbor was one key to the Kingdom, He ordered him to "Go and do likewise."

No, He ordered *us*. We can take or leave it, but there it stands, and will stand.

SUGGESTIONS TO TEACHERS

Teaching about compassion, at first glance, seems almost like talking about motherhood and apple pie. Remember, however, that you and your class do not live in a compassionate world. In fact, it might help get you prepared for this week's lesson by recalling the instances where compassion was lacking in your recent daily experience. A few minutes with the newspaper will quickly confirm that compassion is a commodity in short supply these days.

1. *WHAT DO YOU MEAN?* You and your class need models of compassion. Jesus offers the best and the most. For starters, work with the episode where He raised the only son of the widow of Nain. Remember that Jesus is not trying to startle viewers with a dramatic stunt. This miracle is intended to exemplify the compassion He has toward all. In this case, Jesus has compassion toward a nameless, helpless woman whose sole means of support has been taken from her. The raising of her son is compassion in action. This miracle is, like all Jesus' miracles, an enactment of His teaching on compassion. Help your class to use this story as a way of comprehending what compassion is.

2. *WHERE HAVE YOU KNOWN?* Focus on the question by John the Baptist's followers to Jesus: "Are you the one, or should we look for another?" Note Jesus' answer in which He instructs them to go and tell what they have heard and seen. Jesus is the source of compassion. All of His actions communicate a profound caring toward ones others do not care about. Furthermore, the world around us will appreciate Jesus' compassion only as we put it into action.

3. *WHO IS MY NEIGHBOR?* Allow lots of time to go over the interview between Jesus and the lawyer. You may want to have your class appreciate the evasions of the lawyer by doing some impromptu role-playing or informal *ad hoc* drama in which the lawyer's ideas are spelled out in the contemporary world. Or, have your class members offer examples of self-justification from their experiences, paralleling the lawyer's attempt to justify himself as a compassionate person.

4. *HOW DO I ACT?* Devote plenty of time on the parable of the Good

Samaritan. Bring out the nuances of meaning in the story, such as making a despised Samaritan the hero, the example of a compassionate person. Most of all, concentrate on how compassion is more than feeling. It is doing for your neighbor. "And who is my neighbor?" everyone, like the lawyer, asks. Jesus makes it clear that "neighbor" means *anyone* in need. Compassion is to be shown to anyone, regardless. Let your class suggest examples of forgotten "neighbors" toward whom compassion is to be directed.

TOPIC FOR ADULTS
TEACHING ABOUT COMPASSION

More Than Feelings. In the days of Russian nobility, a Czar's Empress was driven through the subzero cold of St. Petersburg from her warm palace to a comfortable theater to watch a play. The Empress haughtily demanded that the coachman remain in his place, exposed to the cold winds, during the performance so that she would be able to be returned without delay to her palace after the final curtain. The Empress, wrapped in her luxurious furs, swept inside to the royal box, where heating arrangements provided cozy warmth. The play had a sentimental plot, and the Empress wept copiously out of pity for the fictitious characters. Still dabbing at her eyes, she was escorted out to her carriage at the close of the play. As directed, the carriage stood at the door of the theater with the coachman slumped on the seat, holding the reins to the shivering horses. When she ordered the coachman to drive on, there was no response. He had frozen to death while she had shed tears of compassion for the heroine of a play.

Compassion is more than sentiment, more than feelings, more than a few tears. Christ's kind of compassion is remembering the coachman in the cold; it is *doing!*

A Century of Compassion. "If anyone called Lyda Thomas, now in her 100th year, a 'healing presence,' she would undoubtedly wrinkle her face and burst into laughter, a staple of her life.

"But ask the cancer patient, being shielded from hospital visitors, who heard Lyda's voice in the corridor.

" 'Lyda Thomas?' she quavered. 'Let her in. I must see her!'

"Or the epileptic, recently admitted to a rest home, where Lyda visited. She swung Lyda, all 90 pounds of her, off her feet, hugged her and said, 'You'll never know how glad I am to see you!'

" 'Visiting the ill or friendless is no burden to me,' she says. 'It makes me feel alive and fresh.'

"For the past six years Lyda, who has been a widow for more than 30 years, has lived in an apartment in a niece's home in Shaker Heights, Ohio. She keeps her own rooms tidy and insists on sharing the cooking chores.

"Her sweet rolls, cookies, and fancy breads go with her on visits to shut-ins. Her oven's wares were probably most appreciated by patients in a state hospital which she began visiting in 1928, when a relative was confined there. She was dismayed to learn that some patients had no visitors at all.

" 'Their families did not come,' Lyda says, 'They had been shut up and put away to be forgotten, like pieces of old furniture.'

"Lyda went into action. She baked birthday cakes for 'her' patients, some of whom were as young as 14. She brought them magazines and gathered clothing for them from fellow church members.

"When many mental patients were transferred from the hospital to nursing homes, Lyda followed up on her 15 adopted 'children.'

"Even at age 90 she drove to nursing homes in crime-plagued neighborhoods, and once had her car's back seat and trunk cleared of clothing and gifts while she was visiting a patient.

" 'I simply went home for more,' she recalls.

"Lyda was an early patient 'activist,' arguing with nursing home administrators for better treatment of patients. In 1965 the Cleveland Press honored her humanitarianism by naming her an 'Alias Santa Claus.'

"But Lyda Thomas describes the life-style she has followed for nearly a century this way: 'As long as my mind and my body hold out, I'm going to live as I do now—doing all I can for others.' "—Marie Boehringer, *A.D.*, March 1980.

Why We Remember. What do you think of when you hear the names Drew, Vanderbilt, and Stanford? Universities, right? Significantly, each of these great institutions were made possible by multimillionaires who left generous bequests out of compassion for young people who had no opportunities for learning. Few persons remember much about Drew or Vanderbilt or Stanford themselves. Drew himself could barely read, and Vanderbilt and Stanford wouldn't.

Perhaps it is a lesson for us. Not many will remember much about any of us except for the ways we translated our Christian compassion into deeds for others.

Questions for Pupils on the Next Lesson. 1. Why are we so prone to think that we find ultimate security, happiness, and meaning in our possessions? 2. How can you avoid putting all your energies on making a living to the neglect of personal relationships? 3. How can we in our culture best exercise responsibility for the have-nots in the world? 4. Who or what is actually in charge of your life? 5. What are Jesus' warnings about covetousness?

TOPIC FOR YOUTH
CARE FOR OTHERS

Unimportant Obstacle. "Count Alfred von Schlieffen, Chief of the German General Staff from 1891 to 1906, was, like all German officers, schooled in Clausewitz's precept, 'The heart of France lies between Brussels and Paris.' It was a frustrating axiom because the path it pointed to was forbidden by Belgian neutrality, which Germany, along with the other four major European powers, had guaranteed in perpetuity. Believing that war was a certainty and that Germany must enter it under conditions that gave her the most promise of success, Schlieffen determined not to allow the Belgian difficulty to stand in Germany's way. Of the two classes of Prussian officer, the bullnecked and the wasp-waisted, he belonged to the second. Monocled and effete in appearance, cold and distant in manner, he concentrated with such singlemindedness on his profession that when an aide, at the end of an all-night staff ride in East Prussia, pointed out to him the beauty of the river Pregel sparkling in the rising sun, the General gave a brief, hard look and replied, 'An unimportant obstacle.' So, too, he decided, was Belgian neutrality."—From *The Guns of August* by Barbara Tuchman.

Care for Others. In Chiang Mai, Thailand, when a mother died in childbirth, the people were afraid of the spirit of the dead mother, so they would take the baby out in a field and simply let it die of exposure. The McCormick Christian Hospital people said, "Bring these children to us." And, the Thais, trusting that the power of the Christian God was as great as the power of the dead mother's spirit, brought those children, who then had a chance to survive. That is the difference the Christian faith can make in releasing captives of fear and superstition and death.

More Than Charity. "A socially prominent woman of Boston went one day to see a poor widow who at one time performed some domestic service in her home, but who now was seriously ill. The caller was shocked at the evidences of poverty apparent on all sides, and she said, 'I will ask a charitable organization to come and help you.'

"But the woman said, 'Thank you, ma'am! Although I am poor I cannot take charity.'

" 'But,' said the rich woman, 'you have just told me that your neighbors have been helping you. You take things from them.'

" 'Yes,' she answered, 'but that is not charity. They are my friends. They love me and care for me. They know that if they needed help I would do the same for them.' Gifts from a loving heart are welcome; from a cold heart they mean nothing."—From the Sunday School Times.

Sentence Sermon to Remember: To pity distress is but human; to relieve it is Godlike.—Horace Mann.

Questions for Pupils on the Next Lesson. 1. What are examples of how our culture places such heavy emphasis on material possessions? 2. How would you describe your personal struggle with dependence and independence? 2. What is the difference between making a life and making a living? 4. Why do we sometimes imagine that security, happiness, and meaning are to be found in possessions? 5. Who or what do you think is in charge of your life?

LESSON VII—JANUARY 16

TEACHING ABOUT PRIORITIES

Background Scripture: Luke 12:13–40
Devotional Reading: Luke 6:46–49

KING JAMES VERSION

LUKE 12 13 And one of the company said unto him, Master, speak to my brother, that he divide the inheritance with me.

14 And he said unto him, Man, who made me a judge or a divider over you?

15 And he said unto them, Take heed, and beware of covetousness: for a man's life consisteth not in the abundance of the things which he possesseth.

16 And he spake a parable unto them, saying, The ground of a certain rich man brought forth plentifully:

17 And he thought within himself, saying, What shall I do, because I have no room where to bestow my fruits?

18 And he said, This will I do: I will pull down my barns, and build greater; and there will I bestow all my fruits and my goods.

19 And I will say to my soul, Soul, thou hast much goods laid up for many years; take thine ease, eat, drink, *and* be merry.

20 But God said unto him, *Thou* fool, this night thy soul shall be required of thee: then whose shall those things be, which thou hast provided?

21 So *is* he that layeth up treasure for himself, and is not rich toward God.

35 Let your loins be girded about, and *your* lights burning;

36 And ye yourselves like unto men that wait for their lord, when he will return from the wedding; that when he cometh and knocketh, they may open unto him immediately.

37 Blessed *are* those servants, whom the lord when he cometh shall find watching: verily I say unto you, that he shall gird himself, and make them to sit down to meat, and will come forth and serve them.

38 And if he shall come in the second watch, or come in the third watch, and find *them* so, blessed are those servants.

39 And this know, that if the goodman of the house had known what hour the thief would come, he would have watched, and not have suffered his house to be broken through.

REVISED STANDARD VERSION

LUKE 12 13 One of the multitude said to him, "Teacher, bid my brother divide the inheritance with me." 14 But he said to him, "Man, who made me a judge or divider over you?" 15 And he said to them, "Take heed, and beware of all covetousness; for a man's life does not consist in the abundance of his possessions." 16 And he told them a parable, saying, "The land of a rich man brought forth plentifully; 17 and he thought to himself, 'What shall I do, for I have nowhere to store my crops?' 18 And he said, 'I will do this: I will pull down my barns, and build larger ones; and there I will store all my grain and my goods. 19 And I will say to my soul, Soul, you have ample goods laid up for many years; take your ease, eat, drink, be merry.' 20 But God said to him, 'Fool! This night your soul is required to you; and the things you have prepared, whose will they be?' 21 So is he who lays up treasure for himself, and is not rich toward God."

35 "Let your loins be girded and your lamps burning, 36 and be like men who are waiting for their master to come home from the marriage feast, so that they may open to him at once when he comes and knocks. 37 Blessed are those servants whom the master finds awake when he comes; truly, I say to you, he will gird himself and have them sit at table, and he will come and serve them. 38 If he comes in the second watch, or in the third, and finds them so, blessed are those servants! 39 But know this, that if the householder had known at what hour the thief was coming, he would have been awake and would not have left his house to be broken into. 40 You also must be ready; for the Son of man is coming at an unexpected hour."

40 Be ye therefore ready also: for the Son of man cometh at an hour when ye think not.

KEY VERSE: "You also must be ready; for the Son of man is coming at an unexpected hour." Luke 12:40 (RSV).

HOME DAILY BIBLE READINGS

Jan. 10. M. Concerned About Things. Luke 10:38–42.
Jan. 11. T. God's Supply. Luke 11:1–13.
Jan. 12. W. A Test of Genuineness. Luke 11:37–44.
Jan. 13. T. Determining Priorities. Luke 12:1–12.
Jan. 14. F. Full Barn and Empty Life. Luke 12:13–21.
Jan. 15. S. Seek God's Kingdom First. Luke 12:22–31.
Jan. 16. S. Expecting His Return. Luke 12:32–40.

BACKGROUND

Great evangelists preach to great crowds once their popularity is established. That happened to Jesus; Luke tells us of one occasion "when there were gathered together an innumerable multitude of people, insomuch that they trode one upon another . . ." (Luke 12:1). He was surrounded by people so anxious to see Him and hear Him that almost in panic they *crushed* each other. They were often more of a mob than a multitude: this famous spellbinding, wonderworking Man from Nazareth had something that these people wanted. Some wanted healing from sickness; some had tempests in their hearts that they wanted stilled; some had demons they wanted to be driven out. Some came out of sheer curiosity and nothing else. And some came to ask questions.

It would be interesting to make a comprehensive study of the people who came to ask Him questions. What kind of people *were* they? Rich or poor, intelligent or ignorant, respectable or rascals, sincere or hypocrites? And why did Jesus take time out to answer the questions they asked, whatever they were?

Very often, the questioners were men of intelligence, highly placed, respected as leaders like the Pharisees or the rich young ruler. Others were poor in great need both physically and spiritually. In our lesson for today, we have one who was a fool.

NOTES ON THE PRINTED TEXT

Some say that there are only two kinds of people in the world: those who have, and those who have not. The rich and the poor. That isn't quite true, for there are many who are neither rich nor poor, but somewhere in between. But it is true that those who have not always want to have more of this world's goods, and they spend the best part of their lives trying to get more, more, more, and they are unahppy until they get it—and sometimes they are unhappy *when* they get it! One such man fought his way through a crowd around Jesus and asked Him to speak to his brother who was cheating him out of an inheritance. What a demand to make on One who was the very Son of God! What a question to put to the Messiah: "Will you come and speak to my brother, and help me to get my share of the inheritance money?" Jesus seems angry as He tells the selfish little fool that He is not a divider of inheritances, no justice of the people elected to settle petty problems.

We all do it, even yet. We ask God to help us make money, to succeed in business, to get a good mark on an examination, to win a ball game, to do a lot of trivial things which we are quite able to do for and by ourselves. Let our prayers, our requests of God, at least be intelligent and not selfish; God has greater things to do, and He has no time for trifles craved by those who scarcely know Him!

Jesus was not mad; gently, He tells another parable to illustrate what He means by His reply to the man who was interested only in money. He tells of a man who is already rich, already possessed of barns crammed full with all the food he would ever need, a man, with no material needs, struggling to get his hands on more, more, more material things. The man tears down his barns and builds bigger ones, and he gloats about his "security." "And I will say to my soul, Soul, thou hast much goods laid up for many years; take thine ease, eat, drink, and be merry" (verse 19).

His *soul?* This man—whom Jesus called a fool—spoke in infamous ignorance; he did not know the meaning of the word *soul,* and does not appear to even know that he *had* a soul! All he was interested in was his stomach. All he wanted was bigger and better barns. The only one he was interested in was himself; all he wanted to achieve was more possessions as his own, not as gifts from God—*my* barns, *my* goods, *my* soul! Me first, and the rest afterwards. "ME," said someone, "is at the bottom of all sin. One little word, *ME.* It may spell lust, pride, covetousness, self-will, but it is some form of *Me.*"

This man, said Jesus, was a fool. Didn't he know that he might die tomorrow and leave all his overstuffed barns to rot in the sun? Didn't he know that "You can't take it with you?" Couldn't he see that death could separate him from mere *things,* and that a person is rich only when he lives in fellowship with God? You fool! This very night your soul may be required of you; what good are your barns then?

It happens. We once had a fine young friend who slaved night and day for ten years to make a quick fortune and then died at twenty-nine of a heart attack. (His father, who never made a really good salary, is still alive and incredibly happy serving meals to broken and forgotten men on Skid Row and living among them.)

Charles H. Spurgeon said, in one of his famous sermons, "You can use the wealth of this world in the service of the Master. To gain is not wrong. It is wrong only when grasping becomes the main object of life."

Verses 35–48, in Luke 12, are a bit confusing at first glance. The underlying message here may refer to the Second Coming of Christ, or it may refer to the moment when God enters into the life of a man. Either way, these verses cry out with a clear "Be ready for it!" Prepare for it by way of service to God and not to Mammon—not to "the almighty dollar." Be ready for His coming for you will never know exactly *when* He will come. (Many well-meaning Christians have tried to figure out the exact date, but in every instance, they have failed; this is an exercise in futility.) Blessed are those who are ready to greet Him, when He comes into fellowship with them. Their blessedness (and this is an amazing statement) will be found *in their sitting at table and being served by their*

Master. (Now read Luke 22:27, and you will get the whole picture.)

"In the Franklin County Courthouse in Virginia is preserved the will of the man who owned Booker T. Washington. Since most of his property was in slaves, the owner had listed them and set down the price of each one. Opposite the name of Booker Washington he had marked $200. Was this a fair estimate of that youngster's worth? Hardly, for he turned out to be one of America's great men and an educator who inspired his people to seek knowledge. But the plantation owner could not see the essential worth of a black slave. Too often we are in the same position, misled by appearances and blind to unseen value. Like the Rich Fool, we build the big barns and neglect the essentials."—Gerald Kennedy in *The Parables,* by permission of Harper & Rowe, publishers.

SUGGESTIONS TO TEACHERS

Dr. R. Alec Mackenzie, the eminent management consultant, writes extensively and conducts seminars to help business leaders set proper priorities. Dr. Mackenzie discusses how much of most person's time and energies are wasted attending to trivial matters or responding to the urgent rather than the important issues. In one recent training session of forty business leaders, after seeing a film and hearing Dr. Mackenzie's presentations, the persons present listed their own "management sins." The following led the list: Attempting too much at once; Procrastinating. They obviously realized their need for priorities.

Jesus, more than any management consultant, can teach us about priorities. Your lesson will have great practical value for everyone in your class if you heed His words closely.

1. *PERSPECTIVE ON POSSESSIONS.* You could spend the entire lesson period on dealing with Jesus' comments on covetousness and His parable on the rich man (12:13–21). In our consumer society, your people sometimes find it hard to sort out what comes first. A person seems to be measured by what he/she gets or owns. Behind much of the advertising is an appeal to greed. Help your people to examine their priorities regarding possessions and wealth. Point out the name which Jesus laid on the man in the parable: "Fool." Also make clear to your students how the hour eventually comes when everyone must surrender all he/she has. As the Spanish proverb puts it, "There are no pockets in a shroud." Therefore, set priorities now.

2. *PROVISIONS FOR PRESSURES.* Examine with your class Jesus' comments about anxiety and what to seek (12:22–32). It may be helpful to have your people write down the three or four main fears which nag at them. Let them talk over how these sometimes put pressures on their time and energies, and sometimes paralyze action. How do Jesus' teachings in this passage help believers deal with anxieties in their lives?

3. *PLEASURE IN TREASURE.* Your class may have to struggle a bit with "Where your treasure is, there will your heart be also" and Jesus' words on giving to others (12:32–34). Few of them will readily see that sharing sacrificially with others builds up "treasure in the heavens." Jesus' perceptions are always absolutely correct: a person's "heart"—real interests and deepest commitments—will be where his or her treasure is.

And the only permanent treasure is that spiritual wealth accrued through Christlike giving.

4. *PREPARATION FOR THE UNEXPECTED.* Plan your lesson so that you don't skip over Luke 12:35–40 in which Jesus calls His followers to be alert and prepared. The inevitable and unknown time of reckoning comes unexpectedly to everyone. Help your class to understand what it is to be "ready for Christ's coming" each day in life.

TOPIC FOR ADULTS
TEACHING ABOUT PRIORITIES

Priorities on the Altar. "You would consider it sacrilege of the lowest form, if in place of the cross, you found on the altar a bottle of Chanel No. 5, a carton of Lucky Strikes or a box of fine Havana cigars, a Haig and Haig Pinch bottle, or a pair of tickets for box seats at the latest Broadway play. You would rise up in wrathful denunciation of the agnostic who had the gall to put them there; and yet, I say to you, that these are the things which have supplanted the cross on the private altars of many Christian hearts."—*Presbyterian Life.*

Your Vows. A couple was telling me about a nephew who had recently entered a Benedictine monastery, intending to take vows as a monk. They were deeply impressed with the way the young man would have to turn over everything he had to a monastic order. "You wouldn't believe it," they told me, "but he says everything he has belongs to the Lord when he takes his vows." I nodded, then suggested that the same was also true of them—and indeed all Christians.

The definition of a Christian, in fact, could be one who knows he or she belongs to the Lord, and also knows that all that he or she has is His.

When you know that you belong to the Lord, your priorities quickly fall into place!

Time Priorities. We have to establish priorities for serving God in our daily lives. Once this is done, the day's work can produce the greatest things. Take the case of Johann Sebastian Bach, the master musician. For years he was the teacher and organist in St. Thomas's School, Leipzig. For 125 pounds a year he had to train the boy's choir, play at services, weddings and funerals, and—most amazing of all—to produce new compositions every Sunday. They were never published; they were simply written, sung, and then piled into a cupboard to grow old and dusty and forgotten for years. Priceless music—"Sheep May Safely Graze," "Jesu, Joy of Man's Desiring," all kinds of things were written, used, and piled away. In the day's work in Leipzig, he produced 265 church cantatas; 263 chorales; 14 larger works; 24 secular cantatas; 6 concertos; 4 overtures; 18 piano and violin concertos; 356 organ works and 162 pieces for the piano—all in the day's work. So then it is in the day's work we can produce masterpieces and meet God.

Questions for Pupils on the Next Lesson. 1. What are some of the ways in which persons can be "lost"? 2. What are the different kinds of lostness described in the three parables in Luke 15? 3. Why does cutting yourself off from relationships with God and people contribute to a person's sense of lostness? 4. When do you feel most alienated, helpless, and hopeless? 5.

How can your church help the Lord "find" those who are lost through carelessness, bad choices, and self-righteousness?

TOPIC FOR YOUTH
STAY ALERT

A Ton of Squash From a Packet of Seeds. "In the fall of 1976 an East Granby, Connecticut, merchant found himself with some unsold packets of vegetable seeds. Rather than return them for credit, Walter Simmons offered the seeds to the congregation's mission board. At first, the mission board tried to send the seeds overseas. But, fearing that the packets would be confiscated by custom officials, they sent the seeds to the Charles Hall Home for Indian children in North Dakota.

"A year later the director of the home, Pete Brinkerhoff, reported that 100 families in a local co-op had planted the seeds, tended gardens, and harvested the produce: 1,000 pounds of corn, 600 pounds of peas, 300 pounds of string beans, 200 pounds of carrots, 100 pounds of beets, 100 pounds turnips, 1,000 pounds of cabbage, and 2,000 pounds of squash.

"The 100 families returned half of their harvest to the co-op where 296 other low-income families bought the produce for 6 cents a pound. The $318 earned in this way made it possible for the families to obtain potatoes.

"Pete Brinkerhoff estimated that 1,584 persons (four in each of the 396 families) were helped by the gift of seeds. About half the families were Indian people. Loaves and fishes, anyone?"—J. Martin Bailey, *A.D.* magazine, December–January 1977. Copyright *A.D.* Used by permission.

Retrospection. "A salesman came into a client's office one morning," writes William D. Ellis in *Your Personality.* "When he came in, the man at the desk was busily tearing sheets from his calendar pad and throwing them in the waste basket.

" 'Wait,' ordered the salesman. 'Don't you save your check stubs and go over them to see how you've spent your money?'

" 'But these aren't check stubs,' the man at the desk protested. 'They're only days!'

"The salesman looked at him quietly. 'Say that again—slow,' he asked.

" 'Sure.' The man at the desk smiled. 'This isn't money. They're only. . . .' And then the meaning broke through, clear and strikingly."

A Question of Values. Researchers have discovered that Americans spend $20 for flowers for every $1.00 spent for medical research. In other words, we seem to be more interested in memorializing the dead than in helping the living. Remembering Jesus' teaching about priorities, what would you suggest in regard to the way you use your money?

Priorities in Planting. "When planning for a year, plant corn. When planning for a decade, plant trees. When planning for life, train and educate people."—Chinese Proverb.

Sentence Sermon to Remember: Ahab sold himself for a vineyard; Judas, for a bag of silver; Achan, for a wedge and a garment; Gehazi, for silver and raiment. Are you for sale?—Otis Philip Gifford.

Questions for Pupils on the Next Lesson. 1. Do you see value in the people you may not like? 2. When do you feel most alienated from God and others? 3. What are the forms of lostness described in Jesus' three parables in Luke 15? 4. How is your church trying to reach out to those "lost" through their being careless, or making wrong choices, or becoming self-righteous? 5. Is there ever a time when a person can be "too lost" for God to find?

LESSON VIII—JANUARY 23

TEACHING ABOUT LOSTNESS

Background Scripture: Luke 15
Devotional Reading: Luke 15:4–7

KING JAMES VERSION

LUKE 15 11 And he said, A certain man had two sons:

12 And the younger of them said to *his* father, Father, give me the portion of goods that falleth *to me.* And he divided unto them *his* living.

13 And not many days after the younger son gathered all together, and took his journey into a far country, and there wasted his substance with riotous living.

14 And when he had spent all, there arose a mighty famine in that land; and he began to be in want.

15 And he went and joined himself to a citizen of that country; and he sent him into his fields to feed swine.

16 And he would fain have filled his belly with the husks that the swine did eat: and no man gave unto him.

17 And when he came to himself, he said, How many hired servants of my father's have bread enough and to spare, and I perish with hunger!

18 I will arise and go to my father, and will say unto him, Father, I have sinned against heaven, and before thee,

19 And am no more worthy to be called thy son: make me as one of thy hired servants.

20 And he arose, and came to his father. But when he was yet a great way off, his father saw him, and had compassion, and ran, and fell on his neck, and kissed him.

21 And the son said unto him, Father, I have sinned against heaven, and in thy sight, and am no more worthy to be called thy son.

22 But the father said to his servants, Bring forth the best robe, and put *it* on him; and put a ring on his hand, and shoes on *his* feet:

23 And bring hither the fatted calf, and kill *it;* and let us eat, and be merry:

24 For this my son was dead, and is alive again; he was lost, and is found. And they began to be merry.

REVISED STANDARD VERSION

LUKE 15 11 And he said, "There was a man who had two sons; 12 and the younger of them said to his father, 'Father, give me the share of property that falls to me.' And he divided his living between them. 13 Not many days later, the younger son gathered all he had and took his journey into a far country, and there he squandered his property in loose living. 14 And when he had spent everything, a great famine arose in that country, and he began to be in want. 15 So he went and joined himself to one of the citizens of that country, who sent him into his fields to feed swine. 16 And he would gladly have fed on the pods that the swine ate; and no one gave him anything. 17 But when he came to himself he said, 'How many of my father's hired servants have bread enough and to spare, but I perish here with hunger! 18 I will arise and go to my father, and I will say to him, "Father, I have sinned against heaven and before you; 19 I am no longer worthy to be called your son; treat me as one of your hired servants." ' 20 And he arose and came to his father. But while he was yet at a distance, his father saw him and had compassion, and ran and embraced him and kissed him. 21 And the son said to him, 'Father, I have sinned against heaven and before you; I am no longer worthy to be called your son.' 22 But the father said to his servants, 'Bring quickly the best robe, and put it on him; and put a ring on his hand, and shoes on his feet; 23 and bring the fatted calf and kill it, and let us eat and make merry; 24 for this my son was dead, and is alive again; he was lost, and is found.' And they began to make merry.

KEY VERSE: "My son was dead, and is alive again; he was lost, and is found. . . ." Luke 15:24 (RSV).

HOME DAILY BIBLE READINGS

Jan. 17. M. The Lost Sheep. Luke 15:1–7.
Jan. 18. T. The Lost Coin. Luke 15:8–10.
Jan. 19. W. The Lost Son. Luke 15:11–17.
Jan. 20. T. The Father's Compassion. Luke 15:18–24.
Jan. 21. F. The Unforgiving Son. Luke 15:25–32.
Jan. 22. S. To Seek and to Save. Luke 19:1–10.
Jan. 23. S. God Seeks His Sheep. Ezekiel 34:11–16.

BACKGROUND

The experts on Jewish Law were deeply concerned with the size of the crowds that came to hear Jesus preach. This preacher out of Nazareth, they feared, just might incense these crowds to start a revolution; for these were "the lesser people"—the common folk, the uneducated, the easily led. Luke says that there were many publicans (tax collectors) and sinners in these crowds. Of course there were. The crowds were made up of people who were "yet sinners," as they listened. These were the ones He had come to seek and to save.

But, said the legal experts, they were such a *despicable* people. How could so brilliant a man as Jesus associate with them? To the strict, legalistic Jew, such miserable sinners were untouchable; there was no joy in heaven over them; they were better dead. To show them how wrong they were, Jesus told them three parables about lostness, and what God did with the problem of the lost sinner—be he an aristocrat or the lowest of the low.

NOTES ON THE PRINTED TEXT

Sheep get lost out of sheer foolishness. Sheep have a reputation for being *dumb;* they are not as smart as horses or monkeys or dogs; they have a bad habit of wandering away from the flock and getting lost; the shepherd hunts until he finds them. The lostness of the sheep is their own fault.

Jesus told a short story or parable about a woman losing a silver coin. She did *not deliberately* lose it; she just forgot where she had left it. It was nobody's fault that it was lost.

Then He told them about a prodigal son who *deliberately* got lost, or lost himself, by turning his back on his own father. This little literary gem has been called the greatest short story ever written.

The Prodigal Son! That is the name by which we know it, but it is a bad title for such a story. It should be called "The Parable of the Perfect Father." Just as the rescuing shepherd is the hero of the parable of the lost sheep, so here the main, great character is not the heedless, self-serving young fool who broke his father's heart, but the father who never gave up this son as lost.

This father was what we might call "well-off"; he owned a farm large enough to require the labor of slaves. He had two sons. Under Jewish Law, when a father with two sons died, two-thirds of his estate was inherited by the elder son, and one-third by the younger son. Often, the father would divide his estate before he died. The older son was content to wait until the father died; he knew that his security was perfect; he could wait. But the younger son, wearied with labor on the farm, just couldn't wait; he went to ask his father to give him his one-third *now*. He wanted to get away from that farm and see the world and have some fun before he settled down.

It was pure selfishness, and it must have broken the father's heart, but he did it; he gave his ungrateful son the money and watched him go gaily off down the road. He might have refused the son's request, but he was too wise to do that; he knew that the headstrong youngster *had to learn it the hard way*. Like many a modern youth, the boy wanted to do it *his* way; he wanted to be "free." And many a modern father has been forced to let the child he loves find out for himself what a fool he is.

The son got his money; he went far from home, found new friends who flocked to him to help him spend his money. They ate, drank, and made merry—until the money ran out; then the "friends" left him and he took a job feeding pigs just to stay alive. He had struck bottom in his "freedom"; every Jew was forbidden to feed pigs for the law said, "Cursed is he who feeds swine." Was this *freedom?*

The foolish young spendthrift, up to this point, seems to be 50 percent foolish and 50 percent bad, but now he becomes something, someone better. He took a good look at himself; Luke says that he "came to himself." For the first time, he saw himself as he really *was*, and he did not like what he saw, and he saw what he had to do. He walked out of the pigsty, walked down the long road to home, and begged his father's forgiveness. That took courage. Give him credit. For the first time in his life, he humbled himself and asked only that his father let him serve as a slave on the old farm.

At the farm gate, he was welcomed *by a waiting father* who did not scold him but welcomed him, putting on his shoulders a robe (which stood for honor), a ring on his finger (which stood for authority), and shoes on his feet (the children of a Jewish family wore shoes; slaves did not).

Can you see him there, that waiting father whose heart yearned for the saving of his lost son? Can you feel the pain in his suffering heart as he waited the long years that his son was "away"? The "lostness" of the foolish son was nothing in comparison with the sense of lostness in the father's heart.

Why did Jesus tell such a story? He told it hoping that those who heard it would understand that *God is like that waiting father*. He told it as a parable (it was a parable, yes, but it is true of all the human race) to illustrate the glorious truth that God the Father never gives up on any (lost) sinner, that God knows of no total depravity from which a man may not be saved if he has the courage and the heart to "come to himself" and admit his sins and come home to Him for forgiveness and a fresh start. David Redding writes of the coming home of the son to the loving father: "This scene is a supreme moment in all literature, the gem of His Gospel—a God like that. Here the Author had in his head the greatest love story ever told. He would take time later to write it down indelibly in blood and glory. When our modern medicines and washing machines are as obsolete as bloodletting and the 'Old Oaken Bucket'; when our space ships take their place on the shelf beside the steam engine and the buggywhip; when the planet waxes old like a garment, and the last sun sets, this story will still be young."—David A Redding, in *The Parables He Told*, Fleming H. Revell Company, publisher.

The waiting, forgiving Father! The Father of us all "standeth . . . within the shadows" watching, waiting, waiting. Whatever we are, to whatever far country we go, we cannot put ourselves beyond the reach of His loving, forgiving hand.

SUGGESTIONS TO TEACHERS

Your "problem" in today's lesson will be that the three parables containing Jesus' teaching about lostness suffer from overexposure. Each of these three picture stories has been made almost too familiar through retelling. Your task today will be to rescue these powerful parables from the realm of "harmless little Bible stories," as one children's librarian once condescendingly described them in a lecture on suitable reading for youngsters.

Begin by filling in the background on the telling of these parables. Remind your class that Jesus had eaten with sinners and had caused the self-righteous religious folk to murmur. This conflict-laden setting quickly removes the trio of parables from the category of kiddies' literature. Working with these stories by Jesus, you will quickly notice common elements to all three.

1. *SEPARATION.* Ask your class to define *lostness.* You will help them to realize that lostness means being out of circulation, useless, not carrying out the intended function. If time allows, ask your class to relate times when one remembers being lost, such as when a child wandering away, or as an adult making a wrong turn on a trip. Jesus defines our state of being separated or apart from God as "lostness." Is this not what the meaning of sin is? Sin is not being consigned to hell as much as being out of circulation, misplaced, separated from God, from others, from life, from self.

2. *SEARCH.* Call attention to the tireless, relentless effort on the part of the shepherd, the woman, and the father in each of these three parables to reclaim the lost sheep or coin or son respectively. Make starkly clear to your class that the meaning of the Gospel is that God has set aside all duties and dignity to come in quest of reclaiming the "lost." As Jesus says, "For the Son of Man came to seek and to save the lost" (Luke 19:10 RSV). Is each person in your class aware of the seeking love of God expressed through Jesus Christ?

3. *CELEBRATION.* Have you caught the tremendous note of joy throughout this fifteenth chapter of Luke? Point out the party atmosphere that pervades these parables when the owner or parent reclaims what had been lost. No gloom-and-doom faith here! Rather, Jesus stresses how God rejoices when any of us "lost" sons or daughters has been found.

4. *SHARING.* Have your class also note how the shepherd who searches, the woman who sweeps, and the father who seeks all call together family, friends, and neighbors to share their happiness in finding the lost. Likewise, God wants to share His joy. What does each shared joy by God suggest regarding your worship or toward strangers and sinners?

TOPIC FOR ADULTS
TEACHING ABOUT LOSTNESS

Ignore Them and You Ignore Me! "It was headlined in the newspaper, 'Lost Blind Man Ignored.' As the article went, a seventy-year-old blind man got on a bus in Miami to ride to West Palm Beach. About nineteen miles short of his destination, he mistakenly got off the bus. When he discovered that he was in the wrong city, he felt around for a bench and sat down and started asking for help from the passersby. As he later related, 'I cried for people to call the police, but nobody listened. I didn't know where I was, so I prayed and hoped help would arrive.' As it turned out, he sat in that one spot for fifteen hours in temperatures that climbed to near 90° without any food or drink until finally at around 10:30 P.M. police came to help him. Fifteen people passed by this man who was obviously in need of assistance, but they just ignored him."—*Pulpit Helps*, August 1978.

How Do We Explain? Two and one-half billion people on the earth have never heard the name of Jesus Christ. How are we going to explain that to the Lord, when 80 percent of the know-how and money of the Christian world is here in the United States?

Lost Boy Rescued Later Finds Lost Rescuer. After forty years and as many blind alleys, Manuel Alvarez has found his Unknown Soldier.

Alvarez had just one clue to go on in his search for the soldier who rescued him during the Spanish Civil War in 1938 when he was eleven years old and fleeing from the fascist bombs falling on his village, Corbera, in Northern Spain. He was hiding in a pump shack when a bomb hit the water tower directly above. With one leg broken in two places and the other badly lacerated by shrapnel, the boy was swept by the water toward the nearby Ebro River. Alvarez knew that he would be lost forever. A tall man in a military uniform struggled through the torrent, swept Manuel into his arms and said, "*Yo Canadiense,*" Spanish for "I am Canadian." After rescuing the boy from certain death, the soldier took the boy to an aid station and disappeared.

Manuel Alvarez, grateful that he had been found, wanted to find the Canadian who saved him from being lost in the raging waters. Years passed. In 1958, Alvarez emigrated to Vancouver, British Columbia, and eventually became the owner of a car dealership. He still wanted to find his rescuer to thank him.

He knew the soldier was a member of the MacKenzie-Papineau Brigade, a volunteer outfit which sent 1,200 members to Spain to fight with the Loyalists. Only 700 returned. Alvarez was reading a magazine and came across the name of a brigade member he had not already checked. With help, he found Jimmy Higgins, seventy-one, a veteran living in Peterborough, Ontario, who had an unpublished manuscript describing his experiences in Spain. One chapter, entitled The Boy, detailed Higgins's rescue of the boy and the greeting "*Yo Canadiense.*"

Manuel Alvarez's search is complete. The final act will come when he travels to Peterborough to visit the man who saved his life years earlier.

You also were once "lost"—perhaps through carelessness, or through bad choices, or through self-righteousness, or through indifference, or through guilt. Through Jesus Christ, you have been found. You have been rescued. You are no longer being swept to destruction.

Have you, in turn, remembered your Rescuer? Have you found Him?

Questions for Pupils on the Next Lesson. 1. Why do people sometimes want to manipulate circumstances for personal advantage? 2. What is unchristian about identifying security in terms of material possessions? 3. What do you do when you find a compulsion to satisfy your own needs blinding you to the needs of others? 4. How can you prevent your interest in possessions from possessing you? 5. What is mature and responsible stewardship?

TOPIC FOR YOUTH
LOST AND FOUND

Coffee With an 0–6. The twenty-four-year-old soldier had given up. He despaired of getting well or ever walking again. Lost from active duty, the young enlisted man was also lost from life. A crippling ailment had caused his muscles to stop functioning, and the soldier was depressed when Chaplain (Colonel) Ralph Miller walked up to his bed in the 97th Field Hospital in Frankfurt, Germany. The young American heard the Chaplain pray. Before Miller left the bedside, he told the sick man, "When you walk into my office, you—an E-3 (corporal) will get a cup of coffee from an 0-6 (colonel)."

Miller walked away and continued his busy rounds. Weeks passed. Miller, immersed in the hectic schedule of serving at a huge Army hospital, was busy at his desk one day trying to catch up on the paperwork. There had been a series of annoying interruptions when his assistant stuck his head inside the door again telling him that there was a man outside his office who insisted on seeing Chaplain Miller. Miller, tense, busy, and irritated over another interruption, sighed and said, "Send him in." In staggered the enlisted man who had been lost to despair many weeks earlier, unsteadily but on his own two feet. It turned out that the man had propelled his wheelchair nearly a quarter of a mile through the hospital corridors, left the chair and made his way the last twenty feet to Chaplain Miller's office on his own. So grateful at being found by Miller when he had felt so lost, he smiled and asked if the offer of the coffee still stood. Miller handed him a mug and poured the coffee personally.

In the person of Jesus Christ, God has found us when we might have thought we were lost in a hopeless situation. We are found when we are at the point of resigning ourselves to being lost and despairing of being found.

Reward Refused. Little two-year-old Jamie Mokshefski vanished with his baby-sitter from the home of his parents in Colorado Springs, Colorado, in the summer of 1980. A $1,000 reward to anyone having any leads on the child's wherabouts was offered. David Abernethy, thirty-five, of Anahuac, Texas, found little Jamie and took him to the police who returned the boy to his parents. When authorities tried to give the $1,000 to David Abernethy, Abernethy refused the reward. He insisted that the money be turned over to little Jamie's family. "I'm glad to see that he's home okay," said Abernethy. "I saw on television when his father went in to see the boy. That was reward enough to see them back together again."

God wants to see us back together again with Him. It is reward enough to Him to have us found when we are lost or separated from Him. Through Jesus Christ, He has sought and found us when we thought we were lost!

"Zhonggue" Forms of Lostness. The Chinese word for China is *Zhongguo.* This means "middle of the world." The assumption was that the farther away from China one lived, the more barbarian. China was the center of the universe, according to ancient reasoning.

Many people are secretly *Zhongguo*-ians. A *Zhongguo*-type has the notion that everything is intended to revolve around him or her because where he/she happens to be is supposed to be the hub of the universe. Anyone different is believed to be a barbarian. A *Zhongguo*-personality refuses to consider any except himself or herself. *Zhongguo*-kinds of people, in other words, are self-righteous and self-centered. They may reside in any place in the world, not only in China. Some live in your community. Sometimes, you are, in reality a *Zhongguo*-kind of person!

A person with such a set of attitudes—a *Zhongguo*-type—really doesn't need Jesus Christ.

He or she is lost.

But Jesus came to seek and save those who are lost, including us when we become so self-righteous and self-centered that we imagine everything exists for our personal comfort!

Sentence Sermon to Remember: The most amazing thing about God is His patience with all His earthly prodigal sons.—Henry T. Wilkenson.

Questions for Pupils on the Next Lesson. 1. What are your greatest personal gifts from the Lord? 2. What are your biggest limitations? 3. that exactly do you think is meant by the term *stewardship?* 4. How is a Christian supposed to regard his/her material possessions? 5. What does your response to Christ's claims have to do with your personal life-style?

LESSON IX—JANUARY 30

TEACHING ABOUT STEWARDSHIP

Background Scripture: Luke 16:1–13,19–31
Devotional Reading: Amos 5:6–15

KING JAMES VERSION

LUKE 16 1 And he said also unto his disciples, There was a certain rich man, which had a steward; and the same was accused unto him that he had wasted his goods.

2 And he called him, and said unto him, How is it that I hear this of thee? give an account of thy stewardship; for thou mayest be no longer steward.

3 Then the steward said within himself, What shall I do? for my lord taketh away from me the stewardship: I cannot dig; to beg I am ashamed.

4 I am resolved what to do, that, when I am put out of the stewardship, they may receive me into their houses.

5 So he called every one of his lord's debtors *unto him,* and said unto the first, How much owest thou unto my lord?

6 And he said, A hundred measures of oil. And he said unto him, Take thy bill, and sit down quickly, and write fifty.

7 Then said he to another, And how much owest thou? And he said, A hundred measures of wheat. And he said unto him, Take thy bill, and write four-score.

8 And the lord commended the unjust steward, because he had done wisely: for the children of this world are in their generation wiser than the children of light.

9 And I say unto you, Make to yourselves friends of the mammon of unrighteousness; that, when ye fail, they may receive you into everlasting habitations.

10 He that is faithful in that which is least is faithful also in much: and he that is unjust in the least is unjust also in much.

11 If therefore ye have not been faithful in the unrighteous mammon, who will commit to your trust the true *riches?*

12 And if ye have not been faithful in that which is another man's, who shall give you that which is your own?

13 No servant can serve two masters: for either he will hate the one, and love the other; or else he will hold to the one, and despise the other. Ye cannot serve God and mammon.

REVISED STANDARD VERSION

LUKE 16 1 He also said to the disciples, "There was a rich man who had a steward, and charges were brought to him that this man was wasting his goods. 2 And he called him and said to him, 'What is this that I hear about you? Turn in the account of your stewardship, for you can no longer be steward.' 3 And the steward said to himself, 'What shall I do, since my master is taking the stewardship away from me? I am not strong enough to dig, and I am ashamed to beg. 4 I have decided what to do, so that people may receive me into their houses when I am put out of the stewardship.' 5 So, summoning his master's debtors one by one, he said to the first, 'How much do you owe my master?' 6 He said, 'A hundred measures of oil.' And he said to him, 'Take your bill, and sit down quickly and write fifty.' 7 Then he said to another, 'And how much do you owe?' He said, 'A hundred measures of wheat.' He said to him, 'Take your bill, and write eighty.' 8 The master commended the dishonest steward for his shrewdness; for the sons of this world are more shrewd in dealing with their own generation than the sons of light. 9 And I tell you, make friends for yourselves by means of unrighteous mammon, so that when it fails they may receive you into the eternal habitations.

10 "He who is faithful in a very little is faithful also in much; and he who is dishonest in a very little is dishonest also in much. 11 If then you have not been faithful in the unrighteous mammon, who will entrust to you the true riches? 12 And if you have not been faithful in that which is another's, who will give you that which is your own? 13 No servant can serve two masters; for either he will hate the one and love the other, or he will be devoted to the one and despise the other. You cannot serve God and mammon."

KEY VERSE: "No servant can serve two masters; for either he will hate the one and love the other, or he will be devoted to the one and despise the other. You cannot serve God and Mammon." Luke 16:13 (RSV).

HOME DAILY BIBLE READINGS

Jan. 24. M. The Shrewd Steward. Luke 16:1–9.
Jan. 25. T. The Faithful Steward. Luke 16:10–17.
Jan. 26. W. Unconditional Service. Luke 17:5–10.
Jan. 27. T. The Rich and the Kingdom. Luke 18:18–25.
Jan. 28. F. Not to Use Is to Lose. Luke 19:12–26.
Jan. 29. S. Stewardship Determines Destiny. Luke 16:19–31.
Jan. 30. S. A Plea for Justice. Amos 5:6–15.

BACKGROUND

A famous agnostic once said that it was strange to him that while Jesus said that the love of money was the root of all evil, He still talked more about money than about anything else. That statement may be hard to prove, but it is sadly true that Jesus *did* talk a great deal about money—or *possessions* because He had to. Money was the first concern of 90 percent of the people to whom He preached.

In the Parable of the Unjust Steward (in Luke 16), Jesus says so much about money and possessions and people who are concerned with it that all become confused. At first glance the reader is tempted to say, "I just can't believe it: Jesus is giving His approvel to a man who is plainly a crook!" It does seem that way, but, when we look at it carefully, we find Him using this parable to say something about money and the way men use it that is directly opposite to such approval. Once we understand this parable, we will never again be in doubt about the teaching of Jesus on money and possessions.

NOTES ON THE PRINTED TEXT

Read the parable carefully and objectively and you will find that all three of the characters in it are nothing more than scheming scoundrels; there is not a single *good* man in the whole lot. First, there is the master of an estate, a rich master. He was a master or owner of an estate on which he did not live; we would call him an absentee owner. His aim in life was to get rich and stay rich.

Second, there is the steward, or manager, of the estate and of the master's money. In plain English, he was an embezzler, a thief, a "con artist" who also wanted to get rich quick, and so helped himself to money that was his master's and not his. And third, there were the debtors who owed the master money they had borrowed and who couldn't repay it. They became accessories to the steward's crime—not unwillingly.

The master discovered the theft and fired the steward. The steward is down but not out: he goes to those who owe his master money, shows them how to dodge the debts by helping him to "doctor" the ledgers in which the records are kept, and in so doing win them as friends who can help him in his forced "retirement!" That was crooked but clever; he could blackmail those debtors as long as he pleased; they "owed him," and he could make them pay. And strangely enough, when the master discovered the shrewd trick of his steward, he "commended the unjust steward, because he had done wisely: for the children of this world are in their generation wiser than the children of light" (verse 8). It sounds impossible; why should any sensible man commend (approve of) any man who had stolen his money?

But for *what* was the master commending his steward? He was not approving of the steward's *dishonesty,* but for his quick wit in a bad situation. The steward had not panicked; he shrewdly provided for his future welfare. With an ironic humor, Luke (and Jesus) are saying here that the righteous people could learn something from this unrighteous steward—namely, that the unrighteous are often wiser in their ways than the righteous are in *their* ways. "And so perhaps what He meant was to remind His often blundering disciples that in addition to good hearts it was important that they also use their brains. What would *they* do in a crisis? How far could *they* look ahead and find new possibilities when what they had depended upon before was swept away?"—W. R. Bowie. If the Christians were as quick and eager in *their* attempts to be really good and effective Christians, how much more could they accomplish for the Kingdom, and how much better would men and the world be! (Note: Modern Christians spend twenty times more on amusement and cosmetics and sports than they give to Christ's Church!)

Verse 9 is thought by some biblical scholars to be an interpolation added to the parable. It may be that; it certainly adds something quite important to the basic teaching of the parable which deals with worldly cleverness. Verse 9 deals with the "everlasting habitations" in which men live after their earthly life is over. Life there will depend upon what one does in *this* life. If the lust for money and possessions has led a man to ignore God, he can expect little reward in heaven. But if he had used his money to help the poor, if he had made friends by being generous in charity, he will find welcome in the heavenly life. Make life easier for others with your wealth, and *your* life will be rich and blessed.

Money and possessions are not sins in themselves, but they are great *responsibilities;* they can make or break us, depending upon how they are *used.* A. M. Sullivan has written: "There's no such thing as dirty money; the stain is only on the hand that holds it as giver or taker."

Then there is the story told by Henry Van Dyke of the millionaire who reached heaven and found himself assigned to live in a miserable hut while a poor man of his acquaintance lived in a palace. When he objected to such "treatment," an angel said, "We built your eternal home out of all that you sent us to build with!"

In verses 10-12, Luke gives us a series of sayings about money in order that we may not misunderstand the deep, full meaning of the parable; he does not want to leave his readers with the idea that crooked, shrewd, and dishonest men may be honored in either their lives on earth or in their lives to come. He says that a man who does well working at a small job can be trusted to do well in a bigger job. Men are not always promoted because they are shrewd; they are more often promoted because they are able and *honest* men. The same thing holds in the *eternal* life; those who have done well with their wealth, with whatever they have, will be glorified by their Father in heaven. Those who could not be honest in the small matters of earth cannot be trusted with greater responsibilities. Those who have proved themselves untrustworthy about worldly wealth will *not* be trusted with the greater riches of heaven.

Luke ends his explanation of the parable with six words that boggle the human mind and shake the human heart: "Ye *cannot* serve God and mammon." Many of us try to worship both, but it never turns out very well. Frederick Saunders says that "Mammon is the largest slave-holder in the world," and he may be right about that; sooner or later he who worships mammon at all will be worshiping him full-time, and, when that happens, God fades entirely out of his life picture. (A bitter Ralph Waldo Emerson wrote that "The Americans have little faith; they rely on the power of the dollar." Don't curse him for saying that; *is it true?*)

The servants of God are full-time servants; and there is no such thing as a part-time Christian. We serve God full-time or not at all. To compromise, to believe that we can worship both God *and* mammon, is to court slow but certain death for the soul.

And, lest we forget, let us remember that we are *all* stewards of God on this earth.

SUGGESTIONS TO TEACHERS

Stewardship, in most churches, has become a euphemism for money talk and pledge cards. Giving one's money, of course, is an extremely important dimension of discipleship. But *stewardship* means much more.

Your goal as teacher for this lesson is to aid your students to get to the root of the meaning of stewardship. A *steward,* in the Bible and in ancient practice, was one who looked after the interests of the owner. A steward was not the owner but was closer to what we would call the overseer or manager of the properties. Throughout the Bible, humans are meant to see themselves as responsible trustees to God, the sole Shareholder of their lives and of all life. The string of parables in Luke 16 reinforces this idea.

1. *WITH A SCOUNDREL'S RESOURCEFULNESS.* Be sure to do your homework on the parable of the dishonest steward. It can be a slippery one for the person who will not patiently listen. At first hearing, some may conclude that Jesus seems to be glorifying chicanery, or even condoning dishonesty. Check the background material and consult your Bible commentaries so that you understand what Jesus' point is. You will begin to understand that He is saying in effect, "Be as resourceful and quick in your serving God as this scoundrel of an estate-manager was when he had to pay up because his job was in jeopardy." Discuss with your class what imaginative stewardship can be. Bring in examples of persons who showed an originality in serving God. If God is owner of everything in each person's life, what are some innovative ways of living as trustees of one's time, talents, and treasure?

2. *WITH A SERVANT'S SINGLEMINDEDNESS.* Move on during your lesson to the words of Jesus about being able to serve only *one* Master. Generate some dialogue in the group by asking for comments about the rival masters to Jesus which try to exercise control on class members. How are those in your class withstanding (or trying to withstand) the claims of these other masters? What happens when a man or woman tries to please two bosses, Jesus Christ and another "lord?"

3. *WITH A SINNER'S RESPONSE.* Again, the parable of the Rich Man and Lazarus can booby trap the careless teacher. Remember that the point of this picture story by Jesus is not to paint a full-blown canvas of the world-to-come. Jesus is not talking so much about life after death as about life before death, or our stewardship of our lives here and now. Point out the urgency in dealing responsibly with our possessions and sharing with others. The person who fails to do so is missing out on life according to Jesus.

TOPIC FOR ADULTS
TEACHING ABOUT STEWARDSHIP

Title Deed on Your Life. Everything belongs to God. Everything is traced to Him as ultimate Owner. You may recall the episode of the New York law firm engaged to trace and clear the title to some property in New Orleans. A New Orleans attorney traced the title back to 1803, but the New York firm wrote that he hadn't traced it back far enough. In due time, the New Orleans attorney wrote back: "Please be advised that in 1803, the U.S.A. government acquired the territory of Louisiana from the Republic of France by Purchase. The Republic of France acquired the title from the Spanish Crown by conquest, the Spanish Crown having obtained it by one Christopher Columbus, a Genoese navigator, authorized by Isabella, Queen of Spain, who obtained sanction from the Pope, the Vicar of Christ, who is the Son and Heir of the Almighty, who made Louisiana."

Title deed on your life is held by the Creator!

The Only Giver. Repeatedly, the imagery of the New Testament suggests that you have been bought back by God, as if you had been captured or stolen by evil, selfish powers. "You are not your own," the Apostle writes, "you were bought with a price" (1 Corinthians 6:19,20). Through Jesus, God has established His claims on you. You are "redeemed," as the old hymns used to put it, that is "bought back" by the Lord who was willing to pay any price—even to going to a Cross—to welcome you back into a new relationship with Him.

Throughout the New Testament, the early Christian writers think of themselves as Jesus Christ's "servants" or "slaves." They know they belong to Him. They count it joy to be His.

Any person who knows any hint of the grace of the Lord must concur. A person touched by mercy and life can only respond that he or she belongs to Jesus Christ. A Christian can only sing with Isaac Watts in the beautiful hymn, "Love so amazing, so divine, demands my life, my soul, my all."

Perhaps the favorite word by Jesus to denote this ownership and claim by the Lord over us is that of *stewardship.* It is a business-world term from His times. It refers to a nonstockholding manager, a trustee of another's property. A steward was never the owner. He was merely the overseer. Only the Lord, in the case of our lives, has property rights. You and I own nothing. We are simply trustees to look after what is His and which has been entrusted to us for looking after His interests. We are accountable.

Whenever the time comes to speak of money and we ask, "How much do we give?" the reply is that this is not the right question. Rather, "How much have you received?"

The answer, of course, is "EVERYTHING!" Our talk about "giving" is incorrect. It implies ownership. Only God owns. Only God may properly give.

How Much? Personally, I can only testify that I have learned that the old story is true about the wealthy miser who died. The old boy had been known as a selfish penny pincher who never shared. After his funeral, someone asked, "How much did he leave?" Someone answered, "He left it all."

We leave it all ultimately. We Christians especially realize that Jesus who claims it all calls us to be stewards of it all while we are given the use of a few years. Some of us, recognizing that we are stewards even of our time, budget hours as carefully as we budget our dollars for the work of Christ. Some of us, remembering we are stewards of our bodies, give up smoking and destructive drinking, and place in our wills that corneas and bone marrow and kidneys, hearts and transplantable organs be passed on for someone else to use. "We are not our own; we are bought with a price." We are Christ's, and therefore merely stewards of our lives.

Questions for Pupils on the Next Lesson. 1. Why did Jesus not choose to save His skin and stay away from Jerusalem? 2. Why did Jesus weep over the city of Jerusalem? 3. How do you try to resolve the confusion over various choices of life values which you experience? 4. To what or to whom do you find yourself giving your loyalty? 5. What makes you the angriest?

TOPIC FOR YOUTH
GOD IS COUNTING ON YOU

The Lord's Calf. Stewardship has to do with what we do with our lives after we have said *Yes* to Jesus Christ. Stewardship is acknowledging that we have been baptized into a new life, a new relationship in which all we are and own is the Lord's.

However, we are all masters at evasion and excuses. We are like the Ohio farmer my father once encountered. The man had two calves and promised that one should be the Lord's. Everything went well for a time, and the farmer's gift promised to be a good one. However, one day, he found one of the calves dead. At first, he was distressed. But soon he announced to his wife, "Sarah, the Lord's calf is dead."

As Resourceful as a Scoundrel. In a recent year, a study in Los Angeles revealed that nearly 7,000 groups were passing the hat for charities. You probably feel that there are just as many here in our area, and that you are on the sucker list for every one of them plus most of the ones in the rest of the country. Nationally, we Americans donate about 40 billion dollars annually to charities, including religious, educational, medical, and other eleemosynary causes.

Some of these funds will go to groups having little accountability or sense of responsibility, such as the campaign in Philadelphia to get funds to train paraplegics for jobs, find them work, and provide wheelchairs. The charity raised $70,000, but only $181 went to paraplegics. The rest went for "expenses" and salaries. Other monies will go to fakes, such as the two who were going from door to door soliciting for a fund to aid the parents of the unknown soldier. Most of the phonies and dubious campaigns rely on people contributing either out of emotional impulse or sense of duty.

A Christian realizes that everything he/she has belongs to Christ, and that he/she is accountable for what is the Lord's. Being accountable calls for a sense of resourcefulness: putting brains and imagination to work.

Our New Testament Scripture describes a chiseling sneak of a steward. This steward has acted as if the owner's is his own. This dishonest estate-manager is a scoundrel. Nothing in the way of details is given in the parable as to what this embezzling steward does with the money he has cheated the owner out of, but eventually he is found out. He is called to accountability and suddenly realizes he is in a desperate situation. With incredible energy and imagination, he turns to creditors and offers quick, immediate discount settlements in order to raise quick cash. He resourcefully and singlemindedly arranges to cover for his embezzlement.

Expert Excuse Makers. We are experts in excusing ourselves and evading our accountability to the Lord, the Owner of our lives, in the realm of our possessions. For example, one enterprising accountant with expertise in statistics of Presbyterians has figured that if every present-day Presbyterian were on welfare, and tithed his/her welfare check, giving would be increased 35 percent.

Sentence Sermon to Remember: Stewardship is what a man does after he says, "I believe."—W. H. Greever.

Questions for Pupils on the Next Lesson. 1. When do you find greatest confusion over what values to choose? 2. What makes you angriest? 3. How do you handle your anger? 4. What made Jesus angry, and how did He channel His anger? 5. Why did Jesus go to Jerusalem when He could have stayed away and saved His life?

LESSON X—FEBRUARY 6

GOING UP TO JERUSALEM

Background Scripture: Luke 19:28–48
Devotional Reading: Lamentations 3:21–33

KING JAMES VERSION

LUKE 19 29 And it came to pass, when he was come nigh to Bethphage and Bethany, at the mount called *the mount* of Olives, he sent two of his disciples,

30 Saying, Go ye into the village over against *you;* in the which at your entering ye shall find a colt tied, whereon yet never man sat; loose him, and bring *him hither.*

31 And if any man ask you, Why do ye loose *him?* thus shall ye say unto him, Because the Lord hath need of him.

32 And they that were sent went their way, and found even as he had said unto them.

33 And as they were loosing the colt, the owners thereof said unto them, Why loose ye the colt?

34 And they said, The Lord hath need of him.

35 And they brought him to Jesus: and they cast their garments upon the colt, and they set Jesus thereon.

36 And as he went, they spread their clothes in the way.

37 And when he was come nigh, even now at the descent of the mount of Olives, the whole multitude of the disciples began to rejoice and praise God with a loud voice for all the mighty works that they had seen;

38 Saying, Blessed *be* the King that cometh in the name of the Lord: peace in heaven, and glory in the highest.

39 And some of the Pharisees from among the multitude said unto him, Master, rebuke thy disciples.

40 And he answered and said unto them, I tell you that, if these should hold their peace, the stones would immediately cry out.

45 And he went into the temple, and began to cast out them that sold therein, and them that bought;

46 Saying unto them, It is written, My house is the house of prayer; but ye have made it a den of thieves.

47 And he taught daily in the temple. But the chief priests and the scribes and

REVISED STANDARD VERSION

LUKE 19 29 When he drew near to Bethphage and Bethany, at the mount that is called Olivet, he sent two of the disciples, 30 saying, "Go into the village opposite, where on entering you will find a colt tied, on which no one has ever yet sat; untie it and bring it here. 31 If any one asks you, 'Why are you untying it?' you shall say this, 'The Lord has need of it.' " 32 So those who were sent went away and found it as he had told them. 33 And as they were untying the colt, its owners said to them, "Why are you untying the colt?" 34 And they said, "The Lord has need of it." 35 And they brought it to Jesus, and throwing their garments on the colt they set Jesus upon it. 36 And as he rode along, they spread their garments on the road. 37 As he was now drawing near, at the descent of the Mount of Olives, the whole multitude of the disciples began to rejoice and praise God with a loud voice for all the mighty works that they had seen, 38 saying, "Blessed is the King who comes in the name of the Lord! Peace in heaven and glory in the highest!" 39 And some of the Pharisees in the multitude said to him, "Teacher, rebuke your disciples." 40 He answered, "I tell you, if these were silent, the very stones would cry out."

45 And he entered the temple and began to drive out those who sold, 46 saying to them, "It is written, 'My house shall be a house of prayer'; but you have made it a den of robbers."

47 And he was teaching daily in the temple. The chief priests and the scribes

the chief of the people sought to destroy him,

48 And could not find what they might do: for all the people were very attentive to hear him.

and the principal men of the people sought to destroy him; 48 but they did not find anything they could do, for all the people hung upon his words.

KEY VERSE: When the days drew near for him to be received up, he set his face to go to Jerusalem. Luke 9:51 (RSV).

HOME DAILY BIBLE READINGS

Jan. 31. M. *"The Lord Has Need."* Luke 19:28–40.
Feb. 1. T. *A Place to Pray and Teach.* Luke 19:41–48.
Feb. 2. W. *The Question of Authority.* Luke 20:1–18.
Feb. 3. T. *A Parable of Judgment.* Luke 20:9–18.
Feb. 4. F. *Give God His Own.* Luke 20:19–26.
Feb. 5. S. *God of the Living.* Luke 20:27–40.
Feb. 6. S. *The Lord Is Good.* Lamentations 3:22–33.

BACKGROUND

To every life, there is that last mile. There comes a time when our work is done. Jesus has reached that point in our lesson for today. He has done His work on earth; He has healed many of the illnesses of body and mind. He has preached to crowds and won many. He has chosen disciples who will carry on His work after He is gone. To them, He tells one last parable (The Parable of the Pounds, Luke 19:12–27) as they walked the twenty miles from Jericho to Jerusalem.

Why Jerusalem? It seems foolish for Him to go there, for Jerusalem was headquarters for His enemies. The disciples must have wondered about this, but Jesus knew that He *had* to go there for the last dramatic moment of His ministry. Had not the great Prophet Zechariah predicted that He would one day come riding into Jerusalem "upon an ass, and upon a colt the foal of an ass" (Zechariah 9:9)? Riding in *triumph?*

The prophets of old, when the people refused to listen to them, often put on a dramatic performance that they hoped would *make* them understand: there was Jeremiah walking the streets with a yoke around his neck, and Ezekiel shaving his beard in public. Sometimes the dramatization worked, sometimes it failed.

Jesus planned just such a dramatization, at the time of Passover in Jerusalem.

NOTES ON THE PRINTED TEXT

Jesus planned it well. Nearing Jerusalem, He sent two of His disciples to look for a colt tied at the roadside near Bethphage and Bethany; they were to bring the colt to Jesus. If the owners of the colt objected, they were to say to him, "The Lord has need of it." That was a sort of password used between Christians, and it indicates that the owners of the colt were friends or followers who had been forewarned that the Lord had need of a colt that never before had been ridden. Such untrained animals were often ridden in religious celebrations. He would enter the Holy City at the time of the Passover festival, riding not on a prancing horse but upon a lowly donkey. Conquering warriors rode prancing steeds in their triumphal processions, but Jesus wanted to appear in Jerusalem not as a warrior-conqueror, but as a Messiah who would conquer not by the sword but by way of love. He rode to announce Himself not as a king leading armed battalions, but as a King or a Prince of *Peace*.

So He rides down the slope of the Mount of Olives. His disciples have thrown some of their clothing on the back of the colt that He rode and other garments under the feet of the colt. The disciples were ecstatic, shouting "with a loud voice" of the mighty works He had done—so that the Passover crowds would know who He was. The crowds joined the uproar: they sang with the disciples. "Blessed be the King that cometh in the name of the Lord. . . ." The disciples and the crowd may have been singing for different purposes: the disciples sang to honor Him as the Lord of love, but the crowds sang to honor Him as the warrior-restorer of the kingdom of David.

Crowds are fickle in their loyalties. A clever orator can stir them to violence in causes that are wrong; the next day, a different orator can start them fighting for a *just* cause. "Put not your trust in crowds,"' said Anatole France of the people (the crowds), "Today they shout 'Huzzah'; tomorrow they shout 'To the guillotine!' " It was so with Jesus. On Palm Sunday, they hailed Him as King; on Good Friday they approved His Crucifixion.

For the common people who had come to Jerusalem for the Passover feast, this cheering and enthusiasm was great Good News. Even though they did not understand all this Man of Nazareth had said and done, they had in their hearts a renewed hope that He had come to set them free from those who carried Roman swords, to stand again in dignity and power as they had stood in the days of their father David. They had something to cheer about—and some of the Pharisees in Jerusalem didn't like that at all. They came to Jesus and asked Him, supposedly in a plea for "law and order," to rebuke the cheering crowd. If this went on, the people would turn into a mob, and then there *would* be trouble. There could even be riots and revolution.

Jesus rebuked *them* for making such a proposition. If, He said, the disciples and the crowds stopped singing their song of recognition, the very stones in the road would "cry out" (start singing).

The Pharisees, too, had a plan concerning Jesus, a plan they had started to build long, long ago. Their plan was to kill Him in Jerusalem. Jesus knew about that.

So what had Jesus accomplished in this Triumphal Entry into Jerusalem? For one thing, He had thrown down the gauntlet to those who would destroy Him. He might have hidden from them in the hills of Judea, or in the home of some disciple, but no—He rode openly, courageously, in such a manner that the whole city would see Him. Openly and dramatically He declared Himself to be the Messiah; His ride as Messiah challenged them to either accept or reject Him. He set Himself up as rival to all the kings of earth, and especially as Israel's King; He fulfilled the prophecy of Zechariah (14:4) that the Lord (Messiah) this day should "stand . . . upon the mount of Olives." Here He forced the issue; those who wanted to be rid of Him *had* to make a move, one way or the other.

At some time after the Triumphal Entry, He threw another challenge at them. Entering the courts of the Temple, He found a disgraceful situation. Here sat the moneychangers who made an outrageous profit in changing the money of the poor (who had to buy sacrifices for the temple) into one certain, acceptable shekel or half-shekel. They changed "foreign" money into Jewish money with which a temple tax was paid by every Jewish male. A High Priest named Annas supervised this exchange, and he was making a fortune out of it. Added to this were the merchants who sold the sacrificial animals—also at an exhorbitant price. It was a racket; it was plain thievery; it was an oppression of the poor, and it drove Jesus into one of His very infrequent moments of anger. In a rage He drove the changers and the merchants from the temple court, shouting that they had taken a temple which the Prophet Isaiah (56:11) had described as "a house of prayer," and turned it into a "den of thieves" (*see* Jeremiah 7:11). When Jesus, enraged, drove these thieves from the precincts of His Father's House, He brought down upon Himself the enmity of the high officials in the temple (the ordinary priests opposed the practice).

His violent reaction to this robbery gave the officials (who controlled the "business") the obligation of making a vital decision: did Jesus, as Messiah, have the *right* to do what He did, or was He an imposter who must be destroyed? They decided upon His destruction. When Jesus acted as He did, He sprang the trap of His own death. It was an act that aroused the lethal anger of the entrenched business interests of Jerusalem. The late Halford E. Luccock claimed that "Jesus was not crucified for saying 'Consider the lilies, how they grow,' but for saying, 'Look at the thieves in the Temple, how they steal!' " That is truth. It is also truth that Jesus stood ready to die even when He was convicted by a greedy enemy in order that those enemies might be saved from their greed at the foot of the cross.

SUGGESTIONS TO TEACHERS

During these past weeks, you have been tracing Jesus' career with Luke. You should be aware by now that Luke the doctor has not set out a haphazard arrangement of anecdotes. Instead, you should note that, like a skillful surgeon carefully laying out his instruments for surgery, Luke meticulously arranges his materials for examining Jesus' claims. This final unit of study from Luke discloses how Luke views Jesus' final ministry on earth as complete. Your purpose as teacher will be to help those in your class to understand that Jesus accomplished everything that needs to be done to minister to the world.

Today, you and your class will take a new look at the events surrounding Jesus' entry into Jerusalem. Because it's not Palm Sunday, you can find fresh insights on Jesus' coming to the city.

1. *ANNOUNCEMENT OF MISSION.* Research the details of Jesus sitting on the colt, the words of the crowd, etc. Share with your class the way that Jesus was carefully and consciously enacting His claims. The triumphal procession down the Mount of Olives was not an impromptu parade; it was a deliberately presented announcement by Jesus of His arrival as Messiah. Think with your class how Jesus would arrive in your

town. How would He be received? Where would He feel most at home? How do those in your church respect His claims today?

2. *ANGUISH OVER THE METROPOLIS.* Jesus wept over the city of Jerusalem. He ached for His people and lamented their indifference and disobedience toward God. How do Christ's people react toward the population area in which they reside in these times? Do your class members have a deep feeling of heartache over the failure of numbers of people to respond to the Lord? Do Christians care enough for their neighbors to cry? Remind your class members that Jesus claims the city. Christians instead of turning their backs on urban problems must share His concern for the city.

3. *ARDOR FOR MORALITY.* Your lesson also deals with Jesus cleansing the Temple. Go over the details, calling attention to the way Jesus stated, "My house shall be a house of prayer" (19:46). Jesus was not lapsing into a fit of violence but restoring the court of Gentiles into its rightful function—a place where everyone could pray. Encourage your class to consider those who are excluded from participating in the life of your community, such as the handicapped, the elderly, the refugees, etc.

4. *ARRIVAL OF THE MESSIAH.* Jesus teaches in the Temple and clearly regards Himself as the Messiah ensconced in the seat of authority. What does Jesus' authority mean to your congregation and your denomination at this time? What, if He were to teach today, would He be saying to your class?

TOPIC FOR ADULTS
GOING UP TO JERUSALEM

Give Us Some Plow Work. A mission executive tells of an American businessman on a quick sightseeing trip through the countryside of northeastern Thailand in the company of a missionary. Passing through rice fields, he saw an old man behind a primitive plow with a boy pulling it. In Thailand, plows are usually pulled by water buffalo.

In amazement, the traveler stopped and through the missionary talked with the old man. One can imagine his feelings when he heard the story.

"We're a Christian family," the grandfather said, "and our church was destroyed in a communist raid on our village. Our church means the world to us, not just on Sunday, but every day. Each morning before sunrise before we go to the fields, we Christians gathered at the church for prayer. When our church was demolished, it was a part of our daily lives that was lost. We *had* to rebuild it, but we didn't have even enough money to rebuild our own homes properly. We decided that no matter what it cost us we would rebuild the church. When we were asked to make our pledge, the only thing we owned of any value was our water buffalo. We sold the water buffalo and gave the money to the church. Now *we* do the plow work."

The American was shocked. Hunting for appropriate words, he said to the old man through the interpreter, "This was a great sacrifice."

"No!" replied the old man as his deeply lined face wrinkled with a smile, "We don't call it that. In our family, we thought it was fortunate that we had a water buffalo to sell."

Foolish? Some would say so, but it all depends upon our values.

The businessman couldn't forget the old man and the boy who loved

Jesus Christ and His Church so much that they counted it a happy circumstance that they had a water buffalo to give. As he recounted the incident to his pastor, a profound change in his life was evident, for his standard of values had changed. And as he pledged himself to faithful stewardship of his life and substance he said, "My wife and family join me. Give us some plow work for Jesus here in our church."

Essential Quality for a Leader. "The most important quality of a leader," says Henry Kissinger, "is courage. He must act in risky situations on the confidence in his own judgment. The task of a leader is to get his people from where they are to where they have not been. The public does not fully understand the world into which it is going. Leaders must invoke an alchemy of great vision. Those leaders who do not are ultimately judged failures, even though they may be popular at the moment. Leadership is not just something you do as a job."

Ponder Kissinger's words in the light of Jesus going up to Jerusalem. Notice how Kissinger's comments apply completely to Jesus.

No wonder that Jesus is regarded as the greatest leader of all time. He had courage. He acted in the risky situation of the Passover time in the last week of His life. He realized that He was called to get His people to where they had not been, a world they did not fully understand. Jesus, more than anyone before or since, had great vision. Going to Jerusalem to die for the world was more than merely a job.

Negative Critic. Jesus constantly encountered negative critics, some told Him that He shouldn't go up to Jerusalem, because it would merely result in His death. When the crowds cheered and hailed Jesus, the Pharisees criticized Him for not rebuking those who cheered and hailed Him. Jesus' activities in the Temple infuriated the officials, who criticized His teachings and healings.

You will have to learn to live with criticism if you are trying to serve others in Christ's name. Negative critics will always find fault or problems in what you are attempting. At the time that Robert Fulton gave the first public demonstration of his steamboat, one of those "can't be done" fellows stood in the crowd along the shore repeating, "He can't start her." Suddenly there was a belch of steam and smoke and the steamboat began slowly to move. Startled, the man stared for a moment and then began to chant, "He can't stop her."

Questions for Pupils on the Next Lesson. 1. What does the cup at the Last Supper symbolize? 2. How do you deal with betrayal by a friend you have trusted? 3. How do you understand and cope with personal suffering? 4. Why do your deeply held convictions sometimes bring you into conflict with opposing social forces? 5. What does the Holy Communion Service in your church mean to you?

TOPIC FOR YOUTH
JESUS—DEMONSTRATING STRENGTH

Ignorant Professor. A college professor being ferried across a stream asked the boatman, "Do you understand philosophy?"

"No, never heard of it."

"Then one-quarter of your life is gone. Do you understand astronomy?"

"No."

"Then three-quarters of your life is gone."

Suddenly the boat tipped over and both fell into the water. "Can you swim?" asked the boatman.

"No."

"Then the whole of your life is gone!"

You may know more of this world's culture than the professor mentioned above, but if you don't know Christ as your Savior, you will have no real knowledge and no moral strength.

Jesus, demonstrating strength and knowledge of God's will by going up to Jerusalem, is the model for your living and thinking.

Courage of Her Convictions. Some years ago in South America, Chile and Argentina were about to go to war. Armies of both countries had been mobilized, and hostilities were about to break out. Fortunately, the conflict was averted through diplomatic negotiations.

A woman, however, made a suggestion which was laughed at when people first heard about it. The woman persisted, convinced that her Christian faith was stronger than the sneers. Her suggestion was fairly simple: melt down the cannons each nation had hauled up to bombard the other and fashion the metal into a statue of Jesus Christ to be placed at the border of Chile and Argentina. The courage of the woman's convictions as a Christian gradually affected others, and eventually the magnificent statue called *The Christ of the Andes* was erected where the people of both nations could see it. The great statue carries this inscription:

"Sooner shall these mountains crumble than this pact of peace, entered into at the feet of Christ between these two nations, shall be broken."

That pact has never been broken. Christ's strength, symbolized in the statue, preserves the peace.

And all because of one woman, filled with the strength and courage of Christ!

Inscription as Description and Prescription. The words inscribed on the memorial to those in the American, Australian, and British forces in the Southeast Asia Command during World War II could be both a description of Jesus' going up to Jerusalem and a prescription for your living a life of sacrifice for others. The words read:

FOR YOUR TOMORROW, THEY GAVE THEIR TODAY.

Jesus gave His today for your tomorrow. He calls you to take risks in His name. Demonstrating the strength of sacrifical love, He summons you to march steadfastly to the Jerusalems of daily living.

Sentence Sermon to Remember: Every man has his Jerusalem, his sacred city, calling to him from the hilltop where it stands.—Phillips Brooks.

Questions for Pupils on the Next Lesson. 1. What does the broken bread and the poured-out cup at the Communion Service mean to you? 2. Do you truly have a sense of "belonging" to some part of the Christian fellowship? Why, or why not? 3. How does Jesus Christ help you to deal with betrayal by trusted friends? 4. Are there any traditions which have meaning for you? If so, what are they? Why are they important?

LESSON XI—FEBRUARY 13

OBSERVING THE LAST SUPPER

Background Scripture: Luke 22:1–23
Devotional Reading: 1 Corinthians 11:23–26

KING JAMES VERSION

LUKE 22 1 Now the feast of unleavened bread drew nigh, which is called the passover.

2 And the chief priests and scribes sought how they might kill him; for they feared the people.

7 Then came the day of unleavened bread, when the passover must be killed.

8 And he sent Peter and John, saying, Go and prepare us the passover, that we may eat.

9 And they said unto him, Where wilt thou that we prepare?

10 And he said unto them, Behold, when ye are entered into the city, there shall a man meet you, bearing a pitcher of water; follow him into the house where he entereth in.

11 And ye shall say unto the goodman of the house, The Master saith unto thee, Where is the guest chamber, where I shall eat the passover with my disciples?

12 And he shall shew you a large upper room furnished: there make ready.

13 And they went, and found as he had said unto them: and they made ready the passover.

14 And when the hour was come, he sat down, and the twelve apostles with him.

15 And he said unto them, With desire I have desired to eat this passover with you before I suffer:

16 For I say unto you, I will not any more eat thereof, until it be fulfilled in the kingdom of God.

17 And he took the cup, and gave thanks, and said, Take this, and divide *it* among yourselves:

18 For I say unto you, I will not drink of the fruit of the vine, until the kingdom of God shall come.

19 And he took bread, and gave thanks, and brake *it*, and gave unto them, saying, This is my body which is given for you: this do in remembrance of me.

20 Likewise also the cup after supper, saying, This cup *is* the new testament in my blood, which is shed for you.

REVISED STANDARD VERSION

LUKE 22 1 Now the feast of Unleavened Bread drew near, which is called the Passover. 2 And the chief priests and the scribes were seeking how to put him to death; for they feared the people.

7 Then came the day of Unleavened Bread, on which the passover lamb had to be sacrificed. 8 So Jesus sent Peter and John, saying, "Go and prepare the passover for us, that we may eat it." 9 They said to him, "Where will you have us prepare it?" 10 He said to them, "Behold, when you have entered the city, a man carrying a jar of water will meet you; follow him into the house which he enters, 11 and tell the householder, 'The Teacher says to you, Where is the guest room, where I am to eat the passover with my disciples?' 12 And he will show you a large upper room furnished; there make ready." 13 And they went, and found it as he had told them; and they prepared the passover.

14 And when the hour came, he sat at table, and the apostles with him. 15 And he said to them, "I have earnestly desired to eat this passover with you before I suffer; 16 for I tell you I shall not eat it until it is fulfilled in the kingdom of God." 17 And he took a cup, and when he had given thanks he said, "Take this, and divide it among yourselves; 18 for I tell you that from now on I shall not drink of the fruit of the vine until the kingdom of God comes." 19 And he took bread, and when he had given thanks he broke it and gave it to them, saying, "This is my body which is given for you. Do this in remembrance of me." 20 And likewise the cup after supper, saying, "This cup which is poured out for you is the new covenant in my blood."

KEY VERSE: And he took bread, and when he had given thanks he broke it and gave it to them, saying, "This is my body. . . ." Luke 22:19 (RSV).

HOME DAILY BIBLE READINGS

Feb. 7. *M.* *Institution of the Passover.* Exodus 12:1–13.
Feb. 8. *T.* *Plotting Against Jesus.* John 11:45–53.
Feb. 9. *W.* *Judas Agrees to Help Jesus' Enemies.* Luke 22:1–6.
Feb. 10. *T.* *Jesus Prepares for the Passover.* Luke 22:7–13.
Feb. 11. *F.* *The Lord's Supper.* Luke 22:14–23.
Feb. 12. *S.* *The Meal Anticipates God's Kingdom.* Luke 13:28,29; 14:15; 22:28–30.
Feb. 13. *S.* *Memorializing the Supper.* 1 Corinthians 11:23–32.

BACKGROUND

Luke begins his story of the Last Supper with the words, "Now the feast of unleavened bread drew nigh, which is called the passover" (Luke 22:1). That would lead us to think that the Feast of Unleavened Bread and the Passover were one and the same thing. This is not true. The Feast lasted seven days; the meal of the Passover was eaten on the fifteenth of Nisan (April), in commemoration of the deliverance of Israel from Egypt. At the time of that deliverance, we remember, the blood of a lamb was smeared on every Jewish doorpost. They fled from Egypt in such a hurry that they did not have time to bake bread with leaven. Blood . . . bread . . . Passover!

Every Jew within fifteen miles of Jerusalem was required by law to observe the Passover in Jerusalem; this meant, according to some Bible statisticians, that nearly 3,000,000 pilgrims crowded into the Holy City for the Feast. The Roman overlords had misgivings about such crowds in the capital at the same time. In the enthusiasm whipped up at Passover, anything could happen. Jesus knew that, too; He deliberately planned a "happening" that both Roman and Jew were helpless to prevent. The Romans, who now wanted Him arrested, knew it, but were hard put to stop it until one named Judas whispered in their ears.

NOTES ON THE PRINTED TEXT

The Romans, who eventually crucified Jesus, were not the *original* plotters who wanted to see Him die as quickly and quietly as possible. There were others—namely, the chief priests and scribes, who desperately wanted to see Him "out of the way." Jesus was aware of their hatred and their plotting, and now He moved swiftly to arrange one last meeting with His disciples before he could be arrested.

Apparently, He alone prepared the way for the events that were to come; none of His disciples seemed to know anything of His plans, nor were any of them consulted. Secretly, He sent two of His most trusted disciples—Peter and John—into Jerusalem to look for a man carrying a pitcher of water at a certain spot. Such a man would not be hard to find; drawing and carrying water was woman's work, and it wouldn't be hard to spot a *man* carrying water! They spotted him, and he took them to the room in which Jesus planned His Last Supper. It was an *upper* room, probably one frequently used by various rabbis to teach the faith of Judaism; it was reached by way of an outside stairway. It was a room "furnished" with tables and couches for the feast; to it went the two disciples, who made it ready for their Master and His other disciples. The whole thing was done quickly, stealthy, and by night. It sounds like a modern "thriller," doesn't it?

The Supper itself began with the words of Jesus, "I have earnestly desired to eat this passover with you before I suffer. . ." (verse 15 RSV). He knew that never again on this earth, would He eat with them, never again, until "what it represents has occurred in the Kingdom of God" (verse 16 TLB). This was their last meeting before the horror of Calvary. So the Passover meal began, as no other Passover meal had ever begun before this one.

As we have said, Passover celebrated the deliverance of Israel from Egypt. But *this* Passover, with Jesus, celebrated *man's* deliverance from *sin.* In the old Jewish Passover, sacrifices of animals were made at the Temple; in this upper room, Jesus offered Himself as a sacrifice for every living sinner. He took the Passover bread in His hands and broke it into pieces and gave it to the disciples, saying, "This is my body, which is given for you." Broken body, broken on the cross, in atonement for the sins of the *world.* Yes, it was symbolism, but this bread was a symbol invested with new meaning; every time the true disciple partakes of the bread of the Last Supper he knows that he eats of no *common* bread but a bread that stirs in his heart a remembrance of what Christ did that night in Jerusalem.

Then He passed the Passover cup of wine among them, saying, "This cup which is poured out for you is the new covenant in my blood" (verse 20 RSV). Now a covenant is an agreement, or a relationship between man and God. Man, all down the ages, has promised God that he would keep his agreement with Him—and then fallen back into his old sinning with astonishing regularity. The Israelites established a system of sacrifice through which the sinner could restore his old relationship with God. It was an easy way out. Jesus proposed and instituted a new way out: He offered His very blood, His very life, to bring men into a new friendship with the Father, a friendship and fellowship ratified or endorsed by the blood of the very Son of God.

The Last Supper! The final instruction of Jesus, which ends with His words, "This do *in remembrance of me.*" Partake of this Supper regularly, Christian, and you will not forget Him. The pressures of life, the exhaustions of "the rat race" of life, have a way of disappearing when one kneels to take the bread and wine of the Supper.

"When the Christian church celebrates the central act of its worship—whether it calls it Mass, Eucharist, Holy Communion, or Lord's Supper—it points back not only to these events in the Upper Room but to the whole drama of God's redemptive action that Jesus Himself is symbolizing in His words and gestures."—William Hamilton.

SUGGESTIONS TO TEACHERS

Many in your class are faintly embarrassed by the Communion Service. "How should I feel?" "What is happening?" They may be aware that this is one of the few practices in the Church which comes directly from Jesus Christ Himself. They may also realize that sharing the bread and cup is something which every Christian group (except a very few such as the Religious Society of Friends) observes. Nonetheless, some in your class feel a vague uneasiness about participating in something which is not clear.

This lesson on observing the Last Supper will offer a fine opportunity for everyone, yourself included, to grow in understanding of both the Last Supper and Communion.

1. *BACKDROP OF BETRAYAL.* Begin by remarking about the death plots against Jesus at the time of the Last Supper. Point out the atmosphere of violence, fear, and resentment as the disciples gathered. Remind your people that Jesus shared His meal not on a pleasant mountaintop or in a tranquil cathedral but in the midst of people—including a scheming Judas and a vacillating Peter. Take a few minutes in your lesson to reflect on how Jesus insists on relating with us, with all of our weakness and rebelliousness. No person has earned a place at table with Jesus!

2. *ANNOUNCEMENT OF IDENTITY.* Your class should be assisted to comprehend that Jesus made clear who He is at the Last Supper. Today, the Communion service is still an occasion in which Jesus Christ discloses Himself. In the Upper Room, He told the shaky followers that He was the Messiah but that He would be called upon to suffer even to the point of giving up His life for them and others. At the same time, He assured them that God would bring Him victory. Communion continues to communicate the suffering, the death, and the Resurrection-Victory of Jesus Christ.

3. *COMING OF THE KINGDOM.* The Upper Room experience also announced that Jesus' assignment had been completely carried out. The guesswork about God is over. The death and Resurrection of Jesus lets us know the arrival of God's rule in our lives and in the world. Communion, through which food is shared, is Christ's own pledge of God's continuing reign.

4. *ASSURANCE OF ASSOCIATION.* Communion is the fellowship meal with Jesus Christ and His "family." As He assured His followers in the Upper Room that He would dine again with them, through the Communion service, today He continues to promise His presence. The Communion is a continuing expression of association with Jesus Christ in death and victory.

TOPIC FOR ADULTS
OBSERVING THE LAST SUPPER

The Presence of Christ in the Lord's Supper. "I freely accept whatever can be made to express the true and substantial partaking of the body and blood of the Lord, which is shown to believers under the sacred symbols of the Supper—and so to express it that they may be understood not to receive it solely by imagination or understanding of the mind, but to enjoy the thing itself as nourishment of eternal life.

"Now if anyone should ask me how this takes place, I shall not be ashamed to confess that it is a secret too lofty for either my mind to comprehend or my words to declare. And, to speak more plainly, I rather experience than understand it. Therefore, I am here to embrace without controversy the truth of God in which I may safely rest. He declares his flesh the food of my soul, his blood its drink. I offer my soul to him to be fed with such food. In his sacred Supper he bids me to take, eat, and drink his body and blood under the symbols of bread and wine. I do not doubt that he himself truly presents them, and that I receive them."—John Calvin, *Institutes* IV, XVII, 19, and XVIII, 32.

River or Swamp. At the Lord's Table, we discover that only Jesus Christ ultimately can be experienced as Lord and Savior. Replying to those who object to the claim that Jesus only offers new life, E. Stanley Jones writes, "I know what I have written will sound narrow and bigoted to some. They will wave their hands and say: 'Do not all rivers finally run into the ocean? Though they may have wandered through devious ways, they all arrive at last.' But the illustration is not true, for some rivers do not get into the ocean; one runs into the Dead Sea; another starts toward the ocean and is lost in the desert sands of Africa. Nothing is more patent to a real observer than that life very often runs into Dead Seas.

"The fact is that all great truths are narrow. That two and two make four is narrow. Why not be broad and liberal and believe that two and two make five, or even six? That sounds liberal. But put it into mathematical life and test it there—put it into . . . the universe of mathematical truth. Spreading out water beyond certain limits does not make for a wider and finer river—it makes for a swamp."—E. Stanley Jones, *Christ at the Round Table.*

Deceit in Neat Package. As he prepared to leave for work one day in Albuquerque, New Mexico, a taxi driver found a small bag of garbage outside his home. It had been overlooked by the garbage collectors.

Not wanting to leave it out in the heat all day, on the spur of the moment, he decided to dispose of it in a unique way. Wrapping it into a neat package, he placed it on the back seat of his cab.

"It worked," he reported. "In my rear-view mirror, I watched a woman spend five minutes stuffing it into her shopping bag before she got out of the cab. Imagine her surprise when she arrived home with that bag of trash!"

Some of the devil's deceits are wrapped up in neat packages. He lures the unwary with the pleasures of sin which look attractive, but which in the end are only a waste.

Judas discovered this. Betraying Jesus, thereby registering his anger over Jesus' refusal to go along with Judas's idea of the Messiah, and also pocketing thirty pieces of silver for his efforts, was an attractive package. Tragically, however, Judas's deceit in the guise of his neat ploy brought him to inevitable destruction. Not surprisingly, the devil is often referred to in the Bible as "father of lies," and "the deceiver."

Be wary of his neat parcels luring you to betraying your Lord!

Questions for Pupils on the Next Lesson. 1. Do you sometimes find that you don't want to accept responsibility for your behavior? If so, why? 2. How can you maintain a balance between feeling and reason in your actions? 3. What is meant by the claim that "Christ died for your sins"? 4. Why do you sometimes find yourself ignoring injustice when it does not directly affect you? 5. What were some of the unusual events which occurred as Jesus was dying?

TOPIC FOR YOUTH
JESUS—GIVING NEW DIRECTION

Pigs and Beans and Jesus. Rowland Hill, one of England's great preachers of the past, was walking down the street one day when he saw a drove of pigs following a man. This excited his curiosity so much that he decided to follow them.

"I did so," he said later, "and to my surprise, I saw them follow him to the slaughterhouse. I said to the man, 'My friend, how do you get those pigs to follow you here?' He replied, 'I had a basket of beans under my arm, and I dropped a few as I went along, so they followed me here.' "

Rowland Hill would tell this story in his preaching, and then would add: "And so it is that Satan has a basket of beans under his arm; and he drops a few for you as he leads you along to an everlasting slaughterhouse of doom."

What "beans" are being dropped along your pathway to try to lead you to destruction? More important, is Jesus giving you new direction?

Lord's Table Means Fighting Hunger. Williard Avery, a member of the Booneville, Missouri, United Church of Christ, remembered that receiving the bread and the cup at the altar means accepting the new direction which Jesus gives. On the day when his pastor, The Rev. Kenneth Kuenning, discussed the hunger in India, Avery pondered what new direction Christ could give to his small Midwest congregation. After the church service that Sunday, he asked, "Would it be possible for us to bring a family from India to the U.S. to learn modern methods of farming?"

After getting in contact with the Board of World Mission office in St. Louis, Avery, Kuenning, and others in the Booneville church began to plan in earnest to respond to the challenge. Church officials selected a brilliant young Indian Christian named Doraiswamy Kanakaraj from the Christian Agricultural Institute at Katpadi in Southern India to accept Booneville's invitation. Members of the church welcomed Kanakaraj to their community and took him into their homes. Led by Williard Avery, the congregation's members arranged to show "Raj," as he came to be known, aspects of farming and enrolled him in an extensive program. By the end of sixteen months in Booneville, Raj had earned a master's degree and had acquired expertise in agriculture.

Back at Katpadi, Raj was appointed farm manager at the Institute. The modern techniques he taught, however, were resisted by the tradition-bound farmers and older students. Then Raj was advised to work with the younger boys. In time the new methods proved themselves as rice production increased. In 1974, when it came time to select twenty students for Raj's program, there were 860 applications.

Thanks to the continuing interest of Williard Avery and other Booneville friends, Raj returned to Missouri in August 1974 to work toward his doctorate. His American supporters soon realized the need to keep the Kanakaraj family circle intact—while in India, Raj had married Grace Monoyamani, a zoology teacher, and they had a small son and daughter. The Missourians combined efforts to start the "Raj Project," and within a year the Kanakaraj family was reunited.

Home in India, Raj hopes to serve as an agricultural specialist in a new program sponsored by Vellore Christian Medical College in cooperation with the local diocese of the Church of South India.

New Directions From the Lord's Supper. It was the summer of 1942 at La Sang P.O.W. Camp in the Philippines. Forced to work for the Japanese building an airplane runaway for the enemy after surviving the Bataan Death March, Sidney Stewart lay helpless with disease, exhaustion, and starvation.

"One afternoon one of the prisoners came in. He walked over and sat down beside me. There was a smile on his face. 'I brought you something,' he said. 'There's a Jap guard out there who says he knows you real well and he gave me something to give you.'

"He reached down inside his shirt and pulled out two hard-boiled eggs.

"Good old Maurii, I thought. I wanted to give the boy one of the eggs. Without saying a word, I handed him an egg. He laughed. 'No, you keep it,' he said. 'There's a lot of nourishment in those eggs. If you eat 'em you'll get well. The guard said he was going to bring me something like that for you every day. We have to be careful, you know. The other Japs would raise hell if they found out about it. They'd beat him up for doin' it.' "—Sidney Stewart, *Give Us This Day.*

"Because of the guard's sharing, Stewart lived to tell his story. Two eggs bridged cultural differences. Two eggs broke down hatred. Two eggs showed God's love. Two eggs united enemies in communion.

"Communion serves to give each of us a sense of kinship with everyone around this world."—John B. Barker, West Sunbury United Presbyterian Church.

Sentence Sermon to Remember: It is small wonder that this upper room has been a dearer place to Christendom than all the great cathedrals raised by subsequent ages to Jesus' honor.—James S. Stewart

Questions for Pupils on the Next Lesson. 1. Can you name some of those who have suffered on your behalf? 2. How do you best demonstrate concern for other persons' needs? 3. What is the greatest example for someone forgiving another that you remember? 4. What exactly is the meaning of Jesus Christ's Crucifixion to you? 5. What are some of the events that took place as Jesus was dying?

LESSON XII—FEBRUARY 20

SUFFERING CRUCIFIXION

Background Scripture: Luke 23
Devotional Reading: Luke 23:18–25

KING JAMES VERSION

LUKE 23 32 And there were also two others, malefactors, led with him to be put to death.

33 And when they were come to the place, which is called Calvary, there they crucified him, and the malefactors, one on the right hand, and the other on the left.

34 Then said Jesus, Father, forgive them; for they know not what they do. And they parted his raiment, and cast lots.

35 And the people stood beholding. And the rulers also with them derided *him*, saying, He saved others; let him save himself, if he be Christ, the chosen of God.

36 And the soldiers also mocked him, coming to him, and offering him vinegar,

37 And saying, If thou be the King of the Jews, save thyself.

38 And a superscription also was written over him in letters of Greek, and Latin, and Hebrew, THIS IS THE KING OF THE JEWS.

39 And one of the malefactors which were hanged railed on him, saying, If thou be Christ, save thyself and us.

40 But the other answering rebuked him, saying, Dost not thou fear God, seeing thou art in the same condemnation?

41 And we indeed justly; for we receive the due reward of our deeds: but this man hath done nothing amiss.

42 And he said unto Jesus, Lord, remember me when thou comest into thy kingdom.

43 And Jesus said unto him, Verily I say unto thee, To day shalt thou be with me in paradise.

44 And it was about the sixth hour, and there was a darkness over all the earth until the ninth hour.

45 And the sun was darkened, and the veil of the temple was rent in the midst.

46 And when Jesus had cried with a loud voice, he said, Father, into thy hands I commend my spirit: and having said thus, he gave up the ghost.

REVISED STANDARD VERSION

LUKE 23 32 Two others also, who were criminals, were led away to be put to death with him. 33 And when they came to the place which is called The Skull, there they crucified him, and the criminals, one on the right and one on the left. 34 And Jesus said, "Father, forgive them; for they know not what they do." And they cast lots to divide his garments. 35 And the people stood by, watching; but the rulers scoffed at him, saying, "He saved others; let him save himself, if he is the Christ of God, his Chosen One!" 36 The soldiers also mocked him, coming up and offering him vinegar, 37 and saying, "If you are the King of the Jews, save yourself!" 38 There was also an inscription over him, "This is the King of the Jews."

39 One of the criminals who were hanged railed at him, saying, "Are you not the Christ? Save yourself and us!" 40 But the other rebuked him, saying, "Do you not fear God, since you are under the same sentence of condemnation? 41 And we indeed justly; for we are receiving the due reward of our deeds; but this man has done nothing wrong." 42 And he said, "Jesus, remember me when you come into your kingdom." 43 And he said to him, "Truly, I say to you, today you will be with me in Paradise."

44 It was now about the sixth hour, and there was darkness over the whole land until the ninth hour, 45 while the sun's light failed; and the curtain of the temple was torn in two. 46 Then Jesus, crying with a loud voice, said, "Father, into thy hands I commit my spirit!" And having said this he breathed his last.

KEY VERSE: Then Jesus, crying with a loud voice, said, "Father, into thy hands I commit my spirit!" And having said this he breathed his last. Luke 23:46 (RSV).

HOME DAILY BIBLE READINGS

Feb. 14. M. *Jesus Before the Council.* Luke 22:66–71.
Feb. 15. T. *Jesus Before Pilate.* Luke 23:1–5.
Feb. 16. W. *Jesus Before Herod.* Luke 23:6–12.
Feb. 17. T. *Jesus Is Sentenced to Death.* Luke 23:13–25.
Feb. 18. F. *Jesus Is Crucified.* Luke 23:26–43.
Feb. 19. S. *The Death of Jesus.* Luke 23:44–49.
Feb. 20. S. *The Burial of Jesus.* Luke 23:50–56.

BACKGROUND

After the Last Supper came the arrest of Jesus in Gethsemane, His "trials" before Pilate and Herod, and His inevitable conviction and sentence to death by crucifixion. The trials were a farce, an exercise in injustice. He was charged with sedition, with refusing to pay tribute to Caesar, and with setting Himself up as a king. All three charges were plain lies, and both Pilate and Herod knew that they had no reason to convict Jesus, but both gave in to what was plain *political* pressure from the collaborationistic scribes and Sadducees.

The Jews, at this time, did not have the power to inflict capital punishment; that sentence could be inflicted only by a Roman governor and executed by Roman soldiers. That was why the Jews hastened to bring Jesus before Governor Pontius Pilate who alone could send Him to His death. Pilate, who wanted no bad report of his governorship to be sent to Rome, surrendered to the Jewish pressure, "washed his hands" of the whole thing and sent the Prisoner to Calvary's hill. If crucifying this preacher from Nazareth would help him keep things peaceful and under control, then why not put him to death? Why should Pilate worry about this little tempest in Jerusalem?

NOTES ON THE PRINTED TEXT

On Calvary (commonly known as The Skull), Roman soldiers drove in the nails which fastened Him to the cross and raised the cross high so that all could see. That strikes repulsion, even terror, to the heart of the modern reader of the most wicked act in human history. On either side of Him, two others were fastened to crosses; Mark and Matthew call them two thieves, but Luke calls them malefactors (criminals). They may have been members of the Zealot revolutionary party, dangerous to Rome and to Judea, and it was fitting that they die on either side of the Rebel from Galilee. Society has an odd way of putting to death not only those who are violently dangerous and who would drag men down, but often the same society puts to death others who would lift men *up* (Abraham Lincoln, Martin Luther King, for instance) but who in lifting men up conflict with the interests of those who in selfishness "want to keep things as they are."

So there he writhed on a cross He never deserved. All the world knows the story of His agonizing death in bloody, ghastly detail. But not many of us think or talk much of what Christ *did* on that cross before He died. Luke tells us about that; he would, knowing as he did this compassionate Christ. It will help us a great deal if we look at Him on that cross and see Him through Luke's eyes.

We see, first, a dying Man who looked down at the crowd assembled on Calvary, *and thought more about them than He thought of Himself.* "Father," He cried, "forgive them, for they know not what they do!" (verse 34). *Forgive* them?

Who did He mean by *them*? Who, gathered around that crowd, deserved forgiveness? Well, there were the Roman soldiers who nailed Him to the cross. Jesus felt sorry for them because He knew that they were only carrying out orders that they dared not disobey. Personally, they had nothing against Jesus; He was just another criminal of whom they knew next to nothing. Jesus pitied them.

Then there were the people, the crowd. They did not know much either about what was happening. Jesus had been tried in secrecy and condemned by way of political influence and pressure. The people at large were ignorant but not malicious until they were led to madness by those who really hated the Christ. Clever talkers can talk mobs into violence. The people watched and wondered, blind and ignorant of the shameful murder that was taking place; many were probably only curious, who had only come to see a man die. (When Ruth Snyder was electrocuted in Sing Sing prison in New York, hundreds of curious people wrote the prison, asking for "tickets" that would let them watch her die! That was in the *twentieth* century.)

Soldiers and the curious—we might justify or at least understand that they did what they did at Calvary at least partially in ignorance. But that does not apply to those who actually sent Jesus to His death—the scoffing priests and soldiers who shouted in derision, "If you are the Christ and the King of the Jews, *save yourself.*" If God was really with Him, let Him come down from the cross. That was bitter hatred, it was also ignorance. Those who threw the taunt to the dying Christ did not know what He knew—namely, that it was in the divine plan that He die in order to save the taunters and the hardened sinners. He had told His disciples that "He must go unto Jerusalem, and suffer many things of the elders and chief priests and scribes, and be killed. . ." (Matthew 16:21 RSV). Now that was being fulfilled on the cross. He had also told them that he who gives his life to God shall save it—save it to do the work of saving others. Jesus could have avoided the cross; He chose to die upon it so that others might live.

His last act on Calvary was to save one of the criminals dying with Him. One of them was hard, bitter, dying in hatred against those who had put him there. All he wanted was to be taken down from the cross and go back to his old life of crime—he wanted *vengeance,* just as many a convict in a modern prison wants only to get out and get even with those who put him in prison. Jesus did not answer him, but the other criminal did: the other one confessed his guilt. He saw in Jesus something that his criminal companion missed—a strange superhuman power, a Spirit that could conquer physical pain and even death, a power to grant forgiveness and a second chance. Minutes before death took him, Jesus led him to a better life in a better world, or "paradise." His name was Dismas; he has a memorial dedicated to him in a state prison in Dannemora, New York; it is called The Chapel of the Penitent Thief, and it says to every criminal in that prison that it is never too late for the worst of us to turn to Jesus Christ and be set free.

Now came death, welcome death. Jesus breathed His last, and it was finished. At that moment, "the curtain of the temple was torn in two" (verse 45 RSV). Luke here is speaking of a curtain in the Jerusalem Temple which veiled the Holy of Holies into which only the high priest could enter. Now, by way of the dead One on the cross, the curtain that separates the cry of human need from the presence and forgiveness of God had been torn away, and the way was opened to God and salvation. The cross is the key that rips down curtains and opens doors.

It all happened in A.D. 29. If Jesus were to come back to *our* world in A.D. 1983, would it happen all over again? G. Studdert Kennedy wrote a shocking little poem in which he described what might happen to Him in a world that gives millions for war and pennies for Christ; he pictures it happening in Birmingham, England:

When Jesus came to Birmingham, they simply passed Him by.
They never hurt a hair of Him, they only let Him die;
For men had grown more tender, and they would not give Him pain,
They only just passed down the street, and left Him in the rain.
Still Jesus cried, "Forgive them, for they know not what they do,"
And still it rained the winter rain that drenched Him through and through;
The crowds went home and left the streets without a soul to see,
And Jesus crouched against a wall and cried for Calvary.

Is that too much—or do we recrucify Him so, every day, not out of hatred or ignorance but out of sheer disinterest? We say we love Him, but would we climb Calvary with Him, or let Him die there alone, this second time around?

SUGGESTIONS TO TEACHERS

Let's acknowledge from the outset that there is so much packed into Luke 23 that you could spend a month of Sundays on this one chapter. Don't get frustrated if you are not able to teach and discuss everything in this passage. Let's also be alert to how easy it is to get off the subject when working with this lesson material. Spending too much time on Pilate or Herod or Barabbas, for example, can cause you and the class to lose sight of the Cross itself. Remember that the central theme today is the sacrificial death of Jesus Christ!

1. *PARTIES TO HIS EXECUTION.* Give your class some time to do some character studies of some of the personalities which took part in Jesus' death. Perhaps groups of two or three people could read, confer together, and report to the rest of the class on the Temple authorities and how the religious people missed understanding Jesus, on Pilate and how responsible people allow justice to miscarry, on Herod and how some people want to trifle with Jesus. Perhaps, time permitting, your class may

also find it meaningful to look seriously at Simon of Cyrene, the other men crucified that day, the Centurion, the women and followers of Jesus, and Joseph of Arimathea. What similarities are there between these people and your class members?

2. *PAIN OF HIS CRUCIFIXION.* We have sentimentalized the Cross so that it frequently means nothing except a dimestore trinket on a chain. Have your class consider all dimensions of Jesus' going to the Cross and what it entailed, including the physical agony and the emotional pain. Remind your people of the disgrace suffered by a crucified man as well as the indescribable torture of the lingering death. Most of all, make certain that your students grasp that Jesus went through the horrors of the Crucifixion for them!

3. *PROFUNDITY OF HIS SACRIFICE.* The cosmic significance of the Cross must be repeatedly mentioned. The detail of the Temple curtain being torn indicates that Jesus' death opens new access to the Father-God. Jesus' death is for all, for all time, for all of us!

4. *PRELUDE TO THE RESURRECTION.* Luke 50:58 indicates with breathless expectation that there is more to come! Death cannot contain Jesus. From the standpoint of the Resurrection (from which Luke and all other New Testament writers wrote), Jesus suffering Crucifixion was bad news turned to good! Do your class members understand that the Cross is God's own "to be continued" written into the deepest tragedy of history?

TOPIC FOR ADULTS
SUFFERING CRUCIFIXION

Accept the Pardon. In the year 1829, a man named George Wilson, of Philadelphia, committed an act of robbery from the United States mails, killing another person. He was later arrested and brought to trial. He was found to be guilty, and the Judge sentenced him to be hanged.

Some friends intervened in his behalf and were finally able to obtain a pardon for him from President Andrew Jackson. But when he was informed of this, *George Wilson refused to accept the pardon!*

The Sheriff was unwilling to act, for, he reasoned: How could he hang a pardoned man? So an appeal was sent to President Jackson. The perplexed President turned to the United States Supreme Court to decide the case.

Chief Justice Marshall gave his ruling: "A pardon is a piece of paper, the value of which depends upon its acceptance by the person implicated. It is hardly to be supposed that a person under the sentence of death would refuse to accept a pardon, *but if it is refused, it is no pardon.* George Wilson must be hanged."

So George Wilson was executed, although his pardon lay on the Sheriff's desk.

But how much more tragic it is that people ignore or refuse God's offer of pardon.

God asks: "Why will you die?" He says: "I have set before you life and death . . . therefore choose life."

Through Jesus Christ's sacrifice on the Cross, we may be assured that we are unconditionally pardoned and set free to serve.

Faithful Action. "The longer I live, the more I feel that true repose consists in 'renouncing' one's own self, by which I mean making up one's mind to admit that there is no importance whatever in being 'happy' or 'unhappy' in the usual meaning of the words. Personal success or personal satisfaction are not worth another thought if one does achieve them, or worth worrying about it if they evade one or are slow in coming. . . . All that is really worthwhile is action—faithful action, for the world, and in God. Before one can see that and live by it, there is a sort of threshold to cross, or a reversal to be made in what appears to be men's general habit of thought; but once that gesture has been made, what freedom is yours, freedom to work and to love! I have told you more than once that my life is now possessed by this 'disinterest' which I feel to be growing on me, while at the same time the deep-seated appetite, that calls me to all that is real at the heart of the real, continues to grow stronger."—Pierre Teilhard de Chardin, *Letters from a Traveler.*

The Right Answer! A gentleman once asked a group of children what was meant by the word *repentance.* A little boy raised his hand: "Repentance is being sorry for your sins." A little girl also raised her hand. "Well," said the gentleman, turning to her, "what do you say?" "It's being sorry enough to quit," she said.

Questions for Pupils on the Next Lesson. 1. Are you sometimes afraid to admit your doubts? 2. Why are some people unprepared to cope with crises of life? 3. Do you wonder if there can be life beyond death? 4. How did the disciples and followers of Jesus react to the news of the Resurrection? How do you think you would have reacted if you had been present? 5. How do you react to the news of the Resurrection today?

TOPIC FOR YOUTH
JESUS—EXPRESSING LOVE

Christ's Last Will and Testament. He left His purse to Judas; His body to Joseph of Arimathea; His mother to John; His clothes to the soldiers; His peace to His disciples; His supper to His followers; Himself as an example and as a servant; His Gospel to the world; His presence always with God's children!

Unpromising Beginning. Who would have guessed that an ugly eighty-ton load somewhat resembling a stubby fusilage of an airplane propped on top of a trailer pulled by a truck crawling along at three miles-per-hour would be the start of a space voyage? When the "Columbia," the huge new space ship, rolled out of the Rockwell International Assembly line in Palmdale, California, to go to the Dryden Flight Research Center, lumbering so slowly, spectators probably could not believe that it was designed for speeds measuring in the miles-per-second bracket.

Who would have guessed that the horror and ugliness of the Crucifixion of Jesus Christ could have been the step toward the soaring hope of the Resurrection? Who could have surmised that the Cross of Calvary could have been the beginning of the journey of the Rising of Jesus as Living Lord?

Attacking Poverty Is Expressing Love. There are still 1.3 billion people, more than one-quarter of the world population, living in countries where the per capita income doesn't exceed $200 a year.

The aid efforts of most industrial nations are puny, particularly of the United States, which is currently doing less to help combat poverty in relation to its wealth, than any other non-Communist industrial nation.

World Bank figures show the United States last year allocated just 18-hundredths of 1 percent of its gross national product for foreign aid, compared with the average for all industrial countries of 34-hundredths of 1 percent. The U.S. effort was 27-hundredths of 1 percent as recently as 1978.

"Sustaining the attack on poverty is not an economic luxury, something affordable when times are easy and superfluous when times become troublesome," Robert S. McNamara, former President of the World Bank, said. "It is a continuing social and moral responsibility, and an economic imperative—and its need now is greater than ever."

Sentence Sermon to Remember: The Cross of Christ, on which he was extended, points, in the length of it, to heaven and earth, reconciling them together; and in the breadth of it, to former and following ages, as being equally salvation to both.—Samuel Rutherford.

Questions for Pupils on the Next Lesson. 1. What are the principal doubts you have? 2. Do you sometimes feel guilty because you have doubts about the Christian faith? 3. What is the significance of the major events in your life in the light of the Christian faith? 4. Why is the Resurrection so supremely important to the Christian Church? 5. What did Jesus commission His disciples to do at the time of the Resurrection?

LESSON XIII—FEBRUARY 27

STANDING AMONG HIS DISCIPLES

Background Scripture: Luke 24:1–11, 36–53
Devotional Reading: 1 Corinthians 15:1–11

KING JAMES VERSION

LUKE 24 36 And as they thus spake, Jesus himself stood in the midst of them, and saith unto them, Peace *be* unto you.

37 But they were terrified and affrighted, and supposed that they had seen a spirit.

38 And he said unto them, Why are ye troubled? and why do thoughts arise in your hearts?

39 Behold my hands and my feet, that it is I myself: handle me, and see; for a spirit hath not flesh and bones, as ye see me have.

40 And when he had thus spoken, he shewed them *his* hands and *his* feet.

41 And while they yet believed not for joy, and wondered, he said unto them, Have ye here any meat?

42 And they gave him a piece of a broiled fish, and of a honeycomb.

43 And he took *it*, and did eat before them.

44 And he said unto them, These *are* the words which I spake unto you, while I was yet with you, that all things must be fulfilled, which were written in the law of Moses, and *in* the prophets, and *in* the psalms, concerning me.

45 Then opened he their understanding, that they might understand the scriptures,

46 And said unto them, Thus it is written, and thus it behoved Christ to suffer, and to rise from the dead the third day:

47 And that repentance and remission of sins should be preached in his name among all nations, beginning at Jerusalem.

48 And ye are witnesses of these things.

49 And, behold, I send the promise of my Father upon you: but tarry ye in the city of Jerusalem, until ye be endued with power from on high.

50 And he led them out as far as to Bethany, and he lifted up his hands, and blessed them.

51 And it came to pass, while he blessed them, he was parted from them, and carried up into heaven.

52 And they worshipped him, and returned to Jerusalem with great joy:

53 And were continually in the temple, praising and blessing God. Amen.

REVISED STANDARD VERSION

LUKE 24 36 As they were saying this, Jesus himself stood among them. 37 But they were startled and frightened, and supposed that they saw a spirit. 38 And he said to them, "Why are you troubled, and why do questionings rise in your hearts? 39 See my hands and my feet, that it is I myself; handle me, and see; for a spirit has not flesh and bones as you see that I have." 41 And while they still disbelieved for joy, and wondered, he said to them, "Have you anything here to eat?" 42 They gave him a piece of broiled fish, 43 and he took it and ate before them.

44 Then he said to them, "These are my words which I spoke to you, while I was still with you, that everything written about me in the law of Moses and the prophets and the psalms must be fulfilled." 45 Then he opened their minds to understand the scriptures, 46 and said to them, "Thus it is written, that the Christ should suffer and on the third day rise from the dead, 47 and that repentance and forgiveness of sins should be preached in his name to all nations, beginning from Jerusalem. 48 You are witnesses of these things. 49 And behold, I send the promise of my Father upon you; but stay in the city, until you are clothed with power from on high."

50 Then he led them out as far as Bethany, and lifting up his hands he blessed them. 51 While he blessed them, he parted from them. 52 And they returned to Jerusalem with great joy, 53 and were continually in the temple blessing God.

KEY VERSE: "See my hands and my feet, that it is I myself; handle me, and see; for a spirit has not flesh and bones as you see I have." Luke 24:39 (RSV).

HOME DAILY BIBLE READINGS

Feb. 21. M. The Resurrection. Luke 24:1–12.
Feb. 22. T. The Walk to Emmaus. Luke 24:13–24.
Feb. 23. W. Explanation. Luke 24:25–35.
Feb. 24. T. Appearance to His Disciples. Luke 24:36–43.
Feb. 25. F. Commissioning His Disciples. Luke 24:44–49.
Feb. 26. S. The Ascension. Luke 24:50–53; Acts 1:9–11.
Feb. 27. S. Paul's Testimony. 1 Corinthians 15:1–11.

BACKGROUND

There were many in Jerusalem who witnessed the death of Jesus on His cross and who said to each other, "Well, that's the end of *Him!*" We say the same thing today, when someone, good or bad, passes from us. "When you're dead, you're *dead.*" But they were wrong who thought the Nazarene was finished, and we are wrong when we say that death ends everything. Luke's short and sublime account of what happened *after* Calvary was written to *prove* that we are wrong.

On the Sunday following the Crucifixion, two men who had seen and probably followed Jesus were walking toward a village called Emmaus, some seven miles from Jerusalem. We all know the story of Emmaus, and of the two who met a risen Christ on the highway. As Luke tells it, these two (one named Cleopas) rushed back to Jerusalem to tell the eleven disciples (gathered with some others in—the Upper Room?) that He was alive and not dead; they had *seen* Him, talked with Him; so had Peter (Luke does not tell us how or where Peter saw him). They found the disciples to be dispirited, crushed with grief. They had been told that His tomb was empty by the two Marys and Joanna, but they just couldn't believe such "idle tales," or even Peter's words about the tomb.

Then "Jesus Himself stood in the midst of them, and saith Peace be unto you!" And they were terrified.

NOTES ON THE PRINTED TEXT

Why did Jesus appear at this particular moment to a little group of crushed and saddened men?

He appeared, first of all, to prove to them that the Resurrection was a fact and not a fantasy. They were frightened because "they supposed that they had seen a spirit," and spirits made men tremble. It was no spirit: it was the Christ they had seen and heard, Christ *alive.* It was no hallucination, no spectre dreamed up in the minds of distraught men. *Touch* me, if you have difficulty believing that; look at the wounds in my hands and feet! (Remember the similar words that He spoke to doubting Thomas?) He asked them for food, fish and honey, and He ate it in their presence. *Now* do you believe?

Do *we* believe that the Resurrection happened exactly like this? Or do we "have our doubts?" Dr. Ernest Scott, a great theologian, once answered those critics who think that the disciples were duped and that the whole story is a myth. He replied by saying to them, "If you can tell me how belief in His resurrection became *objectified* in millions of His disciples, you will be saying something worth listening to." Jesus Himself objectified His rising from the dead this day when He stood there before them, where thy could see Him with their own eyes.

Jesus wanted them to believe with all their hearts *and minds* that He had conquered death. He also wanted them to be clear concerning the meaning of the cross which preceded His Resurrection, so He reminds them that the cross was the fulfillment of prophecy about Him in the Old Testament. The prophets (particularly Isaiah) had promised one who should come and be "despised and rejected of men; a man of sorrows, and acquainted with grief," one wounded for our transgressions . . . "and with his stripes we are healed" (Isaiah 53). It came out exactly that way through His sufferings on the cross. From the time of Moses and the giving of the Law and the Ten Commandments, Israel had been trying to find out God's will for men. Through the Psalms runs the longing: "My God, my God, why hast thou forsaken me?" (Psalms 22); "Save me, O God, for the waters are come into my soul" (Psalms 69). That longing, that hope for salvation, came at last by way of One who had come in fulfillment of prophecy to release men from the bondage and the shame of sin.

To the Romans who used it, the cross was nothing more than an instrument of punishment for criminals. To the One they crucified, the cross became the key that opened the door to forgiveness and God. Let all disciples base their teaching and preaching on *that!* Go, disciples, go out from Jerusalem to preach this about the cross and the tomb; go as witnesses of these things, which you must surely believe; go as My *witnesses,* and preach repentance and forgiveness of sin in the name of the Crucified One. Go! Don't just sit around talking about it: *go,* beginning at Jerusalem, when I have ascended unto My Father.

Now going out from Jerusalem to preach a risen Christ was anything but easy; it was hard to even contemplate. These disciples would go out as lambs into a world of wolves who despised everything that Christ stood for. Their enemies would be countless. But they would have a secret power—the Holy Spirit—to give them a strength that was not human but superhuman. They would get that strength at Pentecost. They were not to rush out the minute after He had left them; they should have first a waiting time, a quiet, strengthening time, when they would wait for the Spirit to come upon them. We modern Christians should read that twice: we have a great need for quiet times with our Lord if we expect to win out over a sin-smitten world.

Then, says Luke, "he was parted from them, and carried up into heaven" (24:51). There is a bit of confusion in the record, here. Luke tells us in Acts that the post-Resurrection of Jesus lasted forty days, so the Ascension could not have taken place immediately after His final conversation with the disciples. But the Ascension did take place, whatever the time, and it left the disciples not weeping at their separation but with "great joy." That was quite different from the way they had responded to His death on the cross. Now they were glad—glad that He had gone to sit at the right hand of God, glad that He was enthroned in heaven. And glad, even more, that He had at the very last moment on earth given a blessing that would be with them and within them as they spread out to obey His commandment. He was with them in the Spirit, and nothing, no one on earth, could separate them from that.

They went singing back to Jerusalem; they worshiped Him as they walked—past Calvary? Now read the last line in Luke's Gospel. "It is no accident," says one commentator, "that Luke's Gospel ends where it began—in the Temple!" And then they moved out from the Temple to establish a new form of temple known as the Church, in which they preached and led other apostles to preach that the Gospel of their risen Lord "is the power of God for salvation to every one who has faith, to the Jew first and also to the Greek" (Romans 1:16 RSV).

SUGGESTIONS TO TEACHERS

At every British military funeral, the custom is practiced of sounding "Last Post," the sad plaintive notes of mourning and sleep. A time of silence follows. Suddenly, the stillness is shattered with the urgent notes of Reveille. "Arise! A new day has dawned!"

The Resurrection of Jesus Christ is God's Reveille for Jesus Christ and for His followers. Easter is the "great gettin' up day" for Jesus, and the assurance of a new day dawning for the believer.

1. *MYSTERY OF THE MISSING BODY.* Part of the Easter story has to do with the perplexing details of the women finding the tomb empty. Notice how no one was expecting Jesus' Resurrection. Furthermore, everybody was certain that Jesus was actually dead. Help your people to answer the half-baked claims of some ill-informed critics that the Resurrection was a hoax, or that Jesus was not actually dead. Jesus went through all of the total separation of death.

2. *REPORT OF THE RESURRECTED JESUS.* The women hear the announcement of Jesus' Resurrection from the messengers inside the tomb. Impress on your students the importance of progressing beyond curiosity over the missing body to hearing the news that Jesus is alive.

3. *REPAST WITH THE RISEN LORD.* The table fellowship at the inn at Emmaus enabled two followers to discern Jesus alive and with them. Do communion and worship and meals together as a church offer an opportunity to people so that "their eyes were opened and they recognized him" (24:31)? Jesus confirms that He truly is alive as we meet in His name.

4. *ENCOUNTER WITH THE UNBELIEVING ELEVEN.* Ask your people to consider how Jesus makes Himself known today. How do Christians detect His presence as the Resurrected One? Do the gatherings in your church show a sense of expecting to meet Jesus? Have your class talk over the need for belief. Also think together of the times when the Risen Christ was at work undetected.

5. *MISSION TO NEEDY MILLIONS.* Concentrate for a significant part of your lesson on the closing verses of today's scriptural material, especially 24:45–53. Remind your class members of their vital assignment as witnesses of the Resurrection. Is your congregation as a "resurrection community" bringing new life by bringing "forgiveness of sins . . . in his name to all nations" (24:47)?

TOPIC FOR ADULTS
STANDING AMONG THE DISCIPLES

Jesus Alive! "We are committed not to a system but to a Person. Christian excitement centers in Jesus Christ. Systems can disappoint us, but not the Saviour. Let us make certain that our allegiance is not to a particular leader or to some aspect of the church's life. It is our relationship to the Lord that holds us up.

"Never was this brought home to me more forcibly than when my wife and I traveled to the Soviet Union recently. A highlight of that trip was our visit to Lenin's tomb, located on Moscow's Red Square. As we waited in the long line, barely inching forward, I had time to look about me. In the distance I could see St. Basil's Cathedral, the Kremlin, and the flag with the hammer and sickle.

"Ahead of us was the low granite enclosure containing Lenin's body. I counted ten soldiers standing guard around the mausoleum. Finally our turn came.

" 'Two by two,' were the instructions. 'No laughing, no talking, no picture-taking.'

"Through the door, down the steps, around the corner and up the inside steps. How sobering it was to stand gazing upon the remains of the most powerful atheist who ever lived.

"Vladimir Ilyich Lenin lay face up, eyes closed, hands folded. White light seemed to emanate from the body itself. Not a sound broke the cool stillness save the quiet shuffle of feet. I counted 11 more guards inside, making a total of 21.

"Then down more steps and into the sunshine. One thought kept vibrating through my mind as if it were the beat of my heart: 'Lenin is dead; Jesus is alive. Lenin is dead; Jesus is alive!'

"Where do 21 armed troops stand guard over the dead body of Jesus of Nazareth? Where is his glass casket on display that millions might view his remains? There is no place. Nowhere on this planet can the body of Jesus be found because that body is not here. He took it with him when he ascended to be with the Father. His rising from the tomb was a preview of our own resurrection. He is alive, today, now!"—From *Decision* © 1975 The Billy Graham Evangelistic Association. Excerpts from A CHANCE TO START OVER by Roderick Huron.

Proper Game of Joy. "Jurgen Moltmann, in his recent book, *The Church in the Power of the Spirit*, suggests that probably the earliest Easter Epiphanies and celebrations of the Lord's Supper were together (cf. Luke 24:13–43). He states: 'Easter is the feast of freedom, when the risen Christ sits at the table with his disciples . . . with Easter the laughter of the redeemed, the dance of the liberated and the creative play of fantasy begins.' His view recaptures the picture of Easter presented by Hippolytus who refers to Christ as 'the leader of the mystic round dance and the Church is the bride who dances with him.' It also echoes Paul Gerhardt's Easter hymn which proclaims Christ's resurrection as *'ein rechtes Freudenspiel'*—a proper game of joy."—David Shannon.

Closet Christian. "I suppose if you were to notice me at work, shopping, driving down the street, you would just think I was the average person. If you came to know me, you might discover that I go to church regularly, participate in a weekly Bible study, and am a church deacon. By now you would probably think that I was a very devout Christian. WRONG! I am only a closet Christian.

"Why do I call myself a closet Christian? Well, perhaps it can be explained this way. It is true that I have accepted Christ Jesus as my personal Savior, but why don't I exclaim it to my friends, family, associates? Why? Because I am only a closet Christian.

"How do I know I am a closet Christian? That one is easy to answer, I wonder how many opportunities I have had to witness for the Lord, but have let those opportunities pass by. I can't remember the number of times I could have counseled someone to the grace of God, but chose to keep silent. Now don't think that these were great, noteworthy occasions. They were not! Instead the situations were everyday, true-to-life, real world events that you and I and everyone else face daily. The friend whose husband is laid off because of lack of work, but there is no lack of monthly bills; the unmarried girl who discovers she is pregnant and can't decide if she wants to have the baby or have an abortion; the associate who has a drinking problem; the fellow office worker who is constantly depressed and complains about everything. Or, if I can't speak up and tell about how Jesus can and will help us in times of need or trouble, I certainly could inform them of the good things He has done for me. The prayers He has already answered, the blessings He has given us just out of the goodness of His heart. But why don't I pass the information on? Why am I so tight-lipped about the wonders of Christ? Why don't I speak out and tell people about the blessings of the Lord and what a difference He can make in life? Why?

"Is it because I don't want to 'turn people off' to God instead of 'turning them on?' (That's the oldest, cheapest cop-out going.) Is it because I don't want my friends or family to think that I am a 'Jesus freak' or a 'Bible thumper?' Is it because I don't want people to be uncomfortable around me, think that they can't be themselves because of my religious beliefs? Or is it because if I advertise my Christianity and then fall somewhat short of being divine I don't want someone to chide: 'Is that any way for a Christian to act, or talk, or think?' Or is it because I know my shortcomings and if I am a self-professed Christian I would have to work harder at controlling them? It could be any or all of the above, but the fact remains that still I am only a closet Christian."—Mrs. Linda Doddlepke. Reprinted from *The Presbyterian Layman.*

Questions for Pupils on the Next Lesson. 1. Do you find meaning in seeing your life as part of a larger story? Why, or why not? 2. Is your life a continuing rhythm of waiting and doing? 3. What do you think the future holds for you? 4. When was the last time you felt you were going through a time of transition? 5. Do you reassess your goals and activities from time to time?

TOPIC FOR YOUTH
JESUS—LIVING AGAIN

Rouses. The first weeks of World War I were a nightmare for the British troops. The heat, dust, fatigue, and discouragement dragged down the men as they were forced to continue to retreat. Staggering into the town of St. Quentin, the exhausted remnants of two battalions collapsed in the railway station and refused to go farther. They told Major Bridges whose cavalry had orders to hold off the Germans until St. Quentin was clear of troops, that their commanding officers had given the mayor a written promise to surrender in order to save the town further bombardment. Not caring to confront the battalion colonels whom he knew and who were senior to him, Bridges wished desperately for a band to rouse the two hundred or three hundred dispirited men lying about in the square. "Why not? There was a toy shop handy which provided my trumpeter and myself with a tin whistle and a drum and we marched round and round the fountain where the men were lying like the dead, playing the 'British Grenadiers' and 'Tipperary' and beating the drum like mad." The men sat up, began to laugh, then cheer, then one by one stood up, fell in and "eventually we moved off slowly into the night to the music of our improved band, now reinforced with a couple of mouth organs."

Jesus rouses tired, depressed people who have given up. With the insistent, yet comforting call, "I am with you!" He summons persons ready to quit the battle of life to bestir themselves again. His powerful presence and the music of hope against all odds brings men and women to their feet and ready to march behind Him with confidence!

Unbelievable Tale. When the reports of the astronauts on the moon were first made, members of the Flat Earth Research Society, an organization with members throughout the world who firmly reject all evidence that the earth is round, scoffed at the news that men walked on the moon. "Just another Hollywood science fiction tale," the leaders in England stated.

The same attitude unfortunately pervades the thinking of many persons when they are told that Jesus was raised up alive after the Crucifixion. Insisting that the Resurrection of Jesus was a hoax or a fake, they ignore all evidence.

Evidence? The best, the most convincing evidence is not air-tight proofs. It is a changed life; it is a shared love.

Jesus Averts Collapse. After Mahatma Gandhi's release from prison, he asked a missionary what was the reason for the collapse of his movement while he was in jail. The missionary replied that he thought that since life finally came to the level of the habitual thinking, the cause lay back in the thinking of India. In the mind of the Moslem, there is gripping him in the inmost places the thought of Kismet—everything is predestined by the sovereign will of Allah. When he gets under difficulties the tendency is to tap his forehead and say: "What can I do? My Kismet is bad." It is more or less fatalistic, On the other hand, the Hindu has lying back in his mind the thought of Karma—that we are in the grip of the results of the deeds of the previous birth. When the Hindu runs against difficult situations, he usually says: "What can I do? My Karma is bad." It, too, is more or less fatalistic and consequently paralyzing.

Jesus, on the other hand, delivers people from paralyzing fatalism. With Him, they do not sigh "What can I do?" but shout "Because He lives, look what we may do!"

Sentence Sermon to Remember:

The Carpenter of Galilee
Comes down the street again.
In every land, in every age,
He still is building men.
On Christmas Eve we hear him knock;
He goes from door to door:
"Are any workmen out of work?
The Carpenter needs more."
—Hilda W. Smith, in
"The Carpenter of Galilee."

Questions for Pupils on the Next Lesson. 1. What causes you the greatest excitement and what causes you the greatest anxiety? 2. Do you see your life as part of a larger story in the universe? 3. What do you think God has in mind for you in the future? 4. What nagging, unanswered questions keep recurring in your life? 5. When did Jesus tell His followers that they would have to go through a time of waiting?

MARCH–MAY 1983

THE BOOK OF ACTS

LESSON I—MARCH 6

AN EXPECTANT FELLOWSHIP

Background Scripture: Exodus 33:15,16; Luke 1:1–4; 24:36–53; Acts 1
Devotional Reading: Exodus 17:1–7

KING JAMES VERSION

ACTS 1 4 And, being assembled together with *them*, commanded them that they should not depart from Jerusalem, but wait for the promise of the Father, which, *saith he*, ye have heard of me.

5 For John truly baptized with water; but ye shall be baptized with the Holy Ghost not many days hence.

6 When they therefore were come together, they asked of him, saying, Lord, wilt thou at this time restore again the kingdom to Israel?

7 And he said unto them, It is not for you to know the times or the seasons, which the Father hath put in his own power.

8 But ye shall receive power, after that the Holy Ghost is come upon you: and ye shall be witnesses unto me both in Jerusalem, and in all Judaea, and in Samaria, and unto the uttermost part of the earth.

9 And when he had spoken these things, while they beheld, he was taken up; and a cloud received him out of their sight.

10 And while they looked stedfastly toward heaven as he went up, behold, two men stood by them in white apparel;

11 Which also said, Ye men of Galilee, why stand ye gazing up into heaven? this same Jesus, which is taken up from you into heaven, shall so come in like manner as ye have seen him go into heaven.

12 Then returned they unto Jerusalem from the mount called Olivet, which is from Jerusalem a sabbath day's journey.

13 And when they were come in, they went up into an upper room, where abode both Peter, and James, and John, and Andrew, Philip, and Thomas, Bartholomew, and Matthew, James *the son* of Alpheus, and Simon Zelotes, and Judas *the brother* of James.

14 These all continued with one accord in prayer and supplication, with the women, and Mary the mother of Jesus, and with his brethren.

REVISED STANDARD VERSION

ACTS 1 4 And while staying with them he charged them not to depart from Jerusalem, but to wait for the promise of the Father, which, he said, "you heard from me, 5 for John baptized with water, but before many days you shall be baptized with the Holy Spirit."

6 So when they had come together, they asked him, "Lord, will you at this time restore the kingdom to Israel?" 7 He said to them, "It is not for you to know times or seasons which the Father has fixed by his own authority. 8 But you shall receive power when the Holy Spirit has come upon you; and you shall be my witnesses in Jerusalem and in all Judea and Samaria and to the end of the earth." 9 And when he had said this, as they were looking on, he was lifted up, and a cloud took him out of their sight. 10 And while they were gazing into heaven as he went, behold, two men stood by them in white robes, 11 and said, "Men of Galilee, why do you stand looking into heaven? This Jesus, who was taken up from you into heaven, will come in the same way as you saw him go into heaven."

12 Then they returned to Jerusalem from the mount called Olivet, which is near Jerusalem, a sabbath day's journey away; 13 and when they had entered, they went up to the upper room, where they were staying, Peter and John and James and Andrew, Philip and Thomas, Bartholomew and Matthew, James the son of Alphaeus and Simon the Zealot and Judas the son of James. 14 All these with one accord devoted themselves to prayer, together with the women and Mary the mother of Jesus, and with his brothers.

KEY VERSE: "But you shall receive power when the Holy Spirit has come upon you; and you shall be my witnesses in Jerusalem and in all Judea and Samaria and to the end of the earth." Acts 1:8 (RSV).

HOME DAILY BIBLE READINGS

Feb. 28. M. The Presence of the Lord. Exodus 33:12–16.
Mar. 1. T. Proof of the Resurrection. Luke 1:1–3.
Mar. 2. W. The Fellowship of Witness. 1 Thessalonians 1:2–9
Mar. 3. T. All People Are Welcome. Romans 15:7–13.
Mar. 4. F. The Living Hope. 1 Peter 1:3–9.
Mar. 5. S. Living in Readiness. 2 Peter 3:9–14.
Mar. 6. S. Sharing Our Hope. Titus 2:11–15.

BACKGROUND

Luke wrote not one but two of the most valuable books in the New Testament. The first one we know as The Gospel of St. Luke; it tells the story of the life and work of Jesus. The second book picks up the story where the Gospel leaves off; it tells the story of the establishment of the Christian Church, and we know it as The Acts of the Apostles. We might say that Acts is something like the second chapter of a *continuing* story, the last chapter of which has not yet been written.

Generally, Luke is credited with the authorship of both books, though there is still some debate about that. It is also generally conceded that Acts was written somewhere within the last forty years of the first century.

Keep in mind, as you study Acts, that it may be the *most* important book in the New Testament. For one reason, it is the only record of the origins of the Church; there is no other such record in the Bible. For a second reason, without Acts, we might never have had any New Testament at all for it prompted the publication of those letters of Paul written long before Acts was written. Those letters would probably have been lost had not Luke come along to inspire their collection. Without Acts, the New Testament might never have been put together.

NOTES ON THE PRINTED TEXT

Luke addresses both his Gospel and his Acts to one and the same man: someone called Theophilus—"most excellent Theophilus" (Luke 1:3 KJV). There is a clue in that to the purpose of Luke in writing these two books. The Living Bible doesn't name Theophilus; it addresses these two books to a "Dear Friend Who Loves God." This Book of Acts was written for the benefit of just such people—people who loved God and who had heard of Jesus, but who were still plagued with uncertainty about Him and about what they were to do now that His work on earth was over.

They were anxious to know two things: exactly what was the Gospel preached by Jesus, and what were they to do about it?

Jesus tells them that the heart of His faith was the Gospel of the Kingdom of God. That was the central theme of all His earthly ministry. Now the Jews of His day also talked of a coming Kingdom—a *political* kingdom, a restoration of the old Israel, a kingdom which they, as the Chosen People, would dominate. It was a kingdom established by force—and it was *not* the Kingdom preached by a Jesus who taught us to pray: "Thy Kingdom come; *Thy* will be done. . . ." It was a Kingdom of love, not of might; a society worldwide, in which men obeyed the will of God above the will of earthly kings.

And *when*, they asked Him, would that Kingdom come? Some of us are still asking that question, in A.D. 1983, and it is a foolish question, a question to which only God has the answer. Those who were with Jesus at this moment had more justification in asking the question than we have, for they had seen Him risen; they *had* to believe in the Resurrection for they had been alive when it happened.

Would He restore Israel and bring the Kingdom now, immediately after His Resurrection? That was a natural question for them. Gently, Jesus told them that that was not for them to know. No man could know the exact moment when *God* would bring it to pass. Says Dr. Barclay: "There is something almost blasphemous in speculating about that which was hidden even from Christ Himself."

Then what were they to do? They were to go back to Jerusalem and *wait.* Wait for God to inspire them by putting His Spirit upon them. Wait for power to come from Him—the power which came at Pentecost. Without that Spirit, there would have been no Church. It was the Spirit that made them witnesses—no, *martyrs*—giving their very lives for their Christ. It welded them into a society of evangelizing *Christians.* It was the granting of a strength and a glory that was not meant to make them boastful because they had it, but which drove them out as witnesses to win a world for Christ. (We modern Christians might well ask of ourselves, "Now that we have the Spirit and a Church—what shall we *do* with them?")

Now Luke repeats his story of the Ascension. (He is the only Gospel writer who puts this event in story form. Jesus "was lifted up, and a cloud took him out of their sight" (verse 9). Bewildered, those who were with Him on the Mount of Olives stood for a moment gazing into heaven. The gazing did not last long; Luke says that two men in white robes appeared among them to ask an embarrassing question: why did they stand there doing nothing? Did they not know that He would come again? Did they not know that it was in the Father's plan to have Him return to His glory and sit at the Father's right hand? Did they not know that from that place of honor and power, He would give them strength and power to perform their ministry for Him, and, that even unto the end, He would be with them, among them, risen, living on? Don't stand there, doing nothing; go out into all the world. *Go!*

So they returned to Jerusalem; Luke (24:52) says that they "returned to Jerusalem *with great joy.*" He was not gone; He would be with them forever. We can easily imagine them singing as they made their way back to the upper room where they had been with Him before. Luke lists the names of those who were there that day; eleven of His disciples (Iscariot was not there), several women including Mary His mother—and, believe it or not, the brothers of Jesus! These were the sorry characters who were blind to His person and mission while He lived among them, who were hostile to Him and who even thought Him a bit mad—these came now, at the risk of their lives, to enlist in His cause. Once unconvinced, now they had been conquered by His Resurrection, His post-Resurrection appearances, and His Ascension. Those we call cynics or doubters, in our day, may not be convinced of the "happenings" between the death on Calvary and the Ascension on the Mount, but *these* men, these *women* who had *seen* it all had no doubts about it. They did not only *think* He was this or that: they *knew*.

And from the upper room they moved out over the bridge called Samaria to tell the Gentile world about Him.

SUGGESTIONS TO TEACHERS

Have you ever read a fascinating story in a magazine and found the words at the bottom of the column, "To be continued"? You will understand the Book of Acts better if you remember that it is another "installment" in the series which Luke wrote. You and your class have been studying the first part—Luke's account of Jesus' life, teaching, and mission—during the past thirteen weeks. Now you will move into "Part Two" of Luke's writings—the spread of the Gospel from the time of Jesus' Ascension to the time of Paul's arrival and ministry in Rome. You may want to mention at the outset of this series that the final "installment" is still being written, so to speak. This is the story of the continuing growth and development of Christ's Church in the world under the guidance of the Holy Spirit through your class and all Christians today!

Your first three lessons in this series, with the title "Beginning at Jerusalem," focus on the significant events in the birth of the Church. Today's lesson centers on Jesus' followers in the period between Passover and Pentecost. Like theatergoers excitedly waiting for the curtain to rise on the next act of a great play, Jesus' disciples anticipated the next part of God's great drama. You should point your lesson toward helping your people to be an expectant fellowship similar to the earliest believers.

1. *PILLAR OF CLOUD.* The Old Testament references throughout Acts are important. Take time to examine Exodus 33:14–16, in which Moses has an experience of, "My Presence will go with you. . . ." Let your class understand that the earliest Christians understood that through Jesus Christ they had the same experience of, "God is with us." Do your people have the same sense? Note also the claim in Exodus 33 that God's presence is what makes His people distinct from all others. Is this what makes your class and your Church distinctive from other gatherings and associations?

2. *PREPARATION FOR COMING.* Stress how the earliest followers were told that they would receive power when the Holy Spirit came upon them and were to be witnesses of Christ everywhere (*see* Acts 1:8). They also understood that all history was a preparation for the new beginning God was making through Jesus Christ. Discuss what your people are expecting from God, and what they think God is expecting of them. Do your people sense that they are empowered to witness to what God is doing?

3. *PAUSE IN THE CITY.* The Risen Lord orders His people to "wait" for the Promise of the Father (Acts 1:4), that is the empowering Presence of Spirit. Sometimes, we leap impetuously when we should wait expectantly. Invariably, when the Church tries to act without the patient

waiting for guidance and strength of the Spirit, it operates clumsily and ineffectively. Look at the "busy work" of selecting a twelfth apostle which Peter and others went through without waiting (Acts 1:15–26). Talk over with your class the frustrations and impatience of waiting for the Spirit.

4. *PRAYER OF THE COMMITTED.* In spite of resorting to casting lots for a replacement for Judas, the earliest pre-Pentecost believers were a praying fellowship. Zero in on verse 14: "All these with one accord devoted themselves to prayer, together with the women. . . ." Allow plenty of time in your lesson to extract the rich meaning of this verse. Does your class pray "one accord?" (Or, backing up for a moment, do your people really pray at all?) Is your praying inclusive, that is "with the women" and with others in mind? Emphasize that the Spirit's presence and power will be known by believers only when a praying and expectant fellowship is gathered.

TOPIC FOR ADULTS
AN EXPECTANT FELLOWSHIP

Having Terrible Time—Glad God Is Here. "Miserable world conditions shouldn't be considered proof of God's absence, but simply proof of humanity's failure to be aware of the divine presence and to live accordingly.

"The most sublime and victorious life ever lived was that of Jesus Christ, the noblest Man ever to walk this Earth. Jesus suffered adversity and death, but His divine power made every tribulation endurable.

"Though human lives can be transformed by the divine Presence, the world remains filled with hazards, sin, sickness, suffering, and death.

"The early Christians might easily have agreed with Theodore A. Gill, who coined the expression, 'Having terrible time—glad God is here.' He said the writers of the Bible didn't live in ivory towers and speak about the impossible and unreal. St. Paul, for example, wrote many letters, but not in the mood of one on vacation in Bermuda who teases friends back home with this message: 'Having wonderful time—wish you were here.' No, the writers of the Bible often reflected a different mood: 'Having terrible time—glad God is here.'

"No matter how miserable the world may seem to us this Christmas, it can't seem worse than it did to biblical folks when their temple was destroyed and when they were made captives. Even when the Hebrews were hostages in a strange land, they could still sing unto the Lord a new song. St. Paul suffered more than we shall ever be required to suffer, but he was able to declare: 'Blessed be the God and Father of our Lord Jesus Christ, the Father and God of all comfort, who comforts us in all our afflictions, so that we may be able to comfort those who are in any way afflicted, with the comfort with which we ourselves are comforted by God.' "—Rev. Joseph Mohr, *The Morning Call/Weekender*, Allentown, Pennsylvania, December 22, 1979. Reprinted with permission of *Call-Chronicle* Newspapers, Allentown, PA. © 1981.

Shallow Waters. A visitor to Layasia reports watching grown men sitting on the ridges of the twelve rice fields and fishing in a foot of water. Within sight of where they sat, the mighty ocean rolled filled with fish.

Instead, they sat and fished in the shallow rice paddies. They failed to take advantage of the great and nutritious catch waiting for them if they would only throw a net from the beach into the ocean.

Isn't much of our church activity a kind of fishing in the rice fields? We toil over trivia, ignoring the great possibilities around us.

The earliest believers, before the Coming of the Holy Spirit, were inclined to busy themselves in "rice-paddy" activities. When Pentecost came, they launched into the deep for great adventures of faith and great rewards!

Casting Problems. Robert Morley, the famous English actor, once made a quip about a play that folded which also could be applied to Christian congregations. The theatrical production closed after two performances because, according to Morley, "there was trouble casting the audience."

Trouble casting the audience! Isn't this the way those earliest believers were after the Crucifixion and Resurrection? The great drama of God's salvation through Jesus Christ seemed about to fold because of "trouble casting" the audience. In the first Chapter of Acts, the casting problems loom large. When the Holy Spirit was given, however, suddenly there was no trouble casting the audience. Common fishermen and housewives understood the drama!

Is there "trouble casting the audience" in your church?

Questions for Pupils on the Next Lesson. 1. Do you ever long for a sense of empowerment in dealing with life? 2. Was the gift of the Spirit intended for an elite few or for everyone? 3. What were some of the reactions to the experience of Pentecost in the Acts 2 account? 4. Do you think that your church is so bound to the past that it closes its eyes and ears to opportunities for new beginnings? 5. What does the coming of the Holy Spirit mean to you personally?

TOPIC FOR YOUTH
A TIME FOR WAITING

My Tears Count With Him. When she graduated from a suburban Baltimore high school, she was voted the "Most Athletic Girl." She was cute and peppy. That summer, she broke her neck in a diving accident. She was totally paralyzed from the neck down.

During the first months in the hospital, she wanted to die but was so helpless she could not take her own life. She even begged a girl friend to put her out of her misery. Hanging in a canvas Stryker frame in the paraplegic ward, the once-radiant girl was certain that life was completely meaningless. "All those yardsticks for success that had come to mean so much to me were shattered—being pretty and popular, dating the right guys." She felt lost in waves of depression and self-pity.

Today, Joni Eareckson is still totally paralyzed from the neck down and still requires someone to feed her, bathe her, and brush her hair. But Joni has learned that Jesus Christ puts disabled persons to work in ministry. Joni has taught herself to draw and paint, holding the pen or brush between her teeth. She goes on speaking tours. She has written best-selling books and has starred in a film version of her life. Her ministry to those who suffer, especially the handicapped, offers advice to as many as 2,000 letter writers each week.

It has not come easily. "Sometimes, I can't stand being in a wheelchair," Joni says, "but then God's grace takes over. Even in my handicap, God has a plan and purpose for my life." Joni learned sometimes God calls His people to a time of waiting before opening new possibilities. However, His presence and strength are always there. She says that through Jesus Christ, "I know my tears count with Him."

Wanting to Be Different? Many people are waiting for some miraculous change to come in their lives without understanding what or how or why. Some feel insecure. Others are unhappy with themselves. Still others don't like the way they look.

Audrey Hepburn's fans may think she's perfect, but she answered *People*'s question by saying, "You can have three million fans and still be insecure. I was always full of complexes about my feet being too big and about being too tall and skinny."

Though he wears his hard-won laurels proudly, Bill Rodgers would really rather have a pompadour as his crowning glory. "Like Sha Na Na," he says. "I never could get my hair to do that." When asked what he doesn't like about himself, Rodgers said he'd "lop a half-inch off my nose" if he could. Who would he like to look like? "Robert Redford," the marathon man said. "I'd swap with him."

Are you waiting to be someone different? The early believers in Acts 1 were. They prayed. They waited expectantly. When the Spirit was given, they were filled with power and new life. When you wait expectantly and prayerfully, God also gives you a new personality.

Learned Two Things. A French chaplain had listened to confessions of thousands of people over a period of many years. Someone asked him if he had learned anything about people after listening to so many confess to him. "Yes," the priest replied, "I have learned two things. First, most people are not very happy, and, second, we never grow up."

Is this the substance of your "confession"? Are you not very happy? Are you still not very grown up? You may be similar to those in Acts 1 before the gift of the Holy Spirit.

Pray. Wait. Remain with other believers. God showers those who wait faithfully with new joy and maturity. The Holy Spirit comes—always!

Sentence Sermon to Remember: Whenever God gives us a cross to bear, it is a prophecy that He will also give us strength.—Anonymous.

Questions for Pupils on the Next Lesson. 1. Is joy a part of your religious experience? Why or why not? 2. Why do you like to have friends who will keep promises? 3. Does God always keep His promises? 4. Do you ever sense a power beyond yourself at work in your life? 5. What is the meaning of "Pentecost"? 6. How has God given you new beginnings in your life?

LESSON II—MARCH 13

AN EMPOWERED FELLOWSHIP

Background Scripture: Numbers 11:24–29; Joel 2:28–32; Acts 2:1–42
Devotional Reading: Ephesians 1:3–10

KING JAMES VERSION

ACTS 2 1 And when the day of Pentecost was fully come, they were all with one accord in one place.

2 And suddenly there came a sound from heaven as of a rushing mighty wind, and it filled all the house where they were sitting.

3 And there appeared unto them cloven tongues like as of fire, and it sat upon each of them.

4 And they were all filled with the Holy Ghost, and began to speak with other tongues, as the Spirit gave them utterance.

12 And they were all amazed, and were in doubt, saying one to another, What meaneth this?

13 Others mocking said, These men are full of new wine.

14 But Peter, standing up with the eleven, lifted up his voice, and said unto them, Ye men of Judaea, and all *ye* that dwell at Jerusalem, be this known unto you, and hearken to my words:

15 For these are not drunken, as ye suppose, seeing it is *but* the third hour of the day.

16 But this is that which was spoken by the prophet Joel;

17 And it shall come to pass in the last days, saith God, I will pour out of my Spirit upon all flesh: and your sons and your daughters shall prophesy, and your young men shall see visions, and your old men shall dream dreams:

18 And on my servants and on my handmaidens I will pour out in those days of my Spirit; and they shall prophesy:

37 Now when they heard this they were pricked in their heart, and said unto Peter and to the rest of the apostles, Men and brethren, what shall we do? 38 Then Peter said unto them, Repent, and be baptized every one of you in the name of Jesus Christ for the remission of sins; and ye shall receive the gift of the Holy Ghost.

REVISED STANDARD VERSION

ACTS 2 1 When the day of Pentecost had come, they were all together in one place. 2 And suddenly a sound came from heaven like the rush of a mighty wind, and it filled all the house where they were sitting. 3 And there appeared to them tongues as of fire, distributed and resting on each one of them. 4 And they were all filled with the Holy Spirit and began to speak in other tongues, as the Spirit gave them utterance.

12 And all were amazed and perplexed, saying to one another, "What does this mean?" 13 But others mocking said, "They are filled with new wine."

14 But Peter, standing with the eleven, lifted up his voice and addressed them, "Men of Judea and all who dwell in Jerusalem, let this be known to you, and give ear to my words. 15 For these men are not drunk, as you suppose, since it is only the third hour of the day; 16 but this is what was spoken by the prophet Joel:

17 'And in the last days it shall be, God declares,
that I will pour out my Spirit upon all flesh,
and your sons and your daughters shall prophesy,
and your young men shall see visions,
and your old men shall dream dreams;
18 yea, and on my menservants and my maidservants in those days
I will pour out my Spirit; and they shall prophesy.

37 Now when they heard this they were cut to the heart, and said to Peter and the rest of the apostles, "Brethren, what shall we do?" 38 And Peter said to them, "Repent, and be baptized every one of you in the name of Jesus Christ for the forgiveness of your sins; and you shall receive the gift of the Holy Spirit.

KEY VERSE: . . . Not by might, nor by power, but by my spirit, saith the Lord of hosts. Zechariah 4:6.

HOME DAILY BIBLE READINGS

Mar. 7. M. The Promise of the Holy Spirit. John 14:15–24.
Mar. 8. T. The Promise of Peace. John 14:25–31.
Mar. 9. W. When the Spirit of Truth Comes. John 16:4–11.
Mar. 10. T. The Illuminating Power of the Holy Spirit. John 16:12–15.
Mar. 11. F. Filled With the Holy Spirit. Acts 4: 23–31.
Mar. 12. S. The Source and Varieties of Spiritual Gifts. Romans 12:1–11.
Mar. 13. S. The Promised Outpouring of the Spirit. Joel 2:28–32.

BACKGROUND

Every male Jew living within twenty miles of Jerusalem was legally required to attend three great feasts or festivals: the feasts were those of Passover, Tabernacles, and Pentecost. Pentecost was also called, "The Feast of Weeks"; the word itself meant "The Fiftieth," because it was always celebrated on the fiftieth day, or a week of weeks, after Passover. Pentecost commemorated the giving of the Law to Moses; it was also a day upon which sacrifices (two loaves of bread) were offered in gratitude to God for the harvest of their crops.

Pentecost came in June, when the weather was good. Great crowds of pilgrims from all the Mediterranean lands flocked to the city with a population of some 50,000; during the Feast, that population rose to over a million! They were Jews who seemed to come "from the ends of the earth." Somewhere in the city, a small fellowship of Christians was waiting, as they had been told to wait, for the baptism of the Spirit. They prayed as they waited, and their prayers were heard and answered.

NOTES ON THE PRINTED TEXT

Where they were gathered, how many of them there were waiting there at Pentecost, we do not know. All we know is that the promised sending of the Spirit upon them was fulfilled. The Spirit came to them as it had never come before—with a roar like the roar of the wind and with fire. That statement has a Greek and Jewish background: in the Greek and Hebrew language the same word means both "wind" and "spirit." A "mighty" wind sweeps all before it; it is awesome and overwhelming. The Spirit works like a flame: it cleanses, burns away the dross, gives light. And this sudden burst of wind and fire left the fellowship in confusion, almost in panic. They began to "speak in tongues."

This speaking in tongues is still practiced among *us;* there has come a revival of it after twenty centuries. Just what is meant, here in Acts 2, by "speaking in tongues"? Some scholars believe that these excited people having come, Jews and Gentiles alike, from many different countries were speaking many different "tongues," or languages. That seems hardly possible. There were two languages spoken all over Palestine and over the Roman world: Greek and Hebrew (Aramaic); they all had these languages wherever they came from, and it is quite possible that in this moment in Jerusalem these people talked together as a fellowship in either Greek or Aramaic and not in a Babel of dialects or national dialects. And when the Spirit descended upon them, they were ecstatic, rapturous, in a fervor of excitement, and, in that excitement, they poured out words and sounds which no one understood. This, they believed, was something inspired of God, and it was greatly prized and widely practiced. The best description of it is found in 1 Corinthians 14; here Paul seems to be suspicious of the practice; he fears that it might create more confusion than faith, but he accepts it after saying that he would prefer that those in the Christian fellowship speak a language that *all* could understand!

There were many others who were suspicious of this business of "tongues": some non-Christians gleefully announced that these babbling Christians were drunk. Peter, who was there with the other disciples, knocked that idea to pieces with the remark that men did not get drunk at nine o'clock in the morning! What the non-Christians and the Christians alike were seeing here was not a drunken orgy but the fulfillment of a Jewish prophet named Joel, who wrote (as far back as 350 B.C.) that the day would come when the Spirit would be poured out *just as it was being poured out this day*. But there was a new significant "pouring" involved here. The Spirit had always been. In the Old Testament, there are many stories of the Spirit falling upon the leaders of Israel, but never upon all the people. Joel, being a prophet, may have liked that, but he struck a note of revolution when he wrote that the time would come when the Spirit would be poured out "upon all flesh"—upon leaders and commoners, even servants and handmaidens . . . (Joel 2:28, 29). Now Peter, standing up to preach a sermon, announces that this day had come. The time had come when the old prophets would be replaced by new prophets—by *young* men who would have a new and clearer view or vision of the future and of the ways of God with men, while the other men would sit dreaming of the past. Upon the lowest of men, God would bestow the gift of prophecy and preaching. Even upon women! (Women, with the Coming of Christ and the establishment of His Church, were lifted to a higher place than they had ever had before.)

Peter's sermon—the first sermon in Acts and typical of most of the preaching of the early Church—runs from verse 14 to verse 40; it is short, plain, and direct. The other disciples stood with him as he preached, signifying their approval of what he was saying. He started with a quotation from Joel concerning the coming of "the last days" and of the coming of the Day of the Lord—the day when God would intervene in history and exalt Israel to the place of dominion over the world. The listening crowd was glad to hear that "good news"; they had believed in this Coming of the Lord for centuries. Now comes Peter saying that this moment of moments has come in this Pentecostal pouring out of the Spirit. In a beautiful condensation, he reviews the mighty works of Jesus, concentrating on His death and Resurrection. The dying and the rising were God's work, not man's; it was God's hand intervening in man's affairs—God's hand and the Spirit. Halfway through the sermon, he tells them that there is in Jesus a new hope for life after death—something that was not stressed in the Old Testament and by the old prophets who had only a place called Sheol, a place of shadowy, meaningless existence after their earthly life was over. God would not leave them in

Sheol; He would gather them to Him in the glory of heaven. (Read Psalms 16, here.) That was a new hope, and it was intended for all believing men.

God, too, had planned this!

This sermon was anything but casual; it was a thunderclap, and those who were fortunate enough to hear it were "cut to the heart" (verse 37). Evidently they believed in what Peter had said—*but what could they do about it?* (If every converted Christian does not ask that question, it is not a very effective conversion.) What shall we do about it? That gave the fiery Peter a chance to drive home the "clinch line," or "the bottom line" of the whole sermon. What shall you, what *must* you do now? *Repent* of your sins. (Who among *us* has not sinned?) And be baptized, *every one of you.* Cut yourself off from your old corrupt life in a corrupt society, and through baptism stand up cleansed and strengthened in the society, the community, of the Messiah. Then and only then will the power of the Spirit become *your* power; only then will the dead past be buried and forgotten, and only then are we armed with God's weapon of love to fight the battles of tomorrow.

Wait no longer, ye who are in Christ. Now *go.*

SUGGESTIONS TO TEACHERS

Your lesson today is taken from Acts 2, the record of the Pentecost event, the coming of the Holy Spirit upon the earliest believers, and the birth of the Christian Church. Throughout your lesson, stress how the Spirit's coming made these first Christians into an *empowered* fellowship. Point out how Jesus promised, "You shall receive power when the Holy Spirit has come upon you" (Acts 1:8). The Greek word for power is *dynamis,* from which our words *dynamite* and *dynamic* come. You must help your class to understand the promise that the Spirit dynamically empowers believers in these times as well as in Jerusalem nearly 2,000 years ago.

1. *PEOPLE OF PROPHECY.* Have your people turn to Numbers 11:24–29 where the Lord puts the Spirit not only on Moses but also upon the seventy elders, so that "when the Spirit rested upon them, they prophesied" (Numbers 11:25). Here, in the Old Testament, is a foretaste of how God intends His people to be. Everyone is to be filled with Spirit; everyone is to prophesy! Let your class see that the Spirit is not the private gift of God to a few select individuals but an outpouring of His Presence upon a larger body of believers. Furthermore, when the Spirit is known to be among God's people, they speak and act prophetically. As teacher, you may wish to remind your people that *prophesy* does not mean to indulge in crystal-ball gazing about the future but to interpet what God is doing in His world now. Ask you class to think as prophets for several minutes guided by the Spirit and to reflect on a couple of the critical moral issues in our nation or in your community.

2. *DAY OF DREAMS.* You will note that Peter in his sermon quotes Joel 2:28–32. Have your class examine this passage. Remind the class of the importance of having dreams and visions for everyone, especially God's people. Without dreams and visions of the future, people soon lose heart and quit. Point out that the coming of the Holy Spirit gave the faltering early followers of Jesus, such as Peter, a new sense of God's dreams

and visions. Peter and the others were fired with enthusiasm. The Spirit empowered them to appear boldly on the street corners and in the Temple area instead of skulking behind closed doors. The same Spirit empowered them to speak fearlessly about the Good News of Jesus. Take time in your class to share "dreams" and "visions" for your church which each member may share as empowered by the Spirit.

3. *DRAMA OF DISPARATES.* Focus also on the way in which the Spirit enabled persons of astonishingly different backgrounds to understand the Good News through the Galilean believers. "How is it that we hear, each of us in his own language?" they asked (Acts 2:8). The Spirit empowered them to communicate! People from various parts of the entire Roman world, in spite of differences in culture, customs, language, and geography, comprehended that Jesus Christ was for them! The Spirit made it possible for all these differences to be transcended.

How is your church communicating to others? For example, is your congregation speaking "childrenese" to younger members well enough to share the Good News with them on their level?

4. *PREACHER WITH POWER.* Examine the sample of early preaching which Luke inserts in Acts 2. Compare Peter, the preacher, as seen in this section with portraits of him previously, especially before the Crucifixion in Gethsemane and in the courtyard of the high priest's house. Ask your people to remark on the reasons for Peter's new-found sense of confidence and conviction. Also ask them how each of them may "preach" in the Monday-to-Saturday world. Remind them that they also may be empowered!

TOPIC FOR ADULTS
AN EMPOWERED FELLOWSHIP

Speaking in Native Language Today. Albert C. Winn describes the need for an outpouring of the Spirit so that various factions of a denomination can hear in their own "languages." Dr. Winn talks about Southern Presbyterians, but he could be telling about Methodists or Nazarenes or Baptists or the Church anywhere today.

"Southern Presbyterians don't all speak the same language: one part of the church has no conception of how the other parts live and what they are thinking.

"Some Presbyterians speak Large Church and others speak Small Church. We are a denomination of small churches: 75% to 80% of our churches are small and more than half of our individual members speak Small Church. It's tough on them when most of the official communications of the denomination are in Large Church language.

"Things are not all roses for those who speak and understand Large Church language. Much of what is said there is in the Suburban Dialect. Those of us who are in proud old downtown churches that have seen better days wonder if anybody wants to talk *our* language.

"So much of what is said in the dominant Large-Church-Suburban dialect bears a heavy Father-Mother-Dick-Jane-and-Spot accent. A surprising number of widowed, divorced, and never married Presbyterians are hungry for some messages in the Singles Accent.

"Then there is the difficulty that Eastern Seaboard Presbyterians have in understanding the West-of-the-River dialect.

"Presbyterians in the Everglades, South and Central Mississippi, for example, ask entirely different questions from those the rest of the Church asks. Other Presbyterians need extraordinary sensitivity to imagine what life is like there and to understand the heavy accent of Discouragement.

"Then there is Standard Evangelical—'Praise the Lord!'—which turns off those who studied their grammar under the Professors of Social Action. And Social Activistese sounds downright unchristian to the speakers of Standard Evangelical.

"Native American Presbyterians sing in Choctaw. But their English is colored by a special history of misunderstanding and betrayal by their white brothers and sisters. It takes keen ears to hear what they are really saying.

"Hispanic Presbyterians sing in Spanish and they speak a special language called Chicano-Double-Bind. The double bind is being Spanish in a predominantly Anglo culture, and being Protestant in a traditionally Catholic culture. Can we hear and understand the language?

"Black Presbyterians speak in a dialect the rest of the Church thinks it understands. But do we? It's Black-Double-Bind: being Black with all the roots, all the decades of assaults on your basic human dignity, and then being Presbyterian in a Black culture that never heard of anything but Baptists and Methodists and is deeply suspicious whether a predominantly White church . . . can possibly be Christian at all. Can we hear and understand that language?

"Asian-American Presbyterians have one advantage. We of the majority have no illusions that we understand Korean.

"And if you travel overseas to our daughter churches, you of course encounter a welter of foreign languages. But even in translation Younger Church is sometimes so abrasive that we who speak Mother Church stop up our ears and refuse to hear.

"Now onto this pastiche of languages, this Babel of tongues, is overlaid the most esoteric language of all: General Assembly Bureaucratese. It is a language of which the session in my church can understand scarcely a syllable. But what they do understand they don't like.

"It is a miracle of the grace of God, a sign of Pentecost, that despite the confusion of language we are one church, we hold together, we basically wish each other well.

"Why not continue and intentionally enlarge the forum offered to those who write in Small Church and in Downtown and in Single and in Western and in Discouraged and in Black and in Native American and in Evangelical and in Social Activist and in Younger Church? And may we continue to resist, with every fiber of our being, the overlay of Bureaucratese. Then will the saying be brought to pass: 'How is it that we hear, each of us in his own native language? . . . We hear them telling in our own tongues the mighty works of God!' (Acts 2:8,11.)"—Albert C. Winn, *Presbyterian Outlook*, July 28, 1980.

Electronics of the Spirit. "Statesmen in every land are beginning to discover that the human mind, however able and sincere, cannot solve the problems created by the human passions of hate, greed, and fear. It needs an electronic intervention, an experience of the Spirit, a new dimension that can usher in a new age. It is an answer that works."—Frank Buchman.

Questions for Pupils on the Next Lesson. 1. In what ways did early Christians share that we usually do not? 2. What factors contributed most to the rapid growth of the early Church? 3. What were the qualities of leadership among those who headed the early Christian community? 4. What was the place of worship in the early Church, and what is its place in your church? 5. What organizational patterns evolved in the life of the early Church?

TOPIC FOR YOUTH
POWER SOURCE

Power Supply. Although the harnessing of electricity is a modern accomplishment, electricity has been known for 2,500 years! But until a man named Michael Faraday learned how to produce electric current with a generator, electricity was known only in the form of magnetism and was merely a curiosity—not a source of power.

In 1822, Faraday jotted down a challenge to himself: "Convert magnetism into electricity." Scientists of that day believed this was impossible. But Faraday believed God would help him. He set to work. After many experiments, he discovered that electricity could be produced by thrusting a magnet through a coil of wire. He also found out that current could not be produced without motion. Merely holding the magnet within the coil was not enough!

Perhaps the Holy Spirit and His power is only known to you by hearsay. Perhaps you have known about the energizing presence of God, but you have never been electrified into serving Him. Through Jesus Christ, God's power was at work. You must be in motion, however, if you are to receive His power. You cannot passively do nothing. God's outpouring of Spirit empowers those who are ready and active to serve in Christ's name. Are you?

The One Power. "There is one power that surpasses the all-consuming power of time—the eternal: he who was and is and is to come, the beginning and the end. He gives us forgiveness for what has passed. He gives us courage for what is to come. He gives us rest in his eternal presence."—Paul J. Tillich.

Alive! One of the most colorful Christians in the nineteenth century was a black woman named Sojourner Truth. Sojourner Truth was born a slave but became famous as a preacher, as a crusader for women's rights, and an advocate for the abolition of slavery. Although persecuted, this illiterate Christian deplored bloodshed and pleaded for nonviolent, legal methods of crusading for human rights. Her means and words served as a model for Dr. Martin Luther King, Jr., a century later.

Once her fellow distinguished abolitionist and exslave Frederick Douglass was depressed. Despairing of ever seeing success for oppressed black people in this country, Douglass said that perhaps the only hope was for blacks to rise in violent revolt.

Sojourner Truth answered immediately. "Frederick, is God dead?" Aware of the power of the Spirit, she marched off to Washington, not with a rifle, but with a big white banner. Sojourner Truth knew that she was part of an empowered fellowship and also knew her Power Source. Her words and deeds would be celebrated by persons of every race, men and women.

Sentence Sermon to Remember:

Praise the Power that hath made and
preserved us a nation! . . .
And this be our motto: In God is our trust!
The Star-Spangled Banner.

Questions for Pupils on the Next Lesson. 1. What are the qualities of a good church leader? 2. In what ways does the Church help you to grow? In what ways do you help the Church to grow? 3. From reading the Background Scripture for the March 20 lesson, what qualities of the Church helped it to grow so rapidly? 4. Why is worship in the place it is in your life? What are you doing about it?

LESSON III—MARCH 20

AN EXPANDING FELLOWSHIP

Background Scripture: Acts 2:43–6:7
Devotional Reading: Isaiah 44:6–8

KING JAMES VERSION

ACTS 2 43 And fear came upon every soul: and many wonders and signs were done by the apostles.

44 And all that believed were together, and had all things common;

45 And sold their possessions and goods, and parted them to all *men,* as every man had need.

46 And they, continuing daily with one accord in the temple, and breaking bread from house to house, did eat their meat with gladness and singleness of heart,

47 Praising God, and having favour with all the people. And the Lord added to the church daily such as should be saved.

6 1 And in those days, when the number of the disciples was multiplied, there arose a murmuring of the Grecians against the Hebrews, because their widows were neglected in the daily ministration.

2 Then the twelve called the multitude of the disciples *unto them,* and said, It is not reason that we should leave the word of God, and serve tables.

3 Wherefore, brethren, look ye out among you seven men of honest report, full of the Holy Ghost and wisdom, whom we may appoint over this business.

4 But we will give ourselves continually to prayer, and to the ministry of the word.

5 And the saying pleased the whole multitude: and they chose Stephen, a man full of faith and of the Holy Ghost, and Philip, and Prochorus, and Nicanor, and Timon, and Parmenas, and Nicolas a proselyte of Antioch:

6 Whom they set before the apostles: and when they had prayed, they laid *their* hands on them.

7 And the word of God increased; and the number of the disciples multiplied in Jerusalem greatly; and a great company of the priests were obedient to the faith.

REVISED STANDARD VERSION

ACTS 2 43 And fear came upon every soul; and many wonders and signs were done through the apostles. 44 And all who believed were together and had all things in common; 45 and they sold their possessions and goods and distributed them to all, as any had need. 46 And day by day, attending the temple together and breaking bread in their homes, they partook of food with glad and generous hearts, 47 praising God and having favor with all the people. And the Lord added to their number day by day those who were being saved.

6 1 Now in these days when the disciples were increasing in number, the Hellenists murmured against the Hebrews because their widows were neglected in the daily distribution. 2 And the twelve summoned the body of the disciples and said, "It is not right that we should give up preaching the word of God to serve tables. 3 Therefore, brethren, pick out from among you seven men of good repute, full of the Spirit and of wisdom, whom we may appoint to this duty. 4 But we will devote ourselves to prayer and to the ministry of the word." 5 And what they said pleased the whole multitude, and they chose Stephen, a man full of faith and of the Holy Spirit, and Philip, and Prochorus, and Nicanor, and Timon, and Parmenas, and Nicolaus, a proselyte of Antioch. 6 These they set before the apostles, and they prayed and laid their hands upon them.

7 And the word of God increased; and the number of the disciples multiplied greatly in Jerusalem, and a great many of the priests were obedient to the faith.

KEY VERSE: And all that believed were together, and had all things common. Acts 2:44.

HOME DAILY BIBLE READINGS

Mar. 14. M. The First Ingathering of Souls. Acts 2:37–42.
Mar. 15. T. The Faith Through Jesus Christ. Acts 3:11–16.
Mar. 16. W. A Call to Repentance. Acts 3:17–26.
Mar. 17. T. Preaching the Resurrection of Jesus. Acts 4:1–8.
Mar. 18. F. Peter's Defense Before the Sanhedrin. Acts 4:5–12.
Mar. 19. S. The Fearlessness of the Apostles. Acts 4:13–22.
Mar. 20. S. Stephen Before the Sanhedrin. Acts 6:8–15.

BACKGROUND

Peter must have been a powerful preacher to say the least; it is recorded that following his sermon in Jerusalem, some three thousand souls (people) were added to the believers in Christ and were baptized. That is a clear indication that Jerusalem was a shaken, frightened city following Christ's Resurrection. It sounds like fiction, but it is true: "Historically, the emergence of a world figure should be noticed. A fisherman from Galilee, so demoralized a few weeks before that he denied his Master with the crudest language of unregenerate days, had become a power in a hate-ridden city. He was to be a force in the civilized world. A vast church named after him dominates Rome, where the Caesars' triumphal arches crumble and their palaces and fora are broken walls and truncated column shafts."—E. M. Blaiklock in *Acts: The Birth of the Church.*

Now three thousand people is quite a crowd to be saved by the preaching of one sermon. Quite probably, many of those who heard Peter that day had already heard Jesus, and some of them may have been healed by Him, and others may have watched Him die. But the truth remains that whatever their number, they joined the band of disciples in an eagerness to hear more about this Jesus. And it must be added: many of them were *frightened* people.

NOTES ON THE PRINTED TEXT

Luke says that "fear came upon every soul." Why fear? *What* were they afraid of? It was not so much fear as it was a sense of awe as they saw the miracles of healing performed by the apostles. Surely, these apostles must be possessed of a supernatural power to perform such "signs and wonders!" It is no wonder that thousands came in awe to join the fellowship of the apostles and to share with them a new, deeply spiritual life.

If you were privileged to attend a meeting of these apostles and converts in Jerusalem, what would you find them doing? First, you would find them "breaking bread together," going from house to house and sharing their food in a common meal. Eating together was a symbol of their unity and fellowship.

Indeed, you would find them sharing "all things in common" (verse 44). It was said that they sold their possessions and goods and distributed them to all "as any had need." Some cynics like to tell us that this was Communism! It was never Communism; it was *communal,* but it had none of the violence or ungodliness of Communism. It was a sharing, not an inhuman lust for power. They shared what they had with others who had less in fellowship. That did not, however, involve the sale of their houses. It was a noble experiment; unfortunately, it did not last very long.

You would find them worshiping—praying, singing, listening to an exposition of the Scriptures. These first Christians continued to worship in their (Jewish) temples at the regular hour; they still went together to the temple, and they did *not* think of any break with their spiritual, Jewish fathers at this point in time. But, somehow, temple worship did not seem to be enough; they remembered Jesus breaking bread with His disciples not in the temple but in an Upper Room in a private house, and they wished to keep the memory of that Supper alive—*and to establish a family temple in their homes* where they could worship when the temple doors were closed. (It is interesting to observe that our modern Roman Catholic Church is now encouraging group worship in the homes of their people.) And why not? Religion is a seven-day business.

And you would have sensed the beginning of a quarrel among these first Christians. It was not a quarrel with hostile Jews, but a quarrel among themselves. Too often, we think of these early Christians as people "altogether lovely"—as a peculiarly sanctified, perfect, saint-like people, but we are wrong when we do that. There were troubles among them from the start. To understand what they were troubled about, we have to take a glance at their past. The trouble developed, oddly, over sharing their food with one another.

To understand it, we have to go back to the Exile (597 B.C.), following which the Jews were scattered all over the world. Some lived in Rome, some in Alexandria, some in Tarsus from which came Paul; actually they were scattered from India to Rome and perhaps to Spain. Later, there were synagogues formed by the Jews, and these synagogues gave them the only unity they had. In the synagogues were both those who had been born Jews and Gentile proselytes. They all lived in a Greek-speaking world wherever they happened to be. Inevitably, differences arose between the "Metropolitan" (Jerusalem) strict Jews who were *born* Jews and the "Hellenists" (Greek-speaking) converts who had been born and reared abroad. The "hundred-percent," strictly loyal Jews "looked down their noses" at the foreign-born Hellenists; the friction carried over into the early Church in which the Hellenists accused those who distributed bread among the needy of neglecting *their* poor in the distribution. The Hellenist widows, they said, just weren't getting their fair share, and something had to be done about it.

Something was done, and fast. The whole congregation met and elected seven among them who would be charged with the duty of the distribution. The real unity in the church was demonstrated in that election; every one of the seven deacons (from which we get our word *diaconate*) was a *Hellenist* (a word, incidentally, which means "one who lives as a Greek"). Their only requirement was that these seven "overseers of the poor" had to be men of "good report, full of the Spirit and of wisdom" (Acts 6:3). If only *our* church quarrels were settled as easily as this!

So you would find, in this first Church, insistence upon two activities: *preaching* and *serving*. The seven set apart for this work of relief for the poor were preachers as well as "servers of tables" (verse 2). Both of these functions, this Church believed, should be performed by men talented to perform them. Their Church was not to become a social agency, but neither was it to neglect or ignore the material needs of the poor. *Our* modern church, thanks to the labors of the first seven deacons, builds hospitals and orphanages and homes for the aged, as it spreads the Word from its pulpits.

The names of five of the seven are not familiar to us, but there were two who stood out prominently: one was Philip, who was to carry the Gospel into Africa, and the other was a man named Stephen who was to become a martyr, whose blood has been called "the seed of the Church."

SUGGESTIONS TO TEACHERS

What makes a church grow? "Parking!" responds one expert. A large parking lot next to the church plus a highly visible location on a main street is the clue to church growth, states a recent survey. Jazzy programs for the teen-agers and postretirement groups, reports another. An attractive building and winsome preacher are the keys to expanding membership, maintains a denominational leader. What are your ideas on the topic? How about the ideas of your class?

Contrast all of the above studies, reports, surveys, and expert opinions with the scriptural material for today's lesson. You and your class will find it startling to discover that the early Christian church had no parking lots, no million-dollar edifices, no video-taped extravaganzas, no growth gimmicks whatsoever. Only the Spirit! Yet—this early band of believers was a phenomenally expanding fellowship! Several characteristics stand out.

1. *SUPPORTIVE.* As an expanding fellowship, they stood together. They had a sort of common fund for the needs of those in the fellowship. They helped any poor member. They worshiped frequently and regularly together, both in the Temple and in their homes. They created and maintained a support system which reached out to each member. When Peter was released from prison, he immediately made his way to the "house church" or supportive community of friends in the faith. Discuss with your class how your congregation may be more supportive of each member. What in particular can your class members do to build a stronger sense of community within your church?

2. *SERVING.* Call attention to the personal act of service through healing in Acts 3:1–11. Peter and John, although without funds, were not daunted. When a need to serve presented itself in the form of a helpless crippled beggar on the steps of the Temple, they did not shrug, "Sorry, we're broke," or refer the man to a social agency. The early Christians knew that they were empowered to serve and gave the cripple new life. Their personal service in the name of the Servant Lord prompted others to take them seriously—and, more important, to take Jesus Christ seriously. The fellowship expanded. Make time in your lesson period for a serious evaluation of the way your church serves. Do your people primarily come to serve, or to be served?

3. *SHARING.* The early Church grew because the members shared. They shared their money and their food and their homes. They also shared their faith. Energized by the Spirit, they told everyone they encountered what Jesus Christ means to all humans. Have your class read

Peter's impromptu speeches in the Temple after healing the crippled beggar (Acts 3:12–26; 4:8–12, 19–22), and Peter's defense before the authorities (5:29–32). Probe with your class for ways in which each member may share his or her faith with others, both by actions such as sharing possessions with those in need, and by words such as speaking on behalf of justice or witnessing for the faith.

4. *SUFFERING.* Throughout the scriptural passage for today's study, threats, persecution, reports of pain and privation keep recurring. Early Christians were prepared to suffer—and often did—for their faith. No "cheap grace" here, as Dietrich Bonhoeffer called it. Significantly, however, the times of greatest growth in the Church have also been times of gravest peril to believers! Talk over with your class the sacrifices that are required of Christians today. What suffering should believers be prepared to accept today?

TOPIC FOR ADULTS
AN EXPANDING FELLOWSHIP

Theology of Church Growth. Growth in itself may be worth little; the furthering of the growth which comes by the winning of men and women to Christian discipleship is vitally important. If we are not making every effort toward that end, if our numbers decline because we do not greatly care, we have reason to feel guilt and failure.

Brown Barr put it well several years ago when he wrote: "Many churches have applauded a theology of nongrowth. Growth has been seen to be as vulgar and plastic as Disneyland and, furthermore, sure evidence that the Gospel is not being preached with its radical claims. Such defenses seldom recall the text which says, 'The common people heard him gladly.' Applause for the theology of nongrowth will not last long, however. It is almost impossible for a drowning man to clap.

"Suppose the church were ready and willing to suffer or die in order to hear the Good News. Well, the blood of martyrs has often been the seed of the Church. Undeniably we need more of their spirit today.

"The Book of Acts is a dramatic story of Church growth. The Apostle Paul had a passion for it, writing: 'I have become all things to all men, that I might by all means save some.' When our Lord said, 'Go . . . make disciples of all the nations, baptizing them in the name of the Father and of the Son and of the Holy Ghost, teaching them to observe all that I have commanded you,' he was surely not unconcerned for the growth of his church."—J. McDowell Richards, from a letter to *Presbyterian Outlook,* January 12, 1981.

The Irreplaceable Hour. "For us, the greatest and loveliest result of the sabbatical year was that it gave us our lives back. In small measure, that is what the Sunday service is supposed to do every week. It gives us back the week for judgment and forgiveness. The purpose of worship is not to hear a sermon, to sing a hymn or two. It is something much larger, to come in contact with the world as it is and as we want it to be. Both and at the same time. That's why it looks so silly to an outsider and observer who objects to the seemingly easy transition, not knowing that it is not easy at all. It is an ongoing process. Sunday after Sunday after Sunday. It is not a habit, it is discipline and discipleship. In one short hour to moan and to mourn and then to forget oneself and join with joy the others in a mock-up banquet reminding us of bread—hunger, wine—blood, life—death, and resurrection—the hope that defies despair. You don't do that in an hour—the hour becomes only a manifestation of what it takes a lifetime to realize.

"The hour spent in church is irreplaceable. When I now leave for church on Sunday morning and return an hour and a half later, I can hardly believe such a short time has elapsed. What could I have done in that length of time? Read a little, think somewhat, listen to music, finish a review, prepare a meal, yes. But compared to the cosmic importance and personal engagement that has taken place in church—no, it cannot be compared. Church time is eternal."—*Sabbatical Reflections:* The Ten Commandments in a New Day, The Irreplaceable Hour, Brita Stendahl, Fortress Press, 1980. Reprinted by permission.

Vote to Close Church? "Last Sunday, I voted to close the church; not intentionally, nor maliciously; but carelessly, thoughtlessly, indifferently, I voted. I voted to close the open Bible that had been given us by years of struggle and by blood of martyrs. I voted that the children of the Church School no longer be taught the Christian faith. I voted for the degrading influence of sin, the blight of ignorance, and the curse of selfish greed to settle their damning load on the shoulders of an already overburdened world.

"Carelessly, thoughtlessly, lazily, indifferently, I voted.

"For you see, I could have gone and I should have gone, but I didn't. I stayed away from church last Sunday."

Questions for Pupils on the Next Lesson. 1. Is it possible in every circumstance in life to discover opportunities for witness? 2. What are life-renewing situations in your life? 3. How did persecution help the spread of the Christian faith? 4. How have you helped others come to an understanding of the faith? 5. Who are some of the "outsiders" in your community who need to be welcomed into the circle of Christ's people?

TOPIC FOR YOUTH
MEETING NEEDS

Living Faith. The Spirit keeps breaking in on people in surprising ways and in surprising places. The Christian community continues to be an expanding fellowship. Although atheism seems widespread in many areas, the news of Jesus Christ continues to meet deepest human needs. Hans Kung has written a book, *Does God Exist? An Answer for Today* (New York: Doubleday; 1980) in which he states the Gospel refuses to be quenched even in atheistic cultures.

Kung writes: "Atheism as a mass phenomenon . . . is a phenomenon of the most recent times, of our own times." Ludwig Feuerbach, whom he calls "the Church Father of modern atheism," flung a blunt challenge: "Faith has been replaced by unbelief, the Bible by reason, religion and Church by politics, heaven by earth, prayer by work, hell by material wretchedness, the Christian by man." Among those whom Feuerbach influenced were Nietzsche and, portentously, Karl Marx. Yet Father Kung observes: "Nowhere is religion dying out, even in the Communist countries. Persecute it, curtail it, propagandize against it—these they can do; destroy it, they cannot."

Christian Manifesto. "Our Christian obedience demands a simple lifestyle, irrespective of the needs of others. Nevertheless, the facts that 800 million people are destitute and that about 10,000 die of starvation every day make any other life-style indefensible.

"While some of us have been called to live among the poor, and others to open our homes to the needy, all of us are determined to develop a simpler life-style. We intend to reexamine our income and expenditure, in order to manage on less and give away more. We lay down no rules or regulations, for either ourselves or others. Yet we resolve to renounce waste and oppose extravagance in personal living, clothing and housing, travel and church buildings. We also accept the distinction between necessities and luxuries, creative hobbies and empty status symbols, modesty and vanity, occasional celebrations and normal routine, and between the service of God and slavery to fashion. Where to draw the line requires conscientious thought and decision by us, together with members of our family. Those of us who belong to the West need the help of our Third World brothers and sisters in evaluating our standards of spending. Those of us who live in the Third World acknowledge that we too are exposed to the temptation to covetousness. So we need each other's understanding, encouragement and prayers.

"We echo the words of the Luasanne Covenant: 'We are shocked by the poverty of millions, and disturbed by the injustices which cause it.' One quarter of the world's population enjoys unparalleled prosperity, while another quarter endures grinding poverty. This gross disparity is an intolerable injustice; we refuse to acquiesce in it.

"While personal commitment to change our life-style without political action, without personal commitment, lacks integrity.

"We are deeply concerned for the vast millions of unevangelized people in the world. Nothing that has been said about life-style or justice diminishes the urgency of developing evangelistic strategies appropriate to different cultural environments. We must not cease to proclaim Christ as Saviour and Lord throughout the world. The church is not yet taking seriously its commission to be his witnesses 'to the ends of the earth' (Acts 1:8).

"So the call to a responsible life-style must not be divorced from the call to responsible witness. For the credibility of our message is seriously diminished whenever we contradict it by our lives. It is impossible with integrity to proclaim Christ's salvation if he has evidently not saved us from greed, or his lordship if we are not good stewards of our possessions, or his love if we close our hearts against the needy. When Christians care for each other and for the deprived, Jesus Christ becomes more visibly attractive."—From "An Evangelical Commitment to Simple Lifestyle" by the International Consultation on Simple Lifestyle, at Hoddesdon, England on March 17–21, 1980.

Sentence Sermon to Remember: The most acceptable service of God is doing good to man.—Benjamin Franklin.

Questions for Pupils on the Next Lesson. 1. When do you find it easiest and when do you find it hardest to talk about your faith? 2. Do you sometimes find that it is hard to accept people who are different from you? 3. Do you occasionally find it difficult to understand how the Bible relates to your life? 4. Have you ever experienced hardship or suffering because of your faith? 5. Who are some of the "outsiders" in your community?

LESSON IV—MARCH 27

GOOD NEWS FOR OUTSIDERS

Background Scripture: Isaiah 56:3–8; Acts 6:8–8:40
Devotional Reading: Isaiah 56:3–8

KING JAMES VERSION

ACTS 8 25 And they, when they had testified and preached the word of the Lord, returned to Jerusalem, and preached the gospel in many villages of the Samaritans.

26 And the angel of the Lord spake unto Philip, saying, Arise, and go toward the south, unto the way that goeth down from Jerusalem unto Gaza, which is desert.

27 And he arose and went: and, behold, a man of Ethiopia, a eunuch of great authority under Candace queen of the Ethiopians, who had the charge of all her treasure, and had come to Jerusalem for to worship,

28 Was returning, and sitting in his chariot read Esaias the prophet.

29 Then the Spirit said unto Philip, Go near, and join thyself to this chariot.

30 And Philip ran thither to *him*, and heard him read the prophet Esaias, and said, Understandest thou what thou readest?

31 And he said, How can I, except some man should guide me? And he desired Philip that he would come up and sit with him.

32 The place of the Scripture which he read was this, He was led as a sheep to the slaughter; and like a lamb dumb before his shearer, so opened he not his mouth:

33 In his humiliation his judgment was taken away: and who shall declare his generation? for his life is taken from the earth.

34 And the eunuch answered Philip, and said, I pray thee, of whom speaketh the prophet this? of himself, or of some other man?

35 Then Philip opened his mouth, and began at the same Scripture, and preached unto him Jesus.

36 And as they went on *their* way, they came unto a certain water: and the eunuch said, See, *here is* water; what doth hinder me to be baptized?

37 And Philip said, If thou believest with all thine heart, thou mayest. And he

REVISED STANDARD VERSION

ACTS 8 25 Now when they had testified and spoken the word of the Lord, they returned to Jerusalem, preaching the gospel to many villages of the Samaritans.

26 But an angel of the Lord said to Philip, "Rise and go toward the south to the road that goes down from Jerusalem to Gaza." This is a desert road. 27 And he rose and went. And behold, an Ethiopian, a eunuch, a minister of Candace the queen of the Ethiopians, in charge of all her treasure, had come to Jerusalem to worship 28 and was returning; seated in his chariot, he was reading the prophet Isaiah. 29 And the Spirit said to Philip, "Go up and join this chariot." 30 So Philip ran to him, and heard him reading Isaiah the prophet, and asked, "Do you understand what you are reading?" 31 And he said, "How can I, unless some one guides me?" And he invited Philip to come up and sit with him. 32 Now the passage of the scripture which he was reading was this:

"As a sheep led to the slaughter
or a lamb before its shearer is dumb,
so he opens not his mouth.

33 In his humiliation justice was denied him.
Who can describe his generation?
For his life is taken up from the earth."

34 And the eunuch said to Philip, "About whom, pray, does the prophet say this, about himself or about some one else?" 35 Then Philip opened his mouth, and beginning with this scripture he told him the good news of Jesus. 36 And as they went along the road they came to some water, and the eunuch said, "See, here is water! What is to prevent my being baptized?" 38 And he commanded the chariot to stop, and they both went down into the water, Philip and the eunuch, and he baptized him.

answered and said, I believe that Jesus Christ is the Son of God.

38 And he commanded the chariot to stand still: and they went down both into the water, both Philip and the eunuch; and he baptized him.

KEY VERSE: Then Philip opened his mouth, and beginning with this scripture he told him the good news of Jesus. Acts 8:35 (RSV).

HOME DAILY BIBLE READINGS

Mar. 21. *M.* *The Promised Blessings to Outsiders.* Isaiah 56:3–8.
Mar. 22. *T.* *The Gospel Proclaimed in Samaria.* Acts 8:4–8.
Mar. 23. *W.* *The Gift of the Holy Spirit to Gentiles.* Acts 8:14–17.
Mar. 24. *T.* *The Good Tidings of Salvation.* Isaiah 61:1–3.
Mar. 25. *F.* *The Kingdom of God on Earth.* Isaiah 2:1–4.
Mar. 26. *S.* *An Apostle to the Gentiles.* Romans 11:13–16.
Mar. 27. *S.* *Standing Fast Through Faith.* Romans 11:17–24.

BACKGROUND

There was an old road that ran through Bethlehem and Hebron to the main road to Egypt at a point just south of Gaza. Over this road to Egypt moved a teeming traffic of merchants and pilgrims, Jewish and non-Jewish. It was a desert road, along which the travelers moved slowly, thanks to clouds of desert dust and the confusion of a two-way traffic. It was here that an humble little Christian named Philip met a state official from Ethiopia. The people of Ethiopia were actually Nubians, a black-skinned people who had an African background. This particular Ethiopian was a eunuch, one of those emasculated men who served as guards of the harems of high officials and who often rose to high places as trusted officials in government. They were regarded as men unfit to worship in the temples; they were definitely despised "outsiders" among both Jews and non-Jews.

It was such a man that Philip met on the Gaza road—a highly placed chancellor (treasurer) of the exchequer of the ruling Candace (queen) of Ethiopia. The Spirit, or an angel, or the very voice of God sent him out there for a definite purpose: there were those who might be made Christians, though they were only traveling outsiders, and this dark-skinned eunuch (a *Negro?*) was one of them.

NOTES ON THE PRINTED TEXT

Luke says that Philip found this eunuch starting his journey back from Jerusalem to Ethiopia; he was sitting in his chariot, reading a religious scroll. He *must* have been sitting in a *wagon*, rather than a chariot, for no man could stand up driving the horses and read a scroll at the same time! Philip saw him, impulsively *ran* toward him, to walk beside the wagon and listen to what he was reading. He was reading the fifty-third chapter of Isaiah! Reading about a Savior who was led like a sheep to the slaughter and who died, oppressed and afflicted, and never opened His mouth to save Himself from that cruel fate. He read, but he did not quite understand what he read; he confessed this to Philip running beside his wagon, and Philip was invited to get in and ride with him and explain what Isaiah was writing about.

There are three very interesting things about this strange story. One is that the man from Ethiopia was either a proselyte, a non-Jew who had accepted Judaism and been circumcised, or he was known as a "God-fearer" who did not accept circumcision or the Jewish faith but who read the Jewish Scriptures in a continuing search for a God who somehow meant more to him than the gods of his pagan or "outside" Ethiopia. It is possible that besides caring for the queen's business in Jerusalem, he had worshiped in Jerusalem. He had an open, a seeking mind, a *receptive* mind ready and anxious to hear what Philip had to say about the God of Isaiah—and the living Christ.

Second, this is the first time that the great, immortal passages of the 53rd of Isaiah is specifically quoted as a great basic doctrine of the Church that was being born at this moment. The Suffering Servant! That Good News was to spread out from the desert Gaza road to march down the highways of lands "outside" Israel, beyond Jerusalem, to the very ends of the earth. The conversion of the God-seeking eunuch introduced something new, a new *principle*, in the pagan-tired world. The conversion of the Ethiopian is thought by many to have been the first Gentile conversion, but that is not so; Cornelius was the first, but both of them opened doors to the lands beyond Jerusalem.

Then, third, there was Philip. We know too little about Philip the Evangelist; he does not stand out like a giant, as did many of the other early followers of Jesus; he did his work quietly. He helped with the relief of the poor in the Jerusalem Church; he preached in hostile Samaria (Acts 8:4–8), which must have been no easy task; he led a sorcerer to become a member of the Church (Acts 8:9–13). And he *ran* to talk with the eunuch. After that, according to tradition, he led the way in bringing the Gospel to Northeast Africa, and finally settled down in Caesarea, where he played host to the Apostle Paul. (Acts 21:8–15). And he had four daughters who became Christian prophetesses (21:9).

He was a quiet and self-effacing man, but he baptized the eunuch, who went on to evangelize Ethiopia (odd, isn't it, that we do not even know his name?), and that was no mean accomplishment. We have no copies of the sermons Philip preached, and that is to our loss for they must have been good sermons. Philip *lived* his faith; he also moved out among the outsiders of Israel and *talked* his faith. We who are Christians in 1983 should learn something from that—something vitally important. We love our church; we support it financially; we attend its services regularly, but do we realize that Philip and his convert *moved out* among those who were not Christians at all and won them to Christ? The Church of Christ, to them, was not so much a place to come to as *it was a place to move out from.*

We complain today about the Church losing membership at an alarming rate. If we ask ourselves, "Why," one answer *must* be that by and large we have *not* gone after the "outsiders." For one reason or another, we do not talk our faith to those who most need it. Is it too much for us to say that the Church was created for the outsiders, more than for its *insiders?*

SUGGESTIONS TO TEACHERS

The fourteen-year-old son of a Vietnamese refugee family was invited by a schoolmate to attend a local church youth group. Although the young people accepted the newcomer from Vietnam, some of the parents did not. The advisors of the youth group and the pastor received several calls disapproving of the boy's coming to the church youth program. "We're a Christian congregation, and Buddhists and outsiders really don't belong in our program," complained one unhappy parent, not realizing that the Vietnamese boy and his family had been Roman Catholics in Saigon for several generations. The Vietnamese-American quickly "got the message" and stopped coming.

What a contrast between this recent unhappy episode and the attitudes and actions of the Church in Acts! Informed by the Spirit that the Good News of Jesus Christ was meant for outsiders, the earliest Christians seemed to exert all their energies to reach out to "foreigners."

Your lesson for today is the first of four lessons showing how the Spirit impells believers to move beyond old barriers. The Gospel is the news that God through Christ seeks persons of each race, social status, sex, and educational level. In today's lesson, you will stress the Good News for outsiders.

1. *HARBINGER.* Refer to the passage in Isaiah 56:3–8, where God declares that His people are to include all types. His house is to be a "house of prayer for all people," because He intends to bring still other people to join His own chosen people. Remind your class that Jesus quoted this selection from Isaiah when He cleansed the Temple during His final days on earth. Jesus' mission, continuing that of Israel as seen in Isaiah 56, was not only to "his own kind" but also to outsiders. Pick out examples from Jesus' ministry of His profound concern for outsiders. (Luke's Gospel account has many, such as Jesus' interest in women, Samaritans, lepers, etc.)

2. *HERITAGE.* Direct the attention of your people to Stephen and his speech. Point out that Stephen, a "Hellenist" or Greek-speaking Jew, was himself an outsider to the Jerusalem Jews who followed Jesus Christ. Have your class examine Stephen's defense (Acts 7). Help your class to grasp the point that the Christian message is rooted in the Old Testament and is a continuation of God's outreach for the entire world. More important, draw attention to the climax of Stephen's speech in which he emphasizes that God will not allow Himself to be shut up in the confines of a sacred Temple, but extends His Presence through the coming of "the Righteous One" (Jesus) whom the narrow-minded Temple types have killed. This will be a good opportunity for you to stress the ties Christianity has with Judaism.

3. *HERO.* The Good News demands a willingness to sacrifice, just as Jesus Christ sacrificed for us. Persecution quickly hit believers in the early church. Retell the story of Stephen's martyrdom. Also discuss the cost paid by many other early Church people (*see* Acts 8:1–2). Do your class members realize the debt owed to these many nameless ancestors in the faith and countless others? What sacrifices are your people making for the sake of the Gospel so that others will know the Good News?

4. *HERALD.* Devote enough time in your lesson to Philip the Evangelist's preaching missions to outsiders in Samaria. Samaritans, you will

recall, were definitely outsiders in New Testament days! Have your class identify the "Samaritans" in today's culture, such as the poor or the minorities. Look at Philip's alertness in noticing the opportunity to speak to the needs of another outsider, the Ethiopian official (Acts 8:26–40), and his willingness to take the until-then unprecedented step of baptizing an outsider into the fellowship of Christ's people! What exactly is your class and your church doing to reach out to the various kinds of outsiders in your area and in our world?

TOPIC FOR ADULTS
GOOD NEWS FOR OUTSIDERS

Building Links Between Pews and Jails. "Robb and Irene Denney, based in Cordova, California, are a unique couple engaged in a unique ministry of interpretation and reconciliation between prisoners and churchgoers. The program is called, 'Go and Tell Everyone' or 'GATE.' The Denneys go around to churches to tell congregations what it's like to be in jail and what Christians can do to provide a healthy link between the prisoner and the outside world. Robb Denney is particularly equipped to perform this ministry. An ex-offender, Robb puts it this way:

" 'I was released from prison in 1977, nine years after being sentenced to life, and four years after God's love reached me inside the walls and freed me from my prison of sin. I'm a member of a church which befriended, baptized, and assisted me during my imprisonment and afterwards. They also introduced me to Irene, who became my wife two years before I was released.'

"The essence of their ministry is this: 'Christians reached into the prison to give me love and hope. I reached out to ask Christians to give love and support to all prisoners by writing articles for Christian magazines, helping persons who want to get involved become involved by visiting or writing prisoners, becoming friends of a prisoner's family, working through legislation to improve prison conditions, giving parolees jobs, and even helping whole congregations establish their own prison ministries.'

"With strong support from the Cordova congregation, the Sierra Mission Area, and the Synod of the Pacific, and with a boost of a mission development grant from the denomination's Program Agency, GATE's ministry is to expand and become a comprehensive program in criminal justice ministry."—From *Missionscope,* Number 10; December, 1980.

Apostle to African Outsiders. During the first half of this century, Mary Slessor was well known in Scotland as a heroine who risked all in her service to Africans—living in Eastern Nigeria. Today we see her not so much as a pioneer in the geographical sense but in her understanding of African culture. She accepted for herself the standards of housing, food, and other aspects of life of those living in the bush in the Calabar and Cross River areas. By identifying herself with those she lived to serve, she witnessed to the living presence of Jesus Christ. "If I did not know that my Saviour is near me, I would go out of my mind."

Constant tribal warfare and a lack of basic medical knowledge resulted in life being not only short but cruel. Yet, in spite of identifying herself with the people to an extent no other missionary in Nigeria has done, by her character and faith, she opened up the way for the establishment of the Christian Church. Records and numbers did not interest her; such was her complete commitment to an ever increasing circle of friends of different tribes. Through such links she was able to prevent and even stop much intertribal fighting. These were important years for tribes which had suffered severely from the effects of the slave trade—people were still divided as between free and slave. For the longest period in her missionary career, this unique woman, brought up among the slums of Dundee almost entirely on her own, by her motherly care linked to an explosive determination, laid foundations on which African Christian leaders have built.

Whenever Ma Slessor heard a cry for help, either from an individual or a village, she attempted immediately to meet it. But at heart she was no recluse, keeping abreast of what was happening throughout the world and making lasting friendships with those who came from Scotland in her later years to follow where she had led. Honored in her lifetime by the people she had often scolded, she gradually won the respect and admiration of leading colonial civil servants.

Invite Them to See the Splendor. Some of the most gorgeous stained-glass windows are in the synagogue of the Hadassah-Hebrew University Medical Centre in Jerusalem. Created by Marc Chagall, the beauty of the light shining through these colorful designs causes gasps of delight to everyone who sees the windows from the inside. When someone is excited about the loveliness of the Chagall windows, he knows that the only way to convince others of their beauty is to invite them into the synagogue.

Our task as Christian witnesses is not so much to make beautiful windows, but to lead others inside the synagogue where they can see the splendid colors when the light shines through. This is what evangelism to outsiders is all about—to invite everyone to appreciate the significance of Christ's light for themselves.

Questions for Pupils on the Next Lesson. 1. What verified the reality of the Resurrection to Paul? 2. What did conversion entail in the case of Paul? Does conversion have the same implications in our times? 3. What special ministry do you believe Christ has given to you? 4. Is every Christian "called" to some form of service? 5. How can Easter be celebrated in a way that will share the Resurrection news more meaningfully in your church?

TOPIC FOR YOUTH
SHARING GOD'S WORD

Eyes That Cannot See. In the caves of Kentucky and Tennessee, there lives a curious fish. A catfish, it is fully developed in all respects except one. It cannot see. It has eyes, but millions of years in the dark have rendered those eyes useless. The fish depends on its other senses to survive.

The thought of a creature with eyes that could not see stirred me to question how many of us were like that fish—blind to our surroundings.

When the Lincoln Memorial was dedicated in 1922, the blacks who attended the ceremony commemorating the Great Emancipator were segregated in a section about two blocks from the speaker's platform. Most newspapers of the day failed to see the irony of that.

How often we as Christ's people do not *see* those around us—especially outsiders. How frequently we are blind to our surroundings. Countless opportunities to share God's Good News present themselves each week—if we will but look with Christ's eyes!

Understanding God's Word. Mark Twain once said, "Most people are bothered by those passages in Scripture which they cannot understand; but as for me, I always noticed that the passages in Scripture which troubled me most are those which I do understand."

Sometimes, God's Word troubles us so much we don't want to understand it. Or, we try to escape His claims by looking for "problems" in interpreting parts of the Bible we don't like.

One troubling portion of the Bible insists that hearing means sharing God's Good News. The earliest Christians knew this. God's Word calls us to share the hope, joy, and peace of Jesus Christ with outsiders.

Sharing Good News to Outsiders. For nine years, Bill Sample, a police officer, stood watch at a Philadelphia pediatrics hospital. He saw the children come and go, some bald from chemotherapy, some drooped on crutches. He would smile, and they would talk to him. But then some of them wouldn't come any more. And he would check and find that they were dead.

Several years ago, Mr. Sample, with a mortgage and three children of his own, reached into his own pocket to buy a dream for a girl dying of cancer. He sent her to a concert.

Today, Mr. Sample is president of the Sunshine Foundation, a nonprofit organization that he put together in his spare time. Seventy volunteer workers now assemble the dreams: a trip to Disney World, a ride down the Mississippi on a houseboat, a week at the seashore, a trip to the Grand Canyon, or a visit with a far-away friend. For one eleven-year-old with leukemia, it was sharing the bench with the Pittsburgh Pirates baseball team.

Mr. Sample is forty-eight years old, and has been on the Philadelphia police force for twenty-four years. When he is not working as a policeman, he is either asleep or working at the foundation, always in a hurry for fear that death will cancel a trip.

"That really hurts," he said, "because you become attached to them. You try not to, but you do. You go into their houses and you see them lying on the floor in pain. And you talk to them about their trip and they look at you and smile. And the next thing you know they're dead."

Since the fall of 1976, he has helped 500 dying or chronically ill children and their families, many drained financially by the illnesses.

Sentence Sermon to Remember: A church that does not speak to those outside it, but only to those inside, is not the Church Christ expected.—Eugene Price.

Questions for Pupils on the Next Lesson. 1. How did Paul know that the Resurrection of Jesus Christ was true? 2. What does it mean to be "converted"? 3. Do you think God has special plans for you? If so, what are they? 4. Are all Christians chosen for forms of ministry? 5. Does every Christian experience suffering? 6. How have others influenced you in your pilgrimage of faith? How are you influencing others in their journeys?

LESSON V—APRIL 3

CONFRONTED BY THE RISEN LORD

Background Scripture: Acts 9:1–31; 22:1–21; 26:1–23; 1 Corinthians 15:3–11
Devotional Reading: 1 Corinthians 15:1–11

KING JAMES VERSION

ACTS 9 1 And Saul, yet breathing out threatenings and slaughter against the disciples of the Lord, went unto the high priest,

2 And desired of him letters to Damascus to the synagogues, that if he found any of this way, whether they were men or women, he might bring them bound unto Jerusalem.

3 And as he journeyed, he came near Damascus: and suddenly there shined round about him a light from heaven:

4 And he fell to the earth, and heard a voice saying unto him, Saul, Saul, why persecutest thou me?

5 And he said, Who art thou, Lord? And the Lord said, I am Jesus whom thou persecutest: *it is* hard for thee to kick against the pricks.

6 And he trembling and astonished said, Lord, what wilt thou have me to do? And the Lord *said* unto him, Arise, and go into the city, and it shall be told thee what thou must do.

7 And the men which journeyed with him stood speechless, hearing a voice, but seeing no man.

8 And Saul arose from the earth; and when his eyes were opened, he saw no man: but they led him by the hand, and brought *him* into Damascus.

9 And he was three days without sight, and neither did eat nor drink.

10 And there was a certain disciple at Damascus, named Ananias; and to him said the Lord in a vision, Ananias. And he said, Behold, I *am here,* Lord.

11 And the Lord *said* unto him, Arise, and go into the street which is called Straight, and inquire in the house of Judas for *one* called Saul, of Tarsus: for, behold, he prayeth,

12 And hath seen in a vision a man named Ananias coming in, and putting *his* hand on him, that he might receive his sight.

13 Then Ananias answered, Lord, I have

REVISED STANDARD VERSION

ACTS 9 1 But Saul, still breathing threats and murder against the disciples of the Lord, went to the high priest 2 and asked him for letters to the synagogues at Damascus, so that if he found any belonging to the Way, men or women, he might bring them bound to Jerusalem. 3 Now as he journeyed he approached Damascus, and suddenly a light from heaven flashed about him. 4 And he fell to the ground and heard a voice saying to him, "Saul, Saul, why do you persecute me?" 5 And he said, "Who are you, Lord?" And he said, "I am Jesus, whom you are persecuting; 6 but rise and enter the city, and you will be told what you are to do." 7 The men who were traveling with him stood speechless, hearing the voice but seeing no one. 8 Saul arose from the ground; and when his eyes were opened, he could see nothing; so they led him by the hand and brought him into Damascus. 9 And for three days he was without sight, and neither ate nor drank.

10 Now there was a disciple at Damascus named Ananias. The Lord said to him in a vision, "Ananias." And he said, "Here I am, Lord." 11 And the Lord said to him, "Rise and go to the street called Straight, and inquire in the house of Judas for a man of Tarsus named Saul; for behold, he is praying, 12 and he has seen a man named Ananias come in and lay his hands on him so that he might regain his sight." 13 But Ananias answered, "Lord, I have heard from many about this man, how much evil he has done to thy saints at Jerusalem; 14 and here he has authority from the chief

heard by many of this man, how much evil he hath done to thy saints at Jerusalem:

14 And here he hath authority from the chief priests to bind all that call on thy name.

15 But the Lord said unto him, Go thy way: for he is a chosen vessel unto me, to bear my name before the Gentiles, and kings, and the children is Israel:

16 For I will shew him how great things he must suffer for my name's sake.

priests to bind all who call upon thy name." 15 But the Lord said to him, "Go, for he is a chosen instrument of mine to carry my name before the Gentiles and kings and the sons of Israel; 16 for I will show him how much he must suffer for the sake of my name."

KEY VERSE: "And I said, 'Who are you, Lord?' And the Lord said, 'I am Jesus whom you are persecuting.'" Acts 26:15 (RSV).

HOME DAILY BIBLE READINGS

Mar. 28. M. *The Conversion of Saul.* Acts 9:1–9.
Mar. 29. T. *The Authority of Paul's Apostleship.* Galatians 1:11–17.
Mar. 30. W. *The Damascus Road—Revisited.* Acts 22:1–10.
Mar. 31. T. *The Divine Command.* Acts 22:17–22.
Apr. 1. F. *Paul's Defense Before Agrippa.* Acs 26:1–8.
Apr. 2. S. *By the Grace of God.* 1 Corinthians 15:3–11.
Apr. 3. S. *From Persecutor to Preacher.* Galatians 1:18–24.

BACKGROUND

Now we meet Paul. That was his Roman name; his Jewish name was Saul. But what's in a name? Whatever they called him, he remains the Colossus of the early Church, the most dynamic and influential of all the first Christians, the pivotal portrait in the gallery of the first volunteer Soldiers of the Cross.

Born in Tarsus, the capital of Cilicia, he was both a Roman and a Jewish citizen, a citizenship inherited from his father, a maker of tents. At twenty, he was a student in the rabbinical school of the Pharisees, a student with a fine mind and one of the young radical fanatics who, as Pharisees, reacted violently to both the disturber named Jesus and the Church called Christian. "As for Saul, he made havock of the church, entering into every house, and haling men and women committed them to prison" (Acts 8:3). He was in the crowd that stoned Stephen to death; indeed, the executioners who hurled the stones laid their coats at the feet of Paul—a recognition that the wild young student was one of them. Paul came to enjoy the sight, and he went out after it was over, with the approval of the high priest of the moment, to hunt down other "heretics" in Damascus where a group of fugitive Christians had sought refuge from the terrorism of Jerusalem.

But on the Damascus Road, Paul had deep, disturbing thoughts about it—thoughts that opened the way for him to turn from his fanaticism to become a champion of the Christians, and the great leader of their persecuted Church.

NOTES ON THE PRINTED TEXT

Damascus and Jerusalem are something less than 200 miles apart; on such a trip, Paul had time to do a lot of meditating. Surely, all along the way, he kept thinking of the man he had just seen stoned to death while pleading for forgiveness of his executioners. He had never met another like Stephen who could die so beautifully, and that disturbed this Christian hater. And he must have had deep, deep thoughts of the Christ who had inspired this first martyr of the Church. Maybe, after all, Christ was not the man Paul had thought Him to be.

As he mulled it over in his mind, "a light from heaven flashed about him" (verse 3). It was a light so bright that it blinded him. And in the light he heard the voice of the Christ he had despised, telling him what to do (Not what to think or believe, but what to *do,* and that is more than interesting!)

This experience of Paul is, in one sense, as baffling to us as it was to him. First of all, it struck with blinding speed like a flash of lightning, and it was all over almost as quickly and unexpectedly as it came—or, in our modern parlance, like a bolt out of the blue. At least, that is the way it appears to be as we read the Scripture describing it. Many of us believe that *our* conversions to Christ must come that way, too, in a moment of sudden apprehension, and indeed it does often come that way, when many come face to face with Christ. But is it not also possible that behind the sudden recognition as we encounter Him, that there are long days and years in which we are dissatisfied with what we are, and during which we long to be *more like Christ?* Paul struggled long in separating the demands of Jewish law from the demands of his conscience, and the explosion on the Damascus Road came at the end of that fight within himself. He was born to be great, and, across those conflicting years, he knew that in his present state he was *not* great, not satisfied. He spent his early life seeking God's truth—and on this road he came face to face with the truth that was in Christ.

Every one of us faces the fact that a day comes to us when we must decide for or against Christ; to some the truth comes quietly, gently; to others, in a blinding flash. There comes that moment after long debate and hesitation when we say yes or no to this divine intervention into our lives, when a voice from beyond this world speaks, and when a light bursts upon us that changes the whole direction of our lives. It matters little what the *form* of that experience is; what matters is *what the experience does to us.*

Paul did as Christ commanded him that day; staggering about in blindness, unable to eat or drink. Those who were journeying with him led him into the city of Damascus into the house of one Judas, a fugitive Christian, and into the hands of one Ananias. No, this was *not* Ananias the liar, but Ananias a humble Christian sent of the Lord to heal the blindness of Paul and to explain to him his mission for God. Instantly (it was as though scales fell from his eyes) Paul could see, and was immediately baptized (*see* Acts 9:18). Was this Ananias a (professional) faith-healer? Probably not; he was an obscure little disciple who with the help of the Spirit did what God told him to do—to bring Paul back to see those around him and to see clearly that he was God's human instrument to carry the Gospel behind the gates of the Gentile world.

The first words of Ananias to blind Paul were "*Brother* Saul;" Brother? Paul had been sent to throw Ananias into prison, perhaps even to bring about his death, and he was greeted as a brother. If we forget all else about Ananias, remember this: he symbolized the love and forgiveness of the first Christians and the first Church. We hear no more about him following this; he is just one of those "little" men who inspire greatness in "big" men. (Some of the greatest Christians we have had were led by unknown little men to Jesus Christ!) Paul was told of the Lord that he was "a chosen vessel unto me," or a chosen *instrument.* Was not Ananias His instrument, too? What, we wonder, would have become of Paul had it not been for the healing and the brotherhood of Ananias?

SUGGESTIONS TO TEACHERS

"*What if* . . . ?"

What if the Nazis had triumphed in 1945? What would the world be like today? What if the American Revolution had failed? What if Luther had not nailed his ninety-five theses to the Wittenberg Church door in 1517? Think how different our history would have been in each case.

The greatest "*What if* . . . ?" to ponder is the death of Jesus Christ. What if there had been no Resurrection?

For one thing, there would have been no Easter announcement that Jesus lives. There would have been no confrontation with Saul of Tarsus, then the chief persecutor of Christians. Undoubtedly, if there had been no Resurrection, there would be no Christian community. You and your class would not be meeting if there had been no encounter with the Risen Lord.

This Easter, you may well open your lesson discussion by prodding your class to ponder the question, "What if there had been no Resurrection?" Then, relying on the accounts of Paul's conversion in Acts 9, 22, and 26, and his understanding of the Resurrection in 1 Corinthians 15, develop your lesson around the following points.

1. *PERSON TO PERSON.* Call attention to Paul's report of the Risen Christ encountering him on the way to Damascus. The Resurrection is actually a direct personal question by Jesus Christ. "Saul, Saul, why do you persecute me?" the Lord asks. Easter means that God has raised up Jesus alive to address each believer by name. The Resurrection means a firsthand experience with Jesus Christ. Help your people to appreciate the "person-to-person" aspect of the relationship with Him. Without making anyone feel uncomfortable, allow those, who wish, to share what Jesus Christ means to them.

2. *PERSECUTOR TO PARTISAN.* Devote plenty of lesson time to Saul's conversion. Whether sudden (as in the case of Saul and others) or gradual (as in the case of still others) conversion means changing direction. The details of each person's Damascus Road experience vary. However, each Christian is being confronted by the Living Christ. It would undoubtedly be helpful for you to share part of your own personal story of how you have found yourself pushed by Christ into different directions on occasion.

3. *PICKED AS PROCLAIMER.* Be sure to make clear to your class that the Risen Lord always summons a person to share the news of Easter. "I will send you . . . to the Gentiles," Jesus tells Saul on the Damascus Road. Usually, as in Saul's case, Jesus' assignment means to "Gentiles,"

that is, people not part of one's own religious club! Easter means that each Christian believer is picked by the Lord to proclaim Christ's Lordship.

4. *PRESENT WITH PARDON.* The Apostle Paul, your class should recall, was a man with a past. As Saul, he had "shut up many of the saints in prison," voted to have them "put to death," and "persecuted them even to foreign cities" (Acts 26:10,11). How could God ever accept a man guilty of such cruelty who also freely acknowledged he had done "many things in opposing the name of Jesus" (26:9)? The answer: God's conditional pardon through the Cross and Resurrection of Jesus Christ. Christ's appearance to Saul meant mercy. Make certain that your lesson this Easter lays enough importance on God's "amazing grace!"

TOPIC FOR ADULTS
CONFRONTED BY THE LIVING LORD

Christ, Not an Experience. "In 1687 a young Lutheran theologian, August Hermann Franckes, found his academic career interrupted by financial concerns.

"In this frame of mind and heart he arrived in Lueneburg with his goal firmly before him but unable to shake off the mantle of worldliness he had acquired.

"In despair Francke fell to his knees time and time again while a powerful battle raged within him for several days. Finally, he experienced the living God in Jesus Christ. He reported: 'I again fell on my knees on that Sunday eve and cried to God, whom I neither knew nor believed, for salvation from such a sorrowful condition, if there truly was a God. Then the Lord heard me. Then as one turns his hand, so all my doubts were gone, I was sure in my heart of the grace of God in Jesus Christ. I knew God not only as God but rather as one called my Father. All sadness and unrest in my heart was taken away in a moment.'

"His desire for honor in the academic community, the hope for recognition, the seeking for status among the nobility and striving for 'the good life,' all became things of the past. In time, Francke certainly became famous for his scholarship; his name was recognized by church leaders from America to Asia, and he was held in high regard by kings and emperors, but this was not his expressed goal.

"His approach to life eventually resulted in a massive institution, the *Stiftungen,* which housed widows and orphans, educated wealthy and poor alike (including poor girls, a major innovation), established the first Bible institute, sent missionaries throughout the world, effected the humanizing of Prussian law, and touched on the spiritual and physical lives of people throughout Germany.

"As powerful as his conversion experience may have been, Francke saw it as neither an end in itself nor as something to be sought again. It is here that we may profit from Francke's perspective on religious experience.

"He was concerned not to *experience* God, but rather to experience *God.* There is quite a difference! In the former case, one arranges the circumstances of one's encounter with God, waiting for tears, fireworks, a deep sense of sin, excitement, or whatever else has been prescribed by one's religious community or imagination. In such a situation, the possibility of frustration, disappointment, and even bitterness is enormous as is the temptation to create one's own experience.

"In the second circumstance, however, one allows God to set the conditions of the meeting. Here God Himself is the central figure, the beginning and end of an experience that is simply the vehicle for the divine-human encounter. There are no preestablished criteria to be fulfilled. Thus one is less likely to be disappointed by (or proud of) the intensity or drama of the experience. It is also less likely to become the focus of the subsequent Christian life.

"Although Francke referred frequently to his conversion and was ever aware of the presence of the Holy Spirit, we do not find him seeking to duplicate his conversion or manufacture any new experiences. It is all too easy for one's conversion experience, precisely because of its beauty or power, to nudge aside Christ's promises as the source of assurance, comfort, and hope. Religious experience then becomes a drug."—Gary R. Sattler, *Ministry*, November 1980.

No Dead End. "Easter is the ground of everything positive and worthwhile. 'No Resurrection, no Gospel!' wrote Moffatt, and he is right. 'But now is Christ risen!' For me, four implications stand out.

"There is no such thing as a completely closed situation. Christ Risen, is in its midst. His boundless sovereignty opens up all things to unlimited possibilities of redemption.

"Those who live by faith are not fools or dupes. However hard the going, however tempting the way of unfaith, faith must be right! Greatest of all 'signs' is given us that faith is rooted in, and directed towards, no mirage but ultimate reality. Christ Risen's path of faith through life and death has been vindicated by God. In the fate of His faith, our faith is validated!

"Christ rose as victor over the forces of every kind of evil. He triumphed in the power of love. Good Friday comes again as a powerful needed reminder of the Cross-like cost of love we shrink from bearing; Easter, no less, of love's assured eventual victory. We give up too soon, appalled by the seeming weakness and slowness of love. Christ Risen says: 'Keep on! Love must win!'

"And Easter assuredly says: The end is not a dead-end! Death opens the door into God's very presence. Christ is there—and so many we have loved. Such a home we have to go to: such fulfillment, in the fulness of life eternal."—Neil Alexander, *Life and Work*, April 1979.

Enlivened by Risen Lord. Ibsen's Julian said: "Have you looked at these Christians closely? Hollow-eyed, pale-cheeked, flat-breasted all; they brood their lives away, unspurred by ambition; the sun shines for them, but they do not see it; the earth offers them its fullness, but they desire it not; all their desire is to renounce and suffer, that they may come to die."

Hendrik Ibsen the writer of dramas apparently was not a reader of the Resurrection drama. Instead of being people who "brood their lives away, unspurred by ambition," these confronted by the Risen Lord joyously gave their lives away. The early Christians who met the living Christ were spurred by unquenchable ambition to share the news! Their stories read like adventure novels. They radiated a confidence and a happiness. And the reason was that Jesus was alive and with them!

Questions for Pupils on the Next Lesson. 1. Do you sometimes experience tension between old values and new ones? 2. Do you sometimes find that you allow cultural and ethnic differences to block relationships with others? 3. How does the Christian Gospel help people to move beyond prejudicial attitudes toward other groups? 4. Why is a greater sense of inclusiveness and world community vital to the survival of the human family? 5. Has the Christian faith ever reconciled you to someone who was your enemy?

TOPIC FOR YOUTH
ENCOUNTERING CHRIST

Immediate Response. Dorothy Day became an agnostic during her student days at the University of Illinois. "For me Christ no longer walked the streets of this world. He was 2,000 years dead and new prophets had risen up in his place," she later recalled. Among the new prophets who tried to take Christ's place for Dorothy Day were socialist thinkers. She lived as if Christ were long dead. She lived with a Marxist lover, but when she gave birth to a daughter she began to think that she wanted to have the child baptized. "I was not going to have her floundering through many years as I had done, doubting, undisciplined, and amoral. For myself, I prayed for the gift of faith," she wrote many years later.

The gift of faith finally came. Jesus Christ proved not to be 2,000 years dead, but incredibly alive. In 1927, Dorothy Day left her lover and was baptized. For the rest of her life, Dorothy Day the Christian devoted all of her energies as "immediate response to the need of the other person," as she put it.

She started a newspaper that advocated a more equitable distribution of society's goods to help the poor. She opened a soup kitchen and hospitality house for the needy in the poorest slum in New York. Her tireless efforts for justice led to the formation of the Catholic Worker Movement, which took the Gospel literally. Hundreds flocked to help her run her Hospitality Houses in American cities, offering food, shelter, jobs, used clothing, and a practical demonstration of love to derelicts. Her newspaper, *Catholic Worker,* helped make Christ alive to thousands more. Dorothy Day championed such social issues as women's rights, hunger, and peace long before they were "in."

Throughout her long life, Dorothy Day continued to live among the poor in New York, accepting the same poverty and hardship as they. "It's the whole business of accepting the Cross," she would always reply. At her enormously well attended funeral, former Yippie Abbie Hoffman mumbled, "She is the nearest thing this Jewish boy is ever going to get to a saint."

When Christ encounters a person, He makes a radical difference. He starts that person on the road to a kind of saintliness. Has He encountered you?

Living Person. "Without Easter there would have been no Gospels as we know them, no Christian Church, no New Testament, no Lord's Day.

It is because of Easter that we have a Gospel at all: 'If Christ be not risen then is your faith vain.'

"It is worthwhile to remember that the Gospels were written after the Resurrection, and one might say *because* of the Resurrection.

"But for a Christian, it is not enough to believe in the Resurrection—that the Resurrection 'happened;' he must also believe that Jesus Christ is the Resurrection.

"It is not enough to believe in a past event; he must believe, too, in a living person. There can be a difference between belief in the Resurrection and trust in a living Lord.

"Easter then is not just something that 'happened;' it means Someone who is alive for everymore—alive now, today, where you are now.

"We believe that at this Eastertide, as on that first Easter evening, Jesus stands in our midst and says, 'Peace be unto you;' and He calls you by name. And you answer, 'My Lord and my God . . . Into Thy hands . . . Into Thy hands.' No longer now afraid of life or death. Such is our faith, and those who believe in Him with all their heart know it to be true."—Ronald Selby Wright, *Life and Work*, April 1979.

Gift of Himself. A few years ago, a congregation in Frankfort, Indiana, decided it needed a gimmick to perk up church attendance on Easter Sunday. On the Saturday before Easter, 1,000 balloons bombarded Frankfort from an airplane. Each balloon carried a message and some had the added incentive of gift certificates ranging from fifty cents to fifty dollars with the notice, "The certificate must be presented at church school services Easter to be redeemed."

The news of Easter is not a balloon with a gift certificate. It is that Jesus lives. He wants to encounter each person with the gift of His friendship. Does your church present Him as God's gift to every person? Do you act as if He truly is alive? Has He encountered you in love? Do you introduce others to Him?

Sentence Sermon to Remember: Easter is not a passport to another world; it is a quality of perception for this one.—W. P. Lemon.

Questions for Pupils on the Next Lesson. 1. Do you ever feel a conflict between traditional values and Christ's? 2. With what people do you find it hardest to associate? 3. In your community, what are the most notable prejudices that people seem to hold? 4. Do you feel that your church makes a sincere effort to welcome people who are "different"? 5. Do you feel, even secretly, that you have people you regard as enemies?

LESSON VI—APRIL 10

GOOD NEWS FOR FORMER ENEMIES

Background Scripture: Acts 9:32–12:24
Devotional Reading: 1 John 5:1–12

KING JAMES VERSION

ACTS 11 2 And when Peter was come up to Jerusalem, they that were of the circumcision contended with him,

3 Saying, Thou wentest in to men uncircumcised, and didst eat with them.

4 But Peter rehearsed *the matter* from the beginning, and expounded *it* by order unto them, saying,

5 I was in the city of Joppa praying: and in a trance I saw a vision, A certain vessel descend, as it had been a great sheet, let down from heaven by four corners; and it came even to me:

6 Upon the which when I had fastened mine eyes, I considered, and saw fourfooted beasts of the earth, and wild beasts, and creeping things, and fowls of the air.

7 And I heard a voice saying unto me, Arise, Peter; slay and eat.

8 But I said, Not so, Lord: for nothing common or unclean hath at any time entered into my mouth.

9 But the voice answered me again from heaven, What God hath cleansed, *that* call not thou common.

10 And this was done three times: and all were drawn up again into heaven.

11 And, behold, immediately there were three men already come unto the house where I was, sent from Caesarea unto me.

12 And the Spirit bade me go with them, nothing doubting. Moreover these six brethren accompanied me, and we entered into the man's house:

13 And he shewed us how he had seen an angel in his house, which stood and said unto him, Send men to Joppa, and call for Simon, whose surname is Peter;

14 Who shall tell thee words, whereby thou and all thy house shall be saved.

15 And as I began to speak, the Holy Ghost fell on them, as on us at the beginning.

16 Then remembered I the word of the Lord, how that he said, John indeed baptized with water; but ye shall be baptized with the Holy Ghost.

17 Forasmuch then as God gave them the like gift as *he did* unto us, who believed

REVISED STANDARD VERSION

ACTS 11 2 So when Peter went up to Jerusalem, the circumcision party criticized him, 3 saying, "Why did you go to uncircumcised men and eat with them?" 4 But Peter began and explained to them in order: 5 "I was in the city of Joppa praying; and in a trance I saw a vision, something descending, like a great sheet, let down from heaven by four corners; and it came down to me. 6 Looking at it closely I observed animals and beasts of prey and reptiles and birds of the air. 7 And I heard a voice saying to me, 'Rise, Peter; kill and eat.' 8 But I said, 'No, Lord; for nothing common or unclean has ever entered my mouth.' 9 But the voice answered a second time from heaven, 'What God has cleansed you must not call common.' 10 This happened three times, and all was drawn up again into heaven. 11 At that very moment three men arrived at the house in which we were, sent to me from Caesarea. 12 And the Spirit told me to go with them, making no distinction. These six brethren also accompanied me, and we entered the man's house. 13 And he told us how he had seen the angel standing in his house and saying, 'Send to Joppa and bring Simon called Peter; 14 he will declare to you a message by which you will be saved, you and all your household.' 15 As I began to speak, the Holy Spirit fell on them just as on us at the beginning. 16 And I remembered the word of the Lord, how he said, 'John baptized with water, but you shall be baptized with the Holy Spirit.' 17 If then God gave the same gift to them as he gave to us when we believed in the Lord Jesus Christ, who was I that I could withstand God?" 18 When they heard this they were silenced. And they glorified God, saying, "Then to the Gentiles also God has granted repentance unto life."

on the Lord Jesus Christ, what was I, that I could withstand God?

18 When they heard these things, they held their peace, and glorified God, saying, Then hath God also to the Gentiles granted repentance unto life.

KEY VERSE: . . . "Then to the Gentiles also God has granted repentance unto life." Acts 11:18 (RSV).

HOME DAILY BIBLE READINGS

Apr. *4.* *M.* *The Universality of Guilt.* Romans 3:1–11.
Apr. *5.* *T.* *Righteousness by Faith.* Romans 3:21–26.
Apr. *6.* *W.* *The Reign of Grace.* Romans 5:17–21.
Apr. *7.* *T.* *Saved by Grace.* Ephesians 2:1–10.
Apr. *8.* *F.* *Through Jesus Christ.* Ephesians 2:11–18.
Apr. *9.* *S.* *An Habitation of God.* Ephesians 2:19–22.
Apr. *10.* *S.* *A Light to the Gentiles.* Acts 13:44–49.

BACKGROUND

Which was the greater man, Paul or Peter? Paul the scholar, or Peter the fisherman? (We know of one church that settled that problem by calling itself the Church of Saint Peter and Saint Paul.) Both were great, both of great value to God. Paul's value lay largely in his thinking; Peter was an activist; wherever he went, there was *action.*

Acts mentions Peter first as the healer of a man born lame (Acts 3), again in connection with Ananias (Acts 5), again as a fiery disciple who defied a high priest with the words, "We ought to obey God rather than men." To prove that conviction, he had accepted a Roman centurion named Cornelius into the Church without insisting that the centurion be circumcised. He actually *ate* with this Gentile soldier. The church fathers in Jerusalem heard of it and had Peter brought before them to explain how he could do such a thing; it was a blatant denial of Jewish law and authority, and the Jewish Christians were appalled and angry with the rebellious Peter.

NOTES ON THE PRINTED TEXT

Peter came, bringing six other men who would be witnesses to speak in his defense. (It was a custom under Egyptian law that seven witnesses were necessary to prove a case, and the Romans demanded seven "seals" to authenticate a legal document, and Peter knew that his judges would be convinced if he had seven witnesses.) There were two charges brought against him: one, that he had eaten with Gentiles, and second, that he had failed to have Cornelius circumcised.

Yes, said Peter, he had eaten with this Gentile. That could, usually, have been enough to convict any Jew of outrageously breaking the ancestral Law and custom of his (Jewish) people. Jews avoided any contact with a non-Jew; they would not enter a Gentile home; to do that would be to violate a precious *tradition.*

There was the root of it, in that word, *tradition.* In this first Church in the very beginning, all its members were Jews; the Christianity of that time was considered a movement *within* Judaism, so Jewish rules and regulations and customs were preserved. They were Jewish Christians. They must stay that way, and any man who dared break with that little group of superorthodox Jews should be thrown into outer darkness, dismissed, shunned.

Peter, for once with his temper under control, explained why he thought otherwise. He thought otherwise because of a vision he had had in the city of Joppa. (Luke thought this vision so important that he told us about it twice, in Acts 10 and 11.) A net, or sheet, was dropped down before him, a net filled with fourfooted beasts, and wild beasts, and creeping things, and fowls of the air." When a voice (from heaven?) told him to eat of this food—unclean as some of it certainly was—Peter refused: as a Jew, he could not touch unclean food. The voice told him to stop being foolish and eat: "Don't say it isn't right when God declares that it is!" (verse 9 TLB).

It shouldn't be hard for us to interpret this vision, and the voice's (God's) reply. This earth of ours is a vast net filled with good and bad, clean and unclean, righteous and unrighteous humanity. Christ's Church is called to minister not only to the "insiders" in the Church but to the "outsiders" beyond it. Let the Christian understand that, let him see that God has made the decision as to who must be saved: let not the Christian try to play God.

The reply also struck at the old belief that only the Jews were to be honored as the Children of God, and the Gentiles shunned as heretics and unbelievers. "For God so loved the *world*"—not only the Israelites. Shun nobody, Church of God: open the gates wide for all of them, that they may come to stand before the gate of heaven.

When Peter said this, he opened the gates of Jerusalem and let the love and salvation of His Christ spread out across the world like an irresistible flood.

The second charge brought against him was that he did not believe it was necessary for a convert to be circumcised before he could be baptized into the Church. This allegiance to Jewish custom and rituals was organized into what is known in church history as "the circumcision party." Here, at the very beginning, we have the picture of a church in danger of division in the conflict between little organized groups within the membership. The circumcision party might as well have hung a sign out in front of meeting-places of the new Christians, a sign reading, "For Jews Only. None Other Need Apply."

We need not be surprised at that, for wherever you find an idea, a religious conviction, or a ritual in any large group, sooner or later you will find an argument. No two of us think alike; no two Christians are exactly alike; some are strong on ceremony, others are strong on informal worship. Some are ultraconservatives like the circumcision party, and some are moderates in theology and in procedures. That is not altogether bad; human beings being what they are, we should expect it. What is bad about it is that if differences of opinion are allowed to run wild, and given precedence over the preaching and teaching of the Word of God, then the Church will be in trouble and in danger of ruin.

Suppose we put it this way: *it is nothing short of sin and blasphemy for any of us in the Church to put the organization above the the message of God.* Nearly every Church we know, today, has some one individual or group of individuals who are ready to split the Church in order to have things *their* way, even though they may drive people out of the church or shut its doors against people who may have thoughts about religious faith that are different from their own. The great value lies not in how the Church is organized, but in what it teaches about Jesus Christ and in what it does for the community that surrounds it. Quarreling parties within the Church can be plain poison when they substitute a system for the Spirit.

Peter and those who rallied around him, happily, won out against the circumcisionists. They won by simply quoting the promise of Jesus that those baptized with the Holy Ghost were qualified for membership in His Church and His crusade. Peter looked his opponents in the eye and asked them, "Who was I that I could withstand (argue with) God?" That ended the debate. The opposition gave in: "And they glorified God, saying, 'Then to the Gentiles also God has granted repentance unto life' " (verse 18 RSV). Repentance into life, and repentance into the Church of His Son.

It was one of the most momentous decisions the Church ever made, for it saved the Church from becoming nothing more than a little movement within the old Judaism.

SUGGESTIONS TO TEACHERS

Corrymeela is the name of a Christian retreat center on Ballycastle Bay in Northern Ireland. *Corrymeela* means hill of harmony in Gaelic, and tries to be such in that trouble-filled part of the world. Several times each year, Corrymeela brings youths from bitterly separated Protestant and Roman Catholic neighborhoods of Belfast for a weekend together. These "Prods" and "Taigs," as they refer to each other, come to Corrymeela as enemies. Nearly all have participated in violent acts against members of the other community. Most have had a relative or friend killed or badly injured during "the troubles" in strife-torn Northern Ireland. After the weekend retreat, however, these boys discover a kinship with each other. As one priest and pastor agreed after participating in such a retreat with tough youngsters from their parishes, "It could only happen because of the Holy Spirit."

Your lesson this Sunday describes how enemies discover that the Good News of Jesus Christ brings them together, through the power of the Holy Spirit. The Scripture for today offers numerous examples. Use them as illustrations, and prod your class members to understand that your church is meant to be a *Corrymeela*.

1. *NEW VALUES*. Start your lesson by looking at the occasion when Peter found himself at the place where Simon of Joppa worked and lived. Peter would formerly have refused to associate with a leatherworker, a despised "unclean" man who handled dead animals. Guided by the Spirit, he learned that Jesus Christ encouraged him to re-examine his old assumptions. Jesus brings a new set of values. Ask your class to discuss how Christian values differ from society's, especially on such matters as attitudes toward those of other races or color.

2. *NEW VIEW*. Review the story of Peter and Cornelius. Point out to your class that Cornelius, a Roman army man, and Peter, a Galilean nationalist, would have been sworn enemies. Jews despised the Roman oc-

cupation forces, and the haughty Romans loathed the natives. Through Jesus Christ, however, mutual antagonists gained a new view of each other. Elicit from your class examples from members' experiences of how Christ reconciled onetime foes.

3. *NEW VISION.* Peter's change of mind and heart toward his enemies was not easy. In fact, it took a special vision. The Lord pushed Peter into understanding that the Gospel was meant for him to forget his old notions of "clean" and "unclean," and to welcome Gentile believers into Christian fellowship. Point out to your class that a mini-Pentecost followed Peter's welcoming of Cornelius. To Peter's amazement, the Holy Spirit was "poured out even on the Gentiles" (Acts 10:45). Assure your people that fresh outpourings of the Spirit always occur when former enemies are united in Christ.

4. *NEW VITALITY.* Peter was called upon to defend his "rash" act of baptizing Cornelius and reminds his critics in the church that Jesus had promised baptisms or drenchings in the Spirit, and that the Spirit had directed him to welcome Cornelius. Through Peter's vision and sharing, many others in the Jerusalem church grew in vitality. Remind your class that when your congregation is a true hill of harmony, the Spirit brings new power to you.

5. *NEW VIRTUE.* Point out the way in which the early church in Antioch shared with the early church in Judea during a famine in Judea. In spite of differences and tensions within the Church, the Spirit impelled these Christians to be concerned for each other. Does your denomination and your congregation show any genuine concern for those with whom it finds itself in disagreement?

TOPIC FOR ADULTS
GOOD NEWS FOR FORMER ENEMIES

Grace Permits Community. "It is true, of course, that what is an unspeakable gift of God for the lonely individual is easily disregarded and trodden underfoot by those who have the gift every day. It is easily forgotten that the fellowship of Christian brethren is a gift of grace, a gift of the Kingdom of God that any day may be taken from us, that the time that still separates us from utter loneliness may be brief indeed. Therefore, let him who until now has had the privilege of living a common Christian life with other Christians praise God's grace from the bottom of his heart. Let him thank God on his knees and declare: It is grace, nothing but grace, that we are allowed to live in community with Christian brethren."—Dietrich Bonhoeffer, *Life Together.*

Futile Feuding. Most people in the quiet Illinois community of Carlock know nothing of the days when Democrats and Republicans feuded so fiercely that they refused to bury their dead together.

The cemeteries in this central Illinois town, ten miles northwest of Bloomington, offer evidence that the two parties literally took their political battles to the graveyard: Republicans were buried on one side of the road, Democrats on the other. The battle began with the town's founder, Abraham W. Carlock, a staunch Democrat who disliked Republicans.

There was only one cemetery then, a parcel of land donated by Mr. Carlock. But when he refused to expand it until a trust fund for its care was established, John Benson, a Republican rival, quickly offered land for a new graveyard.

The village people took it, and for years Democrats were buried in the first cemetery while Republicans were buried a quarter of a mile down the road in the second. When Mr. Carlock died in 1889, he was buried in the land he had donated, and this inscription was chiseled on his monument: "Here sleeps the old Democrat."

A lot has changed since the nineteenth century. The Carlock family joined the Republican Party and even buried one member of the family on the Republican side of the road.

There are few burials in the cemeteries now. The most recent ones were in the larger, more elaborate, lakeside grounds where once only Democrats were buried. The deficiencies of character we detect in others are frequently our own, which we note in the character and actions of those we dislike.

Best of all, through Christ, we are reconciled. There is Good News for former enemies!

Questions for Pupils on the Next Lesson. 1. Where do you find most meaning in your relationship with the church? 2. What assignments would you like to be given in your church? 3. Do you feel that others in your church share your values? 4. How are you helping others in your church to mature by moving outward toward others? 5. Is your congregation a missionary church?

TOPIC FOR YOUTH
CHANGING DIRECTION

Hatchet Burying. In Georgetown, Delaware, after November election day, Ronald F. Dodd, an undertaker dressed in an elegant black cape and top hat, raised a silver hatchet above his head. Then, as the crowd of more than 20,000 roared its approval, he placed the hatchet in a glass box and buried it with "graveyard sand," not to be resurrected until "the white oak leaves are as large as a mouse's ear."

It was the symbolic centerpiece of Return Day, a biennial custom that dates to 1791 in this Sussex County town of 2,000. For almost two centuries, the state's business has ground to a halt while its residents jam into the town square two days after elections to hear a crier announce the winners and losers.

Television, radio, and newspapers have made the announcements obsolete, of course, but no one cares. On a day when politicians who have snarled and scoffed at each other for months ride down the streets smiling together in carriages drawn by horses and oxen, partisanship is pushed aside.

The events, graced by bright autumn sunshine, got under way with a luncheon of chicken and crabmeat at a local high school. Just off the town square, oxen were roasted on spits.

At 1:30 P.M. sharp, a blast from the town's fire siren signaled the beginning of the parade—a two-hour stream of politicians, fire engines, military color guards, high-school marching bands, floats, motorcycles, and a camel.

This town's Election Day ritual is more than a day of many happy returns. It is also a custom which stems from the way Christian people are intended to change direction toward each other, especially after being adversaries. Former enemies are friends because of the Good News!

Million a Minute. The world is spending $1 million a minute on arms, twenty times more than industrialized nations spend to help poorer countries, the Stockholm International Peace Research Institute reports.

Current worldwide military expenditures total $400 billion and "with the current rate it will top $1 trillion by the end of the century," SIPRI Chairman Dr. Frank Barnaby said.

Barnaby, who is British, said that worldwide military spending is twice as high as the yearly gross domestic product of the whole of Africa, about the same amount as the gross domestic product of all Latin America and twenty times more than the total annual development assistance given by industrialized nations to the developing world.

The two great superpowers account for more than half the world's military spending.

Arms trade with the Third World has increased at an annual rate of 15 percent during the 1970s, Barnaby said, and four countries have supplied 90 percent of the major weapons exported to the Third World.

The United States ranks first, selling 38 percent of the arms imported by the Third World, followed by the Soviet Union at 34 percent, and Britain and France at 9 percent each, he said.

What do these statistics mean to Christians—who are meant to be "peacemakers"? What can Christians do today to change the direction of the world? What is your church doing to make peace and encourage a change of direction?

Bank of Friendship. John Adams and Thomas Jefferson frequently disagreed violently in the early days of the American Republic. In the hard-fought presidential election of 1801, Jefferson defeated Adams. Hurt and angry, Adams retired to his Quincy farm. Neither man had been known for tact, and each had managed to offend the other on many occasions. Fortunately, however, each man intended to live by Christian principles. Within a few years, Adams mended the break with his "enemy." Together, they changed direction and became staunch friends, exchanging many long letters as they grew older. When John Adams's beloved wife Abigail died on November 10, 1818, Jefferson sent Adams a touching letter of consolation. John Adams wrote to his former enemy words which breathe the spirit of Christian forgiveness and appreciation: "While you live, I seem to have a bank at Monticello on which I can draw for a letter of friendship and entertainment when I please." Interestingly, the two doughty old one-time adversaries died on the same day, and that day was July 4th, 1826.

Sentence Sermon to Remember: Five great enemies of peace inhabit with us—avarice, ambition, envy, anger, and pride; if these were to be banished, we should infallibly enjoy perpetual peace.—Petrarch.

Questions for Pupils on the Next Lesson. 1. What are some of the forms of idolatry in our culture? 2. Why should every church be a missionary congregation? 3. Have you ever considered a church-related vocation? 4. How can you and your church reach out to other people more effectively? 5. Why is both prayer and giving so important for Christians?

LESSON VII—APRIL 17

MISSIONARIES ON THE MOVE

Background Scripture: Acts 12:25–14:28
Devotional Reading: 1 Peter 1:19–25

KING JAMES VERSION

ACTS 13 1 Now there were in the church that was at Antioch certain prophets and teachers; as Barnabas, and Simeon that was called Niger, and Lucius of Cyrene, and Manaen, which had been brought up with Herod the tetrarch, and Saul.

2 As they ministered to the Lord, and fasted, the Holy Ghost said, Separate me Barnabas and Saul for the work whereunto I have called them.

3 And when they had fasted and prayed, and laid *their* hands on them, they sent *them* away.

14 8 And there sat a certain man at Lystra, impotent in his feet, being a cripple from his mother's womb, who never had walked:

9 The same heard Paul speak: who stedfastly beholding him, and perceiving that he had faith to be healed,

10 Said with a loud voice, Stand upright on thy feet. And he leaped and walked.

11 And when the people saw what Paul had done, they lifted up their voices, saying in the speech of Lycaonia, The gods are come down to us in the likeness of men.

12 And they called Barnabas, Jupiter; and Paul, Mercurius, because he was the chief speaker.

13 Then the priest of Jupiter, which was before their city, brought oxen and garlands unto the gates, and would have done sacrifice with the people.

14 *Which* when the apostles, Barnabas and Paul, heard *of,* they rent their clothes, and ran in among the people, crying out,

15 And saying, Sirs, why do ye these things? We also are men of like passions with you, and preach unto you that ye should turn from these vanities unto the living God, which made heaven, and earth, and the sea, and all things that are therein:

16 Who in times past suffered all nations to walk in their own ways.

17 Nevertheless he left not himself without witness, in that he did good, and

REVISED STANDARD VERSION

ACTS 13 1 Now in the church at Antioch there were prophets and teachers, Barnabas, Simeon who was called Niger, Lucius of Cyrene, Manaen a member of the court of Herod the tetrarch, and Saul. 2 While they were worshiping the Lord and fasting, the Holy Spirit said, "Set apart for me Barnabas and Saul for the work to which I have called them." 3 Then after fasting and praying they laid their hands on them and sent them off.

14 8 Now at Lystra there was a man sitting, who could not use his feet; he was a cripple from birth, who had never walked. 9 He listened to Paul speaking; and Paul, looking intently at him and seeing that he had faith to be made well, 10 said in a loud voice, "Stand upright on your feet." And he sprang up and walked. 11 And when the crowds saw what Paul had done, they lifted up their voices, saying in Lycaonian, "The gods have come down to us in the likeness of men!" 12 Barnabas they called Zeus, and Paul, because he was the chief speaker, they called Hermes. 13 And the priest of Zeus, whose temple was in front of the city, brought oxen and garlands to the gates and wanted to offer sacrifice with the people. 14 But when the apostles Barnabas and Paul heard of it, they tore their garments and rushed out among the multitude, crying, 15 "Men, why are you doing this? We also are men, of like nature with you, and bring you good news, that you should turn from these vain things to a living God who made the heaven and the earth and the sea and all that is in them. 16 In past generations he allowed all the nations to walk in their own ways; 17 yet he did not leave himself without witness, for he did good and gave you from heaven rains and fruitful seasons, satisfying your hearts with food and gladness." 18 With these words they scarcely restrained the people from offering sacrifice to them.

gave us rain from heaven, and fruitful seasons, filling our hearts with food and gladness.

18 And with these sayings scarce restrained they the people, that they had not done sacrifice unto them.

KEY VERSE: " *'I have set you to be a light for the Gentiles, that you may bring salvation to the uttermost parts of the earth.'* " Acts 13:47 (RSV).

HOME DAILY BIBLE READINGS

Apr. 11. *M.* *The Conversion of Simon the Sorcerer.* Acts 8:9–13.
Apr. 12. *T.* *The Conversion of the Eunuch.* Acts 8:26–40.
Apr. 13. *W.* *The Ministry of Peter at Lydda.* Acts 9:32–35.
Apr. 14. *T.* *Barnabas at Antioch.* Acts 11:19–26.
Apr. 15. *F.* *The Missionaries Driven Out of Town.* Acts 14:1–7.
Apr. 16. *S.* *Through Much Tribulation.* Acts 14:19–22.
Apr. 17. *S.* *The Missionary Report to the Church.* Acts 14:23–28.

BACKGROUND

Antioch, in Syria, was called at one time "The Queen of the East"; some 300 miles from Jerusalem, it was the third largest city in the Roman Empire. The martyrdom of Stephen brought many fugitive Jews to this free city of Antioch, among them Barnabas and Paul. These two did well helping to make it second only to Jerusalem in importance in the Apostolic Church.

Jerusalem, as we know, was the mother church of early Christianity; the church at Antioch sent alms regularly to Jerusalem, but eventually it broke with the conservative teachings of the mother church in favor of a universal evangelism. We can say that Antioch was the door through which the Church moved out into the pagan world.

It had another distinction: Antioch was the city in which the disciples were first called Christians. The Christians called themselves disciples, brethren, saints, believers; others called them "The People of the Way."

Barnabas was the first apostle of Christ in Antioch; Paul was his assistant; they had been in Antioch for a year when the incident in our lesson occurred. Working with them was a group of men who were symbolic of the universal appeal of the Gospel: Simeon was a Jew, active in work among the Romans, and his nickname, "the Black," may mean that he was a Negro; Lucius came from Cyrene in North Africa; Manaen had been a boy companion of Herod the Tetrarch; Saul and Barnabas were Jews. An *international* staff!

NOTES ON THE PRINTED TEXT

Among the men on this staff were some called "prophets," whose duty it was to move out, unattached to any one church, to spread the Good News among strangers. Some others were called "teachers," who instructed the church members in the Gospel. Some of each of these were quite probably among those elected as official missionaries of the Antioch Church. They were traveling men, going not always where they wanted to go but wherever God wanted them to go. We know only of the route upon which Paul and Barnabas, the most prominent of them, set out (which we call the First Missionary Journey of Paul) and came to the city of Lystra, in the Lycaonian section of Galatia. At the gates of Lystra they ran into a strange situation: they were given an enthusiastic welcome that they did not want.

Lystra, apparently, had no synagogue; its people were almost unanimously pagan, worshiping the gods of Rome, But when Paul healed a man born lame and sent him walking down the street, the Lystrians went wild with joy and praise; they thought that the gods had come down to them in physical form, and they shouted that Barnabas (did he wear a huge beard?) was actually the god Zeus, or Jupiter, and that Paul was Hermes, or Mercury, come to earth at long last to work miracles among their devotees. When the local priest of Zeus heard of it, he brought flowers to throw at their feet and offered to bring oxen to be sacrificed at the gates of the city. There is a legend behind that act.

The people of Lystra believed a story that had come down from their fathers. It was a story in which they were told that long ago Zeus and Hermes had come to earth in disguise. Unrecognized as gods, no door in Lystra was opened to them except the doors of two humble peasants, Philemon and his wife Baucis, who were kind to the incognito gods. For that, the whole city was wiped out and every inhabitant slain except Philemon and Baucis, who were richly rewarded. Lystra didn't want that to happen again and so, rather than make another mistake, they accepted the Christian missionaries—as Zeus and Hermes!

The people of Lystra doubtless thought they were paying Barnabas and Paul a great honor when they did this. But the two missionaries saw no honor in it, but only blasphemy. They tore their garments in a typically Eastern protest against anything that was untrue or shameful; then Paul stunned the overenthusiastic Lystrians who were trying to make gods of them. Wrong, cried Paul: We are *men* like you, not gods at all, men with the same passions, men who come as messengers to bring you the Good News of a God above all the little gods you worship.

There are some unique things about the sermon of Paul, which followed this declaration of their humanity. One is that he did not mention the name of Jesus Christ once in that sermon. He talked to these pagans about *God.* They had no God—only gods. So he felt that he must start with giving them a concept of a God of whom they knew nothing. That took courage. He could have responded otherwise to their respect for him; he could have accepted the plaudits of the crowd, and so made himself popular. Many of us would have done that and *do* it. Politicians seeking office love the applause of crowds; men who fight their way to the top in their chosen fields bask in the admiration of lesser men. Movie stars will do almost anything to get in the spotlight. Paul and Barnabas could have done that—but what would have become of them if they had done it? They preferred to follow the humble example of Jesus who spurned the shallow admiration of little minds.

So Paul preached on God to a people who had never heard of Him! (That was a great strength of Paul; he was an artist at adjusting his sermons to the needs of those who were in need; preaching to Jews, he spoke a language that Jews understood; preaching to Gentiles, he spoke in Gentile Greek.) In Lystra, he started not by referring them to the Jewish Scriptures, of which they knew nothing, but by telling them of a God whose love and power were manifested in the works of nature and providence. He pointed to the sea and asked them who made the seas; who but an all-powerful Creator could make an ocean? He talked of the earth on which they lived: who but God could create *that*, and all that lived upon the earth? And the heavens above, the stars in the skies, who? That got through to them; in understanding the creations of such a Creator, they were taking their first step toward Him.

Paul started with God in nature, but he did not stop there; he went on to talk about the nations on the earth, each of which "walked in their own ways" but who were never without His love and interest, never without "witnesses" not only of His power but of His love. His rain from heaven fell upon the just and the unjust everywhere; He gave them fruitful seasons which satisfied their hearts "with food and gladness." Even a Lystrian who had never heard of God would start *thinking* about such a God, once he had heard this. It was a sermon that struck deep into the pagan heart.

Sadly, many in Lystra did not "get it" at all; they could not be restrained from offering their sacrifices to "Jupiter and Hermes." The task of bringing God into the consciousness of different people is no easy task; life-styles are hard to change; we have a saying that "you can't teach an old dog new tricks," and that idea might well be applied to much of our modern world. It means that we still need missionaries with the humility and the courage of Barnabas and Paul who went on undiscouraged out through the gates of Lystra to sow their seed somewhere else. They were sure that *some* of the seed they sowed would take root—and so it did!

They were not pessimistic about Lystra, despite their rejection; there were some who went on from belief in God to fellowship with the Son, who was and is Saviour of all mankind.

SUGGESTIONS TO TEACHERS

When William Carey, the father of the modern missionary movement, first approached church authorities to offer his service to go to India to preach the Gospel, he was turned down. In fact, he was told that his notion of traveling anywhere to share the faith was silly. "Young man," he was advised, "When God sees fit to convert the heathen, He will do it without your help or ours." Fortunately, the poor Baptist cobbler-turned-preacher persevered and, surmounting incredible opposition, finally began his great work in India in 1793. Carey's career stimulated the formation of missionary boards and societies in nearly every denomination in the United States and Great Britain.

Today, however, there is a return of the cynicism and resistance which William Carey faced. Many church people openly question the place of missions to others. Your lesson, based on scriptural records from Acts 12:25–14:28, is meant to force your class to examine the way the early church concerned itself with sharing the faith.

1. *CALLED FOR ORDINATION.* Look at the passage dealing with the way the Church in Antioch set apart Barnabas and Saul for special

duties of spreading the Gospel. The "ordination" of these two missionaries came after fasting and prayer. Saul and Barnabas knew they were chosen, sent, and backed by their fellow believers who had to stay at home in Antioch. Consider with your class the many issues raised in this section, such as the meaning of ordination, the lack of distinction between "clergy" and "laymen," the involvement in mission of *every* Christian in the Antioch congregation. Obviously, this group of Christians had the conviction that it was impelled by the Spirit to move out into the wider world to spread the Word! How about your church?

2. *CARELESS OF OPPOSITION.* Take note of the way Barnabas and Paul faced constant opposition. In fact, they usually risked danger if not death by serving as missionaries. Yet, they remained undaunted. You should allot part of your lesson for a frank discussion with your class on the persecution and problems which every sincere Christian should expect. In fact, you may even go so far as to suggest that if one's Christian life is not encountering some persecution and problems, it is questionable that much missionary effort is being shown! Sustained by the Spirit and inspired by the Lord's command, ". . . I have sent you to be a light to the Gentiles, that you may bring salvation to the uttermost parts of the earth" (Acts 13:47 RSV), you and your fellow missionaries in your class will proceed with your assignment!

3. *CONDITIONED FOR OPPORTUNITIES.* The Antioch congregation, Barnabas, and Paul can serve as a model for every group of Christians today. Basically, every congregation is a missionary society; sensitized by the Holy Spirit, it must be alert to possibilities for service and proclamation. In the case of the Antioch church, it saw an opportunity (1) to send a relief offering to alleviate hunger among fellow Christians in distant Judea (Acts 11:27–29), and (2) to "set apart Barnabas and Saul for the work to which I called them" (Acts 13:2), that is, send the first missionaries. Churches, like any organization, can fall into the rut of dull routine. When worshiping, listening, and praying, however, even the smallest and most insignificant church will find that the Holy Spirit is offering astonishing new opportunities and prodding that church to meet those opportunities! What new opportunities for witnessing do members of your class see the Spirit providing your church?

TOPIC FOR ADULTS
MISSIONARIES ON THE MOVE

Tracy's Trauma. Cyclone Tracy roared through the city of Darwin, Australia, on Christmas Eve, 1974, leveling buildings, hurling cars through the air, beaching ships, and killing scores. The winds came with such force that they registered 185 miles-per-hour on the wind gauge at the Darwin International Airport before they broke the gauge. Nearly everyone of the city's 45,000 people had lost almost everything. On Christmas morning the once-lovely capital of Australia's Northern Territory was a grim shambles.

One of the survivors was the Rev. Douglas G. McKenzie, minister of the Uniting Church. Although he had watched his house disintegrate and his church collapse, Doug McKenzie remembered that he was still a Christian pastor. He saw that his first task was to minister to those who lived through the horrors of Cyclone Tracy, and he helped surviving civil authorities to organize emergency efforts to care for the injured, identify the dead, feed, and clothe, and house people who had nothing left. A missionary on the move, Doug McKenzie is remembered for working around the clock during those first days. (His efforts subsequently won him a silver medal from Queen Elizabeth.) More important, he moved as a Christian missionary among those who were traumatized by the disaster. McKenzie reports that it was the children and men over forty-five who seemed to be affected most. In the case of the over-forty-five men, he points out that this group had lost their sense of purpose because everything they'd worked for had been wiped out within a few hours. McKenzie's missionary efforts to this group of people were especially effective and appreciated, as he shared his sturdy sense of Christian faith. The open-air communion service he held in the wreckage of Darwin the Sunday following Cyclone Tracy was regarded as the start of a new Darwin and the beginning of new lives.

Christians are men and women on the move, especially in times when disasters discourage others. Christians are people who share their faith in words and actions, regardless of circumstances. Christians, in short, are missionaries on the move!

Off the Fence. "Come off that fence. There's no room for fences in the 1980's. Commitment is the opposite of sitting on the fence. It's not that going to church matters of itself—you can worship in a dustbin; but being a Christian has everything to do with making a real church—building and sustaining a community of God's people who can go out in His strength to try and mend a broken world. You can't do that from the fence. You can only build that church by looking beyond the much-maligned church pew to the Christ who gives it meaning. So let's get on with making a church together—a caring church, a generous church, a church which is so busy looking out from Christ to His world that there just isn't time for contemplating the group navel. There's a message for our times in the Gospel and it's time we got off the fence to proclaim it."—Sally Magnesson, quoted by H. C. Donaldson in *The Presbyterian Outlook*, 512 E. Main St., Richmond, Va. 23219. Published weekly. $14 per year. Issue of November 24, 1980.

The Little Boy Who Made the Big Offering. He was attending his church's annual revival services, and as the testimonies and verbal vows of commitment sounded forth from all across the church, his mother noticed that he was becoming increasingly restless. Finally, he broke free from his mother's restraining hand, dashed down the center aisle toward the startled preacher, and lunged for the pile of offering plates on the table. Before anyone could stop him he took the top plate, placed it on the floor before the communion table and *stepped into it!* Turning toward the shocked people in the congregation, he said, "Please! I've heard what you all have been saying you'd give to Jesus. I want to give, too, but I don't have much. I want to give Him all I've got—ME!"

The ultimate in Christlike *self-giving generosity* is to promise to give of yourself generously.

Questions for Pupils on the Next Lesson. 1. Are you inclined to accept others unconditionally or with strings attached? 2. Have you been part of a community in which one group has tried to impose its will on others? 3. Have you ever experienced unconditional love and acceptance? 4. Are you able to make concessions out of sensitivity to others' convictions? 5. What could your church do to build better community feeling in its membership and in the larger community?

TOPIC FOR YOUTH
MOVING FORWARD

Moving Forward on Giving. The Rev. Ron Guinn of the Highland Presbyterian Church in Tyler, Texas, lays it on the line about Christian giving. Although he's writing to his Presbyterian congregation, his words apply to every parish in every denomination.

"And now a word from M. Crunch . . . not, 'Kaptain Krunch,' although the famous statement attacking the nourishment value of breakfast cereals may be pertinent. ('You'll get as much nutrition if you throw the cereal away and eat the box with milk, fruit, and sugar.') The voice we now hear loudly is 'Money Crunch,' an old virus now more virulent. Our presbytery must cut 1980 expenditures 14 percent because we Presbyterians have not given enough to benevolences. Strangely, the crunch comes when the church shows signs of being its most robust in a decade. Reading 500 pages of General Assembly (PCUS) reports enthused me to discover the great variety and innovative programs of witness/service we have in the United States and across the world. I sense that the morale of the General Assembly staff in Atlanta is higher than it's been in years. They certainly are not 'fat cats' either, for one of the disgraces of our church is the ridiculously low salaries we pay those who serve Christ with us in Atlanta. (Just because they live in Georgia, they shouldn't have to work for peanuts.) Closer to home, another health sign is the high quality of men and women coming out of seminary to small rural pastorates of East Texas. What's the bottom line? Dig deeper? Maybe we need to concentrate a little harder. Our giving gets distracted by the junk mail and TV solicitations, kids trading light globes or candy for our door-side contribution to their band, club, or group. Presbyterians are not cookie-pushers, nor do we mail you Indian salt shakers. You have to *want* to give to Christ, nobody makes it easy. The words, '15 percent gratuity added' are found on your restaurant check. Adding 15 percent to your church pledge will be more than a 'tip.' It may tip the balance in funding the work we want to do for Christ as Presbyterians."—Ron Guinn, *Monday Morning,* September 22, 1980.

What's a Missionary or a Minister Really Like? "Have you ever taken a close look at how ministers are portrayed on TV? On the Jell-O commercial, there's a priest named Father Regan. Heavy desserts, he tells us, do just rotten things to his delicate stomach. So his hostess lovingly assures him that she's made Jell-O, a light little dessert guaranteed to treat him gently. On the series, "Little House on the Prairie," there's a pious, sweet-voiced gent who every week climbs into the pulpit and suggests wonderful, honey-tasting thoughts. After church the *real* men of Walnut Grove go out into the *real* world to do whatever the real world calls on them to do, regardless of what the little preacher says. The series

"M*A*S*H" has Father Mulcahey, who feels useful only when he gets to do real doctoring work. And a commercial for a Nashville bank introduces us to a gentle old reverend who attends a Sunday-school picnic for his idea of an exciting afternoon.

"We can blame the media—whoever they are—for giving us this kind of picture of ministers. On show after show, commercial after commercial, ministers are shown as a bunch of bumblers, sissies, and nerds. But what do we think of our real life ministers?

"I once heard this comment about a colleague: 'He's so big and tough-looking. I just can't believe he's a preacher.' People often say to me, 'Here, preacher. You hadn't ought to carry that. It's too heavy for you.' I hear that even from people much smaller than I am. Our ministers have such delicate backs, such delicate ears, and such delicate egos that the least little strain will break them.

"Now, I won't suggest that the church needs an angry army of macho ministers who jump up and slap around their sessions—John Wayne style—to keep them in line. But it says something about how the media think of the church, something of the place Christian faith takes when ministers are pictured as sweet, frail little tweeks who can't hold their Jell-O."—Robert Ensign, Pastor, White County Parish, Sparta, Tenn., *Monday Morning,* December 15, 1980.

Sentence Sermon to Remember: The minister lives behind a "stained glass curtain." The layman has opportunities for evangelism which a minister will never have.—James McCord.

Questions for Pupils on the Next Lesson. 1. Are you sometimes "turned off" by regulations in which you see no meaning? 2. What do you think is expected of a Christian in your daily life? 3. Have you ever known what it is to be accepted and loved without any strings attached? 4. Who are the people you find it hardest to welcome or accept to your circle of acquaintances? 5. What could your church do to show a greater sensitivity toward those of differing convictions?

LESSON VIII—APRIL 24

GOOD NEWS FOR ALL PEOPLE

Background Scripture: Genesis 17:9–14; Acts 15:1–13; Galatians 2:1–10
Devotional Reading: John 10:7–18

KING JAMES VERSION

ACTS 15 4 And when they were come to Jerusalem, they were received of the church, and *of* the apostles and elders, and they declared all things that God had done with them.

5 But there rose up certain of the sect of the Pharisees which believed, saying, That it was needful to circumcise them, and to command *them* to keep the law of Moses.

6 And the apostles and elders came together for to consider of this matter.

7 And when there had been much disputing, Peter rose up, and said unto them, Men *and* brethren, ye know how that a good while ago God made choice among us, that the Gentiles by my mouth should hear the word of the gospel, and believe.

8 And God, which knoweth the hearts, bare them witness, giving them the Holy Ghost, even as *he did* unto us;

9 And put no difference between us and them, purifying their hearts by faith.

10 Now therefore why tempt ye God, to put a yoke upon the neck of the disciples, which neither our fathers nor we were able to bear?

11 But we believe that through the grace of the Lord Jesus Christ we shall be saved, even as they.

12 Then all the multitude kept silence, and gave audience to Barnabas and Paul, declaring what miracles and wonders God had wrought among the Gentiles by them.

13 And after they had held their peace, James answered, saying, Men *and* brethren, hearken unto me:

14 Simeon hath declared how God at the first did visit the Gentiles, to take out of them a people for his name.

19 Wherefore my sentence is, that we trouble not them, which from among the Gentiles are turned to God:

20 But that we write unto them, that they abstain from pollutions of idols, and *from* fornication, and *from* things strangled, and *from* blood.

21 For Moses of old time hath in every city them that preach him, being read in the synagogues every sabbath day.

REVISED STANDARD VERSION

ACTS 15 4 When they came to Jerusalem, they were welcomed by the church and the apostles and the elders, and they declared all that God had done with them. 5 But some believers who belonged to the party of the Pharisees rose up, and said, "It is necessary to circumcise them, and to charge them to keep the law of Moses."

6 The apostles and the elders were gathered together to consider this matter. 7 And after there had been much debate, Peter rose and said to them, "Brethren, you know that in the early days God made choice among you, that by my mouth the Gentiles should hear the word of the gospel and believe. 8 And God who knows the heart bore witness to them, giving them the Holy Spirit just as he did to us; 9 and he made no distinction between us and them, but cleansed their hearts by faith. 10 Now therefore why do you make trial of God by putting a yoke upon the neck of the disciples which neither our fathers nor we have been able to bear? 11 But we believe that we shall be saved through the grace of the Lord Jesus, just as they will."

12 And all the assembly kept silence; and they listened to Barnabas and Paul as they listened to Barnabas and Paul as they related what signs and wonders God had done through them among the Gentiles. 13 After they finished speaking, James replied, "Brethren, listen to me. 14 Simeon has related how God first visited the Gentiles, to take out of them a people for his name.

19 "Therefore my judgment is that we should not trouble those of the Gentiles who turn to God, 20 but should write to them to abstain from the pollutions of idols and from unchastity and from what is strangled and from blood. 21 For from early generations Moses has had in every city those who preach him, for he is read every sabbath in the synagogues."

KEY VERSE: For in Christ Jesus neither circumcision nor uncircumcision is of any avail, but faith working through love. Galatians 5:6 (RSV).

HOME DAILY BIBLE READINGS

Apr. 18. M. God's Promise to Abraham. Genesis 17:1–8.
Apr. 19. T. The Blessings of Obedience. Genesis 28:1–14.
Apr. 20. W. A Great Light in Darkness. Matthew 4:12–17.
Apr. 21. T. A Light to the Nations. Isaiah 42:5–9.
Apr. 22. F. The Truth of the Gospel. Galatians 2:1–5.
Apr. 23. S. The Apostleship to the Gentiles. Galatians 2:6–10.
Apr. 24. S. One Fold and One Shepherd. John 10:14–16.

BACKGROUND

From Moses and the Exodus soon after 1300 B.C. to Jesus preaching in A.D. 26–30, the heart of Jewish faith was in the Mosaic Law. To be a Jew, one must obey every "jot and tittle" of that Law from beginning to end; that was the spiritual and moral pattern of the people through all those generations. If a non-Jew wished to become a Jew, he must first be circumcised into the Jewish faith and accept the Jewish life-style in every particular.

The first Christians were all Jews with few exceptions, and there were those among them who insisted on continuing these requirements. Jesus Himself had been circumcised; Jesus Himself regularly attended worship services in the synagogue, and the great Paul was raised as a Jew and a Pharisee. But now disturbing differences concerning the Law arose; some wanted to keep firm the old allegiance to the Law, some wanted to make certain changes in order to take Gentiles into the Church. That met determined opposition, especially when Peter and Paul welcomed so many Gentiles into the fellowship. This was a dangerous signal to those who wanted to "keep things as they were"; these conservatives were so alarmed by it all that they called for a council to meet in Jerusalem to settle the dispute for once and all.

NOTES ON THE PRINTED TEXT

This was not a council called by the entire Church. It was a meeting of Christian leaders from the two larger churches in Antioch and Jerusalem. Presiding over it was James, the leader of the Jerusalem Christians—the brother of Jesus, and a man so devout that some said he had knees as hard as a camel's because he prayed so often and so long. He was also a strict observer of the Law. He was called James the Just—and his sense of justice made him the perfect man to preside over what promised to be a lively if not a bitter conference.

Now there were three groups or three different schools of thought in this council: the conservatives, the liberals, and the middle-of-the roaders. Peter and Paul were liberals; several of the conservatives were Pharisees, or ex-Pharisees, who were "sticklers" for all-out obedience to the Law; James, as it turned out, was a middle-of-the-roader. They were all *devout and sincere men.*

Peter, Paul, and James the Just! These three dominated the council and, in turn, they made three short speeches which were finally to resolve the bothersome question that just wouldn't go away.

Peter spoke first. He would! Peter was never a man to sit still while something important was about to happen, and, along with Paul and Barnabas, he had been doing something that was *really* important: their work in Asia Minor has been so successful in bringing Gentiles into the Church that the church fathers began to think that the day might come when there would be nothing but Gentiles in their (Jewish) Church! Peter thought otherwise; he thought that the Church of Christ *must* be not a national but a universal Church—a Church of all nations. He got to his feet and dropped a bomb.

It was a bomb thrown straight at the conservative brethren. In paraphrase, it was an embarrassing criticism of the small-minded opponents of Gentile conversions. Did they not know, Peter asked them, that *God* had set him aside for work among the Gentiles, so that "they also could believe?" Did they not know, by this time, that God, who knows men's hearts and who is no respecter of persons, accepted all men, Jewish and Gentile, and that He poured out the Holy Spirit upon the non-Jews as well as upon the Jews? Had not God cleansed the hearts of Cornelius and the Ethiopian eunuch through faith, just as He had cleansed the hearts of the fathers in Jerusalem? What right had they to put upon the necks of the Gentiles a yoke (strict adherence to the Law) that their own fathers had been unable to bear? Who did they think they were playing, God?

Luke says that "all the assembly kept silence" at the end of this tirade. They knew in their hearts that Peter was right, knew that Jew and Gentile alike could be saved only through the grace of Jesus Christ. They were still sitting there, stunned, when Paul took the floor. Paul, and his missionary companion Barnabas. They had a different approach than Peter's; they did not scold or argue, they only told what had happened when they preached in Asia Minor, only told of what had actually *happened* in the hearts and lives of the people. It was no argument; it was pure fact. And just as the businessman of today says that a satisfied customer is his best advertisement, so Paul and Barnabas made it clear that saved souls was the best proof of the Spirit spreading out from behind the walls of Jerusalem toward the end of the earth. The Christians won abroad were walking evidence that could not be denied. God was at work among the Gentiles; they could not deny that, either.

But—what to do now? What must such a council do, having arrived at some agreement among themselves? There were quite likely *some* conservatives who were half convinced, and who would go on mumbling that they would *not* give in to the radical Peter, Paul, and Barnabas. There had to be unity among them if the Church were to go on, but how would they find that unity?

It was James who found the way out, the way to agreement and unity. James the Just, the quiet man with a fair and *open* mind, led them to compromise: they agreed that circumcision was not to be required of the Gentiles. The Jews were not exempt from circumcision, but the Gentiles were required to refrain from eating meat sacrificed to idols and the meat of strangled animals, and from all fornication. These were important regulations to the Jew, and the Jewish group on the council was satisfied with this requirement for the non-Jews.

We say it was compromise; some object to *any* compromise in religious matters. But let us not forget that compromise has been the oil of human history, the lubricant of progress. How many disasters have occurred among nations because one or the other nation refused to compromise and work out their problems in *unity!* Some historian has said that if it had not been for certain "hot heads" on both sides, we would never have had a Civil War in our country. The same truth holds for many a church that has been split apart and all but destroyed because of the stubbornness of a few members who just *had* to have their own way about a church problem, no matter *what!*

But we wonder whether James saw it as compromise. Isn't it possible that James settled here the old Gentile problem once and for all by bringing the council to act in respect and love for each other, and to put the will and purposes of God above the petty quarreling of men who unfortunately did not yet fully understand that it was not enough for men to love God, but that *they must love one another*?

SUGGESTIONS TO TEACHERS

The speakers were "names" in the church conference circuit. Their books and articles were widely read. They had reputations of "always bringing inspirational messages!" When interviewed by the local press just before appearing at a recent rally of church leaders, three of these well-known figures admitted, however, that they had no ties with a local congregation. These three gave the impression that they had outgrown the need to associate with the organized body of Christian believers. Besides, said one with a pious smile, "as soon as the faith becomes institutionalized, it becomes de-spiritualized."

You have undoubtedly run into persons holding such viewpoints. In fact, you may have some in your class or in your congregation. Some of the dropouts from the church in recent years cite these same reasons. Others claim that Gospel must never take any organizational form, forgetting, of course, that Acts shows that the community of the faithful was given an organizational form from the time of the Resurrection. Your lesson is intended to help everyone in your class to sort out the institutional aspects of being the Church, particularly when there are conflicting viewpoints and organizational problems.

1. *SETTLEMENT OF CONFLICT.* Let your class understand that there was conflict even in the early Church. In fact, remind your people that there are inevitable differences present within every group, including your class and your congregation, every married couple, and every family. Conflict is one of the "givens" of associating with other people. Study carefully how the earliest Christians handled the conflict between those insisting that Gentiles be included and those resisting Gentile inclusion. Make sure that your people do not idealize the early Christians. Use the early Church's conflict as a means of getting out in the open some of the issues of conflict within the church today. It may be less threatening to let these issues surface when brought up in the context of the conflict between the Antioch and the Jerusalem factions within the early Church.

1. *SALVATION THROUGH CHRIST.* Trace the theological reasoning of each group in Acts 15. The key issue was whether or not Gentiles should be welcomed without requiring circumcision. In turn, this raised

the question of whether salvation through Jesus Christ was enough, or whether something more—circumcision—was needed. The early Christians finally came to see that circumcision is not indispensible for salvation. What God has done through Jesus Christ saves us, not what humans do to themselves. Discuss in your lesson the sufficiency of God's act through Jesus Christ. Also bring out that frequently church people try to add on their own rules for salvation—usually a series of *Don'ts* required of believers—as if faith in Christ is not enough.

3. *SENSITIVITY AND CHASTITY.* Reserve ample time in your lesson to talk over the way the conflict over including Gentiles in the early Church was resolved through James's wise decision (Acts 15:13–21). Each group was to be especially sensitive to the feelings and backgrounds of the other. The Christians from strict Jewish tradition had sensitivities about associating with pagan cults and abhorred the practices of eating meat from animals strangled in heathen ceremonies, or drinking blood, or participating in idolatrous customs, or countenancing permissive sexual practices. James admonished Gentile believers to respect these sensitivities, and one-time Jewish believers in turn to welcome the uncircumcized as fellow Christians. What does this resolution suggest to those caught in church squabbles today?

4. *SHARING WITH GENTILES.* The uncircumcized non-Jews were welcomed into the fellowship of Christ's community. With a new surge of missionary enthusiasm, the Antioch Christians through Paul and others resolved to share the Gospel with Gentiles! Discuss who the "Gentiles" are whom the Church must address in our culture. What is your congregation doing to reach out to those who differ from others, or who feel estranged from the Church? Remind your class that the Good News is for *all* people!

TOPIC FOR ADULTS
GOOD NEWS FOR ALL PEOPLE

Skunkies and Turtles. "Let us recognize at the start that wherever two or three are gathered together there is going to be a certain amount of anxiety and tension.

"Every book in the Bible speaks of it one way or another. And in Paul's letters to the young churches, he was always concerned about the conflicts these wonderful, struggling, growing, sinful, beautiful, rascal friends were having.

"Dr. John Savage suggests that we all tend to handle our anxieties in one of two ways. He says we are either turtles or skunkies.

"The turtles are those who are most prone to blame themselves. They may say or feel: 'I guess it is my fault . . . no one seems to like me . . . I can't keep up with the changes . . . I just don't have faith.' They say: 'I'm not okay; you're okay.'

"The turtles feel hopeless. The inner self is depleted; I am not able, I can't hack it. I guess it's just me. I give up.

"The skunkies, on the other hand, project the blame outwardly. They say in effect: 'They, them, those did it. If only we had a different minister; if only the true Christians would do something.' They feel—'I'm okay, it's them that are not okay.'

"The turtles feel that they are not good enough for God. The skunkies believe that God has forsaken them. The one feels hopeless; the other, helpless.

"Some of us may be half turtle and half skunkie. In general, we tend to act in one fashion or another when we are filled with anxiety about something that makes us uncomfortable. We lash out at others or blame ourselves. We get angry or feel guilty or both.

"Hey Christian turtles and Christian skunkies: there is a lot wrong in this world. Sometimes it is my fault; sometimes it is your fault. Sometimes the devil has got us all in a twitter . . . and sometimes we don't know who to blame. . . .

"My hurt feelings or yours . . . or whatever else . . . let nothing stand between us and our first and highest loyalty to the God of Jesus Christ . . . and let nothing separate us from one another.

"For our anxiety and pain comes not only from our distance from God but from one another. We cannot live at peace without each other, we cannot live without our brother, sister.

"If we more simply trust God, we will be more gentle with one another. And the fellowship of the Church will become more and more blessed."—John K. Stoner, in a sermon, April 16, 1978.

Bells and Pomegranates. In Hebrew worship, the priest's robe was decorated with golden bells and with pomegranates of blue, purple, and scarlet. The sweet sound of the bells was the outward profession of religion; the pomegranates, the fruit of the tree, were the deeds that should always accompany the spoken words.

It was always intended that these two should go together. Religion is faith and deeds, and in the Christian life what we profess and what we practice are the same in spirit and purpose.

Especially in each congregation, bells and pomegranates must both be shown. The bells of orthodoxy must be matched with the pomegranates of mercy. Love must not only be spoken but also acted—especially within the Church!

Every Christian, when he or she comes to worship, should think of putting on his or her priestly robe with a hem of both bells and pomegranates in order that the Good News for *all* people be both said and lived.

Practical Atheist. A Philadelphia woman was arrested recently who said her "occupation" was shoplifting, and her "avocation" was religion. She told the judge that she considered herself an extremely moral person. She saw no incongruity between her "occupation" of stealing from stores and her "avocation" of religion (her terms). The woman said that her Bible reading gave her great comfort. Her favorite passage was from Psalms 23, which assured her, "The Lord is my Shepherd, I shall not want."

Apparently the woman never considered that the Christian faith means sharing the Good News with all others and building community. The gap between her profession and her practice made her a practical atheist.

You may not be a shoplifter, but when you destroy relationship and community you are denying God's existence.

Questions for Pupils on the Next Lesson. 1. Do you sincerely believe that women may serve effectively as leaders in the church and in the secular world? 2. Have you a regular time and place to worship and study God's Word? 3. How is a person's true identity found? 4. Does your church respond positively to visions of the needs of others?

TOPIC FOR YOUTH
RESOLVING DIFFERENCES

Hardest Instrument. A well-known conductor of one of the world's most famous symphony orchestras was once asked what he thought was the most difficult instrument to play. After some reflection, the conductor answered, "The second fiddle. I can get plenty of first violinists, but to find someone who can play second fiddle with enthusiasm—that's a problem. And if we have no second fiddle, we have no harmony."

In the Church, we can usually find plenty of people to play first fiddle. But how few of us are willing to take on the tasks which offer little recognition? And how few of us can act supportively of others who may get the credit?

Differences within the church often arise over accepting the second-fiddle positions. We resent being made to step to the side of the stage for another and assume a supportive role. Secretly, we think that we deserve applause as a first fiddle-type.

Our differences within the church will be resolved only when we all want Christ only to be given the honor and glory, and be willing to accept routine "second-fiddle" billing for ourselves.

Failure to Resolve Differences Means Catastrophe. Ultimately, our refusal to resolve our differences means resorting to an attempt to destroy the other. In other words, *War.* Whether between fighting factions within a church or nations, the result is catastrophe. Dorothy Sayers says it well: "War is a judgment that overtakes societies when they have been living upon ideas that conflict too violently with the laws governing the universe. Never think that wars are irrational catastrophies: they happen when wrong ways of thinking and living bring about intolerable situations."—Dorothy L. Sayers, in *QUOTE,* May 4, 1975.

New Path. Corrie ten Boom lived in Haarlem, Holland, when the Nazis invaded Holland in World War II. She and her family joined the underground movement to help Jews escape from the country. Later, when this was impossible, they hid Jews in their own homes. Corrie and her family were betrayed by a neighbor in February, 1944, arrested, and shipped off to concentration camps. The next ten months were a nightmare in which Corrie ten Boom's father and sister were tortured and allowed to die, and Corrie was beaten and kept in solitary confinement for four months. Transported to the infamous Ravensburg extermination camp, Corrie lived under daily threat of death and was freed just one week before all women in the camp her age were scheduled to be put to death.

She kept up her Christian witness throughout her months in the prison camps, holding secret Bible meetings and ministering to fellow prisoners. It was after she was released, however, that her faith was most severely tested. One of her first acts was to write to the man who had betrayed the ten Booms, telling him of their imprisonment and the resulting deaths of her father and sister. Corrie ten Boom added, however, "I have forgiven you everything. God will also forgive everything, if you ask Him. I hope the path which you will now take may work for your eternal salvation."

Sentence Sermon to Remember: A small boy, repeating the Lord's Prayer one evening, prayed, "And forgive us our debts as we forgive those who are dead against us."—Francis Roe.

Questions for Pupils on the Next Lesson. 1. Can you be a witness for Christ to your own family members? 2. How may you and other younger members of your Church be involved in ministering and evangelizing? 3. Who, specifically, are the underprivileged in your area? 4. Do you have a regular time for prayer and Bible reading?

LESSON IX—MAY 1

BREAKING THROUGH IN MACEDONIA

Background Scripture: Acts 15:36–17:34
Devotional Reading: John 15:1–8

KING JAMES VERSION

ACTS 16 9 And a vision appeared to Paul in the night; There stood a man of Macedonia, and prayed him, saying, Come over into Macedonia, and help us.

10 And after he had seen the vision, immediately we endeavored to go into Macedonia, assuredly gathering that the Lord had called us for to preach the gospel unto them.

11 Therefore loosing from Troas, we came with a straight course to Samothracia, and the next *day* to Neapolis;

12 And from thence to Philippi, which is the chief city of that part of Macedonia, *and* a colony: and we were in that city abiding certain days.

13 And on the sabbath we went out of the city by a river side, where prayer was wont to be made; and we sat down, and spake unto the women which resorted *thither.*

14 And a certain woman named Lydia, a seller of purple, of the city of Thyatira, which worshipped God, heard *us:* whose heart the Lord opened, that she attended unto the things which were spoken of Paul.

15 And when she was baptized, and her household, she besought *us,* saying, If ye have judged me to be faithful to the Lord, come into my house, and abide *there.* And she constrained us.

16 And it came to pass, as we went to prayer, a certain damsel possessed with a spirit of divination met us, which brought her masters much gain by soothsaying:

17 The same followed Paul and us, and cried, saying, These men are the servants of the most high God, which shew unto us the way of salvation.

18 And this did she many days. But Paul, being grieved, turned and said to the spirit, I command thee in the name of Jesus Christ to come out of her. And he came out the same hour.

REVISED STANDARD VERSION

ACTS 16 9 And a vision appeared to Paul in the night: a man of Macedonia was standing beseeching him and saying, "Come over to Macedonia and help us." 10 And when he had seen the vision, immediately we sought to go on into Macedonia, concluding that God had called us to preach the gospel to them.

11 Setting sail therefore from Troas, we made a direct voyage to Samothrace, and the following day to Neapolis, 12 and from there to Philippi, which is the leading city of the district of Macedonia, and a Roman colony. We remained in this city some days; 13 and on the sabbath day we went outside the gate to the riverside, where we supposed there was a place of prayer; and we sat down and spoke to the women who had come together. 14 One who heard us was a woman named Lydia, from the city of Thyatira, a seller of purple goods, who was a worshiper of God. The Lord opened her heart to give heed to what was said by Paul. 15 And when she was baptized, with her household, she besought us, saying, "If you have judged me to be faithful to the Lord, come to my house and stay." And she prevailed upon us.

16 As we were going to the place of prayer, we were met by a slave girl who had a spirit of divination and brought her owners much gain by soothsaying. 17 She followed Paul and us, crying, "These men are servants of the Most High God, who proclaim to you the way of salvation." 18 And this she did for many days. But Paul was annoyed, and turned and said to the spirit, "I charge you in the name of Jesus Christ to come out of her." And it came out that very hour.

KEY VERSE: There is neither Jew nor Greek, there is neither slave nor free, there is neither male nor female; for you are all one in Christ Jesus. Galatians 3:28 (RSV).

HOME DAILY BIBLE READINGS

Apr. 25. M. The Compassionate Christ. Luke 13:10–13.
Apr. 26. T. Paul Chose Silas. Acts 15:36–41.
Apr. 27. W. A Disobedient Prophet. Jonah 1:1–6.
Apr. 28. T. The Prophet Had a Second Chance. Jonah 3:1–5.
Apr. 29. F. The Unlimited Mercy of God. Jonah 4:1–11.
Apr. 30. S. Go Preach the Gospel. Mark 16:9–16.
May 1. S. The Great Commission. Matthew 28:16–20.

BACKGROUND

Having won the approval of the Jerusalem council to establish churches among the Gentiles, Paul went out on his Second Missionary Journey. With him were Silas and Timothy. They traveled a zigzag course from Antioch to Troas, a chief city and port in the Roman province of Asia. (Paul's plan was to establish churches in the larger cities and have the Word spread from the cities out into the countryside.) "As the crow flies" in a straight line, Troas is located some 600 miles from Antioch, but the missionaries, following this zigzag course in order to establish churches in important cities, traveled much further than that.

Troas is important in Paul's story and in the story of the founding of the early Church: it is "the jumping-off place" between Asia and Europe. Paul had planned to work a while in Mysia, an ancient land in northwest Asia Minor, but the Spirit (God) sent him elsewhere. (Mysia, today, lies within Anatolian Turkey.) He got his travel orders by way of a vision in which an unknown and unnamed stranger from Macedonia came to him, pleading for help.

NOTES ON THE PRINTED TEXT

This man from Macedonia is still a mystery man; we still do not know exactly who he was, but we know that, when he led Paul into Macedonia, he changed the course of early church history as a giant boulder can change the course of a flowing river. Some say that Paul was dreaming here of Alexander the Great. The full name of Troas was Alexandrian Troas, named for the conqueror who dreamed of "marrying the east to the west." That is interesting, but somewhat doubtful. Some others say the man from Macedonia was Luke himself, and that is more probable. Luke may have been a Macedonian. And he was a physician; it is possible that he had been asked to travel with Paul, who was in poor health, and that it was the physician who knew that living in Mysia would not be good for him. It is possible, but it cannot be proved. But we do know that Luke was in Troas with Paul.

Notice now that Luke, in Acts 16, makes use of a new pronoun in telling the story of what happened on this journey: for the first time, he uses the pronoun *we*, instead of *they*. After Paul had had his vision, Luke says "*we* endeavored to go into Macedonia" (verse 10). This is known as one of the "we" passages of Acts. The "we" disappears suddenly after verse

17, but we see it again in chapters, 20, 21 and 27:1–28:16. It is an important *we,* Luke was a companion of Paul in Troas and afterwards, and, in characteristic humility, Luke kept his name out of the story he was telling.

Luke accompanied Paul when they moved out from Troas to Philippi, and it was good that he did; Paul had need of a physician in Philippi where he nearly lost his life.

There was a small colony of Jews in Philippi, but no synagogue in which Paul might have started his preaching. Whenever that happened, the Jews had a way of setting up "places of prayer," usually at some riverside. On the first Sabbath in Philippi, Paul and his companions found such a meeting and "sat down, and spake unto the women which resorted thither" (verse 13). The *women?* Yes—this was a group of women praying; there is no evidence that there was any man in the group. And one of the women was a lady named Lydia, a rich woman, a merchant selling the famous purple cloth of the city of Thyatira, a widow, and a woman who, though a Gentile, was familiar with the Jewish Scriptures and seeking the light which was in Christ. She was won to Christ by Paul who also baptized her and then went with his fellow missionaries to live a while in the house of Lydia. Lydia's house apparently became headquarters of the Church in Philippi.

So the first Christian convert in Europe was a woman! It is worth mentioning that she was a woman rich in this world's goods and unhappy with those goods—a seeker after God. She was also a woman who lived in the very top of the social scale, which reminds us that the message of the Christ leaped all social boundaries and all of the petty distinctions of nationality and race.

On another day, Paul came face to face with another woman living at the bottom of the social scale—a slave girl who would be called a mentally-disturbed woman by any modern physician or psychiatrist. Where Lydia had been a blessing to Paul, this girl was a hindrance. She dogged Paul's footsteps, jabbering in maniacal language. We would call her mentally disturbed; the people of her day called her one in whose body an evil spirit had taken control. Some who were really possessed of the devil took advantage of her disturbances and set her up as one who could go into a trance and mumble predictions of the future. They made good money out of that. She was a pitiful sight, following Paul, seeking deliverance—a nuisance, some would call her, who annoyed the apostle and "grieved" him. There came the day when Paul turned to face her and to cry out against the evil spirit that possessed her: "I charge you in the name of Jesus Christ to come out of her."

It was the confrontation of the evil spirit with the Holy Spirit. The Holy Spirit won the battle. Paul snatched her from the hands of her wicked masters and put her in the hands of the Christ: "And it came out that very hour." Healed, she became the second European convert.

Now suppose we look carefully at these two women. The first thing that is impressive about them is that they *were* women. Up to the time of the coming of Christ, women in both Rome and Jerusalem were expected to be seen but not heard; in most societies, they were little more than chattels—but, with the touch of Christ, they were slowly but surely lifted to a higher place. Woman played a fine part in the life and work of Jesus: think of Mary the Mother, Mary the Magdalene, Mary and Martha, Elizabeth, Anna, the Woman of Samaria, and now the dynamic Lydia and the pitiful slave girl who met Him long after His Resurrection.

We are also impressed by the fact that Lydia and the girl came from opposite ends of the social scale. In spite of this, they were converts who remind the reader of the characters of the Ethiopian eunuch, Saul of Tarsus, Cornelius the centurion—*good* people, *seeking* people, who found what they sought in Him. They were a power in the early Church, and they are a power *now.* The modern church is just beginning to ordain women as ministers in recognition of their priceless contributions to the work of the Church. Women make up the bulk of our church membership; women seem to be more faithful in church attendance, say some, more *religious* than average men. Based on figures and facts disclosed in a recent poll taken by George Gallup, Jr., it appears that "It is not illogical that if women in any given church were to lose interest or become disheartened and drop out, that particular church would not only lose its vitality but be in real danger of losing its future."—From *The Search for America's Faith,* George Gallup, Jr. and David Poling, by permission of Abingdon Press, publishers.

We can thank God and Paul for Lydia and the seeking slave girl. Without them . . . what?

SUGGESTIONS TO TEACHERS

During the past eight weeks, your lessons from Acts have shown the incredible expansion of the early Christian Church, beginning at Jerusalem and breaking through a series of old barriers. The Coming of the Spirit energized the first believers to carry the Gospel beyond the narrow confines of Judea to Samaria, then on to the Gentile world. Your final series of lessons concentrates on the way the Good News broke into the rest of the world.

Your lesson today, as always, should not merely talk about what went on in the past. You as teacher are to introduce your class members to what the Spirit has in mind for the present time and the days to come. In a sense, the Church is always writing the twenty-ninth chapter of Acts! You and fellow Christians are part of the continuing breakthrough of the Gospel into new areas.

1. *SPIRIT'S GUIDANCE.* Have your class trace the way Paul, Silas, and Timothy relied on the guidance of the Spirit in their endeavors. Sometimes, they felt frustrated. For example, they were "forbidden by the Holy Spirit to speak the word in Asia" (Acts 16:6) and also found themselves prevented from entering Bithynia. Sometimes, the Holy Spirit seems to slam doors in the faces of His people! Encourage members of your class to recount such occasions in their lives. Call their attention, however, to the way Paul received a vision to "come over to Macedonia" (16:9). The Lord always opens new possibilities. For Paul and his company, it meant carrying the Gospel to Europe.

2. *START OF A CHURCH.* Devote enough time on the story of Lydia and the women in Philippi to help your class to see an example of the way the Gospel took root in a strange city (16:11–15). Point out that women were often leaders in the Church's ministry. Remind your class also that Paul always started where people were. Even a prayer meeting beside the river was the seed bed for a new Christian community. What are possible avenues to expand the ministry of your church in your area?

3. *SLAVE GIRL'S LIBERATION.* Let your class draw some conclusions from Paul's healing the pathetic slave girl of her emotional illness (16:16-18). How does the Gospel continue to bring new mental health and emotional equilibrium? Make sure that your class also observes the reaction of the girl's owners when she was healed. Whenever faith interferes with business, a reaction follows. Perhaps members of the class can present some examples of how it has cost them or others to accept Christ's presence. Christianity is not always good for business!

4. *SONGS AT MIDNIGHT.* Paul and Silas were attacked by the irate owners of the slave girl, beaten up, falsely accused of disturbing the peace, and chained up in the maximum security section of the Philippian jail. Aching and miserable in the horrors of a dungeon, you would expect them to be cursing or sobbing. Instead, at midnight, they "were praying and singing hymns to God, and the prisoners were listening to them" (16:25). Astonishingly, Paul and Silas continued to trust and to witness even in chains! In the midnights of the various kinds of "prisons," such as pain, loneliness, fear, etc., how do your class members conduct themselves? Can they sing and pray under such circumstances?

5. *SALVATION OF A JAILER.* Stir up a discussion on the jailer's question, "What must I do to be saved?" (16:30). Note Paul's answer. Have your class also comment on the accusation leveled at Paul and Silas the next day: "These men who have turned the world upside down have come here also" (17:6). Could this charge be brought against your church? If not, why not? How does your community perceive your church?

TOPIC FOR ADULTS
BREAKTHROUGH IN MACEDONIA

Answer to Macedonian Call from Russia. "The work of Keston College began after a young Church of England curate received a Macedonian call from the pen and lips of two elderly Russian women. The story is a remarkable one and demonstrates wonderfully the sovereign power of God.

"Michael Bourdeaux began to learn Russian during his military service in 1951. Later, he studied theology at Oxford University and then spent a year in Moscow on the first exchange program ever arranged by the British Government. He grew to love the Russian people and longed to serve them.

"In 1963, when working as a curate in North London, he received, via friends in Paris, a letter written in semiliterate Russian which described the enormity of Khrushchev's new persecution of the Church with detailed account of imprisonments and persecution. The letter was not addressed to him, nor did he know the signatures of the two writers, but he determined to do what he could to help.

"The following year the opportunity arose for Michael Bourdeaux to visit Moscow. He discovered that the church where he had once worshiped had been blown up by the authorities. While he stared at the ruins, he noticed two old ladies also peering through the fence. When he left the site, he followed them and, being careful not to be seen by the police, he spoke to them in Russian explaining briefly why he had come to Moscow. They beckoned him to follow them; eventually they arrived at a house in the suburbs. In an upstairs room, while they spoke more freely together, Michael Bourdeaux explained why he had come to Russia and about the letter he had received. 'Who wrote it?', they asked: hesitatingly, he named the two signatories. Silence, and then a sudden flood of uncontrolled sobbing. 'We wrote that letter . . . we've come to Moscow today for the second time (a distance of 700 miles) to make contact with someone. God sent you to meet us.' They pleaded: '. . . Tell our story. Give the facts exactly as they are. The world must know. You can be our voice where we can't make it heard—others will come forward to help us.'

"During its life, Keston College (of which Michael Bourdeaux is director) has earned an international reputation as an expert and responsible channel of information about religious life in Communist lands. It aims to discover objective truth about religious life in Eastern Europe and other Communist-ruled countries and to make it widely available to Churches, international organizations, and other interested bodies. Its slogan is 'The Right to Believe': it works on behalf of those whose right to express their faith is stifled in their own countries.

"The results of research often lead to the exposure of instances of suppression of religious freedom; but the college's publication also reflects triumphant belief, renewed faith, and the growth of Christian Churches and other religious communities.

"The expulsion of five prisoners of conscience from the Soviet Union at the end of April 1979 in exchange for the release by the United States of two Russian spies, Rudolf Chernyayev and Valdik Enger, brought the plight of many hundreds of people in Russia into the news of the Western world. The best known of the five was probably Alexander Ginzburg, a member of the Russian Orthodox Church who had been active in the Helsinki Monitoring Group compiling reports on Soviet violations of human rights.

"Another was Georgi Vins, who was the first person imprisoned specifically for Christian activity to be expelled from the Soviet Union. The facts about his, and his family's, imprisonment and harassment over many years have, in large part, been made known in the West through the work of Keston College."—Roy Halliwell, *Faith at Work*, April 1980.

The Lord and Revolution. "When so many changes take place, particularly if the world is turned upside down, and if there is a rapid succession of events, we are perplexed and entertain doubts whether all things happen at random and by chance, or are regulated by the providence of God. The Lord, therefore, shows that it is He who effects this revolution, and renews the state of the world, that we may learn that nothing here is of long duration, and may have our whole heart and our whole aim directed to the reign of Christ, which alone is everlasting."—John Calvin, *Commentary on Isaiah* Vol. 2.

Membership Claims. A housewife in a small town in northeastern Pennsylvania was deep-fat frying on her kitchen stove when suddenly the pan of boiling grease caught fire. The woman seized the burning pan and started to rush toward the door. Suddenly she slipped on a spot of hot cooking oil that had spilled. She fell, hurling flaming grease over her face, arms, hands, and upper body. Although she survived, she was terribly disfigured and painfully incapacitated. A long series of expensive operations was required. Two of her neighbors decided to enlist the help of others in the town to raise a fund to help pay the medical expenses. They began to telephone the volunteer fire company people, the president of the Lion's Club, and other local leaders and quickly secured promises of support. However, when they called the pastor of the local church, he told them, "No, she's not a member of this church." It is easy to imagine what most townspeople thought of the church after this rebuff.

The breakthrough of the Gospel into new Macedonias comes whenever an opportunity to serve presents itself. Fortunately, Paul did not tell the man from Macedonia, "No, you are not a member of the Church." Paul went. So also with Christians in every age in every locality!

Are you listening for the calls from Macedonia around you?

Questions for Pupils on the Next Lesson. 1. Which small groups in the church are most meaningful to you? Why? 2. How do you adjust to life's changing situations? 3. Do you think that changing life-styles may require re-examination of certain civil laws? 4. Do you sometimes find it difficult to accept the consequences of living by your convictions? 5. How would you describe the Church at Corinth in contrast to your church?

TOPIC FOR YOUTH
MINISTRY BREAKTHROUGH

Heirs to Riches. "A reward for the sum of $250,000 is offered for actually finding and identifying Helen V. Brach. The offer of reward expires March 25, 1981. Respond to P.O. Box 1663, Chicago, Illinois, 60680."

The advertisement, placed in newspapers in Chicago, Hopedale, Ohio, Rochester, Minnesota, and Fort Lauderdale, Florida, was one more attempt to find an heiress to an enormous fortune.

Helen Vorhees Brach, the daughter of an Ohio coal miner, in 1951 had married Frank V. Brach, then head of the nation's richest candy concern. Mr. Brach died in 1970, leaving her a fortune that is now worth $21 million, plus interest.

At 9 A.M. on February 17, 1977, Mrs. Brach walked out of the Mayo Clinic in Rochester and disappeared soon after.

You are also an heir to the riches of a life with God. Perhaps you have never been aware of your great inheritance. Through Jesus Christ, God has searched for you. Have you allowed the meaning of His ministry to break through in your life? Have you claimed your inheritance? If you have, will you go to other heirs, telling them what is meant to be for them? The great ministry breakthrough began with Jesus Christ, and is meant to continue through you!

Phony Breakthroughs. "People shut their eyes and stop their ears to Jesus every day, choosing instead the peepings and mutterings of some self-styled psychic. Not one word of God's prophecies has ever failed! What is the record of these modern day astrologers, wizards, crystal-ball gazers, and what have you? Let's take a brief look at their record. These prophecies were all given in 1975 and according to them, they were all to come to pass by the end of 1976. It is now 1980. How did they do? Let's take a look.

"1. An Air Force jet will collide with a U.F.O. over the Arizona desert.

"2. Jacqueline Onassis will host her own show on television.

"3. The earth will be contacted by a civilization from outer space.

"4. Fidel Castro will be ousted from Cuba.

"5. A gigantic earthquake will rip the mountains of California open revealing huge gold deposits.

"6. A nuclear submarine will disappear under the Arctic ice cap.

"7. Charles Manson will escape from prison.

"8. Billy Graham will suffer a massive heart attack and will retire from the ministry.

"Not one of these so called 'prophecies' from leading psychics came to pass! Know this: astrological and psychic predictions are pagan in origin and motivated by demonic forces with one thought and purpose in mind: to lead you away from God.

"Does this mean that God wants man to remain in darkness concerning his fate and the fate of the world? Of course not. God has outlined man's history from beginning to end. In speaking of Himself, Jesus said, 'I am Alpha and Omega, the beginning and the end.' The distress of nations with great perplexities that we see today comes as no surprise to God. Two thousand years ago, Jesus prophesied that this is exactly what would happen. Unlike modern day 'prophets' who only point to the Answer . . . Solutions . . . A Way of Escape. 'I am the Way' Jesus says. Not wizards . . . not ouijas . . . not crystal-ball gazers or monthly prognosticators or what have you, but rather Jesus Christ. Hearken to the voice of God today who says to *you,* 'This is my beloved Son. Hear ye Him.' "—Bill Payne, *Highway Evangelist.*

Willing? You say, "But Christ's ministry has not broken through to me." You may feel that there has never been a spiritual breakthrough into your life.

A wise Christian who had also experienced the time when no breakthrough of the Lord's presence and forgiveness had come into his life said later, "I had to become willing to be willing for God to speak to me."

Are you willing to become willing for Him to break through into *your* world?

Sentence Sermon to Remember: The world is my parish.—John Wesley.

Questions for Pupils on the Next Lesson. 1. Where are the greatest areas of conflict in your life? 2. Who are some people you respect for taking a stand for truth and right? 3. Are you willing to take a chance for the sake of being different? 4. What small groups in your church have been meaningful to you? 5. How would you describe the church in the city of Corinth?

LESSON X—MAY 8

CONFLICT IN CORINTH

Background Scripture: Acts 18; 1 Corinthians 1
Devotional Reading: 1 John 3:19–24

KING JAMES VERSION

ACTS 18 1 After these things Paul departed from Athens, and came to Corinth;

4 And he reasoned in the synagogue every sabbath, and persuaded the Jews and the Greeks.

5 And when Silas and Timotheus were come from Macedonia, Paul was pressed in the spirit, and testified to the Jews *that* Jesus *was* Christ.

6 And when they opposed themselves, and blasphemed, he shook *his* raiment, and said unto them, Your blood *be* upon your own heads; I *am* clean: from henceforth I will go unto the Gentiles.

7 And he departed thence, and entered into a certain *man's* house, named Justus, *one* that worshipped God, whose house joined hard to the synagogue.

8 And Crispus, the chief ruler of the synagogue, believed on the Lord with all his house; and many of the Corinthians hearing believed, and were baptized.

9 Then spake the Lord to Paul in the night by a vision, Be not afraid, but speak, and hold not thy peace:

10 For I am with thee, and no man shall set on thee to hurt thee: for I have much people in this city.

11 And he continued *there* a year and six months, teaching the word of God among them.

12 And when Gallio was the deputy of Achaia, the Jews made insurrection with one accord against Paul, and brought him to the judgment seat,

13 Saying, This *fellow* persuadeth men to worship God contrary to the law.

14 And when Paul was now about to open *his* mouth, Gallio said unto the Jews, If it were a matter of wrong or wicked lewdness, O *ye* Jews, reason would that I should bear with you:

15 But if it be a question of words and names, and *of* your law, look ye *to it;* for I will be no judge of such *matters.*

16 And he drave them from the judgment seat.

REVISED STANDARD VERSION

ACTS 18 1 After this he left Athens and went to Corinth.

4 And he argued in the synagogue every sabbath, and persuaded Jews and Greeks.

5 When Silas and Timothy arrived from Macedonia, Paul was occupied with preaching, testifying to the Jews that the Christ was Jesus. 6 And when they opposed and reviled him, he shook out his garments and said to them, "Your blood be upon your heads! I am innocent. From now on I will go to the Gentiles." 7 And he left there and went to the house of a man named Titius Justus, a worshiper of God; his house was next door to the synagogue. 8 Crispus, the ruler of the synagogue, believed in the Lord, together with all his household; and many of the Corinthians hearing Paul believed and were baptized. 9 And the Lord said to Paul one night in a vision, "Do not be afraid, but speak and do not be silent; 10 for I am with you, and no man shall attack you to harm you; for I have many people in this city." 11 And he stayed a year and six months, teaching the word of God among them.

12 But when Gallio was proconsul of Achaia, the Jews made a united attack upon Paul and brought him before the tribunal, 13 saying, "This man is persuading men to worship God contrary to the law." 14 But when Paul was about to open his mouth, Gallio said to the Jews, "If it were a matter of wrongdoing or vicious crime, I should have reason to bear with you, O Jews; 15 but since it is a matter of questions about words and names and your own law, see to it yourselves, I refuse to be a judge of these things." 16 And he drove them from the tribunal. 17 And they all seized Sosthenes, the rules of the synagogue, and beat him in front of the tribunal. But Gallio paid no attention to this.

17 Then all the Greeks took Sosthenes, the chief ruler of the synagogue, and beat *him* before the judgment seat. And Gallio cared for none of those things.

KEY VERSE: "Do not be afraid, but speak and do not be silent; for I am with you, and no man shall attack you to harm you; for I have many people in this city." Acts 18:9,10 (RSV).

HOME DAILY BIBLE READINGS

May 2. M. How Paul Preached the Gospel at Corinth. 1 Corinthians 2:1–5.
May 3. T. Paul at Berea. Acts 17:11–15.
May 4. W. Paul at Athens. Acts 17:16–21.
May 5. T. Fellow Workers With God. 1 Corinthians 3:1–15.
May 6. F. When They Heard the Gospel. Acts 17:32–34.
May 7. S. Paul Works at His Trade. Acts 18:1–4.
May 8. S. Paul Goes to the Gentiles. Acts 18:5–11.

BACKGROUND

From Philippi, Paul moved down the Aegean coast to Athens; it was a rough journey. Hostility and persecution dogged his heels (read Acts 17). He looked forward to a good time in Athens; this was the cultural center of the world, replete with temples and statues and other relics of a golden past, and populated with a people who "spent their time in nothing else, but either to tell, or to hear some new thing" (17:21). Paul brought them something new: Jesus, and His Resurrection. They listened in amused silence as he talked of the Christ, but they roared with laughter at his mention of any resurrection. Sophisticated Athens just couldn't take *that,* and Paul was literally laughed out of town.

Nothing could have hurt him more; even he could have no answer to ignorant ridicule. He left Athens disconsolate and made his way to Corinth, the capital city of Achaia. Corinth was a thriving commercial center, the largest city in the province—and the most wicked city in the Roman Empire.

NOTES ON THE PRINTED TEXT

There was a synagogue in Corinth; Paul began his preaching there to what was apparently a sizable congregation. After what had happened to him in Athens, he might have been careful what he said to the Jews in this synagogue: he might have compromised a little and worked gradually up to his Christian message. But Paul was a man who could never do that. He began immediately with a statement that struck fire in the congregation: he *began* with an insistence that the Messiah of the Jews was Jesus Christ—and immediately there was a loud howl. To talk of Messiahship might have brought laughter in Athens and watchful tolerance from Rome, but in Corinth it brought the fury of deep hatred. Paul found himself put out in the street, ostracized from the synagogue. He moved his "pulpit" into the home of one Titius Justus, who lived right next door to the synagogue, and that was a further insult to the Jews, for Titius had once been *their* convert and a Roman God-fearer. Adding insult to injury, Paul converted Crispus, the leader of the synagogue, who moved with his whole family into the house of Titius Justus! And Paul went on making convert after convert, and that was just too much!

What we should learn from all this is that the traveling missionaries of the early Church did not suffer persecution and deadly opposition as much from the Romans who ruled Palestine as from their own fellow Jews. Rome was fairly tolerant with them; to a Roman, one god was as good as another, and, so long as the God of the Christians *and* the Christians themselves did not interfere with the government of Rome, there was no trouble. The Romans were enemies at a later date, but, in the early days of missionary effort, the enemy was the Jew and not the Roman.

Paul almost lost his temper with these Jews. He was furious; born a Jew himself, he turned in wrath against the Jews of Corinth: "Your blood be on your heads. . . . From now on I will go to the Gentiles" (verse 6). That was typical of him. He was a man with a hair-trigger temper, impatient with opposition and with men who opposed him in any way. That he was the greatest of the apostles, there is no doubt; that he was often too quick with condemnation, there is no doubt, either.

His success in winning Gentiles to the Christian faith drove the unconverted Jews to desperation. As a last resort, they had Paul arrested and brought before the Roman government for judgment. The charge: this fanatical Jew was persuading men to worship God "contrary to the law." Which law? They must have meant the *Roman* law—and they made a bad mistake when they charged that, for Rome had no law about Jewish worship. They made a mistake, too, when they brought Paul before Gallio; they should have known the reputation of this Gallio as a man who had no tolerance for nonsense and ignorance and for the petty quarrels of the Jews under his jurisdiction. Gallio saw what the Jews were up to before the "trial" could even begin. He dismissed the case as one in which he had no jurisdiction and no interest; he refused to be used as a judge of Jewish religion—and he drove the "prosecution" out of his courtroom. Paul didn't have to defend himself, as far as Gallio (a brother of the famous writer Seneca) was concerned.

In spite of what some say about Gallio, we like him. He has been called "a typically arrogant Roman," but we doubt that judgment. It was not arrogance that led him to throw the Jews and their "case" out of his court; he was simply using common sense. He refused to be moved to anger by a regrettable religious fight. He was not stirred to action even when he saw Sosthenes, the chief of the synagogue, beaten by a group of Greeks before his judgment seat. This, to him, was something for the Jews to settle among themselves without bothering *him!* He was simply saying to the quarreling Jews, "This is *your* problem. Settle it among yourselves." He knew that it was a matter that could and should work itself out. And he was right about that.

Read it and profit, you modern Christians who go into courts of law to settle your differences! Christianity is not a matter of law; it is a *faith* that conquers all disputes, a love that conquers all.

SUGGESTIONS TO TEACHERS

You as a teacher probably get tired and discouraged with teaching. Perhaps you wonder whether it's worth bothering with your class week after week.

If it's any consolation to you, you will be interested to know that every Christian leader occasionally asks whether it's worth the trouble to serve, teach, and sacrifice. Your lesson for this Sunday is for you as well as for your class.

You will be working with scriptural material which discusses Paul's "problem church"—the church at Corinth. Let the Bible speak to both you and to your class as you reflect on the conflict in Corinth.

1. *UNLIKELY LOCATION.* A church at Corinth? If you know anything about this ancient sinkhole of vice and depravity, it would have been the last place you would have tried to organize a Christian congregation. Check your Bible commentaries for background material on Corinth. Life in Corinth shocked even the blasé Romans. Yet God intends a witness even in the Corinths of His world. He also has in mind to locate a Christian presence in your area—through you and your fellow believers. You may question the usefulness of what you're doing sometimes, but God means for you and your class to continue your witness, just as He meant for Paul and the handful of rough ex-pagans in the Corinthian Church to witness in that town.

2. *UNFAILING LIKEMINDED.* Paul arrived in Corinth feeling depressed. His work so far throughout Greece had not been as successful as he had hoped. He had been run out of town in many places. He had made little dent in Athens. His missionary companions were elsewhere, and he came to Corinth alone. However, in Corinth, he found Aquila and Priscilla, two of the most stalwart, supportive friends he ever made. Although they shared the common occupation of tentmaking, they applied their main energies in sharing their common faith in Jesus Christ. The Holy Spirit always finds helpers for His faithful. Remind your class that the Lord will unfailingly introduce them to people who are likeminded in a commitment to Christ and His work, if your people only ask and look!

3. *ANTIDOTE TO LONELINESS.* Paul encountered fierce opposition also in Corinth. He knew anxiety. He sometimes felt that he was alone in the effort to teach. Read and reread the Lord's words to Paul: "Do not be afraid, but speak and do not be silent; for I am with you, and no man shall attack you to harm you; for I have many people in this city" (Acts 18:9,10). This message is also for you and every Christian worker! Read on, and note that Paul remained in Corinth instead of quitting. The Lord gives you and your class staying power!

4. *UNEXPECTED LIFT.* Paul later made a trip through Galatia, "strengthening all the disciples" (18–23). He heartened faltering believers. Are you? Are the members of your class? In your pilgrimage of life, you are intended to strengthen other disciples. Discuss ways in which each person can strengthen other believers in your church.

5. *UNBAPTIZED LEARNER.* Time permitting, you can talk with your class about Apollos, the young promising leader in the Church who still had some lessons to learn. Let your class observe the way Priscilla and

Aquila patiently and gently worked with Apollos, bringing him to a more mature understanding of the faith. Think over how important it is to develop new cadres of leaders in your church, and how older members of your congregation have a responsibility to the young Apolloses coming along.

TOPIC FOR ADULTS
CONFLICT IN CORINTH

Let Them Call Themselves Christians. The last thing that the Protestant reformers desired was division or conflict within Christ's Church. They worked to bring about change within the Church, but abhorred the notion of splitting the Church. Luther, in fact, felt so keenly about factions springing up taking his name that he wrote; "In the first place, I ask that men make no reference to my name; let them call themselves Christians, not Lutherans. What is Luther? After all the teaching is not mine (John 7:16). Neither was I crucified for anyone (1 Corinthians 1:13). St. Paul in 1 Corinthians 3:17, would not allow the Christians to call themselves Pauline or Petrine, but Christians. How then should I—poor stinking maggot-fodder that I am—come to have men call the children of God by my wretched name? Not so, my dear friends; let us abolish all party names and call ourselves Christians, after Him whose teaching we hold."—Luther's Works, Muhlenberg Press, 1962.

In your denomination, do you think of yourselves as Christians first?

Not Comparing Ourselves With Others. Bishop Eivind Berggrav of Norway participated with those opposing the Nazis during the Second World War. Arrested, Bishop Berggrav was hideously tortured by the Nazis to try to force him to disclose names of others in the Norwegian Resistance. He stood up to the worst of the pain and threats, and never gave his captors the information they wanted. His years of torture and imprisonment also toughened him as a man of faith, so that, at the end of the War, he emerged as a spokesman against conflict yet an advocate of change. His words and actions were based solidly on the meaning of the Gospel in his own life. Speaking once to a group of young church people, Bishop Berggrav told how members of the worshiping community at the altar could never again act competitively or contemptuously toward each other.

When we kneel before the altar for Holy Communion, it's the proper posture. Berggrav said: "This physical breaking of my stiffneckedness helps remind me who I am and who He is. I am just waiting here for Him. He is descending to meet me with all His gifts, with overflowing grace, which I can't comprehend with my poor little square brain. I know I am not pious and I will try not to make myself look more pious than I am. I just kneel down before You because I want You above everything in the world.

"This Host at the Lord's Supper never rations His gifts. No one can know beforehand what he will get. Sometimes we feel that we are not getting anything at all. We may kneel at the altar, not changed, at least not feeling we are changed, having a most empty sensation. Feelings are never the most important; the most important is often what we don't notice, what we are not aware of. However that is, be assured He never rations His gifts and grace, never! He gives wholly, completely, entirely, to

Thomas and to Peter, to everyone He calls His servants. Even when we are gazing at ourselves in the mirror, and are comparing ourselves with others, and doing the things we ought not to do!"

Unratified Decisions. "Whenever I hear a mere mortal aspiring to speak about the things of God from God's point of view, I am reminded of an anecdote from Vatican II. Two cardinals were discussing the possibility of changing the Roman Catholic teaching which condemned artificial birth control. The hyperconservative of the two said, 'Oh, no, we could not change that. For years we have opposed it. What about all the women we've been sending to hell because they practiced it?' Asked the more moderate cardinal, 'Are you sure God ratifies all our decisions?' " Reprinted from *CONTEXT* by permission of Claretian Publications, 221 W. Madison St., Chicago, Ill. 60606.

Questions for Pupils on the Next Lesson. 1. Do you think that you are able to influence the behavior and decisions of others? 2. Where do you find yourself experiencing the greatest number of competing claims in life? 3. What examples can you recall in which profits and vested interests threatened moral values? 4. When do you find yourself faced with real and difficult decisions between doing good or evil? 5. Why is the struggle with the power of economics so tough in your life?

TOPIC FOR YOUTH
TAKE A STAND

How to Control Your Pitching. Bob Shawkey was a star pitcher for the New York Yankees when they began to dominate baseball in the 1920s.

Shawkey won 198 games in the major leagues. He also pitched for the Philadelphia Athletics, serving under Manager Connie Mack. With the Yankees, Shawkey pitched for Miller Huggins, whom he later succeeded as manager.

In 1923, Huggins named Shawkey to pitch the first game ever played at Yankee Stadium.

He pitched in New York for twelve years and had four seasons of twenty or more victories. He pitched in five World Series, one with the Athletics and four with the Yankees. His major-league record totaled 198 victories and 150 losses, with an earned run average of 3.09.

Shawkey said he could never forget his first start on the mound for Connie Mack in a practice game. "I was wild as a mountain goat," he said, "and my fast ball was whistling by the ears and ankles of the batters, while my curve kept breaking into the dirt. Then I lost my temper, and Mr. Mack waved me out.

"After I cooled off a bit, I asked Chief Bender to show me what was wrong with my curve. 'Sure,' said the Chief, 'I'll show you anything, but first you will have to show me that you can control yourself.' "

Before you can win at anything, you first have to control yourself! Once you allow Christ to control your life, you have that self under control. You are able to take a stand—on the mound in a baseball game, and in the larger contest of life!

Here I Stand. In 1508, Martin Luther was transferred to an Augustinian monastery at Wittenberg and to the post of instructor in logic and physics, then later professor of theology in the university. Wittenberg was the northern capital but seldom the residence of Frederick the Wise. A contemporary pronounced it "a poor, insignificant town, with little, old, ugly wooden houses." Luther described the inhabitants as "beyond measure drunken, rude, and given to reveling"; they had the reputation of being the amplest drinkers in Saxony which was rated the most drunken province of Germany. One mile to the east, said Luther, civilization ended and barbarism began. Here, for the most part, he remained to the close of his day. In this backwater hicktown, Martin Luther announced to arrogant authorities trying to shake him from his reliance on Scripture, "Here stand I!" His stand ignited the movement known as the Reformation.

Sentence Sermon to Remember: I expect to pass through life but once. If therefore, there by any kindness I can show, or any good thing I can do to any fellow being, let me do it now, and not defer or neglect it, as I shall not pass this way again."—William Penn.

Questions for Pupils on the Next Lesson. 1. How would you describe the economic pressures you feel you are under? 2. How do you react when you sense others are trying to manipulate you? 3. Do the "ends" always justify the "means"? 4. What are some of the times when you felt peer pressure when you took a stand differing from your peer group? 5. What philosophies and religious experiences of others would you like to know more about?

LESSON XI—MAY 15

RIOT IN EPHESUS

Background Scripture: Acts 19,20
Devotional Reading: John 17:20–26

KING JAMES VERSION

ACTS 19 23 And the same time there arose no small stir about that way.

24 For a certain *man* named Demetrius, a silversmith, which made silver shrines for Diana, brought no small gain unto the craftsmen;

25 Whom he called together with the workmen of like occupation, and said, Sirs, ye know that by this craft we have our wealth.

26 Moreover ye see and hear, that not alone at Ephesus, but almost throughout all Asia, this Paul hath persuaded and turned away much people, saying that they be no gods, which are made with hands:

27 So that not only this our craft is in danger to be set at nought; but also that the temple of the great goddess Diana should be despised, and her magnificence should be destroyed, whom all Asia and the world worshippeth.

28 And when they heard *these sayings*, they were full of wrath, and cried out, saying, Great *is* Diana of the Ephesians.

29 And the whole city was filled with confusion: and having caught Gaius and Aristarchus, men of Macedonia, Paul's companions in travel, they rushed with one accord into the theatre.

35 And when the townclerk had appeased the people, he said, *Ye* men of Ephesus, what man is there that knoweth not how that the city of the Ephesians is a worshipper of the great goddess Diana, and of the *image* which fell down from Jupiter?

36 Seeing then that these things cannot be spoken against, ye ought to be quiet, and to do nothing rashly.

37 For ye have brought hither these men, which are neither robbers of churches, nor yet blasphemers of your goddess.

38 Wherefore if Demetrius, and the craftsmen which are with him, have a matter against any man, the law is open, and there are deputies: let them implead one another.

REVISED STANDARD VERSION

ACTS 19 23 About that time there arose no little stir concerning the Way. 24 For a man named Demetrius, a silversmith, who made silver shrines of Artemis, brought no little business to the craftsmen. 25 These he gathered together, with the workmen of like occupation, and said, "Men, you know that from this business we have our wealth. 26 And you see and hear that not only at Ephesus but almost throughout all Asia this Paul has persuaded and turned away a considerable company of people, saying that gods made with hands are not gods. 27 And there is danger not only that this trade of ours may come into disrepute but also that the temple of the great goddess Artemis may count for nothing, and that she may even be deposed from her magnificence, she whom all Asia and the world worship."

28 When they heard this they were enraged, and cried out, "Great is Artemis of the Ephesians!" 29 So the city was filled with the confusion; and they rushed together into the theater, dragging with them Gaius and Aristarchus, Macedonians who were Paul's companions in travel.

35 And when the town clerk had quieted the crowd, he said, "Men of Ephesus, what man is there who does not know that the city of the Ephesians is temple keeper of the great Artemis, and of the sacred stone that fell from the sky? 36 Seeing then that these things cannot be contradicted, you ought to be quiet and do nothing rash. 37 For you have brought these men here who are neither sacrilegious nor blasphemers of our goddess. 38 If therefore Demetrius and the craftsmen with him have a complaint against any one, the courts are open, and there are proconsuls; let them bring charges against one another. 39 But if you seek anything further, it shall be settled in the regular assembly. 40 For we are in danger of being charged with rioting today, there being no

39 But if ye inquire any thing concerning other matters, it shall be determined in a lawful assembly.

40 For we are in danger to be called in question for this day's uproar, there being no cause whereby we may give an account of this concourse.

41 And when he had thus spoken, he dismissed the assembly.

cause that we can give to justify this commotion." 41 And when he had said this, he dismissed the assembly.

KEY VERSE: We are afflicted in every way, but not crushed; perplexed, but not driven to despair. 2 Corinthians 4:8 (RSV).

HOME DAILY BIBLE READINGS

May 9. M. John's Disciples at Ephesus. Acts 19:1–7.
May 10. T. In the School of Tyranus. Acts 19:8–12.
May 11. W. The Growth of the Word. Acts 19:13–20.
May 12. T. The All-Night Service. Acts 20:7–12.
May 13. F. Paul's Farewell Address. Acts 20:17–27.
May 14. S. Paul's Message to the Elders. Acts 20:28–35.
May 15. S. They Kneeled Down and Prayed. Acts 20:36–38.

BACKGROUND

As we read the story of the missionary journeys of Paul and his colleagues, we wonder, more and more, how they did it, how they stood up and fought against almost impossible odds. *Wherever they went, there was trouble.* There were threats of beatings, imprisonment, even of death, and still they went on and on, from riots in one city to riots in the next. What held them up? What gave this man Paul the courage to go on?

For one reason, he was possessed of a divine Spirit that gave him a superhuman spiritual strength. No enemy could throw that Spirit in jail or beat it to death; no one can crucify an idea, or imprison a faith. Beyond this, Paul had a great objective beyond these cities in which he suffered much for Christ: that objective was Rome. There is a little remark of Paul slipped into Acts 19 which reveals the goal he was striving toward: "I must see Rome." Rome was the center of the world; he must preach Christ there, for from Rome, if a strong church were established there, the Good News of Christ might well spread across the whole Empire.

Between him and Rome lay Ephesus, the metropolis of the Roman Province of Asia and one of the three great cities of the eastern Mediterranean. Paul went to Ephesus to face trouble not from the Jews this time, but from one of the deities of Rome. The deity was invisible, hidden in a statue, but it was almost strong enough to put an end to Paul.

NOTES ON THE PRINTED TEXT

High on a hill above Ephesus stood one of the seven wonders of the ancient world: the magnificent Temple of Diana. Diana of the Ephesians! She was the most popular of all the Roman deities. At any time of night or day, there was someone saying or shouting, "Great is Diana of the Ephesians." The people bowed to her like so many unquestioning sheep, and the silversmiths of the town made good money selling little silver images of the goddess. The faithful—and the tourists—paid a good price for these statuettes, but Paul didn't buy one. He stood face to face with Diana and preached the Gospel of Jesus Christ, and that started a riot.

The riot was engineered by one Demetrius, who had made a fortune in the trade. We might call him the leader of the silversmith's union. He is known to us as a scoundrel, and that may be true, but, if it is true, he was a clever scoundrel and, to his way of thinking, a man trying to protect his fellow smiths in what he considered a legitimate occupation. He was smart in organizing the opposition to the traveling Christian who threatened to destroy their lucrative business.

First, he appealed to the love of *profit.* He convinced the smiths of Ephesus that Paul was destroying their business in making little of their Diana. No business meant no bread. That is always a good way to rouse a labor riot: threaten the workers with loss of income, and they are ready to do anything.

Once they were mad, he went on to make an appeal to patriotism and religion. All the Roman world worshiped Diana; who was this stranger from Jerusalem to insult both Diana's worshipers and Diana herself? How dare he throw contempt on her temple, and depose a goddess they had honored for centuries?

It is an old, old trick: bring out the flag and wave it to cover up a selfish drive for more profit! Make it a *religious* crusade. If one method fails, the religious method was sure to win. Many a riot, many a war, had been brought on by men hiding selfish interests behind a thin coating of patriotism and religion. Finance, not faith, lies behind many "righteous causes."

Demetrius was an instant hero; he whipped up a maddened mob that turned on the Christians and dragged two of Paul's companions into the city amphitheater. Paul tried to get into the theater, but his friends held him back. The two who were caught faced death, and they would have died had it not been for a city official who stepped in to stop it.

The town clerk (or was he the mayor of Ephesus?), roused by the shouts of "Great is Diana of the Ephesians," saw what was happening; if this went on, his whole city would be in danger at the hands of a wild mob. With a courage rare in politicians, he faced the mob. He was something more than a town clerk; he had the power to enforce the laws and ordinances of the city, and he was probably the one man in the city to whom the mob would listen. He made a very sensible speech, better than the speech of Demetrius, and one that made Demetrius look like a fool instead of a hero.

Whoever he was, this man must have been a spellbinder; he not only got the mob quieted down, but he made out such a good case for Paul and his companions that they stopped yelling compliments to Diana and went home. It took nerve for any man to "lay down the law" to such a roaring crowd, but he did just that.

What, he asked them, were they afraid of? The faith of Diana wasn't being threatened; she was strong enough to overcome the competition of a few wandering Jews without their help. He told them flatly that Paul had done nothing illegal or blasphemous. If he *had* done anything like that, there were courts in Ephesus established to take care of it and either convict Paul or set him free. That was the court's business, not the mob's. The crowd saw the justice of this argument, gave up, and went home.

Now this "town clerk" has been hailed as a hero. He was certainly heroic in the way he handled things, but there may be some doubt as to his motives. This man was a civil servant, holding office by permission of the Romans; he was in charge of keeping law and order in his city—and if there was any one thing that Rome would not tolerate, it was civil disorder. Such disorder could spread like fire, and Rome moved swiftly to put it down. If local Roman officials were weak when such disorder struck, those officials were very likely to lose their jobs. Thus, we may be justified to believe that this official was not only defending Paul that day, but defending *himself* and his position. He could have been speaking in self-interest. Hero or sly politician—which was he?

The clever town clerk alludes to something that dropped from the skies; that was an effort calculated to remind the rioters of the universal power and popularity of Artemis (Diana). Generally, it is thought to have been a meteorite for which a supernatural origin was claimed. It may all have been an object of superstition, but it is no superstition that the little town clerk may have been, symbolically, "dropped from the skies" to overcome a riot and to save the lives of Paul and his two companions. Such things do happen; many a crisis has been met by men who seemed to be created for just such a purpose. In any event, Paul was spared to continue his journey which he did. He shook the dust of Ephesus from his feet and moved on.

What a story this is! What characters were those in the clash between God and Diana: Paul, who remained calm in every crisis; Demetrius, who put profit above honor and faith; the Roman official who unwittingly gave a helping hand to God! It all counts up to a graphic illustration of the gradual defeat of heathenism and the increasing triumph of the cause of Christ. No opposition could prevail against that ultimate victory.

SUGGESTIONS TO TEACHERS

In a magazine article describing the Christian sites in Jerusalem and Bethlehem, the author described himself as a "nonobserving Protestant." It was apparent that for the writer his Christian faith was made up of vague cultural values. He had no church affiliation. At best only passively "Christian," he regarded the Gospel in action as a rather curious set of ceremonies.

Contrast the attitudes of this "nonobserving Protestant" to those of the early believers in Ephesus as described in Acts 19,20. Your lesson today gives a capsulized version of these Christians in action. Appropriately, it is called "Riot in Ephesus." Throughout your lesson, keep asking whether you and other Christians are stirring many riots in your town.

1. *RENEWED PENTECOSTS.* The Coming of the Holy Spirit was not a once-and-for-all event in Jerusalem around A.D. 29 or 30. You will note that new outpourings of the power of the Spirit kept occurring in the early Church. Have your class look at Acts 19:1–8. Recall that these

Ephesian "disciples" already thought that they had some religion, but grew into a deeper faith when the Holy Spirit touched their lives. Sometimes, Christians forget to ask for fresh drenchings of the Spirit. As in Ephesus, however, when they do, they find new means of communicating and prophesying.

2. *RELEASED POWER.* Jean Barker insists that the prime need for most Church leaders is stamina. By *stamina,* she means spiritual, emotional, and physical staying power. Without the power of the Spirit, most believers burn out. Check the stamina of Paul and his friends against yours and that of your friends in the Church. You should observe that their stamina as Christians braced them to withstand efforts to manipulate, buy, control, or coerce them, as in Acts 19:11–20.

3. *RELIGIOUS PATRIOTISM.* Have your class take a long look at the way opposition to the Gospel developed in Ephesus, especially by Demetrius and the silversmiths. There are nearly always vested interests which resent the claims of Jesus Christ. They will oppose the Church. Whenever Christ's message threatens business, watch out! Often, as in Ephesus, a dangerous blend of idolatrous piety and misdirected patriotism will find an opportunity to oppose the Church.

4. *REPRESSIVE PLOTS.* Sometimes, powerful people in the community who feel that the Church is getting in the way of their profits or their plans will accuse Christians of being "unpatriotic." Demetrius's descendants are still at work. Today, they slander some Christians by calling them "un-American" or "Communists." Help your class to understand that Christians must have stamina to stand up to slurs and name-calling, and even lawsuits and reprisals. The opposition to the Gospel is cunning and mean. Be ready!

5. *REFRESHING PRACTICALITY.* As time permits, look at the vignette in Acts 20:7–12 in which a sleepy listener named Eutychus is revived by practical-minded Paul. (Don't be surprised if the account brings some smiles and quips about long sermons and lessons!) Paul's compassion for the young Eutychus and his attention to mundane matters echoes that of Jesus'. Christian believers always have a healthy down-to-earth way of helping!

6. *RECESSIONAL PRAYER.* Devote a few minutes on Paul's touching farewell before embarking for Jerusalem and what he and everyone senses may be a death sentence for the fearless apostle. The main point is that Paul *encourages* others in the faith. Even in facing uncertainty and probably hardship and failure, Paul lends encouragement to fellow believers. Do you and your class do this? The Spirit gives you all stamina to be encouragers.

TOPIC FOR ADULTS
RIOT IN EPHESUS

Oasis of Peace. At first, the neighbors were hostile. Government officials still remain uncooperative. Orthodox religious groups continue to be suspicious. The parents of many of the participants were opposed to the idea. But led by a Christian priest four Jewish families have settled with two Arab families and the family of a British Roman Catholic and his wife and an Israeli Jew on a rocky hillside in what until 1967 was a no man's land between the Israeli and Jordanian lines twenty miles northwest of Jerusalem. They named the place Neve Shalom, or Oasis of Peace, and hope by their example to prove that Arabs and Jews can live together in Israel and that peace in the Middle East can be more than a dream. To bring this about, they have dedicated their settlement as an educational center to build a bridge between Israeli Jews and Arabs.

The leader of Neve Shalom is Father Hussar, who prefers to be called Bruno or Brother Bruno, and who was born in Egypt sixty-nine years ago, son of a Hungarian father and a French mother, both Jews. He is a Roman Catholic priest now and a citizen of Israel. In 1969, he persuaded the head of the nearby Abbey of Latrun, a Trappist monastery, to lease to him the 100 barren acres for 100 years at a rent of twenty-five cents a year. "We managed to pay it all in advance," the priest said.

In 1973, Brother Bruno and the first four families of settlers established themselves on the hill which had no water, no trees offering shade against the cruel sun of the Judean hills, and a road that could be used only in dry weather. Because they had received no permit to settle, they lived in temporary housing which in the priest's case was a huge packing case.

The first Israeli family came in 1976. Brother Bruno dates the real beginning of the community to that time. Despite a lack of cooperation from the Israeli Government, which the priest attributes to suspicion by Orthodox Jews of the Catholic Church's role, Arabs and Jews managed to encounter each other in peace. "Days that began in fear ended with exchanges of addresses and mutual visits," the priest recalled.

Fifteen Jewish and fifteen Arab schools now send classes to meet here with each other, each pair at least five times a year for a day, to learn to know each other and through teaching and games to break down the stereotypes that cause hostility and distrust.

In spite of opposition and suspicion, every Christian is called to build oases of peace wherever he or she may live. Sometimes, these efforts may bring riots. Sometimes, they may be misunderstood. Nonetheless, believers are "Neve Shalom" people!

Lesson of History from Ephesus. "The clear lesson of history is that when church and state go to bed together, . . . they do not produce offspring. The lesson of history is that one always rapes the other."—Dr. William Self, Atlanta Southern Baptist minister, *QUOTE*, November 1, 1980.

Conflicting Loyalties. A conflict of loyalties sometimes occurs in the course of the day's business. An employee is asked to do something that his conscience does not approve. His wife and children are dependent on him and his earnings. What is he to do? Register a protest? Give up the job? Tell himself that the employer is responsible, not the employee? In 1742, John Woolman, the Quaker, was a clerk in a store. He kept a journal and in it set down this entry:

"My employer, having a Negro woman, sold her, and desired me to write a bill of sale, the man being waiting who bought her. The thing was sudden; and though I felt uneasy at the thought of writing an instrument of slavery for one of my fellow creatures, yet I remembered that I was hired by the year, that it was my master who directed me to do it, and that it was an elderly man, a member of our Society, who bought her; so through weakness I gave way and wrote it; but at the executing of it I was so afflicted in my mind, that I said before my master and the friend that I believed slave-keeping to be a practice inconsistent with the Christian religion. This, in some degree, abated my uneasiness; yet as often as I reflected seriously upon it I thought I should have been clearer if I had desired to be excused from it, as a thing against my conscience; for such it was."

Questions for Pupils on the Next Lesson. 1. Why does a sense of personal integrity strengthen a person to face personal crises? 2. Do you have a sense of personal mission in life? 3. Are you satisfied with the direction your life has been taking? 4. Do you have trouble handling anger? 5. What are the times in your life when you, like Paul, sense you are "on trial"?

TOPIC FOR YOUTH
CAUGHT IN THE MIDDLE

Bowing Down in the House of Rimmon. "Naaman, the Syrian, cleansed of his leprosy, swore that he would thenceforth be loyal to the God of Israel, but he had hardly done so before he realized that when he went back to Syria he would have to go with his master in the line of duty into the temple of Rimmon, and when his master bowed down to worship Rimmon, he would be expected to do likewise. One can symphathize with Naaman's dilemma. There was the duty he owed to the God of Israel and the duty he owed to his monarch, the king of Syria. 'Bowing down in the house of Rimmon' has become a proverbial expression to denote the danger and dishonesty associated with compromise. Yet when loyalties conflict, how is compromise to be avoided?"—Robert McCracken, *Putting Faith to Work.*

Pressures of Greed and Glory. On November 22, 1980, a fire swept through the huge MGM Grand Hotel in Las Vegas, Nevada, destroying the luxurious $100 million structure and killing over 100 persons. While the heat and flames were taking the lives of helpless guests and consuming the building, many persons in the giant casino of the MGM Hotel insisted on continuing at the gambling tables or slot machines. The fire to those wanting to remain in the casino was more of an annoyance than a threat. Many of these gamblers did not want to leave a winning streak or to quit while they were behind. Most had to be herded outside moments before the advancing flames began to melt the casino's 1,000 slot machines. Some of the displaced gamblers headed directly across the street to the Barbary Coast Casino to resume playing.

Sometimes, we are so eager to make easy money or get quick glory that we will sacrifice anything—even our safety and sanity—to get them. We are all caught in the middle in the glittering, luxurious existence in our culture between various conflicting values. The story of Ephesus is repeated every day in our lives.

Jesus Christ enables us to sort out our values when we are caught in the middle!

Bad Bids. There is an old story about a man who bought a parrot at an auction after some spirited bidding. "I suppose this bird talks," he said to the auctioneer.

"Talk?" replied the auctioneer. "He's been bidding against you for the past ten minutes."

Sometimes we are surprised at the way we seem to be caught in the middle by unexpected forces working against us. Like the man at the auction, we often find that we have not been very alert.

We particularly are prone to underestimate the way the powers of evil and greed are bidding against us. As in Ephesus, voices of selfishness will be heard opposing us.

Sentence Sermon to Remember: Paul and Demetrius, like two antler-locked stags, are still fighting it out.—Frank S. Mead, in *Who's Who in the Bible.*

Questions for Pupils on the Next Lesson. 1. Have you ever had to take a stand on an unpopular moral issue? 2. What are some concrete examples of God's leadership in your life? 3. What long-range goals are you setting for yourself in the light of your Christian faith? 4. What do you do when your standards and values are challenged by your peers? 5. When do you feel you are most "on trial" for your faith?

LESSON XII—May 22

ON TRIAL IN JERUSALEM

Background Scripture: Acts 21:1–26:32
Devotional Reading: Acts 21:7–14

KING JAMES VERSION

ACTS 22 30 On the morrow, because he would have known the certainty wherefore he was accused of the Jews, he loosed him from *his* bands, and commanded the chief priests and all their council to appear, and brought Paul down, and set him before them.

23 1 And Paul, earnestly beholding the council, said, Men *and* brethren, I have lived in all good conscience before God until this day.

2 And the high priest Ananias commanded them that stood by him to smite him on the mouth.

3 Then said Paul unto him, God shall smite thee, *thou* whited wall: for sittest thou to judge me after the law, and commandest me to be smitten contrary to the law?

4 And they that stood by said, Revilest thou God's high priest?

5 Then said Paul, I wist not, brethren, that he was the high priest: for it is written, Thou shalt not speak evil of the ruler of thy people.

6 But when Paul perceived that the one part were Sadducees, and the other Pharisees, he cried out in the council, Men *and* brethren, I am a Pharisee, the son of a Pharisee: of the hope and resurrection of the dead I am called in question.

7 And when he had so said, there arose a dissension between the Pharisees and the Sadducees: and the multitude was divided.

8 For the Sadducees say that there is no resurrection, neither angel, nor spirit: but the Pharisees confess both.

9 And there arose a great cry: and the scribes *that were* of the Pharisees' part arose, and strove, saying, We find no evil in this man: but if a spirit or an angel hath spoken to him, let us not fight against God.

10 And when there arose a great dissension, the chief captain, fearing lest Paul should have been pulled in pieces of them, commanded the soldiers to go down, and to take him by force from among them, and to bring *him* into the castle.

REVISED STANDARD VERSION

ACTS 22 30 But on the morrow, desiring to know the real reason why the Jews accused him, he unbound him, and commanded the chief priests and all the council to meet, and he brought Paul down and set him before them.

23 1 And Paul, looking intently at the council, said, "Brethren, I have lived before God in all good conscience up to this day." 2 And the high priest Ananias commanded those who stood by him to strike him on the mouth. 3 Then Paul said to him, "God shall strike you, you whitewashed wall! Are you sitting to judge me according to the law, and yet contrary to the law you order me to be struck?" 4 Those who stood by said, "Would you revile God's high priest?" 5 And Paul said, "I did not know, brethren, that he was the high priest; for it is written, 'You shall not speak evil of a ruler of your people.' "

6 But when Paul perceived that one part were Sadducees and the other Pharisees, he cried out in the council, "Brethren, I am a Pharisee, a son of Pharisees; with respect to the hope and the resurrection of the dead I am on trial." 7 And when he had said this, a dissension arose between the Pharisees and the Sadducees; and the assembly was divided. 8 For the Sadducees say that there is no resurrection, nor angel, nor spirit; but the Pharisees acknowledge them all. 9 Then a great clamor arose; and some of the scribes of the Pharisees' party stood up and contended, "We find nothing wrong in this man. What if a spirit or an angel spoke to him?" 10 And when the dissension became violent, the tribune, afraid that Paul would be torn in pieces by them, commanded the soldiers to go down and take him by force from among them and bring him into the barracks.

11 And the night following the Lord stood by him, and said, Be of good cheer, Paul: for as thou hast testified of me in Jerusalem, so must thou bear witness also at Rome.	11 The following night the Lord stood by him and said, "Take courage, for as you have testified about me at Jerusalem, so you must bear witness also at Rome."

KEY VERSE: I can do all things in him who strengthens me. Philippians 4:13 (RSV).

HOME DAILY BIBLE READINGS

May 16. *M.* *Paul's Journey to Jerusalem.* Acts 21:1–6.
May 17. *T.* *The Warning of the Holy Spirit.* Acts 21:7–15.
May 18. *W.* *Paul Rescued From the Mob.* Acts 21:26–36.
May 19. *T.* *Paul Before the Sanhedrin.* Acts 23:1–8.
May 20. *F.* *The Promise of the Lord.* Acts 23:9–11.
May 21. *S.* *Paul's Defense Before Felix.* Acts 24:10–21.
May 22. *S.* *Paul Appeals to Caesar.* Acts 25:7–12.

BACKGROUND

Paul's third and last missionary journey took him from Corinth through Philippi, Troas, Miletus, Patara, Tyre, Ptolamais, and Caesarea—to Jerusalem. At Miletus he told his companions, "I go bound in the spirit unto Jerusalem, not knowing the things that shall befall me there" (Acts 20:22). At Tyre, he was warned against going to the Holy City; his disciples begged him not to go (21:4). But he went; when Paul made up his mind, that was *it.* He went for several reasons: he wanted to celebrate the Feast of Pentecost in Jerusalem; he wanted to take to the church fathers in the city a collection he had raised among the Gentile Christians for the support of the mother church; he wanted to report on his successes among the Gentiles. It wasn't so much that he *wanted* to go as that he felt that he *had* to go, even though in going he was facing violence and perhaps even death at the hands of hostile Jews. The Spirit, he said, *made* him go.

The mob was waiting for him. By the end of a week, they began to shout for his blood; he was accused of betraying the faith of their Jewish fathers and of having taken a Gentile (Tophimus) into their Temple, and *that* was an unforgivable sin. He was rescued by the commander of the Roman garrison, who had him brought in chains to the Castle of Antonia. On the steps of the Castle, he asked the permission of the commander to address the mob. Permission was granted, and he turned to face the mob.

NOTES ON THE PRINTED TEXT

Paul's speech, in defense of his conversion and his call from God to preach to the Gentiles, is a masterpiece; read it in Acts 22. But no defense, however brilliant, could quiet that mob; it cried out for his execution as a traitor to the old faith. To find out the truth or error of what they were saying, the Roman commander took him into the Castle and ordered that he be lashed. Lashing was frequently used, in those times, to force the "criminal" to confess. Bu the Roman officer overlooked one little detail; Paul was not only a Jew, but a Roman citizen, and it was against Roman law to whip a citizen. The great Cicero had said, "It is a misdeed for a Roman citizen to be bound; it is a crime for him to be beaten; it is almost as bad as to murder a father to kill him."

The Roman knew that all too well, and for a moment he was terrified. If he whipped this citizen, he could be dismissed and even put to death by his superiors in Rome. So he did what Gallio had done in Corinth; he told the Jews to take their "criminal" before their Sanhedrin, and try him there. It was a religious case, and not one to be tried before a Roman judge.

So Paul was taken before the Sanhedrin—the supreme court of the Jews. There he stood—one lonely little Christian taking on both the Jews *and* the Romans! He was perhaps the most courageous man in the New Testament. With an audacity that set the courtroom in an uproar, he started his defense by insulting Ananias, the high priest and chief officer of the Sanhedrin. This was not the dishonest Ananias of Acts 5, but he was still dishonest and worse; he had the reputation of being a thief and a quisling serving the Romans instead of his own people. Paul started out by insulting him and the whole Sanhedrin; he called them, "Brethren," when he should have addressed them as "Rulers of the people and Elders of Israel." For that, Ananias had him slapped on the mouth—which was an act contrary to the law, and Paul promptly reminded him of that: "What kind of judge are you, to break the law yourself by ordering me struck like that? . . . God will slap you, you whitewashed wall" (verse 3 TLB). Actually, Paul was calling him a whitewashed tomb, or sepulcher, which was an insult par excellence. Paul bowed meekly (?) in apology—and then turned to throw the whole court into confusion.

On this Sanhedrin sat Pharisees and Sadduces, both of whom held places of power in the Jewish religious structure—and who differed with each other on various doctrines and procedures. The worst of these differences was one regarding the doctrine of the Resurrection. The Pharisees believed in the resurrection of the dead; the Sadducees did not. Paul was familiar with that old Pharisee-Sadducee debate, and he "threw a bomb" at them by claiming that he was on trial before them for believing in the resurrection of the dead. It was a brilliant move. The result was bedlam before the trial could even get started. The Pharisees on the Sanhedrin were forced to approve of that statement; they saw nothing evil in the prisoner who was also a Pharisee. But the Sadducees roared like a lion caught in a trap, and their roaring struck fire among the audience in the court. It was so violent that the Roman soldiers had to come in and rescue Paul; they took him back to Antonia Castle. The mob dispersed and went home.

It is an old, old trick: if you can get your enemies fighting among themselves, you have won the battle! A Sanhedrin divided against itself was made powerless; a house divided against itself cannot stand. Paul had beaten them, badly.

But was it only Paul who was responsible for this? Is it not possible that the Roman commander wanted to get rid of the troublesome Paul by bringing him before the Sanhedrin? Did the Roman willingly and purposely bring Paul before that court in order to get more information about him and then turn him over to the Roman procurator when he came to Jerusalem? That would take all responsibility for the Jewish rebellion from the commander's shoulders. It could been that way.

But the problem wasn't solved even now by this maneuver. The question still remained—what were they to do with Paul *now?* They couldn't keep him in the castle forever; somehow, they had to get him out of Jerusalem. The Romans governing Jerusalem were worried about that—but Paul wasn't. He put his trust in God, and God spoke to him in a vision: "Be of good cheer, Paul: for as thou hast testified of me in Jerusalem, so must thou bear witness also at Rome" (verse 11).

Rome! Did Paul recall now words he had previously spoken: "I must also see Rome?" It was a long, long journey to Rome, and many strange things happened along the way, but Paul set out immediately, not by his own will but by the will of God; he moved out on the last lap of his life and his ministry.

SUGGESTIONS TO TEACHERS

A billboard in western Pennsylvania carried the following message: IF YOU WERE ARRESTED FOR BEING A CHRISTIAN, WOULD THERE BE ENOUGH EVIDENCE TO CONVICT YOU? Most people dismiss this as a hypothetical question. Actually, however, every Christian is "on trial" every minute. And this is the thrust of today's lesson.

The Scripture for this lesson presents Paul on trial in Jerusalem, but it also gives valuable insights into how your class's people conduct themselves while "on trial" in your community.

1. *READINESS.* "I am ready not only to be imprisoned but even to die at Jerusalem for the name of the Lord Jesus," announces the apostle (Acts 21:13). This is not cheap bravado. Neither is it empty rhetoric. Reminiscent of Paul, Dietrich Bonhoeffer once stated, "When Jesus calls a person, He calls him to come out and die!" Help each person to reflect on and reexamine his or her commitments to Christ. Does each have the "even to die" for Jesus Christ level of consecration?

2. *RECONCILIATION.* Paul and James, the head of the Jerusalem Christians, and other church leaders with whom he had not been on close terms, met together. In spite of differences of opinion on many matters, they acknowledged their common bonds in each other through Jesus Christ. Part of all Christians' "trial" in these times means demonstrating in specific ways the one-ness of Christ's people. Roman Catholics, Eastern Orthodox, and many Protestant denominations have serious divergencies of viewpoints, but no Christian is excused from seeking actively to be reconciled to others.

3. *REPUTATION.* Read the charges brought against Paul by his adversaries. Note that Paul's enemies accused him of emphasizing Jesus as Lord, "but whom Paul asserted to be alive" (Acts 25:19). Would your foes pick up the fact that you asserted Jesus Christ to be alive, if they caught a few snatches of your conversations and a few glimpses of your commitment in action? Ask each person to ask himself or herself for what he/she thinks he/she is most noted.

4. *REASSURANCE.* Spend enough time on Paul's defense before Agrippa (Acts 26) to catch some of the important sayings. For instance, Acts 26:22 states Paul told the audience and Agrippa, "To this day I have

had the help that comes from God . . . saying nothing but what the prophets and Moses said would come to pass . . ." (26:22). Paul was constantly reassured by the Spirit, the Helper. Paul's message was the assurance that the ancient promises had been fulfilled in Jesus Christ. Discuss with your class what gives your people the greatest reassurance in times of difficulty. Comment on the unfailing help through Christ which always comes to Christians who trust.

5. *RESOLUTION.* Paul, you should point out, was not content until every person heard the News of God's great act of mercy through Jesus Christ. He stood up to the mighty Agrippa and said boldly, "I would to God that not only you but also all who hear me this day might become such as I am" (26:29). Do your students have that kind of resolve to share the News of Jesus Christ? What exactly do your people wish for in their lives?

TOPIC FOR ADULTS
ON TRIAL IN JERUSALEM

The God in Whom I Hope. "In February 1945, I was taken prisoner by the British, and for over three years I was moved about from camp to camp in Belgium, Scotland, and England. In April 1948, I was one of the last to be 'repatriated,' as the phrase goes.

"The breakup of the German front, the collapse of law and humanity, the self-destruction of German civilization and culture, and finally the appalling end on 9 May 1945—all this was followed by the revelation of the crimes which had been committed in Germany's name—Buchenwald, Auschwitz, Madenek, Bergen-Belsen, and the rest. And with that came the necessity of standing up to it all inwardly, shut up in camps as we were. I think my own little world fell to pieces then, too. The 'iron rations' (Multmann refers here to the only books he had in prison, Goethe's poems and the works of Nietzsche) I had with me were quickly used up, and what remained left a stale taste in my mouth. In that Belgian camp, hungry as we were, I saw how other men collapsed inwardly, how they gave up all hope, sickening for the lack of it, some of them dying. The same thing almost happened to me. What kept me from it was a rebirth to new life thanks to a hope for which there is no evidence at all.

"It was not that I experienced any sudden conversion. What I felt all at once was the death of all the mainstays that had sustained my life up to then. It was only slowly that something different began to build up in their stead. At home, Christianity was only a matter of form. One came across it once a year at Christmas time, as something rather remote. In the prison camps were I was, I only met it in very human—all too human—form. It was nothing very overwhelming. And yet the experience of misery and forsakenness and daily humiliation gradually built up into an experience of God.

"It was the experience of God's presence in the dark night of the soul: 'If I make my bed in hell, behold, thou art there.' A well-meaning army chaplain had given me a New Testament. I thought it was out of place. I would rather have had something to eat. But then I became fascinated by the Psalms (which were printed in an appendix) and especially by Psalm

39: 'I was dumb with silence, I held my peace, even from good; and my sorrow was stirred (but the German is much stronger—"I have to eat up my grief within myself"). . . . Hold thou not thy peace at my tears; for I am a stranger with thee, and a sojourner, as all my fathers were.' These Psalms gave me the words for my own suffering. They opened my eyes to the God who is with those 'that are of a broken heart.' He was present even behind the barbed wire—no, most of all behind the barbed wire. . . .

"This experience of not sinking into the abyss but of being held up from afar was the beginning of a clear hope, without which it is impossible to live at all. At the same time, even this hope cut two ways; on the one hand, it provided the strength to get up again after every inward or outward defeat; on the other hand, it made the soul rub itself raw on the barbed wire, making it impossible to settle down in captivity or come to terms with it.

"God in the dark night of the soul—God as the power of hope and pain; this was the experience which moulded me in what are a person's most receptive years, between eighteen and twenty-one. I am reluctant to say that this is why I became a Christian, because that sounds like joining a party. Because I believe that I owe my survival to these experiences, I cannot even say that I found God there. But I do know in my heart that it is there that He found me, and that I would otherwise have been lost."—*Experiences of God*, by Jurgen Moltmann. Copyright 1980. Reprinted by permission of Fortress Press.

Certificate of Martyrdom. Long-suffering saints may at last claim recognition.

If they have had three tragic events in their life, they're eligible for a "Certificate of Martyrdom" from the Church of World Peace in Denver, Colorado.

The martyrdom certificate contains these words: "The suffering you have had to endure at the hands of life has been almost more than any one person can bear. Rarely has such a noble soul been forced to put up with such undeserved agony. In recognition of your extraordinary plight, the Church of World Peace hereby awards this Certificate of Martyrdom. Your name shall remain in the Church Archives in perpetuity."

Yes, there is a $5 fee. One wonders whether parting with the sum will qualify as one of the tragic events—or only mark one as a proverbial fool soon parted from his money.

Prayers in Trial. A woman recalls that whenever she saw her mother on her knees she knew that something terrible had happened in the family. Prayer was using God like calling the Fire Department, and when the crisis is over going back to the same old way.

Real praying starts *before* the times of trial come. Genuine prayer means dealing with the things that cause the crisis in the first place. Christians do not pretend they can get along on their own strength, then pray for God to get them out of a jam. Praying is in the midst of trial and in the times of no trials.

Questions for Pupils on the Next Lesson. 1. Do you have a basis for positive daily living, particularly in facing difficulties that can thwart your life? 2. How can you keep yourself from rejecting spiritual values which are the basis for a meaningful life? 3. How do you deal with tough choices in knowing where to focus your energies and concern? 4. Have you ever been sidetracked from your plans? 5. Are you able to witness when you're under adversity?

TOPIC FOR YOUTH
FACING TRIALS

One-Handed Leaders. After a day of conferences on the pros and cons of war tactics, Gen. Dwight Eisenhower made an amusing observation about some staff members.

"These fellows give me a set of facts and we are just about ready to make a decision. But then they say, 'However, on the other hand.' You know, I *do* need to find a couple of one-handed leaders!"

In our times of trial, there eventually comes the time when we must make a decision about whether or not we will be faithful as Christians. We can procrastinate by telling ourselves, ". . . on the other hand. . . ." Finally, we must decide if we will be responsible to the Lord and to each other. We must be "one-handed leaders."

Cheapy Church. A ministerial association in a certain community sponsored a city-wide religious survey. Each person interviewed was asked to state what church he or she was affiliated with, if any. One card was processed which indicated that a certain family's religious preference was the "Penny Cost Church."

Many Christians are members of such a denomination since they do not want to make any deep commitments. The Christian faith costs!

You will face many trials in which you will be able to tell yourself that you cannot afford to sacrifice your money, or your time, or your energies for Christ's work. Remember, however, what the faith you hold has cost Jesus Christ, and also what it has cost many others such as the Apostle Paul.

Choose! There was the case of Pizarro, the famous Spanish explorer in South America. At a certain point, he drew a line on the ground; he pointed out that on the north there lay Mexico with its comparative safety and its security; on the south there lay Panama with all its dangers. "Let each man choose," he said, "as befits a brave Castilian," and they flocked to take the harder but the more glorious way.

Sentence Sermon to Remember: The prophet and the martyr do not see the hooting throng. Their eyes are fixed on the eternities.—Benjamin N. Cardozo.

Questions for Pupils on the Next Lesson. 1. Have you been sidetracked from your intentions to serve Christ very many times? 2. What are the most annoying restrictions you feel in your life? 3. Do you feel that, in the light of what Christ gave up for you, that your restrictions may be for the best? 4. How can witnessing in adversity help you to mature? 5. Do you find yourself frequently on the defensive? If so, why?

LESSON XIII—MAY 29

PAUL IN ROME

Background Scripture: Acts 27,28
Devotional Reading: Ephesians 4:1–6

KING JAMES VERSION

ACTS 28 11 And after three months we departed in a ship of Alexandria, which had wintered in the isle, whose sign was Castor and Pollux.

12 And landing at Syracuse, we tarried *there* three days.

13 And from thence we fetched a compass, and came to Rhegium: and after one day the south wind blew, and we came the next day to Puteoli:

14 Where we found brethren, and were desired to tarry with them seven days: and so we went toward Rome.

15 And from thence, when the brethren heard of us, they came to meet us as far as Appii forum, and The three taverns: whom when Paul saw, he thanked God, and took courage.

16 And when we came to Rome, the centurion delivered the prisoners to the captain of the guard: but Paul was suffered to dwell by himself with a soldier that kept him.

17 And it came to pass, that after three days Paul called the chief of the Jews together: and when they were come together, he said unto them, Men *and* brethren, though I have committed nothing against the people, or customs of our fathers, yet was I delivered prisoner from Jerusalem into the hands of the Romans:

18 Who, when they had examined me, would have let *me* go, because there was no cause of death in me.

19 But when the Jews spake against *it,* I was constrained to appeal unto Caesar; not that I had aught to accuse my nation of.

20 For this cause therefore have I called for you, to see *you,* and to speak with *you:* because that for the hope of Israel I am bound with this chain.

21 And they said unto him, We neither received letters out of Judea concerning thee, neither any of the brethren that came shewed or spake any harm of thee.

22 But we desire to hear of thee what

REVISED STANDARD VERSION

ACTS 28 11 After three months we set sail in a ship which had wintered in the island, a ship of Alexandria, with the Twin Brothers as figurehead. 12 Putting in at Syracuse, we stayed there for three days. 13 And from there we made a circuit and arrived at Rhegium; and after one day a south wind sprang up, and on the second day we came to Puteoli. 14 There we found brethren, and were invited to stay with them for seven days. And so we came to Rome. 15 And the brethren there, when they heard of us, came as far as the Forum of Appius and Three Taverns to meet us. On seeing them Paul thanked God and took courage. 16 And when we came into Rome, Paul was allowed to stay by himself, with the soldier that guarded him.

17 After three days he called together the local leaders of the Jews; and when they had gathered, he said to them, "Brethren, though I had done nothing against the people or the customs of our fathers, yet I was delivered prisoner from Jerusalem into the hands of the Romans. 18 When they had examined me, they wished to set me at liberty, because there was no reason for the death penalty in my case. 19 But when the Jews objected, I was compelled to appeal to Caesar—though I had no charge to bring against my nation. 20 For this reason therefore I have asked to see you and speak with you, since it is because of the hope of Israel that I am bound with this chain." 21 And they said to him, "We have received no letters from Judea about you, and none of the brethren coming here has reported or spoken any evil about you. 22 But we desire to hear from you what your views are; for with regard to this sect we know that everywhere it is spoken against."

thou thinkest: for as concerning this sect, we know that every where it is spoken against.

23 And when they had appointed him a day, there came many to him into *his* lodging; to whom he expounded and testified the kingdom of God, persuading them concerning Jesus, both out of the law of Moses, and *out of* the prophets, from morning till evening.

23 When they had appointed a day for him, they came to him at his lodging in great numbers. And he expounded the matter to them from morning till evening, testifying to the kingdom of God and trying to convince them about Jesus both from the law of Moses and from the prophets.

KEY VERSE: Let it be known to you then that this salvation of God has been sent to the Gentiles; they will listen. Acts 28:28 (RSV).

HOME DAILY BIBLE READINGS

May 23. M. *The Dilemma of the Governor.* Acts 25:21–27.
May 24. T. *Paul's Advice to the Centurion.* Acts 27:9–11.
May 25. W. *A Word From the Lord.* Acts 27:21–26.
May 26. T. *Except These Abide in the Ship.* Acts 27:27–36.
May 27. F. *The Shipwreck.* Acts 27:37–44.
May 28. S. *On the Isle of Melita.* Acts 28:1–7.
May 29. S. *Paul's Ministry in Rome.* Acs 28:30,31.

BACKGROUND

Paul could never have dreamed of what was to happen to him on the long road to Rome.

First, there was a plot to kill him. Forty desperate Jews banded together and swore that they would neither eat nor drink until they had killed him. When the Roman commander discovered the plot, he hustled Paul out of the city under strong military guard to Caesarea, where he would be under the care of the Roman governor, Felix.

Felix was a repulsive character and a cruel, scheming governor: he threw Paul into jail and kept him there until he was succeeded as governor by Porcius Festus. Festus was a frightened little man anxious to curry favor with the Jews who shouted their false charges against Paul in his court. He hesitated to make any final decision as to the guilt or innocence of Paul until Paul, knowing that he would get no justice here, cried out, "I appeal to Caesar!" That put Festus in a bad position. If he sent this innocent man to Rome, he would disclose his inability to handle the matter, and Rome would not like that. But in the end, he had no choice; he *had* to respect the appeal of a Roman citizen—and he put Paul aboard ship for Rome.

Aboard ship, a prisoner, Paul won the respect of the Roman officer sent along to "guard him," saved the lives of the crew when the ship was wrecked in a storm at sea, and spent three months winning converts on the island of Melita (Malta). Another ship took them to Puteoli in Italy, one hundred and fifty miles from Rome.

NOTES ON THE PRINTED TEXT

One wonders what Paul was thinking as he started down the last leg of his journey to Rome. Luke doesn't give us much of a clue here; in the fewest possible words, he pictures the journey by sea to Puteoli, and the "foot journey" after that, but there are fascinating little touches in the story that Luke may never have intended to be fascinating. One is that the ship that took them from Melita to Puteoli had as a figurehead on its bow two figures of two Roman mythology—Castor and Pollux—who were the friends or gods of sailors. That's interesting, for this was a most friendly ship, in contrast with the first ship that had brought them to Malta. Paul was treated like a gentleman and a friend; it was almost a pleasant "cruise ship." There is no indication that Paul was downcast; he was going where he had always wanted to go.

From this point on, there were other things that must have warmed the heart of the apostle. On the dock at Puteoli, he found friends waiting to welcome him. Says Luke, "We found brethren" there. They may have been Christian converts living in the city, or they could have been friends who had come all the way from Rome. Paul must have remembered the words of God to him as he entered Corinth: "I have much people in this city" (Acts 18:10). He had many friends in many places that he never knew anything about until he met them!

The historian now is concerned with the reception given to Paul by three groups of people: those in the imperial city, those in the Church, and last but hardly least, the Jews.

The Romans bore no hatred for this man; they did not wish to persecute him. They accepted him simply as the leader of a (Jewish) faith in which they had little interest. The soldiers assigned to guard him were not his enemies, they became his friends, even when they were chained to him! They made it possible for him to stay seven days in Puteoli, preaching and teaching. Then, on the road to Rome, the (Christian) brothers of the city came out to meet him at the Forum on the Appian Way (forty-three miles from Rome) and at The Three Taverns (thirty-five miles out). Paul thanked God for them and "took courage" to go on. Then he reached the Eternal City, where the Romans generously allowed him to live wherever he pleased, but guarded by a soldier who must have hated being chained to a man he respected. Three days after his arrival, he asked the Jewish leaders to come and hear what he had to say. He told them of the unjust treatment he had received at the hands of the Palestinian Jews and insisted that he was still a loyal Jew held in chains only because he was completely devoted to the preaching of Jesus as Messiah—the hope and dream of all Israel.

That brought a mixed reaction. Some of the Jews accepted it and found no evil in him; others rejected him and his teaching. It was then that Paul, severe in his courage and consecration, issued a word of defiance to the rejecting Jews: He quoted their own prophet Isaiah (Isaiah 6:9,10), who had prophesied that doom awaited an Israel that heard the Word and warning of God and refused to understand them. Let the Jews who heard Paul understand that this was happening *now* with their rejection of Jesus as Messiah. Some Jews would be saved, but the nation would be rejected. "Be it known therefore unto you, that the salvation of God is sent unto the Gentiles, and that they will hear it" (Acts 28:28).

There was little comfort in that for the Jews, but it had to be said, had to be believed. It was an inspired insight into the future: *the Jewish re-*

jection of Jesus had thrown open the door to the Gentiles.

That ends the story as told by Luke. He does not go on to tell what happened to Paul after that; he does not describe his death and for a very good reason. Luke wrote Acts as a *history* and not as a biography of Paul—a history which tells us how the Church was founded, and how it broke out of the walls of Judaism to conquer the Gentile world and became a *universal* brotherhood. Luke says only that Paul spent the next two years in Rome; that is all.

How did Paul die? We have only a tradition about that, one which says that he was beheaded in Rome, and that may well be. In modern Rome, there is a splendid Church bearing a glorious name: it is called The Church of St. Paul's Without (beyond) the Walls. It is quite likely that Paul died near this spot, but in *our* Church, he is still tremendously alive; without him there might not be any church at all beyond the walls.

SUGGESTIONS TO TEACHERS

Luke is not writing an action-thriller. Although Acts 27,28 shake and roar with excitement, Luke wants to show that the mighty acts of the Spirit have succeeded even in bringing the Church to the world's mightiest capital—Rome! Your lesson should be organized to show that, in spite of difficulties and hardships, Christians may witness boldly and confidently because they know that ultimately the Gospel will triumph everywhere.

1. *PRACTICALITY OF MIND.* The gift of faith means good judgment. Being a believer never means being "out of touch" with practical matters. In fact, as with Paul on the journey to Rome, being a Christian seems to bestow good sense in such things as alerting the centurion that the ship's crew was secretly preparing to abandon ship (Acts 27:31), urging everyone to eat during a prolonged storm (27:33), gathering wood for a fire after shipwreck on the rainy, cold coast of Malta (28:3), and healing ill people on the island (28:8). Remind your class that Christians are meant to have their faces lifted upward, but their feet planted firmly on the ground, serving in practical ways.

2. *PARAGON OF ENCOURAGEMENT.* Paul, in spite of terrifying storms and shipwrecks on inhospitable coasts, in spite of personal discomfort and threat of execution in Rome, consistently tries to minister to others. In his urging others to take nourishment during the two-week spell of bad weather, he set an example of trust in the Lord by "giving thanks to God in the presence of all" so that "they were all encouraged and began to eat some food themselves" (27:35,36). Remark about ways in which Christians may encourage others in these times.

3. *PREPAREDNESS TO MINISTER.* Like Paul, Christians must stay alert to find opportunities to minister wherever they find themselves. There is no script or manual to state exactly how each person may serve in each set of circumstances. In unsettled and unsettling times such as these (our "storms at sea" when the world seems headed toward shipwreck), tell your people that they are called to be Christians regardless. Every believer may be useful and helpful somewhere in the Lord's service!

4. *PRESENTATION BEFORE CAESAR.* Luke shows how Paul even-

tually arrives in Rome to testify to the hope and power of the Gospel. Paul, although a prisoner, comes to the world capital as a conqueror. Like his Lord, he is a conqueror in chains. Although Paul's personal story is left without being concluded, God's story is told everywhere, including the mighty center of the Empire. Luke would have his readers understand that the Gospel overcomes all obstacles and ultimately spreads to every place on earth. Urge your hearers to contemplate the way in which they and Christians today are inheritors of that promise and that program! Like Paul, they are to spend all energies "preaching the kingdom and teaching about the Lord Jesus Christ" (28:31).

TOPIC FOR ADULTS
PAUL IN ROME

Foundation. Henry Thoreau once remarked it is all right to build castles in the air provided we put foundations under them. It is commonplace to suggest the foundation is the most important part of the structure, yet we continually need to be reminded of it. "The foundation is often quite unnoticed and disregarded," says Frederick Meek, "because the superficial observation of our society tends to pay much more attention to external impressions than to hidden quality and strength. And yet for lasting stability and strength there is nothing as important as the unseen foundation which the casual passerby is sure to miss."

Paul arrived in Rome, conqueror in chains but victorious nevertheless because his life was founded on Jesus Christ. With such a foundation, he could accept whatever befell him—death or life.

Pliable Heart. Paul did not know what would happen when he appealed to Caesar and was taken to Rome. He was prepared to face torture in the arena, if necessary, for the sake of the Gospel. Paul knew he was led and accompanied by the Spirit. He made his mark on Christians in his day and in subsequent days. A generation later, Irenaeus, renowned bishop of the early church, wrote this:

"Keep your heart soft and pliable for Him. Retain the form in which the Artist fashioned you, having moisture in yourself, lest, becoming hard, you should lose the marks of His fingers.

"But should you prove hardened and reject His artistic work and prove ingrate for being made man, with your ingratitude you have also lost His art and your life.

"For to make is the property of God, but to be made that of men."

Able to Risk Failure. "I can 'afford to fail,' since something good will be resurrected out of my failures, thereby rendering them other than simply failures. And grace has a lot to do with that.

"Grace means that there are two further consequences. One, I would describe by the phrase, 'little deaths, big resurrections'; by this I mean that a personal disappointment or miscalculation, a 'little death,' can be the occasion for a 'big resurrection,' the emergence of new possibilities, new hopes, a new life, in ways far beyond our calculation or miscalculation. It happens all the time: some unexpected and creative use is made of something we diffidently offer, and the realization that it is so comes as a pure gift. We discover that although grace did not seem apparent it was still there, transforming for good what we were fearful had only been for ill (Genesis 50:20).

"The other consequences of being able 'to afford to fail' is the discovery that we never do anything alone; not only do our actions always have consequences for others, but others can pick up and use and complete whatever it is we have initiated. The 'results' may be the work of other hands than ours, but in this we can rejoice."—Robert McAfee Brown, *Creative Dislocation—The Movement of Grace*, Abingdon, 1980.

Questions for Pupils on the Next Lesson. 1. Do you find many situations in your life where you are able to speak for God? 2. Do you wish you had more meaningful worship experiences? 3. Who is most supportive of you when you must wrestle with obstacles that test your faith? 4. Who are a few of the persons you know who are called of God and consecrated to His service? 5. How effective are you in being in a supportive role of others?

TOPIC FOR YOUTH
NO LIMIT ON FREEDOM

Freedom to Grow Has Pain. "When nine-year-old Scott Deindorfer asked a number of famous Americans their favorite sayings, actress Mary Tyler Moore replied, 'I guess my favorite quotation comes from my ballet teacher, who said to me: "If it doesn't hurt, you're not doing it right." I think you can apply this admonition to a great deal more than dance!'

"Every dancer and every athlete knows that muscles grow and harden only from exercise. Our minds, our knowledge and understanding, and consequently the quality of our lives follow the same growth pattern. Psychological growth is the result of learning experiences, but, like our muscles, our minds atrophy from inactivity, while vigorous exercise is often painful.

"Since we have a natural tendency to avoid pain, it requires a sufficient amount of self-discipline, dedication, or motivation to overcome the resistance to exercising our muscles and our brains and to do the things necessary to grow to our potential. As the great German writer Goethe put it, 'Everybody wants to be somebody; nobody wants to grow.'

"The kinds of growth experiences that are the most painful, and, consequently, the ones we are most inclined to shy away from are those that result from failure and defeat. At first this does not seem to pose much of a problem. If you have ever watched a young child learn to walk, you know that failures far outnumber successes. But this does not deter many youngsters for long. They get up, take a tenuous step, fall down, get up, and try again. If they waited until they could do it right the first time, they might never learn to walk."—From TAKING CHANCES by Robert T. Lewis. Copyright © 1979 by Robert T. Lewis. Reprinted by permission of Houghton Mifflin Company.

No Limit on Freedom. Sometimes, we never dream what great things God has in store for us for the future. We cannot see possibilities with Him for ourselves. We cannot understand the freedom which He gives us to *be* and to *do*.

We are often like the two caterpillars who were crawling across the grass when a butterfly flew over them. They looked up, and one nudged the other and said, "You couldn't get me up in one of those things for a million dollars!"

Free to Fail. The Apostle Paul could come to Rome because he was free to fail. Perhaps, in one sense, he did fail. We don't know for sure, but we think he probably died a martyr's death in Rome. Yet, in a greater way, he succeeded because he knew Christ gave him the freedom to try, to fail, but to be loved and enabled to go on.

Once, a young would-be writer came to Thomas J. Watson, the genius who headed IBM. The young man asked Watson for advice on how to succeed at writing.

Watson said that writing was not exactly his field, but offered him excellent counsel. "How many rejected manuscripts do you have?" Watson asked.

"A whole desk full," replied the dejected writer.

"That's fine," boomed Watson. "Every one of those manuscripts was rejected for a reason. Have you pulled them to pieces looking for that reason? You can be discouraged by failure, or you can learn from it. So go ahead and make mistakes, because that's where you'll find success. On the far side of failure!"

Sentence Sermon to Remember: They never fail who die in a great cause.—George Gordon Byron.

Questions for Pupils on the Next Lesson. 1. Do you have opportunities to speak on behalf of God? 2. How can you influence others in more positive ways? 3. Who helps support you when you're in times of crisis and need? 4. In what areas do you feel the strongest peer pressure—drugs, sex, alcohol, cheating, driving, or where? 5. Who looks to you for leadership?

JUNE, JULY, AUGUST 1983

OLD TESTAMENT PERSONALITIES

LESSON I—JUNE 5

AARON: SPOKESMAN AND PRIEST

Background Scripture: Exodus 4:10–17,27–31; 17:8–13; 28:1–4; 32:1–6; Leviticus 8:6–12; Numbers 20:22–29
Devotional Reading: Exodus 32:30–35

KING JAMES VERSION

EXODUS 4 14 And the anger of the LORD was kindled against Moses, and he said, *Is* not Aaron the Levite thy brother? I know that he can speak well. And also, behold, he cometh forth to meet thee: and when he seeth thee, he will be glad in his heart.

15 And thou shalt speak unto him, and put words in his mouth: and I will be with thy mouth, and with his mouth, and will teach you what ye shall do.

16 And he shall be thy spokesman unto the people: and he shall be, *even* he shall be to thee instead of a mouth, and thou shalt be to him instead of God.

27 And the LORD said to Aaron, Go into the wilderness to meet Moses. And he went, and met him in the mount of God, and kissed him.

28 And Moses told Aaron all the words of the LORD who had sent him, and all the signs which he had commanded him.

29 And Moses and Aaron went and gathered together all the elders of the children of Israel:

30 And Aaron spake all the words which the LORD had spoken unto Moses, and did the signs in the sight of the people.

17 9 And Moses said unto Joshua, Choose us out men, and go out, fight with Amalek: to morrow I will stand on the top of the hill with the rod of God in mine hand.

10 So Joshua did as Moses had said to him, and fought with Amalek: and Moses, Aaron, and Hur went up to the top of the hill.

11 And it came to pass, when Moses held up his hand, that Israel prevailed: and when he let down his hand, Amalek prevailed.

REVISED STANDARD VERSION

EXODUS 4 14 Then the anger of the LORD was kindled against Moses and he said, "Is there not Aaron, your brother, the Levite? I know that he can speak well; and behold, he is coming out to meet you, and when he sees you he will be glad in his heart. 15 And you shall speak to him and put the words in his mouth; and I will be with your mouth and with his mouth, and will teach you what you shall do. 16 He shall speak for you to the people; and he shall be a mouth for you, and you shall be to him as God."

27 The LORD said to Aaron, "Go into the wilderness to meet Moses." So he went, and met him at the mountain of God and kissed him. 28 And Moses told Aaron all the words of the LORD with which he had sent him, and all the signs which he had charged him to do. 29 Then Moses and Aaron went and gathered together all the elders of the people of Israel. 30 And Aaron spoke all the words which the LORD had spoken to Moses, and did the signs in the sight of the people.

17 9 And Moses said to Joshua, "Choose for us men, and go out, fight with Amalek; tomorrow I will stand on the top of the hill with the rod of God in my hand." 10 So Joshua did as Moses told him, and fought with Amalek; and Moses, Aaron, and Hur went up to the top of the hill. 11 Whenever Moses held up his hand, Israel prevailed; and whenever he lowered his hand, Amalek prevailed. 12 But Moses' hands grew weary; so they took a stone and put it under him, and he sat upon it, and Aaron and Hur held up his hands, one

12 But Moses' hands *were* heavy; and they took a stone, and put *it* under him, and he sat thereon; and Aaron and Hur stayed up his hands, the one on the one side, and the other on the other side; and his hands were steady until the going down of the sun.

13 And Joshua discomfited Amalek and his people with the edge of the sword.

on one side, and the other on the other side; so his hands were steady until the going down of the sun. 13 And Joshua mowed down Amalek and his people with the edge of the sword.

28 1 And take thou unto thee Aaron thy brother, and his sons with him, from among the children of Israel, that he may minister unto me in the priest's office, *even* Aaron, Nadab and Abihu, Eleazar and Ithamar, Aaron's sons.

2 And thou shalt make holy garments for Aaron thy brother, for glory and for beauty.

3 And thou shalt speak unto all *that are* wise hearted, whom I have filled with the spirit of wisdom, that they may make Aaron's garments to consecrate him, that he may minister unto me in the priest's office.

28 1 "Then bring near to you Aaron your brother, and his sons with him, from among the people of Israel, to serve me as priests—Aaron and Aaron's sons, Nadab and Abihu, Eleazar and Ithamar. 2 And you shall make holy garments for Aaron your brother, for glory and for beauty. 3 And you shall speak to all who have ability, whom I have endowed with an able mind, that they make Aaron's garments to consecrate him for my priesthood."

KEY VERSE: "He shall speak for you to the people; and he shall be a mouth for you, and you shall be to him as God." Exodus 4:16 (RSV).

HOME DAILY BIBLE READINGS

May 30. *M.* *Speaking for God.* Exodus 4:10–12.
May 31. *T.* *Willingness to Be Chosen.* Exodus 4:12–17.
June 1. *W.* *God's Credible Witness Through Persons.* Exodus 4:27–31.
June 2. *T.* *Obedience Brings Victory.* Exodus 17:8–13.
June 3. *F.* *Consecration Involves Community.* Exodus 28:1–3.
June 4. *S.* *Worshiping False Gods.* Exodus 32:1–6.
June 5. *S.* *Preparing for Ministry.* Leviticus 8:6–12.

BACKGROUND

In this last quarter, we are to meet a group of Old Testament personalities who offer us good examples of the *people* of the Book. Purposely, most of them are seldom the subjects of Sunday-school lessons; they are people who *supported* greater men in the work that the great were called of God to do. Some are remembered because they were *good;* others because they were poor examples to follow. The Bible is a very honest Book; if a biblical character was a good man or woman, he or she is pictured as good; if he or she were bad, the Bible tells the sad truth about them. Some were saints and some were unrepentant sinners; the Book never lies about them.

We start our study with Moses and his brother Aaron. Moses was, and still is, considered one of the Bible's greatest, a mountain of a man, the deliverer of Israel. But Moses, alas, had his bad moments. When God called upon him to go back to Egypt and bring his people out to freedom, he was full of excuses; he simply didn't want to go. Why *me,* he asked God. Who am I for such a mission? The Israelites and the Egyptians will laugh at me. They will not believe me. I am not an eloquent man. I could never convince Israel to come out of Egypt, etc., etc., ad nauseam.

And the Lord was angry with Moses—but He had just the man to do what Moses was afraid to do. This was Aaron, his own brother, a man almost obscured by the shadow of Moses.

NOTES ON THE PRINTED TEXT

Aaron had one great gift. God said to Moses, "I know that he can speak well" (Exodus 4:14). He could speak well enough to become the spokesman of Moses, his younger brother. Moses was ordained of God to "be as God to him," to speak to him as God would speak. Aaron would be the bumper between the elders and the people of Israel, between Pharaoh and the Israelites. He was to do what the fiery Moses could not do: talk in low key, reasonably, convincingly.

He was also one set aside to do the *praying.* He was a Levite—no, the senior member of that distinguished tribe of high priests which held sway over Israel for sixteen hundred years. Actually, Aaron was consecrated to a higher order than the Levites, who performed the menial tasks in connection with the furnishings and service of the Tabernacle. But he is still considered as the first head of the Hebrew priesthood, and that is important. Moses was the prophet; Aaron was the priest. When that designation was made, two vital institutions were established in Israel: prophetism and priesthood. In time, both institutions worked in perfect concert. The prophets prophesied; the priests kept the prophecies alive in the temples of Israel, just as the priests and ministers of our time keep the faith alive and active in the Church. Both prophet and priest are necessary to inspire and organize the people of God.

Aaron is seen at his best during a battle between Israel and the Amalekites—an old enemy of Israel, and said to be the descendents of Esau (Genesis 36:12), which would seem to make them distantly related to Israel! In this crucial battle, Moses, with Aaron and Hur, climbed a hill to watch the bitter fighting that involved the annihilation of Israel. As the story goes, when Moses held up his hands, Israel prevailed; when he dropped his hands, the Amalekites drove back the army of Israel. When his hands grew weary, Aaron and Hur stood at his side and held up his hands—and Joshua, in command of the army, mowed down the enemy as a scythe mows hay. That finished the Amalekite threat.

It is a good story, but it has some dubious aspects and interpretations. The great Moses seems a minor character; God does not enter the picture until the battle is won (verse 14). And we can wonder why Joshua seems to get no credit at all for really winning the fight. Still, it gives us a good picture of Aaron as the supporter of Moses, doing what had to be done in the crisis. In more ways than one, it was Aaron who saved Israel and Moses from failure if not from destruction.

"He was eloquent but unstable; witness his erection of the golden calf and his ridiculous explanation. He was often weak in danger and irresolute; witness his willingness to let Miriam take the whole blame for their foolhardy little rebellion. He was strong as long as he had Moses to lean upon. But when left to himself, he was quite apt to fail. Some men are valuable, but we cannot trust them far.

"His life is a study in chaos. Promise and uncertainty fought for him.

Uncertainty won. He died in disgrace, stripped of his robes and office. The mind of Moses dominated him and left him weak."—F. S. Mead, in *Who's Who in the Bible.*

Still, we had better be merciful, and not judge him before we judge ourselves. Too often, God needs humble supporters behind men called great, and too many of us fail Him there. We cannot all be leaders, but we can all do *something.*

SUGGESTIONS TO TEACHERS

Pat McConnell, brother of the well-known Methodist Bishop, Francis McConnell, used to laugh and describe himself as the victim of the second handshake. When Pat McConnell was introduced, people would politely greet him and casually accept his handshake. Almost invariably, however, someone would mention, "Reverend Pat McConnell here is the brother of Bishop McConnell." Whereupon the persons just introduced to Pat McConnell would seize Pat's hand and pump it vigorously—as if they had not shaken hands a moment earlier!

Lesser-known brothers often suffer from the "second handshake" syndrome. Aaron, Moses' brother, is another example. Your lesson will discuss this interesting and important figure in the Bible who was often overshadowed by a more famous brother. Throughout the lesson, you should point out ways in which each Christian is also called to be a spokesman and priest for the Lord.

1. *SPOKESMAN.* Aaron stands with his brother and offers his gifts of being able to speak in public in place of the tongue-tied Moses. Aaron obviously is a leader. He is also obedient to the Lord. Furthermore, Aaron has the courage to tell "all the words which the Lord had spoken to Moses" (Exodus 4:30). Ask your people whether they are willing to speak up for the Lord, especially when it takes courage!

2. *SUPPORT.* Have your class examine the Scripture passage (Exodus 17:8–13) in which Aaron props up Moses' arms during Joshua's crucial battle with the Amelekites; Aaron had an important part in making possible the victory. Although it might have seemed inconsequential, Aaron's supporting Moses' arms helped the Lord's cause to win. How often people such as those in your class are called upon to carry out apparently insignificant responsibilities but which prove to be extraordinarily significant to God's work! Have your people select examples from their experience, such as parenting or teaching. Have your class members note also how they may not get the credit or limelight that the Moses-types often receive! But that is not the important thing!

3. *SERVER.* Just as Aaron was selected and set apart as a priest, so every Christian is chosen and consecrated through baptism to be part of a community of priests. Remind your class that priests in Exodus 28:1–4 were ordained to serve the Lord. Impress on each person in your class that whether homemaker, bricklayer, student, bank president, or whatever, he or she is called by Christ to serve in His name. Discuss where the "parish" is for each Christian in your class.

4. *SINNER.* Aaron tragically weakened and went along with the crowd when it clammered for a golden calf like other people had as a worship-object. Take some time to talk over the pressures to "go along"

with the crowd which beset those in your class. Most important, point out that God's grace through Jesus Christ means a new beginning. We Christians are people with a second chance!

5. *SUCCESSOR.* Look at the Numbers 20 selection with your class, and have it noticed that Aaron helped train and install another, Eleazar, to take his place before he died. God gives us each a limited time to serve, then intends that we prepare others to take the responsibilities. How effectively is your church calling and training your Eleazars to succeed you and your generation?

TOPIC FOR ADULTS
AARON: SPOKESMAN AND PRIEST

The Time to Speak. Ever since the time of the Nazi atrocities, people have asked, "Why didn't decent, God-fearing people speak out? How could the people of a nation that produced great theologians, writers, and composers also create Auschwitz, Buchenwald, and the Holocaust?"

Looking back on the Nazi era, many Germans and others note that there were too few who were spokesmen and priests for God. Intimidated into silence, or indifferent to the issues, many decided not to speak out. There were few Aarons who acted as God's speakers. Says Pastor Martin Niemöller, the German theologian, "First the Nazis went after the Jews, but I was not a Jew, so I did not object. Then they went after the Catholics, but I was not a Catholic, so I did not object. Then they went after the Trade-Unionists, but I was not a Trade-Unionist, so I did not object. Then they came after me, and there was no one left to object."

God's Intolerance. "A pulpit is not a place to declare war, but it is a place to remind people who their God is. A pulpit is not a place to solve an international crisis, but it is a place to remind people that their God is a God of justice and to be mightily feared. . . . Jesus did not come with a geopolitical solution. But He did come to remind us that God is intolerant of oppression and is on the side of its victims."—Charles A. Perry, Provost, Washington Cathedral, in *Cathedral Age,* Spring 1980.

Testimony of an Ex-Hostage. Colonel Thomas Schaefer was held hostage in Iran for 444 days before being released in January, 1981, with the other fifty-two Americans held captive by Iranian militants. Like all of the hostages, Col. Schaefer conducted himself in ways that exemplify the best in American character. Col. Schaefer and the other hostages have not talked much publicly of their ordeal. Speaking for many of the fifty-two held for the 444 days of terror and uncertainty, Col. Schaefer has commented on the way their faith sustained them:

"I wonder how I could have gone through that experience without my God," states Col. Schaefer. Many times during the days of his captivity, he recalls, "I got to my knees and said, 'God, I need your help.' " Thomas Schaefer further testifies, "God was no further than a prayer away."

After 444 days in the hands of the Iranian militants, this Air Force Colonel chooses to relate the personal knowledge he has of God's strength and guidance. Like Aaron, Schaefer acts as a spokesman and priest for God. Do you?

Questions for Pupils on the Next Lesson. 1. In a world where people are often fickle and insensitive, how can you learn to trust others? 2. Whom do you usually turn to for advice, and why? 3. What qualities in another person inspire trust and friendship? 4. Do you sometimes have trouble accepting persons of a different culture? 5. What was the wisest advice you were ever given?

TOPIC FOR YOUTH
AARON: GIFTED SPOKESMAN

Now Communicates the Gospel. Joe English made tours and cut records as a drummer-vocalist for former Beatle Paul McCartney and the renowned British rock 'n' roll group Wings. He and Wings appeared before 3 million people and recorded more than twenty gold and platinum albums. Joe English, with fame and riches, left the choice position of vocalist-drummer because, as he puts it, "The Lord was knocking at my door." English still has the greatest respect for Paul McCartney and Wings and adds, "There was no falling-out, and I didn't get fired." He says he "ended up by retiring from the ranks of the superstars" in order to communicate the Gospel through music. Now operating out of Nashville with his own band, he plays and writes and makes albums to share the Good News of Jesus Christ.

There are many ways of being a gifted spokesman for the Lord. Aaron used speeches. Joe English uses rock. If you know the Lord has knocked on your door—which He's constantly doing—you'll use your gifts to tell others about Him!

Cell Block Spokesman for the Lord. Author of the widely-read *Pilgrim's Progress* and other religious books, John Bunyan was an English Baptist dissenter. Bunyan, a tinker's son, was from the lower classes and lived a reprobate boyhood. At seventeen, he served in the Parliamentary Army against King Charles I and was deeply affected by the death of a comrade and by the pageantry of the military. Returning home in 1646, he went through a severe emotional crisis, part of which was described in *Grace Abounding.* His bad dreams, guilt, and mental torment led the illiterate young man to careful religious investigation. John Bunyan finally, in 1653, joined a nonconformist congregation at Bedford and began to preach. The death of his first wife in 1656 drove him to deep Bible study and unleashed a zeal in preaching.

Bunyan was at first treated with contempt by the Establishment, then with uneasiness, as his speaking had a profound effect in the Bedford area. In 1660, with royalty restored in England, Bunyan was thrown into Bedford jail where he spent most of the next twelve years. He worried about his four small children, including a blind daughter, and his new wife but refused to agree to stop preaching as a condition for his release from jail. He tried to support his family while in jail by making shoelaces, and began his writing.

Released in 1672, he was jailed a second time not long afterward. During this term, he wrote his allegorical masterpiece, *Pilgrim's Progress,* which became an immediate best seller when published in 1678. After his final release, he was respected as an author and preacher. He died in 1688 from a chill incurred during a freezing rain while riding to bring about a reconciliation between a son and an angry father.

Center of Conversation. What, or who, do you like most to talk about? Yourself? or, the Lord?

Mae West, the self-centered, sultry-voiced actress, was her own favorite topic of conversation. She surrounded herself with admirers (usually musclemen, who in her later years were often a half-century younger than she). When the subject of the talk switched from Mae West to something else, such as world affairs, she would hum softly until the conversation returned to the one matter that interested her. Once the great Greta Garbo came to meet her. Mae was polite, but not particularly interested in the Swedish actress and spent the evening talking about herself and her career. As one reporter once described Mae West shortly after her death in 1980, "Her narcissism was as all-encompassing as a baby's."

Are you, like Mae West, merely a spokesman for yourself and your career? Do you want to hum until the conversation revolves around you? Or have you grown up to realize that the Good News is Jesus Christ, and not your minor accomplishments? What are you communicating? Of whom do you choose to speak mostly?

Sentence Sermon to Remember: Before we can speak God's message, we must learn to listen. The opened ear comes before the opened mouth.—A. B. Simpson.

Questions for Pupils on the Next Lesson. 1. For what are you willing to sacrifice? 2. In what areas in your life, do you feel you have important responsibilities? 3. Are you truly able to rejoice in the good fortune of others? 4. Why do you find it is sometimes difficult to accept advice from parents and family members? 5. To whom do you turn for advice, and why?

LESSON II—JUNE 12

JETHRO: WISE ADVISER

Background Scripture: Exodus 2:15–3:1; 4:18; 18:1–27
Devotional Reading: John 1:43–51

KING JAMES VERSION

EXODUS 18 13 And it came to pass on the morrow, that Moses sat to judge the people: and the people stood by Moses from the morning unto the evening.

14 And when Moses' father in law saw all that he did to the people, he said, What *is* this thing that thou doest to the people? Why sittest thou thyself alone, and all the people stand by thee from morning unto even?

15 And Moses said unto his father in law, Because the people come unto me to inquire of God:

16 When they have a matter, they come unto me; and I judge between one and another, and I do make *them* know the statutes of God, and his laws.

17 And Moses' father in law said unto him, The thing that thou doest *is* not good.

18 Thou wilt surely wear away, both thou, and this people that *is* with thee: for this thing *is* too heavy for thee; thou art not able to perform it thyself alone.

19 Hearken now unto my voice, I will give thee counsel, and God shall be with thee: Be thou for the people to God-ward, that thou mayest bring the causes unto God:

20 And thou shalt teach them ordinances and laws, and shalt shew them the way wherein they must walk, and the work that they must do.

21 Moreover thou shalt provide out of all the people able men, such as fear God, men of truth, hating covetousness; and place *such* over them, *to be* rulers of thousands, *and* rulers of hundreds, rulers of fifties, and rulers of tens:

22 And let them judge the people at all seasons: and it shall be, *that* every great matter they shall bring unto thee, but every small matter they shall judge: so shall it be easier for thyself, and they shall bear *the burden* with thee.

23 If thou shalt do this thing, and God command thee *so,* then thou shalt be able to endure, and all this people shall also go to their place in peace.

24 So Moses hearkened to the voice of his father in law, and did all that he had said.

REVISED STANDARD VERSION

EXODUS 18 13 On the morrow Moses sat to judge the people, and the people stood about Moses from morning till evening. 14 When Moses' father-in-law saw all that he was doing for the people, he said, "What is this that you are doing for the people? Why do you sit alone, and all the people stand about you from morning till evening?" 15 And Moses said to his father-in-law, "Because the people come to me to inquire of God; 16 when they have a dispute, they come to me and I decide between a man and his neighbor, and I make them know the statutes of God and his decisions." 17 Moses' father-in-law said to him, "What you are doing is not good. 18 You and the people with you will wear yourselves out, for the thing is too heavy for you; you are not able to perform it alone. 19 Listen now to my voice; I will give you counsel, and God be with you! You shall represent the people before God, and bring their cases to God; 20 and you shall teach them the statutes and the decisions, and make them know the way in which they must walk and what they must do. 21 Moreover choose able men from all the people, such as fear God, men who are trustworthy and who hate a bribe; and place such men over the people as rulers of thousands, of hundreds, of fifties, and of tens. 22 And let them judge the people at all times; every great matter they shall bring to you, but any small matter they shall decide themselves; so it will be easier for you, and they will bear the burden with you. 23 If you do this, and God so commands you, then you will be able to endure, and all this people also will go to their place in peace."

24 So Moses gave heed to the voice of his father-in-law and did all that he had said.

KEY VERSE: "You and the people with you will wear yourselves out, for the thing is too heavy for you; you are not able to perform it alone. Exodus 18:18 (RSV).

HOME DAILY BIBLE READINGS

June 6. M. Caring for Others. Exodus 2:17–21.
June 7. T. Meeting God in Daily Life. Exodus 3:1.
June 8. W. Recognizing the Signs of God. Exodus 4:8.
June 9. T. Rejoicing in Deliverance. Exodus 18:1–12.
June 10. F. The Good Stewardship of Time. Exodus 18:13–27.
June 11. S. Responsible Decision Making. Exodus 18:19–28.
June 12. S. Delegating Authority. Exodus 18:24–27.

BACKGROUND

Jethro (whose name meant *excellence*) was a noble shepherd-priest of a Midianite tribe called Kenites. The Kenites were coppersmiths—a tribe of prosperous traveling tinkers or gypsy smiths famous for their artistry with copper and iron. It was to the home of Jethro that Moses fled after he had killed the Egyptian taskmaster (Exodus 2:12). Moses married Jethro's shepherdess daughter, Zipporah, who bore him two sons; he stayed in the home of Jethro for forty years, until he was called by God to lead the Hebrews out of Egypt.

That was a good marriage; it gave Moses not only a good wife but an "excellent," understanding father-in-law who played a great role in the life of the great deliverer. Fathers-in-law, as well as mothers-in-law, can often be more of a hindrance than a blessing; here, it was all blessing.

In our lesson, we find Moses and his people at the foot of Sinai; they have made a successful escape from Egypt. Hearing of it, Jethro, taking with him Zipporah and her two sons, goes out to meet Moses at the foot of the mountain.

NOTES ON THE PRINTED TEXT

What a gathering that was! Jethro, a priest with complete devotion to God, offers sacrifices of thanksgiving to God and then sits down with the family and the leaders of Israel to partake of the sacrificial feast. We might call it a Thanksgiving Day dinner. After all the trials and tribulations and sufferings of the Exodus, we have a scene in which there was affection, sympathy, and love. But it was more than just a nice family gathering.

The next day, Jethro and Moses sat down to talk about what was to be done now that Israel was free. Jethro was more than happy with the accomplishments of his indomitable son-in-law, but there was one thing that worried him. To put it in the fewest possible words, Moses was working himself to death. At the risk of making himself obnoxious, Jethro says to Moses, "Thou wilt surely wear away, both thou, and this people that is with thee: for this thing is too heavy for thee; thou art not able to perform it thyself alone" (verse 18).

What was Moses doing to deserve that friendly criticism? He was doing many things that he should *not* have been doing. His main error was that of a top executive who tries to do everything and fails to assign minor tasks and responsibilities to capable assistants. Moses was wearing himself out doing things that others could do just as well as he could and who should be doing them.

This was particularly evident in the area of justice. Moses was sitting, day after day and night after night, as a sort of Chief Justice of a Supreme Court. Week in and week out, he was surrounded by crowds of people who came to him with minor grievances that could have been settled in a local court. People with petty grievances, like disputes over the right to draw water or law suits against debtors who owed a debt of small change. The strength of the great leader was being overtaxed and the patience of the people was being exhausted as they waited for justice in an over-crowded court.

Moses, warned Jethro, should not be concerned with trivialities; he was called for a greater work—the work of leading people in the ways they should go in company with God. He should be teaching the people the will of God for them, teaching ordinances and laws laid down by Him.

There was a better way. Jethro offered two suggestions: let Moses present only *serious* cases to God in prayer, and let him establish a series of courts presided over by men of ability—like *our* series of courts which run from local magistrate courts to district courts to supreme courts. He should set up "rulers (judges) of thousands, and rulers of hundreds, rulers of fifties and rulers of tens" (verse 21). These judges would have to prove to the people that they were fit to rule, fit to judge, God-fearing, truthful, and hating covetousness (strong enough morally to refuse a bribe in any case or any court). And Moses, great and powerful as he was, heeded the advice of his father-in-law, and "did all that he had said."

Several lessons are offered here to the modern reader. One is that Moses shows himself to be a great *administrator* here and demonstrated his humility in accepting Jethro's advice. He proved his wisdom when he set up a system of justice which made a distinction between enacting laws and administering justice.

He did not inaugurate these reforms as a dictator; he established them by way of a democratic method: he left to the people the privilege of selecting their own rulers and judges. And even before they established themselves in the Promised Land, his people had a system of law and order that has been imitated all across the centuries.

This is all history. But we are more interested in the characters of the two men in this lesson than we are in historical events. We see in Moses the perfect leader: highly talented and deeply consecrated. He was never too proud to take advice from lesser men; he did not rule as a tyrant, but as a servant of God and servant of God's people. There was no selfishness in him.

And Jethro? Amos R. Wells thinks of Jethro as a labor organizer, and that is not as strange as it seems. Says Wells: "Really, it is supremely selfish as well as supremely foolish to insist on doing yourself all the work in sight. In few ways, can you help men more than by setting them at honorable tasks. An organizer of labor is the highest type of laborer. To every man his trade. When the merchant spends hours at home in tinkering with the faucets and painting the kitchen ceiling and mending the front steps, he not only wrongs the plumber, painter, and carpenter . . .

but he generally wastes more than he saves, in time and temper as well as in money.

"Find out what God has put you into the world to do, and then do it. Whatever else you do, do that. Get the help of others in doing it, and utilize them to the full. Moses for the mount, and not for the police court!"—From *Biblical Miniatures*, by Amos R. Wells.

If Jethro were a member of your church, what suggestions do you think he might make about how you run that church?

SUGGESTIONS TO TEACHERS

Have you ever noticed that people often need to turn to someone for advice? "Dear Abby" and "Ask Ann Landers" and a dozen syndicated counsel-giving columnists receive thousands of letters. Palm readers and fortune-tellers enjoy a brisk business. Your pastor tries to answer an astonishing number and variety of questions from those wanting advice.

Where do you suggest people go when they feel overwhelmed by decisions and problems? What do you think such people should look for in an adviser? This is the overview of your lesson for this Sunday. Jethro, a wise adviser, offers meaningful insights.

1. *HOSPITABLE.* Jethro welcomes a stranger. He offers hospitality to a foreigner. Significantly, that stranger-foreigner eventually marries one of his daughters. Jethro's graciousness not only brings him a fine son-in-law, Moses, but also deeply influences the course of history. Use some of your class time to discuss the place of ***hospitality*** in the life of Christians. Who are the strangers in our society today? What exactly is required of Christians in regard to practicing hospitality today (*see* 1 Peter 4:9, Hebrews 13:2, etc.)? How may welcoming refugees be a form of hospitality?

2. *HOPEFUL.* Jethro is a trusting, generous relative. When Moses announces his intention of returning to Egypt, Jethro does not try to hold him back. He will not control or direct his son-in-law. He thinks the best and hopes the best. Jethro can serve as model for us in our family relationships. Allow the class to reflect on the way God is eternally hopeful for us. We in turn may live with hope for others—including those in our own families about whom we sometimes have our doubts. How high are the "hope level" and "trust level" in the families represented in your class?

3. *HUMBLE.* Jethro hears about Moses' claims about encountering the Presence of the Lord in the burning bush. Jethro believes his son-in-law. He recognizes that Moses has had an authentic spiritual experience. Jethro affirms Moses' faith. Suppose Jethro had not encouraged Moses? What might have happened if Jethro had disparaged Moses' stammering report of God's call through the burning bush? Jethro wisely counseled Moses to take seriously the call of the Lord. Is your church humbly listening to the younger members of your congregation when they try to share their faith-experiences? Are there Jethros among your church family who are encouraging growth in faith for the budding Moseses in God's community in this generations?

4. *HELPFUL.* Jethro gently teaches Moses how to delegate duties when he finds the distraught son-in-law trying to do too much. Jethro helps Moses to learn to trust others, to organize a group of "elders," and

to share responsibility with them. Jethro has the wisdom to assist Moses. He also has the wisdom to approach Moses in a way that will not belittle or threaten Moses. Discuss the key traits of a good adviser with your class. How is the Holy Spirit the One who gives advice today? (Remind your people that the Spirit is called "the Counselor" throughout the New Testament!) How may the Holy Spirit advise us today?

TOPIC FOR ADULTS
JETHRO: WISE ADVISER

Influence of an Adviser. Alan Paton, the noted author, tells of the influence of Railton Dent in his life.

"He was I think the most upright person I ever was to know, and his influence on me was profound. He did not make me into a good man; that would have been too much. But he taught me one thing, the theme of which will run through this book, with undertones (or overtones, I never know which) of victories, defeats, resolutions, betrayals, that life must be lived in the service of a cause greater than oneself. This can be done by a Christian for two reasons: one is obedience to his Lord, the other is purely pragmatic, namely that one is going to miss the meaning of life if one doesn't.

"How Railton Dent taught me this, I don't quite know. I suppose that my reverence and affection for him was so great that I caught it from him. And I must have caught it thoroughly, because in the course of my life which I have not considered conspicuously good, I have never given up trying to be obedient, nor have I ever lost the pragmatic belief that I was going to miss something of the greatest importance if I did not treat my life as not being altogether my own property."—Alan Paton, *Towards the Mountain.* Copyright © 1980 by Alan Paton (New York: Charles Scribner's Sons, 1980). Reprinted with the permission of Charles Scribner's Sons.

Tomorrow's Another Day. Leo Durocher, manager of the old New York Giants, gave a weeping rookie named Willie Mays some support after Mays had gone one and sixteen in his major league debut. "Tomorrow's another day, kid, and you're going to be playing centerfield tomorrow."

God offers each of us the same new start. We are given a fresh, clean, new day to begin a day that offers new tensions, new problems, new situations, to be sure—but also a day offering new opportunities, new beginnings, and new joys.

God has the same kind of trust in us as Durocher had in Mays. Don't waste your days. Use them wisely in His service.

Power of a Jethro. Often teachers and other adults active in working to advise the young feel discouraged and ineffective. Says Locke Bowman, who has been a Jethro to a generation of young Moseses in the Church:

"Teaching is, by its own nature, not a profession that yields a lot of tangible returns—and especially not in the first decade or so. . . . The teacher who has simply tried to be faithful in activating thought and whose life is given to helping students to create for themselves frequently is never able to know whether anything at all has resulted from the work. Students are rarely inclined to tell their teachers what they have been learning (creating inwardly). Indeed, the students may not even realize that it was a teacher who got something going for them; that may be a fact lying dormant and unrecognizable for years to come. Small wonder, then, that we 'lose heart' and feel lonely in a ministry of teaching. Did our Lord feel less lonely, less deserted?"—*Teaching Today: The Church's First Ministry*, Locke E. Bowman, Jr., Westminster Press.

Questions for Pupils on the Next Lesson. 1. Why are people sometimes afraid to risk to obtain their goal? 2. Do you honestly find yourself developing patience as you work to fulfill your major goals? 3. To what are you most loyal? Why? 4. Have you ever found yourself holding an opinion not shared by the majority and under pressure to go along with the rest? 5. Under what conditions do you find the greatest strain on your trust in God's promises?

TOPIC FOR YOUTH
JETHRO: SHARE THE LOAD

The Hassle Factor. Most persons aren't always sure what decision to make. Where do you turn when you have to make important choices? For example, let's say you have to make up your mind whether to take a certain job in a certain town. To help advise you, Indiana University professor Richard Farmer has come up with a new rating called the Hassle Factor to help resolve such perplexing decisions. *The Hassle Factor* lists a dozen things that influence the quality of life and suggests that each be assigned a value from one to ten, depending on how important it is to you. Farmer's factors are bureacracies, shopping, security, medicine, commuting, repairmen, neighbors, utilities, pollution, recreation, education, and climate. After rating the importance of each factor, you then rate its local quality on a zero-to-ten scale. The two ratings are multiplied for a total score for each factor. The Hassle Factor index for the area you are considering is the total of all factors divided by the total possible score. To Farmer, any place "that is 84 percent hassle-free is a fairly pleasant place to live."

Even with such tools as Professor Farmer's *Hassle Factor*, you still need a Jethro. You still need advice. You still need someone who will share the load. Your Church, through trusted pastors, teachers, and leaders, may be trusted to provide the "Helping Factor"—the way Jesus Christ helps you and intends you, in turn, to help others. In spite of the hassles of life, He stands as The Counselor!

Stop Digging. We all must learn to wait for God's counsel. Sometimes, we insist on trying to check on what God's doing.

One day, a young minister ran into an older friend. The older Christian asked how things were going. "I'm so discouraged," admitted the young pastor. "I've been working in that church for over two years. I have struggled. I've done everything I think I should have, but there's simply nothing happening. Nothing. I'm about ready to quit."

"Cal," replied the wiser, older Christian, "You're sure you're preaching the Gospel?"

"Yes, sir."

"You're sure you're sowing the seed of God's Word, Cal?"

"I know I am!"

"Then," smiled the Jethro to this young Moses, "stop digging it up to see if it has sprouted!"

Main Business in Life. Dr. William Osler, the celebrated Canadian-born physician and professor of medicine at McGill, the University of Pennsylvania, Johns Hopkins, and Oxford, wrote authoritative books on diseases of children and scientific treatises on illness of the digestive system. Dr. Osler claimed that the turning point in his future, which aided him to become one of the most famous and respected surgeon-teachers in the world, came when he read some words from Thomas Carlyle. Osler, accepting Carlyle as his Jethro, quoted Carlyle's words: "Our main business in Life is not to see what lies dimly at a distance, but to *do* what lies clearly at hand."

Christ calls you not so much to peer into the impossible future but to serve Him by doing what you can where you are, starting now.

Sentence Sermon to Remember: A helping word to one in trouble is often like a switch on a railroad track—but one inch between a wreck and smooth rolling prosperity.—Henry Ward Beecher.

Questions for Pupils on the Next Lesson. 1. Do you sometimes lack the courage to disagree with the crowd? 2. Have you ever found satisfaction in being in a supporting role? 3. Why does it require patience to be loyal to a cause or a person? 4. What are the biggest risks in your life? 5. Why are Christians often out of step with society?

LESSON III—JUNE 19

CALEB: LOYAL AND PATIENT

Background Scripture: Numbers 13:1–6,30–33; 14:24; 32:10–12; Joshua 14:6–15
Devotional Reading: Acts 11:19–26

KING JAMES VERSION

NUMBERS 13 30 And Caleb stilled the people before Moses, and said, Let us go up at once, and possess it; for we are well able to overcome it.

31 But the men that went up with him said, We be not able to go up against the people; for they *are* stronger than we.

32 And they brought up an evil report of the land which they had searched unto the children of Israel, saying, The land, through which we have gone to search it, *is* a land that eateth up the inhabitants thereof; and all the people that we saw in it *are* men of a great stature.

33 And there we saw the giants, the sons of Anak, *which come* of the giant: and we were in our own sight as grasshoppers, and so we were in their sight.

14 24 But my servant Caleb, because he had another spirit with him, and hath followed me fully, him will I bring into the land whereinto he went; and his seed shall possess it.

32 10 And the LORD's anger was kindled the same time, and he sware, saying,

11 Surely none of the men that came up out of Egypt, from twenty years old and upward, shall see the land which I sware unto Abraham, unto Isaac, and unto Jacob; because they have not wholly followed me:

12 Save Caleb the son of Jephunneh the Kenezite, and Joshua the son of Nun; for they have wholly followed the LORD.

JOSHUA 14 8 Nevertheless my brethren that went up with me made the heart of the people melt: but I wholly followed the LORD my God.

9 And Moses sware on that day, saying, Surely the land whereon thy feet have trodden shall be thine inheritance, and thy children's for ever, because thou hast wholly followed the LORD my God.

REVISED STANDARD VERSION

NUMBERS 13 30 But Caleb quieted the people before Moses, and said, "Let us go up at once, and occupy it; for we are well able to overcome it." 31 Then the men who had gone up with him said, "We are not able to go up against the people; for they are stronger than we." 32 So they brought to the people of Israel an evil report of the land which they had spied out, saying, "The land, through which we have gone to spy it out, is a land that devours its inhabitants; and all the people that we saw in it are men of great stature. 33 And there we saw the Nephilim (the sons of Anak, who come from the Nephilim); and we seemed to ourselves like grasshoppers, and so we seemed to them."

14 24 "But my servant Caleb, because he has a different spirit and has followed me fully, I will bring into the land into which he went, and his descendants shall possess it."

32 10 "And the LORD's anger was kindled on that day, and he swore, saying, 11 'Surely none of the men who came up out of Egypt, from twenty years old and upward, shall see the land which I swore to give to Abraham, to Isaac, and to Jacob, because they have not wholly followed me; 12 none except Caleb the son of Jephunneh the Kenizzite and Joshua the son of Nun, for they have wholly followed the LORD.' "

JOSHUA 14 8 "But my brethren who went up with me made the heart of the people melt; yet I wholly followed the LORD my God. 9 And Moses swore on that day, saying, 'Surely the land on which your foot has trodden shall be an inheritance for you and your children for ever, because you have wholly followed the LORD my God.' "

KEY VERSE: " 'Surely the land on which your foot has trodden, shall be an inheritance for you and your children for ever, because you have wholly followed the Lord my God.' " Joshua 14:9 (RSV).

HOME DAILY BIBLE READINGS

June 13. M. Spies Sent to Canaan. Numbers 13:1–3,17–20.
June 14. T. An Evil Report of the Land. Numbers 13:20–33.
June 15. W. The Challenge to Caleb and Joshua. Numbers 14:1–10.
June 16. T. God's Promise Regarding Caleb. Numbers 14:10–24.
June 17. F. God Recognizes Caleb's Faith. Numbers 32:10–15.
June 18. S. Hebron Given to Caleb. Joshua 14:6–14.
June 19. S. Prayer for Deliverence. Psalms 142.

BACKGROUND

Moses led his Israelites from Sinai to Kadesh in the wilderness of Paran; here they were standing at the gates of Canaan, and on the threshold of the Land of Promise pledged to Father Abraham. That was not too long a march, but there was trouble, smoldering rebellion and talk of going back to Egypt. One would have thought that, once they got that close to the Promised Land, they would have rushed in and taken it. But—no. On the brink of victory, they hesitated, and fear got a good grip on them, and they "played for time." They suggested that Moses send spies into the Land to find out more about it before they marched in. They were a frightened lot, and Moses must have been ashamed of them, but he was wise enough to realize that what they suggested was really good strategy. No good commander marches into strange territory until he has learned at least a little of what he is going to be up against when he gets there! So Moses appointed twelve spies to go in and study the land and report to him of what they found there, in terms of a good arable land on which to settle, and how well it was defended against invasion. One spy for each of the twelve tribes. They went in and studied the country from the wilderness in the south to Hamath in the extreme north, and they came back with an alarming report—and the biggest cluster of grapes ever heard of anywhere, as proof that this was a land of milk and honey, a rich, good land. But!

What a "but"! It cost them forty years, and death in the wilderness for almost all of them. He who hesitates is *lost!*

NOTES ON THE PRINTED TEXT

Ten of the spies agreed that they had seen a fertile land; the grapes and the other fruits they brought back testified to that. *But* their forty days in the new land had shown them something else; the land was fruitful, yes, but the people living there were "something else." They were a mighty people, living in well-fortified cities. All up and down the land they saw strange people called Ahimanites, Sheshites and Talmites—all families descended from a mystical and mysterious people called Anakim, a race of physically powerful giants about whom true and false tales were spread in the land. Giants! The spies saw them, and trembled in fear and felt like so many grasshoppers in their presence. Ten out of the twelve spies spread that report among the people, and the people believed it and flew into a panic. Why, they screamed, had God—and Moses—brought them here to die at the hands of these giants? Why were they to be denied this "land of milk and honey," which now became in their eyes and their fear a land that "devours its inhabitants" (fails to support them)? Fear swings a terrible whip; it can make cowards out of men born strong.

We once heard a famous marathon runner say, "If a man thinks he is licked in the race of life, he *is* licked." If he faces an enemy or a problem feeling that he is a grasshopper facing a giant, he is beaten before he begins. Israel, in accepting the reports of the ten spies (the *false* reports born of fear) stood on the threshold of complete annihilation. Fortunately for them, there were two among the spies with the courage of heroes: Caleb and Joshua. They practically called the other spies liars, reminded the weak in heart that God loved them and that God had promised to give them this land at the gates of which they now stood, that God would go with them if and when they entered it, and that to rebel against God now meant nothing but destruction.

That was the pity of the whole thing: Israel was not only rebelling against Moses; *she was rebelling against God.* "Fear not the invisible giants, Israel: fear God and go in and possess the land He has promised to give you." So said Caleb.

So one man stood up for God, one who was different from the rest of them in that "he had another spirit with (within) him"—the very spirit of complete faithfulness to God in *every* situation. What a minority Caleb was! A minority of one, in the eyes of the people, but an unconquerable majority of two in the eyes of God. That proves something: the minorities who live and fight on God's side have an amazing ability to win.

Studs Terkel, in a thrilling book entitled *American Dream: Lost and Found,* makes a statement hard to forget. He says that, "The world has always been saved by an Abrahamic minority." That statement is packed with truth. If we had been alive at the time of the American Revolution, how many of us would ever have thought that a string of little colonies along the Atlantic coast could defeat mighty England? How many, the day Jesus was crucified, would have believed that the faith of twelve humble disciples could topple the Roman Empire? Truly *active* Christians have always been a minority, but look at what they have accomplished!

Caleb was never honored as a great hero by his people; he lived quietly and went on humbly "wholly following the Lord." For that, the Lord rewarded him, allowed him, along with Joshua, to enter the Promised Land; the others, those who were twenty years old or older, died in the wilderness as God had promised! (Numbers 14:29). Forty-five years later, Caleb comes to Joshua asking for a land-grant in the hills of Hebron. He got it along with a war; he had to fight "the sons of Anak" to hold it.

Humble, yes; but he was more than great because, almost alone, he always looked forward to Canaan and never back to Egypt. That is a habit peculiar to God's minority.

SUGGESTIONS TO TEACHERS

A famous track coach once remarked that he always found plenty of competitors for the dashes. His hardest job was to encourage and train takers for the long-distance runs. This coach stated that few seemed to want to build up the stamina and put up with the tedium of a series of laps or cross-country runs.

The same could be said of the Christian life. Discipleship is more like a grueling long-distance marathon than a short sprint. It is often lonely. It demands commitment and patience. Your lesson on Caleb illustrates these dimensions of living as God's person.

1. *MINORITY.* As Judah's tribal representative on the team of twelve spies, Caleb is sent on a long reconnaissance mission into the Promised Land. Nearly all of the others lack the "long-distance runner" aspects of faith that Caleb has. They are ready to quit. They bring back a majority report dripping with pessimism. Only Caleb and Joshua persist in believing in possible victory. Caleb realizes the loneliness and unpopularity of being in a minority. Your class must grow in appreciating that Christians are often forced into positions of bringing in a minority report. Frequently, our society belittles or ignores our claims for God and the Promised Land. Have your class members bring out occasions when they have had to endure the loneliness and unpopularity of holding a view or taking an action which has not been accepted by most others.

2. *MALIGNED.* Caleb had a confidence born from his faith in the Lord. Therefore, he courageously urged a decisive advance into the Promised Land. He finds himself opposed by petty, fearful types who finally resort to spreading lies and rumors. Your class should remember that God's men and women are sometimes opposed and maligned. The class should remind itself of the experience of Caleb, the prophets—and Jesus. God's people must be prepared to face slander and endure lies.

3. *MEASURED.* The Lord states, "Caleb, because he has a different spirit and has followed me fully, I will bring into the land" (Numbers 14:24). Caleb's attitude ultimately brings him victory—entrance to the Promised Land of Canaan. It took many years of waiting. It required trust in God's promise. It demanded patient waiting and working. Eventually, Caleb's loyalty and patience were vindicated. He measured life's course from God's perspective. Point out the need for such loyalty and patience with the Lord on the part of each Christian believer in these difficult times.

4. *MAGNANIMOUS.* Although Caleb had to wait forty-five years before he received a plot of real estate in the Promised Land (he was given Hebron), he unswervingly lived with the knowledge that God keeps His commitments. He believed that God is good! State to your class the certainty that we Christians have in God's goodness through Jesus Christ. The Lord of the universe has spelled out His magnanimous mercy through the Incarnation, Crucifixion, and Resurrection.

TOPIC FOR ADULTS
CALEB: LOYAL AND PATIENT

Life's Encounter. A Christian man or woman knows that God has revealed Himself in Jesus Christ, and that man or woman will be loyal and patient in spite of life's adversities. As John Krumm states, "Revelation means the involvement of God in human history. Revelation is God's entrance into history, bearing in a personal way all the pain and ugliness and sin of it. The orthodox Christian, confident that life is fundamentally an encounter with a personal God, is of all men the most flexible, the most resilient, least likely to be overwhelmed in despair or reduced to panic when favorite doctrines and ideas must be discarded or radically revised."—John M. Krumm, *Modern Heresies,* Seabury.

Phony Predictions. Christians are sometimes unsettled by the shrill predictions of self-styled Bible "experts." On Sunday, January 25, 1981, some believers were startled to read a half-page advertisement in the *New York Times* by a St. Petersburg, Florida, man "proving" that before June 20, 1981, the "Rapture" would take place. By *Rapture,* this author meant, "the removal from the earth of all living people that have accepted Jesus as the Personal Saviour and been born again." The same writer, computing dates from what he claimed to be "prophecies" in Scripture and a list of recent world events, attempted to frighten readers into joining his cause before the 1981 deadline.

As any person familiar with Church history knows, the screaming headlines from the St. Petersburg voice are simply part of a long list of those setting dates and deadlines for the Lord and His people. Believers in every age must have Caleb's qualities of loyalty and patience under stress and provocation. Christians must remember that God has His own schedule, but He does not give Scripture as a cryptic message from which we decode a secret time line. Like Caleb, we are intended to work steadily and confidently with the Lord each day, leaving the future in His hands.

Delight and Rejoice. John Adams, the great American President and statesman, had suffered a long seige of ill health. By 1814, he was also nearly blind and could not enjoy his books. Wracked by a persistent cough and fever, he realized that old age was leaving him weaker and less resistant to sickness. Most of his closest associates and friends had died. Adams, however, was undaunted. The old Massachusetts elder statesman had once studied for the ministry and retained a deep faith throughout his long life. In 1814, in spite of his pain, weakness, and loneliness, Adams wrote, "Yet I delight and rejoice in life."

With a Caleb-like loyalty and patience because of the Lord, Adams could continue to delight and rejoice in life. So may, indeed, so *must* every Christian!

Questions for Pupils on the Next Lesson. 1. What are some of the occasions when you have had to serve as a leader and other times when you have had to be in a supporting role? 2. Where do you find encouragement and support in order to fulfill the demands placed on you? 3. Have you ever sensed the need to take a prophetic stand? 4. Why are some people reluctant to share credit and recognition? 5. Do you sometimes feel the need for credit and recognition? If so, what do you do?

TOPIC FOR YOUTH
CALEB: LOYAL AND PATIENT

George Johnson's Confidence. In 1928, an Indian trapper named George Johnson bought a new Chevrolet and had it delivered by boat to his place in Tesline Lake, in northern Canada's Yukon. George Johnson's neighbors hooted. After all, there were no roads near his place. Johnson assured them that someday there would be. As the years went past, the neighbors often smiled as they pointed to the Chevy at George Johnson's. George finally began to use the car as a duck blind. He insisted, however, that the day would come when he would be vindicated. During World War II, the Alcan Highway was built as a military supply line to protect Alaska and the Aleutians from Japanese attack. In 1948, the road was opened for civilian traffic. George Johnson was the first tourist on the Alcan. As he drove his 1928 Chevrolet out of the driveway from his place at Tesline Lake on to the highway, his previously dubious neighbors gathered and cheered. George Johnson's faith in the future was proven correct!

Christians have an even deeper sense of certainty for themselves and the future. Like Caleb, who patiently and loyally stuck to his faith in the Lord through many ups and downs, believers in our day must live with the laughter and sneers of others. But God always vindicates those who trust in Him.

Confidence in the Church. Perhaps you find it hard to be patient with the Church. Your loyalty may be wavering. The following true story may help you to gain a better perspective.

In the days when Napoleon Bonaparte cast his imperial shadow across most of the map of the Western world, he found himself unhappy with many of the policies of the Church. Napoleon made a number of demands on the Pope and clergy. One day, the Emperor summoned Cardinal Ercole Consalvi, the papal Secretary of State. Napoleon had another order to have delivered to Pope Pius VII and gave the Cardinal a long lecture on the Emperor's policies.

"Do you know that I can destroy your church?" shouted the fiery Napoleon.

Consalvi dared a small smile.

"Your majesty," replied the Cardinal, "not even we priests, in eighteen centuries, have been able to do that."

You may find new loyalty and patience, like Caleb, by remembering that God continues to have plans for His community, in spite of what some leaders may do.

Persevering in Loyalty and Patience. The young dentist was broke and discouraged. He felt rejected. He finally had to admit that he was a failure in dentistry. Discarding his career hurt his pride. Life seemed to grow worse when he became seriously ill. Recovering from the long illness, he began to write. He patiently felt that he would find a purpose in his life. His tales of the West helped him forget his own inner ache. The young ex-dentist's loyalty to the ideal that the Lord had a purpose for him encouraged him to send some of his stories to a publisher. Soon he began to find funds and recognition from his writing. He took the name *Zane* from his birthplace of Zanesville, Ohio, and Zane Grey's great list of titles of adventure in the Old West such as *The Last of the Plainsmen* and *Riders of the Purple Sage* won him a place of deep affection in the hearts of readers everywhere.

Sometimes, like Caleb, you may be a small minority in which nearly everyone and everything is against you. Persevere in loyalty and patience! God remembers and helps!

Sentence Sermon to Remember: The greatest contributions in man's upward march have been made not by unbelieving majorities, but by believing minorities.—Anonymous.

Questions for Pupils on the Next Lesson. 1. When was the last time you spoke any words of positive encouragement to anyone? 2. Do you find yourself sometimes serving both as a leader and as a supporter? Are you able to be comfortable in both roles? 3. Does your church help you realize that it is acceptable to celebrate God's goodness? 4. Where do you get the recognition you need? 5. Why are some people loath to give recognition and credit to others?

LESSON IV—JUNE 26

DEBORAH: SUPPORTER AND LEADER

Background Scripture: Judges 4,5
Devotional Reading: Acts 16:11–15

KING JAMES VERSION

JUDGES 4 4 And Deborah, a prophetess, the wife of Lapidoth, she judged Israel at that time.

5 And she dwelt under the palm tree of Deborah, between Ramah and Bethel in mount Ephraim: and the children of Israel came up to her for judgment.

6 And she sent and called Barak the son of Abinoam out of Kedesh-naphtali, and said unto him, Hath not the LORD God of Israel commanded, *saying*, Go and draw toward mount Tabor, and take with thee ten thousand men of the children of Naphtali and of the children of Zebulun?

7 And I will draw unto thee, to the river Kishon, Sisera the captain of Jabin's army, with his chariots and his multitude; and I will deliver him into thine hand.

8 And Barak said unto her, If thou wilt go with me, then I will go: but if thou wilt not go with me, *then* I will not go.

9 And she said, I will surely go with thee: notwithstanding the journey that thou takest shall not be for thine honour; for the LORD shall sell Sisera into the hand of a woman. And Deborah arose, and went with Barak to Kedesh.

14 And Deborah said unto Barak, Up; for this *is* the day in which the LORD hath delivered Sisera into thine hand: is not the LORD gone out before thee? So Barak went down from mount Tabor, and ten thousand men after him.

15 And the LORD discomfited Sisera, and all *his* chariots, and all *his* host, with the edge of the sword before Barak; so that Sisera lighted down off *his* chariot, and fled away on his feet.

16 But Barak pursued after the chariots, and after the host, unto Harosheth of the Gentiles: and all the host of Sisera fell upon the edge of the sword; *and* there was not a man left.

5 1 Then sang Deborah and Barak the son of Abinoam on that day, saying,

2 Praise ye the LORD for the avenging of Israel, when the people willingly offered themselves.

3 Hear, O ye kings; give ear, O ye

REVISED STANDARD VERSION

JUDGES 4 4 Now Deborah, a prophetess, the wife of Lappidoth, was judging Israel at that time. 5 She used to sit under the palm of Deborah between Ramah and Bethel in the hill country of Ephraim; and the people of Israel came up to her for judgment. 6 She sent and summoned Barak the son of Abinoam from Kedesh in Naphtali, and said to him, "The LORD, the God of Israel, commands you, 'Go, gather your men at Mount Tabor, taking ten thousand from the tribe of Naphtali and the tribe of Zebulun. 7 And I will draw out Sisera, the general of Jabin's army, to meet you by the river Kishon with his chariots and his troops; and I will give him into your hand.' " 8 Barak said to her, "If you will go with me, I will go; but if you will not go with me, I will not go." 9 And she said, "I will surely go with you; nevertheless, the road on which you are going will not lead to your glory, for the LORD will sell Sisera into the hand of a woman." Then Deborah arose, and went with Barak to Kedesh.

14 And Deborah said to Barak, "Up! For this is the day in which the LORD has given Sisera into your hand. Does not the LORD go out before you?" So Barak went down from Mount Tabor with ten thousand men following him. 15 And the LORD routed Sisera and all his chariots and all his army before Barak at the edge of the sword; and Sisera alighted from his chariot and fled away on foot. 16 And Barak pursued the chariots and the army to Harosheth-hagoiim, and all the army of Sisera fell by the edge of the sword; not a man was left.

5 1 Then sang Deborah and Barak the son of Abinoam on that day:

2 "That the leaders took the lead in Israel,
that the people offered themselves willingly,

princes; I, *even* I, will sing unto the LORD;
I will sing *praise* to the LORD God of Israel.

bless the LORD!
3 "Hear, O kings; give ear, O princes;
to the LORD I will sing,
I will make melody to the LORD,
the God of Israel.

KEY VERSE: "If you will go with me, I will go; but if you will not go with me, I will not go." Judges 4:8 (RSV).

HOME DAILY BIBLE READINGS

June 20. M. *The Canaanite Oppression.* Judges 4:1–3.
June 21. T. *Deborah and Barak.* Judges 4:4–9.
June 22. W. *Defeat of the Canaanites.* Judges 4:10–16.
June 23. T. *The End of Sisera.* Judges 4:17–22.
June 24. F. *God Is Our Refuge and Strength.* Psalms 46:1–7.
June 25. S. *Deborah and Barak Thank the Lord.* Judges 5:1–5.
June 26. S. *Bless the Lord for Victory.* Judges 5:6–18.

BACKGROUND

Women in the Old Testament are too often described as "second-class citizens," as mere chattels with few "rights" of their own. That simply is not true. There were women in early Israel who rose to places of great respect above the men of the times, and Deborah was one of them. She was the wife of Lapidoth (poor man, that is all we know about him) and she was the first prophet to succeed Moses. She was the only female judge in Israel, and she was famous early in life and influential as a judge who, like all judges, sat at the gate of her city and held court. Her decisions in that court were fair and intelligent. Occasionally she was called upon to hear complaints about atrocities inflicted upon the Israelite homesteaders by the Canaanites.

As judge she was just; as prophetess her predictions were fulfilled; and, as coordinator with a soldier named Barak, she won a victory that ended the threat of the Canaanites forever and united the scattered Jewish tribes as no one before her had been able to do. Greatest among the women of her day was Deborah.

NOTES ON THE PRINTED TEXT

Deborah used to sit under a palm tree in the days when she was a judge in the hill country of Ephraim. That is a lovely touch in her story: it is a scene of peace and justice. But even in those quieter days, the blood of this woman boiled at the spectacle of Israel writhing under the heel of "King" Jabin of the Canaanites who ruled by terror over a space of twenty years. Deborah had good eyes; she saw the end of Israel if Jabin were to rule much longer. The suffering Hebrews lacked a leader to bring them out of their lethargy and to go out to meet Jabin's troops in battle. Such a battle seemed to them to be impossible; they were not strong enough, etc., etc.

But Deborah had the strength and the vision that they lacked. When she could stand it no longer, she sent for an outstanding soldier named Barak. Deborah never planned to lead a rebellion, herself, against Jabin; she knew nothing of military strategy, but she knew that she had her military leader in Barak; she sent for him and told him that, if he could raise an army of ten thousand men, she could promise him a victory over the army of Sisera, Jabin's general in the valley near Megiddo. Barak said he would go out and fight on one condition: that Deborah go with him. She went. She became a flaming torch, an ancient Joan of Arc putting courage into the hearts of weak men. She stirred the old fighting spirit in the tribes of Ephraim, Benjamin, West Manasseh, Zebulun, Naphtali and Issachar. They gathered, ten thousand strong, on or near the slopes of Mount Tabor.

Down below on the plain of Esdraelon, General Sisera waited for them; Josephus, the great Jewish historian, says that Jabin had three hundred thousand foot soldiers at his command, ten thousand horsemen and three thousand iron chariots (with knives spinning at their hubs). But we must be careful about these figures in "thousands upon thousands," which appear often in the Old Testament. It is not quite likely that the Canaanite had three hundred thousand at the foot of Tabor, but he did have those terrifying chariots, plus the high morale that came out of previous victories. Surely, they could annihilate this little band of rural rebels led by a woman!

Down from Tabor, in a wild roar, swooped the army of Barak; they struck at the rear of Sisera's men in a surprise attack, routed them, sent the terrified horses who drew the chariots into panic. They had assistance in this attack that they never expected: one of those sudden storms of rain and hail broke over the Canaanites, blinding their archers and concealing their enemies—and they broke and ran. The host of Sisera was wiped out; "and there was not a man left" (verse 16). Even Sisera perished: another woman, Jael, drove a tent pin through his head.

Two women and a man! Deborah was the inspiration, Jael was the assassin, Barak was the soldier. The place was Esdraelon. And there is a legend which says that the last battle in the world, the Armageddon that will preceed the millennium, will be fought there. It could be. Many strange things happen in this warring world which are puzzling beyond all sense and explanation. This was certainly true in this story of Deborah. Barak won a great victory on a field that was stained with the blood of a thousand battles; he won because he trusted the faith and vision of Deborah, and that is the gist of the whole story. Had it not been for Deborah, Barak would never have marched. But it is Deborah we remember; she represents the host of those through whom the greater host of men hear the voice of God and learn of His will for them. No wonder Barak refused to fight unless Deborah went with him. No wonder that many mothers still name their daughters *Deborah*, never Jael, and no fathers ever name their sons *Barak*.

We wonder: what would Deborah be doing if she were alive today in our "man's world"? Can we imagine her as a quiet little housewife? Or would she still be a judge in one of those courts dealing with the problems of homes and children? Or a Congresswoman wielding real influence in the governing bodies of our land? Women judges, in our time, have won respect, and so have women legislators. So have women who have become ordained ministers in our churches! Dr. Deborah might have easily become one of those!

But in another sense, Deborah is still with us, still a woman giving inspiration to men in positions of power and to generation after generation of the children of men. "The place of women" is a subject that has been argued ever since Eve. More and more, as time flies by, woman has risen to higher and higher places and greater respect and love. Mary Carolyn Davies has put it well when she says that, "Women are doormats and have been—the years these mats applaud—they keep the men from going in—with muddy feet to God."

SUGGESTIONS TO TEACHERS

Today's lesson is intended to be more than the biography of a brave woman. It is also meant to show that a leader must be a supporter, and a supporter must be a leader. Deborah, Barak, and Jael exemplify the way in which God's people are both supporters and leaders of each other.

1. *ACKNOWLEDGED.* Deborah provides you and your class a unique opportunity to be reminded that the Bible puts women in important leadership roles. In spite of the discrimination against women that continues, even in the Church, the Scriptures offer many examples of women as leaders. Deborah is one. People went to her for help in making important decisions. The nation looked to her as a leader.

2. *APPOINTS.* Deborah selects Barak to be commander-in-chief of the nation's army. She does more than appoint; she also accompanies him when requested. Deborah supports her commander by going in person to the battlefield when Barak needs her encouragement. Deborah, a superb example of a good leader, gives support and counsel to those serving with her. Like true leaders in God's work, she has no *prima donna* complex. The main thing is to carry out God's will. Let the implications of Deborah's example soak into the thinking of your class.

3. *ATTACKS.* Deborah's unshakable confidence in God steadies her, Barak, and the army. When the mighty enemy under the terrible Sisera threatens Israel, Deborah rallies the troops; "Up! For this is the day in which the Lord has given Sisera into your hand. Does not the Lord go out before you?" (Judges 4:14). God-fearing Deborah commands Barak to attack and brings about a stunning victory. The woman or man who knows the Lord will not be daunted by any threats but will press ahead. It would be profitable to take some lesson time to think of the "Siseras" and the "900 chariots of iron" which sometimes appear to be ready to overwhelm us individually or to threaten the future of the Church. Of what are members of your class most frightened? What sinister powers seem to be more than your congregation or denomination can handle? How may your trust in the power of the Living Lord enable your church to withstand "Siseras" and "iron chariots"?

4. *ACCLAIMS.* Have your class look at the Song of Deborah in Judges 5. Read it first as one of the earliest and greatest pieces of Hebrew poetry. Also read it for its message. Deborah sings of the Lord's strength and goodness. Credit for the startling victory over Sisera and his 900 iron chariots must be given to God, not to Israel or Barak or Deborah! Hers is the hallmark of a true leader: the humility to acclaim God and not one's own accomplishments. Are your class members willing to recognize the Lord as the One to whom all praise, honor, and glory are due?

5. *AFFIRMS.* The Song also applauds Jael. Time permitting, you can go over the details of how this heroine coolly faced the terrorism of Sisera. This story offers your class still another example of the way women may be affirmed as well as men in the story of God's people.

TOPIC FOR ADULTS
DEBORAH: SUPPORTER AND LEADER

"As Soon As. . . ." Shopping-bag ladies are social outcasts who walk the streets of most major cities, but few of the people who look at them with pity or disgust know anything about them. Nor did Ann Marie Rousseau when she began teaching art at a shelter for homeless women in Manhattan.

"But so many of the women said they had spent time in the streets that I decided to interview those still out there," said Miss Rousseau.

In all cities, the women share common fears. "They are in constant danger of sexual attack, no matter how old, ugly, or dirty," said Miss Rousseau, "and they're all targets of thieves who believe the myth about their having lots of money. They stay awake all night because it's too dangerous not to," she said. About 40 percent had alcohol-related problems.

Shopping-bag women are ashamed of their sorry state, but most believe their condition is only temporary. Even people who have been on the street ten years say they'll get back on their feet as soon as they can get a check or a job.

The "as-soon-as-I-can-get . . ." syndrome prevails also beyond the circle of shopping-bag women. How often you or I say, "As soon as I get a better job," "As soon as I get a raise," "As soon as I get settled," "As soon as I get. . . ." Then, at that distant point, we are sure that everything will be fine. As soon as we acquire this or achieve that, we will be happy.

The Deborahs of the world, supported and led by the Lord, don't have to make excuses or fantasies about the future. Deborahs are doers for God. They lead. They support. Today.

Knows Deep Channel. Captain Eliot Winslow owns a fleet of six tugboats in Maine. He is often called to assist in launching ships. In Bath, Maine, the shipyard is sixteen miles up the Kennebec River from the ocean. However, high ocean tides push saltwater upstream to the launching site. When the tides flow in or out, the river is particularly treacherous. Dangerous rocks protrude from the shore and river bottom which can rip open the ship of a careless skipper. Captain Winslow has navigated these waters for many years.

Recently, the Bath shipbuilding company launched an enormous container ship, and Captain Winslow and his tugs were called to assist. The container ship, longer than three football fields laid end to end, had to be nudged carefully from the shipyard and down the river. A bridge, carrying automobile and railroad traffic, stands only 400 yards downstream from the launching site. The huge hull had to be guided by Eliot Winslow's tugs around this obstacle.

The wife of the admiral for whom the new container ship had been named was standing on the bridge of the tug with Captain Winslow. Marveling at his skill as he quietly gave commands to his tugs to ease the enormous ship safely past the bridge and down the narrow rocky banks of the Kennebec, she said, "I suppose, Captain, that you know every rock in this river."

Winslow was silent for a long while before answering, "No," he replied, "I don't know where all the rocks are, but I do know the deep channel."

Captain Winslow, who had to serve both as a leader and a supporter, knew where the safe depths were and could guide his craft to its destination without disaster. The same is true in life. We may not know where all the dangers are, but when we know the deep channel of God's care and guidance, we may launch forth in confidence. Faith in this Lord means such a certain channel. These waters run deep, and we may sail with safety! We also may be both leader and supporter.

Head Count. "Women constitute more than half the population of the United States and nearly 40 percent of the labor force, yet, according to the government's latest employment figures, they represent barely 5 percent of the nation's lawyers, 3 percent of all dentists, 4 percent of the architects, and 1 percent of all engineers. There are, for example, 35,501 major airline pilots in this country—only 1 of them is a woman. What do all the working women do? Well, they are secretaries (2,638,033), typists (920,612), keypunch operators (244,674), cleaners and charwomen (252,423), registered nurses (807,350), bank tellers (214,879), file clerks (292,252), waitresses (907,466), and teachers (2,064,228). The question remains: Whose world is it?"—*Today's Health,* May 1975.

Questions for Pupils on the Next Lesson. 1. What was Jephthah's rash vow? 2. How have rash promises had dire consequences in your life? 3. What are some of the most serious promises you have made during your life? Why were they important? 4. What allies does your church seek to serve it in various undertakings? 5. Why must a Christian have both zeal and wisdom?

TOPIC FOR YOUTH
DEBORAH: ENCOURAGING WORDS

Who Is She? A park ranger found a woman about thirty, near death, naked and suffering from exposure in dense underbrush at High Taylor Birch State Park in Fort Lauderdale, Florida, on September 19, 1980. Rushed to a hospital, doctors restored her health in due time. Her memory, however, was gone. The attractive, obviously well-educated woman had no identifying marks on her body. Her fingerprints were not in any files. Her speech revealed no regional accent. "I try to remember and I can't," said the woman; "I just feel left alone in the world . . . just trying to go about my life the best I can." Doctors began calling her Jane Doe. In February 1981, Jane Doe went on national television in an effort to find people "who know me better than I know myself." After more than 500 inquiries, the woman was reunited with her family. She has not regained her memory.

The unfortunate woman suffered from amnesia. Others, although not technically ill, suffer from what we could call "spiritual amnesia" in that they apparently forget their roots with God. They lose a sense of their identities as His daughter or son. They experience feelings of anxiety and confusion. They don't realize that their pasts are rooted in God's love.

They lack the security of being part of His family. They want the sense of purpose for the future which remembering Him brings.

God has already spoken encouraging words about you through Jesus Christ. He has told you that you belong to Him. Therefore, you begin to know who you are. You may be encouraged by being comfortable with Him and with yourself.

Once you know this, you are encouraged to encourage others! You are encouraged to bring an identity as God's son or daughter to those you meet! No anonymous Jane Doe or John Doe with the Lord! You and all the men and women you know are led and supported to become persons in Christ.

Busy Bees. Bee experts point out that bees make less honey amidst the abundance of early spring flowers than later on. The reason is that honey bees find themselves flying about in the general abundance and failing to pause long enough to gather precious nectar. Therefore, they produce a small quantity of honey in their hives.

If we are so distracted by the abundance of activities and anxieties around us, we will never pause long enough to gather strength from the Lord. We will not be encouraged by Him. Without His encouragement, we can produce little. We are unable to encourage others. Like the bees flitting busily among the flowers without pausing, we will not be a source of encouragement for those near us. We fail in our destiny.

The Christian life means taking a lesson from Deborah, the woman close to the Lord in Judges. Encouraged by the Lord, Deborah encouraged others. Your encouraging words to others will come only when you hear the encouraging Word God has spoken to you in Jesus Christ.

Well-Laid Keel. The old fisherman at Boothbay Harbor, Maine, had been seriously ill. His doctor was surprised at his tremendous strength—both physical and spiritual. After the old lobsterman recovered, the physician commented that he was astonished at the stamina and resiliency of the old salt. The fisherman, who usually had little to say, replied with typical down-east brevity, "Yup. I've a well-laid keel."

What a picturesque way of describing the basis for one's spiritual life also! The keel of a ship or boat is the most basic and important part of the hull. If it is strong and carefully constructed, the vessel will endure the pounding of waves and jarring of rough use for many, many years. A person who firmly establishes his or her faith in the powerful certainty of God's providence will endure almost anything.

Do you have a "well-laid keel" of trust in the living, loving Lord?

Sentence Sermon to Remember: All virtuous women, like tortoises, carry their houses on their heads, and their chapel in their hearts, their danger in their eyes, and their souls in their hands, and God in all their actions.—Jeremy Taylor.

Questions for Pupils on the Next Lesson. 1. What are some examples of unfortunate consequences because of poor decisions you have made? 2. Why is it so hard to face the consequences of some rash decisions we have made? 3. Why do we often want immediate satisfaction and overlook the undesired consequences? 4. What was the rash decision that Jephthah made? 5. What are the most important promises you have made or expect to make? Why?

LESSON V—JULY 3

JEPHTHAH: ZEAL WITHOUT WISDOM

Background Scripture: Judges 11:1–12:7
Devotional Reading: Matthew 26:30–35

KING JAMES VERSION

JUDGES 11 7 And Jephthah said unto the elders of Gilead, Did not ye hate me, and expel me out of my father's house? and why are ye come unto me now when ye are in distress?

8 And the elders of Gilead said unto Jephthah, Therefore we turn again to thee now, that thou mayest go with us, and fight against the children of Ammon, and be our head over all the inhabitants of Gilead.

9 And Jephthah said unto the elders of Gilead, If ye bring me home again to fight against the children of Ammon, and the LORD deliver them before me, shall I be your head?

10 And the elders of Gilead said unto Jephthah, The LORD be witness between us, if we do not so according to thy words.

29 Then the Spirit of the LORD came upon Jephthah, and he passed over Gilead, and Manasseh, and passed over Mizpeh of Gilead, and from Mizpeh of Gilead he passed over *unto* the children of Ammon.

30 And Jephthah vowed a vow unto the LORD, and said, If thou shalt without fail deliver the children of Ammon into mine hands,

31 Then it shall be, that whatsoever cometh forth of the doors of my house to meet me, when I return in peace from the children of Ammon, shall surely be the LORD's, and I will offer it up for a burnt offering.

32 So Jephthah passed over unto the children of Ammon to fight against them; and the LORD delivered them into his hands.

33 And he smote them from Aroer, even till thou come to Minnith, *even* twenty cities, and unto the plain of the vineyards, with a very great slaughter. Thus the children of Ammon were subdued before the children of Israel.

34 And Jephthah came to Mizpeh unto his house, and, behold, his daughter came out to meet him with timbrels and with dances: and she *was his* only child; beside her he had neither son nor daughter.

REVISED STANDARD VERSION

JUDGES 11 7 But Jephthah said to the elders of Gilead, "Did you not hate me, and drive me out of my father's house? Why have you come to me now when you are in trouble?" 8 And the elders of Gilead said to Jephthah, "That is why we have turned to you now, that you may go with us and fight with the Ammonites, and be our head over all the inhabitants of Gilead." 9 Jephthah said to the elders of Gilead, "If you bring me home again to fight with the Ammonites, and the LORD gives them over to me, I will be your head." 10 And the elders of Gilead said to Jephthah, "The LORD will be witness between us; we will surely do as you say."

29 Then the Spirit of the LORD came upon Jephthah, and he passed through Gilead and Manasseh, and passed on to Mizpah of Gilead, and from Mizpah of Gilead he passed on to the Ammonites. 30 And Jephthah made a vow to the LORD, and said, "If thou wilt give the Ammonites into my hand, 31 then whoever comes forth from the doors of my house to meet me, when I return victorious from the Ammonites, shall be the LORD's, and I will offer him up for a burnt offering." 32 So Jephthah crossed over to the Ammonites to fight against them; and the LORD gave them into his hand. 33 And he smote them from Aroer to the neighborhood of Minnith, twenty cities, and as far as Abel-keramim, with a very great slaughter. So the Ammonites were subdued before the people of Israel.

34 Then Jephthah came to his home at Mizpah; and behold, his daughter came out to meet him with timbrels and with dances; she was his only child; beside her he had neither son nor daughter. 35 And when he saw her, he rent his clothes, and

35 And it came to pass, when he saw her, that he rent his clothes, and said, Alas, my daughter! thou hast brought me very low, and thou art one of them that trouble me: for I have opened my mouth unto the LORD, and I cannot go back.

said, "Alas, my daughter! you have brought me very low, and you have become the cause of great trouble to me; for I have opened my mouth to the LORD, and I cannot take back my vow."

KEY VERSE: There is a way which seems right to a man, but its end is the way to death. Proverbs 14:12 (RSV).

HOME DAILY BIBLE READINGS

June 27. *M.* *Choosing a Leader.* Judges 11:1–11.
June 28. *T.* *Message to a King.* Judges 11:12–28.
June 29. *W.* *A Tragic Vow.* Judges 11:29–40.
June 30. *T.* *The Way of Wisdom.* Proverbs 14:8–18.
July. 1. *F.* *The Value of Wisdom.* Proverbs 3:13–24.
July 2. *S.* *Unwise Promises.* Matthew 26:30–35.
July 3. *S.* *God's Wisdom.* 1 Corinthians 1:18–31.

BACKGROUND

The tribal heroes of early Israel were sometimes good and capable and sometimes shallow and unworthy of any hero worship. During the period of the Judges (419 years), between Joshua and Samson, we have an array of independent warring chieftains who were indeed both good and bad. Up to the time of Jephthah in our lesson for today, we find Othniel (good), Ehud (bad), Shamgar (good), Barak and Deborah (good), Gideon (very good), Abimelech (very bad), and Tola and Jair (useless). When we come to Jephthah we have a man never born to be a judge or a hero, but an outlaw and an accidental hero who was both good *and* bad. His story is a fascinating riddle.

At the moment of his rise to power, Israel was once more at war, this time against the Ammonites. The war was the result of a dispute over land—the land east of Jordan. The Ammonites claimed that this was *their* land; they had been its first settlers, and the Israelites were intruders who had no right whatever to the land. When they ran out of arguments, as is usually the case, they went to war.

The tribes of Israel were ready and eager to fight, but they had one very serious difficulty: they had no capable leader, no experienced chieftain to direct the fighting.

NOTES ON THE PRINTED TEXT

The call to lead the troops of Israel against those of Ammon fell upon a man whom *we* might think the last man in Gilead worthy of the honor: this was Jephthah, an outlaw, who had been driven from the home of his father. Judges 11:1 calls him "a mighty man of valour, and he was the son of an harlot." That says much in the fewest possible words. Jephthah was the illegitimate son of a good father and a harlot mother. He was despised in that family by his legitimate brothers, who hated him not because of his mother but because he grew up to be a man of formidable physique and strong, independent mind. They were less admirable than he was, but, like the brothers of Joseph, they wanted to be rid of him in order that they might inherit their father's estate.

Jephthah had three choices as to what he could do, as he left his father's house: he could live as a hermit in the wilderness or the desert, he could become a common laborer, or he could seek refuge with one of the roving bands of ex-soldiers or lawless men who lived on what they could steal at the point of the sword. Jephthah chose the bandit's way. Before long, he was recognized and feared as the most powerful terrorist in the land.

Then came the trouble with the Ammonites who were making life unbearable for the Israelites—including the vicious brothers who had driven him into the wilderness. They came begging to the harlot's son; they "ate crow" bitterly, but they had no choice. This despised brother was their only hope. Jephthah could have berated them and refused to help them, but he was not that brand of man. He came home to Gilead, got his army organized for the battle, and prepared to move.

Before he moved, he went to his knees and made a promise to the Lord: if the Lord would deliver the children of Ammon into his hands (help him win this battle), then "whatsoever cometh forth of the doors of my house to meet me, when I return in peace . . . shall surely be the Lord's, and I will offer it up for a burnt offering" (verse 31). That raises some questions. Did Jephthah know and worship Israel's God, or was he following the old pagan practice of trying to bribe the gods? And did he promise to sacrifice *something* ("Whatsoever") or *someone* (some *person*)? Our Revised Standard Version of the Bible says it was "*whoever* comes forth from the doors of my house. . . ."

Either way, Jephthah went out and won his battle, came home in triumph—and saw his daughter come out of his house "with timbrels and with dances." He could not run to meet her, to hold her in his arms; he could only weep, brokenhearted, could only cry out, "Alas, my daughter, thou hast brought me very low. . . ." It was a moment of unspeakable horror; his bitter cup overflowed.

But read on. He was brought very low, but "I cannot take back my vow." And he kept it, and thereafter "lived in a world of moan." Grim as it seems, as foolish as his vow was, he kept his word—kept it because his daughter insisted that he keep it! Here the emphasis shifts from father to daughter. Here a battle more desperate than the battle Jephthah had just won gave way to a greater battle in the heart and soul of a girl! Who could blame her if she had fled into the wilderness to save herself from a death she did not deserve? She did not do that. She insisted that the vow be kept—and, when she did that, she roused the mind of Israel to put a stop to such sacrifice. If this sacrifice of an innocent was necessary or acceptable, then their Jehovah was no better than the pagan Baal who seemed to love human sacrifice. Overwhelmed by the spectacle of the dying girl, the people remembered that in their ancient law (in Leviticus 27:5), it had been laid down that such a vow as Jephthah made could have been redeemed by the payment of ten shekels!

What the daughter did brought about the end of human sacrifice in Israel forever. This girl, not a victim but a martyr, accomplished that.

Jephthah was great. He was also courageous, rash, and short-sighted, and faithful to a vow. The daughter was loyal, loving, tragically beautiful; she gave her one life for her people. Was God pleased with her sacrifice—or more pleased with her contribution to the future of her people? Which think you the greater, the father or the daughter?

SUGGESTIONS TO TEACHERS

A well-known children's bedtime story describes an elephant who has too much zeal and too little wisdom. The impetuous elephant decides to help a chicken hatch her eggs. When the elephant sits on the nest, however, he smashes the eggs.

Starting this new unit this Sunday on Persons Choosing Priorities, you will open with the story of a man who "smashes the eggs," so to speak, by having zeal without wisdom. You and your class may be repelled by some of the gory details in the biblical passages. Remember, however, that the Bible is realistic about us humans. It tells it "like it is" about all people. And the Bible also states plainly the way God persists in involving Himself in our human story.

1. *HUMBLE ORIGINS.* Why did God choose Jephthah? Look at his background: son of a prostitute. The lesson must be brought home to every person in your class that God works with unpromising material. He uses persons from poor origins and humble backgrounds. The Lord chose and worked through Jephthah. Have your class recall other such cases from the Bible, such as Moses the fugitive, David the shepherd boy, Mary and Joseph (poor people of Nazareth), the apostles. Since this Sunday is nearest July 4th, some may also remember heroes and heroines of insignificant homes who seemed to have been raised up by God in times of national crises. Emphasize mostly the fact that each one in your class, regardless of his or her background, is selected by the Lord for some special service.

2. *HISTORIC APPEAL.* Jephthah begins well, and tries to avoid bloodshed by appealing to history (Judges 11:12–28). He has a sense of the past. He uses this in his discussions with the Ammonite king. Jephthah also has a sense of God's working through history. He calls on this in trying to negotiate with the king of Ammon. Do members of your class have a sense of the past in which they are mindful of God's guidance? Help your people to understand that God's activities may be discerned for the present by noting these in the past, especially in the biblical story.

3. *HORRIBLE OATH.* Jephthah makes a reckless promise. Although he realizes he has made a rash vow, he insists on fulfilling it because he feels his honor is at stake. How often we end by killing our children in wars because we think our national honor is at stake. And is our pride over race not sometimes causing us inadvertently to cause the deaths, emotionally if not physically, of youngsters who happen to be non-white? A misplaced sense of honor, zeal without wisdom, remind your class, can ultimately bring ruin and death to our most precious possessions—our children!

4. *HATEFUL EPHRAIMITES.* Talk with your class about coping with the Ephraimites. This surly group, resentful because they thought they had been deprived of the spoils of victory, made problems for Jephthah. Everyone has some "Ephraimites" in his or her life—people who dislike

or oppose you, or people who carry grudges against you for no reason. Discuss how Christians deal with such sullen and annoying persons.

TOPIC FOR ADULTS
JEPHTHAH: ZEAL WITHOUT WISDOM

Zeal Without Wisdom. William Goodloe started from his home in Marywood, a suburb of Chicago, to the commuter station to catch the train to downtown Chicago, where he works as a computor operator. As he approached, he saw a long freight train slowly creeping by. It looked miles long and was moving so slowly that Goodloe worried that he would miss his train. As he waited, he heard the bell in the station announcing that his commuter train was coming in. Goodloe did what he had done several times before; he scrambled on board a flat car on the freight train and started to work his way past some truck trailers on the flat car, intending to jump off on the other side. This time, however, just as he was getting on board, the freight train started to pick up speed. By the time he got past the trailers, the train was going faster. When Goodloe looked down at the ground, he realized the freight was moving so fast that it would be dangerous to jump. He stayed on the freight train. He didn't worry, however. When the train came to the next station and slowed or stopped, Goodloe figured he would get off. The freight train didn't stop at the next station, but roared through at forty miles an hour. It grew colder, but Goodloe still didn't get upset. When the freight pounded through Geneva, the last commuter stop, Goodloe began to realize he was in trouble. By that time, his flatcar was hurtling along at sixty miles an hour, vibrating and almost rocking him off the train. The icy wind tore through his clothing. The train finally slowed down as it approached the Mississippi River. Goodloe jumped. He was nearly 180 miles from home with $1.45 and a brown-bag lunch in his pockets. When he was picked up by a police car from Clinton, Iowa, while hiking along the highway, he was suspected of shooting a policeman in a nearby Iowa town the day before. He finally called his wife back home in Maywood, who drove the 180 miles to pick him up, but he never got to his job at Pandick Press Midwest, Inc. in Chicago that day. His zeal to catch his train without the wisdom of waiting for the freight train to pass cost him a day's work, and could have cost him injury or death.

In God's service, zeal must also be accompanied with wisdom. When it doesn't, we end farther from our destination—as did Jephthah.

Zeal With Wisdom and Wisdom With Zeal. It is now becoming apparent to many American citizens that we cannot renew the spirit of this nation without reviewing gratefully its splendid traditions, learning from them and building on them. George Santayana is right: "Those who disdain history are bound to repeat its mistakes." A nation that loses touch with its founding principles is not only ungrateful but, in time, becomes irresponsible, unable to cope with present and future demands on it. Christopher Lasch argues in his seminal study, *The Culture of Narcissism,* that a "denial of the past, superficially progressive and optimistic, proves on closer analysis to embody the despair of a society that cannot face the future."

"It is equally true that a church that forgets its living traditions will not establish new beachheads in this world for God. . . . God acted as He did in Jesus because He had been acting with the same mind in dealing with the people of Israel for centuries. God is not schizophrenic. The God of the Old Testament and the God of the New Testament are one and the same God.

"God is the same yesterday, today, and tomorrow. The New Covenant can be fully understood only in the context of the Old Covenant. The two high points in God's liberating work, the Exodus and the Resurrection, are a single beachhead of grace. From Genesis to Revelation, the Bible teaches that history is going somewhere because God is acting in it. Revelation and history are inseparable. In the Christian faith, memory and hope complement each other. There can be tradition without mission (nostalgia); the church through the ages has demonstrated that. But there can be no surging mission apart from sound biblical tradition (memory); the long history of the church demonstrates that too. . . ."—Wallace E. Fisher, *Because God Cares: Messages for Lent and Easter*, Augsburg Publishing House, 1981.

Founding Fathers' Mixture of Zeal and Wisdom. On this Independence Day weekend, it is particularly appropriate to remember that the patriotism of the Founders of our nation was zeal for the country informed by the wisdom of knowing that God is the Ruler of all nations. George Washington understood this well. In his inaugural address at the Old City Hall in New York, on April 30, 1789, Washington stated: "It would be peculiarly improper to omit, in this first official act, my fervent supplications to that Almighty Being who rules over the Universe, who presides in the Councils of Nations, and whose providential aids can supply every human defect, that His benediction may consecrate to the Liberties and Happiness of the people of the United States a Government instituted by themselves for these essential purposes."

In your devotion to the nation and its flag, do you have this type of zeal and wisdom?

Questions for Pupils on the Next Lesson. 1. What are some of the personal encounters with God that you have experienced? 2. Do you feel that you are ready to deal with the activity of the Holy Spirit in your life? 3. What examples can you relate of people whose moral weaknesses have caused them to become careless in dealing with serious responsibilities? 4. Why do vengeance and desperation cause self-destructive behavior? 5. How did Samson's weakness allow him to handle serious matters carelessly?

TOPIC FOR YOUTH
JEPHTHAH: A POOR PROMISE

Saw Themselves. Sometimes we don't like Scripture because we find we see ourselves portrayed in its story. We don't like discovering ourselves in this way.

It is like what happened to a couple of artists recently. Anthony Siani and Jacob Silberman didn't like what they saw when they gazed at a painting called, "The Mugging of the Muse" by a fellow artist named

Paul Georges. Siani and Silberman claimed that the two muggers in the painting bore a distinct resemblance to them. They didn't like seeing themselves in this way and hired a lawyer. The jury in court agreed with them and awarded them $30,000.

In the Bible, we discover that *we* are pictured. Through the episodes of Jephthah's life, including his rash promise, we see the consequences of hasty and poor decisions. Part of the reason why we must continue to work seriously with Scripture is that we may see ourselves as the persons the Creator knows us to be, and take steps to become the persons He also hopes that we will become.

Body Beautiful. Your promises to the Lord to be a responsible Christian require some hard decisions. Decisions about how you spend your money, for instance. How much should you spend on yourself? How much to help others?

Statistics indicate that most people decide to be more preoccupied with their body beautiful than with Christian caring. Estimated consumer expenditure on cosmetics and personal hygiene products in a recent year came to the following:

Women's hair products—$1,913.4 million
Cosmetics—$2,656.8 million
Diet Aid—$388.8 million
Skin preparations—$1,552.4 million
Women's fragrances—$1,828.3 million
Feminine hygiene—$770.1 million
Personal cleanliness—$1,454.1 million
Oral hygiene—$1,453.6 million
Foot products—$199.3 million
Men's toiletries—$852.0 million

What kind of promises are you making to the Lord? Rash, silly Jephthah-like promises? Or meaningful, permanent Jesus-like promises?

Zeal With Wisdom. This Fourth of July weekend celebrates the Independence Day of our nation. Some will use it to glorify military exploits. Others will want us to use the occasion to make rash commitments by force of arms, like Jephthah.

A newspaper headline appeared not long ago which read: "Soldiers are itching for a manageable war." They were discussing a war in which only several thousand would be killed and only 10,000 wounded. "America would be stronger for it," they say. The fact is it could happen now.

"War fever," it has been called.

If a manageable war is essential to keep America strong, an enemy can be found somewhere, and war fever can get us involved. But the most dangerous enemy today is not an enemy nation but war itself. War is mankind's real enemy, said a reputable religious journal some years ago. War is the monster that can destroy us.

War fever means: "We have met the enemy and he is us."

Sentence Sermon to Remember: The fear of the Lord, which is the beginning of wisdom, consists in a complete devotion to God.—Otto Zockler.

Questions for Pupils on the Next Lesson. 1. What exactly was Samson's weakness? 2. How did his weakness cause him to handle serious matters carelessly? 3. Why is the desire for vengeance ultimately so destructive? 4. What are the most self-destructive patterns you see in lives of young persons today? 5. What are occasions in which you have sensed the movement of God in your life?

LESSON VI—JULY 10

SAMSON: UNFULFILLED DESTINY

Background Scripture: Judges 13–16
Devotional Reading: Acts 15:6–11

KING JAMES VERSION

JUDGES 13 2 And there was a certain man of Zorah, of the family of the Danites, whose name *was* Manoah; and his wife *was* barren, and bare not.

3 And the angel of the LORD appeared unto the woman, and said unto her, Behold now, thou *art* barren, and bearest not: but thou shalt conceive, and bear a son.

4 Now therefore beware, I pray thee, and drink not wine nor strong drink, and eat not any unclean *thing:*

5 For, lo, thou shalt conceive, and bear a son; and no razor shall come on his head: for the child shall be a Nazarite unto God from the womb: and he shall begin to deliver Israel out of the hand of the Philistines.

24 And the woman bare a son, and called his name Samson: and the child grew, and the LORD blessed him.

25 And the Spirit of the LORD began to move him at times in the camp of Dan between Zorah and Eshtaol.

16 15 And she said unto him, How canst thou say, I love thee, when thine heart *is* not with me? Thou hast mocked me these three times, and hast not told me wherein thy great strength *lieth.*

16 And it came to pass, when she pressed him daily with her words, and urged him, *so* that his soul was vexed unto death;

17 That he told her all his heart, and said unto her, There hath not come a razor upon mine head; for I *have been* a Nazarite unto God from my mother's womb: if I be shaven, then my strength will go from me, and I shall become weak, and be like any *other* man.

28 And Samson called unto the LORD, and said, O Lord GOD, remember me, I pray thee, and strengthen me, I pray thee, only this once, O God, that I may be at once avenged of the Philistines for my two eyes.

29 And Samson took hold of the two middle pillars upon which the house stood, and on which it was borne up, of the one

REVISED STANDARD VERSION

JUDGES 13 2 And there was a certain man of Zorah, of the tribe of the Danites, whose name was Manoah; and his wife was barren and had no children. 3 And the angel of the LORD appeared to the woman and said to her, "Behold, you are barren and have no children; but you shall conceive and bear a son. 4 Therefore beware, and drink no wine or strong drink, and eat nothing unclean, 5 for lo, you shall conceive and bear a son. No razor shall come upon his head, for the boy shall be a Nazirite to God from birth; and he shall begin to deliver Israel from the hand of the Philistines."

24 And the woman bore a son, and called his name Samson; and the boy grew, and the LORD blessed him. 25 And the Spirit of the LORD began to stir him in Mahaneh-dan, between Zorah and Eshta-ol.

16 15 And she said to him, "How can you say, 'I love you,' when your heart is not with me? You have mocked me these three times, and you have not told me wherein your great strength lies." 16 And when she pressed him hard with her words day after day, and urged him, his soul was vexed to death. 17 And he told her all his mind, and said to her, "A razor has never come upon my head; for I have been a Nazirite to God from my mother's womb. If I be shaved, then my strength will leave me, and I shall become weak, and be like any other man."

28 Then Samson called to the LORD and said, "O Lord God, remember me, I pray thee, and strengthen me, I pray thee, only this once, O God, that I may be avenged upon the Philistines for one of my two eyes." 29 And Samson grasped the two middle pillars upon which the house rested, and he leaned his weight upon them, his right hand on the one and his left

with his right hand, and of the other with his left.

30 And Samson said, Let me die with the Philistines. And he bowed himself with *all his* might; and the house fell upon the lords, and upon all the people that *were* therein. So the dead which he slew at his death were more than *they* which he slew in his life.

hand on the other. 30 And Samson said, "Let me die with the Philistines." Then he bowed with all his might; and the house fell upon the lords and upon all the people that were in it. So the dead whom he slew at his death were more than those whom he had slain during his life.

KEY VERSE: A man without self-control is like a city broken into and left without walls. Proverbs 25:28 (RSV).

HOME DAILY BIBLE READINGS

July 4. M. A Promised Birth. Judges 13:1–14.
July 5. T. A Good Beginning. Judges 13:15–25.
July 6. W. An Unwise Marriage. Judges 14:5–20.
July 7. T. Treachery Produces Treachery. Judges 15:1–15.
July 8. F. Secret Strength. Judges 16:1–14.
July 9. S. A Tragic Ending. Judges 16:15–30.
July 10. S. Walk by the Spirit. Galatians 5:13–24.

BACKGROUND

The author or authors of Judges were fond of an oft-repeated formula of "sin—judgment—and deliverance." This is the basic theme of our lesson for today, and it is illustrated in the amazing story of Samson, who in physical strength would have been a good match for the Philistine Goliath. But he happened to come many years before Goliath appeared—about the first quarter of the twelfth century B.C. Some scholars say the Philistines came from as far away as the Dalmatian coast (now Yugoslavia) and fought their way to Palestine (which is named for them!). They settled in a strip along the Mediterranean coast where they established armed cities from which they made periodic raids into Israelite territory and were a plague and a threat to Israel up to the time of David; in fact, they were never quite conquered.

They were good at making iron swords and spearheads, and they had a good supply of iron in their war-loving hearts. Israel fought a long guerrilla war with the Philistines with neither side gaining any great advantage. Israel's lack, in this long fighting, was a lack of leadership—at least until a man named Samson was born. Samson never claimed to be a judge but became the hero of the storytellers who wandered across the land. He remained in Jewish history as a semi-serious Hercules who made life miserable for the Philistines.

NOTES ON THE PRINTED TEXT

The brief account of Samson's birth reminds us of the story of Abraham and Sarah and the birth of their son Isaac. The father of Samson was Manoah, whose wife was barren. As it was with Sarah, an angel appeared to announce the birth of a son. It was a highly unusual birth; the mother took what was known as the Nazarite vow for her son. "A Nazarite was a man set apart and dedicated to God, distinguished from his fellows by abstinence from strong drink, by letting his hair grow long, and by keeping out of contact with dead bodies. . . . Such Nazarites might be so dedicated for a limited time or for life. This child was apparently to be subjected to a lifetime vow. The baby so born was said to be a promised deliverer."—Eric C. Rust. And even though the child never took the vow, he was encouraged to grow up as an austere Nazarite.

He grew up, but hardly in any austere fashion. As the old folk-tales told it, the child became almost a monstrosity of a man, with a superhuman strength and the mind of a rather deadly practical joker, playing grim jokes on the Philistines. He married a Philistine woman in defiance of all Jewish laws and regulations, and that may have accounted for the ease with which he frequently entered Philistine territory. But wife or no wife, those Philistines were his enemies, and he acted accordingly. He slaughtered a thousand Philistines with the jawbone of an ass; he caught three hundred foxes, tied their tails together, and set them loose in the Philistines' cornfields; he stole the great gates of the city of Gaza like a boy let loose on Hallowe'en. His strength became a legend, probably enlarged upon as time went by. Physically, the Bible has no stronger man.

But there was a fatal weakness behind the great strength: Samson had what we would call a weakness for women. The record written in the Book of Judges says that "The Spirit of the Lord began to move him at times in the camp of (the tribe of) Dan . . ." which is probably intended to mean that his enormous strength was being used of the Lord to put down the pestiferous Philistines; but even if that is true, there was no prodding of the Holy Spirit in his behavior with the Philistine woman named Delilah. Delilah was certainly a beautiful harlot whose charms lured the great Samson to his death. She made the mighty one look like a fool as she wheedled out of him the secret that his strength lay in his long (Nazarite) hair. The hair was the symbol of his allegiance to his God, and, if a razor were to touch his head and his hair be cut, his strength was gone. Delilah schemed to have that hair cut, and that was the end of the man's strength.

Some writers, more sentimental than sensible, suggest that Delilah really loved him. That is possible but not probable for Delilah coldly sold him into the hands of her fellow Philistines. She was the tool of the Philistines, and she loved money and was ready to do anything to get it. She shed no tears as they put out his eyes and set him turning the mill stones in the prison at Gaza (the city from which he had once stolen their gates!). For eleven thousand pieces of silver, she betrayed and sold him. She made a better deal than Judas made when he sold Jesus Christ, and she showed no signs of remorse, as Judas did. She shed no tears as Samson toiled "Eyeless in Gaza at the mill with slaves."

Samson got his revenge; a man of his mind *would* get that. When they took him into the Temple of Dagon in chains to make fun of him, he brought down the temple on their guilty heads, "killing more than those whom he had slain during his life" (verse 30 RSV). In this last moment of his life, we hear him pray for the first time: "O Lord God, . . . strengthen me . . . only this once . . . that I may be at once avenged of the Philistines" (16:28).

Some think the story is a bit of humor, but it isn't. It is sad, tragic, a recital concerning a degenerate woman who gained a bloody fortune and a man who might have done great things for his God but gave his life to his own amusement. Still, Samson had at least a few virtues. He stood and fought when even Judah's mighty tribe ran from the field. He worshiped God once while they deserted to idols. In the midst of a nation disrupted, he was a militant, solitary, defiant soul.

His feuds were personal, his story an accumulation of village tales. Read it with one eye open to pity, the other to Samson's background.

He might have delivered Israel from the hands of the Philistines, but somehow he failed to understand that *only with God* he could have done it.

SUGGESTIONS TO TEACHERS

Every town has a few "might-have-been's." The bars of every skid row have a shabby alcoholic who occasionally will find a piano and astonish listeners with renditions of Chopin from memory, or a shaking drifter who carries a shoebox filled with yellowing clippings of his once-promising pitching career in the minors. Today's lesson centers on another "might-have-been." Samson, the promising leader, wasted his talents degenerating into a vengeful playboy.

1. *VALUED.* No child was ever more wanted or loved than Samson. His doting parents were so grateful to God for Samson that they made promises to the Lord. They saw their boy as a miraculous gift. Point out to your class that each of the people in your class is also a unique gift from God. Every person in your classroom is valued deeply by God. You may even wish to have class members tell what they regard as special about each other, and what particular gifts from God each brings.

2. *VENGEFUL.* Samson's insistence upon revenge, especially through costly and elaborate practical jokes such as tying foxes' tails together to flaming torches to burn the fields of the Philistines, dissipated his talents and energies. These escapades did nothing to help his nation or other people. Vengeance is a luxury no one can ever afford. In Samson's case, it eventually brought about his own ruin. Use time in today's lesson period to talk together of why Jesus prohibits vengeance. Check the New Testament teachings on revenge, especially in Matthew 5.

3. *VULNERABLE.* Every person has certain areas in which he or she is vulnerable. Samson's weakness was women. However, instead of recognizing his area of vulnerability and taking steps to guard himself from being destroyed by it, he foolishly repeated his past mistakes. Finally, Delilah took fatal advantage of Samson's weakness. Point out to those in your class that every Christian must seek to recognize his or her areas of weakness. In one person, it may be gossiping. For another, it may be a tendency to become deeply depressed. Others may have to guard themselves against temptation to be promiscuous, or to be violent, or to drink excessively. The point is that every person must be aware of these points of being vulnerable and to plead with the Lord for strength to withstand the onslaught of temptation. Above all, remind your class that the Lord is stronger than any temptation. When we humans admit our weakness, we may receive His strength.

4. *VANQUISHED.* Samson ended by destroying himself. His superb physique and immense strength, which could have been used to fulfill his

destiny as a great leader in Israel, brought him a tragic ending even if he did bring down the Philistine palace. When any one of God's people does not try to fulfill his or her destiny by using the strength and power God has given him or her, that person concludes his or her life on a note of tragedy instead of victory. You may wish to have each person in your class list on a paper what each believes his or her unique destiny is, or to write the three greatest gifts he or she thinks that God has blessed him or her with. Ask whether each feels he or she is fulfilling that destiny or using those gifts.

TOPIC FOR ADULTS
SAMSON: UNFULFILLED DESTINY

Unfulfilled Destiny. Oswald Mosley was born into the privileged class in England. Educated in the finest schools and universities, gifted with a first-rate mind, and connected by blood ties or friendship to the Establishment, Mosley was regarded as one of the most promising leaders in Great Britain. He married the daughter of Lord Curzon, once Viceroy of India, Mosley's wedding, attended by King George V and most of the royal family, was the social event of the year. Mosley ran for Parliament and was elected. He quickly emerged as a brilliant young leader. Later, he switched to Laborite. He made such a vivid impression that it was said that he could have been the leader of either party. He was knighted, and was addressed as "Sir Oswald Mosley."

Instead of becoming one of Britain's respected leaders, during the 1930s, Mosley attached himself to the British Union of Fascists. His extraordinary talents were turned to demonic purposes. He became leader of what he said would be the New Order, modeled on Hitler's Germany and Mussolini's Italy. His bigotry sent his blackshirts storming through Jewish sections of London, burning and beating. In 1938, he married again, this time in Germany, where the beaming head of state present was Adolf Hitler himself. Mosley continued to spread his poison against Jews and to organize his paramilitary blackshirts in England. When World War II broke out, he was interned as a potential traitor. Mosley shrilly protested that he was misunderstood until his death in 1980. His own son Nicholas, however, offered a more telling judgment: "I see clearly that while the right hand dealt with grandiose ideas and glory, the left hand let the rat out of the sewer."

Samson was also a man with great promise who never fulfilled his destiny. You are a person who also has a destiny. Will you be aware of the potential you also have to end destructively? Will you take seriously the dream of God and His people for you and your future?

Floe's Flow. A couple of winters ago, Lake Erie froze. Fishermen drove snowmobiles and trucks onto the ice, cut holes in the ice with chain saws, set up shanties to protect themselves from the cold wind, and lowered their fishing lines into the cold waters. One weekend, nearly 500 fishermen took to the ice along the shores of Jerusalem Township, Ohio. Many drove five miles out on the pack to find suitable spots on the white expanse to bring in catches of perch, bass, walleyes, and muskies to fill their freezers back home. One Sunday morning, no one noticed when the ice pack began imperceptibly to separate from the shore and start to drift out into the lake. By the time the flow became an immense ice island ten miles long and five miles wide, with 100 yards of dark water between it and the Ohio shore, the alarm was given. Fortunately twenty rescue boats and a helicopter came to take the fishermen off the crunching floe. The cars, trucks, snowmobiles, fishing gear, shanties, and buckets of freshly-caught fish, however, could not be taken aboard and were abandoned on the ice.

Sin is a separation from God and others. Like the fishermen on the ice floe slipping almost unnoticeably from the security of the shore, we may be gradually separated from the Lord. The gulf may be imperceptible at first, because we are intent on our own pleasure and greed. Like Samson, drifting from the destiny of standing securely with God, we can eventually drift into the cold darkness of isolation from God's purpose.

Skilled Barbarians. "The biggest failing in higher education today is that we fall short in exposing students to values. We don't really provide a value framework to young people who more and more are searching for it.

"This situation has come about because the modern university is rooted in the scientific method, having essentially turned its back on religion. I'm not hostile to the scientific method—it is a marvelous means of inquiry, and it has been highly productive—but it really doesn't provide a value system. It has taken a long time for that to become apparent because our traditional value system survived intact for such a long time.

"Since World War II, however, we've seen the greatest disintegration of the social consensus and the most accelerated pace and degree of change in human history. As a result, all our institutions have lost a coherent set of values—including universities. . . .

"The failure to rally around a set of values means that universities are turning out potentially highly skilled barbarians: People who are very expert in the laboratory or at the computer or in surgery or in the law courts but who have no real understanding of their own society. We are not turning out very self-confident people, and in a democracy that is a potentially catastrophic problem because our society depends on people who are not passive but active, who are prepared to make choices and take responsibility. That requires individuals who have self-confidence—and to have that confidence requires a value structure.

"I hear kids today who lack that confidence asking: 'Why should I work? Where's it all going? What does it all mean? I don't have any control over anything. I don't understand anything. Why not just slide along?' "—Steven Muller, President, Johns Hopkins University, Baltimore, *U.S. News and World Report*, November 10, 1980.

Your motto should most appropriately be "To Christ be true." With Him, you have control of yourself, of life, of the future because you are controlled by Him.

Destroyed by Greed. Langley Collyer and his brother Homer inherited a fortune and a beautiful mansion in a fashionable part of New York City. Instead of using their money wisely, however, they bought and hoarded possessions. They lacked all self-control when it came to using their inheritance responsibly. The two brothers never married but lived as miserly recluses. Gradually, their mansion became filled with their accumulated treasure. Turning away from contact with the outside world, they grew more and more eccentric. Their greed seemed to possess them. The huge rooms became so piled with things they bought and clung to that the two men were only able to move through narrow tunnel-like passageways in the clutter. One day in 1947, Langley Collyer, the elder brother, was carrying a tray of food through one of the rooms piled high with hoarded possessions. Somehow, he jarred the tall heap and was knocked down by a collapsing pile of newspapers, a sewing machine, three breadboxes, and heavy suitcases filled with metal scrap. Felled by the avalanche of possessions, the helpless man finally died. His brother Homer, unable to reach him and unable to break out, also perished.

Questions for Pupils on the Next Lesson. 1. What are the greatest problems in raising children today? 2. How are the adults in your church fostering religious development in younger persons? 3. In what different ways do you sense God's response to your prayers? 4. Does prayer bring you a sense of release and fulfillment? 5. Does God ever ignore expressions of genuine faith?

TOPIC FOR YOUTH
SAMSON: LACKING SELF-CONTROL

Troll Tale. In *Peer Gynt*, the play by Hendrik Ibsen, in one scene, Gynt lives among the trolls. The trolls are mythological figures in Scandinavian folklore. Usually they are evil and destructive spirits. Gynt asks the trolls what the difference is between humans and trolls. The trolls respond, "To thyself be enough" is their motto. It is not, as one would expect, "To thyself be true," but "To thyself be enough." Peer Gynt, not liking the rigid requirement of being true to himself, welcomes the new principle of self-sufficiency. He pursues it. And he continues pursuing it to the point of strangulating himself.

Samson's story in the Bible could be given the subtitle of "To thyself be enough." Lacking self-control, this undisciplined giant ended a blinded, disgraced might-have-been leader of Israel.

Samson the Pretender. For most of his young life, Samson had been pretending to be tied to God. He had kept the outward form of his Nazarite sect but actually had been coasting on his parents' faith. Like the person who has evaded all responsibilities of Christian discipleship by explaining, "Oh, but I was baptized a Presbyterian," or "But I used to go to church every Sunday as a kid back in Kalamazoo," or "My father was a deacon, my mother sang in the choir, and Aunt Bessie taught Sunday school for fifty-five years," Samson thought it was enough to have religious connections. Actually, of course, Samson's Nazarite affiliation had sunk from being empty ritual to silly superstition.

Still not suspecting Delilah's duplicity, Samson spent a passionate evening with her, then heaved into a deep sleep. He groggily opened his eyes when Delilah shrieked that the Philistines were coming. To his horror, he found that his girl friend had shaved him completely bald! Powerless, he was jumped and subdued by a band of Philistines. He struggled frantically, but he could not prevent them from gouging out his eyes.

More than Samson's strength was gone. "He did not know that the

Lord had left him" (Judges 16:20). Samson had defected from serving God. And God, for Samson, finally ceased to exist.

There seems to be a spiritual law which implies that one may lose a sense of the reality of the Wholly Other through prolonged refusal to obey Him. As the fragile mystic, Simone Weil, once put it, "If we remain deaf, He comes back again and again like a beggar, but also like a beggar, one day He stops coming."

Sentence Sermon to Remember: The past is littered with the wreckage of nations which have tried to meet the crises of their times by physical means alone.—Raymond B. Fosdick.

Questions for Pupils on the Next Lesson. 1. What is the biggest promise you hope to keep? 2. What do you think can fill the voids of life? 3. Do you feel that God may ignore expressions of genuine faith? 4. What is the way to inner peace?

LESSON VII—JULY 17

HANNAH: A PROMISE KEPT

Background Scripture: 1 Samuel 1:1–2:10
Devotional Reading: Luke 1:8–20

KING JAMES VERSION

1 SAMUEL 1 9 So Hannah rose up after they had eaten in Shiloh, and after they had drunk. Now Eli the priest sat upon a seat by a post of the temple of the LORD.

10 And she *was* in bitterness of soul, and prayed unto the LORD, and wept sore.

11 And she vowed a vow, and said, O LORD of hosts, if thou wilt indeed look on the affliction of thine handmaid, and remember me, and not forget thine handmaid, but wilt give unto thine handmaid a man child, then I will give him unto the LORD all the days of his life, and there shall no razor come upon his head.

19 And they rose up in the morning early, and worshipped before the LORD, and returned, and came to their house to Ramah: and Elkanah knew Hannah his wife; and the LORD remembered her.

20 Wherefore it came to pass, when the time was come about after Hannah had conceived, that she bare a son, and called his name Samuel, *saying*, Because I have asked him of the LORD.

24 And when she had weaned him, she took him up with her, with three bullocks, and one ephah of flour, and a bottle of wine, and brought him unto the house of the LORD in Shiloh: and the child *was* young.

25 And they slew a bullock, and brought the child to Eli.

26 And she said, O my lord, *as* thy soul liveth, my lord, I *am* the woman that sood by thee here, praying unto the LORD.

27 For this child I prayed; and the LORD hath given me my petition which I asked of him:

28 Therefore also I have lent him to the LORD; as long as he liveth he shall be lent to the LORD. And he worshipped the LORD there.

2 1 And Hannah prayed, and said, My heart rejoiceth in the LORD, mine horn is exalted in the LORD; my mouth is enlarged over mine enemies; because I rejoice in thy salvation.

REVISED STANDARD VERSION

1 SAMUEL 1 9 After they had eaten and drunk in Shiloh, Hannah rose. Now Eli the priest was sitting on the seat beside the doorpost of the temple of the LORD. 10 She was deeply distressed and prayed to the LORD, and wept bitterly. 11 And she vowed a vow and said, "O LORD of hosts, if thou wilt indeed look on the affliction of thy maidservant, and remember me, and not forget thy maidservant, but wilt give to thy maidservant a son, then I will give him to the LORD all the days of his life, and no razor shall touch his head."

19 They rose early in the morning and worshiped before the LORD; then they went back to their house at Ramah. And Elkanah knew Hannah his wife, and the LORD remembered her; 20 and in due time Hannah conceived and bore a son, and she called his name Samuel, for she said, "I have asked him of the LORD."

24 And when she had weaned him, she took him up with her, along with a three-year-old bull, an ephah of flour, and a skin of wine; and she brought him to the house of the LORD at Shiloh; and the child was young. 25 Then they slew the bull, and they brought the child to Eli. 26 And she said, "Oh, my lord! As you live, my lord, I am the woman who was standing here in your presence, praying to the LORD. 27 For this child I prayed; and the LORD has granted me my petition which I made to him. 28 Therefore I have lent him to the LORD; as long as he lives, he is lent to the LORD."

And they worshiped the LORD there.

2 1 Hannah also prayed and said,
"My heart exults in the LORD;
my strength is exalted in the LORD.
My mouth derides my enemies,
because I rejoice in thy salvation.

2 *There is* none holy as the LORD: for *there is* none besides thee: neither *is there* any rock like our God.

2 "There is none holy like the LORD,
there is none besides thee;
there is no rock like our God."

KEY VERSE: "For this child I prayed; and the Lord has granted me my petition which I made to him. Therefore I have lent him to the Lord." 1 Samuel 1:27,28 (RSV).

HOME DAILY BIBLE READINGS

July 11. *M.* *Hannah Weeps.* 1 Samuel 1:1–8.
July 12. *T.* *Hannah Makes a Promise.* 1 Samuel 1:9–18.
July 13. *W.* *Hannah Has a Son.* 1 Samuel 1:19–23.
July 14. *T.* *Hannah Keeps Her Promise.* 1 Samuel 1:24–28.
July 15. *F.* *Hannah Praises God.* 1 Samuel 2:1–11.
July 16. *S.* *God Seeks a Faithful Priest.* 1 Samuel 2:26–36.
July 17. *S.* *Samuel Answers God's Call.* 1 Samuel 3:1–10.

BACKGROUND

Hannah appears on the scene at a time in which the high standards of morality and spirituality set up by Moses had seriously lapsed. Contact with the Canaanites had all but destroyed such standards, but there were homes and people who struggled to keep the values of their faith alive and active. The home of Elkanah of the tribe of Ephraim was like that. It was a pious home.

Elkanah had two wives. Yes, this was bigamy (to us), but it was accepted and practiced widely in Israel. The reason it was so accepted was that the worst thing that could happen to a man was to die without sons to perpetuate his name. To die childless was to have one's name and family wiped out. To be certain of an heir, or heirs, the men took unto themselves not one but two or more wives.

The Chinese have an ancient adage which says that, "Two women under the same roof means trouble," or words to that effect. It worked that way in Elkanah's house. His two wives, Hannah and Peninnah, had trouble getting along together; the trouble was that Peninnah gave children to her husband, and Hannah gave him none. This disturbed Hannah, who had to suffer the constant taunts and ridicule of Peninnah, who was jealous of Hannah's position as Elkanah's favorite wife.

Once every year the family went up to the sanctuary at Shiloh, at the time after harvest, to thank God for His blessings. Hannah, after long years of suffering at the hands of Peninnah, went one year with another thought in mind: she would pray for a child.

NOTES ON THE PRINTED TEXT

Hannah's prayers are not recorded in the Bible, but they must have been fervent and even desperate prayers, for Eli, the high priest at Shiloh, thought that she was drunk! (That would have been nothing unusual; many of them got drunk at these festivals of thanksgiving.) She prayed *silently,* muttering to herself. The constant friction with Peninnah was taking its toll; Hannah never fought back, never stooped to Peninnah's level, but the abuse tore at her heart. She could not eat. She could only pray. More than life itself, more than anything else in the world, she wanted that child.

Eli rebuked her, but she explained it all to him, and he understood, and he prayed with her and for the coming of that child. In his presence, she made her vow: if the Lord God would bless her with a man child, she would give him to the Lord "all the days of his life, and there shall no razor come upon his head" (verse 11). (This was an approved custom for those who were wholly dedicated to God.) And she prayed on, and on, and on after she left Shiloh, and in time the child came, and she named her man child *Samuel*, which meant "asked of the Lord."

Even though she could not have known at this time what a man her Samuel was destined to be, she surrounded him with her love; she never left him to others. She even refused to make another trip to Shiloh, because her baby had not yet been weaned. Then came the day when she had to fulfill her vow; it must have been a stab in her heart to give up her child, but she was heroic enough to do as she had promised with him. She gave him into the hands of Eli at Shiloh—no, into the hands of God. She went back home alone, and every step must have been a step of pain. Such mothers do not give up their children easily.

Year after year, as the boy grew in stature and in favor with Eli and with God, Hannah made little robes for him to wear as he went about his duties in the temple. Larger and longer robes she sewed and took to Shiloh.

The perfect mother! Womanly, candid, graceful, she typifies the ultimate mother love in spiritual joy and renunciation. Persistent, praying prayers fragrant with simple faith: such was Hannah, mother of Samuel. "Hannah, like Mary, gave her child to God, and after she did that, slipped into the background and became immortal through her son."—Edith Deen in *All the Women of the Bible.*

Some commentators seem less than enthusiastic about this story. Some call Hannah purely selfish, say that she wanted this child in order to "get even" with the despicable Peninnah. But when we see what she did with that child, the criticism seems ridiculous. Few mothers have the courage to give up their children so soon after birth. If it were a selfish act, it was a noble selfishness. Other critics, writing in our day, ask if it is right for any mother to decide what her son shall do and be even before he is born. But what *Christian* mother does not want her son to know God and love and follow Him, whatever he does or wherever he goes? There is nothing selfish in a mother who keeps her promise to God whatever it costs her in sacrifice and loneliness.

Now read Hannah's song of joy, in 1 Samuel 2. Could a self-centered woman sing a song like this? Could it not be that Mary the mother of Jesus knew the song of Hannah before she sang her glorious Magnificat? Hannah and Mary had much in common when they gave their sons to God at such a cost.

Samuel Taylor Coleridge touched the heart of the matter when he wrote that

A mother is a mother still,
The holiest thing alive.

SUGGESTIONS TO TEACHERS

"I'm only a housewife." "I'm just a salesman." How many times have you heard these words?

These comments ("I'm only a . . .") reveal the sense of failure and insignificance that so many people feel about themselves. In a society where persons are perceived primarily as commodities to be used, exploited, even bought and sold, many humans regard themselves as measly nobodies.

Your lesson today is aimed at those in your class who see themselves as "merely a . . ." bit of surplus fixture in the world. You will work with Hannah's story, the account of a woman who kept her promises because she knew God kept His promises.

1. *NUMB IN MISERY.* Let the full impact of Hannah's loneliness and unhappiness sink in on your class. Point out how she was a victim of put-downs. Tell your class that Hannah was so misunderstood that she was accused of drunkenness when she was found moving her lips in silent prayer. Help your class to appreciate the depths of Hannah's feelings of failure because she had not had any children. With Hannah's example before your class, encourage the class to reflect on times in the lives of each member when they have had feelings similar to Hannah's.

2. *KNOWN BY THE MAKER.* As teacher, be sure you make clear to your class that the Lord remembered Hannah. He responded with a promise of a son. Stress that God does not make promises lightly, but always stands by them. As Hannah learned to trust God to keep His word, each believer today may trust Him to be true to His promises. You should emphasize that Jesus Christ is God's promise to us, the "Word made flesh."

3. *NAME WITH MEANING.* God keeps His word. He sends Hannah a son. Hannah, grateful for the way the Lord has been part of her story, names the baby *Samuel.* Your class should be told the meaning of *Samuel:* "Name of God." Hannah names God into her life and her son's life. You as teacher should bring up occasions in which you could name the Lord as present and involved in your story in the past. As you realize His involvement in your past, you can take hope that He will also stand with you in the future. Have your class relate occasions in which they can name God as One at work in the events of the past.

4. *NOTES FOR THE MAGNIFICAT.* Be sure those in your class read the lovely hymn of praise by Hannah in 1 Samuel 2:1–10. Have them comment on the parallels between Hannah's Song and Mary's *Magnificat* ("My soul doth magnify the Lord" Luke 1:46–55). Are your people able to sing joyously because of the Lord's good gifts? What are reasons for breaking into such happy hymns today?

TOPIC FOR ADULTS
HANNAH: A PROMISE KEPT

Inscribed on the Altar. In the ancient church of Saint Sophia in Istanbul, Turkey, a curious legend is told. When the Emperor Justinian, a sixth-century Roman ruler professing Christianity, decided to build a temple for worship in his capital, Constantinople, he decreed that the edifice be made so ornate and huge that people would remember him forever. Architects and builders were gathered. After many years, the great temple was ready to be dedicated. Enormous crowds assembled. An impressive worship began. The great moment came when the Emperor, clothed in regal robes, pulled back the curtain to uncover the great altar. The magnificently carved marble glistened. The congregation looked in awe. Suddenly, Emperor Justinian spoke angrily. Who, he demanded was the name engraved over the altar? Why was his name replaced by this woman's name? Who was she?

The crowd stirred with fear, knowing that the Emperor's whims were not to be taken lightly. People whispered, asking who was the unknown woman whose name was carved high above the altar. "Find the woman whose name is on the altar," ordered Justinian, "and bring her to me!"

Court officials searched for days before they finally located the woman living in a peasant hut along the road to the royal stone quarries. She claimed she had no idea how her name could be written on the altar. "I am too poor, I could contribute nothing for its construction."

Under severe questioning, however, this peasant woman admitted that one day she saw the oxen pulling a heavy load of stones for Saint Sophia stumble and stop from fatigue in front of her hut. The woman, pitying the exhausted creatures, grabbed some straw from her thin mattress and gave it to the oxen to eat. Refreshed, the weary beasts struggled on again. All she had been able to give toward the beautiful cathedral was a handful of straw from her mattress.

The Emperor listened to her story. Suddenly, his face brightened. Here, he announced was a miracle. Her name was rightly inscribed, apparently by angels, on the great arch above the altar because she had given more than he!

Like Hannah, this woman had remembered and kept God's promises.

Need for Reward. Psychologists point out that many persons think that they deserve rewards for what they do in everyday life. Secretly telling themselves that they have earned a reward for completing a project or doing some service, they go on eating binges, buy a trinket, or slip into fantasy worlds.

Some professional women who are emotionally healthy, balanced persons, laugh about their need to reward themselves. "I eat peanut clusters. Now I can indulge myself. All during my singing career, I had to be strict with myself," admits opera star Beverly Sills. Tennis champion Billy Jean King admits, "I go on a culture binge—theater, ballet, movies." On one weekend, Miss King rewarded herself with fifteen movies.

Do you feel that you have to indulge yourself as a reward for serving or working? Or, do you find your satisfaction in knowing that you keep your promises to the Lord. Is doing His will reward enough?

Hannah learned this. Have you?

What's in a Name? Hannah and the Hebrews took naming a child seriously. *Samuel* means "Name of God," and the boy Samuel could not help but remember he carried a divine promise in his very name.

L.R.N. Ashley, former President of the American Name Society, agrees that names have great importance in shaping the identity of a person. "Parents should be very careful about naming their children;

names have much to do with how people learn to cope with the world," states Ashley. Self-respect, acceptance by peers, superiors, teachers, and a positive self-image come from a name which a child feels comfortable with or accepts with pride."

In a sense, every Christian believer is a *Samuel* or bears the name of the Lord. *Christian* literally means "Miniature Christ." Each person who is baptized as a Christian is given the name of Jesus' own family, and may properly affirm the identity which belonging to Jesus Christ brings.

Next time you wonder about your name, whether it is Sylvester or Hortense, or John or Mary, remember that your real name is *Christian!*

Questions for Pupils on the Next Lesson. 1. How does lack of communication between adults often lead to problems? 2. Why are people sometimes reluctant to follow another person's advice? 3. How do you respond to the issue of faith healing? 4. Why did Naaman at first reject Elisha's instructions? 5. What was Naaman's attitude toward the God of Israel after his healing?

TOPIC FOR YOUTH
HANNAH: KEEPING A PROMISE

Promise Kept. A woman in South Wales made promises to the Lord to be a faithful wife and caring mother. She prayed regularly and attended the tiny chapel in her Welsh mining village. Desperately poor, she worked hard to provide for her baby. She never complained, however, but told others that her child was God's gift.

One wintry night, she became lost in a blizzard and was unable to find her way home. The next morning a search found her snow-covered body. They were surprised to discover that she was not wearing any coat or shawl or dress, but was clad only in ragged undergarments. When they lifted her body, they discovered the reason. The woman had carefully wrapped all of her clothing around the body of her baby, then tenderly crouched over the infant to shield him from the wind and snow. Rescuers found that the baby was still living, and hurried him to warmth and safety. The infant survived. Later, he became Prime Minister of Great Britain during World War I. That Welsh woman, mother of David Lloyd George, kept her promises to the Lord, even to the point of death, so that her child could live.

Promise to Keep. What promises have you made to God, to others, to yourself? Have you kept them?

Paul Rokich made a promise when he was a six-year-old boy in 1939 and first saw the burnt-over, washed-out barren slopes of the Oquirrh Mountains, the 10,000-foot-high, twenty-five-mile-long mountain range across the Salt Lake Valley from Utah's capital city. Young Paul Rokich promised that he would restore the range so terribly ravaged by fire, flood, logging, and overgrazing.

Rokich learned that the mountains had once been a botanical showcase, called "the Lily Range" by naturalist John Muir because they were so lovely. Rokich began to sneak up to the mountain to plant grass and trees. The previous owners, a copper company, refused to give him permission to trespass, but Rokich hiked up by night to continue his planting. After Kennecott Copper bought the Oquirrh area, Rokich got permission to climb with his seedlings and shovel legally. Evenings, Saturdays, and holidays, Paul Rokich persisted in bringing green to the mountain. He managed a store and worked at construction to support his family and buy his seeds and saplings. Locals began to refer to Rokich as "Utah's Johnny Appleseed."

As the fire-blackened peaks and flood-ravaged gullies began to be covered with trees, grass, and flowers, the elk, deer, and eagles started to return. Finally, in 1974, the Kennecott people decided to pay Rokich for what he had been doing on his own and hired him as "environmental technician."

Paul Rokich snorts at the title and attention given him. He is simply keeping his promise.

Promise Without Pillars. When the famous architect Sir Christopher Wren was hired to design and build the great Corn Market in London, he presented a design which showed no pillars holding up the roof. He promised they would not be needed, but the Fathers could not conceive of such a thing and insisted on pillars. Finally, the architect yielded and agreed to give them pillars, though he still insisted they were not necessary. But sometime afterward it was found that he had won after all, for he made the pillars one half inch shorter than the roof. There they stand, but they serve no useful purpose for the roof has never sagged.

Wren's promise was kept in every way. God's promises stand even firmer and stronger. Because of His promise, you may make and keep promises to others, even when you may be slighted or slandered.

Sentence Sermon to Remember: The promises of God are just as good as ready money any day.—Billy Bray.

Questions for Pupils on the Next Lesson. 1. Why does failure to listen always bring communication problems? 2. Does your need to feel important and independent sometimes make you feel you don't want to follow instructions given by others? 3. Why did Naaman not want to follow Elisha's advice? 4. What is your opinion of faith healing?

LESSON VIII—JULY 24

NAAMAN: RELUCTANT FOLLOWER

Background Scripture: 2 Kings 5
Devotional Reading: John 3:1–12

KING JAMES VERSION

2 KINGS 5 1 Now Naaman, captain of the host of the king of Syria, was a great man with his master, and honourable, because by him the LORD had given deliverance unto Syria: he was also a mighty man in valour, *but he was* a leper.

2 And the Syrians had gone out by companies, and had brought away captive out of the land of Israel a little maid; and she waited on Naaman's wife.

3 And she said unto her mistress, Would God my lord *were* with the prophet that *is* in Samaria! for he would recover him of his leprosy.

4 And *one* went in, and told his lord, saying, Thus and thus said the maid that *is* of the land of Israel.

5 And the king of Syria said, Go to, go, and I will send a letter unto the king of Israel. And he departed, and took with him ten talents of silver, and six thousand *pieces* of gold, and ten changes of raiment.

9 So Naaman came with his horses and with his chariot, and stood at the door of the house of Elisha.

10 And Elisha sent a messenger unto him, saying, Go and wash in Jordan seven times, and thy flesh shall come again to thee, and thou shalt be clean.

11 But Naaman was wroth, and went away, and said, Behold, I thought, He will surely come out to me, and stand, and call on the name of the LORD his God, and strike his hand over the place, and recover the leper.

12 *Are* not Abana and Pharpar, rivers of Damascus, better than all the waters of Israel? may I not wash in them, and be clean? So he turned and went away in a rage.

13 And his servants came near, and spake unto him, and said, My father, *if* the prophet had bid thee *do some* great thing, wouldest thou not have done *it*? how much rather then, when he saith to thee, Wash, and be clean?

14 Then went he down, and dipped himself seven times in Jordan, according to

REVISED STANDARD VERSION

2 KINGS 5 1 Naaman, commander of the army of the king of Syria, was a great man with his master and in high favor, because by him the LORD had given victory to Syria. He was a mighty man of valor, but he was a leper. 2 Now the Syrians on one of their raids had carried off a little maid from the land of Israel, and she waited on Naaman's wife. 3 She said to her mistress, "Would that my lord were with the prophet who is in Samaria! He would cure him of his leprosy." 4 So Naaman went in and told his lord, "Thus and so spoke the maiden from the land of Israel." 5 And the king of Syria said, "Go now, and I will send a letter to the king of Israel."

So he went, taking with him ten talents of silver, six thousand shekels of gold, and ten festal garments. 9 So Naaman came with his horses and chariots, and halted at the door of Elisha's house. 10 And Elisha sent a messenger to him, saying, "Go and wash in the Jordan seven times, and your flesh shall be restored, and you shall be clean." 11 But Naaman was angry, and went away, saying, "Behold, I thought that he would surely come out to me, and stand, and call on the name of the LORD his God, and wave his hand over the place, and cure the leper. 12 Are not Abana and Pharpar, the rivers of Damascus, better than all the waters of Israel? Could I not wash in them, and be clean?" So he turned and went away in a rage. 13 But his servants came near and said to him, "My father, if the prophet had commanded you to do some great thing, would you not have done it? How much rather, then, when he says to you, 'Wash, and be clean?' " 14 So he went down and dipped himself seven times in the Jordan, according to the word of the man of God; and his flesh was restored like the flesh of a little child, and he was clean.

the saying of the man of God: and his flesh came again like unto the flesh of a little child, and he was clean.

KEY VERSE: So he went down and dipped himself seven times in the Jordan, according to the word of the man of God: and his flesh was restored like the flesh of a little child, and he was clean. 2 Kings 5:14 (RSV).

HOME DAILY BIBLE READINGS

July 18. *M.* *The Priest Tests for Leprosy.* Leviticus 13:9–17.
July 19. *T.* *A Syrian Maiden Suggests a Cure.* 2 Kings 5:1–7.
July 20. *W.* *Naaman Is Cured of Leprosy.* 2 Kings 5:8–14.
July 21. *T.* *Elisha Refuses a Present.* 2 Kings 5:15–19a.
July 22. *F.* *A Deceitful Servant Becomes a Leper.* 2 Kings 5:19b–27.
July 23. *S.* *Jesus Recalls Naaman.* Luke 4:16–28.
July 24. *S.* *Jesus Sends Ten Lepers to the Priest.* Luke 17:11–19.

BACKGROUND

No love was lost between Israel and her neighboring state of Syria. A series of wars was fought between the two nations, wars which often were no more than border raids between the rival kings fought for possession of territory in northern Transjordan. In one of these conflicts, Naaman, the Syrian commander-in-chief of the army, won a victory which left Israel as little more than a vassal of Syria. This made Naaman a great hero in Syria and a despised conqueror in Israel.

In 2 Kings 5:1, there is a line that puzzles us. It reads: "Now Naaman, captain of the host of the king of Syria, was a great man with his master, and honourable, because by him the Lord had given deliverance (victory) unto Syria." The thought here is that, in the Israelite mind, the God of Israel came to be understood as a *universal* God, the Giver of victory to the Syrians as well as to the Israelites. In Jewish history, God made use of heathen nations as "the scourge of God," to bring Israel back into obedience to Him.

In the story of Naaman, we have the story of God bringing the great Syrian commander through a period of wonder if not disbelief to the status of a dedicated but hesitant follower of the God of Israel. That happened because of the faith of a young girl captured during the battle with the Syrians, and because, great as he was, Naaman was a leper.

NOTES ON THE PRINTED TEXT

Leprosy! There were different forms of leprosy; the word in the Bible is a general one, describing numerous skin diseases. Naaman may not have had the dreaded, incurable "white" leprosy but some lesser form of it. Nevertheless, his reaction to the realization that he had any form of leprosy would be *our* reaction: he looked in alarm for a cure of the disease, for someone who could help him. He found the someone in his own household—in the little Jewish maid of his wife. This girl is the most unhonored personality in the Old Testament; we do not even know her name—but *she* knew of the work of a prophet in Israel: Elisha. If her master Naaman would go to this Elisha, the prophet could "recover him of his leprosy" (verse 3). "She had grown up . . . within the radius of Elisha's fame. What stories she had heard! The children had mocked Elisha because of his bald head, and he had called up bears from the wood to devour them; Elisha had sprinkled some salt into the bitter undrinkable water at Jericho and it had been healed. Elisha had promised the childless Sunamite a son, and the child had been born in due time, and then he had died and Elisha had restored him to life. There was no end to the legend of Elisha, there was no limit to Elisha's power. The healing of a leper would be nothing to him!"—Norah Lofts, in *Women in the Old Testament,* by permission of the Macmillan Company, publishers.

It might have meant nothing to Elisha, but it meant a great deal to Naaman, who got into his chariot and drove into the Israel which he despised. He carried with him a letter of introduction from Syria's king to the king of Israel. That was not exactly a good move, for the king of Israel took one look at the letter and saw in it a trick on the part of the Syrian king to make him look foolish by asking him to do something that was impossible—cure a case of leprosy! He would have told Naaman to get in his chariot and go back where he came from had he not heard from Elisha who asked that the Syrian officer be sent to his home in Samaria.

That, to Naaman, was an insult: being a great man, he had thought that the prophet would come out to meet *him.* It was a violation of protocol. Didn't Elisha know who he was? Naaman was furious when Elisha casually sent a messenger to tell him to go and bathe seven times in the river Jordan. That would heal his leprosy. The Jordan? That muddy, unimpressive stream? If he had to bathe in a river, he could do that in the beautiful, sparkling rivers of Damascus. If all he needed was a bath, he could take a bath in his own house! His temper flared again, and he made ready to go back to Syria. He had taken the insult of Elisha, and he had stood at Elisha's door and offered him much money, a gift (bribe!) of some $20,000 in silver and $60,000 in gold, plus ten suits of clothes, and the foolish prophet had refused to accept it. Insult piled on insult!

Fortunately for the rich and proud Naaman, his own servants managed to "cool him down," regain his senses, and do as Elisha had told him to do. They reasoned with him: if this prophet had ordered him to do some *great,* spectacular thing, would he not have done it? Why quibble over a river? Why let foolhardy pride stand in the way of a cure? He could at least *try* to do as Elisha commanded; it could do no harm. They were convincing: he dipped himself seven times in Jordan, and "his flesh was restored like the flesh of a little child, and he was clean" (2 Kings 5:14).

And what does all this mean to *us?* There is more than one good lesson in it. One is that God can and often does work miracles in little things as well as in big things; that idea runs through the whole Old Testament. Another teaching is that God (working through Elisha) requires humble obedience to His commands. God can work and heal through a little slave girl and through a prophet despised by Naaman, as the prophet of an "enemy" people.

Naaman's illness was cured, and, more important, his eyes were opened. A pagan, he had found a *universal* God who could do things that merely national gods could not do. Finding that he could not bribe either God or God's prophet, he turned to prayer; thereafter there was no God but Elisha's God. Thereafter, whenever he went with King Behadad to the Temple of Rimmon, Naaman prayed to Jehovah.

There was another "little thing" in this story that carries good evidence of Naaman's conversion. He asked that he be allowed to carry "two mules' burden of earth" from Samaria to Damascus, so that he might worship the God of Israel on Israel's soil even when he was required to go with his king into the temple of (pagan) Rimmon. "The Great Omaiyid Mosque at Damascus, today the city's most magnificent structure ranking in sanctity with the Dome of the Rock at Jerusalem and the mosques of Mecca and Medina, is built (according to tradition) on the site of the temple of Rimmon where Naaman deposited his load of earth."—*Harper's Bible Dictionary.* And on the traditional site of his house in Damascus there is a leper hospital.

There is no monument to honor the little maid who was really responsible for it all.

SUGGESTIONS TO TEACHERS

Many people think that faith is a TV spectacular: God intervening amidst flashing fireworks and rolling kettledrums; a person reacting sensationally by writing a religious bestseller, and building a hospital in Calcutta. This is what Naaman thought. He wanted a religious extravaganza. Faith, he imagined, had to be supercharged drama.

Your lesson today examines this reluctant follower who cannot bring himself to believe that the Lord usually works in and through the commonplace. Remember that many Christians are secret Naamans; keep in mind that many even in your class privately imagine that their Christian life lacks validity because it is mostly everyday stuff of caring and serving in your local community.

1. *ONE LITTLE ISRAELITE GIRL.* Devote some of your lesson to the episode of the Israelite slave girl in Naaman's household. Note the power of even one believer. Even in captivity, this little girl remains faithful to the Lord and continues her witness. She obviously thinks of herself as "God's agent in Syria." The little slave girl suggests that Naaman visit her spiritual leader back in her homeland. Talk with your class about the power of the witness of one person. Also discuss with your class the various forms of "captivity" or "service in Syria"—perhaps an unpleasant job or a difficult domestic situation—which seems to be the lot of some of your people. How, like the Israelite girl, may your class members remain loyal to the faith in such settings?

2. *SEVEN DIPS IN THE JORDAN.* Naaman takes the Israelite slave girl's advice and consults the Hebrew holy man. However, when told to dip himself in the puny Jordan, Naaman scoffs. Naaman demands dramatic duties and sensational settings. He has to learn that God does His work without hoopla. Naaman has to learn to obey! Remind your class of these truths for your people. Isn't worship, for example, apparently as pointless as dipping into the Jordan? What will ever happen by gathering in church with those hypocrites on Sunday at 11? Or, why go through what seems to be the useless exercise of praying? Or working with the Bible, so filled with difficult-to-understand ancient history? Aren't these

forms of dipping seven times in the Jordan for your people? Stress to your folks the need for obedience today!

3. *SIX THOUSAND PIECES OF SILVER.* Naaman finally dipped himself in the Jordan as commanded by Elisha—and discovered that he was cured! Profoundly grateful, he tries to press payment on the prophet. Elisha refuses. However, Elisha's wily, greedy servant has no such scruples. Reflect with your class on the way "love of money" can be the downfall of anyone, including religious people. Contrast Elisha and Gehazi (*see* 2 Kings 5:18–27). The Lord's true prophets refuse to become peddlers of God's favors!

4. *TWO LOADS OF EARTH.* Naaman takes home two muleloads of earth from Elisha's area as a reminder of the Lord and His goodness. In effect, Naaman sets up a shrine where he resides to worship the Lord. Turn the talk in this part of your lesson to ways in which each person may "take home" the meaning of his or her faith. How is the Lord truly worshiped in the Monday-through-Saturday setting for each person? How does each member of your class create space for God in the midst of a crowded daily schedule? How may every Christian carry home something of the sacred from each Sunday?

TOPIC FOR ADULTS
NAAMAN: RELUCTANT FOLLOWER

With a Pickle Relish Hairdo. Many persons have the notion that they fail at being Christians unless they perform dramatic stunts. A couple of years ago, for instance, three sisters in Lansing, Michigan, were arrested for what they insisted was the only way to spread the Word of God. Slathering their bodies with mustard and mayonnaise, and piling pickle relish in their hair, the trio drove their van to a local police station and started to preach. The startled police took Doshaline McCuin, Charlene Roper, and Sandra Lewis into custody for indecent exposure and joyriding. The three young divorcees, who share a house and a fanatic devotion to certain religious television shows, claimed they were seized by religious fervor. The three insist that "normal" ways of following the Lord, such as are advocated by most Christians in Lansing or Ingham County, are not good enough for them.

Naaman, who disdained Elisha's advice to bathe in the waters of the Jordan, wanted a "pickle-relish-in-the-hair" kind of religion. He mistakenly assumed that he had to go through sensational acts to win God's favor. Genuine faith often means "bathing in the Jordan" in the sense of doing the undramatic and obeying the advice of the Lord.

More Than Meets the Eye. Of all the creatures in the animal world, the llama, the yak, and the camel are among the most unimposing. People think more of flashy colorful animals, talk of putting a tiger in their tank, and get a sense of power from driving a car called a Cougar. No automobile will ever be named "the Yak." The ungainly camel is the butt of jokes about being put together by a committee. No ball club has ever identified with the ugly South American beast and dubbed itself the "Llamas."

Yet, the llama, the camel, and the yak are among the best providers in the animal world. In the lands in which they are found, they offer the natives nearly every need. Their hair is woven into cloth for clothing and tents. Their skins become coats and blankets. Their meat and milk provide nourishment. In the Andes Mountains, in the Tibetan wastelands, and in the bleak deserts, life could not be conducted without the llama, the yak, and the camel respectively.

These three ungainly-looking animals give us a lesson. The exciting-looking and dramatic-sounding person is not necessarily the one who is needed most. The man or woman who provides for others, faithfully carrying out his duties day in and day out, is the person who is ultimately most appreciated. People like Naaman who want to be tigers and cougars in their response to God could better take a lesson from the humbler and plainer camel, yak, and llama.

Checkbook Biography. There is a great contrast between the way Elisha the prophet and his servant Gehazi regarded money and possessions. Elisha possessed; Gehazi was possessed by his money. Elisha gave; Gehazi grabbed.

Your stewardship of your money is a confession of your faith. It reflects accurately how serious you are about your life before Christ.

A noted biographer has described how he researches the lives of the people about whom he writes. He has no problem collecting information on the person's public career—birth, parents, childhood events, education, significant occurrences throughout the subject's lifetime, etc. To get "inside" the person, however, proved to be elusive. For a long time, he struggled to find ways by which he could discover what truly showed what the subject's values and faith were. Finally, he discovered the technique of examining the checkbook stubs. Here, this writer claims, is an infallible method of ascertaining the character of a person.

Your checkbook gossips about you. Your use of your money is the mark of your faith in a way little else is.

Questions for Pupils on the Next Lesson. 1. How does an adult Christian express his or her commitment to community? 2. Who were the most influential persons in your life? Why? 3. Why do you sometimes find it difficult to accept criticism? 4. Why does everyone need a firm value system? 5. Do you see yourself primarily as a leader or a follower? Why?

TOPIC FOR YOUTH
NAAMAN: A PROBLEM WITH PRIDE

Problems With Pride. "Joel Quiñones, after a career of crime and imprisonment in both Mexico and the United States, was converted to Christ. After Bible school and service as a pastor, he went back to the prisons, this time as Mexico's only prison chaplain. What has happened since? Ed Whitford, of Tecate, California, sent us these stories from that ministry—we know you will want to pray for these people.

" 'At the age of fifteen, I began to use drugs and live a base life, given to vice. There was no peace or hope. My mother told me that she was expecting to hear of my death because I was killing myself. I told her I wanted to die drugged. But the message reached me that I could obtain pardon through Jesus Christ. Now I am preparing to work for God to help people know that Jesus Christ died for us and that we can have eternal life.'—Raymundo Rodriquez Delgado.

" 'I was a professional fighter for eighteen years, but was also in prison and lived a life full of sin and perversity. One day I came to know Christ as my personal Savior, and a wish to serve God was born in my life. The doors of the City of Refuge were opened, and I am preparing to carry the Gospel to those who find themselves in prison.'—Ernesto David Hernandez.

" 'I was a convict in Islas Marias and a sick alcoholic. Alcoholism led me to a life of desperation and uncertainty about my future life. Someone came into my life in the most critical moments of my existence and there was born in my life an immense desire to live. This Person is Jesus Christ, the Son of God who has transformed me from a sinner degraded by vice to a true man and servant of Him. My reason for being in the City of Refuge is that God has called me to prepare my life spiritually and in the knowledge of the Word of God in order to approach those who suffer because they believe that no longer is there hope for them in the condition of life they live, as at one time I lived.'—Ysidro Vásquez Duarte.

"And the ministry of Jesus Christ goes on as one person reaches another, and that person in turn speaks of Christ to someone else. We rejoice at what God is doing. He has His people everywhere."—Excerpts from TO PRISON WITH THE GOSPEL by H. Norman Wright, June 1980, *Decision* © 1980 by The Billy Graham Evangelistic Association.

Decal Vision. Our pride sometimes keeps us from looking ahead. We get so obsessed with our own accomplishments that we cannot see where we are heading.

One of the characters on the television program "M*A*S*H" compared people who are so stuck on themselves to those who have their automobile windows plastered with decals of places they have visited and sights they have seen. Said the "M*A*S*H" character, "Their windows are so covered up with where they've been that they can't see where they're going."

Are you so covered with pride over what you've done that you see only the decals of accomplishment? Have you obscured your vision of God and your future by plastering the windshield of your soul with conceit and vanity?

Naaman had to "clean the windshield," so to speak, by forgetting his proud past and stopping his arrogant attitude before he could receive healing. You also must leave your pride behind before Jesus Christ can give you new life.

Appreciated. Naaman learned not to take others for granted. When he finally mastered this important lesson, he was cured of his disease and was given a faith in God. Appreciating others was a key factor in his recovery and in his religion.

During the long transit strike in New York city in the summer of 1980, the managers of one of New York's largest financial houses discovered that absenteeism actually decreased. Everyone expected that the difficulties in getting to work each day would mean many would find excuses not to come to their jobs. Furthermore, contrary to fears, work was carried out at quality and quantity levels higher than before the strike. Experts started to analyze the reasons.

The most important factor in the low absentee rate and the high production rate, the researchers discovered, was that managers showed appreciation to their employees. Managers made a point of thanking workers personally and sent special letters of thanks. Workers were grateful not to be treated as if they were just part of the landscape.

Do you show your gratitude to God, and to others?

Sentence Sermon to Remember: Bless the Lord . . . Who forgiveth all thine iniquities, who healeth all thy diseases.—Psalms 103:1,3.

Questions for Pupils on the Next Lesson. 1. Do you find that you sometimes have difficulty in determining what your true priorities are? 2. How do you set your priorities in life at this time? 3. What changes in society would you like to work to effect? 4. Do you sometimes find that you must choose between being well liked and doing what is right? 5. Who are the people who have influenced you most? Why?

LESSON IX—JULY 31

JOASH: A KING LED ASTRAY

Background Scripture: 2 Chronicles 24
Devotional Reading: Matthew 27:3–10

KING JAMES VERSION

2 CHRONICLES 24 1 Joash *was* seven years old when he began to reign, and he reigned forty years in Jerusalem. His mother's name also was Zibiah of Beer-sheba.

2 And Joash did *that which was* right in the sight of the LORD all the days of Jehoiada the priest.

3 And Jehoiada took for him two wives; and he begat sons and daughters.

4 And it came to pass after this, *that* Joash was minded to repair the house of the LORD.

5 And he gathered together the priests and the Levites, and said to them, Go out unto the cities of Judah, and gather of all Israel money to repair the house of your God from year to year, and see that ye hasten the matter. Howbeit the Levites hastened *it* not.

6 And the king called for Jehoiada the chief, and said unto him, Why hast thou not required of the Levites to bring in out of Judah and out of Jerusalem the collection, *according to the commandment* of Moses the servant of the LORD, and of the congregation of Israel, for the tabernacle of witness?

7 For the sons of Athaliah, that wicked woman, had broken up the house of God; and also all the dedicated things of the house of the LORD did they bestow upon Baalim.

17 Now after the death of Jehoiada came the princes of Judah, and made obeisance to the king. Then the king hearkened unto them.

18 And they left the house of the LORD God of their fathers, and served groves and idols: and wrath came upon Judah and Jerusalem for this their trespass.

19 Yet he sent prophets to them, to bring them again unto the LORD; and they testified against them: but they would not give ear.

20 And the Spirit of God came upon Zechariah the son of Jehoiada the priest, which stood above the people, and said unto them, Thus saith God, Why trans-

REVISED STANDARD VERSION

2 CHRONICLES 24 1 Joash was seven years old when he began to reign, and he reigned forty years in Jerusalem; his mother's name was Zibiah of Beer-sheba. 2 And Joash did what was right in the eyes of the LORD all the days of Jehoiada the priest. 3 Jehoiada got for him two wives, and he had sons and daughters.

4 After this Joash decided to restore the house of the LORD. 5 And he gathered the priests and the Levites, and said to them, "Go out to the cities of Judah, and gather from all Israel money to repair the house of your God from year to year; and see that you hasten the matter." But the Levites did not hasten it. 6 So the king summoned Jehoiada the chief, and said to him, "Why have you not required the Levites to bring in from Judah and Jerusalem the tax levied by Moses, the servant of the LORD, on the congregation of Israel for the tent of testimony?" 7 For the sons of Athaliah, that wicked woman, had broken into the house of God; and had also used all the dedicated things of the house of the LORD for the Baals.

17 Now after the death of Jehoiada the princes of Judah came and did obeisance to the king; then the king harkened to them. 18 And they forsook the house of the LORD, the God of their fathers, and served the Asherim and the idols. And wrath came upon Judah and Jerusalem for this their guilt. 19 Yet he sent prophets among them to bring them back to the LORD; these testified against them, but they would not give heed.

20 Then the Spirit of God took possession of Zechariah the son of Jehoiada the priest; and he stood above the people, and said to them, "Thus says God, 'Why do you trans-

gress ye the commandments of the LORD, that ye cannot prosper? because ye have forsaken the LORD, he hath also forsaken you.

gress the commandments of the LORD, so that you cannot prosper? Because you have forsaken the LORD, he has forsaken you.' "

KEY VERSE: " 'Why do you transgress the commandments of the Lord, so that you cannot prosper? Because you have forsaken the Lord, he has forsaken you.' " 2 Chronicles 24:20 (RSV).

HOME DAILY BIBLE READINGS

July 25. M. The Way of the Wicked. Psalms 1.
July 26. T. Trust in the Lord. Psalms 4.
July 27. W. The Shield of Favor. Psalms 5.
July 28. T. Walking Blamelessly. Psalms 15.
July 29. F. Forgiven Transgressions. Psalms 32.
July 30. S. Walking in Integrity. Psalms 26.
July 31. S. Trust not in Princes. Psalms 146.

BACKGROUND

Both Israel and Judah, we are told, very often did that which was evil in the eyes of their God; mixed in with a few good kings or queens at one period, there was a whole string of kings who were perhaps more responsible for evil than were the people of their kingdoms. Rulers often set a bad example which leads their people to believe that if their rulers sin, it is all right for *them* to sin. Immorality in high places leads to immorality among people in low places.

There was, for instance, the miserable Athaliah, a "queen" who seized the throne of Judah after her son Ahaziah had been killed by Jehu of Israel; she put to death "all the royal seed," but she missed putting to death the young son and prince named Joash, and she was killed by the supporters of young Joash. Actually he was rescued from the slaughter by the wife of Jehoiada, the high priest of Jerusalem, who hid him in a bed chamber of the royal palace. He stayed concealed in the Temple precincts for six long years. When he was seven years old, he was brought out of hiding by Jehoiada, who announced that this boy was the rightful king of Judah. The high priest was clever; he gathered around him a well-equipped little army to take care of any opposition that might develop.

A boy king!

NOTES ON THE PRINTED TEXT

The boy king stayed close to the high priest, who trained him well for his task, and even supervised the selection of wives for him to insure the royal succession (verse 3). And Joash, boy that he was, "did that was right in the sight of the Lord all the days of Jehoiada the priest." There was much to be done; the Temple was in a sad state of ruin, and too many of his subjects were worshiping Baal. At the prodding of Jehoiada, he made war on Baal and reduced the worship of the pagan god, but, right here at the beginning of his reign, he made a sad mistake. He failed to destroy the "high places" where Baal was worshiped. (Or did the high priest make that mistake?) Then he turned to rebuild the Temple. He raided the temples of Baal and brought back the loot that had been stolen by the Baalites and rededicated it to the worship of God. That was good.

Better still was his proclamation that he sent out all over the land of Judah, asking for money to finance the restoration of *their* Temple. And just outside the Temple gate, he set up a chest in which those who had loved the Temple could drop their contributions for its restoration. It was a great idea; it was not long before the chest overflowed. (We know a fine modern preacher who imitates this idea of Joash; one week each year, he sets a chest before the altar of his church, and it overflows!)

The people liked it and liked their young king for doing it, but the priests and the Levites did not think much of it. Having failed themselves to restore the Temple, they were chagrined at the success of Joash, and they took their time in promoting the crusade; but, grudgingly, they "went along" with it.

Then, suddenly, calamity struck. Just when things were going well, Jehoiada died. To the young king, this was like cutting off his right arm. He had leaned on the high priest and moved as Jehoiada directed him to move. He leaned too much; alone, he was forced to choose his "advisers" from among the princes of Judah, and the princes swept down on him like wolves on a sheepfold. They flattered him with soft, pretty speech; they led him back to compromise with the people of Baal. Poor Joash! He was not made of the stuff of strong kings; without Jehoiada, he was weak. Zechariah, the son of Jehoiada, tried his best to bring him back to his senses and to his loyalty to God, but he got nowhere; he was forced to tell the weakening king that because he had forsaken his Lord, the Lord had forsaken him. In Zechariah, Joash saw a threat to his power, a rebel leading the people to riot and revolution and so he did away with Zechariah. At the court of the Temple, he had stoned to death the son of the man who had secreted him in the Temple and made him king.

That same year Hazael of Syria made war against Judah, and Joash bought him off by giving him as tribute the treasures of the palace and the Temple. Then two of his servants came by night into his bedroom at Milo and killed him.

When John Wilkes Booth killed Abraham Lincoln, the assassin shouted, "Sic semper tyrannis," which meant "Thus always to tyrants." The murderers of Joash might have had the same thought in mind when they stabbed him to death, but if they did, they were wrong. Joash was no tyrant. He was a fool who seems to have had no sense of values whatever; he was a weakling who had nothing more than a casual acquaintance with God; he was a reed in the wind of circumstance, easily swayed first one way and then another. He was a king to be admired for only a few years of his reign and pitied for the apostacy of his later years. If his story tells us anything at all, it tells us that we are fools when we put our trust in princes, and that God is absolutely just in His judging of men, and that He demands loyalty from every last one of His servants, from kings to commoners. Joash might have been a good and great king but, like some other heads of state in the long sweep of history, he wanted only power, and God snatched that power from his hand and left him only a bitter memory in the minds of a people who wanted to love him.

SUGGESTIONS TO TEACHERS

A novelist writing after World War I remembered the person he had been before being thrown into the horrors of the trenches. Realizing that he had lost the ideals and resolve of his youth and noting that he had acquired a cynicism and hardness, this writer dedicated one of his books: "To the man I used to be."

Unfortunately, this could be the inscription for the life of many of God's people. How often a person begins well, then seems to fall away from his or her original standards and intentions! This is the story of Joash, who might have reflected at the close of his life that he was no longer the man he used to be.

Your lesson should be pointed toward helping your class members remain the persons Christ intends them to be.

1. *REMINDER TO A PRIEST.* You can illustrate Joash's outstanding start as king by describing the way he even reminded Jehoiada, the priest, of a forgotten temple tax. Joash has zeal for the Lord. He stands for justice. He also humbly accepts the priest's guidance. You may wish to comment on the place of people of God in the political life of every nation. Without being partisan, Christians should serve as the "conscience" of the country and its leaders. Both king and "conscience" or ruler and prophet must be in dialogue if a nation is to be obedient to God.

2. *RENOVATION OF THE TEMPLE.* Joash also restores the Temple to its former state of beauty. This ruler rightly recognized that he is ruled by God. Although king, Joash knows that he must bow to a higher Ruler. He correctly resists the temptation to exalt and worship himself. Take a few minutes to work on the notion of who is *de facto* ruler in the life of your church and in the lives of each of your class members. Determine who those rulers may be by listing priorities of time, energy, and money, that is, the "temple" or shrine to which each church or churchmember is consecrated.

3. *RENUNCIATION OF GOD.* After Jehoiada's death, Joash allows himself to be led astray by others. He begins to listen to human voices instead of to the divine voice. Heeding the wrong voices, he ignores the Lord. What are the most influential voices for those in your class? How does a Christian "listen" to God's voice today?

4. *REVERSAL OF POLICIES.* Renouncing God means reversing His policies. Examine Joash's record from the point where he began to listen to the leaders instead of to the Lord. Notice also how "they forsook the house of the Lord" (2 Chronicles 24:18). When the people no longer worshiped the Lord, they forsook Him for other deities.

5. *RESULTS OF APOSTASY.* The dreary saga of Joash concludes with Joash ignoring the Lord's messengers, even Jehoiada's son Zechariah, and resorting to murder to silence Zechariah. Joash's death at the hands of a small Syrian force was seen as divine justice at work. Discuss the significance of God's providence in human affairs. What is God doing these days? Do your class members firmly believe that God continues to direct and control the ultimate outcome of history?

TOPIC FOR ADULTS
JOASH: A KING LED ASTRAY

The Old Man You'll Meet. "You're going to meet an old man someday! Down the road ahead—ten, twenty, thirty years—he's waiting there for you. You'll be catching up with him!

"What kind of old man are you going to meet? That's a rather significant question!

"He may be a seasoned, soft, gracious fellow—a gentleman who has grown old gracefully, surrounded by hosts of friends who call him blessed because of what his life has meant to them.

"He may be a bitter, disillusioned, dried-up, cynical old buzzard, without a good word for anybody—soured, friendless and alone.

"The kind of old man you will meet depends entirely on you. Because that old man will be you. He'll be the composite of everything you do, say, and think—today and tomorrow. His mind will be set in a mold you have made by your attitudes. His heart will be turning out what you've been putting in.

"Every little thought, every deed, goes into the making of this old man. He'll be exactly what you make him—nothing more, nothing less. It's up to you. You'll have no one else to credit or blame.

"Every day in every way you are becoming more and more like yourself, think more like yourself, talk more like yourself. You're becoming yourself more and more.

"Live only in terms of what you're getting out of life and the old man gets smaller, drier, harder, crabbier, more self-centered.

"Open your life to others, think in terms of what you can give to life, and the old man grows larger, softer, kindlier, greater.

"A point to remember is that these things don't always show immediately, but they'll show up sooner than you think. These little things, so unimportant now—attitudes, goals, ambitions, desires—they're adding up inside, where you can't see them, crystallizing in your heart and mind. Someday you'll harden into that old man, and nothing will be able to soften or change then.

"The time to take care of that old man is right now—this week, today. Examine his motives, attitudes, goals. Check up on him. Work him over while he's still plastic, still in a formative condition. The day comes, awfully soon, when it's too late. The hardness will have set in, worse than paralysis. Character crystallizes, sets, jells. That's the finish.

"Any wise man takes personal inventory regularly. We all need to in the light of Christ and His Word. You'll be much more likely to meet a splendid old fellow at the proper time—the fellow you'd like to be.

" 'Be not deceived; God is not mocked: for whatsoever a man soweth, that shall he also reap' (Galations 6:7)."—Richard C. Halverson, in *PERSPECTIVE.*

Led Astray. Napoleon Bonaparte, the Emperor, once slept in Nazareth in the Holy Land during his campaign through Syria. He claimed to have dreams of serving Christ. However, the remainder of his life was a trail of blood and death from the Pyrennes in Spain to the frozen depths of Russia. Millions died or were maimed. Cities and countrysides were devastated.

At the end of his career standing on his lonely wave-washed rocky island in the South Atlantic, where the nations he tried to conquer had imprisoned him, Napoleon paid this tribute to the other Conqueror who also had slept at Nazareth: "I die before my time. My body will be given back to the earth to be done with as men please, and to become the food of worms. Such will be the fate of him who has been called the Great Napoleon. What an abyss between my deep misery and the eternal Kingdom of Christ, which is proclaimed, loved, and adored, and is extending over the whole earth!"

Bible of History. "The law of judgment and punishment runs through the history of the nations. The time at length comes, the hour at length strikes, when God says, 'Now will I rise . . . ; now will I be exalted: now will I lift up myself.' These 'risings' of the Almighty, when he doeth terrible things in righteousness, are a sublime page, not only in the book of divine revelation which we call the Bible, but also in the book of man's history; for even if men will not read the inspired Bible, God makes a Bible out of history.

"Take the history of our own country. As nations go, our history is a very brief one, yet long enough to display the law of righteousness and the punishment of God upon sin. Three quarters of a century before the stroke of judgment fell, Thomas Jefferson, writing his *Notes on the State of Virginia* on the tilting rock at Harper's Ferry, which overlooks the junction of the Shenandoah and Potomac Rivers, commented on the institution of Negro slavery which had sprung up and flourished in America, saying, with a prophet's voice and vision, 'I tremble for my country when I reflect that God is just.' In 1859 at Charlestown, not far from Harper's Ferry, where Jefferson wrote those prophetic words, an old man was led down the steps of the jail to be hanged by the neck until dead. As he left the prison he handed to his guards this last message to his countrymen: 'I, John Brown, am now quite certain that the crimes of this guilty land will never be purged away but with blood.' Then came the bloodiest day of the Civil War; and the rock where Jefferson wrote his *Notes* and the ground where the gallows stood on which John Brown was hanged shook and quaked with the concussion of the guns firing across the Potomac in the battle of Antietam. When the moon came up over the mountains that night, it looked down upon a strange scene. The rows of standing corn, swept by the sleet of lead, lay prostrate and trampled; the trim hedges and fences were broken and scattered; the orchards were mangled and splintered. In the great barns, the surgeons with bare and bloody arms cut and sawed by the flickering light of the lantern, while the cattle looked on with dumb awe. And down by the river banks, and in the river, and under the bridges, and along the roads and lanes, and in the trampled grain, and beneath the splintered trees, thousands of young men, most of them under twenty-one, lay still and rigid, their white faces pleading a mute protest to the autumnal moon. Had John Brown's prophecy about the atonement of blood come true? Abraham Lincoln must have realized that it had, for less than three years afterward, when he delivered his Second Inaugural Address, he spoke of the war then raging as the punishment that had come to both North and South because of the offense of slavery:

" 'Fondly, do we hope, fervently do we pray that this mighty scourge of war may speedily pass away. Yet, if God wills that it continue until all the wealth piled by the bondsman's two hundred and fifty years of unrequited toil shall be sunk, until every drop of blood drawn with the lash will be paid by another drawn with the sword, as was said three thousand years ago, so still it must be said, "The judgments of the Lord are true and righteous altogether." ' "—Clarence E. Macartney, *Mountains and Mountain Men of the Bible.*

Questions for Pupils on the Next Lesson. 1. What are the qualities that make for strong and lasting homes? 2. Have you found worth in and been able to have companionship with persons of other races and nationalities? 3. How is the quality of your life influencing others? 4. Why was Naomi's plight so bitter? 5. What resources is your church bringing to help strengthen home and family relations?

TOPIC FOR YOUTH
JOASH: LED ASTRAY

Missed Opportunity. An old man made an appointment to call on the painter-poet Dante Gabriel Rossetti. When the man arrived, he opened a portfolio of drawings and spread them in front of Rossetti who quickly saw that they were of poor quality: he told the man that they had no value. The old man reached into his case and laid out another packet of sketches which he said had been done by a student. Rossetti looked at them with enthusiasm. Turning to the elderly man, Rossetti said that the student had great promise and should be encouraged to continue with his art. Suddenly, the aged one choked up with tears. "I, I was that student once," he croaked.

Like Joash, this man had allowed himself to be led astray from using his gifts as God's person.

No Small Potatoes. A soldier on fatigue duty was asked to sort out and peel a huge pile of potatoes. The supervising sergeant told him to put the edible ones to his right, and to the left the inedible ones. Two hours passed before the sergeant's return. He found the soldier completely immobile, with the mound of potatoes untouched. "What's wrong" he asked, "don't you like work?" "It's not the work, Sarge," the soldier said, "it's the decisions that's killin' me."

Joash also found it was the decisions that killed him. The basic decision for Joash—and for you—is to honor and serve the Lord. Not making that fundamental decision can immobilize you from right decision-making for life.

Bumper Sticker Creed. A magazine cartoon shows a bumper sticker behind a forlorn driver's car: "Honk if you believe in anything." That slogan could have been Joash's final epitaph. This young man of immense promise started by believing in the Lord and allowed himself to be led astray so that he ended by believing in nothing.

What one line would you as a Christian put on a bumper sticker to sum up your belief?

Sentence Sermon to Remember: Whenever you face a decision, you have three chances: Do what you please; do what others do; or do what is right.—A. Banningism.

Questions for Pupils on the Next Lesson. 1. Are you willing to cross racial and national barriers in friendships? 2. Do you sometimes feel that God is against you? 3. Why do you sometimes have difficulty in appreciating the value of hard work? 4. Do you think that faithfulness is rewarded? 5. Why was Naomi's situation so sad and bleak?

LESSON X—AUGUST 7

NAOMI AND RUTH: SHARED LOYALTY

Background Scripture: Ruth
Devotional Reading: Luke 10:38–42

KING JAMES VERSION

RUTH 1 16 And Ruth said, Intreat me not to leave thee, *or* to return from following after thee: for whither thou goest, I will go; and where thou lodgest, I will lodge: thy people *shall be* my people, and thy God my God:

17 Where thou diest, will I die, and there will I be buried: the LORD do so to me, and more also, *if aught* but death part thee and me.

18 When she saw that she was stedfastly minded to go with her, then she left speaking unto her.

19 So they two went until they came to Beth-le-hem. And it came to pass, when they were come to Beth-le-hem, that all the city was moved about them, and they said, *Is* this Naomi?

20 And she said unto them, Call me not Naomi, call me Mara: for the Almighty hath dealt very bitterly with me.

3 1 Then Naomi her mother in law said unto her, My daughter, shall I not seek rest for thee, that it may be well with thee?

2 And now *is* not Boaz of our kindred, with whose maidens thou wast? Behold, he winnoweth barley tonight in the threshingfloor.

3 Wash thyself therefore, and anoint thee, and put thy raiment upon thee, and get thee down to the floor: *but* make not thyself known unto the man, until he shall have done eating and drinking.

4 And it shall be, when he lieth down, that thou shalt mark the place where he shall lie, and thou shalt go in, and uncover his feet, and lay thee down; and he will tell thee what thou shalt do.

5 And she said unto her, All that thou sayest unto me I will do.

4 13 So Boaz took Ruth, and she was his wife: and when he went in unto her, the LORD gave her conception, and she bare a son.

14 And the women said unto Naomi, Blessed *be* the LORD, which hath not left thee this day without a kinsman, that his name may be famous in Israel.

15 And he shall be unto thee a restorer

REVISED STANDARD VERSION

RUTH 1 16 But Ruth said, "Entreat me not to leave you or to return from following you; for where you go I will go, and where you lodge I will lodge; your people shall be my people, and your God my God; 17 where you die I will die, and there will I be buried. May the LORD do so to me and more also if even death parts me from you." 18 And when Naomi saw that she was determined to go with her, she said no more.

19 So the two of them went on until they came to Bethlehem. And when they came to Bethlehem, the whole town was stirred because of them; and the women said, "Is this Naomi?" 20 She said to them, "Do not call me Naomi, call me Mara, for the Almighty has dealt very bitterly with me.

3 1 Then Naomi her mother-in-law said to her, "My daughter, should I not seek a home for you, that it may be well with you? 2 Now is not Boaz our kinsman, with whose maidens you were? See, he is winnowing barley tonight at the threshing floor. 3 Wash therefore and anoint yourself, and put on your best clothes and go down to the threshing floor; but do not make yourself known to the man until he has finished eating and drinking. 4 But when he lies down, observe the place where he lies; then, go and uncover his feet and lie down; and he will tell you what to do." 5 And she replied, "All that you say I will do."

4 13 So Boaz took Ruth and she became his wife; and he went in to her, and the LORD gave her conception, and she bore a son. 14 Then the women said to Naomi, "Blessed be the LORD, who has not left you this day without next of kin; and may his name be renowned in Israel! 15 He shall be to you a restorer of life and a nourisher of your old age; for your daugh-

of *thy* life, and a nourisher of thine old age: for thy daughter in law, which loveth thee, which is better to thee than seven sons, hath borne him.

16 And Naomi took the child, and laid it in her bosom, and became nurse unto it.

17 And the women her neighbors gave it a name, saying, There is a son born to Naomi; and they called his name Obed: he *is* the father of Jesse, the father of David.

ter-in-law who loves you, who is more to you than seven sons, has borne him." 16 Then Naomi took the child and laid him in her bosom, and became his nurse. 17 And the women of the neighborhood gave him a name, saying, "A son has been born to Naomi." They named him Obed; he was the father of Jesse, the father of David.

KEY VERSE: "Entreat me not to leave you or to return from following you; for where you go I will go, and where you lodge I will lodge; your people shall be my people, and your God my God." Ruth 1:16 (RSV).

HOME DAILY BIBLE READINGS

Aug. 1. M. Three Widows. Ruth 1:6–14.
Aug. 2. T. A Kind Kinsman. Ruth 2:1–13.
Aug. 3. W. A Happy Mother-In-Law. Ruth 2:14–23.
Aug. 4. T. An Act of Love. Ruth 3:1–13.
Aug. 5. F. A Grateful Man. Ruth 3:14–4:6.
Aug. 6. S. Witnesses of Mercy. Ruth 4:7–12.
Aug. 7. S. Blessings of the Lord. Ruth 4:13–17.

BACKGROUND

Last Sunday we had a lesson rife with apostasy, violence, murder, and faithlessness. Now we have something that is the exact opposite of all that: the story of Ruth and Naomi. No lovelier story has ever been written in any age by any man.

Sometime during the period of the judges, famine struck Palestine, and a little family living in Bethlehem, to escape death by starvation, fled to Moab; the family consisted of Elimelech the father, Naomi the mother, and Mahlon and Chilion, their sons. They did well in Moab, even though they were foreigners in a strange land, until the day came when Elimelech died and Naomi was left with her two sons, who by this time had married two Moabite girls named Ruth and Orpah. That left Naomi alone without husband or sons. She could remain in Moab, but there she would be a Jewish widow who would be anything but popular among the Moabites. Or she could go back to Bethlehem. When her two sons died, the decision had to be made, and she decided to go back to her old home with her two daughters-in-law. The famine had passed; there was food in Bethlehem.

Three women, Naomi and Orpah, and Ruth.

NOTES ON THE PRINTED TEXT

Somewhere along the road, Orpah changed her mind. She wept when she did it, but—she wanted a husband, and she saw little chance of finding a *Jewish* husband; she preferred a husband in Moab to exile with Naomi and Ruth. She had a choice between love for Naomi and love for her own people. Naomi was magnificent when this happened; she urged both girls to choose to go with her or go back, and she kissed Orpah good-bye. Then she asked Ruth if she, too, would like to go back. It was at this moment that Ruth proved herself to be one of the noblest of Old Testament women; in the words that are as beautiful as they are moving, she spoke to Naomi: "Intreat me not to leave thee . . . I will go; and where thou lodgest, I will lodge, thy people shall be my people, and thy God my God" (Ruth 1:16). So they went on to Bethlehem, both courageous, both brokenhearted.

They reached Bethlehem at the time of the harvest. Bethlehem welcomed them, but Bethlehem couldn't believe that this was Naomi who had gone from them so long ago. They watched her weep; they heard her say that they should call her not Naomi but *Mara*, a name which meant "bitter," for God had struck her bitter blows. Who can blame her? Widows are born to weep.

Now in Bethlehem, there lived a man named Boaz. Boaz was a wealthy man with many fields of growing corn; he also happened to be a kinsman of the dead Elimelech. It was the law that the nearest of kin of a dead man should care for the widow. Boaz kept that law. He provided for the lonely women; he told the servants of his fields that they were to leave more than a little of their corn for Ruth in the corners of the fields, when they reaped the harvest. The servants didn't like that, for Ruth was a *foreigner*. But whatever she was, there was also that law in the old law code of Deuteronomy which permitted the needy stranger, orphan, or widow to gather what was left by the harvesters. Ruth became a laborer in the fields under the protection of the gentle Boaz.

She needed protection for a young *foreign* woman stood in danger of being molested by the laborers. There was often drunkenness among them, and there was always bitterness and hatred and racial and religious discrimination. Boaz warned them to leave her alone, and they obeyed for they knew that Boaz, under the law, was the kinsman-redeemer of both Naomi and Ruth. Sometimes, property was spoken of as being "redeemed"; this emphasized the idea of "purchase," or "buying back," and there was property involved here—the property of Mahlon, Ruth's dead husband. The settlement of that estate raised a problem that was quickly solved by Boaz, who married Ruth to rescue (redeem) her from her widowhood.

This marriage was accomplished through the love of Naomi who "arranged" it. Knowing that during the threshing season the workers often slept on the threshing floor to protect the grain, Naomi "prepared Ruth as a bride," and sent her out to sleep at the feet of Boaz; when he awoke, she pleaded with him to spread his cover over her. ("This act of covering with the skirt was a familiar one in the ancient Near East and was symbolic of protection; it was especially associated with marriage."—Eric C. Rust.)

Boaz welcomed it. He loved this girl. This girl gave him a son, and they named him Obed, and this son was to become the father of Jesse, who was the father of David, who . . . !

It is all a story of love overcoming selfishness on the part of Ruth, Naomi, and Boaz. Naomi gave up much for the sake of Ruth; it was fitting when the child came, that Naomi held the baby Obed in her arms and became his nurse. It was providential that Boaz should redeem his Ruth. It is startling to find this Moabite girl challenging the old national and religious prejudices in a day when such prejudice and bigotry ran wild among nations. It was God's purpose that a childless Moabite widow, an alien to the People of God, was to become a progenitor of the line of David, an ancestress of Another born in Bethlehem who was to be Savior of the world and who saw Moabites and Israelites not as enemies but as potential children of God.

A fine American preacher poignantly wonders, "We have improved on Ruth's sickle, but have we improved on Ruth?"

SUGGESTIONS TO TEACHERS

Blood is not necessarily thicker than water. Through the water of baptism, we discover we are brought into a relationship with a new "family." We find ties as close as those we have to blood relatives and ties sometimes closer than those of family kin. God's own community gives us a new set of relations!

Your lesson today illustrates how this happens and what it means. The shared loyalties between a mother-in-law and daughter-in-law, Naomi and Ruth, offers you and your class a beautiful model of God's new and greater family.

1. *FIDELITY IN FRUSTRATION.* Let the full pathos of Naomi's situation be made clear to your class by giving all the details of her grief-filled story. Remind your people that being God's person does not mean being exempt from suffering or hardship. In fact, you may find that some in your class will want to reflect on the fact that the innocent often have rough going. Don't try to offer neat "reasons" or "explanations" for such suffering. Turn them to the Cross. Let the full impact of the mystery and meaning of Jesus' suffering be considered. Naomi, everyone may note, foreshadowed Jesus by remaining faithful in spite of hurts.

2. *FAMILY IN FUTILITY.* What is a family? Or, ask your class, exactly who is "family" for each person in the class? Point out the way in which Naomi and Ruth, in spite of the potentially sticky relationship of being "in-laws" only, found that they were brought close to each other in times when life seemed futile. The mother-in-law jokes simply don't always hold true, especially for God's people. Through a shared faith, people with a potentially adversarial relationship are brought close to each other. Is not this what your congregation should be? Discuss ways in which your church may be "family" to those on its rolls.

3. *FAITH FOR A FOREIGNER.* Naomi's faith rings true, so true that daughter-in-law Ruth, the nonbeliever from Moab, decides to make it her own faith. How attractive is your faith for the "foreigners" around you, such as the young people, the skeptics, the strangers in your community? How winsome is your witness to Jesus Christ to those within your own family? Do they see the Lord and His working through your life? Point out to your class that God is deeply concerned about the "foreigners" of every kind, and calls His people to welcome these foreigners to their midst.

4. *FORWARD WITH A FUTURE.* With the play on words through the literal meaning of *Naomi* in Hebrew (it means "pleasant"), the story of Naomi and Ruth tells us that life is constantly moving from bitter to pleasant with the Lord. In Ruth's case, she even becomes the great-

grandmother of David, and also an ancestress of Jesus. With God, even apparently insignificant Moabite widows become part of the great drama of salvation. Help your class members to appreciate how the Lord brings each believer into the ongoing story of His love story with the human race.

TOPIC FOR ADULTS
NAOMI AND RUTH: SHARED LOYALTY

Antidote to Loneliness. "She was the loneliest woman in the town, and her friends were greatly concerned. 'She does not snap out of it,' they said. 'But she and her husband were so devoted, and you cannot expect her to recover too quickly.'

"Then one day she took her grief to a strange preacher who happened to be visiting in her city. Following her visit, she acted on his advice and arranged a dinner party for some young business-women who lived in hotels and ate at restaurants. The affair was so successful and the merry laughter of the young women was so contagious, that she was lifted out of her gloom and everyone had a grand time.

"Catching a glimpse of what the program might mean to her, she began arranging other parties, dinners, and evenings. Her guests were always those who could never hope to repay her with similar invitations.

"Her kindly way and sweet spirit captivated the girls, and some of them began confiding in her. Soon she found herself at the center of an inspiring group and, almost before she realized it, she had risen above her melancholy and was living in a spirit of triumph.

"In both cases, redemption had come when the grieving forgot their grief and began giving themselves. There is something about that kind of giving which always acts as a solvent of despair and a creator of joy."—Roy L. Smith, "Lose Your Grief In Giving," *Christian Advocate,* May 6, 1954.

Future Possibilities. "The woman was bending over to water some tiny flowers which were growing as part of a large nativity scene inside the entry way of the sister house of a German order of deaconesses in West Berlin. The scene held before the viewer a panorama of excitement surrounding the birth of Christ. It included the wise men, the shepherds, village folks, and, of course, the tableaux of Mary, Joseph, and the baby Jesus. The scene was exquisite in its detail and it carried such a visual impact that for a moment I forgot it wasn't Christmas. When the sister had finished her work, we talked and she explained to me that the scene is maintained throughout the year because of the message of hope it brings for all the times of our lives.

"There are events along the way which mark a change in a person's life, a new time, a rebirth. Hope is born at the beginning time and at many other times of renewal in a man's or woman's history.

"There was something else the German sister said about the hope of Christmas. It is for *all* the times of our lives. I wonder if that means that hope doesn't have to do just with the future, but also with the past. So often, the two are separated in order to make room for hope. The past has to be forgotten to accommodate future possibilities."—Neil R. Paylor, in *PANORAMA*, December 1980, published by Pittsburgh, Pennsylvania, Theological Seminary.

The Precious Present. "Don't wait for gifts tomorrow; recognize them today since they are all about us. There are times to be redeemed, a world to be transformed, yes; but there are also events to be embraced, little events as well as big ones, and persons to be given affirmation and affection. Although the quantity of those moments is finite, the quality those moments can have is infinite. We embrace them when we affirm the small things that give time its blessed quality—a glance, a sound, a touch, a tiny ritual (the meaning of which perhaps only one other person knows). Such things are complete in themselves. But there is a further blessedness. They not only invest the now with preciousness in its own right, but also they give a new quality to the moments that precede and follow the now—an eternity momentarily glimpsed and forever retrievable through another gift, memory."—R. M. Brown, *Creative Dislocation,* Abingdon, 1980.

Questions for Pupils on the Next Lesson. 1. Why is it so disturbing to hear of indiscriminate conduct and behavior of unprincipled persons in high office? 2. Are families of spiritual leaders exempt from temptations? 3. Why is the story of Eli's sons so sad? 4. Is there any correlation between the behavior of religious leaders or national leaders and the course of a nation?

TOPIC FOR YOUTH
NAOMI AND RUTH: SHARED LOYALTY

Shared Loyalty of Marriage. Through the Lord, we share many important loyalties. Naomi and Ruth illustrate the shared loyalty of friendship.

Marriage is another shared loyalty. As you consider your relationship with others, remember that the relationship between two partners who are in love is also a loyalty shared with God.

Temple Gairdner, a missionary who built a lasting relationship of mutual loyalty in his marriage, composed a prayer as he prepared for his wedding. An excerpt of this prayer has these words which sum up the shared loyalty between husband, wife, and Christ: "That I may come near to her, draw me nearer to Thee than to her; that I may know her, make me to know Thee more than her; that I may love her with the perfect love of a perfectly whole heart, cause me to love Thee more than her and most of all.

"That nothing may be between me and her, be Thou between us, every moment; that we may be constantly together, draw us into separate loneliness with Thyself. And when we meet breast to breast, O Lord, let it be upon Thine own."

Stress Test. How do you handle stress? Some people try to cope with stress in strange ways. One of the weirdest recent ideas is called a flotation tank. You pay $25 to climb into a big wooden box in which eight inches of water at 93° temperature is mixed with 800 pounds of salt. For the next sixty minutes, you float in total darkness. Its promoters tell you that this is the best way to relieve the stress you feel! (Some who have tried it say that it's more like being sucked into the sweeper bag!)

Contrast this gimmicky solution with the way Naomi and Ruth handled their stress of losing husbands, being alone, and facing an uncertain future. Naomi and Ruth shared loneliness, but they also shared a loyalty to the Lord which made them loyal to one another. Their shared loyalties gave them strength to withstand stress.

Blossoming Life. Helen Keller became deaf, blind, and dumb through an illness early in her life. In spite of these severe handicaps, she was taught to speak, write, and live a useful life by an inspired teacher named Anne Sullivan. Miss Keller and Miss Sullivan grew to share a loyalty to the Lord and to each other which enabled each of them to bring immense blessings to others. Helen Keller, asked whether she resented her handicaps, said, "I have, like other people, made resolutions which I have broken or only half kept; but one which I send you . . . is the keynote of my life. It is this—always to regard as mere impertinences of fortune, the handicaps which were placed upon my life almost at the beginning. I resolved that that should not crush or dwarf my soul, but rather be made 'to blossom, like Aaron's rod, with flowers.' "—Helen Keller

Sentence Sermon to Remember: Love laughs at barriers—*all* barriers.—Anonymous.

Questions for Pupils on the Next Lesson. 1. How should we judge adults? By their words or by their actions? 2. How much should youth rebel against the authority of their parents? 3. Does doing evil always lead to being punished? 4. Can close personal relationships be destructive as well as supportive? 5. Why is the story of Hophni and Phinehas so sad?

LESSON XI—AUGUST 14

HOPHNI AND PHINEHAS: CORRUPT PRIESTS

Background Scripture: 1 Samuel 1:3; 2:12–17,22–25; 4
Devotional Reading: Acts 5:1–12

KING JAMES VERSION

1 SAMUEL 1 3 And this man went up out of his city yearly to worship and to sacrifice unto the LORD of hosts in Shiloh. And the two sons of Eli, Hophni and Phinehas, the priests of the LORD, *were* there.

2 12 Now the sons of Eli *were* sons of Belial; they knew not the LORD.

13 And the priest's custom with the people *was, that,* when any man offered sacrifice, the priest's servant came, while the flesh was in seething, with a fleshhook of three teeth in his hand;

14 And he struck *it* into the pan, or kettle, or caldron, or pot; all that the fleshhook brought up the priest took for himself. So they did in Shiloh unto all the Israelites that came thither.

15 Also before they burnt the fat, the priest's servant came, and said to the man that sacrificed, Give flesh to roast for the priest; for he will not have sodden flesh of thee, but raw.

16 And *if* any man said unto him, Let them not fail to burn the fat presently, and *then* take *as much* as thy soul desireth; then he would answer him, *Nay;* but thou shalt give *it me* now: and if not, I will take *it* by force.

17 Wherefore the sin of the young men was very great before the LORD: for men abhorred the offering of the LORD.

22 Now Eli was very old, and heard all that his sons did unto all Israel; and how they lay with the women that assembled *at* the door of the tabernacle of the congregation.

23 And he said unto them, Why do ye such things? for I hear of your evil dealings by all this people.

24 Nay, my sons; for *it is* no good report that I hear: ye make the LORD's people to transgress.

25 If one man sin against another, the judge shall judge him: but if a man sin against the LORD, who shall entreat for him? Notwithstanding, they hearkened not unto the voice of their father, because the LORD would slay them.

REVISED STANDARD VERSION

1 SAMUEL 1 3 Now this man used to go up year by year from his city to worship and to sacrifice to the LORD of hosts at Shiloh, where the two sons of Eli, Hophni and Phinehas, were priests of the LORD.

2 12 Now the son of Eli were worthless men; they had no regard for the LORD. 13 The custom of the priests with the people was that when any man offered sacrifice, the priest's servant would come, while the meat was boiling, with a three-pronged fork in his hand, 14 and he would thrust it into the pan, or kettle, or caldron, or pot; all that the fork brought up the priest would take for himself. So they did at Shiloh to all the Israelites who came there. 15 Moreover, before the fat was burned, the priest's servant would come and say to the man who was sacrificing, "Give meat for the priest to roast; for he will not accept boiled meat from you, but raw." 16 And if the man said to him, "Let them burn the fat first, and then take as much as you wish," he would say, "No, you must give it now; and if not, I will take it by force." 17 Thus the sin of the young men was very great in the sight of the LORD; for the men treated the offering of the LORD with contempt.

22 Now Eli was very old, and he heard all that his sons were doing to all Israel, and how they lay with the women who served at the entrance to the tent of meeting. 23 And he said to them, "Why do you do such things? For I hear of your evil dealings from all the people. 24 No, my sons; it is no good report that I hear the people of the LORD spreading abroad. 25 If a man sins against a man, God will mediate for him; but if a man sins against the LORD, who can intercede for him?" But they would not listen to the voice of their father; for it was the will of the LORD to slay them.

4 11 And the ark of God was taken; and the two sons of Eli, Hophni and Phinehas, were slain.	4 11 And the ark of God was captured; and the two sons of Eli, Hophni and Phinehas, were slain.

KEY VERSE: For the Lord knoweth the way of the righteous: but the way of the ungodly shall perish. Psalms 1:6.

HOME DAILY BIBLE READINGS

Aug. 8. M. The Wicked Sons of Eli. 1 Samuel 1:1–3.
Aug. 9. T. The Sins of Hophni and Phinehas. 1 Samuel 2:12–17,22–25.
Aug. 10. W. The Capture of the Ark. 1 Samuel 4:1–10.
Aug. 11. T. The Doom of Eli's House. 1 Samuel 2:27–36.
Aug. 12. F. Philistines Return the Ark. 1 Samuel 6:1–15.
Aug. 13. S. Good and Evil Ways. Psalms 1.
Aug. 14. S. Men Good and Evil. Jeremiah 17:5–10.

BACKGROUND

Shiloh was an important sanctuary town established by Israel in the hill country of Ephraim between Bethel and Lebonah. It was here that Joshua brought the tribes of Israel at the end of their conquest of Canaan; here they cast lots for the assignment of land to each of the tribes. During the period of the Judges, it had become Israel's headquarters; in Shiloh the Ark was set up in the Tabernacle. A staff of resident priests, like Eli and his two sons Hophni and Phinehas, became the administrators of the sacred place; to them came the people for worship and offerings of sacrifice. The priest Eli welcomed a boy named Samuel to the sacred precincts and wielded great influence upon him as he grew to manhood.

Eli was as near being a living saint as any among the men of Israel. No one could doubt his piety and consecration—but in his old age, at the time Samuel came to him, he was a victim of old age, timid and weak. His sons were "something else." They were degenerate, immoral, and plain wicked, a blasphemous pair who took advantage of their decrepit father, who outraged their God and turned Shiloh into a place to be despised. They remain in history as examples of the hard truth that the wearing of a robe does not make any man a priest.

NOTES ON THE PRINTED TEXT

How does it happen that two brothers reared in the same home can become diametrically different kinds of men: that one brother can become a minister and the other a menace to society and a disgrace to his parents? How could it happen that the two sons of Eli were to be so different from Samuel?

The narrative calls the two sons of Eli "the sons of Belial," which meant that they were figurative sons of Satan. How did they get that way with such a father? Certainly a God-fearing man like Eli could never have taught them anything even approximate to evil, but evil they were, both of them. They grew up in Shiloh and they were educated for the priesthood by the proper authorities, but, somewhere along the line, they came to realize that there was power in the priesthood that was anything but the power of the God they pretended to serve. There were certain privileges granted to them that were not granted to the people who supported them, and it was a power often turned to satisfy the greed of priests who never should have become priests. In modern language, we call it clericalism, which means the abuse of power by priests or ministers who at heart are not men of God but men of greed and avarice. That is sad, but it is true; even today, we occasionally find a bad apple in the ecclesiastical barrel who, unless he is exposed and eliminated, can bring disgrace upon the Church.

There were two vicious sins practiced by Hophni and Phinehas. One was the sin of treating with contempt the offerings of the people who came to worship. It was customary—no, it was a rule—that the priests of Shiloh be paid for their services by sticking a fork into the pot where the sacrifice (the meat of lambs, sheep, or oxen) was being cooked; whatever the fork happened to hit and hold became the food of the priest. It was a "pot luck" system, and many priests did not like it; they wanted the choice cuts of the meat. This, they said, was one of the privileges of the clergy. Let the people have what was left over!

It was a disgusting performance to the Jews, who saw this practice as one which took meat before the sacrifice was offered to God. It was a sin compounded by priests who threatened to take what they wanted when they wanted it by force if necessary (1 Samuel 2:16). They were not only cheating men; they were treating God with contempt. They were taking for themselves meat which was offered to God. It is a sin not confined to an errant and traitorous priesthood, but common among careless Christians who believe that because they are Christians they have certain privileges which are doubtful indications of their lack of consecration to their Christ. It reminds us of a man we once knew, a member of the Church, who told us flatly that the thing for every man to do was to make a fortune *first,* and then give back to God a pittance of his wealth for His work! That is anything but Christian; it is a sin that must give pain to the heart of God. (There is nothing wrong with making a fortune; it *is* wrong to make of it the first priority of a man's life.)

The second evil of Hophni and Phinehas was that of adultery. Both of these priests were undoubtedly married men, but they were not satisfied with that: "They lay with the women that assembled at the door of the tabernacle of the congregation" (verse 22). These may have been women who came to worship, or women who served in the Tabernacle. At its worst, it could have been rape; at its best, it was a direct insult to the God worshiped in that Tabernacle, and a sin so low and vicious that, said Eli, God could and would punish. It was bad enough for man to sin against men, but when a man sins in this manner against the Lord of the Tabernacle, "who can intercede for him"? Who but God can punish a man who insists upon insulting God and His commandments?

Eli pleaded with them, but they paid no attention to him. It made no difference whether they listened or not, "for the Lord was already planning to kill them" (1 Samuel 2:25 TLB). This was the Jewish faith: God was the ultimate judge, and God would ultimately punish. He punished Hophni and Phinehas, who later went into battle against the Philistines at Aphek, "protecting" the Ark! They died as they had lived: terribly.

God is no respecter of persons, be they priests or lowly laymen. God demands payment and repentance for our sins, large and small. A man may escape judgment by his fellowmen, but moral and spiritual treason is judged finally not by men but by God. God lays down moral and spiritual rules which we must choose either to ignore or obey. If we disobey, there is a price to be paid in a wasted life and in a loss of fellowship with God.

Eli, poor man, failed to build any stately mansions in the souls of his sons, but he did build them in those long years while he was training Samuel, who became what he had hoped his sons would become. The house of Eli fell, disappeared from future history, but Samuel lived on and brought glory and honor to his name.

SUGGESTIONS TO TEACHERS

Americans were shocked when two young California men in positions of responsibility were convicted in 1981 of passing military secrets to the Russians. Both of these men were from affluent, upper-class homes and had received excellent educations. Both were awarded positions of trust in the military. Both had been raised in a tradition of patriotism. In fact, one was the son of an F.B.I. agent. When the shabby deed of peddling classified information to Russian embassy agents in Mexico City became known, most citizens felt a mixture of anger and disappointment. How could two such promising young men, enjoying all the advantages and privileges they had been given, degenerate into such corrupt characters?

Hophni and Phinehas, sons of the great priest Eli, offer some insights into the way any person may sink into corruption. These two, like the pair of Californian Army officers caught selling secrets, are not to be studied as curiosities, but as examples of "There but for the grace of God go I." Your lesson can proceed along these lines.

1. *CHAMPIONS OF THE CREATOR.* Consider what Hophni and Phinehas were meant to be. Look at their family pedigree. Think what hopes and dreams their father, Eli, had for them, and the expectations the people had of them. Think also of the Lord's plans for Hophni and Phinehas. They were priests. In this lesson, you could profitably take time to have each member ponder the hopes, expectations, and dreams which the Lord has for him or her. Remembering that every Christian is part of the new priesthood, ask each to reflect on what being such a priest means to him or her, to Christ, to others in the Church, and to outsiders.

2. *CAUSE OF CORRUPTION.* 1 Samuel 2:12 has a devastating comment about Hophni and Phinehas: "They had no regard for the Lord." Not surprisingly, Hophni and Phinehas bullied others, acted greedily, and descended into sexual misconduct. The root of all corruption is having no regard for the Lord. Allow sufficient lesson time to discuss thoroughly what it means to have regard for the Lord.

3. *COLLAPSE OF COMMUNITY.* The correlation between the leaders' morality and the community's morale must be underscored. When the spiritual leaders and religious people act in immoral ways as did Hophni and Phinehas, the entire community suffers a decline. You as teacher must make clear to your class that each person carries heavy re-

sponsibilities not only for themselves personally but also for the ethical climate of the entire community. Discuss the implications of the responsibilities of personal morality of each Christian today in the face of the popular Playboy morality.

4. *CHARACTER OF CALUMNY.* Finally, remind your class that Hophni's and Phinehas's immoral ways brought about the deterioration of their nation, and also their own personal deaths. Deterioration and death: the inevitable results of having no regard for the Lord. Actually, of course, Hophni and Phinehas had been taking their own lives by slow degrees long before the Philistine spears cut them down. Help your class to reflect on the ways the Living Christ helps each member to avert such disaster in his or her own life.

TOPIC FOR ADULTS
HOPHNI AND PHINEHAS: CORRUPT PRIESTS

When Greed Becomes a God. Hophni and Phinehas were priests, but the god they served was greed. Their greed corrupted them and finally destroyed them. It can happen to anyone, even a religious person.

Several years ago, a certain Mrs. Garrett died, leaving $17 million but no will or relatives. The result was the most extensive, bitterly fought and circus-like inheritance case in history. In the mad scramble for slices of the fortune, people smeared the name of the deceased and committed practically every crime, including murder. At least 26,000 persons from almost every state and from twenty-nine foreign countries claimed the fortune. Three persons were murdered in quarrels, a dozen died in disgrace before they could be brought to trial, and two killed themselves. Even one saintly-looking old country preacher accepted a bribe for handing over the church records to a fortune hunter.

Lost Colony. A group of English settlers arrived in the New World in 1621 and laid out a town on the James River, upstream ten miles from Jamestown. They built houses, storage buildings, stables, and a fort. The new settlement was named Wolstonholme Towne. The new town never prospered, however. The settlers were not prepared to handle the hot summer climate and the hostile Indians. One of the most crippling events for Wolstoneholme Towne was the arrival of a shipload of adulterated beer which greedy, unscrupulous merchants in England had dispatched to the unsuspecting colonists. The people of Wolstoneholme Towne quaffed the poisoned beer, and many became sick and died. Others, already weakened from starvation and dysentery, were made weaker. When Indians overran the village, killing fifty-eight of the 140 settlers, the survivors fled. Wolstoneholme Towne was abandoned. Part of the cause of the destruction of this community was the corrupt collection of men which sent the shipload of bad beer. Greed invariably brings ruin to a community as well as to individuals.

"Dephosphorization." Steel magnate Andrew Carnegie became a millionaire many times over, but gave away most his fortune. The one-time bobbin boy, who rose from poverty to become one of the richest men in the world, used the analogy of steel making for his giving. Steel is made, Carnegie pointed out, by removing certain substances inherent in iron ore. It is particularly necessary to burn off phosphorus from the iron ore

to get good iron castings. Carnegie stated that human nature must be "dephosphorized" also by having the impurities of greed removed. Only when this form of corruption is taken out of a person's character can humankind improve, Carnegie insisted.

Hophni and Phinehas unfortunately never learned that the Lord had to "dephosphorize" their characters.

Questions for Pupils on the Next Lesson. 1. How do your relationships with others help you to discover your true identity? 2. How can being an unselfish friend help you to grow in your ability to trust? 3. How can you witness to your faith through your relationships with others? 4. Why does a capacity for intimacy add a dimension of depth and richness to life? 5. What are the most basic qualities for a genuine friendship?

TOPIC FOR YOUTH
HOPHNI AND PHINEHAS: CORRUPT LEADERS

People as Instruments. Hophni and Phinehas were priests who forgot that people were persons, not objects. Although sons of the great and godly Eli, they became cruelly corrupt. Their nation suffered as a result. They are a lesson to every one of us and to every nation.

In Cambodia, new leaders are practicing a terrible form of corruption and cruelty, causing the deaths of millions. These leaders, the Khmer Rouge, have introduced a new vocabulary in which words have a dehumanized ring. These terms have become euphemisms for atrocities. The Cambodians had never used them before. For instance, the Khmer Rouge uses the word *Angka,* the word for the Khmer Rouge regime itself, meaning simply "the organization," for all purposes. No explanations are ever given for policy, simply "*Angka* says" or "*Angka* orders." People are never regarded as human beings but are referred to as *opekar,* which means simply "instruments."

When people are called instruments, fear, suspicion, brutality, and death follow. Hophni and Phinehas, like the Khmer Rouge today, became such corrupt people that they assumed their organization was not accountable to anyone and that they could treat others as mere instruments.

Guard against the *Angka* and *Opekar* tendencies in yourself and in the national leaders.

Leading Astray the Mentality of Peoples. Like Hophni and Phinehas in Old Testament times, corruption among the leaders of today may bring ruin. One of the corrupting notions affecting the thinking of most people, including leaders in government, religion, and business, is the idea that bigger and better weaponry will solve all problems. The thought that opponents may be threatened or destroyed corrupts us all. Speaking to this issue before his death, Pope Paul VI said words that need to be heard and heeded:

"You cannot love with weapons in your hands. Long before they mete out death and destruction, those terrible arms supplied by modern science foment bad feelings and cause nightmares, distrust, and designs. . . . They lead astray the mentality of peoples."—Pope Paul VI, *QUOTE,* April 1, 1980.

Just and Caring God. In the face of the Hophnis and Phinehases of the world, we sometimes think that there is no future. We see so much corruption that we are sometimes inclined to believe that God either does not care or that He is not able. When confronted with such observations one time, the late Dr. Albert Einstein replied, "God is subtle, but He is not malicious."

God subtly and lovingly persists in working in this world of corrupt persons. He promises through Jesus Christ as well as through the story of His covenanted relationship with Israel that He brings new hope and new beginnings.

Sentence Sermon to Remember: We cannot break God's laws—but we can break ourselves against them.—A. Maude Royden.

Questions for Pupils on the Next Lesson. 1. How do you support and encourage your friends? 2. How do your friends and family support and encourage you? 3. Do genuine friendships and relationships mean you must sometimes give up some of your rights? 4. How does true friendship lead a person to see potential good in others? 5. Do your relationships with others help you to realize your relationship with God? 6. Do you sometimes experience tension between loyalty to friends and loyalty to parents?

LESSON XII—AUGUST 21

JONATHAN AND DAVID: LOYAL FRIENDS

Background Scripture: 1 Samuel 18:1–9; 19:1–7; 20:1–42; 23:15–18; 2 Samuel 1
Devotional Reading: 1 Thessalonians 3

KING JAMES VERSION

1 SAMUEL 18 1 And it came to pass, when he had made an end of speaking unto Saul, that the soul of Jonathan was knit with the soul of David, and Jonathan loved him as his own soul.

2 And Saul took him that day, and would let him go no more home to his father's house.

3 Then Jonathan and David made a covenant, because he loved him as his own soul.

4 And Jonathan stripped himself of the robe that *was* upon him, and gave it to David, and his garments, even to his sword, and to his bow, and to his girdle.

19 4 And Jonathan spake good of David unto Saul his father, and said unto him, Let not the king sin against his servant, against David; because he hath not sinned against thee, and because his works *have been* to thee-ward very good:

5 For he did put his life in his hand, and slew the Philistine, and the LORD wrought a great salvation for all Israel: thou sawest *it*, and didst rejoice: wherefore then wilt thou sin against innocent blood, to slay David without a cause?

6 And Saul hearkened unto the voice of Jonathan: and Saul sware, *As* the LORD liveth, he shall not be slain.

23 15 And David saw that Saul was come out to seek his life: and David *was* in the wilderness of Ziph in a wood.

16 And Jonathan Saul's son arose, and went to David into the wood, and strengthened his hand in God.

17 And he said unto him, Fear not: for the hand of Saul my father shall not find thee; and thou shalt be king over Israel, and I shall be next unto thee; and that also Saul my father knoweth.

18 And they two made a covenant before the LORD: and David abode in the wood, and Jonathan went to his house.

2 SAMUEL 1 26 I am distressed for thee, my brother Jonathan: very pleasant hast thou been unto me: thy love to me was wonderful, passing the love of women.

REVISED STANDARD VERSION

1 SAMUEL 18 1 When he had finished speaking to Saul, the soul of Jonathan was knit to the soul of David, and Jonathan loved him as his own soul. 2 And Saul took him that day, and would not let him return to his father's house. 3 Then Jonathan made a covenant with David, because he loved him as his own soul. 4 And Jonathan stripped himself of the robe that was upon him, and gave it to David, and his armor, and even his sword and his bow and his girdle.

19 4 And Jonathan spoke well of David to Saul his father, and said to him, "Let not the king sin against his servant David; because he has not sinned against you, and because his deeds have been of good service to you; 5 for he took his life in his hand and he slew the Philistine, and the LORD wrought a great victory for all Israel. You saw it, and rejoiced; why then will you sin against innocent blood by killing David without cause?" 6 And Saul hearkened to the voice of Jonathan; Saul swore, "As the LORD lives, he shall not be put to death."

23 15 And David was afraid because Saul had come out to seek his life. David was in the Wilderness of Ziph at Horesh. 16 And Jonathan, Saul's son, rose, and went to David at Horesh, and strengthened his hand in God. 17 And he said to him, "Fear not; for the hand of Saul my father shall not find you; you shall be king over Israel, and I shall be next to you; Saul my father also knows this." 18 And the two of them made a covenant before the LORD; David remained at Horesh, and Jonathan went home.

2 SAMUEL 1 26 I am distressed for
you, my brother Jonathan;
very pleasant have you been to me;
your love to me was wonderful,
passing the love of women.

KEY VERSE: Then Jonathan made a covenant with David, because he loved him as his own soul. 1 Samuel 18:3 (RSV).

HOME DAILY BIBLE READINGS

Aug. 15. *M.* *David's Abilities Recognized by Saul.* 1 Samuel 17:50–58.
Aug. 16. *T.* *Jonathan's Covenant With David.* 1 Samuel 18:1–5.
Aug. 17. *W.* *Cause of Saul's Jealousy.* 1 Samuel 18:6–10a.
Aug. 18. *T.* *Jonathan Reconciles Saul to David.* 1 Samuel 19:1–7.
Aug. 19. *F.* *Jonathan's Plan to Protect David.* 1 Samuel 20:12–17.
Aug. 20. *S.* *Jonathan Accepts David as His King.* 1 Samuel 23:13–18.
Aug. 21. *S.* *David's Lament for Jonathan's Death.* 2 Samuel 1:23–27.

BACKGROUND

The period of the Judges lasted 410 years; it ended with the coronation of Saul, the son of the Benjamite Kish as the first king of Israel. It was Samuel who anointed him king at the command of God. It seemed like a good choice; this Saul was the scion of a wealthy family, a born aristocrat, a man with prestige. He was young and "goodly: and there was not among the children of Israel a goodlier person than he: from his shoulders and upward he was higher than any of the people" (1 Samuel 9:2).

The Philistines and the Ammonites were making life miserable for the Israelites at this time, and a man of Saul's stature was sorely needed. He was not long in proving his ability and courage; he defeated the Ammonites at Jabesh-gilead, and an exultant people acclaimed him as their king. He set up his capital at Gibeah. He waged war against the Philistines; with the aid of his son Jonathan, he defeated them at Michmash, that made him a hero almost worshiped all across the land. What a future he had!

It would have been a great reign but for one fatal flaw: Saul was over-temperamental. (Someone has described temperamentality as nine-tenths temper and one-tenth mental.) The young king alternated between bursts of energy and fits of depression which got him into trouble with Samuel . . . and with his son Jonathan . . . and with a shepherd-boy from Bethlehem named David.

NOTES ON THE PRINTED TEXT

Worried by these fits of temperament and convinced that an evil spirit possessed the king, certain of his aides suggested that they knew of a young boy in Bethlehem who was a "cunning" player on the harp, and "a comely person, and the Lord is with him" (1 Samuel 16:18). Such a musician might have a cure for the king's despondency; music did have a way of "soothing the savage beast."

David came. Saul loved him at first sight and made him his armor-bearer (bodyguard). For a while, the shepherd boy quieted the tortured heart of the king but not for long. There came the day when young David went out with his sling-shot and killed the Philistine giant Goliath, and that made *him* a man whose praises were sung loudly and too often for the king, who quickly saw in the shepherd boy an interloper who might just dethrone him. Saul had been told that this David was "a mighty valiant man, and a man of war," but he did not quite realize how mighty he was. David killed Goliath—and the stone that killed the Philistine also killed the happy relationship between the king and the shepherd boy.

Now Saul was insanely jealous—and afraid! The people in the streets were shouting that Saul had slain his thousands, and David his tens of thousands. That was more than Saul could tolerate; he went so far as to hurl his spear at David (fortunately, he missed), and in time made him an outlaw hiding in the desert places and the caves in the hills. To him in his hiding-places came Jonathan, son of Saul and rightful heir to the throne. Jonathan did his best to placate his father, the king, but that was a hopeless endeavor for Saul was beyond reason now. Back and forth Jonathan shuttled, between the man in the caves and the man on the throne, doing his best to put an end to the conflict. As the conflict went on, "the soul of Jonathan was knit with the soul of David, and Jonathan loved him as his own soul" (1 Samuel 18:1). They made a covenant: Jonathan would continue living in the palace with his father, and David would remain an outlaw—and hopefully, one day, become Israel's second king. Jonathan went so far as to give David his prince's robe, his sword, and his bow. When he did that, he was saying to David that he was surrendering his claim to the throne. And he further promised that if he heard his father planning to kill him, he would tell David in time to escape.

What a friendship that was! There is nothing quite equal to it in the rest of the Old Testament. Jonathan, at the risk of his own life, more than once saved the life of David; can friendship go farther, deeper, than that? Torn between two loyalties, he gave his loyalty to David because he knew that David was right and that his father was wrong. He took a great chance when he did that, for at that time he had everything to lose and nothing to gain; he gave up all hope of ever becoming king of Israel and put himself in a position in which he might be slain by his own father.

This is the essence of true friendship: *selflessness.* Friendship is not something by which we may gain anything; it is not something to be used for our own benefit. It is a covenant of love between well-meaning men.

In a heartbreaking lament (2 Samuel 1:26), David calls this friendship love. Jonathan was dead when David said that, slain with his father and two brothers at the battle of Mount Gilboa; but love, or friendship, is not killed in the killing of a man. This friendship was one never forgotten by the people of Israel; their Jonathan remains one of the noblest of their heroes. "Though the sacred anointing oil of coronation never fell upon Jonathan's brow, he was nonetheless anointed with an oil even more sacred. For the throne of love is the mightiest of all thrones, and the lordliest of all empires is the empire of unselfishness."—Amos R. Wells.

Jonathan died for his father and renounced his throne to his friend. In some ways, Jonathan was more akin to Christ than David was.

SUGGESTIONS TO TEACHERS

"The language of friendship is not words but meanings," wrote Henry David Thoreau. Jesus regarded His associates as friends and their relationship as one of friendship, saying, "I have called you friends" (John 15:15). The language of that relationship continues to be more than words.

David and Jonathan had a friendship in which the language was meanings rather than words. Your lesson today uses their friendship as a model. As you lead the discussion for this Sunday, weave in the significance of Jesus the Friend. In fact, you may wish to read again the comments about us being His friends in John 15.

1. *REQUEST.* The David-Jonathan friendship has meaning because of the way each had the interests of the other at heart. Looking at 1 Samuel 19:1–7 and other references, you will observe that Jonathan interceded for his friend David many times. A friend has a concern for the other. Jesus had such a concern for His friends, and even went through the terrible trials of Gethsemane and Calvary for them—and us, His friends today. The Spirit continues to intercede on our behalf (Romans 8:26). Take time also in your lesson to have your people talk about interceding for others in prayer. Have them consider the place and the power of intercessory prayer for friends of Jesus Christ everywhere.

2. *RESCUE.* Jonathan saves David's life. A friend cares. A friend brings new life. Remembering the Christlike concern of Jonathan for his friend David, try to direct the thinking of your people to ways of "saving lives of friends," especially Jesus' friends today. Are they not the poor, the hungry, and the oppressed? How is your church expressing Christ's type of friendship to these persons, His friends? Remind your class also that friendship is still shown not so much in words as in meanings such as food, medicine, tools, jobs, and books.

3. *RISK.* Jonathan and David were willing to put their lives on the line for each other. Jonathan, in fact, was even willing to step aside as heir to the throne for the sake of David, thus risking the displeasure of Saul. As teacher, you should help your class to understand the meaning of the covenant between David and Jonathan. Remind your class that this was a pact involving the Lord, and therefore more than a mere human agreement. You may wish to discuss the risk in every human relationship, including marriage, or church membership. In these, all parties are covenanted with God and with one another. This sacred bond is what keeps them together. A covenant between the Lord's people and Him enables persons to take the risk of relating with one another.

4. *REQUIEM.* The sad ending of Saul and his sons, including Jonathan, made David mourn deeply. "I am distressed for you, my brother Jonathan," David cries (2 Samuel 1:26). Human relationships eventually are changed as death comes. Friends die. Those closest to us are no longer with us. You and your class may wish to talk about the fact of death and separation. However, make the class period on this topic more than a rehash of now familiar "death and dying" seminars. Concentrate on the hope brought by the Risen Lord. What does the Resurrection suggest in regard to mourning and funeral practices for Christians in these times?

TOPIC FOR ADULTS
JONATHAN AND DAVID: LOYAL FRIENDS

What It Means. There are some things which you cannot explain. Friendship is one. It is like trying to explain a beautiful piece of music. Once, for example, Ludwig von Beethoven played a new sonata for an acquaintance. After Beethoven finished the final note, the other person asked, "What does it mean?" Beethoven returned to the piano, played the entire sonata again, then said, "That is what it means." This is the kind of response one must make when asked, "What does a friendship mean?"

This is especially true of the friendship with Jesus Christ. As with any meaningful relationship, it cannot be dissected or analyzed without destroying it. The only way to enjoy His friendship is to be His friend. The only way to understand Beethoven's sonata is to hear it. The only way to know the meaning of grace is to accept it.

The Loneliness of God. A lovely story is being circulated about the Polish Jew who stopped praying because of what took place during the Holocaust. He had experienced firsthand the horrors which carried away six million Jews from Europe during World War II, and announced that he could never again approach God "because of what happened at Auschwitz." Sometime later, however, this Jewish man began to pray again. Someone asked him, "What made you change your mind?"

The Jew answered quietly, "It suddenly dawned upon me to think how lonely God must be. Look with whom He is left. I felt sorry for Him."

As that Jew discovered, God wants us to be friends with Him. Through Jesus Christ, we Christians know that He has come, with arms extended in love, offering to be our Friend and pledging to be loyal.

The Sorrow of Separation. Human relationships can be so precious and filled with love that when they are interrupted by death, the survivor feels desperately alone. David felt this after Jonathan's death. Martin Luther also felt this. When his favorite daughter, Magdalena, died at the age of fourteen, Luther was almost broken. "God," he said, "has given no bishop so great a gift in a thousand years as He has given me in her." He prayed night and day for her recovery. "I love her very much, but, dear God, if it is Thy holy will to take her, I would gladly leave her with Thee." And he said to her: "Lena, dear, my little daughter, thou wouldst love to remain here with thy father; art thou willing to go to that other Father?" "Yes, dear father," Lena answered, "just as God wills." When she died, he wept long and bitterly. As she was laid in the earth, he spoke to her as to a living soul: "Du liebes Lenichen, you will rise and shine like the stars and the sun. How strange it is to know that she is at peace and all is well, and yet be so sorrowful!"

Questions for Pupils on the Next Lesson. 1. Why are celebrations important, both on an adult and an intergenerational level? 2. What does the Jewish Feast of Purim mean? 3. What do you do to exercise your civic responsibilities? 4. Do you sometimes shrink from taking courageous stands because you fear risking your career and status? 5. Why is the question, "What's in it for me?" inappropriate for a Christian when faced with a call to serve human needs?

TOPIC FOR YOUTH
JONATHAN AND DAVID: LOYAL FRIENDS

What Kind of Friends? Everyone, of course, needs friends. How does one choose friends?

Scottish poet Robert Burns remembered the casual way he gathered friends in his younger days, and the harm they caused him. When as a young man in Irvine learning the trade of flax-dressing, Burns came under the influence of a fellow worker named Robert Brown. Burns quickly recognized that Brown's standards toward women were disgustingly low, but allowed himself to be pulled into Brown's circle of playboy acquaintances. Years later, regretting the attitudes which Brown had fostered, Burns berated himself for not being more selective of his friends, "Brown's friendship did me a mischief," the poet later wrote.

David and Jonathan offer a model of friendship which did each the favor of deeper faith. Their relationship was grounded in an awareness of their mutual friendship with the Lord. As a result, the friendship brought them not only closer to God but also closer to each other.

Choose your friends on the basis of God's friendship toward you. Develop ties with others who help both of you to develop deeper ties toward the Lord.

Everything You Need? Frank Steklacic, fifty-four-year-old owner of a car wash, had never been particularly well-off. He played the state lottery, however, in the hope that he would be better off in his life in North Warren, Pennsylvania, near the New York State border. On January 31, 1981, Steklacic won the $1 million lottery drawing. After the drawing in the Harrisburg state capitol rotunda, Steklacic announced to reporters, "Thank God, I now have everything I need in life."

Everything? Perhaps everything that money can buy. After all, Mr. Steklacic will collect $1,000 a week for life from the Pennsylvania Lottery. But is a million bucks everything he needs in life?

Will Frank Steklacic's million get him friends? Will his newly-acquired fortune bring him better relationships with his family and friends? Can Mr. Steklacic buy a sense of acceptance by God, or purchase peace of mind, or pay for a sense of loyalty from others?

Consider your priorities in life again. What do you really need? What are you doing to develop relationships between those who are most loyal to you?

Businessmen Praying Together. Groups of businessmen are meeting regularly in prayer groups in most large North American cities. Over thirty such prayer and Bible study groups meet each week in New York City alone. The movement growth has purposely been kept quiet and unobtrusive.

"Businessmen turn to this group because of a desire for fellowship with those who have a common understanding of the pressures of business life," said Homer R. Figler, a senior consultant and principal of Ernst and Whinney, the accounting firm. "Even one's own family can't appreciate the stresses, so we need to find those who can help us apply faith to the work place. The business world has a set of standards that are quite different from Christian standards. And it is easier for a person to coexist by getting involved in one of these prayer groups. He draws a kind of strength from them.

"I think the best way to describe most of those involved is that they see Christ as a central focus of their lives."

Dr. Figler is also a psychologist and author of "Overcoming Executive Mid-Life Crises."

"As far as I'm concerned, my faith has no value unless my work has value," says Terry L. Nagelvoort, a soft-spoken securities analyst with Cyrus J. Lawrence. "I have to pull my own weight in my organization. I have to be productive on the job, just as St. Paul had to make good tents. Then when someone is going through a rough time, I have a basis to share the love of Christ with him."

Do you have loyal friends who pray with you and for you when you're going through a rough time?

Sentence Sermon to Remember: A friend is the one who comes in when the whole world has gone out. Even as David thanked God for Jonathan and praised him in well-remembered lines, so have we abundant reasons to thank God today for friends and to resolve to keep these friendships in constant repair.—Edgar DeWitt Jones.

Questions for Pupils on the Next Lesson. 1. What are some of the good and not-so-good family influences you have experienced? 2. Have you ever been called upon to take a stand because of your convictions as a Christian? 3. What purpose do you think God has in mind for your life? 4. Is there anything worth risking your life for?

LESSON XIII—AUGUST 28

MORDECAI AND ESTHER: CHALLENGE AND COMMITMENT

Background Scripture: Esther
Devotional Reading: Psalms 31:19–24

KING JAMES VERSION

ESTHER 2 7 And he brought up Hadassah, that *is,* Esther, his uncle's daughter: for she had neither father nor mother, and the maid *was* fair and beautiful; whom Mordecai, when her father and mother were dead, took for his own daughter.

4 13 Then Mordecai commanded to answer Esther, Think not with thyself that thou shalt escape in the king's house, more than all the Jews.

14 For if thou altogether holdest thy peace at this time, *then* shall there enlargement and deliverance arise to the Jews from another place; but thou and thy father's house shall be destroyed: and who knoweth whether thou art come to the kingdom for *such* a time as this?

15 Then Esther bade *them* return Mordecai *this answer,*

16 Go, gather together all the Jews that are present in Shushan, and fast ye for me, and neither eat nor drink three days, night or day: I also and my maidens will fast likewise; and so will I go in unto the king, which *is* not according to the law: and if I perish, I perish.

8 3 And Esther spake yet again before the king, and fell down at his feet, and besought him with tears to put away the mischief of Haman the Agagite, and his device that he had devised against the Jews.

4 Then the king held out the golden sceptre toward Esther. So Esther arose, and stood before the king,

5 And said, If it please the king, and if I have found favor in his sight, and the thing *seem* right before the king, and I *be* pleasing in his eyes, let it be written to reverse the letters devised by Haman the son of Hammedatha the Agagite, which he wrote to destroy the Jews which *are* in all the king's provinces:

6 For how can I endure to see the evil that shall come unto my people? or how can I endure to see the destruction of my kindred?

REVISED STANDARD VERSION

ESTHER 2 7 He had brought up Hadassah, that is Esther, the daughter of his uncle, for she had neither father nor mother; the maiden was beautiful and lovely, and when her father and her mother died, Mordecai adopted her as his own daughter.

4 13 Then Mordecai told them to return answer to Esther, "Think not that in the king's palace you will escape any more than all the other Jews. 14 For if you keep silence at such a time as this, relief and deliverance will rise for the Jews from another quarter, but you and your father's house will perish. And who knows whether you have not come to the kingdom for such a time as this?" 15 Then Esther told them to reply to Mordecai, 16 "Go, gather all the Jews to be found in Susa, and hold a fast on my behalf, and neither eat nor drink for three days, night or day. I and my maids will also fast as you do. Then I will go to the king, though it is against the law; and if I perish, I perish."

8 3 Then Esther spoke again to the king; she fell at his feet and besought him with tears to avert the evil design of Haman the Agagite and the plot which he had devised against the Jews. 4 And the king held out the golden scepter to Esther, 5 and Esther rose and stood before the king. And she said, "If it please the king, and if I have found favor in his sight, and if the thing seem right before the king, and I be pleasing in his eyes, let an order be written to revoke the letters devised by Haman the Agagite, the son of Hammedatha, which he wrote to destroy the Jews who are in all the provinces of the king. 6 For how can I endure to see the calamity that is coming to my people? Or how can I endure to see the destruction of my kindred?" 7 Then King Ahasuerus said to Queen Esther and to Mordecai the Jew, "Behold, I have given Esther the house of

7 Then the king Ahasuerus said unto Esther the queen and to Mordecai the Jew, Behold, I have given Esther the house of Haman, and him they have hanged upon the gallows, because he laid his hand upon the Jews.

8 Write ye also for the Jews, as it liketh you, in the king's name, and seal *it* with the king's ring: for the writing which is written in the king's name, and sealed with the king's ring, may no man reverse.

Haman, and they have hanged him on the gallows, because he would lay hands on the Jews. 8 And you may write as you please with regard to the Jews, in the name of the king, and seal it with the king's ring; for an edict written in the name of the king and sealed with the king's ring cannot be revoked."

KEY VERSE: ". . . Who knows whether you have not come to the kingdom for such a time as this?" Esther 4:14 (RSV).

HOME DAILY BIBLE READINGS

Aug. 22. M. The Luxury-Living King of Persia. Esther 1:1–12.
Aug. 23. T. Mordecai Prepares Esther for Presentation. Esther 2:2–11.
Aug. 24. W. Esther Shown Grace and Favor. Esther 2:15–20.
Aug. 25. T. A Jewish Program Planned. Esther 3:8–15a.
Aug. 26. F. Esther Plans to Defy Persian Law. Esther 4:5–16.
Aug. 27. S. Esther and Haman's Opposing Plans. Esther 5:6–14.
Aug. 28. S. Esther Saves (Thousands of) Jewish Lives. Esther 8:5–16.

BACKGROUND

Nebuchadnezzar the Second ("the Great") conquered and sacked Jerusalem in 582 B.C., and left it nothing more than "a wilderness of thorns and briars," and took its people captive in Babylon. Two lesser kings followed him and then his empire fell under the power of Persia (today we call it Iran). As we pick up the story in the Book of Esther, we find a King Ahasuerus ruling the world "from India even unto Ethiopia . . . an hundred and seven and twenty provinces . . ." (Esther 1:1). He also inherited the Judean captives of Nubuchadnezzar, but, under Persian rulers, these Jews were more refugees than captives; on the whole, they were treated well. One of them, a man named Mordecai (a Benjamite) who had once saved the king from a plot to kill him, won the favor of the king (Esther 2:21–23). He must have been envied by his fellow Jews, for he moved about in an atmosphere of palatial luxury; a world of marble pillars, beds of gold and silver, pavements of red, blue, white, and black marble. Wine was served in vessels of gold and "served in abundance"; it was often a drunken court. Mordecai was also the cousin and foster father of a Jewish girl named Hadassah (a Jewish name meaning "Myrtle," which was changed to the Persian name of Esther, which meant "star"). That was more than appropriate, for the Jewish orphan girl was to become the star of one of the most charming romantic stories in the Old Testament.

One thing we must understand as we read the story of Esther; we are reading not verified history, but *historical fiction.*

NOTES ON THE PRINTED TEXT

King Ahasuerus had a wife who was called the most beautiful woman in the Persian world. He loved her. He was so proud of having her as his queen that he once asked her to parade her charms before a motley crowd of the officials of his court who, like the king, were drunk with wine from their golden cups. Queen Vashti refused to do it—and for that the king divorced her and sought another queen who would do as he ordered her to do. That involved a parade of beauties from all over the empire, and that gave the Jew Mordecai the chance for which he had been waiting.

Mordecai had great influence among the captive Jews, and he longed for the day when they would be not only respected in Persia but set free. Now he could do something for his people, and he did it cleverly: he had Esther "presented" to the king as a queen candidate. The king quite probably didn't even know that this beautiful young girl (aged fifteen) was a devout Jewish girl. He saw only her charm and loveliness, and, on that basis, he made her queen of one of the most powerful empires in the world.

Esther never wanted to be queen; it was forced upon her by her cousin Mordecai. With her at the court of the king, he had one who could "get the king's ear," and at that particular time that was important, for the Jewish people were far from popular with the Persians. The Israelites were miserable; they were despised exiles in a foreign land. If Esther would only go and plead for her people with the king who loved her, their lot might be easier.

But—she would be risking her life if she went unbidden to the king. To approach him without being invited to do so could cost the life of the unwelcome one.

Now enters the villain of the drama: Haman the Agagite (an Amelekite) who had pushed his way up to the position of prime minister to the king. Haman hated the Jews with a venomous, lethal hatred, and he actually plotted the murder of every Jew in Persia. He paid the capricious (or drunken) king the equivalent of twenty *million* dollars to cover the expenses of the slaughter which was scheduled for the twenty-eighth day of February of the following year. When Mordecai heard of the plot, he rent his clothes and put on sackcloth and ashes—and sent for Esther. He asked her to go and beg the king to stop the massacre.

This she did not want to do; it was too dangerous to approach the king in such a manner and with such a request, especially if he were drunk, but the patient Mordecai convinced her that she owed a greater loyalty to her people than she owed the Persian king. He made her see that she had "come to the (Jewish) kingdom for such a time as this" (Esther 4:14). He also told her that if such an insane slaughter was started, she would be killed along with every other man and woman of Jewish faith in the empire. It was then that she uttered the words that have immortalized her in Jewish history: "I go in unto the king . . . and if I perish, I perish."

She went to the king—cleverly. She arranged two banquets to which she invited Ahasuerus and Haman. What a dinner the second dinner was! Both Mordecai and Haman were there. No love was lost between these two; Haman had already built a gallows on which he planned to hang Mordecai, but Mordecai had other plans. When the king asked his beautiful Esther what he could give her to prove his love for her, she fell weeping at his feet and answered him: "We are sold, I and my people, to be destroyed, to be slain, and to perish. . . . The adversary and enemy is this wicked Haman" (Esther 7:4,6). Immediately, the king ordered Haman to be hanged on the gallows he had reared for Mordecai. So perished Haman, the Hitler of his day.

So endeth the story.

Once more, let us remember that it is a *story* and not a historical event. There are several evidences of this. For one thing, there is no mention in any authoritative history that any king named Ahasuerus (Xerxes) ever had a queen named Esther or Vashti. There are several exaggerations in this otherwise beautifully written book: the erection of a gallows eighty-three feet high (5:14), the six-months feast (1:4), a year's beauty treatment for the court maidens (2:12), and the twenty-million-bribe to the king to conduct the pogrom (3:9). The Book of Esther contains no explicit religious or ethical teachings; the name of God never appears anywhere in the story. As great a Bible scholar as Martin Luther felt that the book should never have been included in the Scriptures. It bristles with hatred and revenge; Esther even wanted to see the *sons* of Haman hanged. It is a story full of intrigue and death.

But when all this has been said, the story still has great positive truth. It is a condemnation of anti-Semitism; it is the story of an Esther who had great courage, beauty, charm, and character. Esther's faults are outweighed by her self-denial. She was as virtuous as she was fair, dutiful to both her foster father and her king, loyal to her people—and to her God. It is impossible to think of her as one who never prayed, though prayer is not mentioned in the story. She offered to lay down her life for her friends. Greater love hath no man than this.

There are some scholars who feel that the unnamed author of the book was more patriotic than religious. Others believe that the purpose of the Book of Esther may have been to propagandize the Feast of Purim, for which there are no other sanctions. "The Jews then in Persia celebrated their deliverance from the wholesale massacre that had been planned by Haman. And they called the celebration a Purim Festival, because Haman had cast 'pur' (a lot) to ascertain a favorable day for carrying out his plot to destroy the Jews. To this day, the Purim Festival is celebrated on the fourteenth and fifteenth of March when the Roll of Esther is read in Jewish synagogues all over the world. Queen Esther's last decree was that the feast be held annually, and it was written in the book (Esther 9:32). It became a law that stands even today."—Edith Deen in *All The Women of the Bible,* by permission of Harper & Row, publishers.

It may be historical fiction, but God is in it and behind it.

SUGGESTIONS TO TEACHERS

Every February or March, your Jewish neighbors observe the Feast of Purim, celebrating the story of Esther. You may find it enlightening to talk with a rabbi or Jewish friends to hear afresh the significance of Mordecai and Esther and their deliverance of God's people from genocide. Be sure that you as a teacher read the details yourself in the Book of Esther.

Your lesson can take several directions. Here are some "starters" for you and your class to consider.

1. *CONVICTIONS.* Describe how and why Mordecai, Esther's cousin, refused to bow down to Haman, the Persian official. Discuss the need for convictions. In an age where "anything goes" and "it makes no difference what you believe," what are the bottom-line convictions for Christians today? Why? You may wish to have each member list his or her basic convictions for which he or she would be willing to face imprisonment, torture, or death.

2. *COURAGE.* Mordecai and Esther each repeatedly showed they had the moral courage to match their convictions. Esther could easily have passed herself off as a Persian instead of acknowledging that she was a Jew. She and her cousin, Mordecai, were willing to speak up for the Lord, although they realized it could bring frightful consequences. Being God's person, however, does not always mean saving your own hide. Remind your people that Jesus could have saved His life. The hardest kind of courage is moral courage, the willingness to take a stand for the Lord. Where may your people be called to exhibit such courage in these days?

3. *CALL.* Mordecai and Esther remembered their heritage as the Lord's people. Mordecai, in fact, reminds his cousin that God might have placed her as queen "for such a time as this" (Esther 5:14) in order to save her people from the terrible pogrom. Do your people see God at work in their own lives? Do they sense the "call" the Lord has given them? You may profitably use a portion of your lesson time today to reflect on the way in which each person baptized into the community of faith is called and placed in a position of responsibility.

4. *CONSCIENCE.* Take a look at the way by which Mordecai is a reminder to Haman that ultimate allegiance belongs to the Lord, not to Haman or any human leader. (The Book of Esther has some delightful touches in which Haman's gloating victory is spoiled by seeing old Mordecai refusing to bow down to him.) Mordecai, in effect, is the conscience of the community, a walking memo that the Almighty is almighty. Stress to your people that the Church and each member is intended by God to be the conscience of the community today. We as God's people have a mandate to remind all authorities that God is the supreme authority, and that all powers, rulers, and authorities must bow to Him.

5. *COMMITMENT.* When the Jews are marked for slaughter, Queen Esther identifies herself with them and finally averts the massacre. She does more than try to protect herself or her cousin. She risks her life to bring justice and deliverance for all the oppressed. With Esther as a model, think with your class on the call to commitment each Christian has to stand with the oppressed. How may committed Christians identify with the hungry, for example? What forms of commitment to others may those in your church show that are not being shown?

TOPIC FOR ADULTS
MORDECAI AND ESTHER: CHALLENGE AND COMMITMENT

Unpopular Stand. Billy Graham is out of step with many of America's politically active, aggressive, opinionated religious leaders on television. "I have two primary objectives in the balance of my days of active ministry," Graham says. "One is to keep on doing what I've been doing—preaching the Gospel in auditoriums and on television all over the world.

Second, I want to work for world peace. I feel that the arms race is way out of hand, and that I can make a small contribution in talking to all sides on this thing."

Billy Graham's endorsement of nuclear disarmament and the Salt II treaty has taken immense moral courage and has not won him applause in many circles. "I don't believe in unilateral disarmament," says Graham. "I am not a pacifist. There is a possibility in working out some sort of an arrangement of arms control and hopefully, someday, a SALT X—the destruction of nuclear and chemical weapons which can destroy the human race. Somebody said that if the '60s were the age of rebellion, and the '70s were the age of frustration, the '80s will be the decade of survival. I am cautiously optimistic.

"It was a mistake to identify the Kingdom of God with the American way of life," says Graham. "I've come to see that other cultures have their own way that may be of just as great a value. I think we consume too much, and I think we have become too materialistic."

Like Mordecai and Esther, Billy Graham is willing to show his commitment, even if it costs him popularity. Are you?

Identified With Poor. John Wesley, founder of the Methodist Church, lived abstemiously and instructed his preachers to also adopt a frugal life-style. "Give all you can," he urged them. Wesley and his earliest circuit riding preachers never took more than eight ounces of meat per day, nor more than twelve ounces of vegetables. He wanted to have his people continue to identify with the poor masses. Wesley himself never weighed more than 120 pounds, yet at eighty-four years of age, he was still able to preach to 4,000 miners in a Welsh town at 4 A.M.

Does your life-style reflect your commitments as a Christian? How do you identify with the hungry and the poor of the world?

Call for More Mordecais. Mordecai had the courage and commitment to be equal to the challenge facing his people who were facing destruction. At great risk, Mordecai spoke out. He refused to bow to the popular leaders.

God calls persons today to be like Mordecai in the face of human disaster through nuclear war. Both superpowers, Russia and the United States, have between them stored over 50,000 nuclear weapons—enough to destroy the world at least a dozen times. Each nation today spends over $100 million a day enlarging its nuclear arsenal. Although the nuclear device over Hiroshima killed over 110,000 humans, this type of bomb is now considered so small and insignificant that it is not included in any recent disarmament discussions or SALT agreements.

With the possibility of nuclear war growing, and the threat of widespread human deaths from such war increasing, every Christian must be a Mordecai.

Questions for Pupils on the Next Lesson. 1. Has everything had its beginning through God? 2. Some say that you can describe God but cannot define God. Do you agree or disagree? 3. Is it possible for God to be all powerful, all loving and all wise? 4. What is the place in the universe for humans? 5. What does the Creation story in the Bible suggest the reason for your existence is?

TOPIC FOR YOUTH
MORDECAI AND ESTHER: SHARED COMMITMENT

Commitment That Cost. According to sportswriter John Holway, only a handful of men have changed the direction of baseball. They include Al Spalding, the early pioneer, Babe Ruth, who made offense supreme, Judge Kennesaw Mountain Landis, who restored the sport's integrity after the scandals in 1919, Branch Rickey, who devised the farm system, and "Happy" Chandler, who opened the doors of baseball to players of all races in the major leagues.

A. B. "Happy" Chandler upset the barons of baseball in 1945 by defying the unwritten rules barring black baseball players from joining a major league ball club. At that time, Chandler was commissioner of baseball. For years, clubs and owners had resisted any attempt to put black and white players together on the same field. In fact, Landis, Chandler's predecessor, had even ordered all barnstorming white players to stop playing against blacks while wearing their major league uniforms. Although there were dozens of outstanding black ballplayers such as Satch Paige, Buck Leonard, Josh Gibson, and Cool Pappa Bell, they were prevented from playing with any but an all-black ball team. Chandler resolved to change that.

In 1945, Chandler gave the green light to a young athlete name Jackie Robinson, who happened to be black, to sign on with Branch Rickey at that time owner of the old Brooklyn Dodgers. Chandler knew that it would be an unpopular decision, but he never wavered. He paid for his stand. In 1951, when his contract as baseball commissioner ran out, he was voted out and replaced by Ford Frick. Although "Happy" Chandler's historic and courageous stand now is forgotten because a new sports generation has come along, he deserves to be elected to the Cooperstown Hall of Fame as much as others who have been honored. The "Happy" Chandlers and men and women like Mordecai and Esther, however, do not care about being enshrined. They only want to live responsibly before God and others!

Busboy's Perception. "To the Editor: Few experiences underscore the need for America to tighten its collective belt more than that of working in a restaurant.

"On weekends, I work as a busboy in a moderately priced, high-cholesterol establishment that specializes in prime ribs and lobster tails. The number of overweight people who frequent this restaurant is simply amazing (and I am sure that busboys in restaurants across the country witness the same phenomenon).

"People are overweight for a variety of reasons, many of which are truly unfortunate. But what is the significance of all this excess flesh? It is evidently indicative of serious personal problems, but, more importantly, it is indicative of problems of social consequence: misguided and wasted energy, the inequitable distribution of food and resources and thus the striking contrast between the overfed and the underfed. And it signifies a collective hunger emanating more from the spirit than from the flesh.

"In order to remedy this situation, we must learn to channel our appetites and our energies in more productive directions. But before taking this step, we must recognize that we face a serious problem, that of overconsumption. Thus, let us readopt the once-heralded value of moderation, before circumstances force us to do so."—Jonathan B. Harris, in a letter to the Editor, *The New York Times*, January 25, 1981. © 1980 by The New York Times Company. Reprinted by permission.

Simplified Living. To identify more closely with others who know want, as Mordecai urged Esther to do, we must commit ourselves to standing with them as closely as possible, not trying to excuse ourselves from their discomforts.

Albert Einstein, the great physicist, believed in doing this. During his time at the Princeton Institute, he insisted that the least would really suffice, and hesitated to have a salary set for himself. He and the trustees finally agreed that the great Nobel Prize winner would have a checking account instead of being given a salary, and the trustees would see to it that enough funds would be deposited in the checking account. At the end of twelve months, the trustees discovered that Einstein had spent only $1,700. As he had insisted, the least would really do.

How closely to do you identify with those in want? Enough so that you have resolved that the least for yourself will do?

Sentence Sermon to Remember: Loyalty that will do anything, that will endure anything, that will make the whole being consecrate to Him, is what Christ wants. Anything else is not worthy of Him.—Burdett Hart.

Questions for Pupils on the Next Lesson. 1. What, according to the Bible, is the purpose of your life and all human existence? 2. How does God intend us to relate with nature? 3. What are the greatest realities of life? 4. What are some of the claims for your supreme commitment? 5. How does our universe reflect the power and glory of God?